International debt rescheduling has been marked by complex bargaining both historically and in the contemporary epoch. In this process, there has been significant variation in the amount of economic adjustment undertaken by debtors, the concessions made by private lenders, and the type of intervention by creditor governments and international organizations. Professor Vinod K. Aggarwal develops an original formal model that explains these phenomena and predicts debt rescheduling outcomes over the last 170 years in Mexico, Peru, Argentina, and Brazil.

The theoretical core of *Debt Games* develops a pathbreaking "situational theory of bargaining," consisting of two components. The first element, a situational theory of payoffs, focuses on each actor's individual situation, defined by its political and economic characteristics. The effects of these individual situations in constraining actors' basic goals are examined to construct "debt games," which are then solved to predict debt rescheduling outcomes. The second element, a situational theory of change, shows how actors attempt to improve their negotiating position to secure more favorable future outcomes. Professor Aggarwal rigorously tests this model in 61 cases, which include all instances of Mexican and Peruvian debt rescheduling from the 1820s to the present, and Argentina and Brazil in the 1980s and 1990s. The rich empirical material draws on archival research, interviews, and an exhaustive analysis of secondary sources.

This novel combination of formal modeling, game theory, and historical analysis yields a valuable study that points to future directions for research in international political economy, the modeling of international bargaining, and the systematic use of case materials for theory testing.

Debt games

Debt games

Strategic interaction in international debt rescheduling

VINOD K. AGGARWAL
University of California, Berkeley

Published by the Press Syndicate of the University of Cambridge
The Pitt Building, Trumpington Street, Cambridge CB2 1RP
40 West 20th Street, New York, NY 10011–4211, USA
10 Stamford Road, Oakleigh, Melbourne 3166, Australia

First published 1996

Printed in the United States of America

Library of Congress Cataloging-in-Publication Data

Aggarwal, Vinod K.

Debt games : strategic interaction in international debt
rescheduling / Vinod K. Aggarwal.

p. cm.

Includes bibliographical references and index.

ISBN 0–521–35202–9 (hc). – ISBN 0–521–55552–3 (pb)

1. Debt relief. 2. Loans, Foreign. 3. Debts, External.
I. Title.
HG3891.5.A379 1996
336.3′435 – dc20 95–30406
CIP

A catalog record for this book is available from the British Library.

ISBN 0–521–35202–9 Hardback
ISBN 0–521–55552–3 Paperback

To Sonia

Contents

Preface

This book examines international bargaining over debt rescheduling among debtors, lenders, governments, and international organizations. It examines the cases of Mexico and Peru over the last 170 years, and focuses on Argentina and Brazil in the 1980s and 1990s. Although my primary objective has been to understand this important empirical problem, my research has also been driven by what I find to be several theoretical lacunae in the literature on international politics and economics.

Recent studies by political scientists and economists who emphasize single variable explanations of international political and economic phenomena provide a valuable corrective to the excessive eclecticism of historical studies. By focusing on the theoretical mileage that a particular factor gives us, these scholars have allowed us to move away from primarily descriptive studies to more analytical accounts of international political and economic events. But the pendulum now seems to have swung too far in the direction of unicausal explanations. As a result, we have seen fewer integrative approaches that carefully build on the fertile insights of these analysts. In my earlier work on international regimes, *Liberal Protectionism*, I made an effort to construct a synthetic account of the evolution of such arrangements. In this new book on debt rescheduling, although my focus is not on international regimes, I have pursued my earlier interest in integrated explanations by developing a more formal and rigorous explanation to explain international bargaining outcomes. By systematically showing how we might incorporate both political and economic variables that point to the role of both international and domestic factors in developing my model, I have made an effort to build on the insights of scholars who have focused on specific variables in their studies.

The recent emphasis on game theoretic approaches to international political and economic relations has yielded a host of important insights on strategic action among different types of actors. This work has advanced our understanding of how decisionmakers respond to differing constraints and incentives in an interdependent context when their choices are influenced by what they think their counterparts are likely to do. At the same time, I am concerned by the excessive focus on method and technique at the expense of empirical relevance and applicability. In attempting to show how game equilibria might be found through various mathematical techniques, some have lost sight of the more fundamental issue of how such bargaining games may be constructed in the first place. While finding solutions to bargaining problems is no doubt a crucial task, our primary mission as scholars of international political economy must be to carefully specify the problem to which we subject our analytical techniques. In this book, I make an effort to derive actors' preferences over outcomes by drawing on basic economic and political variables. This approach allows me to specify the debt games in which actors find themselves and then to analyze these games for equilibria to predict actors' likely policy choices.

In this context, much recent work on optimal strategies in iterated Prisoner's Dilemma games has given us considerable insight into prospects for cooperation in international politics. These studies have also shed light on the role of institutions in facilitating mutually beneficial outcomes. Yet a key question with respect to ongoing strategic interaction has been overlooked by many analysts. Often, rather than restricting themselves to strategic choices within a context of repeated games, actors have attempted to alter the bargaining games in which they find themselves. An important focus of this book is to examine the changes they try to implement to improve their bargaining position as well as the types of resources that decisionmakers utilize in this effort.

Finally, while we have gained much from "illustrative" case studies that draw upon theoretical insights, the systematic testing of hypotheses has often been slighted. While all scholars need not be involved with all facets of the collective research enterprise, I feel that it is incumbent upon those who develop formal models to devote intellectual resources to the central enterprise of connecting our theoretical insights with the real world. By examining debt rescheduling in 61 cases across both time and countries in this book, I hope to provide a more substantial test of my modeling effort.

My own efforts to address some of these concerns represent only one step in the direction in which we must collectively go. While I am less concerned with advancing the specific formulation of my model, I do hope that the general thrust of this book will contribute to setting a course to better understand the complex international political economy of which we are a part.

Portions of the empirical material in this book and some of the theoretical ideas have appeared earlier. A version of the theoretical argument on deriving game payoffs presented in Chapter 3 and its application to a few cases from Mexico's debt rescheduling history appeared as "Interpreting Mexico's Historical Debt Crises," in Barry Eichengreen and Peter Lindert, eds., *The International Debt Crisis in Historical Perspective* (Cambridge, Mass.: MIT Press, 1989). Much of the co-authored chapter with Maxwell Cameron on contemporary Peruvian debt rescheduling has appeared as "Modelling Peruvian Debt Rescheduling in the 1980s" in *Studies in Comparative Development*, Summer 1994.

In writing this book, I have incurred many debts. In contrast to the regrets that many countries have had after borrowing from the banks, I am pleased to acknowledge the considerable aid I have received from a large number of individuals and institutions. My only hope is that my creditors will be generous in providing me with a sufficiently long repayment schedule to service my obligations.

My greatest debt is to the many scholars and students at Berkeley, as well as the institutional support that this university has provided me over the years in completing the bulk of this work. Several colleagues in the Department of Political Science contributed to this project in many different ways. David Collier has pushed me to clarify my ideas and writing and has provided moral support. His vast store of knowledge of Latin America has also helped to enrich my empirical work. Ernst Haas inspired me to combine theoretical analysis with rigorous empirical research. Gregory Luebbert, whose untimely death took from me a close friend and brilliant colleague, challenged me to be bold and innovative. I am also grateful to Kenneth Waltz, Harold Wilensky, Martin Landau, Ruth Collier, George Breslauer, and Steve Weber for many valuable discussions. Colleagues in other departments also helped guide my thinking. In particular, I am indebted to John Harsanyi for illuminating the intricacies of game theory and thankful to Barry Eichengreen and Albert Fishlow for sharing their knowledge of international debt problems with me.

I am grateful to many current and former Berkeley graduate students for their research help and comments on the manuscript. I have co-authored the chapter in this book on Peruvian debt rescheduling in the 1980s and 1990s with Maxwell Cameron. His insights and intricate knowledge of Peru have greatly strengthened the empirical analysis in that chapter. And I benefited greatly from the help that Cédric Dupont, although not formally a Berkeley student, provided me when he spent a year at the university. Cédric, who worked with me first as a research assistant at the Graduate Institute of International Studies in Geneva, and now as my professional colleague, helped me to clarify my thinking on game theory, and willingly read numerous drafts of my theoretical chapters. Gregory Linden's expertise in the technical aspects of game theory proved to be of great help in tying my work to mainstream treatments of debt rescheduling.

I greatly appreciate the editing assistance I received from Jenny Lind. Faith Raider willingly and skillfully has edited the entire manuscript. Her talent in eliminating jargon is much appreciated. I also received a great deal of help from many other graduate students at Berkeley. These include Leslie Armijo, Eileen Doherty, James Fearon, Amy Gurowitz, Ronald Gutfleish, Wade Huntley, David Kang, Timothy Kessler, James Mahon, Carol Medlin, Deborah Norden, Elizabeth Norville, Amy Rauenhorst, Kenneth Shadlen, David Stuligross, Arun Swamy, Takahiro Yamada, and Yu-Shan Wu. I am pleased to recognize the contributions of two former undergraduates, Theodore Chan and David Platt, who helped in many facets of this work. Others who were involved with various phases of the project include Heidi Assigal, Shashikala Bhat, Roger Chan, Ben Chu, Colin Forth, Amy Gurowitz, Stacy Kravetz, In Lee, Muir MacPherson, Rose Razaghian, and Andrew Wong.

Finally, at Berkeley, the Institute of International Studies and Center for Latin American Studies generously provided me with travel grants to conduct research and helped to fund several of my graduate assistants. In addition, I greatly benefited from the rich resources at the main university library as well as the specialized Latin American collection of the Bancroft Library.

In the early stages of my research for this book, the Rockefeller Foundation granted me a generous fellowship that allowed me to conduct interviews with participants in the contemporary debt crisis. This support also enabled me to spend a productive year as a Visiting Fellow at the Brookings Institution. In conducting my research, I interviewed over 70 bankers and officials from debtor and creditor countries, and international organizations. Because they requested anonymity, I cannot mention them by name. I am grateful, however, to their willingness to graciously share their experiences and insights with me.

Several professional colleagues and friends commented on large parts of the manuscript. My greatest debt is to my friend and fellow scholar Pierre Allan, who helped me to hone my ideas on modeling international bargaining. In addition, he and I collaborated on part of the research in Chapter 4 on types of resources that actors might use to improve their bargaining position. We have also worked together on developing the more general approach to examining international bargaining outcomes that I discuss in my concluding chapter. For all his help, and particularly his friendship, I am deeply grateful. Mark Zacher and I spent many hours together as I attempted to work out an approach to understanding the problem of examining debt rescheduling. His generosity in offering advice despite his own busy schedule is much appreciated. Robert Keohane continues to help me with his keen insights and has provided me with much needed advice as my work has moved in new theoretical and empirical directions. My academic career has been greatly enriched by his sustained support.

While teaching at the Graduate Institute of International Studies in Geneva, I benefited from a grant that I received with Pierre Allan from the Swiss National Science Foundation that partially supported this work. In Geneva, I received valuable research assistance from Brook Boyer, Lars-Erik Cederman, Catherine Kuchta, and Stephanie McLeod.

I am pleased to recognize the many individuals in the broader community of scholars who have contributed to this enterprise. These include Christopher Achen, Jonathan Bender, Bruce Bueno de Mesquita, Stuart Chemtob, William Cline, Benjamin Cohen, Henry Ergas, Kenneth Flamm, Alexander George, Paolo Guerrieri, Peter Katzenstein, Stephen Krasner, David Laitin, Robert Lawrence, Jeffrey Leonard, Peter Lindert, Urs Luterbacher, David Mares, James Morrow, John Odell, Guillermo O'Donnell, Samuel Pickens, Robert Pringle, Duncan Snidal, Robert Solomon, John Steinbruner, Shibley Telhami, Daniel Verdier, and Kent Weaver.

A few changes in the final version of this book were completed while I was a Visiting Fellow at the East-West Center in Honolulu. For providing me with the opportunity to avail myself of a very hospitable working environment, I am grateful to Charles Morrison and Michel Oksenberg, the Director of the Program on International Politics and Economics and the former President of the Center, respectively. I also benefited from the research assistance of Kristine Davidson and Sylvia Donati.

I would like to thank Alex Holzman and Frank Smith of Cambridge University Press for their support of this enterprise. Their encouragement and rapid response to my queries greatly eased the publication process.

My family has been a source of enormous support. I had innumerable discussions with my brother, Sudhir Aggarwal, which helped me to clarify many of my ideas. My sister, Bina Murarka, has been an important source of encouragement. Both my mother, Saroj Aggarwal, and father have supported this complex enterprise from its inception. My father, Om Aggarwal, has been a continuous source of intellectual and moral support. Without his help, I would not have been able to complete this book. My wife, Nibha Aggarwal, has been understanding of the demands that this book has made on both of our lives. Although this project has been in progress since well before the birth of our five-year-old daughter Sonia, her growth has markedly outpaced that of the book. She has also been a stern taskmaster despite her young age. When I took breaks from my writing, she would say: "Daddy, go to work." I hope that she will someday find the hours I have taken from our time together to have been productively spent.

[illegible]

Overview

If the 1970s are remembered in international finance as the halcyon days of international lending, the 1980s and 1990s will be recalled as the turbulent years of international debt rescheduling. From the Philippines to Brazil to the Ivory Coast, the rescheduling of sovereign loans has become the major occupation – and preoccupation – of international bankers. But this pattern of boom and bust in lending is not unique to this epoch; borrowing cycles have occurred in both the nineteenth and twentieth centuries.

The financial crises that the world faced in the 1820s and 1830s, for example, resemble the entanglements of today in many respects. After the French successfully floated indemnity loans in 1817 and 1818, other countries rushed into the borrowing market. Brokers for these loans earned huge profits, which immediately made lending exceptionally attractive. As lenders scrambled to offer funds, many countries in the Americas and Europe leapt to secure loans. In the ensuing melee, countries often misrepresented the intended use of their newly acquired monies. For example, the Greek government easily secured loans by claiming that they would be used to bolster military defenses and keep the country free from Turkish rule. Yet only a portion of the proceeds were used for this claimed purpose:

> The greater part went to various intermediaries [such] as the Greek commissioners to pay them for their arduous labors in negotiating the loan, several well-known English Philhellenes, to compensate them for their losses in the falling securities market, Admiral Cochrane to enable him to spend the rest of his life at ease and several Brooklyn shipbuilders to pay them for frigates, most of which never saw service in the cause. The Greek government did not pay interest on these bonds for over half a century.[1]

Conversely, unscrupulous adventurers offered bogus bonds for the reckless investor. One house even floated a bond issue for a nonexistent "Kingdom of Poyais."[2] Even when countries were straightforward and lenders were legitimate, few of the investment houses made decisions based on sound economic, political, and financial information. A lack of prudent financial sense characterized the era.

As with the 1820s, our current debt problem has been exacerbated by unwise lending, uninformed borrowers, and the misdirection of funds to private coffers where they would not be used to stimulate the economies of debtor countries. Disproportionate profits in both the 1820s and the 1970s encouraged loans that might not have proliferated had bondholders correctly assessed the risks attached to lending. Bankers in both eras assumed that because the sovereign debt was

[1] Edwards (1938), p. 18.
[2] Jenks (1927/1973), p. 45. See the list of loans in Hobson (1914), p. 10.

backed by governments, and thus had a sharply different character than domestic loans, it would always be safe. Yet historical experience suggests the opposite: the fact that sovereign debt lacks collateral makes it risky because enforcing norms of repayment is very difficult.

International debt rescheduling, both in earlier epochs and our present one, has been marked by a flurry of bargaining. In this process, significant variation has emerged over time and across cases in the extent to which debtors have undertaken economic adjustment, banks or bondholders have written down debts, and creditor governments and international organizations have intervened in negotiations. My focus in this book is on explaining this complex rescheduling process, rather than on seeking to account for why countries and creditors have faced the same loan problems time and again. To predict the results of negotiations, my central objective is to develop and apply a "situational theory of bargaining" – focusing on an actor's basic bargaining constraints – to explain why bargaining outcomes have varied.[3] I then use game theory to predict the likely outcome of their strategic interaction. My theory, which involves both a static and a dynamic component, allows us to steer a course between the Scylla of purely aggregate-level analysis and the Charybdis of unique historical analysis of individual cases. This approach enables us to generalize about the debt rescheduling process and to show how it varies with the traits of the participants. Why, for example, in the 1940s and 1950s did Mexico secure high concessions from bondholders for debt going back to the turn of the century while Peru secured a less favorable agreement in 1953? And why did Mexico undertake high adjustment in the early 1980s, whereas Argentina and Brazil often found themselves in deadlock with the banks?

The static portion of my theory, the "situational theory of payoffs," allows us to construct bargaining games between debtors and lenders based on fundamental political and economic variables.[4] I use the term "situation" to refer to the three variables of domestic coalitional stability, issue capabilities, and overall capabilities that I assume will constrain actors' basic goals. By solving these games for equilibria using standard game theoretic techniques, and by taking into account the implications of potential intervention by third parties, I am thus able to predict debt bargaining outcomes.

[3] I am not using the term "bargaining" here in the technical sense developed by John Nash (1950) and others. Whereas I consider all strategic interaction situations as bargaining situations, Nash (1950), Harsanyi (1977), and others restrict it to cases where both parties to a negotiation are able to gain from their interaction. This would rule out a game such as Deadlock (see Chapter 2) since it does not have a "bargaining range" in utility terms. A bargaining range requires that "there be a possibility of negotiated compromise that both parties would prefer to no agreement at all" (Snyder and Diesing, 1977, p. 52). On this point, see Harsanyi (1977), p. 12, and Rapoport and Guyer (1966), p. 203. This issue is discussed at length in Chapter 2.

[4] The word "situation" is sometimes associated with a pure microeconomic approach with an emphasis on constraints generated by an actor's position in a system (Latsis, 1976). While some have used this notion to focus only on international constraints (Keohane, 1984, pp. 26–28), I use the word "situation" to refer to constraints on decisionmakers emanating from both the international and domestic realm.

The dynamic element of my approach, a "situational theory of change," helps to show how bargaining outcomes might vary over time as a result of actors' efforts to change their bargaining situations or serendipitous events. Intended situational change efforts include attempts by bondholders to secure allies, secret debt buybacks by Peru and Mexico, and appeals to international law. Serendipitous events or shocks include such things as the discovery of guano in Peru and oil in Mexico, the rise of particular leaders, earthquakes, or a sudden fall in oil prices.

The approach and organization of the book

My investigation of international debt rescheduling focuses on two key elements: the development of theoretical tools to understand debt bargaining outcomes, and the exploration of the utility of these tools to understand debt rescheduling from an empirical perspective in a large number of current and historical cases.

I present the theoretical portion in Part I of the book, which consists of four chapters. Chapter 1 begins by characterizing debt bargaining outcomes by the degree to which debtors agree to undertake economic adjustment that may further debt repayment, and the extent to which lenders agree to grant lending concessions. I then focus on the structural characteristics of four commonly identified time spans over the last 170 years (1820s–1860s, 1860s–1914, 1920s–1950s, and 1970s–1990s) to investigate debt rescheduling outcomes. The nested systems approach I use to examine these four time periods (or what I term "epochs")[5] focuses on the interlinked overall international, economic, and financial systems.[6] I characterize these systems by focusing on the types of actors, the number of major powers, and the presence or absence of international regimes or organizations.[7] Based on this structural-systemic approach, I find that epochs exhibit some distinctive characteristics that allow us to partially predict some characteristics of debt rescheduling outcomes for the particular epoch. The first epoch, for example, was characterized by newly independent states that were quite unstable politically. In the first three epochs, the debt was held primarily by bondholders rather than banks. The fourth epoch saw the active participation of international organizations.

[5] Because I do not investigate the origin and evolution of what some scholars have termed "debt cycles," I use the term "epochs" to refer to my structural analysis of these four time periods.

[6] See Aggarwal (1983) and (1985) for a more detailed discussion of a nested systems approach.

[7] The idea of a "systemic analysis" is based on microeconomic theory. The basic argument is that the aggregate behavior of the system and the behavior of firms (or states) will be influenced by the structure of the system. In microeconomics, market structure is determined by the number of major firms, for example, monopoly, oligopoly, or atomistic markets. Similarly, in the international system, we can examine the effects of unipolarity, bipolarity, multipolarity, and so on in terms of the distribution of capabilities among states. Waltz has pioneered this approach in international relations, defining the structure of a system along the three dimensions of types of units, distribution of power, and hierarchy or anarchy. I modify this approach somewhat in looking at nested systems. For a detailed discussion of these points, see Waltz (1979) and Chapter 2 in this book.

A focus on epochal factors, however, takes us only part of the way toward understanding the rescheduling process. Unlike the high degree of similarity in the pattern of borrowing and timing of default within a particular epoch, rescheduling patterns do not show the same consistency. Instead, I find significant variation of outcomes even within individual epochs, thus highlighting the need to move beyond a purely epochal analysis of debt rescheduling to a focus on specific bargaining episodes involving debtors, lenders, creditor governments, and international institutions.[8]

The second through fourth chapters present the core of my situational theory of bargaining to explain debt rescheduling cases. My goal is to explain all cases with the same variables, rather than to construct a unique explanation for each. To this end, Chapter 2 argues that it is most useful to focus on the bilateral relationship between individual debtors and groups of lenders. Intervention by creditor governments and international organizations can then be examined in terms of the extent to which they play a role in pressing either one or both of these actors to pursue particular policies. With this perspective in mind, I then show how bargaining efforts between a debtor and lenders can be modeled as a bargaining "game." In particular, I present some basic ideas of game theory, and review alternative modeling approaches. To predict how actors in specific games will attempt to choose the best strategy to optimize their gains, I focus on the concept of a "Nash equilibrium" solution.

The third chapter tackles what I consider a fundamental but consistently neglected issue in game theoretic analysis. Whereas most analysts either establish the payoffs of the games they analyze by assumption, or simply by inferring the payoffs from the outcomes they observe, I attempt to derive these payoffs by using what I term a "situational theory of payoffs." I first argue that actors have a number of goals. For debtors, in a crisis, these goals include a desire to (1) secure additional funds, (2) minimize the political and financial costs of adjustment, and (3) minimize penalties by maintaining good relations with lenders. By contrast, following a debt crisis, lenders generally (1) hesitate to commit additional resources, (2) wish to encourage debt-servicing, and (3) worry about possible penalties imposed by debtors. These goals will be prioritized by actors depending on their "individual situation," defined here as a function of three key factors: direct debt rescheduling related resources, overall capabilities, and domestic coalitional stability.

Actors' moves are guided by a consideration of both goals and constraints. The leaders of a politically unstable coalition, for example, will generally hesitate to undertake drastic adjustment programs that would create intense political conflict. Hence, we will see variation in actors' valuation of different outcomes.[9]

[8] For analytical convenience, I refer to bondholders or banks as "lenders," debtor countries as "debtors," countries where the lenders are located as "creditor governments," and international institutions such as the IMF or World Bank as "international organizations."

[9] It is important to keep in mind that this variation in constrained preferences does not imply that actors' *basic* preferences or goals vary in the model. See Chapter 2 for a more detailed discussion of this point.

These valuations generate the range of payoffs of the debt games that I construct to examine bargaining outcomes. This chapter also examines the role that creditor governments or international organizations might have in the rescheduling process. In my model, these actors' decisions to intervene depend on their relative weighting of strategic, political, and economic factors.

Finally, Chapter 4 moves beyond static game representations to consider the evolution of bargaining outcomes. My "situational theory of change" argues that actors who fare poorly in negotiations are highly motivated to alter their bargaining situation – despite having reached an initially stable equilibrium. In such cases, actors might attempt to alter the course of future negotiations by manipulating either their own or their opponents' situation. The conditions under which actors are likely to do so, and the constraints that they face in such efforts, are issues I investigate in detail in this chapter.

Figure O.1 summarizes the theoretical approach and the chapters in which the different portions of my argument appear.

Parts II–V of the book examine 61 cases of debt rescheduling by focusing on specific rescheduling episodes from the four epochs. These cases were chosen for several purposes: to include sufficient variation in outcomes to provide a significant test of the ideas developed here, to see if decisionmakers learn from their predecessors' experience, and to examine some of the most crucial episodes of international debt rescheduling. I look at all episodes in Mexico and Peru across the epochs from the 1820s to the present and at Argentina and Brazil in the 1980s and 1990s. In terms of significance, Peru was one of the largest borrowers in the world in the 1850s and 1860s, while Brazil and Mexico have been the largest debtors in our present epoch. The cases I have chosen pose a rigorous challenge to my model by forcing it to cope with bargaining episodes that span the last 170 years and a diverse set of countries.

Finally, the conclusion reviews my findings and examines both the success rate of the model as well as the cases where it failed to accurately predict outcomes. In addition, I consider other lessons that emerge from my analysis of the case studies. I end with a discussion of how the model might be enriched and consider how it might be applied to other areas in international politics and economics.

An overview of the modeling approach

I use the following questions to contrast my approach with that of others: (1) Why develop a model? (2) Why use game analysis? (3) What variables affect actors' valuations of outcomes? and (4) Why look at actors' efforts to promote changes in their situation?

First of all, why develop a model? I view a model as a tool to provide insight into the complexities of international negotiations. Without such formalization, it is difficult to systematically evaluate competing predictions and explanations. My model, like all others, omits many aspects of the debt negotiation process; but it should help to pinpoint essential elements in debt rescheduling, and to

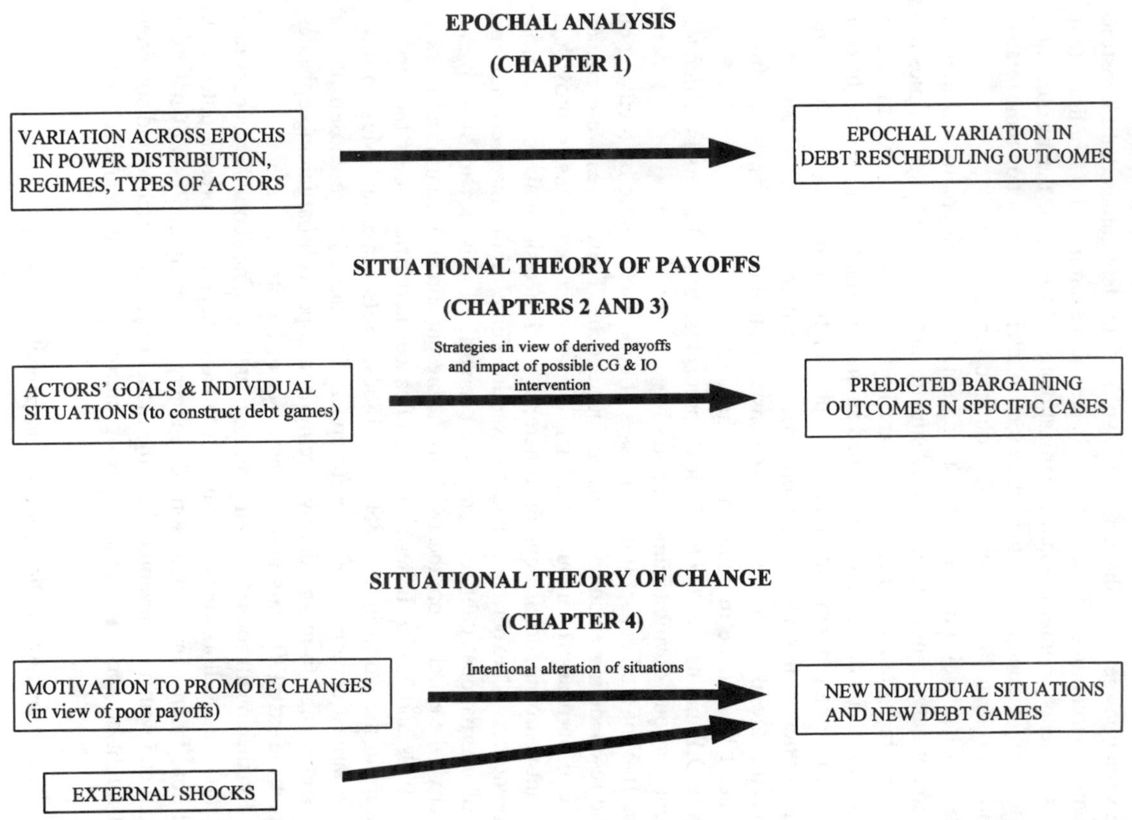

EPOCHAL ANALYSIS

(CHAPTER 1)

VARIATION ACROSS EPOCHS IN POWER DISTRIBUTION, REGIMES, TYPES OF ACTORS → EPOCHAL VARIATION IN DEBT RESCHEDULING OUTCOMES

SITUATIONAL THEORY OF PAYOFFS

(CHAPTERS 2 AND 3)

ACTORS' GOALS & INDIVIDUAL SITUATIONS (to construct debt games) → (Strategies in view of derived payoffs and impact of possible CG & IO intervention) → PREDICTED BARGAINING OUTCOMES IN SPECIFIC CASES

SITUATIONAL THEORY OF CHANGE

(CHAPTER 4)

MOTIVATION TO PROMOTE CHANGES (in view of poor payoffs) → (Intentional alteration of situations) → NEW INDIVIDUAL SITUATIONS AND NEW DEBT GAMES

EXTERNAL SHOCKS → NEW INDIVIDUAL SITUATIONS AND NEW DEBT GAMES

Figure O.1. *A conceptual map to analyze debt rescheduling*

simplify the examination of "What if?" questions, thereby introducing greater analytical rigor and clarifying issues of policy. I have chosen to build a relatively simple model in order to facilitate empirical analysis and to focus on elements that can be operationalized in view of available data. Once this model has proven to be effective for empirical analysis, we can later introduce greater sophistication into the effort.[10]

Second, why use game theoretic analysis? In debt negotiations, as in most other types of international bargaining, protagonists interact with one or more opponents who are presumed to be rational in the specific sense that each player chooses a policy favoring its own interests, while anticipating that its opponent will respond in kind. Game theory allows us to model this strategic and rational decisionmaking problem by considering what actors expect to gain as a result of different combinations of their own and their counterpart's policy choices. Depending on how these "payoffs" are ordered in different situations, rational actors should behave in predictable ways.

Although this seems obvious, much work in international relations fails to explicitly recognize this strategic dependence. For example, although Bruce Bueno de Mesquita's outstanding study *The War Trap* provides an approach to analyzing actors' preference orderings, he "combines" them through an expected utility approach to find outcomes resulting from actors' interaction. This mode of analysis is appropriate for examining individual decisionmaking under conditions of risk or uncertainty – but not for actors involved in a situation of strategic interaction.[11] Actors contemplating a decision to go to war will likely consider their opponents' reactions, which in turn will depend on their opponents' reciprocal expectations. Recognizing this omission, in his recent co-authored work with David Lalman, Bueno de Mesquita develops a game theoretic model that incorporates strategic interaction.[12]

Analysts of international conflict are not the only ones who often fail to examine strategic interaction. Scholars studying the development and stability of international regimes often assume that a single power will simply impose its will on others,[13] without focusing on the bargaining involved in such cases.[14] A new strand of research has questioned the analytical foundations of "hegemonic stability" theory, and has argued that strategic interaction among a few major powers can also lead to the formation of international regimes.[15] This analytical

[10] As an example, the conflict modeling pursued by Bruce Bueno de Mesquita (1981) and Bueno de Mesquita and Lalman (1986 and 1992) can be seen to be a progressive research program despite criticisms of its earlier formulations.

[11] See Harsanyi (1977) for a good discussion of decisionmaking models. The formulation he uses is similar to the one described at length by Luce and Raiffa (1957). I elaborate on these distinctions in Chapter 2.

[12] Bueno de Mesquita and Lalman (1992). [13] See, e.g., Krasner (1976).

[14] See Aggarwal (1985) for an analytical discussion and tracing of the bargaining process in such cases.

[15] See Keohane (1984) and Snidal (1985b). Keohane provides an institutional maintenance argument based on information theory to suggest the possibility of stability with multiple powers. Snidal provides a more formal game theoretic approach to this question.

examination of strategic interaction has markedly contributed to our understanding of the development of such arrangements.

The third question, on choosing variables to derive actors' payoffs, is central. Studies that examine bargaining outcomes and then simply reinterpret them in "preference" and "game" terms are helpful only for illustrative purposes. Much more useful is considering how actors order their preferences in light of the constraints they face. Game theory, as such, is of no help in deriving actors' payoffs for different policy choices: it is simply one approach to rigorously analyzing players' interaction in view of specific payoffs.[16]

Unfortunately, most studies operate under the assumption that empirical situations can be modeled with a few specific types of games – without investigating the basis for actors' payoffs. The most popular game analyzed in the literature is the Prisoner's Dilemma (PD). Yet many cases of international bargaining do *not* have payoffs of the type found in this game. Unless one derives payoffs carefully, game analyses are either harmful – because they might misrepresent the true payoffs in a bargaining situation – or next to useless because they simply restate in game theoretic terms what we already know about the negotiations in a particular case. Hence, I expend considerable effort in deriving and justifying my choice of payoffs for particular bargaining situations.

Many excellent studies in international relations have shed some light on how one might specify actors' preferences, although for the most part, these works have emphasized the role of one variable. For example, in his important study of the patterns of openness in world trade over the last 150 years, Stephen Krasner postulates the basic goals that all states are likely to pursue, and then generates an informal rank ordering of countries' payoffs by focusing on the influence of the country's position in the international system.[17] He argues that large and small states will prefer open trading systems whereas medium powers will generally be more protectionist. Yet Krasner does not examine the impact of domestic coalitions or actors' beliefs on their ordering of preferences except in an ad hoc manner to explain significant anomalies in the findings.

Others, such as Peter Katzenstein, have looked at internal state structures as determinants of actors' preferences. His analysis of European foreign economic policies examines the relationship between state and society as the key explanatory factor.[18] But recognizing the inadequacy of a purely domestic focus, in a more recent study on small European states, Katzenstein incorporates the effect of the international system on state policy choices.[19] In this vein, work by Robert

[16] Pierre Allan (1983) in his study of decisionmaking was one of the first scholars in international relations to raise the issue of examining the origin of payoffs. In this work, he shows how bargaining games might vary solely as a result of changes in overall actors' power capabilities. Duncan Snidal also points to the need to develop payoffs systematically (1985a), but does not formally attempt to do so in this work. See also Oye (1985a) for a discussion of the basis for defining payoffs.

[17] Krasner (1976), pp. 319–322.

[18] See Katzenstein (1976) and his edited volume (1977) on foreign economic policies of the major Western European countries.

[19] See Katzenstein (1985).

Putnam also provides a highly promising approach to combining international and domestic political explanations. His analysis of international bargaining,[20] using what he terms a "two level" games approach (one game is international negotiations and the other domestic negotiations), provides some heuristic value. Still, Putnam does not present a systematic methodology to reconcile the competing constraints that actors face, thus limiting the utility of this approach.

Ernst Haas, Judith Goldstein, and others have concentrated on cognitive consensus or ideological predilections to examine actors' preferences,[21] yielding useful insights into bargaining behavior. Nonetheless, as Haas notes, combining this approach with international power explanations provides a more satisfactory explanation of international regime change than simply examining actors' cognition.

While every approach gives some insight into the analysis of actors' behavior, we need to move beyond simply picking a favorite variable by finding a procedure capable of integrating several important factors.[22] My effort focuses on variables that reflect international and domestic concerns to describe the "individual situation" of actors. By formally hypothesizing how actors might differently weight their goals in response to changes in these variables, I provide a more systematic approach to determine actors' valuation of outcomes.

Fourth and finally, scholars using game theory in international relations have generally failed to examine possible shifts in actors' positions. Actors will obviously bargain to obtain the most favorable outcome when faced with the urgent need to make a strategic choice. But if they are dissatisfied with the outcome,[23] they may try to manipulate the constraints they face – despite having arrived at what scholars find to be the mathematically determined equilibrium for their bargaining situation. Specifically, I argue that actors receiving poor payoffs are highly motivated to change their situation and will draw upon three types of power resources to do so:[24] (1) international arrangements (through appeals to principles and norms or rules and procedures), (2) capabilities (issue-specific and those in other areas), and (3) alliances (with non-state and state actors). A more detailed discussion of these power resources and the constraints that actors face in using them is found in Chapter 4.

In short, my basic objective in this book is to develop both a static and a dynamic model to explain debt rescheduling outcomes. While I draw upon game theoretic and other rational choice tools in this effort, my primary concern is

20 See Putnam (1988) and Evans, Jacobson, and Putnam (1993).

21 Haas (1980), Goldstein (1993). Also see work by Rothstein (1984) and Young (1980).

22 Cohen (1990), p. 269, in a review of a large number of studies on trade, notes that "What is needed is a methodology that considers domestic- and system-level variables simultaneously, rather than sequentially, and specifies whatever interactions there may be among all relevant variables in a rigorous manner." Some studies, such as Odell (1982), have attempted to examine the interplay of different variables in explaining foreign policy. This work does not, however, explicitly address the question of deriving game payoffs.

23 David Laitin has referred to such equilibria as "unhappy equilibria." Personal communication.

24 This idea of three power resources in negotiations was first discussed in Aggarwal and Allan (1983). See also Allan (1984) and Aggarwal (1987).

with setting up the problem correctly: that is, I wish to carefully specify the payoffs that underlie game analyses and also show how they might change as a result of either intentional actions or exogenous shocks.

Caveats

Some caveats about my own analytical efforts are worth mentioning. First, I do not theorize about why the factors underlying different historical epochs change over time. This is doubtless an interesting and essential issue, but for the purposes of this book, I regard these changes as given.

Second, the book provides a detailed analysis of the bilateral bargaining processes and outcomes; it does not seek historical completeness or to discover unknown facts for each bargaining episode. My analysis is based in part on an exhaustive analysis of available secondary sources for all countries, both in English and Spanish, entailing a total of over 800 articles and books. However, I found that secondary sources were often inadequate for my needs. Thus, I used extensive primary source material in the Bancroft Library at Berkeley for the first two epochs, and obtained several hundred pages of original documents from the National Archives in Washington, D.C., for the Peruvian and Mexican cases in the 1930s–1950s. The current cases also draw upon about 70 interviews which I conducted personally with bankers, debt negotiators from the four countries, and officials from creditor governments and international organizations. Thus, in addition to the findings that result from the application of my models, I have compiled and synthesized a very substantial body of empirical material on the four countries.

Third, I formally derive actors' valuations of different outcomes in view of the constraints they face, but from an empirical standpoint, our inability to observe such payoffs directly complicates the testing of the model. Consequently, our assessment of the model's validity rests on the degree of agreement between predicted game outcomes (based on the derived payoff structure and bargaining choices) with the outcomes we actually observe. But by examining the cases in detail through a tracing of the bargaining process, I am able to develop some insight into why the model does not work in particular cases.[25]

Finally, although many comparative and historical analytical studies implicitly code cases, they often do not specify the rules they use to do so. While some may question my coding of the dependent and independent variables, I have attempted to lay out the coding rules as clearly as possible to enable others to replicate – and challenge – my analysis and interpretation of events.

To summarize, my work makes three specific contributions to the study of international debt crises and to the broader scope of international relations analysis. First, unlike most social scientists (and some economists), I try to specify how actors will value different bargaining game outcomes. Moreover, in contrast to

[25] See George (1979) and Aggarwal (1985).

most economic work on debt rescheduling, I do not simply assume that all debtors and lenders are alike and that they will single-mindedly pursue the goal of securing additional loans or repayment. Instead, I show how their valuation of outcomes depends on a combination of economic and political variables that reflect domestic and international considerations. Second, although I consider static game equilibria, I also attempt to develop an approach that analyzes changes in game structures. Third, I go beyond a purely theoretical modeling effort to focus on a large set of bargaining cases, thus providing a genuine empirical test of the model's utility. I hope that this approach will allow us to develop better models to examine international political and economic interactions, as well as to enable us to learn systematically from our past experience in coping with debt crises.

PART I
Argument

1 Examining the importance of epochs

Politicians and scholars are fond of extolling the study of history, invoking the oft-quoted words of Santayana, "Those who cannot remember the past are doomed to repeat it."[1] Yet what historical wisdom should one remember? The teachings of history are often difficult to fathom because each analyst's theoretical and ideological preconceptions color the interpretation of events. At the extreme, some have found history's lessons so elusive that they come to agree with Hegel, who noted that "What experience and history teach is this – that people and governments never have learned anything from history, or acted on principles deduced from it."[2]

While the study of the history of debt crises yields no absolute truths, there is little doubt that ignorance of historical patterns has proved costly. Almost without exception, modern bankers have made mistakes as a result of their unfamiliarity with the turbulent history of international lending. Few lenders in the 1970s, for example, knew that sovereign countries had frequently defaulted on their debt payments in the past. Many American bankers even remained unaware that several American states defaulted in the nineteenth century. Hence, Hegel notwithstanding, some attention to historical events would appear to be in order.

This chapter examines four epochs of indebtedness, default, and rescheduling experience from the late 1820s to the present in an effort to uncover some general systemic factors that affect debt rescheduling bargaining and outcomes. In brief, I find that certain elements (which I will refer to as "epochal characteristics"), when combined with cyclical arguments about lending, account for a great deal of the ebb and flow of indebtedness and default. With respect to variation in debt rescheduling, epochal factors and cyclical characteristics prove much less powerful. Although they do provide some interesting insights, we must turn to a more focused bilateral approach to develop an adequate explanation of debt rescheduling patterns.

My analysis in this chapter consists of six sections, the first of which considers the specific dependent variables that I seek to explain. These variables are the degree to which countries agree to undertake adjustment and the willingness of banks or bondholders to make loan concessions. In this context, I also explore how creditor governments and international organizations might intervene in negotiations to promote an outcome different from one that involves only lenders and debtors.[3] The second section presents some arguments about how epochal characteristics might theoretically influence bargaining outcomes. The final four

[1] George Santayana, 1905. [2] Hegel, 1832.

[3] I define creditor governments as countries, aside from the debtor country, whose nationals are involved as lenders.

sections contain a broad-brush analysis of the four historical epochs examined in this book. In short, this chapter provides the basis for both the theoretical and empirical examination of debt rescheduling episodes that are the focus of this study. To complete my theoretical picture, Chapters 2 through 4 develop my analysis of bilateral bargaining episodes.

Policy choices in debt rescheduling: the dependent variables

Debtors and lenders are the key actors in my analysis. Although these bargainers might in principle consider a large number of issues in negotiations, for the most part they focus on only a few. Leaders of debtor countries must settle on the degree to which they must implement adjustment measures in their economies when pressed by lenders to service their debt. In simplified terms, debtors must choose among one of the following three strategies: (1) pursue no or little adjustment of their economy, (2) accept a medium or moderate degree of adjustment, or (3) promote a high degree of adjustment. Adjustment refers to economic changes that make debt servicing more likely and can include macroeconomic policy changes, trade promotion efforts, and the like.[4]

Similarly, bankers' or bondholders' committees must decide on the degree and types of concessions they will make in lending to or in rescheduling debts with borrowers. Like debtor countries, they are also faced with three possible strategies: "no or low," "medium," or "high" concessions. These three choices are distinguished in this study by considering the extent to which agreements include such elements as a reduced interest rate on rescheduled debt, the amount of debt lenders are willing to reschedule, the amount of new funds and trade credits advanced, and the length of the grace period before payment must recommence.

We must keep in mind, however, that often creditor governments or international institutions play a role in the rescheduling process. If they do intervene, for example, creditor governments must decide on whose behalf they will intervene in order to advance their own agenda. They might choose to support private lenders, debtor countries, or even some combination of the two, based on a number of political and economic factors.

Characterizing epochs and examining their possible effects

Distinguishing between epochs

Some scholars have argued that the occurrence and resolution of debt crises are best explained by a focus on cycles of lending and retrenchment in developed countries. For example, both Carlos Marichal and Christian Suter suggest that fluctuations in lending cycles related to the world economy, rather than individual policy choices of states, account for debt crises.[5] Based on patterns of lending,

[4] The coding of debtors' and lenders' choices are presented in the Appendix of this chapter.

[5] Marichal (1989) and Suter (1992). On cycles more generally, see Kindleberger (1978). I return to this issue in discussing my findings in the conclusion.

default, and rescheduling, both scholars identify four different cycles, namely the 1820s to 1860s, 1870s to the First World War, the interwar period, and the 1970s to 1990s. As I will show, this argument is quite effective in explaining patterns of lending and default, but much less powerful in predicting the outcomes of rescheduling negotiations.[6]

Other scholars have distinguished among different periods of lending and debt problems by focusing on the changing types of lenders in each epoch, suggesting that the earlier epochs' bondholders were fundamentally different than bankers in later epochs. Albert Fishlow, for example, argues that debt crises were more easily resolved and debtors fared better when facing bondholders in earlier epochs than when loans came from banks. He also notes that the merchant banks that negotiated with debtors in the past were less concerned about fully recovering debt payments, compared to the commercial banks of today.[7] Others suggest that the nature of the creditor governments involved have affected the rescheduling process, with the British being more practical and facilitating reschedulings in the nineteenth century as opposed to the less experienced Americans in the twentieth century.[8] Some argue that creditor governments have increasingly intervened to prevent default in the present epoch because creditors' banking systems are now at risk.[9] In addition, in contrast to the generally sanguine view of the role of international institutions, some see the presence of the International Monetary Fund (IMF) and other financial organizations in the present epoch as detrimental to rapid resolution of debt problems.

Explanations based on the characteristics of the actors or their differential interests across time help us to understand some parts of the rescheduling process. But these characteristics do not by themselves fully account for historical differences. For example, there are many cases in which bondholders were not willing to accept reduced payments on loans. Also, creditor governments did sometimes intervene forcefully in debt negotiations in the past, albeit not generally for systemic financial concerns.[10]

The approach that I follow to distinguish among epochs in this chapter can be characterized as a modified systemic approach, or what I have termed "nested systems."[11] I take the time periods identified by cycle theorists and others, and then emphasize their systemic level characteristics by differentiating among the

[6] Eichengreen and Portes (1986) discuss the role of domestic politics in the likelihood of default. Their study suggests that a cyclical approach does not fully explain the likelihood of default. While the notion of cycles is interesting, as Eichengreen (1993), p. 359, has noted, cyclical analysis should identify "an impulse, a propagation mechanism, a dissipation mechanism, and a recurrence mechanism."

[7] Fishlow (1985b), p. 91. On the problems that bondholders have in negotiating with debtors because of their large numbers, see Whitehead (1989), p. 234.

[8] Among others, see Fishlow (1985b) and Eichengreen (1991).

[9] Lipson (1989) and Eichengreen (1991), p. 164. Although I have also made a similar argument, I note (1989) that intervention has been more frequent in the past (aside from direct gunboat diplomacy) than some have suggested.

[10] See Aggarwal (1989) and Eichengreen and Portes (1989).

[11] See Aggarwal (1983) and (1985).

overall security, economics, and international financial systems. Taken together, these interconnected or nested systems can be used to structurally characterize epochs of debt rescheduling. Moreover, in contrast to Kenneth Waltz's view that the only dimension on which the international system has changed over the last 200 years is the overall distribution of capabilities,[12] I also consider variation in the other two dimensions of system structure that he identifies. Thus, I focus on changes in the types of units in various systems. In addition, in examining the hierarchy/anarchy dimension of systems, I also consider how international organizations or regimes influence actors' behavior.

In short, in the historical analysis that follows, I focus on the four historical epochs of the 1820s to 1860s, 1870s to the First World War, the interwar period, and the 1970s to 1990s based on the following characteristics: (1) the distribution of capabilities in the three different systems enumerated above, (2) the different types of lenders and debtors involved, and (3) the presence or absence of international regimes as a constraint on actors' behavior.[13]

Before turning to an analysis of lending, default, and rescheduling patterns on this basis, I think it is a useful conceptual exercise to consider the implications of four possible epochal findings to gauge what type of analysis might be most illuminating.

Epochal versus a bilateral focus on debt rescheduling

If we discovered that bargaining outcomes differed considerably within epochs, but there is not much difference between the average outcomes across different epochs, analysis of a sample of bargaining cases from any epoch would suffice to understand the mechanics of debt rescheduling. Epochs wouldn't matter. By contrast, if typical outcomes varied from one epoch to another, but variation within an epoch was small, our focus would be entirely on epochal factors, with the analysis of bilateral bargaining quite uninteresting.

The analysis in this chapter will demonstrate that debt rescheduling over the last 170 years approximates a third case, in which average bargaining outcomes do vary by epoch but bilateral bargaining cases within epochs also exhibit high variability.[14] For example, most states tended to follow similar roads to default in the first epoch and were resistant to pursuing economic adjustment. But whereas Mexico pursued a strategy of low adjustment in the 1840s, at the same time, Peru and some other debtors agreed to quite high adjustment and came to

[12] Waltz (1979).

[13] Regimes can be defined as sets of implicit or explicit principles, norms, rules, and decision-making procedures around which actors' expectations converge in a given area of international relations. Principles are beliefs of fact, causation, and rectitude. Norms are standards of behavior defined in terms of rights and obligations. Rules are specific prescriptions or proscriptions for action. Decisionmaking procedures are prevailing practices for making and implementing collective choice (Krasner, 1983b, p. 2). I have argued (1985) that we should distinguish between meta-regimes (principles and norms) on the one hand, and regimes (rules and procedures) on the other.

[14] There is the possibility of combining these four types so that we might find that some epochs have high variation but that others do not. This would lead us to emphasize either epochal or bilateral factors depending on the combination.

terms with their lenders by the 1840s. By contrast, Mexico did not come to a final resolution of its default until the 1880s. In the 1980s, almost all debtors turned to the IMF at some point. But whereas some followed adjustment programs quite assiduously, others such as Peru and Brazil broke with the IMF, pursued independent strategies, and refused to undertake adjustment.

The large variance both between and within epochs justifies the joint consideration of epochal factors and bilateral bargaining analysis. Certain regularities exist within each of the four epochs examined here. However, focusing only on epochs obscures important differences in debt negotiations, especially in terms of the degree of adjustment and concessions undertaken by debtors and lenders, and the extent to which creditor governments intervened in negotiations.

Epoch 1: British lending to the Americas, 1820s–1860s

Two major episodes of increased lending characterize the first epoch: the 1820s, with heavy borrowing by the newly independent Latin American countries, and the 1830s, with loans to American states that chose to borrow in financial markets independently of the Federal government. In addition, European countries such as Spain, Portugal, Greece, Russia, and Turkey borrowed throughout the time period.

This section identifies the following epochal characteristics. The British were one of five major powers in the system, although they dominated the world economy, with the French a close second in overall financial and economic matters. Lending occurred through bond flotations led by merchant banking houses in the London and Paris financial markets. In some cases, these banks actually held bonds in their own accounts, but for the most part holdings were widespread among the public. Debtors, especially in Latin America, were in general domestically unstable, which led to a high number of defaults and rescheduling difficulties. With respect to the international financial organizations or arrangements, no strong regime existed at this time.[15] Bilateral debt bargaining depended on the power of the respective actors, be they bondholders, creditor governments, or debtors. There were no multilaterally based rules or procedures (or even norms) that effectively constrained bargaining outcomes.

Default came rapidly for most states within only a few years of their loan flotations. The duration of debt rescheduling before a final resolution, however, varied considerably. Some negotiations lasted over 60 years.

Epochal characteristics

Although during the 1820s to 1860s, Great Britain rose to a position of international economic hegemony, Great Britain did not predominate in the overall distribution of capabilities as it did in the narrower issue-areas of economic

[15] Although some, such as Charles Lipson (1985), have argued that a strong international regime to regulate portfolio lending existed at this time, I suggest below that this is a mistaken notion.

interaction, such as trade or finance. A balance of power among the five great countries – England, France, Prussia, Russia, and Austria – continued until the First World War. With England at the helm, this "concert of Europe," cobbled together at the Congress of Vienna in 1815, was committed to maintaining an "equilibrium of forces among the major powers" in order to "resist unilateral attempts at domination."[16] As Gordon Craig and Alexander George wrote:

> In every crisis that threatened the peace between 1815 and 1854, the British were represented and played a leading role in finding a solution short of war . . . The European concert was able, with British participation, to demonstrate its effectiveness in preserving the Vienna balance and the public order.[17]

Great Britain's international economic dominance during this period is undeniable. To a great extent, the British economy – Britain's relations with its colonies and trade partners – was synonymous with the international economy during this early stage of industrialization. In the British textile market in 1840 alone, Europe bought 200 million yards in 1840, and Latin America, Africa, and Asia provided an even larger market, buying 529 million yards. One scholar notes:

> Within these (underdeveloped) areas British industry had established a monopoly by means of war, other people's revolutions, and her own imperial rule . . . Latin America came to depend virtually entirely on British imports during the Napoleonic Wars, and after it broke with Spain and Portugal, it became an almost total economic dependency of Britain . . . India was systematically deindustrialized and became in turn a market for Lancashire cottons . . .[18]

By 1848, Britain traded twice as heavily as France, its nearest competitor.[19]

In finance, London dominated lending until the French began to compete from the middle of the 1840s through the 1850s. The City of London enjoyed vast economies of scale, access to British capitalists' profits, and, although it rarely used it, naval protection for its loans. Britain was the primary lender in Latin America, issuing some £26 million worth of bonds from 1822 to 1825.[20]

Initially, only a few major banking houses were involved in the lending business, with Baring Brothers and N.M. Rothschild among the most important. Later, other less reputable lenders including mercantile firms saw profitable opportunities in the bond market and jumped into the market for Latin American flotations.[21] These actors were intermediaries who profited on transactions, but they generally did not suffer direct losses when loans fell into default. Because bankers were held more accountable to investors and needed to protect their reputations, they were more inclined to make good loans. In many cases, however, contrary to many analysts' view of this epoch, underwriting houses often did hold loans on their own account. Thus, the widely perceived difference between banks that hold debt on their own books (as is generally the case in the present

16 Craig and George (1983), p. 30. 17 Craig and George (1983), p. 32.

18 Hobsbawm (1969), p. 53. 19 Hobsbawm (1969), p. 72.

20 Computed from Corporation of Foreign Bondholders (1878), pp. 52–53. Also see United Nations (1955).

21 Jenks (1927/1973), p. 48.

epoch) and private bondholders (who held the bulk of debt in previous epochs) does not always apply.

On the debtor side, newly established Latin American states sought financing for two major expenses: paying for their wars of liberation and covering current governmental costs. Because these objectives did little to increase debt servicing capabilities, debt repayment was unlikely. The borrowers often seemed relatively unconcerned with the damage to their credit rating that default would incur. The American states and Argentina were exceptions: the former often borrowed for public works, while the latter used funds to open up the country's interior to agricultural development.

Finally, scholars disagree whether an international regime guided finance during this era. Charles Lipson, for one, has argued that a strong regime guided states with respect to the appropriation of foreign investments, including portfolio investment in the period until the First World War.[22] If this is correct, analysis of bilateral bargaining would be superfluous because the rules of the regime would directly determine outcomes.

Yet the evidence does not support Lipson's contention. A regime is strong if its norms and rules constrain bargaining outcomes differently than, for example, the threat of force or the relative balance of capabilities between debtors and lenders. An examination of the facts suggests, however, that neither creditor governments, bondholders, nor borrowers were strongly bound by norms and rules during this era.

To illustrate the problem with Lipson's argument, let us posit that a strong regime did indeed exist. If so, what was its nature – that is, what objectives did it promote?[23] Two possibilities exist: the regime was interventionist (encouraging creditor government involvement and/or providing specific rules for working out problems between debtors and lenders); or it was laissez-faire. We can quickly rule out the first possibility. The regime, such as it was, did not promote government intervention or force actors to follow specific rules and procedures in negotiations. Lipson himself notes that even Britain directly intervened only infrequently following bond defaults. As for rules governing direct negotiations, the most careful legal scholar of bond defaults, Edwin Borchard, argues that "the judicial remedies of a bondholder in the forum of either the debtor or the creditor are exceedingly tenuous and in most cases practically unavailable."[24] But what about a strong *non*-interventionist regime? In this case, presumably, creditor governments have an interest in adhering to a set of norms, rules, or procedures relating to debt conflicts between bondholders and borrowers. Yet the British appeared to be motivated by a desire to promote the larger principles of open trade and investment protection (principles, one should note, that were not necessarily accepted by less developed countries). Britain thus chose to shoulder "the immediate costs of occasional bond defaults,"[25] rather than put a damper on

[22] Lipson (1985), p. 142. [23] See Aggarwal (1983) and (1985) for these distinctions.
[24] Borchard (1951), p. 171. [25] Lipson (1985), p. 45.

international trade. British intervention in bond cases was therefore limited by a practical consideration – and *not* by rules forbidding intervention. Lipson asserts that the persuasive power of bondholders' collective resources over debtors also "maintained the regime." That is, debtors came to agreements because of the possibility of a cutoff of future lending. But this notion hardly qualifies as proof of the existence of a strong regime; it simply points to the debtors' recognition of a credible economic threat from the bondholders.

The lack of established regime rules and procedures, then, is clear. But what about norms and principles, or what I elsewhere refer to as a "meta-regime"?[26] I have been unable to identify any coherent norms and principles that would qualify as a meta-regime in the debt issue-area in this epoch. On the other hand, there may well have been a meta-regime for the general protection of property rights, with some agreement on rules and enforcement among the major powers.[27] This could qualify as a general regime on investment, wherein the weak might be able to profit more from negotiations than we would predict from simple power calculations.

A brief comparison with another issue-area will clarify my point about regime constraints. In the 1960s and early 1970s bilateral agreements in textile trade were quite uniform and were in accord with the provisions of the textile regime. Moreover, weak countries could often appeal effectively to regime provisions in their bilateral negotiations to secure more satisfactory arrangements. By contrast, in international finance during the 1800s, power considerations consistently dominated both negotiations and outcomes.

Patterns of lending and default

The new Latin American countries drew heavily on London markets in order to raise the funds needed to cover immediate financial needs. Between 1821 and 1825, they contracted £48 million worth of debt.[28] As Latin American states increased their borrowing, however, they found themselves in worsening financial straits because funds went to cover consumption rather than investment. They were soon forced to borrow new capital to pay off old loans. Investors feared that these states would default, and they pressured the British government to remedy the situation. But the government showed no inclination to take action in the matter; although it entertained supplicants, it "would not move officially."[29]

In January 1826, B.A. Goldschmidt and Co., agents for Colombia, suspended payments on the 1820 Colombian loans. Within two years of the financial panic of 1825 caused by falling commodity prices and the failure of cotton trading firms, Spain, Portugal, Greece, and every country in Latin America, save Brazil, were in default on their debt payments. The British government still refused to intervene. In fact, *The Times* (of London) editorialized on April 23, 1829, that

[26] Aggarwal (1983) and (1985).
[27] On this point, I am more in accord with Lipson's (1985) perspective.
[28] Levi (1880), p. 186. [29] Jenks (1927/1973), p. 118.

"the government would depart from every profession which it has made . . . if it hazarded an hour of national peace, or wasted a shilling of public money to secure the fulfillment of contracts which it neither invited nor guaranteed."[30]

The banks were the target of mounting criticism for their role in the foreign loan business. The House of Lords even discussed a proposal that the government should outlaw the export of capital. The practice of foreign lending was subject to the further criticism that it supported despotic regimes, but practically no effort was made to place the system under government control.[31]

Both the banks and the debtor countries were to blame for the debt fiasco. On the one hand, debtor countries had borrowed beyond their means. On the other hand, in their haste to find new outlets for their capital, bankers did not dwell on the feasibility of loan repayments when making the loans. In fact, one scholar noted that "the more a country borrowed, the better its credit, it seemed."[32] To pay back their debts, these developing countries would have had to export more than they imported; in practice, they were running trade deficits.

Meanwhile, the agents who sold loans to individual bondholders faced another default, this time in the United States. In New York, the state-owned Erie Canal, built with funds derived from bond sales in the 1820s, had earned sufficient revenue to both pay back the debt incurred and return a handsome profit to bondholders.[33] Other states, encouraged by the Erie Canal windfall, decided to build public works financed by public borrowing. Overconfidence was contagious among borrowers. The Governor of Kentucky, remarking on the 1839 inauguration of a public works program involving a $6 million loan issue, said, "What is this sum to the resources and wealth of the state of Kentucky whose taxable property is now valued at $275,000,000?"[34]

The states' debts soared from $13 million to about $170 million between 1820 and 1838. President Jackson estimated that European holdings of American state and corporate stocks and bonds amounted to about $200 million in 1839.[35] These loans were not, however, guaranteed by the Federal government, which also engaged in foreign borrowing. The English were particularly eager to float loans because of increasing interest rates. These loans were made in dollars, but payments were to be guaranteed at fixed rates of exchange.[36]

Disaster soon loomed. The U.S. trade deficit increased as the national income rose, with the demand for manufactured imports growing more quickly than the demand for its raw-material exports. By 1836, the U.S. deficit rose to $60 million. The federal government financed its growing deficit by short-term debt.[37] From 1835 to 1837 the U.S. experienced a cotton boom as exports doubled to $70 million per annum. This temporary boom, along with the Jackson

[30] *The Times* (London), April 23, 1829. [31] Edwards (1938), pp. 23–25.
[32] Jenks (1927/1973), p. 47. [33] Edwards (1938), p. 146.
[34] Edwards (1938), p. 46. [35] Hobson (1914), p. 111.
[36] The interest rate ranged from 5% for state loans slated for development projects to almost 10% for loans to some Southern banks.
[37] Jenks (1927/1973), p. 84.

Administration's decision in July 1836 to demand that purchasers of public lands pay in gold, set the stage for collapse.[38]

The Bank of England responded to its own problem of decreasing reserves (which had fallen from about $55 million in 1834 to under $7 million two years later)[39] by raising the discount rate from 4 to 5%. In August 1836 it stopped accepting American paper. Credits for British cotton importers vanished, which further depressed the price of cotton, already fallen by half in the U.S. As earnings from this primary export product fell sharply, so did the country's ability to service its debts.[40]

The state of the U.S. economy quickly went from bad to worse. The cotton price collapse precipitated the downfall of Southern banks that had financed the crops. These banks then suspended specie payments, causing a run on cash from March through May 1837. The states subsequently wavered in both their ability and their willingness to pay back their debts. For instance, the state of Louisiana would have had to levy a tax of $3 (a large sum for that time) on every resident in order to meet its interest payments. If the state had imposed such a tax, however, its settlers would have merely moved west.[41]

In February 1840, the state of Pennsylvania failed to meet its semiannual payments. A month later, the U.S. Senate adopted resolutions disavowing federal responsibility for state debts. Nine states in total failed to meet their interest payments. Two states, Michigan and Mississippi, repudiated them outright. Florida claimed that it was a ward of the federal government and thus did not have the ability to contract debts. The other states – Indiana, Illinois, Louisiana, Arkansas, and Maryland – simply stopped paying. Barings sought a transnational alliance with the Whigs, who introduced a measure in Congress intending to force the federal government to assume these debts. That proposal failed, however.

In February 1841, the Bank of the United States stopped paying dividends to its British stockholders entirely. Trade between Europe and the Americas plummeted, to the detriment of both continents. Annual British exports to the U.S. fell from $62 million in 1836 to an average of $31 million from 1837 to 1842. As U.S. cotton exports dropped, British unemployment rates rose to 25 to 30% in the textile producing region of Lancashire.[42] When American agents attempted to secure a loan in London during this period, they were sharply rebuffed. *The Times* summed up British sentiment: "the people of the United States may be fully persuaded that there is a certain class of securities to which no overabundance of money, however great can give value; and in this class their own securities stand preeminent."[43] The lending boom had ended.

Patterns of rescheduling

Although there were similarities in the timing of borrowing and the patterns of default during this first epoch, the same cannot be said for the ensuing patterns

38 Jenks (1927/1973), p. 86. 39 Levy-Leboyer (1982), p. 68.
40 Levy-Leboyer (1982), pp. 70–74. 41 Jenks (1927/1973), p. 102.
42 Levy-Leboyer (1982), p. 88.
43 *The Times* (London), February 5, 1842, quoted in Jenks (1927/1973), p. 106.

of debt rescheduling. With respect to this issue, we see much less consistency across cases, whether we focus on structural variables or economic cycles. The timing of rescheduling varied considerably: Chile came to an agreement in 1842, reschedulings by an assortment of other Latin American states occurred in the 1850s, 1860s, and 1870s, and a final resolution of the continent's defaults arrived only with the Mexican agreement of 1888.[44] In Peru, for example, guano initially appeared to be the saving grace for bondholders.[45] An export boom, combined with a stable government, allowed Peru to settle with bondholders in 1849, but Peru later went in and out of default over the next two decades after contracting additional loans in the 1850s and 1860s. During the long negotiations that finally led to Mexico's 1888 settlement, it faced, among other crises, loss of territory to the U.S. and occupation by European states in an effort to force debt repayment.

The outcomes of debt agreements depended on such factors as the political stability of the countries, their financial resources, and the demands of their creditors. During this long time period, some settlements were initially favorable to debtors but proved unstable (several Mexican cases), other debtor countries agreed to harsh terms, and still others achieved agreements with little difficulty. In the absence of formal international rules and procedures on rescheduling, this epoch also saw pressure by the French, British, and American governments on debtor countries. The harshest measures were taken by the French with the installation of Maximilian as Emperor of Mexico in the early 1860s.

In the United States, money for the incomplete public works projects had to be raised locally, while British opportunists bought off the old debt at outrageous discounts. In due time U.S. cotton exports resumed, and the British paid for these exports with old American bonds. Dividend payments were eventually resumed by all but the three states that had repudiated their debts.[46]

In short, despite a similarity across countries in borrowing patterns and in the onset of financial problems, debtors and lenders came to agreements at very different times. Often, they had quite dissimilar results and varying degrees of creditor government intervention.

Epoch 2: railroads and lending, 1865–1914

Three important changes demarcate the transition to the second epoch in the mid-1860s. First, much British capital flowed into railway construction in England in the 1840s and early 1850s. The Indian rebellion in 1857 subsequently created a major movement of British capital to India for public works projects until 1865.[47] As a consequence, lending to other less developed areas did not flourish again until after 1865.

Second, the French ceased to be a major competitor to Britain by the end of

44 For a description of the differences in the timing of outcomes, see Marichal (1989), pp. 58–61.

45 "Guano" (bird droppings) was an actively sought-after material for fertilizer.

46 Jenks (1927/1973), p. 107. 47 Jenks (1927/1973), p. 207.

the 1860s, a decline exacerbated by their military defeat at the hands of Prussia in 1871. The London and Paris markets handled comparable amounts of money in the late 1860s, but the British had moved decisively to a preeminent position by 1885, issuing twice as many foreign loans as the French.[48]

Third, both the lenders and debtors changed significantly. Bondholders in Britain organized the Corporation of Foreign Bondholders in 1868, a move that sparked similar arrangements in other countries. This forum provided a central negotiating body for bondholders. In addition, Latin American debtors in particular were relatively more stable and more concerned with developmental borrowing than they had been in their first foray into financial markets in the 1820s.

In previewing specific epochal characteristics and outcomes, we find that Britain's overall position began to erode gradually after 1873. It remained dominant in economic and financial matters, with its leadership role in financial markets only moderately challenged by competitors in the early 1900s. Bondholders continued to dominate portfolio lending, although in some cases, crises involving bank-held debt (for example, the Barings Crisis) also occurred. Although more stable than the newly independent Latin American countries of the 1820s, borrowers of this epoch fared little better in avoiding default.

The spectrum of varying debt resolutions in this epoch is particularly striking, ranging from joint military intervention (Venezuela, 1902–1903), an international commission to manage rescheduling (Turkey and Egypt), customs management by creditor governments (Nicaragua, Haiti, and Santo Domingo at various times), a governmental bailout of a major lender (Barings Brothers in the Argentine case), to straightforward debt rescheduling (Ecuador).

Epochal characteristics

Turning first to security affairs, in terms of overall structure, the system remained multipolar. Britain continued to play its role as the lead country in the European balance of power. But the fluidity of this system declined with the formation of both the Triple Alliance among Austria, Germany, and Italy and the Triple Entente among France, Russia, and Great Britain. The onset of more rigid alliance politics increased the need for management of blocs, which in turn increased the difficulty of crisis management in the period before the First World War.

In overall economic matters, Britain continued to stand out, although not as strikingly as in the financial arena. Per capita growth rates remained below those of the U.S. and Germany throughout the period.[49] In foreign trade, despite a slow decline, Britain remained at the center of the international system, accounting for about 38% of total manufactured exports around 1880. This figure dropped to slightly over 30% on the eve of the First World War.

Regarding the international financial system, this epoch stands out as a time of overwhelming British dominance in international financial affairs. In Latin America in 1914, total foreign investments in billions of dollars were as follows:

[48] Fishlow (1985a), p. 53. [49] Floud and McCloskey (1981), pp. 8–9.

Britain, 3.7; the U.S., 1.7; France, 1.2; Germany, 0.9; and all others combined, about 1.0. Although these figures reflect clear British predominance, the total net worth of British world assets by 1913 as compared to other countries is even more striking: Britain accounted for over $20 billion worth of assets in 1913 out of a combined total of $32 billion for all European countries and the U.S.[50]

Turning now to actor characteristics, countries increasingly borrowed for infrastructural development (railroad expenditures constituted over 40% of invested debt) although many still sought to finance current governmental expenditures.[51] Lenders, meanwhile, had succeeded in organizing bondholders' associations in Britain, France, and Belgium. This improved the bondholders' abilities to negotiate and effectively suppressed efforts by speculators and issuing bankers to represent them, eliminating middlemen who did not always keep bondholders' best interests in mind.

Lastly, the second epoch still lacked a debt regime. Little innovation occurred in the development of international arrangements in finance. Instead, any intervention in debt rescheduling was still undertaken unilaterally by the governments of the major creditor countries.

Patterns of lending and default

In the 1860s, the boom in lending to Latin America was accompanied by huge capital flows to Egypt and Turkey. The interest in lending was stimulated "by cheap steel, ocean-going steamships, effective refrigeration, and new mining techniques."[52] With capital flowing both East and West from London, a loan mania was particularly evident from 1870 to 1873. It seemed that during this period "[a]ny government which claimed sovereignty over a bit of the earth's surface and a fraction of its inhabitants could find a financial agent in London and purchasers for her bonds."[53]

This boom marked the first of three cycles of lending, retrenchment, and default that preceded the First World War.[54] In 1872, Costa Rica, Santo Domingo, and Paraguay fell into default, and were quickly followed by Bolivia, Guatemala, Liberia, and Uruguay.[55] By 1873, a cyclical downswing began that would bring on "one of the great periods of structural adjustment in the international economy."[56] Overcapacity in agriculture and industry, particularly in iron and steel, propelled a plunge in prices.

Questions of impropriety in the issuing of loans brought on a British Parliamentary investigation in 1875. The committee criticized almost everyone involved.

[50] Fishlow (1985a), p. 388.

[51] Fishlow (1985a) argues that debtors can be divided into the uses to which they put funds: development or current revenue. In the first category are Australia and most of the Latin American countries; in the second most Eastern European and Middle Eastern countries.

[52] United Nations (1955), p. 4. [53] Jenks (1927/1973), p. 282.

[54] See Feis (1930) for the classic study of European lending during this period.

[55] Jenks (1927/1973), pp. 291–292.

[56] Gourevitch (1986), p. 74. See his discussion in Chapter 3 for an excellent analytical discussion of comparative European and American responses to the crisis of 1873–1896.

Expressing opinions similar to those widely held in relation to the most recent crisis, the report noted:

Your Committee feels that it is not their duty to apportion the blame to the different actors in the transactions; to a great extent they agree in the opinion of the Secretary to the Honduras legation, that "the fault of the failure falls with equal force upon all who have interests, rights, claims, complaints, or any participation whatever in these matters. It is a kind of original sin, which reaches even the most innocent who have anything to do with this undertaking."[57]

The next upswing in lending occurred in the mid-1880s. From 1886 to 1890, some £130 million worth of calls for portfolio investment were recorded in the London market, while from 1891 to 1895, the total dropped to only £26 million.[58] This falloff in lending can be attributed to the Baring Crisis in 1890 involving Argentina and Barings, the leading British merchant bank. Although the Bank of England mounted a successful rescue operation to back Argentina, a crisis involving such a prestigious British bank dampened enthusiasm for lending to Latin America. In addition, the Greek default in 1893, and growing debt servicing problems in other borrowing countries, served to bring this second cycle of lending to an end.

The last cycle preceded the outbreak of war at the turn of the century. British investment, concentrated in the first seven years of the 20th century, was matched by sizable French, German, and for the first time, American lending. In Latin America alone, the nominal value of French investments increased from about \$400 million to about \$1.2 billion in 1914.[59] Pre-war German investments in this region amounted to \$900 million. American portfolio investments grew from about \$50 million in 1897 to just under \$1 billion by 1914, with Latin America accounting for some 40% of that total.[60]

Patterns of rescheduling

Most countries in these regions fell rapidly into default with the crisis of 1873. Only Argentina, Brazil, and Chile were spared. As in the first epoch, resolution of debt crises varied considerably, in terms of such measures as sales of assets (the Egyptian case), write-downs of debt, and variation in timing running from 1879 to the 1890s. The cycle of lending that reached its height in the 1880s was followed by a decade of rescheduling involving the repeated issuance of new bonds. Defaults by Venezuela resulted in armed intervention and a forced rescheduling in 1904, and customs management by the United States was imposed in Nicaragua, Haiti, and Santo Domingo at various times in the early twentieth century.

In the second epoch, cyclical factors, although highly significant, are less powerful explanations of default than in the first epoch. Economically stronger states often were able to cope with decreased lending, and such countries as

[57] United Kingdom (1875), p. xlv. [58] Simon (1968), p. 23.
[59] Feis (1930), p. 51. [60] Estimated from Lewis (1938), p. 606.

Canada, the United States, and Australia, for example, resisted default altogether. With respect to rescheduling, although the Council on Foreign Bondholders played an active role in many negotiations, we still see considerable variations in outcomes, particularly in terms of the role of creditor governments in the negotiations. In short, individual variation in the position of the key actors in this epoch are important for explanations of rescheduling outcomes.

To take a concrete example, borrowing by both Nicaragua and Costa Rica during this period shows initial similarities.[61] Each country used their loans for developmental purposes rather than revenue financing. Britain served as creditor for both nations and the Corporation of Foreign Bondholders handled loan renegotiations. Despite these parallels, both countries ended the epoch with markedly different rescheduling experiences.

In 1886, Nicaragua borrowed £285,000 at 6% interest in order to finance the development of its railways. In 1904, the government sought foreign capital again, this time borrowing from the United States. The loan was for $1 million, also at 6% interest, repayable in five years. In 1909 Nicaragua made its third venture into the international capital market, floating bonds for £1.25 million. This loan was used to retire the 1886 bonds, repay the 1904 loan, and finance new railway projects. When Nicaragua faced financial problems, the Corporation of Foreign Bondholders agreed to a renegotiated 5% return on the 1909 loans as an alternative to default.

Costa Rica did not fare as well as Nicaragua during this epoch. It incurred its first foreign debt in 1871 by borrowing £1 million from London at 6%. This was followed in 1872 by another London loan for £2.4 million at seven percent. Both loans were used for the construction of railway lines, and both went into default in 1874. Eleven years later a new settlement was negotiated, which lasted until 1895. Another round of renegotiation in 1897, and subsequent default in 1901, led to a final settlement in 1911 in which £2 million worth of refunding bonds were issued at 5%.

The divergence of these two nations' paths in the debt rescheduling process illustrates my argument that a strictly epochal account of foreign lending is insufficient to explain and predict the outcome of debt negotiations.

Epoch 3: the U.S. at the center, 1920s–1960s

The third epoch in international finance encompasses the period of rapid lending in the 1920s followed by default in the 1930s and rescheduling efforts that lasted into the 1960s. The greatest historical changes over this period – impelled by the First World War and completed by World War II – were the decline of the British Empire and American financial ascendance. The mode of financial intermediation remained the same: banks continued to float borrowers' bonds, but in this era, New York emerged as the center of finance.

[61] This section draws heavily on United Nations (1955).

Epochal characteristics

The international system overall remained multipolar, although the U.S. began to emerge as the key player from the standpoint of overall resources. But as a military power, the U.S. would only shift into high gear with the onset of the Second World War.

In overall economic terms, Britain's heyday had passed. By the late 1920s, its share of world industrial production had dropped below 10%, in contrast to 11.5% for Germany and 42.5% for the U.S.[62] Although Britain still retained the largest share of industrial exports, these comprised primarily the products of mature industries such as textiles, which faced growing competition from Japan and other countries.

Britain's decline as a financial power stemmed in part from its decision to finance its deficit by printing money during the First World War. By the war's end, the U.K. found itself awash in liquidity. The pound's value had dropped from $4.866 to $3.40; if the British had attempted to return to the pre-war gold standard, a serious deflation would have been necessary. Instead the international monetary system shifted to a "gold exchange standard," under which both gold and foreign exchange served as a nation's reserves against its own currency. Only the sterling area's demand for the sterling as a reserve currency steadied the shaky pound, as Britain struggled in vain to regain its financial leadership.

During this same period, the U.S. first exercised its growing international financial strength. It emerged from World War I as a creditor country that enjoyed a strong demand for its goods. Despite evidence of the increasing importance of the U.S. to international capital flows, American leaders failed to recognize that continuing their traditionally isolationist foreign economic policies could have serious effects abroad with repercussions at home. The U.S. maintained a protectionist policy that did not allow other countries to service their debts through the export of goods. Furthermore, U.S. centrality in the system was such that when domestic financial speculation grew – as in the late 1920s – the internal demand for funds diverted lending that was needed internationally. Driven by lending rather than by trade, the system was fragile. This fragility, combined with American reluctance to assume leadership and British inability to continue leading, eventually led to an international crash.[63]

American investment in Latin America grew dramatically during the period: from 1914–1919, investment increased by 50%, and from 1919–1929, by more than 100%. This capital flowed overwhelmingly into public coffers; as much as 80% of American funds went toward the purchase of publicly floated bonds. By 1930, 14 out of 20 Latin American countries had floated new bonds. During the depression, however, little new capital flowed into the area, which led to defaults on previously amassed external debt. In Europe, the U.K.'s investment ceased to grow, as a small new outflow was offset by equivalent funds returning

[62] League of Nations (1942), pp. 128 and 157–158.
[63] See Kindleberger (1973a) for a discussion of this period.

due to amortization on bonds and other investments. On the continent, France no longer invested new funds because of the depreciation of the French franc. War-weakened Germany also no longer lent to anyone, but other European creditors maintained or slightly increased their Latin American holdings.[64]

As in the previous two epochs, bondholders held their investments directly, and formed private bodies to coordinate actions aimed at regaining their investments when defaults occurred. Once U.S. loans became important the government promoted an American "Foreign Bondholders' Protective Council, Inc.," a counterpart to the British Council of the Corporation of Foreign Bondholders. And like Great Britain, the U.S. government mostly shunned intervention. In March 1922, the U.S. State Department explicitly refused to pass judgment on the economic merits of specific foreign loans (but continued to occasionally indicate its views on specific loans). In the early thirties, official scrutiny ended altogether.[65]

The end of the First World War saw additional countries joining the sovereign borrowing bandwagon. Most capital flowed from the U.S. (the new center of international finance) to Europe (especially Germany), and to Latin America and Canada (as before the war). Instead of financing developmental projects such as railroads, the foreign capital bolstered reserves, balanced governmental deficits, and financed current expenditures.[66]

The third epoch also saw a significant role for the League of Nations in rescheduling for some European countries. In many respects, League loans to Eastern European countries aimed at stabilizing their economies resemble current IMF programs, complete with austerity targets and conditionality. The League did not, however, play a role with respect to Latin American debts.

As a result of the 1922 Genoa Agreement to stabilize currencies, under the auspices of the League of Nations, central banks loaned the Austrian government $260 million to support its currency. In a move similar to the U.S. Treasury's action in the current epoch to help several Latin American debtors, the Bank of England granted an advance to Austria, enabling it to use the designated funds months before the League loan was actually issued.[67] When Hungary, Italy, Yugoslavia, and Greece received loans, a growing group of central banks participated in these international efforts carried out under League of Nations authority. Leading commercial banks were also involved. J.P. Morgan participated in the effort, which offered $435 million in 1924 alone.[68] Other loans were put together outside the League for countries such as Poland and Rumania.

Conditions were imposed on state borrowers, just as they are today. The Financial Committee of the League based these loans on recipient attempts to get its "house back in order." These programs usually required the government to balance the budget, curtail economic expansion, and align prices. They also required central banks to operate independently from governments, and to carry

[64] United Nations (1955), pp. 7–9. [65] United Nations (1955), p. 9.
[66] Fishlow (1985), pp. 73–74. [67] Einzig (1932), p. 13. [68] Brandes (1962), p. 158.

adequate reserves.[69] As in later criticisms of the IMF, the League was accused of being too intolerant.

It was said and not without reason, that the principles of the Finance Committee of the League . . . were too dogmatic, and failed to take into consideration the difference between a financially developed and underdeveloped country . . . The insistence of the authorities for instance, in the case of Bulgaria and Estonia that the central banks should be controlled by private shareholders instead of the government has caused both countries considerable inconvenience as it was not in accord with local conditions.[70]

Governments in need of assistance became increasingly unwilling to submit to these conditions. Desiring a measure of policymaking control, they sought representation in the committees that made the decisions. In fact, the Danish National Bank rejected League conditions and instead stabilized its exchange rate with the aid of credits by the Hambros Bank of England and several American banks.[71]

Almost all League loans went into default by 1932 as the world economy turned sour. The Bank of England promoted the development of a League Loans Committee to assist recovery of lost payments and capital on these loans. Despite this committee's efforts, very little debt servicing took place.[72]

Patterns of lending and default

The United States, predominant creditor of the 1920s, sent abroad nearly $9 billion from 1919 to 1929, accounting for about two-thirds of all investment.[73] Lending fluctuated considerably during this period, with major declines in 1921, 1923, 1926, and 1928. Some observers remained optimistic about continued lending, but by 1929, borrowers paid over a billion dollars more in interest, dividends, and amortization than they received in new loans and investments. The last severe drop in 1928 (due to the diversion of funds to the U.S. stock market) crushed the servicing prospects of both European and Latin American borrowers. Lending picked up in 1930 and 1931, but was too little too late. The deflationary shock to the world economy had taken its toll: depression had set in.

By 1933, 12 Latin American countries and nine European countries suspended at least part of their debt servicing. They were joined by Germany in 1933.[74] Although some Latin American countries restored partial servicing in the mid-1930s, by 1937, 85% of these bonds had gone into default.[75] In 1935, slightly over $1.5 billion of a total $1.866 billion in outstanding bonds were in default. The amount in default declined to $750.5 million by 1945, before falling to $127 million by 1952.[76]

[69] Clarke (1967), pp. 42–44. [70] Einzig (1932), p. 17.
[71] Einzig (1932), pp. 17–18. [72] Borchard (1951), p. 215.
[73] Aldcroft (1977), p. 241. The following discussion of lending draws on this excellent review of financial markets in the 1920s. For other analyses of this period, see the citations in this work.
[74] Winkler (1933). [75] See Felix (1984) and his references on bond defaults.
[76] United Nations (1955), p. 157.

Patterns of debt rescheduling

Terms of rescheduling varied considerably in this epoch. Some countries, such as Argentina, the Dominican Republic, and Haiti, met most of their servicing and principal obligations. At the other extreme, Brazil and Mexico offered bondholders only a small percentage of their outstanding claims. In rescheduling negotiations, both the American and British bondholders' committees played the central negotiating role. In addition, the newly created World Bank's reluctance to make loans to countries that had not reached settlements undoubtedly stimulated rapid settlement at the end of the period. In an unmistakably clear message to Ecuador, for example, the Bank pointedly stated that it "would not feel it right to extend credit facilities to the Ecuadorean Government until the latter enters into negotiations with the [British] Council and gives assurances which the Council can consider adequate."[77] Similar pressure by the American Export-Import Bank also encouraged the rapid post-war settlements. As in the last epoch, a comparison of two case studies, Bolivia and Panama, will illustrate how similarities in patterns of borrowing and default give way to significant differences in rescheduling.

The Bolivian case followed a pattern typical of Latin American defaults in the thirties. The nation began the twenties with negligible debt.[78] By 1930, however, Bolivia had amassed an $80 million debt, predominantly borrowed on the U.S. market. Like other countries, as Bolivia borrowed more externally, internal borrowing decreased dramatically in relative importance. In 1920 external debt was only 28% of total public debt, but by 1930 it had risen to 89% of total public debt.

Like many developing nations, Bolivia's economy was dependent upon one primary commodity export (tin, in Bolivia's case). When the price of primary commodities collapsed in 1929, Bolivia saw the value of its tin exports fall from $36.6 million to $17 million in only one year.[79] The drop in the price of tin created an overall government revenue decrease of 28%.[80] Bolivia's Siles government, on the verge of being ousted because of social unrest, used the last foreign loan it received to prevent default in mid-1930. The military government that overthrew Siles in late 1930 attempted to negotiate a refunding loan. But this attempt, coupled with sharp cuts in military spending, proved insufficient to spare Bolivia from earning the dubious distinction of the first Latin American country of this epoch to default in 1931.[81] It did not take actions to resume payment on its foreign debt until 1948.[82]

Another Latin American nation, Panama, entered the international capital arena with an issue placed in the United States in 1914. From 1923 to 1929 Panama's foreign obligations swelled to $21.3 million, $17.5 million for which the government was directly responsible. The Canal Annuity and the Constitutional Fund

[77] Corporation of Foreign Bondholders (1948), quoted in United Nations (1955), p. 12, n. 38.
[78] Discussion in this paragraph draws heavily on Contreras (1990), p. 267.
[79] United Nations (1955), p. 43. [80] Contreras (1990), p. 281.
[81] Contreras (1990), p. 281. [82] United Nations (1955), p. 43.

guaranteed the debt service payments of these issues. The stagnant world economy of the early thirties, coupled with a dispute over the gold value of dollars paid in the Canal Annuity, however, led Panama to discontinue its interest payments in May of 1933 within two years of Bolivia.[83]

Panama began to reschedule its debt service payments as early as 1940, and soon floated a new $4 million loan on the U.S. market. This speedy rescheduling during a time of international economic difficulty was greatly aided by a U.S. decision to raise the Canal Annuity from $250,000 to $430,000, an important concession because the Canal Zone accounted for 15% of Panama's national income.[84]

This epoch showcases the strikingly similar timing with which nearly all debtor nations discontinued debt service in the face of the tightening capital market. The amount of time it took for these nations to reschedule their debts, as well as the nature of the agreements they eventually concluded, however, varied significantly. Bolivia, for example, did not begin to reschedule its payments until 1948, while Panama, with its close ties to the United States, was able to begin rescheduling eight years earlier. Countries such as Peru and Ecuador did not conclude accords until the early and mid-1950s. Moreover, whereas Mexico was permitted to write down most of its debt to less than 10 cents on the dollar and voided most of its interest arrears, others did not receive any reduction of the principal and only received moderate reductions in outstanding interest.[85]

Epoch 4: the current crisis and beyond, 1970s–1990s

OPEC's successful manipulation of oil prices in 1973–1974 has been seen justifiably as one of the most significant events in political relations between developed and less developed countries (LDCs). The impact of this price increase on the international financial system has been equally striking. Bank lending to developing countries grew throughout the 1960s – accounting for some 33% of total lending. But the magnitude of LDC and Eastern Bloc debt has grown particularly rapidly since the first oil crisis as petrodollars were recycled. In 1973, the medium- and long-term debt of LDCs (over one year in maturity) was $97.3 billion; by the end of 1981, it had soared to $425.2 billion. Concurrently, Eastern Bloc debt grew tenfold from approximately $8 to $80 billion. The total outstanding debt of LDCs and Eastern Bloc countries now approaches one trillion dollars. In Latin America, Asia, East Europe, and Africa, countries have sought to reschedule their loans, with strategies and outcomes ranging from outright defaults, as in Bolivia, to continued rescheduling accords as in Mexico, Argentina, Poland, and Venezuela.

[83] United Nations (1955), p. 124. [84] United Nations (1955), pp. 124 and 128.
[85] See United Nations (1955), p. 11 and Marichal (1989), pp. 212–213.

Epochal characteristics

What is the international distribution of capabilities in our own epoch? Considering the sum of overall economic, political, and military resources, the world is bipolar, although with the demise of the Soviet Union, it looks increasingly unipolar at the international overall level. Because Russia continues to possess significant numbers of nuclear weapons, however, many agree that a bipolar structure persists.

By contrast if we look only at the international economy, the U.S. still remains dominant, but Japan and Germany have emerged as significant economic powers. Although analysts have frequently pointed to the decline of American hegemony, reports of American demise are premature. In the financial realm, American banks occupy an important role: they accounted for 35.7% of total international lending to Argentina, Brazil, and Mexico, the major borrowers in Latin America. In addition, much of this debt has been concentrated in the hands of a few large North American creditors, so that their perspective on rescheduling has a disproportionately large impact on negotiations. The European banking community, on the other hand, has played a more significant role in financing Eastern Europe.

Unlike earlier epochs, today the banks as corporations hold responsibility for the money they lend, instead of playing middlemen to bondholders who earn profits and absorb the bulk of losses. Many analysts have argued that this change is of great significance for at least three reasons. First, individual corporations wield much more power than individual bondholders (especially since many of the corporations deeply involved in the current debt crisis are among the largest), and thus can make their demands more forcefully. Second, a relatively small number of corporations threatened with bankruptcy can organize themselves for collective action more readily than thousands of individuals facing losses. And finally, because corporate losses threaten both national and international financial systems, creditor governments are motivated to become more actively involved in rescheduling. In fact, as I shall argue, these apparent changes have not been as significant for debt rescheduling outcomes as many believe.

Turning to borrowers, developing countries have been the most significant debtors in our own epoch. In many cases, the countries that needed to reschedule their debts in this epoch are the same debtor countries that owed money and sought adjustments in the nineteenth century: Mexico, Brazil, and Argentina, among others. Although considerably more stable as nation-states than the developing countries of the early nineteenth century, many of the same problems of poor fiscal management beset these countries in the twentieth century.

Finally, with respect to international regimes, the most influential international organization in debt rescheduling has been the International Monetary Fund.[86] The IMF was designed primarily to fund loans to countries suffering from temporary balance-of-payments disequilibria. Over time, the Fund's role

[86] The World Bank has begun to take a more active role in the debt crisis but remains secondary to the International Monetary Fund.

has shifted because of its inability to cover the sizable shortfalls suffered by many third world countries, and because of increased availability of funds on the private capital market (mainly petrodollars recycled through the unregulated Eurocurrency markets). Recently, the IMF has come to serve as an arbiter of creditworthiness on private markets; and private lenders have sought to link further lending to Fund approval. As we shall see in the examination of our cases, the IMF has also played a key role in monitoring debt rescheduling agreements.[87]

Whereas the IMF and other international organizations influenced debt rescheduling throughout the 1980s, the most significant move toward regime creation came with the March 1989 announcement of a new plan by U.S. Treasury Secretary Nicholas Brady. He placed the U.S. firmly behind the process of debt reduction. Based in part on a plan proposed by Japan and France in 1988, Brady proposed that debt reduction and/or debt service reduction be combined with increased lending and continuation of growth-oriented economic adjustment. The U.S. endorsed debt reduction as necessary to help reforming countries break out of the debt cycle, viewing excess debt and net transfer of resources as stifling economic recovery in countries that could otherwise serve as important export markets.

The Brady Plan, as it came to be known, was not the first to employ "voluntary debt relief," a strategy that had been attempted earlier in the form of debt-equity swaps and the debt-bond program of 1988. The crucial change involved designating the IMF and World Bank (along with creditor and debtor governments) guarantors of both principal and interest payments on the exit bonds.[88] Moreover, this plan called for the banks to waive the sharing and negative-pledge provisions that had allowed free-riders to continue collecting interest without participating in new arrangements.[89] IMF Managing Director Michel Camdessus endorsed Brady's proposal. Camdessus had also come to side with the debtors, stressing that countries willing to enact domestic reforms "need to be able, from the outset, to count on a more adequate alleviation of the present drag of debt-service payments on their adjustment efforts."[90]

Neither Brady nor Camdessus proposed an abandonment of debtor adjustment and economic reforms. Quite the contrary, reduction would be exclusively available to countries with records of consistent economic reform, but with persistently stagnating economies such as Mexico. Debt reduction was designed to serve as both a complement and an incentive to adjustment. But the proposal represented a more flexible position on debt rescheduling for the IMF. Among other measures, it permitted the conclusion of adjustment programs – even in the presence of interest arrears. At the meeting of the Interim Committee of the Board of Governors, in April 1989, the Finance Ministers supported Brady's proposal, recommending that the Fund apply its resources to facilitate debt reduction for countries implementing economic reforms.[91]

[87] For a discussion of the role of the Fund in the debt crisis, see Aggarwal (1987).
[88] *The Economist*, March 18, 1989, pp. 17–18. [89] *The Economist*, March 18, 1989, p. 110.
[90] *IMF Survey*, March 20, 1989, p. 91. [91] *IMF Survey*, April 17, 1989, p. 113.

Under the Brady Plan, we have entered a distinct phase in debt rescheduling.[92] Although there has been some variation in both the timing and provisions of the accords, we have seen considerable uniformity in debt rescheduling. The Brady approach has brought bilateral debt rescheduling efforts more into the fold of an "international debt regime." Negotiations are still on a case by case basis, as has been the norm for textile negotiations under the Long Term and Multi-Fiber Arrangement, but bargaining has taken on a distinct set of features. All Brady Plan agreements have called for a basic menu of options: interest or principal reduction, new money in one form or the other, and sustained participation by the United States and the IMF. Moreover, at least with respect to major debtors, the average reduction in debt obligations has been in the range of 30 to 35%. In the past, whereas IMF and creditor government intervention was common, debtors and lenders could not count on an ongoing commitment on the part of these actors.

Although the Brady Plan does not contain formal rules, it does have clear principles, norms, and procedures. These provide participants with a greater sense of certainty and an expectation that the regime will regulate and control the behavior of all actors in a sustained fashion. While the Brady Plan has not dramatically affected the amount of capitals flows between debtors and lenders – at least in the short run – the development of a meta-regime and partial regime has altered actors' behavior in debt negotiations. Thus while the impact that the Brady Plan has had on negotiations in view of its limited direct financial importance at first glance is puzzling, analytical insights from the study of international regimes illuminate this phenomenon. The Brady Plan helps to diminish moral hazard and uncertainty, allows actors to control one another's behavior through norms and procedures, and constrains actors because of the nested connections among different international arrangements.[93] In bilateral negotiations, banks and debtors have thus been willing to be considerably more concessionary toward each other than might otherwise have been the case. As I will show in my discussion of bilateral negotiations under the auspices of the Brady Plan, this arrangement considerably alters our expectations of actors' behavior and payoffs in debt games.

Patterns of lending and default

The onset of debt problems in the 1980s has been similar to those of previous epochs.[94] As before, growing trade and increasingly available private funding from flush banks encouraged countries to borrow. An important departure from previous epochs, however, has been the development of new financial markets and mechanisms that have accelerated the lending drive. These mechanisms include the aforementioned Eurocurrency market and the advent of loan syndication.

[92] For an excellent discussion of the implications of the Brady Plan, see Clark (1993).

[93] See Keohane (1984) on transactions costs arguments and Aggarwal (1983, 1985) on control and nesting considerations.

[94] For a good discussion of parallels in this regard, see Marichal (1989), p. 233.

During the 1960s, most lending to the developing countries came from public institutions such as the World Bank and the Inter-American Development Bank, as well as from creditor governments. After the 1973 oil crisis, however, international banks became flush as oil producing countries poured their money into these banks, expanding the funds available in the Euromarket. This market, earlier known as the Eurodollar market, had developed in the 1960s and early 1970s as the U.S. ran trade deficits and expanded its money supply after overspending in Vietnam and at home. The Eurocurrency market readily accomplished the task of recycling the vast inflow of funds. Newly creditworthy developing countries in Latin America, Asia, and Eastern Europe faced serious balance of payments problems as their oil bills increased. As governments found economic adjustment to be politically unpopular, the international banks provided a welcome source of capital. At the same time, even oil-rich countries borrowed money, in anticipation of rapidly growing future revenues.

Lending in the 1970s was accelerated by an incentive system created through the loan syndication process. Although banks lent on their own account, they could often garner large fees with less risk by arranging loans involving large numbers of banks. These so-called lead banks, with regional and smaller banks in tow, searched far and wide for lending opportunities.

The banks found a ready market in places such as Latin America. Countries in this region had a high demand for funds as state-owned enterprises and other public actors expanded their activities.[95] The lending system entailed recycling funds from OPEC countries to banks to developing borrowers, who then sold goods to developed countries, allowing them to pay for their oil imports. It worked smoothly at first. By the second oil shock of 1979, however, which jacked prices up to a high of $35 a barrel in 1981, concern grew among some analysts that the process would prove unsustainable. Yet the renewed inflow of funds into international banks after the post-1979 oil crisis compelled the banks to continue high rates of lending or refuse deposits. But as countries faced pending loan repayments, they turned increasingly to shorter term borrowing, aggravating the need for continued access to capital.[96] At the same time, the aggregate amount of loans skyrocketed. Latin American debt grew from $75.4 billion in 1975 to nearly $315 billion by the end of 1982. By 1983, external debt had reached 325% of the region's exports of goods and services as compared to 166% in 1975.[97]

By 1981, the crisis began to take shape. Faced with strong inflationary pressures, the U.S. pursued tight monetary policies that both drove up interest rates on existing loans (which had been made at floating rates) and induced a recession in the developed countries, thus hurting export prospects for the debtors. In addition, capital flight from many debtor countries exacerbated the crisis as did worsening terms of trade for debtors. For non-oil producing debtors, these shocks,

[95] On this point, see Frieden (1981).

[96] In Latin America, short-term debt as a proportion of imports grew to 65% in 1981 from 26% in 1975. Inter-American Development Bank (hereinafter, IDB) (1984a), p. 16.

[97] See IDB (1984a), pp. 3 and 12.

combined with steep oil prices before 1981, were threatening. For oil exporters such as Mexico, the effect of an oil price plunge in 1981, higher interest rates, and worsening export prospects proved lethal. Although Mexico was not the first to seek bank rescheduling (Poland and Argentina needed to reschedule as early as 1981), its massive debts of over $80 billion proved too much for the existing rescheduling mechanisms to handle. By August 1982, Mexico neared complete default. As banks continued to retrench, Brazil, Argentina, and other major debtors found themselves in similar crises. By 1983, over 25 countries were in arrears, initiating more than a decade of rescheduling efforts which is only now drawing to a close.

Patterns of debt rescheduling

During this epoch, the pattern of debt rescheduling has evolved considerably.[98] In the early stages of the debt crisis, we saw crisis-based active intervention by creditor governments and the IMF. More recently, we have seen a more regularized, regime-like approach to rescheduling.[99]

From late 1982 to early 1983, all actors dealt with the debt problem as an immediate fire-fighting problem. The banks were initially reluctant to provide new inflows of funds to debtors. Prodded by the U.S. and IMF, however, they provided "jumbo loans" of several billion dollars to Mexico, Brazil, and other major debtors, in exchange for promises to implement austerity programs under IMF supervision. In these cases, the IMF and the creditor governments also imposed conditions on the banks, forcing them to provide new funds in accordance with IMF guidelines. Although debtors talked loudly about forming a cartel, in practice these actors failed to unite because they worried that they would have to eventually compete for future funds, their adjustment efforts came at different times, and their individual financial positions varied greatly.[100] Meanwhile, creditor governments worried about the health of banks. Concerned that payment delays might set off a chain reaction of collapsing banks because of their high levels of outstanding debt as a proportion of capital,[101] creditor governments worked to ensure payments from debtors.

After the immediate crisis was allayed by 1984, Mexico, followed by other major debtors, began to negotiate multiyear rescheduling agreements, or MYRAs. Each set of negotiations with a debtor was explicitly treated by both public and private creditors as unique. Attempts by debtors to discuss more general across-the-board forms of relief were continuously rebuffed. But as debtors adjusted under IMF auspices, they faced growing political instability as their policies

[98] Good recent surveys of debt rescheduling and adjustment in this epoch include Cooper (1992), Haggard and Kaufman (1992), and Biersteker (1993).

[99] For a discussion of rescheduling in the early stages, among many others see Lipson (1985) and Aggarwal (1987). The latter phases or stages of debt rescheduling are treated with a broad brush in Economic Commission for Latin America and the Caribbean (hereinafter ECLAC) (1990).

[100] For a discussion, see Aggarwal (1987), Chapter 4.

[101] By the end of 1982, developing country loans represented nearly 290% of the top nine U.S. banks' capital.

sparked recessions and massive unemployment. By 1984, it became clear that the crisis was not simply one of illiquidity; stop-gap lending would not resolve the problem. Without prospects for either funding on a larger scale or some debt alleviation through write-downs, the debt burden of these states continued to grow. In the meantime, economic decline continued, with Latin American debtors' GDP per capita in 1985 8% lower than in 1980.[102]

As crisis loomed, U.S. Secretary of the Treasury James Baker announced a new plan in late 1985 at the joint annual World Bank and IMF meetings.[103] His proposal was a three-part plan for lenders: First, commercial banks were asked to provide $20 billion in additional loans to 17 debtors over the next three years. Second, he called on the World Bank and the Inter-American Development Bank (IDB) to increase their commitments to these debtors by $9 billion, also over the next three years. Third, he suggested that the anticipated $2.7 billion in repayments to the IMF go to help the poorest (mainly African) debtors. In exchange for this new stream of funding, debtors were to adopt market-oriented policies such as the promotion of increased domestic savings, encouragement of foreign investment, deregulation, privatization, trade liberalization, and so on.

In practice, the Baker Plan proved deficient. Although many debtors did attempt significant adjustment, and the lenders did come forth with the loans after significant arm-twisting, the continued net outflow of capital in the form of repayments on debt continued to seriously damage the debtors' economies. Faced with declines in commodity prices, and then in oil prices, debtors failed to stage a sustained recovery.

In February 1987, the Brazilians declared a moratorium and Mexico, among other debtors, continued to suffer a financial crisis. The U.S. modified the Baker Plan to incorporate options such as debt-equity swaps, debt-for-bond exchanges, and exit bonds (which allowed recalcitrant banks to swap their debt for guaranteed bonds at lower rates). Although none of these measures actually alleviated the ongoing problems, they would set a precedent for the upcoming Brady Plan.

In May 1987, Citicorp increased its loan loss reserves by 150%, and other banks soon followed. In the second quarter of 1987, U.S. banks registered a loss of $11 billion as they added $21 billion to loan loss reserves. Although such losses were unprecedented since the Great Depression, they served to strengthen the banks' positions in negotiations with debtors as the banks' balance sheet improved. Initially, this action decreased American concern about the debt crisis and only hardened its position toward the debtors as risk to the financial system as a whole dropped. But as Mexico, Argentina, and Venezuela faced growing political problems, the U.S. was forced to respond by adopting a plan to deal with the debt problem on a longer term basis.

After 1989, under the Brady Plan, agreements have been concluded by all major Latin American debtors and a few other countries in other regions of the

[102] ECLAC (1990), p. 10.

[103] For discussions of the Baker Plan, among others, see Aggarwal (1987) and ECLAC (1990).

world accounting for over 80% of problem debtors.[104] In each case, the accords have been marked by relatively similar provisions on debt restructuring involving principal write-downs, lower fixed interest rate bonds, and disbursement of new money. The agreements have generally been backed by funds provided by international organizations and creditor governments. Most accords seem to have led to successful restoration of normal financial relations, although the success of the arrangements has clearly been influenced by a fall in interest rates since 1989. Although large-scale capital flows have not resumed directly from banks, increased confidence by the financial community has led to an inflow of capital into these countries' equity markets. In the eyes of most analysts, the current epoch's debt crisis has now been resolved. Yet the recent shift in financing from bank debt to "hot" money flows into the stock and bond markets of debtor countries has threatened their recovery – as illustrated by the December 1994 Mexican financial crisis.

Conclusion

This chapter has developed the notion of historical epochs characterized by specific systemic factors. My objective has been to ascertain the extent to which epochal analysis of 170 years of debt crises allows us to account for possible variation in the manner countries reschedule their debts.

I characterize epochs in terms of the distribution of capabilities in the overall, economic, and debt system, the types of units involved in debt negotiations, and the presence or absence of international norms and rules.[105] My objective has been to gain insight into the degree to which debtors make economic adjustments, the degree of lending concessions by bondholders or bankers, and the extent of government or international organization intervention in debt negotiations.

Although an epochal analysis with a focus on lending booms and busts proved helpful in accounting for patterns of borrowing and the timing of default, we saw much less consistency across cases of rescheduling within epochs. Thus, to understand debt rescheduling, it is essential to develop a model with a more precise focus on case-specific negotiations – a theoretical task I take up in the next three chapters. Still, it is valuable to review the epochal-based insights, albeit limited, that come from this chapter.

Considering all four epochs together, both the similarities and changes in several structural characteristics appear to account for some of the variation in

[104] Clark (1993).

[105] An alternative aggregate level approach would be to examine significant cognitive shifts over time. For example, one could examine differences in epochs by examining whether beliefs about the need to service loans (or not service them, for that matter) have shifted over time, either among debtor countries or among lenders. There also do not appear to be significant differences in creditor government behavior, although full-fledged occupation has clearly not occurred. But even in the past, such intervention was rare and generally tied to other political objectives. Although my investigation of debt rescheduling over time in this chapter does not provide an in-depth analysis of cognitive changes, I have failed to detect any such shifts over the last 170 years.

rescheduling. Turning first to the distribution of capabilities in the overall, economic, and financial systems, the entry of new lenders as a result of changing economic fortunes appears to be important. For example, the Mexicans were encouraged to conclude an agreement with their bondholders in 1888 (ending their longstanding default from the early 1820s) in anticipation of loans from newly emerging lenders.

Changes in the overall distribution of capabilities proved significant to a degree in altering the incentives of creditor governments to foster debt settlements, particularly during and after the Second World War. For example, the U.S. became highly interested in resolving outstanding problems with Latin American debtors, and made it clear to American lenders that they would not pressure debtors to come to a settlement. In fact, by making loans to these countries or other economic arrangements, the U.S. partially undercut the bondholders' ability to pressure the debtors.

Often, the more significant influence concerns the number of powers actively involved in a particular region, rather than the distribution of capabilities as a whole. Thus, in the mid-nineteenth century in Latin America, the most important powers jockeying for position were the U.S., Great Britain, and France. Rescheduling outcomes were influenced by such intrigue, as with the French intervention in Mexico in the 1860s, but power plays did not have a uniform effect on rescheduling outcomes. More recently, with the economic rivalry among powers in the 1980s and early 1990s, the U.S. appears to have been motivated to promote debt reduction as a response to Japanese and French initiatives for debt reduction, resulting in the Brady Plan and the agreements it spawned.

With respect to changing capabilities of debtors, newly independent countries behaved somewhat differently than more established ones. Thus, in the first epoch, debtors were anxious to borrow money and promised to reschedule because of their dire need for funds, both to defend their borders and also simply to raise revenue domestically. But when it came to the actual implementation of rescheduling accords, most countries failed to deliver on their promises because of their high degree of domestic instability and lack of financial resources.

With respect to the type of lenders, the shift from bondholders to bankers has been given significant prominence in the literature. Many scholars argue that, among other implications, the change has led to less willingness of lenders to accept debt reduction. However, this factor is not as important as has been suggested. In part, much analysis of debt rescheduling has ignored the fact that bankers sometimes held a great deal of the bonds they floated on behalf of debtors themselves. Thus, the notion that the current epoch is radically different in this respect from earlier epochs may not provide as much explanatory power as some have suggested. Instead, as I shall argue based on theoretical and empirical analysis in the chapters that follow, the degree of cohesion among the lenders, be they bankers or bondholders, would appear to be the more important factor.

This shift in types of lenders has also been used to account for the greater degree of intervention by creditor governments in the current epoch. While this pattern does appear to be related to the greater concern of creditor governments about the stability of financial systems, these governments often intervened in the past for a host of reasons.

One of the most significant developments has been the role of international organizations. In the third epoch, the League began to play some role in reschedulings, but its actions were quickly overwhelmed by the global depression of the 1930s. By contrast, in the fourth epoch, the IMF (and the Bank for International settlements [BIS] to a lesser extent) played a significant role from the outset, and continuously affected the nature of rescheduling agreements. More recently, with the linkage of creditor governments and financial organization policies through the Brady Plan, we have seen a move toward uniformity in outcomes, although the timing of agreements has differed somewhat.

To summarize: aggregate level analysis does indeed provide considerable insight into the lending and default process. It proves much less powerful for analyzing debt rescheduling, at least until the last few years. At the same time, the factors we have used in examining debt rescheduling at an aggregate level help in pointing to the variables that we need to incorporate in our effort to model specific debt negotiations. It is to this task that we now turn.

APPENDIX

Coding of lending concessions and economic adjustment

1. Lending Concessions

No/Low Concessions: same terms, no new funds

Medium Concessions: significant rescheduling package with new money, some interest reductions or principal write-down, some new funds

High Concessions: debt forgiveness, significant interest rate reduction, large new lending

2. Economic Adjustment

No/Low Adjustment: no or minor policy changes

Medium Adjustment: some efforts to cut money supply or fiscal deficit, partial assignment of revenue

High Adjustment: cut in money supply and fiscal deficit, high assignment of other revenues to lender

Note: The coding of lenders' and debtors' behavior will be dependent on the epochal context. In addition, both adjustment and lending concessions for a particular case are considered in relation to other outcomes.

2 Debt games and play: toward a model of debt rescheduling

We have seen how an epochal analysis sheds some light on patterns of debt rescheduling. But given the consistently high variation in the nature and timing of agreements in different epochs, we must move to a less aggregate analysis to predict rescheduling outcomes. This and the subsequent two chapters draw on insights from game theory and theories of political economy to develop a model of bilateral debt negotiations between lenders and debtors, which also allows for possible intervention by creditor governments and international organizations.

Scholars have increasingly turned to game theory to understand strategic interaction among actors.[1] Although this approach has successfully provided insights into many questions in international relations and political economy, it has not been without its detractors. Critics of the use of game theory argue that among other problems, analysts often fail to justify their use of game theoretic approaches, do not make their assumptions clear, and are attracted to technically sophisticated models solely for form's sake at the expense of empirical applicability.

Two additional problems have also tarnished the reputation of the game theoretic approach. First, scholars often simply rework their analysis of an empirical bargaining situation in game theoretic language, failing to provide any additional insight. The basic problem stems from an arbitrary or post-hoc assignment of particular payoff orderings to bargainers. Unless theorists derive utilities from knowledge of actors' characteristics,[2] such efforts simply become misguided attempts to generate sophisticated games that are not empirically applicable. Second, scholars often assume that payoffs remain static. Rather than assuming that actors repeatedly face the same game payoffs, we must consider how games might change over time.

This chapter begins the task of addressing these criticisms. The first two sections provide an introduction to the key concepts of normal form games and Nash equilibrium, which can be skipped by those who are already familiar with them. In the third section, I begin my modeling effort by considering assumptions about the rescheduling process by specifying the actors and issues involved in negotiations. This section also presents the basic game I use to analyze debt rescheduling. Chapters 3 and 4 will complete my argument.

[1] For a good basic discussion of game theory see Davis (1983). More advanced works include von Neumann and Morgenstern (1944), Luce and Raiffa (1957), Harsanyi (1977), Friedman (1986), Harsanyi and Selten (1988), Fudenberg and Tirole (1991), and Myerson (1991).

[2] For an important exception to this point, see Allan (1983). For a discussion of this question, see Snidal (1985a). Also see Powell (1994).

Rational choice theory

Why is a game theoretic approach most appropriate to analyze bargaining between debtors and lenders? And how might we incorporate intervention by creditor governments and international organizations into a bargaining game? In order to answer these questions, we must examine the assumptions we make about the character of the decisionmaking environment.[3]

Let us assume that an actor has to choose between alternative actions and that the consequences of each choice is known (presumably because they cannot be influenced either by chance or by the action of other individuals). This case is defined as decisionmaking under conditions of *certainty*. An actor's rational choice in this instance would be the action that gave that actor the highest utility.

If the outcomes of some or all of the actor's alternative actions depend on chance events, but the actor knows the objective probabilities of each outcome, this case is defined as decisionmaking under *risk*. In this situation, the rational decisionmaker calculates the expected utility corresponding to each alternative action and chooses the action for which the expected utility is the highest.

By contrast, under conditions of *uncertainty*, actors do not know the probabilities associated with the outcomes of their choices. If they can assign subjective probabilities to these outcomes, however, the expected utility approach can still be fruitfully employed. Bruce Bueno de Mesquita and his colleagues use this approach in analyzing international conflict and foreign policy choices.[4]

The implied assumption in modeling decisionmaking in the three cases examined above is that strategic interaction does not determine outcomes: these approaches presume that actors make an independent assessment of probabilities without considering strategic play.

Yet in a situation in which actors' choices are *interdependent*, a game theoretic approach provides us with the best analytical tool. In such cases, the most effective strategy often depends on what the decisionmaker expects his opponent to do, while he assumes that the opponent is making similar calculations. Thus, in contrast to individual decisionmaking theory, in which an actor assumes that his counterpart does not adjust his strategy in response to his best guess about what his opponent will choose, such calculations are essential for choosing a strategy in interdependent decisionmaking situations.

In my analysis of international debt rescheduling, I assume that debtors and lenders interact strategically; thus their choices cannot be considered independently. In most debt rescheduling situations, this would seem to be an appropriate assumption, as bargainers appear to choose policies in view of what their opponents are likely to do, both for initial choices and possible retaliatory moves. To examine intervention decisions by creditor governments and international

[3] For a good discussion of decisionmaking theory see John Harsanyi (1977), particularly pp. 8–11. I follow his distinctions in the analysis below.

[4] See, e.g., Bueno de Mesquita (1981); for an analysis of foreign policy choices, see Bueno de Mesquita, Newman, and Rabushka (1985).

		Lender	
		High Concessions (HC)	Low Concessions (LC)
Debtor	High Adjustment (HA)	Successful rescheduling	Unilateral adjustment
	Low Adjustment (LA)	Debt repudiation	Breakdown

Figure 2.1. *An illustrative normal form rescheduling game*

organizations, however, I model their choices as decisionmaking under certainty for reasons that I elaborate on in Chapter 3.

An introduction to some basic game theory concepts

Although game theory has become a highly technical subject, readers unfamiliar with the subject need only concern themselves with some simple concepts to understand the basic thrust of the modeling used in this book.[5] The first part of this section reviews some basic game theory ideas using examples from debt rescheduling. The second part discusses one popular approach to solving games for equilibria, the Nash solution.

Normal form games

I begin with some definitions and examples of normal form games in the context of debt rescheduling.[6] By way of definition, a normal form game specifies (1) the players involved in the game, (2) the actions or strategies available to the players, and (3) the utility or payoffs each actor would receive as a result of both his and his opponent's choice. For illustrative purposes, I will work with a simple debt rescheduling game involving a debtor and a lender, before working with a more realistic depiction of the rescheduling negotiations.

Consider the single-shot debt game in Figure 2.1 that has a single lender and debtor, each of whom must choose between only two actions.[7] The debtor may choose to sharply adjust its economy (HA), or to not adjust it (LA); the lender

[5] Those interested in the technical issues of comparing alternative rescheduling models should consult the Appendix to the book and its footnotes for further references.

[6] I focus this section on so-called normal form games. This type of game represents the strategies available to each actor as complete plans of action specified in advance that respond to every possible contingency in the game. Such games are more compact representations of a more extensive game tree, which explicitly models every option available to each actor at every decision node in the game. See the discussion in the third section of this chapter.

[7] The following illustrative games of debt rescheduling draw heavily on Aggarwal (1987).

		Lender	
		C_2 High Concessions	D_2 Low Concessions
Debtor	C_1 High Adjustment	3,3	1,4
	D_1 Low Adjustment	4,1	2,2

Figure 2.2. *Prisoner's dilemma (debtor's preference ordering: D_1C_2 > C_1C_2 > D_1D_2 > C_1D_2; lender's preference ordering: D_2C_1 > C_2C_1 > D_2D_1 > C_2D_1)*

may either make high concessions on existing debt while providing additional loans (HC), or refuse to make any concessions (LC). The combination of each actor's two options result in four possible outcomes from debt rescheduling negotiations:

1. "Successful rescheduling," whereby the lender provides new money or reduction in the principal or interest rate, while the debtor follows adjustment polices designed to improve its ability to repay;
2. "Debt repudiation," whereby the debtor refuses to adjust while the lender (at least initially) keeps the debtor liquid by providing additional capital;
3. "Unilateral adjustment," whereby the debtor country takes significant steps to improve its ability to repay and continues servicing the debt, while the lender fails to make concessions; and
4. "Breakdown," whereby the debtor repudiates its obligations and the lender does not provide additional funds.

So far, we have undertaken three of the steps required to define a normal form game: we have specified the players and indicated the strategies available to each. As a final step, we assign values to the outcomes we identified that represent debtor and lender payoffs for different strategy combinations. In each case, the first number in any cell (the intersection of row and column) refers to the debtor's payoffs, and the second number refers to the lender's. A high number signifies a better payoff (e.g., 4) than a low number (e.g., 1). Consider the game presented in Figure 2.2 which is commonly referred to as the Prisoner's Dilemma.

This type of payoff structure has been analyzed frequently in terms of the following story. Two prisoners are charged with committing armed robbery.

Although the District Attorney (DA) possesses only enough evidence to send the prisoners to jail on a lesser charge, if he succeeds in eliciting a signed confession from them, they will receive lengthy jail sentences. His problem, then, is to get the prisoners to confess. The clever DA attempts to do this by interrogating the prisoners in separate rooms and telling each that if he turns state's evidence, he will go free. The four possible outcomes arise from both prisoners' different strategies concerning confessing or not: both may "defect" by confessing (D_1,D_2); both may "cooperate" and refuse to give evidence against the other (C_1,C_2); and one or the other may turn state's evidence and go free while sending his counterpart to jail for a lengthy term (C_1,D_2 or D_1,C_2). Equating cooperation (not confessing) with undertaking high adjustment and concessions, and defection (confessing) with low adjustment and concessions yields the matrix in Figure 2.2.

In this situation (assuming a one-shot game) it is likely that both prisoners will confess, resulting in a payoff of 2,2 instead of a mutually advantageous payoff of 3,3.[8] Unless a player is convinced the other will not confess, it is to his advantage to confess. Because there is no way to bind the other actor in this game, both actors' dominant strategy is to confess, causing both to be worse off than had they both held to their innocence. In short, the payoffs here lead to a game of "Prisoner's Dilemma" because both would ideally like to cooperate but fear that they will be "suckered" if they do.

Similarly, if debtors believe they could survive without additional bank funds, and that doing so would be less harmful than adjusting their economies under IMF strictures, like the prisoners, their dominant strategy would be defection (D_1).[9] And banks may decide they would benefit more by not lending further and writing off the existing debt instead of committing additional funds to debtors who they feel would not pay them back.

When the debtors are more willing than banks to see a breakdown in negotiations – faced with the alternative of economic adjustment without lending concessions – then they can tough it out, converting the game into one with a clearly asymmetrical outcome: Called Bluff (see Figure 2.3). Here, the debtor's payoffs are ordered as in a Prisoner's Dilemma situation, in which mutual defection is preferable to capitulation to the opponents' demands. On the other hand, for the banks, a breakdown of negotiations is the worst option. The payoffs in such a game are as shown in the figure.

This is not a symmetrical game.[10] The debtor can stick to its strategy of playing D_1 with confidence, since this is its dominant strategy. The lender, on the other hand, is afraid to play D_2 since this would lead to a (D_1,D_2) outcome

[8] This describes a "Pareto superior" situation. In general, Pareto superiority means that the situation of at least one player can be improved without worsening the others' situation.

[9] See Kaletsky (1985) for the argument that the debtors may be better off repudiating their debt instead of submitting to harsh adjustment programs – even if no additional funds are immediately forthcoming. It is important to keep in mind that refusing to cooperate would not obviate the need for some type of economic adjustment.

[10] For lenders, the game is Chicken (see below), and for the debtor, the game is Prisoner's Dilemma.

		Lender	
		C_2 High Concessions	D_2 Low Concessions
Debtor	C_1 High Adjustment	3,3	1,4
	D_1 Low Adjustment	4,2	2,1

Figure 2.3. *Called Bluff (debtor's preference ordering:* $D_1C_2 > C_1C_2 > D_1D_2 > C_1D_2$*; lender's preference ordering:* $D_2C_1 > C_2C_1 > C_2D_1 > D_2D_1$*)*

which is the worst outcome for the lender but which is not as bad for the debtor. Indeed, if the lender threatens to play D_2, then the debtor can call the lender's bluff – hence the name of the game. If both actors know the payoff structure, the lender will know that the debtor will play its dominant strategy of defection, and the lender will thus be forced to play a cooperative strategy, yielding it a payoff of 2.

Argentina has at times adopted this debtor's strategy of refusing to undertake adjustment, demonstrating a lack of concern over the consequences. This strategy is illustrated by the following threat issued by one of Argentina's ambassadors:

> It is good for my country to be so isolated . . . We can go to East Germany, Bulgaria, Hungary. If we are pushed to buy more imports from the Soviet Union, we will and it won't be our fault . . . Frankly, no one will tell you the government is making contingency plans. But they are.[11]

Let us now turn to a case where the solution to the game is harder to determine. The debt rescheduling game with the payoffs shown in Figure 2.4 represents the common game known as Chicken. Here, there are four options: (1) both the lender's and debtor's first choice is to hold their ground and force the other to capitulate (D,C); (2) each has the same second choice whereby both bear some portion of the adjustment burden (C,C); (3) choice three is shouldering the brunt of the adjustment burden alone (C,D); and (4) lastly, both believe that the worst outcome for each would be a breakdown in negotiations (D,D), whereby both would suffer considerably.

The story behind the game of Chicken illustrates the trade-offs well. Two drivers race their cars on a collision course down the center of a road from

[11] *Wall Street Journal*, June 26, 1984.

		Lender	
		C_2 High Concessions	D_2 Low Concessions
Debtor	C_1 High Adjustment	3,3	2,4
	D_1 Low Adjustment	4,2	1,1

Figure 2.4. *Chicken (debtor's preference ordering: $D_1C_2 > C_1C_2 > C_1D_2 > D_1D_2$; lender's preference ordering: $D_2C_1 > C_2C_1 > C_2D_1 > D_2D_1$)*

opposite directions. The one who swerves and "chickens out" will get a payoff (2) lower than that given to the other driver who persists (4). If both swerve, the damage to each of them would be limited to harming their reputations (3,3). But if neither swerves, the ensuing collision will be disastrous for both (1,1).

Although both players are tempted to refuse to swerve (defect) in order to maximize their payoffs (4), fear of the consequences of such mutual defection counteracts this temptation. The chief difference between a PD and a Chicken game is that in PD the worst outcome is unrequited cooperation (ending up a sucker, that is, cooperating although your opponent defects, C,D); mutual defection (both confessing to the District Attorney, D,D) is only the second worst outcome. In Chicken the reverse is true: collision (D,D) is the worst and chickening out (C,D) is the second worst. Choosing strategies in this game is more complicated than in the PD case because neither has a dominant strategy; in other words, a player's expectation of what the other is likely to do heavily influences one's choice.

To cope with such games, and others as well, a useful concept called the "Nash equilibrium" has been developed. This notion, discussed in the next section, predicts that in pure strategies,[12] we would have two equilibria in a Chicken game, one at D_1C_2, and another at C_1D_2. I next examine the logic of this solution concept.

Predicting game outcomes: the Nash solution concept

To find solutions to various games, we need to make assumptions about the conditions under which they are played. The premise of "noncooperative games" is that agreements between actors are not enforceable – although actors are able to communicate. The obverse, "cooperative games," are cases in which actors

[12] "Pure strategies" refer to cases where an actor must pick a single strategy, rather than randomizing with some probability over a collection of strategies (known as "mixed strategies").

		Column		
		C_1	C_2	C_3
	R_1	3, 5	7, 3	4, 6
Row	R_2	7, 2	5, 8	5, 6
	R_3	2, 4	9, 6	8, 2

Figure 2.5. *Examining best reply strategies*

can bind each other to the strategy they choose.[13] Because debt rescheduling games are generally characterized by a lack of an authority who can force both parties to adhere to any agreement between them, these games are essentially noncooperative in nature.[14]

Let us examine a formal solution for two-person noncooperative games. As in our rescheduling game above, I depict a matrix in which the columns and rows represent alternative strategies. In this case, we have two players, R and C, and I assume that both players are rational: that is, I assume they will choose the strategies that yield the maximum payoff, while knowing that the opponent is similarly motivated.

John Nash was the first to introduce a solution concept for noncooperative games based on the concept of equilibrium points (EPs).[15] An EP is a payoff pair resulting from two strategy choices such that neither player has an incentive to change his strategy – hence the notion of equilibrium. To help understand the concept of an EP, I will first consider the meaning and implications of a "best reply" by a player to a strategy chosen by his opponent.

Consider Figure 2.5, in which the players R and C each have three strategies to choose among. I denote the strategies available to R by R_1, R_2, and R_3 and those to C by C_1, C_2, and C_3.

A player's "best reply" strategy to any given strategy his opponent chooses is one that gives him the highest payoff among all available payoffs corresponding to his opponent's choice. In this case, suppose R were to choose R_2. How would C respond, supposing she knows in advance that R will choose R_2? Player C will

[13] In some discussions, there is often confusion about whether the distinction between cooperative and non-cooperative games should rest on the ability of actors to communicate and/or bind themselves to a course of action. In light of the ability of bargainers to engage in deceptive communication, the appropriate distinction between these types of solutions should be the ability to bind actors to a course of action, not communication. See Harsanyi (1977).

[14] Of course, at times major powers or international institutions may play an arbitration role, but, in general, they are unable to bind actors to a solution through a rule system.

[15] Harsanyi (1977), p. 274.

look at her own payoffs from row R_2, which are (2), (8), or (6), corresponding to her selection of the columns marked C_1, C_2, and C_3, respectively. C's best reply will naturally be C_2, because this choice gives her the best payoff (8). Similarly, against R's choice of R_1 the best reply is C_3, and against R_3 the best reply is again C_2.

I assume that both players know the payoff matrix and can determine the best reply to each other's strategy choices. Hence if R committed to playing R_2 in the above game, he knows that C will reply by choosing C_2. The strategy pair (R_2,C_2) yields a payoff of 5 to R and 8 to C. Naturally, because R can see that C will choose C_2 against R's selection of R_2, it is not in R's interest to choose R_2. Player R will want to shift from R_2 to R_3, so as to get a payoff of 9 instead of 5. Consequently, we can say that the pair (R_2,C_2) is not an equilibrium point because one of the players, player R, will want to change his choice from R_2 to R_3 against C's choice of C_2.

Assume now that R has settled on R_3 as the best reply against C_2. Is C motivated to change his strategy from C_2 to some other column against R's choice of R_3? We can see that C's best reply against R's choice of R_3 is still C_2, because it gives him the highest payoff (6), among the possible payoffs in row R_3. Thus, C is unmotivated to move away from C_2 against strategy R_3. This pair (R_3,C_2) is a strategy pair such that R_3 is the best reply against C_2 and at the same time C_2 is the best reply against R_3. The pair (R_3,C_2) is thus an equilibrium point because neither player is motivated to change his strategy.

This game has only one equilibrium, but this need not be so for other games. In the Chicken game of Figure 2.4, both (D_1,C_2) and (C_1,D_2) share the property that, if it were the game outcome, neither player would want to unilaterally deviate. Such multiple equilibria complicate the prediction of game outcomes.

In sum, an equilibrium point in a two-player game is defined as a strategy pair such that each player's choice is a best reply to the opponent's choice. We can easily see that such a pair has the property that the first number of the payoff pair in that cell is the highest of all first numbers in the column and the second number is the highest of all the second numbers in the row.[16]

A game model of debt rescheduling

To this point, we have been working with a simplified illustrative game of debt rescheduling to illuminate some points about game theory. When formally

[16] Note that the equilibrium point is the straightforward generalization of the well-known concept of "saddle points" in two-person zero-sum games. In such games, the entries in the matrix are single numbers representing payoffs to R and losses to C, and the saddle point has the property that an entry is both the highest in the column and the lowest in the row. In fact the zero-sum game can be written in the same form as nonzero-sum games in which the second number of the payoff pair for each cell is simply *equal* in value and *opposite* in sign to the first number. In this case, the total payoff for whatever choices are made by R and C is always zero. The requirement that the payoff to C (as the second number) be the highest in the row means that its opposite in sign (the first number, and payoff to R) is the lowest in the row while at the same time the highest in the column. This is the property of a saddle point.

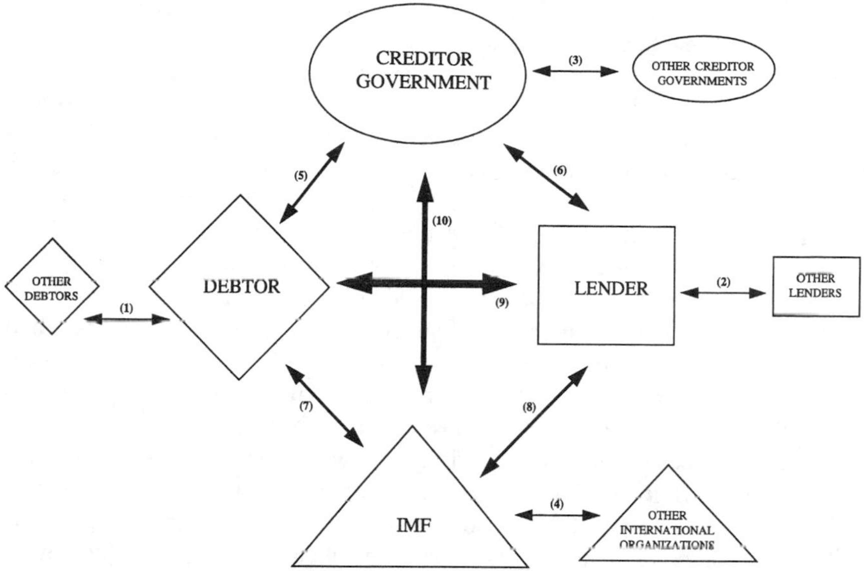

Figure 2.6. *The actors and potential bargaining relationships in debt rescheduling*

modeling debt rescheduling negotiations, however, we must specify carefully (1) the relevant actors, (2) the actions available to them, (3) the context of their strategic action, and (4) how they value the possible outcomes resulting from their interaction in view of their basic goals and the constraints they face. The first three questions are taken up in the discussion that follows, while the last is deferred to the next chapter.

Assumptions in modeling debt rescheduling

In my discussion of epochs, I noted that four types of actors have participated in debt rescheduling: debtors, lenders, creditor governments, and international organizations. To model debt rescheduling, we must find a way to systematically incorporate the influence of these actors and their relationships (as depicted in Figure 2.6).

The figure illustrates 10 possible bargaining relationships: Among similar actors, we have interaction (1) among debtors, (2) among lenders, (3) among creditor governments, and (4) among international organizations. In addition, we have six remaining interaction possibilities among pairs of different types of actors. Although one could analyze each of these relationships, doing so would needlessly complicate the model. Fortunately, we do not have to examine each in detail.

In practice, the debt rescheduling issue-area initially encompasses the terms of rescheduling (which include spreads, fees, and repayment arrangements),[17] the amount of new loans made available to debtors, and the type of adjustment debtors must follow (if any) as part of their arrangements with lenders. This characterization of issues involved in negotiations relies on the empirical pattern observed among bargainers: in general, they restrict their discussion to these financial matters and to concern about future relationships with their counterparts. As long as actors involved in negotiations accept the bounds of the issue-area, negotiations will revolve around the resolution of such issues, and the types and numbers of actors involved in negotiations should remain the same.[18]

Empirically, most private debt rescheduling discussions have initially involved debtor countries, and bondholders or bankers on the lending side. Banks (and bondholders) have generally succeeded in forming unified coalitions to bolster their position. By contrast, debtors have historically failed to unite in a common negotiating front, although in the 1980s they made efforts to do so.[19]

By linking debt to security or trade issues, however, debtors and lenders have often attempted to involve creditor governments in negotiations. When debtors have succeeded in linking debt to a creditor government's national interest, these governments have at times provided financial aid and also pressured private lenders to make concessions to debtors. Yet creditor governments have also faced appeals from their bankers (or bondholders) to become involved as their allies in debt negotiations.[20] Private lenders have often called on their governments to enforce contractual provisions of their loans, cloaking their pleas for creditor state intervention by invoking the "national interest." At times, of course, creditor governments have become involved in debt negotiations of their own volition to meet their own political or economic objectives.[21]

Lastly, in times of perceived threat to the international financial system, international institutions such as the IMF, the World Bank, or the League of Nations have become actively involved in the debt rescheduling process. In particular, these institutions have often responded to pressures from creditor countries that wished to encourage specific policies in debtor countries without being directly associated with their promotion.

My characterization of the issues and the primary actors involved in debt

[17] "Spreads" refer to the difference between the bank's cost of funds and the interest rate charged to the borrower. "Fees" are charges for managing and initiating loans.

[18] In more technical language, the bounds of the issue-area can be determined by "cognitive consensus" among actors on which issues are interlinked. For a theoretical discussion of this point, see in particular Haas (1980). Also, see Aggarwal (1985), in which I examine this notion in the context of international trade.

[19] Lipson (1985) examines bank efforts to unite in the 1980s; Aggarwal (1987) analyzes the differential success of banks and debtors in uniting.

[20] Bulow and Rogoff (1989b) formalize a three-way bargaining game in which sufficiently large gains from trade allow the banks and debtors to secure "side payments" from creditor governments.

[21] Naturally, creditor governments may not always see eye-to-eye on debt rescheduling issues and are likely to bargain among themselves over the sharing of costs in rescheduling. See Wellons (1985) on differences among creditor government approaches to rescheduling in the 1980s. Fishlow (1985) examines differences among governments in earlier debt rescheduling episodes.

rescheduling allows my analysis to be simplified from Figure 2.6 into the interaction depicted in Figure 2.7. I begin with the assumption that lenders sometimes unite, but that debtors do not.[22] I use a game theoretic approach to model interaction between single debtors and groups of lenders. To introduce possible intervention by creditor governments and international organizations, I model their behavior as decisionmaking under certainty. If these actors choose to intervene, I assume that they do so with full knowledge of what equilibrium outcome is likely in view of the interaction between private actors. Based on cost/benefit calculations that depend on factors discussed in the next chapter, these intervening actors may use political influence or economic side-payments to try to alter the equilibrium outcome to one different than the two-actor Nash equilibrium. For now, I defer discussion of the effects of intervention by creditor governments or international organizations and focus on a single debtor and a group of lenders.

What are the actions or strategic choices available to a debtor and lenders? In keeping with my empirical objectives as discussed in the Overview and Chapter 1 on policy choices, I am interested in predicting the debtor's willingness to adjust its economy and the degree to which lenders are likely to make concessions. These possible choices can be categorized for debtors as "no/low," "medium," and "high" adjustment and similarly for lenders as "no/low," "medium," and "high" concessions.

With respect to the context within which these choices of adjustment and concessions are made, I make two additional assumptions, one with respect to the likelihood of additional moves following the basic adjustment and concessions decision, and a second with respect to the information available to actors when they make their moves.

From my perspective, debt rescheduling games are more than just a one-shot affair. The basic moves of adjustment or concessions are not the only possible moves in the game. Actors are clearly aware that there is a possibility of additional future moves if either of them responds to the other's basic choice. This reaction could take the form of some kind of retaliatory measure, such as the expropriation of assets by the debtors, the restriction of trade credits, or the blocking of future loans by lenders. In addition, actors will consider how their play might lead to possible future situational changes that are adverse to their interests and incorporate these concerns into their initial evaluation of outcomes. These considerations are formally discussed in the Appendix to the book.[23]

In terms of information distribution, I assume a situation of complete information, that is, a case where each player knows both players' payoffs and the rules of the game, but not the initial choice of the other player.[24] I presume that

[22] This assumption provides a realistic base-line for this study and leaves open the possibility of investigating other possible interactions among actors in the empirical portion of the study.

[23] The Appendix will be more comprehensible to readers who have read Chapters 3 and 4 as well.

[24] The following discussion of information conditions and of the extensive form game developed below draws heavily on Aggarwal and Dupont (1992).

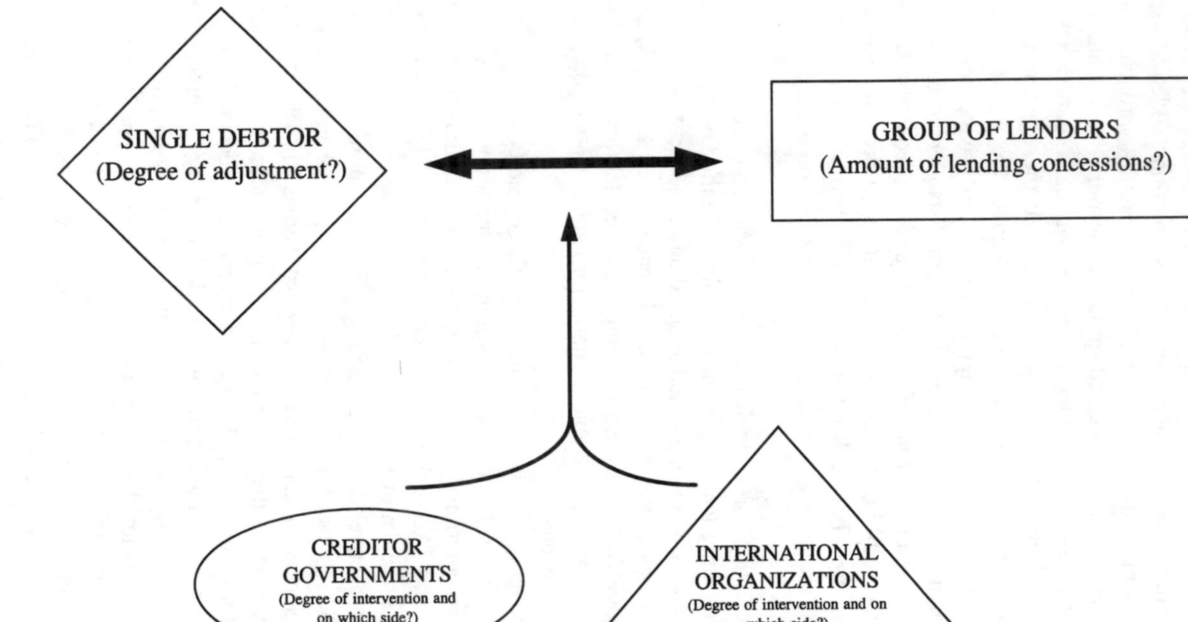

Figure 2.7. *The analytical model*

when the debtor and the lenders make their adjustment or concession moves, they cannot be certain the other will follow through on his commitment. Thus, at least initially, the game appears simultaneous.[25] An alternative approach would be to assume that actors not only do not know each other's initial choices, but also lack information about each other's preference orderings. Such an incomplete information approach would asssume that actors do not know the game payoffs of the bargaining situations in which they find themselves.[26]

My decision to use complete information may actually more closely approximate decisionmaking behavior in the context of international debt rescheduling than using incomplete information. As we shall see in the empirical cases, actors generally have a good sense of the kinds of actors they face in negotiations. In addition, for empirical purposes, complete information models provide a much more operationally tractable approach than incomplete information frameworks to analyze the implications of interaction among different kinds of actors. I return to this issue of assuming complete or incomplete information conditions in Chapter 15.

The debt game

The assumptions I have made so far allow us to construct the basic game used in this book to examine debt rescheduling. I begin by illustrating the strategic interaction I have described in extensive form. An extensive form consists of three elements: (1) the players, (2) the game tree, and (3) the players' payoffs. In turn, the game tree illustrates (a) when each player has a move, (b) what each player can do at each of his opportunities to move, (c) what each player knows at each of his opportunities to move, and possibly (d) the probability distribution over any exogenous events (moves by "Nature"). Points c and d are known as the information conditions in the game.[27] I depict the players and their possible moves in a debt rescheduling game in Figure 2.8.

In the extensive form game, the debtor chooses among the options of high, medium, or no/low adjustment. Similarly, the lenders, uncertain of what the debtor will do (as illustrated by the dashed connecting line between the lenders' choice nodes), must choose between making high, medium, or no/low concessions. Following these initial choices, I have illustrated actors' possible future concerns by an ellipsis (. . .) following adjustment and concession moves. An examination of these concerns is presented in the next chapter and the Appendix.

Although the extensive form captures the moves and countermoves involved in a debt game, I find that it is more useful and simpler to work with the

[25] Kletzer (1989), p. 211, in a less compact model of debt renegotiations focusing on economic variables with both complete and incomplete information, argues that simultaneity is a more realistic assumption than sequential play in games of complete information.

[26] The derivation of payoffs for actors in different bargaining situations is the topic of the next chapter.

[27] For more on this and information sets see Fudenberg and Tirole (1991), pp. 77–82; Harsanyi (1977), pp. 88–94; Kuhn (1953); Luce and Raiffa (1957), pp. 39–49; Myerson (1991), pp. 37–46; Shubik (1982), pp. 39–45.

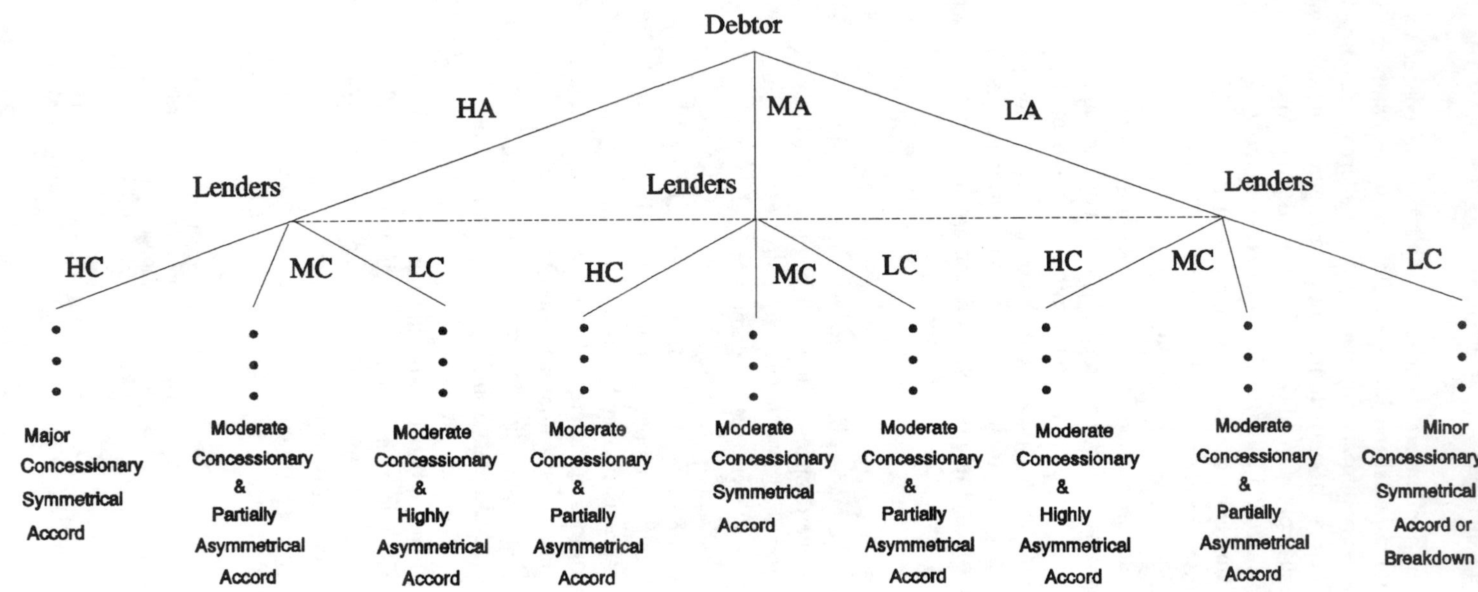

Figure 2.8. *An extensive form debt rescheduling game*

		Lenders		
		High Concessions with Future Concerns (HC...)	Medium Concessions with Future Concerns (MC...)	Low Concessions with Future Concerns (LC...)
Debtor	High Adjustment with Future Concerns (HA...)	Major concessionary & symmetrical accord	Moderate concessionary & partially asymmetrical accord	Moderate concessionary & highly asymmetrical accord
	Medium Adjustment with Future Concerns (MA...)	Moderate concessionary & partially asymmetrical accord	Moderate concessionary & symmetrical accord	Moderate concessionary & partially asymmetrical accord
	Low Adjustment with Future Concerns (LA...)	Moderate concessionary & highly asymmetrical accord	Moderate concessionary & partially asymmetrical accord	Minor concessionary & symmetrical accord or breakdown

Figure 2.9. A *normal form debt rescheduling game with types of outcomes*

corresponding normal form game of this debt game. Elsewhere, in collaborative work with Cédric Dupont, I have developed a formal correspondence between the extensive and the normal form game and shown the trade-offs in using one form over another.[28] I follow standard methods to transform the extensive form game in Figure 2.8 into normal form. Figure 2.9 shows the debt game in normal form that I work with for empirical purposes. In the normal form game, strategy choices for the debtor are now presented as (HA...), (MA...), and (LA...) and for the lenders as (HC...), (MC...), and (LC...). As with the extensive form game, the ellipsis incorporates the notion of future concerns. The possible outcomes of actors' strategic interaction are depicted in the nine cells as in the illustrative game in Figure 2.1 of this chapter. Moreover, the normal form game as depicted captures the situation of what can be termed "complete but not perfect information" that I illustrated in the extensive form game. This normal form game provides the basis for the empirical analysis of debt rescheduling in Parts II, III, IV, and V of this book.

[28] See Aggarwal and Dupont (1992).

Conclusion

In this chapter I have completed the first task necessary for developing a model of debt rescheduling. I began by noting that game models are particularly useful for analyzing strategic interaction, wherein a player's optimal strategy depends on what his counterpart is likely to do. I argued that it is useful to consider the rescheduling process primarily as a two-party game, with one actor being a single debtor and the other a group of lenders. Possible intervention by creditor governments or international organizations can then be incorporated into the game to examine how these actors might push the equilibrium outcome in the two-actor game away from a Nash equilibrium. With this approach in mind, I then presented the basic outlines of my model of debt rescheduling in both extensive and normal form.

Three tasks now remain. First, I must show how payoffs can be specified in different bargaining games between debtors and lenders. Second, we must consider the types of calculations that creditor governments and international organizations make when deciding whether or not to intervene in negotiations and on whose side. And third, we need to consider how payoffs might change over time. The first two tasks are taken up in the next chapter, and the third is the subject of Chapter 4.

3 A situational theory of payoffs and intervention decisions

In the last chapter, we saw how game theory can illuminate the bargaining strategies available to debtors and lenders in debt games. Although game theory provides some heuristic insight into strategic interaction in general, we must move beyond this valuable but limited tool to find a way to predict actors' payoffs in debt games. Essentially, we should avoid being misled by the word "theory" in game theory. To complement this tool, we need an empirically based theory drawn from international relations and economics that will help us specify actors' payoffs. Game theory can only help us predict the actual outcomes of international bargaining once payoffs have been derived.[1]

This chapter begins the substantial task of developing a situational theory of payoffs that will enable us to derive actors' payoffs in debt games. To this end, the next section develops a simple utility equation to help assess how a debtor and lenders will calculate the consequences of selecting a policy choice in view of its competing goals. I then provide the crux of my situational theory of payoffs by identifying different variables that reflect international and domestic concerns, and the individual situations created by specific combinations of them, that influence an actor's decision to prioritize one goal over another. In the third section, I use the concept of individual situations to develop some hypotheses about how actors in different individual situations will *weight* their goals. To estimate this weighting, I give numeric values to actors' concerns in each situation. The final section focuses on the factors that influence whether or not creditor governments and international organizations intervene in debt rescheduling games.

Assessing debtors' and lenders' valuation of outcomes

This section examines how a debtor and lenders evaluate the utility of competing policy combinations. A debtor may pursue high, medium, or low levels of economic adjustment; similarly, lenders may opt for high, medium, or low levels of concessions. I begin with a utility function that specifies actors' basic goals as well as variables that represent the weights that reflect how they are likely to

[1] Aggarwal and Dupont (1992) argue that specifying game payoffs is a considerably simpler task for nuclear deterrence issues than for political-economic issues. On this point, see also Powell (1994), p. 320. The need to develop a theoretical basis for payoffs has been raised by several authors including Allan (1983), Snidal (1985a), Oye (1985a), Milner (1988), Cohen (1990), Krasner (1991), and Powell (1994). Cohen (1990), pp. 277–278, puts it best when he notes that "The limitation of even the most ambitious applications of game theory lies in the tendency to concentrate on what comes out of state conceptions of self-interest rather than what goes into them."

emphasize their different goals. The actual weights of these variables will be a function of the constraints arising from an actor's individual situation based on economic and political factors, a topic I turn to later in the chapter. Once these weights have been specified, I can then show how actors are likely to rank different possible outcome combinations of adjustment and lending concessions.

To construct utility functions, we first must make some assumptions about debtors' and lenders' goals. As noted in the Overview, leaders of debtor countries will (1) wish to secure additional funds, and (2) minimize the political and financial costs of adjustment. By contrast, following a debt crisis, lenders will (1) be wary of committing additional funds, and (2) promote debtor adjustment to increase the probability of debt servicing. In addition to these basic goals, owing to the possibility of continued interaction in the debt game, debtors will be concerned about minimizing penalties and maintaining good relations with lenders. Similarly, lenders will worry about possible penalties imposed by debtors and will also be concerned about maintaining good relations with debtors. Note that I do not consider these latter concerns about the future as substantively "primitive" objectives. Rather, they derive from the context of the actors' interaction over time.

The utility equations

I assume that it is possible to quantify lenders' concessions to a debtor and the domestic adjustment undertaken by debtors, as well as the concern that the debtor and lenders have for maintaining good relations with each other. Let L, A, G, and H, represent, respectively, lending concessions, domestic adjustment, and the debtor's and lenders' level of concern for maintaining good relations.[2] The payoffs for the debtor and lenders are obtained by calculating the values of U_{Debtor} and $U_{Lenders}$: these terms represent the utilities of the debtor and of the lenders for different policy combinations of concessions.[3]

$$U_{Debtor} = aL - bA + cG$$

$$U_{Lenders} = yA - xL + zH$$

(Here a, b, c are the weights assigned to the three goals by different debtors and x, y, z are those assigned by different groups of lenders. All weights are greater than zero.)

Before determining how to assign appropriate weights in these equations, we must first consider how the utility functions work. A debtor's utility for a particular policy combination of adjustment and lending concessions is equal to the weighted sum of three numbers: L, the amount of loan concessions; A, the costs of adjustment; and G, the value of maintaining good relations. Similarly, the

[2] I also assume that L, A, G, and H are real-valued non-negative numbers. I use two different variable notations for goodwill because the goodwill of debtors and lenders will be different. See the discussion below.

[3] Although countless functional forms are possible, I use the weighted functions shown in Figure 3.1 to capture the essence of actors' concerns in debt rescheduling and for the sake of simplicity.

lenders' utility will be equal to the weighted sum of three values: A, the benefits of a debtor agreeing to adjust; L, the cost of providing loan concessions; and H, the value of maintaining good relations.

Note that the debtor's utility increases with higher levels of lending concessions, decreases with its need to undertake adjustment, and increases with actions to promote good future relations. Conversely, the lenders' utility increases with higher levels of adjustment and decreases with the need to make lending concessions, but similarly increases with goodwill gestures.

The terms G and H can be interpreted as summary terms that capture actors' concerns about possible penalties or retaliation that result from their actions in the debt game, as well as possible changes in the structure of the bargaining game in the future.[4] Banks, for example, might worry that rescheduling negotiations might become linked to security or other issue-areas in which they may have a disadvantage. Equally, they might fear that playing too aggressively could lead to situational change efforts by debtors that might prove detrimental to them over the longer run. The Appendix to this book discusses concerns about penalties and game change in greater detail.

We can rewrite G as the term (A/L) – 1 for debtors. Debtors recognize that lenders will generally favor a higher value for adjustment as compared to additional lending. Thus, as the amount of adjustment that a debtor agrees to undertake increases relative to lending concessions, the amount of goodwill that the debtor "receives" from the lender also increases.[5] Similarly, goodwill for lenders, H, can be measured by the ratio (L/A) – 1. Because debtors prefer greater lending concessions to increased adjustment, lenders secure greater goodwill as the ratio of lending concessions to adjustment increases. Inserting these terms into the basic utility functions gives us the following:

$$U_{Debtor} = aL - bA + c(A/L - 1)$$

$$U_{Lenders} = yA - xL + z(L/A - 1)$$

(Here a, b, c are the weights assigned to the three goals by different debtors and x, y, z are those assigned by different lenders and all weights are greater than zero.)

These points are best understood by considering the numerical values I assign to the different options and the resulting utility calculations.[6] Numerical values for lending concessions and for adjustment are assigned as follows:

[4] The latter issue of possible situations is the topic of Chapter 4.

[5] I have subtracted one from the ratio of A/L so that when adjustment efforts and lending concessions are equal, the goodwill term will have no effect (G = 0). One could conceive of other functional forms as well that might increase the value that we place on possible retaliatory measures versus goodwill.

[6] In assigning specific numerical values, I assume that we can compute a cardinal utility function for the different bargainers, and not simply an ordinal utility function. This allows us to readily incorporate the weights that actors assign to different goals.

L = 3 when L is high (high lending concessions = HC)
= 2 when L is medium (medium lending concessions = MC)
= 1 when L is low (few or no lending concessions = LC)

A = 3 when A is high (high degree of adjustment = HA)
= 2 when A is medium (some degree of adjustment = MA)
= 1 when A is low (little or no adjustment = LA)

In accord with these assigned values, the values for goodwill concerns will be:

G ranges from 2 (when A is 3 and L is 1) to – 2/3 when A is 1 and L is 3

and

H ranges from 2 (when L is 3 and A is 1) to – 2/3 when L is 1 and A is 3

As an example of the function I have built so far, let us evaluate two policy choices by a debtor faced with a high concession strategy by the banks: (1) (HC...), (HA...) (high concessions with concerns about future actions; high adjustment with concerns about future actions) versus (2) HC... , LA... (high concessions with concerns about future actions; low adjustment with concerns about future actions). I assume for simplicity that the values of a, b, and c are 1 (that is, each of the debtor's goals is equally weighted).

U_{debtor} for HC..., HA... $= 1 \times 3 - 1 \times 3 + 1 \times (3/3) - 1 = 0$

and

U_{debtor} for HC..., LA... $= 1 \times 3 - 1 \times 1 + 1 \times (1/3) - 1 = 1\frac{1}{3}$

This illustrates the simple idea that with equal values for a, b, and c (namely 1), the debtors will prefer HC..., LA... (with a value of $1\frac{1}{3}$) to HC..., HA... (which has only a value of 0).

Before turning to the procedure for determining the weights, some points about my model are in order. I chose the specific formulation and values with two objectives in mind. First, the utility equation provides a simple method to rank different policy combinations, thus allowing us to derive and not simply assume actors' payoffs in my games. Second, the model makes straightforward assumptions that can be easily interpreted both analytically and empirically. Should the model's limitations become constraining, future formulations may incorporate more sophisticated assumptions and complex considerations.

Weighting actors' goals: overall capabilities, issue-resources, and coalitions

So far I have been treating the weights (a,b,c) and (x,y,z) as exogenous. When this is so, all debtors and all lenders are alike. This is the approach used in most economic work on international debt,[7] but it is inadequate. For example, leaders of a debtor country with an unstable domestic coalition will be more reluctant to carry out adjustment programs than leaders of strong coalitions because of the increased danger of potential political fallout. It is precisely this type of political concern that will become the basis for deriving situation-specific weights for the utility function.

Any attempt to evaluate the factors that influence how actors weight their goals must sift through almost endless possibilities. We could, for example, consider leaders' characteristics, the dominant party's ideology in debtor countries, countries' or banks' capabilities in the international system, and so on. With a multitude of available options, we must balance competing desires for parsimony, predictive power, and empirical observability.

In my integrated approach, I use three variables to shed light on actors' valuation of different outcomes. From the Realist school, which focuses on general power considerations, I borrow the notion of actors' overall capabilities and apply it to debt negotiations. From the modified strucuturalist perspective, I consider issue-specific or "debt resources" in bargaining.[8] Lastly, a domestic politics argument contributes the consideration of actors' coalitional stability. This notion is helpful when looking both at lenders' willingness to make additional loans and debtors' concern with undertaking economic adjustment.

Realism: overall capabilities

Realists focus on the importance of power in predicting actors' behavior.[9] Relative capabilities will obviously influence bargaining outcomes, but actors' overall resources are most relevant for constructing their preference ordering over outcomes, independent of strategic interaction. Thus, I focus on actors' overall levels of capabilities to capture the concern that actors will have about possible future actions in a debt rescheduling game that might spill over to other issues.

In this connection, we can direct our attention to issues such as trade, political stability, immigration, security, and so on. High dependence on trade, for example, may reduce debtors' propensity to take precipitous actions in debt negotiations for fear of retaliation. Lenders that fear repudiation may be able to help debtors increase their exports, in order to facilitate debt servicing, by encouraging their countries' markets to open or by pressing other countries to liberalize their trade policies.

In sum, goals in one issue may affect the pursuit of goals in another area of concern. Pressures from other arenas may even supersede those created by the

[7] Although the use of a minimally specified utility function (e.g., Kletzer, 1989) can be seen as implicitly recognizing the possibility of individual variation among debtors, these differences generally have no effect on the outcome in such models.

[8] See Keohane and Nye (1977) and Aggarwal (1985), among others, for an issue-specific approach to capabilities.

[9] A more theoretically refined version of realism has been developed by Kenneth Waltz (1979) and has acquired the label "structural realism."

game at hand. Actors' resources in other areas will thus influence their calculations in debt rescheduling games.

Modified structuralism: defining debt rescheduling resources

Power resources are not always fungible, particularly in the short run. Once an issue-area has been specified, the capabilities relevant to negotiations in that area can be examined separately from other possible resources. Following the logic of this approach, we must first describe the actors' perception of an issue-area to identify the resources that will influence their valuation of outcomes. I took this first step in Chapter 2 when defining the issue-area of international debt rescheduling. For this basic, unlinked issue-area, we can look at debtor and lender resources as follows.

Debtors will be concerned about maintaining general financial solvency and will consider their ability to obtain other sources of financing besides loans when determining to what extent they must cooperate with lenders.[10] For their part, lenders will consider their financial resources – namely their ability to do without debt servicing and to write down assets – in deciding which goals to emphasize. For example, bank managers will be concerned about their capital base and the amount of losses they can sustain without being replaced by disgruntled stockholders.

Issue-area definitions may not, or course, remain constant.[11] As I and others have argued, connections among issues may change, leading to either a broader or narrower agenda of negotiations, and this is an issue I consider at length in Chapter 4.

Theories of domestic politics: coalitional stability

Within debtor countries, the ins and outs of bureaucratic politics, new leaders, party competition, or a new consensus on policy tools can potentially affect which outcomes the debtors will prefer. In the analysis that follows, I will focus on the domestic support (or lack thereof) that debtor governments can expect for their bargaining positions. I argue that such support stems from the strength or weakness of the domestic coalition they represent. This emphasis on coalitional stability reflects my assumption that domestic conditions strongly constrain decisionmakers; bargainers' valuation of outcomes will depend not only on their debt-related resources and overall capabilities but also on the reactions they think their bargains will elicit on their home front.

For lenders, I take a somewhat different approach that does not parallel exactly my analysis of debtors. In this case, I focus on the extent to which the lenders as a group have a stable coalition, rather than focusing on each lender's internal stability. Although I will point to important internal differences among

[10] This idea corresponds to what economic models typically call the "reservation utility." See Kletzer (1989) and Bulow and Rogoff (1989b) for examples.

[11] Keohane and Nye (1977), Haas (1980), Baldwin (1980), Aggarwal (1983, 1985), and Keohane (1984).

lenders when relevant, the group focus is my point of departure. Recalling Figure 2.7, I suggest that it is advantageous to consider lenders as varying in their degree of unity but to regard debtors as individual actors.

Leaders of debtor countries will never be eager to incur adjustment costs. But in some cases, depending on their coalitional stability, the political cost they will be forced to bear will be lower. Debtor countries' negotiators must consider whether an agreement to pursue economic adjustment (which might include increasing prices, lowering wages, etc.) will lead to domestic turmoil. This could take the form of rioting, work shutdowns, or other forms of dissent – all of which could potentially lead to leaders losing power. The primary means to predict whether adjustment will lead to political chaos is to measure the debtors' coalitional stability.

Two key elements are used to operationalize this concept: (1) the incumbency expectations of the leader or group in power, and (2) the ability of leaders to control potential opposition to their policies.[12]

The first element, incumbency expectations, refers simply to the likelihood that the leaders will be in power for some time. If there is a constant threat that a coup or other political upheaval will occur, leaders will be highly unwilling to pursue unpopular adjustment programs. In addition, leaders will fear being replaced by political antagonists who might fundamentally challenge the legitimacy of their regime. To pose a question, do the terms of the political debate foster an expectation among leaders that they will be able to serve out their terms of office?

The second basis for predicting the political costs of adjustment is leaders' ability to control potential opposition. By their very nature, adjustment programs mandate sacrifices on the part of competing societal factions – labor, small businesses, large industrialists, or consumers in general. Almost inevitably, the sharing of costs in such cases will be unequal, creating resentment and political conflict.

In examining leaders' ability to control opposition, it is important to distinguish between industrial and pre-industrial societies. In pre-industrial societies, where workers, peasants, or other interest groups of the modern period have not been incorporated into the political system, we must use a different notion of stability than in societies which have begun the process of industrialization. In these cases, leadership challenges might arise from a variety of sources, such as factional strife, military coups, or private armies, and in fact often hinge on the probability that the leader(s) will live to complete the term of office. Stated differently, in pre-industrialized societies, threats to incumbency arise more often than not from counter-elites of one sort or another rather than from organized societal groups, as occurs more typically in the cases of countries which have begun to industrialize.

Industrializing societies may be partially or fully mobilized. Where societal groups such as peasants and workers have been incorporated into the political

[12] I would like to thank David Collier for this conceptualization.

system, they exert a special kind of influence over the policy process not present in pre-industrialized societies; consequently, we require different indicators of adjustment potential. Although physical survival may continue to be an issue in these modern societies, and incumbency expectations may be as volatile as in pre-mobilized societies, the sources of potential opposition will differ. Threats to incumbency arise most typically from either the army or organized labor, although business groups, intellectuals, and the middle classes have also frequently been sources of opposition to reform and, hence, to the leadership attempting to implement austerity measures. In many cases, these potential sources of opposition have been controlled by strong executive systems or corporatist mechanisms which shape the ways in which these groups can or cannot exert pressure to resist change. In other cases, fractionalized party systems make it nearly impossible for a leader to form the coalitional support he needs to impose the costs of reform; consequently, incumbency expectations are low.

My approach to measuring coalitional stability stands in contrast to efforts that focus on state strength or solely on the political popularity of specific leaders. In my view, more important than the power of the state is the interrelationship of state and society and the mechanisms of state and society interactions. It follows from this perspective, then, that even authoritarian states may face important opposition, as we will see in many of the cases examined in the empirical portion of this book.[13]

Turning briefly to lenders' coalitions, we consider the extent to which bankers or bondholders have formed strong ties among themselves in the negotiations. In some cases, different bondholder groups have competed for bondholders' representation. In addition, at times, private entrepreneurs or investment banks have themselves tried to lure bondholders into organizing, often to promote their own agenda.

I measure the stability of lenders' coalitions by the level of competition for representation and the extent to which institutionalized forums have been established to channel bondholders' demands. For banks in the modern era, the analogues of bondholder groups are the advisory groups of large banks that were created to negotiate with debtors. Competition among different banks can especially undermine efforts to maintain coalitional stability.

Deriving payoffs: combining goals and constraints

Having described bargainers' goals and the constraints decisionmakers face during bargaining, we can now derive actors' valuation of possible outcomes. This can be accomplished by specifying connections between the bargainers' characteristics and the outcomes they prefer.

[13] See Haggard (1985) for a good discussion of the success of different regime types in promoting adjustment.

Issue and Overall Capabilities		Coalitional Stability? Yes	No
	Issue strength, Overall weakness	IS 1	IS 2
	Issue weakness, Overall strength	IS 3	IS 4
	Issue strength, Overall strength	IS 5	IS 6
	Issue weakness, Overall weakness	IS 7	IS 8

Figure 3.1. *Individual situations (IS)*

Categorizing constraints on actors: defining individual situations

I first catalogue the full range of "individual situations" that either a debtor or lenders might find themselves in, defined by domestically and internationally relevant factors. For this purpose, the three factors specified in the previous section – overall capabilities, debt resources, and domestic coalitional strength – will be treated as dichotomous variables. In my empirical analysis, I will consider intermediate values of these three factors when appropriate. Figure 3.1 illustrates the various possibilities.

Each individual situation comprises a combination of the values of the three variables. For example, IS 8 describes a situation of an unstable coalition, few debt-related resources, and overall weakness in negotiations with the banks – a situation which describes Argentina during part of the late 1980s. The types of indicators I use to code each of the three aspects of actors' situations are presented in the Appendix to this chapter. IS 7 describes holders of Mexican bonds in the 1830s and early 1840s: they had managed to develop a united negotiating front but possessed few debt-related resources or overall capabilities.

Analyzing the effects of different individual situations on actors' weighting of goals is crucial for understanding the development of their preferences over outcomes. These preference orderings derive from an actor's position with respect to the three factors described, independent of its counterpart's position with respect to these same factors. In other words, I do not compare relative capabilities or the relative coalitional stability of different actors, but rather evaluate each actor's resources and coalitional stability separately.[14] Actors may

[14] It is, however, sometimes difficult to distinguish between overall and relative capabilities.

thus fall in any of eight individual situations; paired with another actor, they can be in any of the 64 joint situations.

My use of individual situations is similar to the game theoretic notion of "types" of actors. Rather than the commonly used cases of "hawks" and "doves," however, I distinguish among a larger number of types. Depending on what one assumes about the information that actors have when they are engaging in strategic interaction, they may or may not know the type of opponent against whom they are playing. Games in which an actor is unsure about his opponent's type are called games of incomplete information. I do not use this type of model here for two reasons. First, in my empirical analysis, I have found little evidence that actors are unaware of their opponents' type. Second, because of the large number of types, incomplete information models would be unwieldy for my empirical work.[15] Therefore I use complete information as a basic assumption in this book.

Weighting actors' goals for individual situations

How will an actor's individual situation determine the weighting of its goals? To answer this question, we must examine the independent effect that each of the three factors – coalitions, debt resources, and overall capabilities – will likely have on each of the three goals. Second, I will consider the secondary effect of the combinations of variables on different goals.

Turning first to the primary effect of each variable, I argue that for debtors (1) greater coalitional stability will be associated with lower costs for undertaking adjustment policies, (2) higher debt-related capabilities will shield debtors from the need to make additional adjustments, and (3) greater overall capabilities will decrease debtors' concern about the costs of non-cooperation.

Similarly, I expect that lenders with stable coalitions will be more willing to make loan concessions, whereas unstable coalitions of lenders will worry that providing additional loans or concessions will simply enable the debtor to pay other creditors.[16] This will naturally increase the reluctance of any individual creditors to provide additional loans and concessions. This notion also applies to bondholders. Referring to competition among bondholding groups, the Chase National Bank argued in the 1930s that:

> In such a situation [where the combined claims of different groups of bond creditors represent a burden which, if unmodified, is too great for the debtor to bear] no group is

[15] Such models are not only complex but also yield indeterminate results. In discussing the idea of a Bayes-Nash equilibrium, Varian (1990), p. 281, notes that "The idea of Bayes-Nash equilibrium is an ingenious one, but perhaps it is too ingenious. The problem is that the reasoning involved in computing Bayes-Nash equilibria is often very involved . . . there is considerable doubt whether real players are able to make the necessary calculations . . . Since we generally don't observe players' beliefs about the prevalence of various types of players, we typically won't be able to check the predictions of the model." For a more detailed discussion and illustration of the problems of using incomplete information models in debt rescheduling, see Aggarwal and Dupont (1992).

[16] For analysis of the implications of lenders' stability on debt rescheduling, see Sachs (1984), Krugman (1985), Lipson (1985a), Eaton, Gersovitz, and Stiglitz (1986), Aggarwal (1987), Caskey (1989), and Fernandez and Kaaret (1992), and Kaneko and Prokop (1993).

inclined to grant a concession unless all other groups make corresponding concessions to the end that the aggregate of concessions may meet the assumed abilities of the debtor.[17]

In addition, lenders who are financially secure (that is, with high debt-related capabilities) will likely be more aggressive in their demands. They are generally somewhat less concerned with immediate loan servicing because they can afford to look at the long term. Finally, lenders who are weak in overall capabilities will be more concerned with their future relationships with debtors than those who can resist coercive efforts by debtors. For example, banks that have subsidiaries in debtor countries will be worried about expropriation of their assets.

These general principles provide a base for assessing how debtors and lenders weight their goals in different individual situations. To a limited extent, the interaction of these three factors will also influence the weights assigned to these goals. For example, if a decisionmaker in a debtor country has a weak domestic coalition and is in danger of being displaced domestically, I would expect that in addition to eschewing stringent economic adjustment programs, he or she will be less fearful of retaliation by foreign lenders than might otherwise be the case – if adjustment comes at the cost of domestic political support.

I now turn to an analysis of how actors will likely prioritize their goals by considering both the primary and interactive effects of the three variables that define different individual situations. I will first consider the utility equation values for debtors (a, b, and c), which refer respectively to the weight assigned to their concern with lending concessions, adjustment costs, and concern with future relations. I will briefly discuss my rationale for each individual debtor situation below, and then I will do the same for lenders (with weights x, y, and z).

For analytical purposes, the weights can be divided into the categories of low, low-medium, medium, medium-high, and high. I have assigned numerical weights from one to five to each of these concerns. The key feature of this range is that it makes the weights important relative to the variables of lending, adjustment, and goodwill, without completely dominating them. Although I make the logic of my coding as explicit as possible, I do not claim that the assigned values are indisputable. Part of the function of the empirical case analyses will be to improve our understanding of these relationships for future studies of international negotiations. Figure 3.2 lists the weights that will be used in the utility function for each of the eight types of debtor.

IS 1. In this situation, I expect debtor leaders to assign a relatively low weight to new borrowing and a low-medium weight to adjustment. They could adjust relatively easily in light of their domestic coalitional stability, but are not in great need of funds. Furthermore, we expect decisionmakers in this case to have a medium-high concern with maintaining future relations, because the country's overall weakness makes it susceptible to outside pressure. Coalitional

[17] Quoted in Borchard (1951), p. 312 from Foreign Bondholders Protective Council (1937), p. 288. Bracketed clarification by Borchard.

CAPABILITIES	COALITIONAL STABILITY? Yes	COALITIONAL STABILITY? No
Issue strength, Overall weakness	IS 1 a: low = 1 b: low-medium = 2 c: medium-high = 4	IS 2 a: low = 1 b: high = 5 c: medium = 3
Issue weakness, Overall strength	IS 3 a: medium-high = 4 b: low = 1 c: low = 1	IS 4 a: medium-high = 4 b: high = 5 c: low = 1
Issue strength, Overall strength	IS 5 a: low = 1 b: low-medium = 2 c: low = 1	IS 6 a: low = 1 b: high = 5 c: low = 1
Issue weakness, Overall weakness	IS 7 a: high = 5 b: low = 1 c: medium-high = 4	IS 8 a: high = 5 b: high = 5 c: medium = 3

Figure 3.2. *Weights for different individual situations (IS) – debtors (a = borrowing need, b = unwillingness to adjust, c = concern about future relations)*

stability gives leaders greater concern about the long-run implications of their policy choice. The shadow of the future looms large: they worry about the consequences of their actions for subsequent negotiations.[18]

IS 2. Here, coalitional instability raises the costs of domestic adjustment, and also decreases decisionmakers' concern for the future compared to IS 1. Hence the high value for "b" and medium value for "c." The value of "a" is likely to stay the same as in IS 1.

IS 3. In this case, the lack of financial resources and need for funds will lead to a higher value by leaders for "a," probably a medium-high assessment. It is unlikely to be "high" because the actor's overall strength might be used to compensate for its issue-weakness. In this case, the political costs of adjustment are lower than in IS 1 because decisionmakers can justify an agreement to undertake an economic adjustment program, given their need for funds. The

[18] See Axelrod (1981) for a discussion of this notion.

value of "c" will be relatively low, however, because the debtor is in a strong overall position and does not fear retaliation.

IS 4. This case presents a more difficult situation for debtors. In this case, they lack funds and thus will tend to place at least a medium-high value on securing loan concessions. Because of the effect of coalitional instability, I do not expect it to be high. As in IS 2, domestic circumstances lead to an unwillingness to adjust. And similar to IS 3, the overall strength also fosters little concern with the future, an effect that is in this case reinforced by the coalitional instability.

IS 5. Debtors in this situation are in the strongest position. They are not in dire need of funds (low "a"). Although we might expect the concern with both adjustment and future relations to be similarly low, I argue that unwillingness to adjust will be low-medium. My reasoning is that although their strong domestic coalition will permit them to adjust, leaders will not feel compelled to do so because of their strong financial position. Consequently, in this case, it will be hard for them to justify following policies of economic adjustment.

IS 6. This situation is straightforward. In view of the difficulty of adjustment, the political costs assigned to "b" should be high. And given its issue strength and lack of a stable coalition, debtors' concern with securing funds and future relations should be low.

IS 7. In this case, the debtor is eager to borrow funds, reflected in the "high" value assigned to "a." Adjustment costs in this case are relatively low because of the domestic political stability. But a debtor's concern with future relations is also quite high, in light of its overall weakness and the coalitional stability that gives its leaders a long-run perspective.

IS 8. Debtors here are weak on all dimensions. As in IS 7, its lack of financial resources makes it anxious to borrow. And although it is weak overall and likely to fear its opponent's actions, the much higher costs of political adjustment make it more focused domestically, and less concerned with international matters.

I next turn to a specification of lenders' weights (x, y, and z), in Figure 3.3. Given the parallel construction of the utility functions for both debtors and lenders, the values for lenders (x, y, and z) are the opposite of the debtors for adjustment and lending. Values for future concern, however, will be the same.

IS 1. This first case presents a situation wherein lenders are willing to make loan concessions because they are coalitionally stable. At the same time, because they are not desperate for loan servicing, such concessions will be harder to justify to their stockholders or bondholders. Consequently, I code "x"

		UNIFIED LENDERS?	
		Yes	No
CAPABILITIES	Issue strength, Overall weakness	IS 1 x: low-medium = 2 y: low = 1 z: medium-high = 4	IS 2 x: high = 5 y: low = 1 z: medium = 3
	Issue weakness, Overall strength	IS 3 x: low = 1 y: medium-high = 4 z: low = 1	IS 4 x: high = 5 y: medium-high = 4 z: low = 1
	Issue strength, Overall strength	IS 5 x: low-medium = 2 y: low = 1 z: low = 1	IS 6 x: high = 5 y: low = 1 z: low = 1
	Issue weakness, Overall weakness	IS 7 x: low = 1 y: high = 5 z: medium-high = 4	IS 8 x: high = 5 y: high = 5 z: medium = 3

Figure 3.3. *Weights for different individual situations (IS) – lenders (x = unwillingness to make loan concessions, y = need for servicing, z = concern about future relations)*

as low-medium. The issue-specific strength corresponds to low concern with debt servicing. Finally, in light of the lenders' stable coalition and overall resources, I expect a medium-high concern with goodwill.

IS 2. In this instance, lenders are unwilling to make concessions owing to their coalitional instability but are highly dependent on receiving servicing. Their value for concern for future relations will be medium, due to their overall weakness, but as in the case of debtors, they are somewhat less concerned about retaliation than we might expect because of their coalitional instability.

IS 3. Here, lenders are very willing to make loan concessions because of their coalitional stability. They are also highly concerned with loan servicing due to their financial weakness, but their overall strength compensates in part, leaving them a medium-high concern. With respect to future relations, their overall strength causes them to value it very slightly.

IS 4. Lenders are unwilling to make loan concessions as a consequence of their unstable coalition. They will also have a medium-high concern for servicing due to their need for funds. This value will not be high, however, because as in IS 3, their overall strength partially compensates for their need for funds. The value for concern with future relations is also the same as in IS 3: low.

IS 5. Lenders are in a very strong position. They are willing to make concessions because of their strong coalition, but their positive financial situation causes lenders to consider them of low-medium value. Lenders' concern for both servicing and goodwill will be low because of their issue and overall strength.

IS 6. IS 6 is similar to IS 5, except for the lenders' high level of unwillingness to make concessions due to their unstable coalition.

IS 7. In this case, lenders are ready to make loan concessions, and are highly concerned with debt servicing because of their poor financial situation. Lenders will also worry about possible retaliation because of their overall weakness: their strong coalition encourages them to focus on the long run.

IS 8. Here, we have a situation in which weakness in both the coalitional and issue-area dimensions causes high valuations for unwillingness to make concessions and need for servicing. Because the coalition is unstable, lenders will assign only a medium value to maintaining good future relations.

Specification of payoffs to construct a game

Using the utility equations that tie together actors' goals and constraints of their individual situations, we can now generate an example of a debt game. Consider the following illustration, based on the values that debtors and lenders place on basic goals as shown in the fully specified utility equations, as well as the weightings presented in Figures 3.2 and 3.3.[19]

Debtor Individual Situation: 7
(Coalition stable, Issue weak, Overall weak)
Borrowing Need a: 5 Adjustment Unwillingness b: 1 Goodwill c: 4
Lender Individual Situation: 6
(Coalition unstable, Issue strong, Overall strong)
Lending Unwillingness x: 5 Assets Concern y: 1 Goodwill z: 1

[19] Although the calculations are straightforward, they are somewhat tedious. Consequently, I have used a simple program, developed with the assistance of Wade Huntley, to calculate the values quickly. The program is obtainable from the author for readers interested in examining the implications of different weightings. It also provides a ready means for examining the implications of other formulations of the utility functions.

I first calculate examples of lenders' valuation of payoffs in IS 6.

$$U_{(lenders)} = y * A - x * L + z * [(L/A) - 1]$$

$$\begin{aligned} U_{(lenders)} \text{ for HA..., LC...} &= 1 * HA - 5 * LC + 1 * [(L/A) - 1] \\ &= 1 * 3 - 5 * 1 + 1 * [(1/3) - 1] \\ &= -2.67 \end{aligned}$$

and

$$\begin{aligned} U_{(lenders)} \text{ for LA..., LC...} &= 1 * LA - 5 * LC + 1 * [(L/A) - 1] \\ &= 1 * 1 - 5 * 1 + 1 * [(1/1) - 1] \\ &= -4 \end{aligned}$$

and

$$\begin{aligned} U_{(lenders)} \text{ for HA..., HC...} &= 1 * HA - 5 * HC + 1 * [(L/A) - 1] \\ &= 1 * 3 - 5 * 3 + 1 * [(3/3) - 1] \\ &= -12 \end{aligned}$$

The results are what we might expect from standard economic modeling of lenders' behavior. That is, of these three possible outcomes, the best from the lenders' perspective is when the debtor undertakes high adjustment but the lenders make only low loan concessions (HA..., LC....) for a value of –2.67. If both actors fail to make adjustment or concessions, the lenders receive a payoff of –4, which is worse than when the debtor undertook adjustment. The lenders do not find the HA..., HC... outcome attractive because they have little interest in making loan concessions and are not worried about future relations.

I next calculate examples of a debtor's valuation for two different possible outcomes for IS 7.

$$U_{(debtor)} = a * L - b * A + c * [(A/L) - 1]$$

$$\begin{aligned} U_{(debtor)} \text{ for LA..., HC...} &= 5 * HC - 1 * LA + 4 * [(A/L) -1] \\ &= 5 * 3 - 1 * 1 + 4 * [(1/3) -1] \\ &= 15 - 1 - 8/3 \\ &= 11.33 \end{aligned}$$

$$\begin{aligned} U_{(debtor)} \text{ for HA..., HC...} &= 5 * HC - 1 * HA + 4 * [(A/L) -1] \\ &= 5 * 3 - 1 * 3 + 4 * [(3/3) - 1] \\ &= 12 \end{aligned}$$

These two examples show the ranking for two outcomes for a debtor in IS 7. In this case, the debtor values the combination of high adjustment and lending concessions now plus future interaction (HA..., HC...) at 12, and no/low adjustment and high lending concessions (LA..., HC...) at 11.33. Here, high borrowing need, relatively high willingness to undertake adjustment, and a strong concern about future relations will lead the debtor to prefer making high adjustment rather than low adjustment if it believes the lenders will make high concessions.

Preference ordering (Debtor IS 7, Lender IS 6)

	Cardinal		Ordinal	
	Debtor	Lenders	Debtor	Lenders
HA...; HC...	12	–12	9	2.5
IIA...; MC...	9	–7.33	5	6
HA...; LC...	10	–2.67	6	9
MA...; HC...	11.67	–12.5	8	1
MA...; MC...	8	–8	4	4.5
MA...; LC...	7	–3.5	2.5	8
LA...; HC...	11.33	–12	7	2.5
LA...; MC...	7	–8	2.5	4.5
LA...; LC...	4	–4	1	7

Cardinal Payoff Matrix JS 7–6

Lenders IS 6

		HC...	MC...	LC...
	HA...	12, –12	9, –7.33	**10, –2.67**
Debtor IS 7	MA...	11.67, –12.5	8, –8	7, –3.5
	LA...	11.33, –12	7, –8	4, –4

Note: Nash equilibrium bolded.

Ordinal Payoff Matrix JS 7–6

		Lenders IS 6		
		HC...	MC...	LC...
	HA...	9, 2.5	5, 6	**6, 9**
Debtor IS 7	MA...	8, 1	4, 4.5	2.5, 8
	LA...	7, 2.5	2.5, 4.5	1, 7

Note: Nash equilibrium bolded.

Figure 3.4. *An example of full preference orderings and a game*

Standard economic models of international debt would assume that less adjustment would always be preferred by debtors. In my model, stable but very weak debtors are sufficiently concerned about their ongoing relationship with lenders to want to match high concessions.[20]

The complete cardinal preference orderings and game for these individual situations are presented in Figure 3.4, referred to as joint situation (JS) 7–6. In addition, I also convert the cardinal values to ordinal ones for ease of presentation. The ordinal conversions are arrived at by simply ranking the cardinal values on a 1 to 9 scale. In the case of ties, I simply use an intermediate value for both. For example, I use an ordinal value of 8.5 if the top two values are the same. If three values are identical, for instance the top three, then I simply use an ordinal value of 8 for the top three numbers 3 and then a value of 6 for the next highest value.

In the empirical chapters, I will use both cardinal games and their ordinal conversions.

The role of creditor government intervention and international organizations in affecting bargaining outcomes

We have now constructed debt games between a debtor and lenders to which we can apply the concept of Nash equilibrium. Yet intervention by creditor governments (CGs) or international organizations (IOs) that are interested in furthering their own agenda may radically alter the outcome of two-party negotiations, pushing the parties away from the Nash equilibrium. In my empirical analysis,

[20] In the language of game theoretic approaches in security studies, such actors are "doves." See, e.g., Bueno de Mesquita and Lalman (1992).

therefore, I consider how intervention by CGs and IOs might shift negotiation outcomes.

When looking at the decisions of both CGs and IOs compared to those of debtors and lenders, there is an important difference in the way I calculate the strategy they choose. For CGs and IOs, I follow a simple utility maximizing decision rule under certainty to describe their behavior. That is, unlike for debtors and lenders, I assume that a CG's or IO's decision to intervene is *not* based on calculations of strategic interaction. This is clearly a significant simplification that may not fully represent the complex decisions of creditor governments, but it still introduces significant aspects of their behavior into the model. Moreover, because of the highly complex nature of the factors influencing behavior, I do not specify exact values to predict intervention, but instead present a qualitative algorithm outlining the calculations CGs or IOs are likely to make when deciding whether or not to intervene.[21]

I begin with a CG's decision to intervene, based on its perceived benefits and cost of intervention. First, the CG begins its benefit calculations by considering the likely outcome of bargaining between debtors and lenders without any intervention. It knows its utilities both for this expected outcome and for its preferred outcome. These utilities will be based, in view of its particular situation, on three goals: financial gain, political stability, and maintenance of overall security interests. The difference between the valuation of the preferred outcome and of the expected outcome without intervention equals the total *gross* benefits of intervention. Second, CGs always estimate the *costs* of intervening in a particular situation. For example, intervention against a powerful debtor country will be more costly than intervention against a less powerful one. This calculation of costs will include the opportunity cost of resources that would be expended by intervention.

Finally, I postulate that CGs, as rational actors, will follow a simple decision rule: maximize the difference between benefits and costs, that is, the *net* benefits. Assuming that the CG cannot foresee all the complications that might arise from intervening, the rule implies that CGs will start with the lowest cost intervention and escalate from there. I identify five levels of intervention available to CGs: (1) avoiding intervention, (2) using their diplomatic offices to encourage a settlement, (3) more actively using their diplomats to formally mediate or arbitrate disputes, (4) threatening economic sanctions, and (5) intervening militarily.[22]

How might CGs estimate the benefits and costs of intervention? Turning to benefits first, I assume that the decision to help their lenders is based on such criteria as (1) the amount of money loaned by banks domiciled in the CG to the particular debtor as compared to the total amount of loans made by the CG's

[21] The remainder of this discussion will describe only the creditor governments' decisionmaking process. Factors relevant to international organizations (to the extent that they act independently from creditor governments or other countries) differ in some ways, but the qualitative approach is identical. Examples of international organizations' decision calculi appear in the empirical chapters.
[22] These stages closely follow the patterns of intervention discussed by Borchard (1951), p. 235.

lenders to all debtors, and (2) the amount of the CG's lenders' loans to the debtor in proportion to the total amount of loans made by all lenders. The first factor is an indicator of the vulnerability of the lenders located in the CG, the second influences the CG's level of interest in taking the lead in rescheduling matters as the primary government actor.

In addition, CGs have security interests (and systemic concerns) that lead them to favor their own private lenders. Their overall security interests depend on epochal factors such as the types of political alliances CGs have with other major powers, the number of competing major powers in the system, and the importance of international financial institutions and of economic competition with other CGs.

The outcome of debt rescheduling on lenders can impact CG security interests in several ways. As an example, decisions by a debtor and its lenders to engage in equity swaps, whereby lenders receive assets in debtor countries, will influence the terms of competition among creditor governments. Also, active intervention by one creditor government to aid its banks can put the banks in non-intervening countries at a considerable financial disadvantage. The decision by Japanese banks in the late 1980s to pool their developing country loans under the guidance of the Japanese government for rescheduling purposes has had strategic implications for U.S. interests in its own banks.

With respect to their relationship with debtors, CGs are concerned with the impact of debt rescheduling on their trade relations, political alliances, ideological concerns, and possible spillovers to areas such as immigration. Severe economic adjustment programs generally lead to sharp cuts in imports and to increased efforts by debtors to promote their exports, both of which are likely to strain trade and other relations between the CG and the debtor. Recently, the increased immigration pressure from Mexico that has resulted in part from its economic problems has led some analysts to call for a more active role by the U.S. government to aid Mexico. A similar argument has been made with respect to the fragility of democracies in Latin America and the deleterious effects of continued adjustment programs on governmental stability. With respect to overall security concerns, threats by debtors to turn to a particular CG's rival will often engage their strategic interests (as Argentina did a few times with respect to the U.S.-USSR relationship and as Mexico often did in the nineteenth century by turning to the U.S. against the European powers and vice versa).

Finally, regarding CG calculations, we can consider how their security concerns might lead them to take an impartial stance from which they nonetheless pressure both debtors and lenders to follow specific policies. I suggest that when CGs have little concern with security issues, but high concern with economic costs, they push both debtors and lenders to higher levels of adjustment and lending concessions. This allows CGs to reduce the possible costs of adjustment problems in debtor countries and financial risks to lenders – assuming they believe that adjustment programs will not fundamentally undermine the debtor and lending concessions will not bankrupt the lenders.

But what happens when security concerns are high? Then I expect the CG to be reluctant to see debtors being forced to pursue possibly destabilizing adjustment and their lenders to absorb costs that might undermine their international competitiveness. In such cases, CGs may step in to foster a "low adjustment, low lending concessions" outcome and be willing to absorb the costs of this result.

Turning briefly to the costs of intervention, I make three assumptions: (1) costs progressively escalate as one moves up the ladder from diplomatic intervention to military involvement, (2) these costs will vary depending on how far the CG determines debtors or creditors need to be pushed (that is the "distance" between the CG's preferred outcomes and the expected outcome), and (3) costs vary with the degree of debtors' or lenders' resistance, which in turn depends on their relative capabilities to resist.

In sum, the CGs' decision on whether or not to intervene in different cases depends on the potential benefits (determined by their security, political, and financial concerns) minus the costs they face in promoting the preferred outcomes. Because I assume that CGs want the biggest benefit for the lowest cost, we expect them to intervene at progressively more costly higher levels over time when initial efforts are unsuccessful, keeping in mind the net benefits they will receive. Naturally, should CG concerns change during a negotiation period, this will lead to a revised intervention decision.

Conclusion

This chapter has developed a situational theory of payoffs. With the help of a utility function, I showed how a debtor and lenders' basic goals could be combined with their differing characteristics in international debt negotiations to derive their valuation of outcomes. In examining actors' attributes, I considered three variables: overall capabilities, debt-specific resources, and coalitional stability. By dichotomizing these variables, I constructed eight ideal-type individual situations in which actors might find themselves. Based on some theoretical assumptions, I then specified the likely weights that both debtors and lenders would assign to their basic goals in view of their individual situations. I then showed how we could derive actors' valuations of payoffs in different cases, and illustrated how we might use these payoffs to construct a debt rescheduling game.

The last section of the chapter investigated the factors that are likely to affect the decision calculus of creditor governments and international organizations in considering whether or not to intervene in a debt game. I illustrated my argument with a focus on the strategic, political, and economic considerations that will influence creditor governments' calculations of the costs and benefits of intervention. The remaining theoretical task is to consider how actors' individual situations might change, either as a result of their own efforts or as a consequence of external shocks.

APPENDIX

Indicators of coalitional stability, issue capabilities, and overall capabilities for debtors and lenders

Indicators for debtors

I. Coalitional stability

- Frequency of executive turnover
- Ability to cope with organized interest groups
- Factional divisions
- Recognition by other countries

II. Issue capabilities

- Reserve situation
- Sources of foreign exchange (e.g., exports)
- Fiscal organization (income tax, import duties, and other taxes)
- Capital flight
- Budget situation
- Other sources of funds available to the debtor internationally (International Monetary Fund, World Bank, creditor governments)
- Inflation
- Currency devaluations

III. Overall capabilities

- Overall trading relationships and the need for access to markets
- GDP
- State of development of the country (including scientific know-how and the education system and reliance on foreign technology)
- Overall reliance on foreign investment
- Attachable assets
- Military capabilities
- Diplomatic recognition by major creditor government
- Overall size of debt
- Commodity dependence and fluctuations in prices

Indicators for lenders

I. Coalitional stability

- Banks' unity as indicated by groupings or organizations of lenders
- Variation in degree of debt exposure, loan-loss reserves, host country regulations

II. Debt-related resources

- Balance sheet (loan-loss reserves)
- Rate of return and options for other investments
- Dispersal of bond holdings
- Diversified financial resources
- Degree of exposure and size of debt*

* The degree of exposure and size of debt can reflect both issue specific and overall vulnerability.

III. Overall capabilities

- Ability to block loans, trade, and investments
- Help from creditor governments or other interest groups (already formed alliances are taken into account)
- Protective measures provided by international agreements and norms
- Attachable assets
- Primary capital
- Degree of exposure and size of debt*

Note: As discussed in the text, some indicators apply to specific epochal time periods. In addition, not all indicators are available for every period of negotiations.

4 A theory of situational change

Until now, we have assumed that actors' individual situations do not change throughout their negotiations. This assumption is rather unrealistic. It is likely that the strength and stability of their domestic support, issue-area needs, and overall capabilities will vary during prolonged negotiations. Such changes may come about through the actors' own efforts because of dissatisfaction with bargaining outcomes, or as a consequence of exogenous shocks.[1]

The possibility that the domestic and international constraints to which bargainers respond might vary – and hence, that bargainers' valuation of outcomes will change – provides the rationale for the four sections of this chapter. First, under what circumstances are actors likely to actively attempt situational changes? Second, upon what resources can they draw to pursue such goals? Third, how might shocks affect their situational constraints? Fourth, what factors constrain actors' ability to successfully use power resources to manipulate their environment?

The first section of this chapter argues that actors dissatisfied with the outcome of a particular game may endeavor to change the game itself by altering their or their opponent's individual situation, and not simply their strategy within a particular game. If they are sufficiently motivated, as indicated by their payoffs, they can draw upon the power resources of international norms and rules, capabilities, and alliances in an effort to fundamentally alter their situation.[2] This possibility of actors initiating change is the topic of the second section. If changes take place, actors' preference orderings are likely to change, and thus their optimal strategies may change as well. Section 3 briefly considers how external shocks might affect actors' individual situations. In concluding, the fourth section shows how both the "nature of goods" involved in the negotiations and the "connections among issues" will constrain actors' efforts to promote situational change.

Three points are worth noting before we proceed. First, actors anticipate the results of each bargaining round (in view of my assumption of complete information). Thus, although they may search for ways to improve their position, unless they are successful in changing their or their opponent's situation, they will continue to play the same game (additional rounds). Second, the approach

[1] Examining change in bilateral bargaining for issue-specific systems is more important than in larger systems. A metaphor is useful for illustrating this point. If we conceive of the overall system as a large ocean, then many changes are required before the body of water is significantly affected. By contrast, issue-specific systems are more like ponds. Their character may be quickly transformed with relatively small variations. Thus, the transformation of the overall system is a much slower process. Hence, we can often understand much of its behavior with static analysis.

[2] See Aggarwal and Allan (1983), Allan (1984), and Aggarwal (1987) for a discussion of power resources.

developed here is only partially predictive: because I do not attempt to derive what aspects of their situation actors are likely to succeed in altering, the analysis should be considered primarily interpretive. Third, I distinguish situational change efforts from purely "tactical" maneuvers, that is, attempts to improve one's payoff within an existing game structure. These tactical efforts generally are likely to provide only a temporary improvement in one's payoffs because actors will know their "best replies" and thus converge on the Nash equilibrium.

Demands for situational change

Actors will be motivated to promote situational changes when dissatisfied with the outcome of their bargaining efforts in a particular game. We can develop a rough measure of this dissatisfaction by examining the actors' payoffs. Looking at the outcome of a particular bargaining round, if an actor receives a low utility payoff (say, 1 to 3 on the 1 to 9 ordinal scale), we will assume the actor will be highly motivated to change its situation. For actors who receive middle level payoffs (4–6), the decision to promote changes will be based on the availability of low cost opportunities to improve outcomes. On the other hand, high payoffs (7–9) should dampen an actor's enthusiasm for manipulating the situation. Although these cutoff points are somewhat arbitrary (particularly in the transition from one category of motivational interest to another), they provide us with a useful starting point.

Using power resources to promote situational change

A desire to promote change is only the first step. Unless bargainers have some power base from which to draw, their attempts to alter their bargaining situation will prove futile. I argue that bargainers can employ three forms of power to achieve situational change: the implicit and explicit norms and rules that guide their relations with their opponents, their own capabilities, and resources they can draw upon from potential state and transnational allies. Employing any of these forms of power, actors may try to alter either their own individual situation or that of their opponent. Naturally, both types of alterations will change preference orderings, thereby possibly leading to different bargaining outcomes.

Norms and rules

When participants agree on international principles, norms, rules, and procedures (which together comprise international regimes), each party may make an effort to apply such arrangements in its own favor. For example, detailed rules and procedures apply to the contractual arrangements for assembling an international loan. If the parties continue to respect these rules, actors can try to invoke them to their advantage.

Of course, a stable international regime can often be used by an actor to alter another actor's individual situation. Using the weapon of diplomatic recognition, governments dealing with debtor nations under disputed leadership have often recognized the factions that were most willing to continue debt servicing. This proved very effective in Mexico in the mid-1800s. Diplomatic recognition from the U.S. in this case helped provide legitimacy to leaders attempting to enhance their political power, and it proved to be an effective means of altering Mexico's preferences.

Sometimes principles and norms (what I refer to as a meta-regime) may exist without a specific regime to implement them. These are cases in which the parties agree upon principles and norms, but not on more specific rules and procedures.[3] If only a meta-regime exists, participants may feel – or expect others to be – "morally" constrained when dissent on a relevant issue arises.[4] In debt negotiations, participants have at times agreed that fraudulently contracted debt should be treated differently than properly contracted loans. In the initial stages of debt renegotiations in the 1980s, Argentina's democratic government argued that it should not be responsible for obligations incurred by its previous military dictatorship.

Regimes (i.e., rules and procedures) can also exist without a meta-regime. IMF conditionality agreements appear to be of this nature. Debtors often strongly dispute the normative validity of IMF programs, which call for harsh economic adjustment as a condition for receiving funds. Given the need for the IMF's imprimatur before debtors can secure funds from banks, when making agreements, borrowers grudgingly follow detailed rules and procedures that have little constraining moral value, but that are enforced through the IMF's threat of loan suspension.[5]

Finally, if there is little shared agreement among opponents, and no rules or procedures, appeals to morality or law have little efficacy. For example, if debtors reject the existing international arrangements as wholly illegitimate, banks must turn to capabilities and alliances to enforce compliance.

Capabilities

Either material or informational resources can be used to affect the behavior of other actors and to alter an actor's situation. To judge the utility of resources in different cases, we must examine the types of issues and actors involved. Except for military resources, which tend to be more fungible in world politics, it is often difficult to judge the efficacy of a particular type of capability in the

[3] Such a situation could arise at different stages. Three possibilities are (1) because of an inability of participants to expend the necessary resources or partially surrender their autonomy to codify rules and procedures for action; (2) when parties are willing to expend resources and surrender some autonomy to support an acceptable agreement – but are unable to agree on its form; and (3) because the regime collapses due to dissension among the participants over implementing the meta-regime.

[4] Countries currently bargaining over nuclear materials are constrained in their actions by a basic acceptance of a meta-regime for non-proliferation; yet rules and procedures on preventing the proliferation of nuclear weapons have fallen into disrepair.

[5] I am not suggesting that borrowers are always opposed to IMF programs. Frequently, an IMF program allows leaders to use the IMF as an international "whipping boy" to evade criticism for programs they themselves wish to pursue.

abstract.[6] Actors can attempt to draw upon a wide variety of power resources in their efforts to promote change. The efficacy of such efforts will depend on their opponent's ability to counter with capabilities of his or her own – be they specific to the issue being manipulated or to other issue-areas.

How might capabilities be used to promote situational change?[7] In putting together a "jumbo loan," for example, large banks, faced with an unstable coalition of allied banks, chose to threaten recalcitrant banks by warning them that they would be excluded from future domestic and international loan opportunities. In addition large banks have threatened to break essential correspondent relationships needed by small banks to conduct their business. Large banks in the current debt crisis have sometimes ensured cooperation by their smaller coalition partners in even more aggressive ways. Small banks reluctant to contribute additional funds to a jumbo loan have been warned that the large bank will call into default a non-performing loan in which a small bank has a large position. By taking a hit on such a loan – an unimportant part of a large bank's portfolio – this action could jeopardize a small bank's profits. Lenders could also, of course, use overall capabilities to destabilize a debtor's government and encourage the formation of a different coalition more favorable to their interests.

Debtors can bolster their capabilities by asking allies to provide them with financial aid in order to improve their issue-specific situation. A debtor can also use its capabilities to invest in import substitution to enable it to become more autarkic and less vulnerable to potential threats from lenders or creditor governments. Naturally, the latter policy will only prove effective over the long run, and may lead to other undesirable economic outcomes.

Alliances

Debtors and lenders can draw upon third parties – state or non-state actors – to alter their bargaining situations. Debtor countries seeking allies have often turned to other countries or to transnational allies, such as exporters or multinational corporations with strong interests in the debtors' economic stability.[8] Argentina, for example, has discussed the possibility of a united front with Brazil, Mexico, and other major debtors. Private creditors have also sought allies to bolster their power, often attempting to involve creditor governments in debt rescheduling. Of course, creditor governments have not always been eager to become involved, often wishing to avoid state-to-state negotiations. In both nineteenth-century and contemporary debt renegotiation talks, creditor governments have at times refused to intervene, hoping to avoid excessive politicization that might transfer costs to them and interfere with their own goals.

6 See Baldwin (1986) for a discussion of this issue. This work is based in part on his earlier papers in which he discusses this question at length.

7 This discussion of capabilities draws on my discussion in Aggarwal (1987), pp. 23–25.

8 The first case, the pursuit of states as allies, has been discussed extensively in the literature on international relations. The second, the use of transnational allies, has been discussed by Keohane and Nye (1972).

In the current epoch, large banks have called upon the U.S. Federal Reserve and the IMF to pressure recalcitrant banks into contributing to jumbo loans. A U.S. government official summed up the predicament of reluctant banks, "Whatever their legal rights, they don't want to annoy the Federal Reserve; it pays to maintain good relations with the Fed."[9] In 1982 and 1983, officials from the Bank of England also helped large banks bolster the stability of their coalition by "encouraging" lending. One banker who had been pressured said he thought that his bank's license would be in danger if they did not cooperate.[10] Even a bank as large as Lloyds is susceptible: in contributing its share of the Mexican jumbo loan, it complained, "We are only doing this because the Bank of England asked us to."[11]

External shocks and situational change

Actors may act to change their individual situations. A second way that situational change occurs is when exogenous shocks affect the three independent variables that define individual situations (overall capabilities, issue-capabilities, and coalitional stability). Changes in the international system generally affect actors differently. A shock such as an oil price increase, for example, might make some debtors more willing to cooperate with banks while causing others to be less forthcoming. Some changes, however, might help all negotiating parties. For instance, a decline in interest rates eases the debtors' repayment burden, while the banks still profit through the spreads they charge on their loans.[12]

Further examples of situational changes include windfalls such as the discovery of new resources. Yet in debt rescheduling, seemingly serendipitous events have often occasioned a backlash, that is, increased demands from creditors. The Chilean experience shows that even victory in war can be to one's disadvantage: after winning important mining areas from Peru in the War of the Pacific (1879–1883), the Chileans found the French government knocking at its door on behalf of its bondholders. The French insisted that Chile assume responsibility for a large portion of Peru's debt! Although by definition these and other such exogenous events are outside of the model, I will discuss their impact on actors' bargaining situations in the empirical chapters.

Constraints on the promotion of change

When attempting to use power resources to foster change, actors face two types of constraints: the type of "goods" with which they are dealing and the "connections" among issues. The nature of these constraints partly determine the obstacles actors face when they try to change situations. Below, we will see that both the types of goods and the connections among issues will affect efforts to alter all

[9] Interview in Washington, D.C. [10] *Euromoney*, January 1983, p. 41.

[11] Quoted in Delamaide (1984), p. 113.

[12] In other scenarios, some actors may lose because of interest rate changes.

three aspects of actors' individual situations: their coalitions, issue-area needs, and their overall capabilities.

Goods as constraints on situational change

The importance of distinguishing between different types of goods in international politics and economics has been recognized for some time. Analysts have made distinctions between public and private goods based on the different constraints they place on efforts to achieve collective action.[13] *Public goods*, such as national defense, allow some individuals to benefit without paying for the provision of these goods. In the case of alliance formation, we find that although participants demonstrate interest in the alliance, they will tend to contribute less than their fair share by understating their true preferences and hoping that others will take up the slack. Examples of how this free-rider problem might be overcome include such obvious means as forced taxation or coercion by a large alliance partner. *Private goods*, by contrast, are produced by entrepreneurs who do so as a means to profit. In this case, only consumers who pay for the good may consume it – thus eliminating their ability to free-ride.

In international debt rescheduling, the importance of this distinction between types of goods can be seen in efforts by banks to form coalitions, by the struggle between labor and business in avoiding the costs of adjustment programs, and so on. However, further differentiation among types of goods is useful in understanding constraints on situational change.

Instead of simply referring to public goods at one extreme and private goods at the other – with "mixed" goods between these two – I identify two additional categories: *collective goods*[14] and joint goods with exclusion (which I term "*patented*" *goods*).[15] This classification of goods is based on two properties: (1) whether other actors can be excluded from consuming the goods produced, and (2) whether consumption by one actor does not diminish the amount available to others (jointness).[16] Although Snidal has examined the importance of these two characteristics in defining types of goods, his analysis does not clearly distinguish between the production of goods and their consumption.[17] By examining consumption and production separately, we can determine how bargaining

[13] For discussion of lenders' coalitions, see pp. 66–68.

[14] Hardin (1982) has distinguished between public and "collective" goods, but this usage is confusing since Olson (1965) (and other scholars) have used the terms interchangeably. A better term might be "crowded" goods. Others use the term "common pool resources."

[15] I have coined the term "patented" to indicate the property of exclusion with jointness. Olson (1965) uses the phrase "inclusive group" to refer to these goods. An example of this is software, a product which is reproducible in mass quantities, but retains its value through legal protection. My discussion of goods and the term "patented" appears in Lipschutz (1991) without attribution. Lipschutz acknowledges his error in the December 1993 issue of *Evaluation Review*.

[16] See Samuelson (1954), Head (1972), Snidal (1979).

[17] In his table on p. 543, Snidal (1979), who refers to what I term "patented" goods as "mixed goods," argues that if there is no jointness and exclusion is impossible, no goods will be produced. This point collapses the production and consumption of goods, leading to an incorrect conclusion. Such goods are produced, as discussed below.

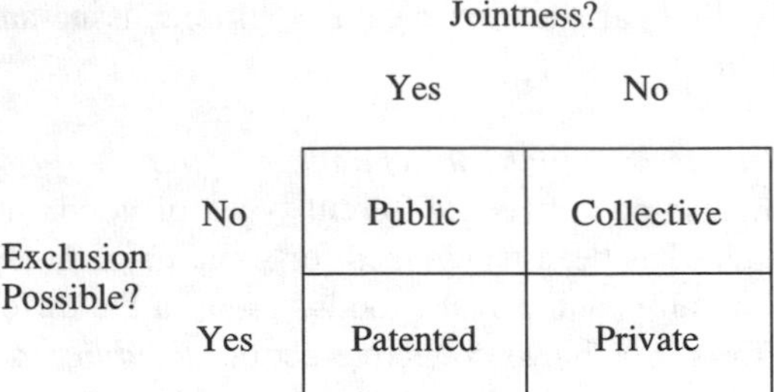

Figure 4.1. *A consumption-side analysis of goods*

will be affected by the incentives provided by different types of goods. Figure 4.1 illustrates the four types of goods.

Public goods are characterized by jointness and the near impossibility of excluding actors from consuming the good produced. For example, if Mexico improves its economic performance to the point where it can service all its debts, a public good has been produced because there is jointness in its consumption. Here, one creditor's consumption does not diminish that of the other creditors, and no one can be easily excluded from enjoying the fruits of this new-found financial stability.

Collective goods differ from public goods because they do not exhibit jointness – even though exclusion is still not possible. If a debtor has only limited debt servicing capabilities and only certain banks have contributed to a jumbo loan, but these creditors cannot restrict repayments to only themselves, the banks have produced a collective good. As we shall see, some banks have suggested that debtors should only conduct subsequent business with those who helped them in their time of need, which would turn jumbo loans into a private good and prevent free-riding by penalizing non-participants.

Patented goods are characterized by both jointness and excludability. Bankers' research in assessing credit risk is an example of a patented good. Although more than one actor can benefit from (or consume) this information, such information provides banks with a competitive advantage and thus will not be readily disseminated.

The last case is the well-known example of private goods. A loan is a private good if, for example, banks advance additional funds to the debtor with the understanding that the debtor will use the increased revenues from the loan to service its debt to the lending banks – and no one else.

If we combine the preceding analysis of the consumption of goods with an analysis of their production, we will see how different types of goods influence actors' efforts to promote situational change. Among the four types of goods, "patented" goods are the most attractive for potential producers. Because these goods are excludable, they eliminate the possibility of free-riding. Producers can set a price according to market conditions, and earn a return. Because patented goods exhibit jointness, no amount of consumption by existing consumers will create "congestion," that is, deter new consumers from paying for and consuming the good.[18] Producers are potentially able to reap high profits because the bulk of their cost is fixed, independent of the number of goods they sell. When producers wish to consume the good themselves, their own use will not be hampered by others' consumption.[19]

Producers of private goods receive profits equal to total revenue minus the cost of production. Because these goods cannot be extended to others at zero or very low marginal cost, entrepreneurs will produce these goods to the point where marginal revenue equals marginal cost. If a producer also desires to consume the good, he will experience some loss of revenue but a gain in utility from this consumption.

Public goods attract free-riders, not customers, because exclusion is not possible. Once the good is produced at some fixed cost to the producer, it extends to all without additional cost. But because consumers can partake of the good without paying, it generates no revenue. On the other hand, free-riding by others does not diminish one's own consumption of the good. Depending on the good's utility, then, it may be worthwhile to produce it.

Finally, collective goods are highly unattractive to producers. Because of their non-excludability, free-riders will be common. In addition, because of the lack of jointness, these free-riders encroach on the producer's ability to benefit from his own production. Non-production is most likely in this case because it gives producers the greatest incentive to become free-riders themselves.[20]

So far, this analysis has established a comparison of incentives for actors to produce different types of goods. From most to least desirable, these are patented goods, private goods, public goods, and collective goods. Let us now consider some more detailed examples about how the nature of goods affects actors' attempts to alter their own or their opponent's individual situations.

If a lender wishes to promote a strong coalition of banks, it must be aware of the types of goods involved in the particular debt rescheduling in question. We saw above that lenders must develop a mechanism to exclude free-riders in a jumbo loan to a debtor. From a consumption standpoint, the attempt to tide over debtors with a jumbo loan can be considered a collective good. Non-contributors to the jumbo loan, who have provided earlier funding to the debtor, cannot generally be excluded from being repaid in the future by debtors. The growing demands on the debtor from multiple lenders will "crowd" the advantages gained from making a jumbo loan because debtors generally are limited in their repayment

[18] This point applies within reasonable limits. Extensive consumption of the good could make it less desirable for other reasons.

[19] Snidal (1979) refers to these goods as "mixed" goods, arguing that "they have varying degrees of public and private properties" (p. 543). This is clearly true, but he does not fully address the incentives for producing these goods.

[20] Snidal (1979) suggests that this category of goods (which he does not name) will not be produced. However, governments commonly provide goods such as highways where exclusion is difficult but crowding takes place.

abilities, especially when faced with a financial crisis. Unless either an exclusionary or a coercive mechanism is developed, attempts to build a strong coalition will collapse because of the detrimental free-riding that could take place in the good's production. For example, bankers might try to solicit contributions to a joint project from their reluctant peers by threatening to exclude their banks from future participation in loan syndications. (Of course, for international loans, this might be seen as a blessing in disguise!) If an exclusion mechanism is developed, this could change the good from collective to private. Banks could attempt to privatize the good by asking the debtor not to repay any banks that do not contribute to the jumbo loans.

The problem of finding producers' incentives for different types of goods is not restricted simply to lenders trying to maintain coalitional stability. Debtors also face this problem, both internally and internationally. Because I have analyzed the failure of a debtors' cartel elsewhere, I will focus here on debtors' internal coalitional stability.[21] As Kaufman has remarked, adjustment programs can be considered public goods.[22] When an austerity program is implemented, both labor and business will struggle to shift the burden of adjustment to the other actor. I argue, however, that this problem might be better analyzed as one involving collective goods. For example, in such a case not only would business free-ride on "adjustment" given the opportunity, but it might even endanger the provision of such goods by failing to cooperate in the adjustment program. If business simply raised prices to compensate for a devaluation as labor wages fell, for instance, the net effect could be the failure of the adjustment program. In this sense, corporatist structures are useful mechanisms for overcoming this type of free-riding because they incorporate all potential free-riders in the production of the good.

Coalitions are not the only area in which the types of goods involved can affect one's situation. If a debtor government tries to improve its issue-resources, perhaps by increasing its foreign exchange reserves, the nature of the goods involved might pose a problem. Consider the public good of foreign exchange convertibility. A government may agree to convert local currency to dollars to maintain domestic investors' confidence in their economy and prevent capital flight. For the most part, the willingness to carry out such a conversion can be considered a public good. Exclusion is difficult since anyone may be allowed to exchange currency and there is no crowding as long as there is no financial panic. But such a good can quickly become a collective good that the state can no longer afford to produce. Increasing foreign exchange reserves in a situation in which private actors are eager to convert their holdings to dollars will quickly crowd the good, preventing the government from maintaining convertibility or from increasing its foreign exchange reserves. Governments in such cases may attempt to cope by imposing exchange controls. Yet even this action could fail to halt the outflow of capital without more severe methods of control, such as

[21] See Aggarwal (1987), Chapter 4. [22] Kaufman (1985).

the nationalization of banks. By taking this measure, governments may succeed in transforming a public good into a private state good.

Similar problems with goods may affect a bank's ability to increase its issue-capabilities. A particular bank may decide to decrease its reliance on sovereign debt servicing by raising capital in financial markets. Yet when a single bank takes such action, its efforts to use this situational change to promote its interests more aggressively in negotiations with a debtor will fail if other banks do not follow suit. Thus, unless all banks take comparable action, the bank raising capital will find that the joint nature of its alliance in bargaining with debtors impairs its ability to take unilateral action.

Lastly, the nature of goods can impede actors' efforts to alter their overall capabilities. Consider a debtor government trying to improve its overall economic position in order to be more independent from pressure by lenders. If it uses its power resources to secure the "good" of an opening of markets for its products in developed countries, it may find that private exporters simply utilize additional foreign exchange earnings to increase their foreign holdings. In such cases, the combination public/collective good produced by the debtor government's attempt to open markets does not benefit the country as a whole. Hence, additional controls on private actors are necessary for governments to gain from their efforts.

The nature of goods is also important with respect to bargaining by debtors. Debtors can free-ride on other debtors who have expended their power resources to secure a favorable arrangement with creditors. Rescheduling agreements often create precedents that creditors may find hard not to follow. Pressure from domestic interest groups may force a debtor's leaders to seek identical terms – even if they themselves recognize that their position is different. This can work to a debtor's advantage if it can convince creditors that the government's hands are tied domestically.

If banks have only a limited capacity to award concessions to debtors, then a favorable rescheduling accord will be seen as a collective good. Thus, debtors who successfully secure better terms may actually decide to assist creditors in discriminating among debtors, in an effort to preserve the "total amount of concessions" for their own future consumption.[23] If creditors could clearly discriminate among debtors based on their performance (without creating rising expectations among more recalcitrant ones), they could also transform the good into a private one.

Issue-connections as constraints on situational change

When trying to alter their situation, actors will be affected by the contours of the debt rescheduling issue-area. As with goods, actors will be constrained by existing issue-connections, and may also attempt to manipulate these connections

[23] It might be possible to manipulate the technological characteristic of "jointness" to affect the type of goods that exist. By and large, this would appear to be difficult to do. See Head (1972).

Table 4.1. *Static connections among issues*

Objective reality	Decisionmakers' perceptions	Basis for issue connections	Outcome
Connected	Connected	Knowledge	Issue-area
Connected	Unconnected	None	Externality
Unconnected	Connected	Misperception	Internality
Unconnected	Unconnected	None	Independent

to achieve changes in their overall capabilities, issue-needs, and coalitions. How they can do this and what effect this might have on their situations is the question we will examine next.[24]

For ease of exposition, we first examine static connections among issues – that is, in which actors are not actively manipulating issue connections. Table 4.1 describes such connections among issues with respect to the following four areas: (1) "objective reality," as it relates to connections among issues, (2) the extent to which decisionmakers involved in negotiations believe such connections exist, (3) the basis, if any, for treating issues as connected, and (4) the resulting outcome. This categorization allows us to examine the types of connections that an actor might make. It also illuminates the connections between the theoretical concepts of externalities, issue-areas, and so on.[25]

Earlier chapters have already discussed the first case, which results in formation of an issue-area. To reiterate, in this situation actors recognize that they interact on several issues, and we must analyze negotiation behavior in all of the issues considered together. When issue-areas are defined this way (whereby experts agree that issues are connected or "objective" connections exist), both the "issue-packaging" and any agreements involving these issues will be more enduring.[26]

The second case, the "externality" outcome, arises when policymakers do not initially realize that their actions regarding one issue may have some bearing on another. They may recognize this over time and try to incorporate the externality into their bargaining calculations.[27] The U.S. government increasingly saw the

[24] For good discussions of issue-linkages, see Tollison and Willet (1979), Haas (1980), Oye (1983), Stein (1980), and Sebenius (1984).

[25] At this point, we are not concerned with the distinction between what can be termed "parallel" versus "nested" issues. Parallel issues refer to "horizontally" arranged issues in the sense that there is no hierarchy of goals associated with them. By contrast, "nested" issues are arranged so that goals in higher level issue-areas may supersede goals of actors in the lower level issues. Issue-area expansion can take place among parallel or nested issues. We might expect the types of new actors or goals that become engaged in these two cases to be different. I do not pursue this analysis formally here, but will examine such differences in the case studies.

[26] See Haas (1980).

[27] In economic terms, the analogue is for the firm to internalize the externality by taking it into account in its production function.

Table 4.2. *The dynamics of issue-linkage*

Objective reality	Target decisionmakers' perceptions	Basis for issue connections	Linkage type	Outcome
Connected	Connected	Knowledge	Substantive link	Stable issue-area
Connected	Unconnected	Power	Failed substantive (perceived as tactical)	Temporary solution to externalities
Unconnected	Connected	Misunderstanding	Failed tactical link (perceived as substantive)	Unstable issue-area
Unconnected	Unconnected	Power	Tactical link	"Contingent" (to independent with power change)

connection between trade protection and debt servicing in the 1980s and early 1990s – although it has met with little success in resisting the protectionist trend.

If decisionmakers perceive their behavior as being contingent on others' actions, but experts do not see causal connections, then negotiations might be packaged in an unstable manner. Because the connections among issues are in the minds of decisionmakers, I refer to this case as an "internality." In some cases, policymakers' experts might correctly understand the fallacy of this issue packaging and try to separate causally unconnected issues from the issue-area.

Lastly, an "independence" situation exists if issues are simply unconnected and everyone recognizes this fact. In this case, measuring the relevant single-issue power resources is relatively simple. Yet actors here may still engage in power-based (that is, tactical) linkages to other issues in an effort to improve their bargaining position.

Having examined static connections among issues, we will now consider actors' efforts to alter such interconnections in Table 4.2. In the four cases of manipulation that will follow, I assume that the target actor behaves as though the issues are linked. My focus here is whether the resulting links are perceived as tactical or substantive by the target decisionmakers – that is, those actors whom the originator of the linkage effort is trying to influence. Tactical links have no intellectual coherence; by contrast substantive linkages are connections among issues based on consensual knowledge.[28] In addition, I will look at the resulting outcome of these linkage attempts.

[28] See Oye (1979) and Haas (1980) on linkages.

The first type of linkage, labeled "substantive," results in the creation of a stable issue-area. This outcome arises from bargaining whereby one actor convinces the other of the impact of externalities surrounding a particular set of negotiations, which leads to their packaging additional issues together (and moving from the second to the first type of static connection). Substantive linkages should lead to more stable agreements (although not necessarily less conflict) because all actors will accept this type of issue packaging as a logical connection of issues. Tradeoffs can then be made rationally based on different actors' objectives.

More complicated is the second type of manipulated linkage, "failed substantive linkage." Here, even though experts agree that two issues are interconnected (such as access to markets for trade and the ability to service debt), policymakers in the target country do not recognize the issues as substantively linked. Instead, they perceive the issues as only tactically related. Without changes, even though the target actor treats the issues as connected, this will prove to be only a temporary solution to the externalities problem. Such a situation may provide hope for the actor trying to establish the links (the "linker"). When the policymaker's initial reaction is a rejection of substantive connections among issues, experts in both countries may play a prominent role in swaying decisionmakers' opinions.[29]

The third type of linkage, misperceived tactical linkages, will only generate confusion. In this instance, policymakers in the target country will see the issues as substantively linked – even though they are only linked tactically. This moves negotiations from static connection type four to type three, the internality. Although the target decisionmakers' own experts will attempt to dissuade their policymakers from accepting the linkage, target decisionmakers may accept some type of joint agreement and consider the issues in question as a package. Clever manipulation by the actor attempting to make the link could produce much more favorable outcomes than might otherwise be the case. But because it is based on a misunderstanding, this is probably an unstable situation and unlikely to endure.

The last type of link, tactical linkage, may foster even greater conflict. This method of connecting issues is a pure power play. If it is used as a positive inducement, it can diminish conflict. But if used as a stick, tactical linkages will create sharp conflict in negotiations and most likely lead to unstable agreements.[30]

To manipulate issue connections, actors draw upon a variety of resources, such as transmitting information to other actors about the spillover effects from one issue to another. For example, Mexico could convince the U.S. government

[29] Naturally, the same argument applies to organizational units besides countries – for example, banks. Transmitting information about causal links among issues may have an important effect on the bargaining process. In particular, skill in explaining the logic of one's position will affect the success of bargaining efforts. Transnational coalitions among like-minded experts may develop and influence outcomes (Haas, 1980, Sebenius, 1984, Rothstein, 1984).

[30] Haas (1980).

that immigration relates directly to the debt issue; it could use this information as leverage to bring the U.S. over to its side against the banks. This would alter the American coalition and possibly increase Mexico's overall capabilities in negotiations with the banks if the U.S. granted significant aid. Debtors may also change the issue-area by threatening to declare a debt moratorium unless given access to developed countries' markets. Brazil, for example, has claimed that its ability to pay its debt depends on liberalized trade measures – or at least, on the absence of additional restrictions on its manufactured exports. Allies may also prove helpful in promoting connections among issues and in altering debtors' overall capabilities. Although debtors have not succeeded in banding together in the current debt crisis, they would improve their overall position if they could convincingly connect the debt crisis to the wider international problem of development.[31] During some of the rescheduling discussions, debtors have tried to turn the debt issue into a North-South issue of systemic inequity. The U.S. government and commercial banks have naturally resisted this effort. It is in their interest to maintain the current contours of the debt rescheduling issue-area, which favor their bargaining position.

Conclusion

This chapter has completed my discussion of a situational theory of bargaining by examining how actors can alter their game payoffs. I have argued that if bargainers receive poor payoffs, they will be motivated to alter either their own or their opponent's individual situation. To promote such changes, I suggested that they can draw upon three types of power resources to improve their position: norms and rules, capabilities, and allies. Situational changes can also come about through exogenous shocks. As I noted, the discovery of new resources, the onset of wars, and changes in the political stability of countries can affect debt negotiations, but are not events that I attempt to predict in my modeling effort. The last issue I considered in this chapter concerned the nature of goods and the role of issue connections. By categorizing both types of goods and issue linkages, I showed some of the calculations actors need to make to improve their situation.

Based on the situational theory of payoffs discussed in this and the previous two chapters, we now turn to an examination of empirical cases of debt rescheduling. Parts II, III, and IV analyze debt rescheduling in Mexico and Peru for three epochs, running from the 1820s to the 1860s, 1860s to the 1910s, and 1910s to 1950s. Part V, which focuses on the fourth epoch, from the 1980s to the 1990s, includes an analysis of Mexico, Peru, Argentina, and Brazil.

Within each epoch, separate rescheduling episodes are divided into different *bargaining periods*, with bargaining periods defined by changes in situational

[31] See, e.g., the study by Brazil's former central banker, Carlos Langoni, on the debt/development crisis (1985).

factors. Each period consists of two parts: a *play phase*, when actors play a particular game with a given set of payoffs, and a *change phase*, where actors' individual situations change, either as a result of their own efforts or due to exogenous shocks. Although actors may attempt to make situational changes during the play phase as well, unless they succeed, by definition, they remain in the same game.

The play phase may sometimes comprise a few bargaining *rounds*, because negotiators may often take some time to arrive at the Nash equilibrium. Thus each "bargaining period" within an epoch corresponds to a different game (with its own specific payoffs) and change efforts; a "round," by contrast, corresponds to one or more negotiating episodes within a period. For example, in the Mexican rescheduling episode in the first epoch, which lasts from 1827 to the 1860s, I look at three periods, with a few rounds in each one. In sum, the book examines 61 "cases" or periods in total.

PART II

Epoch 1: 1820s–1860s

5 The intersection of high and low politics: Mexican debt rescheduling, 1824–1867

My analysis of Mexican rescheduling begins with the country's political independence from Spain in 1821. As with most new-born countries, Mexico experienced the growing pains of domestic turmoil as it sought to establish itself as a sovereign country. In Mexico's case, the gap between gaining independence and sustaining a financially and politically viable nation-state was large. In its first 35 years, Mexico experienced more than 40 changes of political leadership along with chronic financial problems. Unable to raise revenues domestically, Mexico contracted sterling loans in 1824 and 1825 to meet its general financial needs and procure military equipment for defense against possible reconquest. Servicing these bonds with Mexico's own revenues, however, proved impossible. For the first few years payments came from the reserve funds of the banking houses that floated these loans on the London market. When these funds ran out in 1827, Mexico ceased its debt service.

This breach of contract was the first in a 60-year sequence of readjustment schemes and suspensions in debt servicing. Mexico also incurred other foreign debts in connection with property losses of foreign nationals, which resulted in years of convention negotiations with Great Britain, France, the U.S., and Spain. The type and severity of the breaches of contract varied, but suspension of interest payments and government intervention affecting security pledges were common. Solutions to the problems frequently included interest capitalization (converting overdue interest into principal), but on the whole, the most popular approach was debt conversion. This tactic alleviated debt burdens in the short run by reducing payments on interest, by changing the timetable for the resumption of bond servicing, and by altering the assignment of revenues. It was not until an era of peace and strong government under President Porfirio Diáz in 1885, however, that Mexico's leaders devised a comprehensive scheme of financial readjustment to settle these early foreign loans.

From the start, the issue-area of negotiations only implicitly linked debt and trade matters. Mexico's debt servicing and loan securities were tied to its customs revenues, but despite this connection, the "debt issue-area" for negotiation purposes excluded trade. Debt negotiators haggled over the amount and type of customs revenues to be pledged toward debt servicing, but they rarely discussed Mexican trade itself. In this sense, both the Mexican government and its creditors perceived the debt-trade linkage as tactical rather than substantive. The negotiations of the initial loan agreements failed to address the more substantive linkage between debt and Mexican trade: namely that improvements in the Mexican trade balance would improve the government's ability to satisfy debt servicing payments.

My analysis divides the rescheduling negotiations for Mexico's debts incurred at the beginning of this first epoch into five separate periods that span two different epochs. Focusing on the first epoch, this chapter examines the first three periods, while Chapter 8 covers the remaining two periods.[1] The three periods in this chapter are demarcated as follows: The first series of negotiations begins with a default on the original contract in 1827 and ends in 1847 with an 1846 agreement on the conversion of old bonds. The second period encompasses new agreements by Mexico on the London debt (following the conclusion of Mexico's war with the United States in 1848) and runs through the negotiation of the "Convention debts" with several foreign powers in the late 1850s and early 1860s. The third period begins with the French installation of Ferdinand Maximilian as the Emperor of Mexico in 1863 and ends with his overthrow in 1867.

Period one, 1827–1847: from default to conversion

In 1824, Mexico contracted its first bond loan of £3.2 million ($16 million) through the London financial house of Goldschmidt and Company.[2] Of this amount, Mexico received only $6 million in cash after discounting on the bonds, servicing withholdings, and commissions. The following year, Mexico contracted another bond loan issue through Barclay, Richardson, and Company in London for the same amount. For both bond loans, Mexico pledged one-third of its custom duties as security.[3] In October 1827, when the sum retained by the bond issuing houses to pay interest and amortization charges ran dry, the Mexican government found itself bankrupt. The government suspended interest payments before it had even spent a single peso from purely Mexican revenue sources. In two years, the new loans had sharply increased Mexico's debt burden while its productive capacity stagnated. Worse, negotiating readjustments of this "London debt" would plague Mexico for the next 60 years.

Given Mexico's relative instability and its fear of reconquest by Spain, borrowing was partially linked to security issues. Some Mexicans believed borrowing on the London market was a means of encouraging British support for Mexican independence, which would buffer aggressive Spanish advances. As Francisco de Borja Migoni, a Mexican official who negotiated the first loan in London, put it:

> Any nation which lends money to another nation acquires an interest in the continuance of the latter's independence. The English government protects the interests of its people,

[1] Chapter 8 also examines debt negotiations during Porfirio Diáz's long reign (the "Porfiriato").
[2] At this time, the peso was equal to one dollar. [3] Payno (1862), Appendix I, no. 2.

and if the English people have funds in Mexico, I ask you: Will not Mexico be given some slight consideration by the government?[4]

The proposed loan was quickly approved by the Mexican Congress, serving also as an expedient to raise revenue.

Identifying individual situations

To analyze the actors' valuation of possible outcomes, we must identify Mexico's and the bondholders' individual situations. In addition, we focus on the interests of creditor governments to predict the likelihood of their intervention in negotiations. To briefly summarize actors' situations, Mexico was coalitionally unstable, issue weak, and overall strong (IS 4). The bondholders were relatively united, but weak in debt-related and overall capabilities (IS 7). In this first period, Britain cared less about the servicing of loans to Mexico than with securing markets for British industry by countering the U.S. and maintaining good relations with Mexico. The last thing the British wanted was an American excuse to expand into Mexico to "protect Mexican sovereignty." In the following sections, I will discuss the basis for these codings.

Mexico. During the first period, Mexico experienced tremendous factional strife, revolutionary uprisings, changes in government administrations, and wars with outside powers. The formation of the Mexican Republic created a conflict between Federalists and centralists. In addition, throughout these years, liberals and conservatives struggled for power, embroiling Mexico in frequent civil war. Yet struggles over political ideologies were less disruptive than the political ambitions of its leaders, each vying to become President of Mexico. Constant leadership changes produced a shaky political situation and an unstable domestic coalition.[5]

Mexico owed its independence from Spain in large part to Agustín de Iturbide, a military man who renounced colonial rule to join the resistance. In 1821, he came to power based on a precarious alliance between Mexican conservatives and the liberals. Strengthened by this coalitional support, Iturbide and the Mexican revolutionaries forced an end to Spanish rule after more than 11 years of struggle. Iturbide's subsequent decision to create a hereditary monarchy in Mexico, however, and to install himself as Emperor in May 1822 proved ill-advised. This action destroyed the shaky alliance that had brought him to power.

In a parallel twist of fate, Antonio López de Santa Anna, Iturbide's commander in the key port and city of Veracruz, led a liberal uprising against the new monarchy. By February 1823, Santa Anna forced Iturbide to abdicate his throne. With General Santa Anna's blessing, a provisional three-man military junta came to power as the interim government. Yet this new group proved no

[4] Quoted in Turlington (1930), p. 22, without a footnote to indicate the source. See also the discussion by Payno (1862), p. 2.

[5] The following discussion of Mexican politics draws mainly on Bancroft (1885), pp. 376–443, and Meyer and Sherman (1987), pp. 294–354.

more stable than the short-lived "empire." Following passage of a new constitution that created the Republic of Mexico, Guadalupe Victoria was elected president in 1824.

Victoria's administration, faced with an expensive army, a colonial debt of 76 million pesos, and an inability to raise revenues, began the cycle of Mexican foreign debt by turning to London for loans. These loans were seen as a panacea for Mexico's financial difficulties – a misleading hope at best.[6] Although Victoria managed to complete his presidential term despite an attempted coup by his own vice-president, he would be the last president to do so until Benito Juárez managed the same feat 40 years later.[7] The pattern of coups (often by vice-presidents from the opposing faction) continued throughout this first period. As one study writes, "Mexican history from 1833 to 1855 constantly teetered between simple chaos and unmitigated anarchy."[8]

Mexico's financial position was as dismal as its politics. The government found it impossible to raise enough revenue to cover national expenditures. Commerce, agriculture, mining, and industry desperately needed assistance after stagnating during the 11-year revolutionary struggle. The new Mexican government, concerned about the continued threat of Spanish reconquest, also needed to pay troops and maintain supplies. Throughout the 1820s, rumors persisted that Spain would attempt to recapture its most important American colony. In 1829, rumor gave way to reality when Spanish forces landed in Tampico. Beyond simply repelling real or imagined invasions, of course, a strong military also enabled Mexican leaders to maintain their power by quelling rebellions in the countryside.

The Mexican economy consistently failed to provide its government with a stable source of revenue. This situation was particularly acute in the gold and silver mining industries of Mexico – the chief source of revenues for the Spanish colonial administration. The revolutionary war had caused mines to close as workers left to fight. In 1809, in colonial Spanish America, the mines produced \$26 million worth of gold and silver compared to a mere \$6 million excavated by the state of Mexico in 1821.[9] In 1822, the Mexican government estimated that its national deficit in the next year alone would run close to 20 million pesos.[10] In 1825, even after the foreign bond loans, the budget deficit remained at approximately 8 million pesos.[11]

The trade picture was not much brighter. When Mexico floated its second loan in 1825, its imports numbered almost five times its exports (24 million versus 5 million pesos, respectively). This dismal performance continued throughout the period. In 1843, imports still greatly exceeded exports (22 million versus some 12 million pesos). The trade deficit, combined with the government's

[6] See the discussion below of Mexico's financial problems.

[7] Although this was Juárez's third term, his first two were as a rival parallel "government" to Maximilian and his conservative predecessors.

[8] Meyer and Sherman (1987), p. 324. [9] Meyer and Sherman (1987), p. 304.

[10] Romero (1871), p. 72. [11] Romero (1871), p. 81. See also Parkes (1938/1969), pp. 178–179.

inability to raise sufficient revenues through a tax on sales, import duties, or governmental monopolies, produced a nearly bankrupt treasury. The government budget deficit reflected this sorry state of affairs.[12]

In terms of overall capabilities, Mexico was relatively powerful. President Victoria, in office from 1824 through 1828, maintained a standing army of some 50,000 men.[13] Moreover, Mexico had little to fear in the form of retribution from bondholders. The creditors could not attach any foreign assets because Mexico possessed few such assets or investments abroad, and the bondholders could not disrupt Mexican trade, commerce, or access to foreign capital. Most important, bondholders were unable to secure assistance through an alliance with the British government. The Foreign Office viewed Mexico's default as a private matter in which the British government had no responsibility or authority to interfere, except in giving its "friendly support."[14]

Lenders. During this first period, a group of British bondholders formed the first "Committee of Mexican Bondholders"[15] – the sole organizational body representing the interests of lenders. The Committee's leader, John Marshall, addressed the bondholders' claims to the Mexican government and actively sought assistance from the British government.

The bondholders found themselves weak in debt-related capabilities. The committee of bondholders did not have reserve funds to cover possible losses on their Mexican loans. In fact, salaries and expenses of the Committee members and bondholder representatives were tied to Mexico's debt service payments. Commenting on Mexico's failure to meet its debt service, one bondholder wrote that Mexico "has inflicted upon us an injury – not confined to the speculators in stocks, but involving numberless families throughout the United Kingdom . . . largely affecting the prosperity of our merchants and manufacturers."[16]

As we have seen, lack of active support from the British government weakened the bondholders in overall capabilities. Moreover, as ordinary citizens, the bondholders had little control over the international financial system of the time. In 1827, the bondholders had to accept Mexico's inability to make debt payments and could do little to end the continuing default.

Creditor governments. My analysis of the factors influencing creditor government intervention predicts British reluctance to intervene in debt negotiations throughout this period, despite their substantial economic involvement in Mexico. As noted, British policy was to challenge American interests and

[12] Note that the problem of revenue generation has continued to plague Mexico to this day. See the discussion of Mexico's debt problems in the 1980s and 1990s in Part V of this study.

[13] Meyer and Sherman (1987), p. 319.

[14] *British and Foreign State Papers* (hereinafter, *Bri. For. State Papers*), vol. 18, 1830–1851, pp. 1012–1014.

[15] This first "Committee of Mexican Bondholders" was dissolved in 1836 when Mexican bondholders joined forces with other Latin American bondholders in the "Committee of Spanish-American Bondholders." A second "Committee of Mexican Bondholders" was formed in 1850.

[16] Wyllie (1840), p. 2.

influence in Latin America, particularly in Latin American commercial markets. Furthermore, economic penetration from German capital and French commercial interests also shaped British policy.[17] Although the British government was initially interested in providing a solution to debt problems, its policy of protecting its own strategic interests first and foremost left bondholders suffering from a lack of government support.

Although the British government would have liked to extend a loan to Mexico in order to combat American influence in the region, its fear of excessive involvement prevented it from doing so. In proposing British recognition of Mexico in late 1824, George Canning, the Foreign Secretary, remarked, "I believe we now have the opportunity (but it may not last long) of opposing a powerful barrier to the influence of the U.S. by an amicable connection with Mexico . . ."[18] Lionel Harvey, one of a three-member British commission sent to investigate the situation in Mexico after the revolution, exceeded his authority by guaranteeing a loan to Mexico in the name of the British government before he was quickly recalled.[19]

The British fears of American dominance in the area were not assuaged by the announcement of the Monroe Doctrine. In December 1823, due to his worry that European struggles might spill over into the "New World," President James Monroe proclaimed that the Western Hemisphere should no longer be a region of European competition.[20] Through this declaration, pushed by his Secretary of War, John Calhoun, and supported by Secretary of State John Quincy Adams, Monroe set the stage to increase American influence in the region.[21]

Monroe's declaration caught Foreign Secretary Canning off guard. In 1822, Canning had tried to persuade the Americans to make a joint pronouncement on non-intervention in an effort to undercut the French. Richard Rush, the American Minister in London, refused to do so – unless the British recognized the Latin American states. This demand killed the proposal. Canning managed to respond quickly to the U.S. action, however, by publicizing a memo written with the French accepting the policy of non-intervention. Through a classic use of "spin control," he tried to turn this foreign policy setback to his advantage by suggesting publicly that he had pushed the Americans to this action. Privately, of course, Canning was furious because he wished to keep the Americans from securing favorable access to the Latin American markets. Continuing for much of the nineteenth century, competition between the U.S. and Great Britain would deeply influence events in Mexico. As Charles Broughton, who served under both Canning and William Pitt the Elder, told Migoni in a fit of hyperbole: Mexico, because of its situation, would ultimately "hold the balance of all the Nations of America."[22]

[17] Parkes (1938/1969), pp. 190–191. [18] Temperley (1925), p. 553.
[19] Rippy (1929/1964), p. 250.
[20] It is important to recall that a second central focus of the Monroe Doctrine was to dissuade the Russians from maintaining a presence on the American continent.
[21] The following draws from Perkins (1927).
[22] *La Diplomacía Mexicana* (1910/12/23), pp. 163–167, cited in Turlington (1930), p. 31.

Cardinal Payoff Matrix,
No Intervention Expected

		Lenders IS 7		
		HC...	MC...	LC...
	HA...	−3, 12	−6.5, 11.67	−9, 11.33
Mexico IS 4	MA...	−1.67, 9	−2, 8	−5, 7
	LA...	**6.33, 10**	2.5, 7	−1, 4

Note: Nash equilibrium bolded.

Ordinal Payoff Matrix,
No Intervention Expected

		Lenders IS 7		
		HC...	MC...	LC...
	HA...	4, 9	2, 8	1, 7
Mexico IS 4	MA...	7, 5	5, 4	3, 2.5
	LA...	**9, 6**	8, 2.5	6, 1

Note: Nash equilibrium bolded.

Figure 5.1. *Play phase, period one: 1827–1846*

Debt game and predicted outcome

Based on Mexico's classification as coalitionally unstable, weak financially but strong overall (IS 4), and the bondholders as stable but issue and overall weak (IS 7), I predict the game and outcome shown in Figure 5.1.

From a purely deductive standpoint, we would expect Mexico to play a strategy of no adjustment. Regardless of the bondholders' choice, the debtor achieves its optimal payoff by not adjusting. If the bondholders could be certain that Mexico would (and could) carry out a high adjustment policy, they would not be inclined to make any lending concessions. But, if they expect Mexico to make only some or no adjustments as is the case here, then the bondholders will play a strategy of high concessions to obtain the best outcome possible for their interests. This pair of strategies – high concessions, low or no adjustment – is the Nash equilibrium of the game.

Given the interests of the British government discussed above, we expect that its leaders would remain neutral in debt negotiations. British intervention should not change the Nash equilibrium of the matrix by fostering greater or lesser cooperation. Our prediction for this period, even with intervention, thus remains at the equilibrium outcome of no adjustment by Mexico and high concessions on the part of British bondholders.

The negotiations and outcome

We can divide our analysis of the negotiations during this first period from the 1827 default to the 1846 conversion into three bargaining rounds, based on various agreements. The first round begins in 1827 and ends with the conversion of 1831. The second round encompasses the negotiations from that time until 1842 when another debt rescheduling and bond conversion agreement was carried out. Finally, the third round runs from 1842 to the final debt conversion and interest capitalization in 1846. Throughout these three rounds we will see that the actual outcomes correlate to the predicted absence of debtor adjustment and high concessions by bondholders. We also find that involvement of the British and other creditor governments increased from the first to the third round. But as expected, the outcome of the negotiations remained at the predicted equilibrium point, despite growing British interest.

Round one. When in October 1827, the Mexican government failed to meet interest payments due on its London debt, the government cited as the main reason for the default an exhausted public treasury, depleted after years of revolutionary struggle. In fact, prior to the default, no government revenues had ever gone toward servicing the foreign debt. Earlier interest payments had been made by small sums from the initial loans (reserved explicitly for debt servicing) and by advances from Baring Brothers, Mexico's new financial agents.

Despite the default, the Mexican government made clear its intention to fulfill its obligations and maintain Mexico's reputation and credit abroad. As a sign of good faith, in November 1827 Mexico assigned to debt service all export duties on gold and silver, as well as one-eighth of all maritime customs duties. In 1828, to further appease the bondholders, the Mexican Congress passed an act proposing the capitalization of all overdue interest on the foreign debt. These pronouncements of good faith prevented creditor governments from assuming a more active, interventionary role. To jump ahead of our analysis for a moment, the Mexican Minister of Foreign Affairs wrote to the British government in 1833 that, despite its desire to meet its commitments, the country's resources and the public treasury were "inadequate to the expenses indispensably requisite to the existence of the nation and to pay its debt."[23] By arguing that they were

[23] Turlington (1930), p. 64.

simply unable to fulfill the terms of their contract – but that they had every intention of doing so at the first possible opportunity – Mexico temporarily placated the bondholders.

Continued instability worsened Mexico's ability to resume its debt agreements and servicing. In late 1828, new revolutionary uprisings stirred the Mexican countryside. The following year, a virtual civil war surrounded the presidential succession. In July 1829, Mexican troops repulsed a Spanish invasion of the port of Tampico. Finally, in late 1829, General Anastasio Bustamante, a former Mexican Vice-President, led a successful revolution against President Vicente Guerrero and installed himself as President the following year.

Although Mexico survived these crises, foreign confidence in the nation waned. When the value of Mexican bonds fell sharply, the Mexican government considered a secret plan to make a large purchase of the bonds at their low price and resell them at the inflated price that would result from the initial large purchase. This strategy – which the bondholders would have undoubtedly regarded as cheating – was not carried out.[24]

In 1830, to show Mexico's good faith in the debt matter, the government invited the bondholders to name their own agents to collect the proceeds generated from the assigned customs duties of Mexican ports.[25] In June, John Marshall, chairman of the newly formed Committee of Mexican Bondholders, solicited assistance from the British Foreign Office. Only a year earlier, the Foreign Office issued a pronouncement on its policy regarding debt negotiations, arguing that the government had neither the right nor the authority to interfere because the debt issue had arisen "out of the speculations of a private nature."[26] But with Marshall's solicitation, the Earl of Aberdeen, representing the Foreign Office, authorized the British Vice-Consuls at Tampico and Veracruz to receive and remit funds assigned for the bondholders. In addition, Richard Packenham, British Chargé d'Affaires in Mexico, was allowed to second "any proper representations" the bondholders might make to the Mexican government.[27] Although these moves signalled a significant shift in Britain's non-interventionist policy, the Earl of Aberdeen declared that no British official would serve as an agent to the bondholders.[28]

In October 1830, following negotiations between William Manning (the Committee's representative) and the Mexican Minister of Finance, the Mexican Congress passed a law allowing the government to enter into an agreement with the bondholders for the issue of new bonds and the capitalization of interest. The arrangement called for the issue of all bonds to satisfy all interest due up to 1831, and half of the interest coming due five years thereafter. Bondholders of the Goldschmidt loan received new 5% bonds at the rate of 1,000 pesos' worth

[24] A high official of Mexico suggested a similar plan for Mexico in the current crisis – interview, 1987.

[25] Turlington (1930), p. 58. [26] *Bri. For. State Papers*, vol. 28 (1839–1840), p. 970.

[27] *Bri. For. State Papers*, vol. 28 (1839–1840), p. 970.

[28] *Bri. For. State Papers*, vol. 28 (1839–1840), p. 972.

of bonds for 625 pesos of interest due; the Barclay bondholders received new 6% bonds at a rate of 1,000 pesos for 750 pesos. For the payment of the unfunded half of the interest due from 1831 through 1836, one-sixth of the maritime customs duties at Veracruz and Tampico was designated for collection by two officials, one named by the government of Mexico, one by the Committee of Bondholders.[29]

New bonds to capitalize interest due prior to 1831 were issued immediately. Bonds for the capitalization of half of the interest coming due from 1831–1836 were to be issued periodically during those years. The new bonds were to bear no interest until 1836. The agreement increased Mexico's bonded indebtedness by nearly 8 million pesos. On the other hand, Mexico benefited from the five-year postponement of the interest due on the new bonds, which represented overdue interest as well as half of the London debt interest scheduled due within the next five years.

At the end of the first round in 1831, the bondholders had made high concessions, agreeing to accept new bonds and a five-year postponement on their interest due. Mexico received this five-year reprieve by pledging future revenues to their creditors, but undertook no painful financial adjustments to improve its creditworthiness.

Round two. Mexico met its obligations, including the delivery of assigned customs for one year, before failing to meet its debt service commitments and, once again, defaulting on the London debt. As before, internal strife and poor public finances explain Mexico's failure to satisfy its creditors. General Santa Anna, the popular Mexican liberator who overthrew Emperor Iturbide in 1823 and defended Mexico against the Spanish in 1829, continued his fight for Mexico's freedom by leading the revolution against President Bustamante in 1832. After Bustamante's overthrow, the liberals elected Santa Anna president in 1833. Yet, he quickly tired of presidential duties, and after a year, left the post to his liberal vice-president, Valentín Gómez Farías. Santa Anna, however, would return to the presidential post some 11 times for brief interludes. In fact, he switched from his liberal position and took up the conservative banner to displace Farías and return to power. In 1836, he replaced the Mexican Constitution of 1824 with a newer and more conservative one to promote his vision of a centralized state. The struggle between conservatives and liberals continued throughout the remaining half of the nineteenth century. Between 1833 and 1853, the Mexican presidency changed hands over 30 times with an average term lasting seven and a half months.[30]

By emphasizing what they claimed was a temporary setback in debt servicing, the Mexican government hoped to maintain its advantageous position against the bondholders. In 1833, as a sign of good faith, Mexican President Gómez Pedraza

[29] From *Legislación Mexicana*, vol. 2, p. 289, cited in Turlington (1930), p. 61.
[30] Meyer and Sherman (1987), p. 324.

ordered a short-term rerouting of 6% of the maritime customhouses proceeds to pay interest on the foreign debt. This pledge, however, turned out to mean very little. In 1833, only 4 to 5% of these revenues went toward interest payments, and in 1834, the percentage was reduced to 0.5%. Thus out of all the customs duties from the two ports, only 20,678 pesos went to Mexico's foreign creditors. In 1835, this amount was further reduced to 1,309 pesos, and finally, in the following year, no interest payments arose from these revenues.[31]

Mexico's poor economic performance, unresponsiveness to requests for debt servicing, and uncertainty about its actual financial condition caused some bondholders to question the Mexican government's sincerity. As one bondholder wrote:

> the war also deprived them of the means of paying their foreign creditors . . . but the same excuses cannot now be alleged: the conviction has become general . . . that the question is no longer of ability, but of will; the gross attempts at compositions with the creditors to whom they owe liberty and independence, have disgusted all of Europe.[32]

In June 1836, the bondholders of Mexico's London debt dissolved their independent committee. In its place, to increase their leverage, the bondholders joined with the creditors of several other defaulting Latin American countries to form the "Committee of Spanish American Bondholders." By doing so, the bondholders of the Mexican debt consolidated their interests with bondholders of other states including Colombia, Peru, Chile, Argentina, and the Central American countries.[33]

Assuming that Mexicans were able but unwilling to pay, the new committee began to actively solicit assistance from the British government. At the first meeting, the Committee of Spanish American Bondholders decided they would

> confidently rely on the active support of His Majesty's Government in this object, to which they humbly consider themselves entitled on every principle of justice and protection; it being manifest, that whether a foreign nation unlawfully detains the property of British subjects, or unjustly withholds from them the performance of engagements into which it has voluntarily entered, the wrong and the injury alike, and the claim for redress equal.[34]

During this time, the Mexican government continued its desperate search for new funds to fill its bankrupt treasury. The government resorted to short-term, high-interest loans from Mexican capitalists, as well as to other internal forced loans. These measures, however, failed to provide enough capital to cover government expenditures. The Mexican government also explored the possibility of loans from the U.S. government or from American private capitalists. Certain American officials seized on the idea as a means of obtaining Northern Mexican territory. United States Chargé d'Affaires Colonel Anthony Butler suggested in a letter to President Jackson in 1833 that if such loans were secured upon

[31] Payno (1862), p. 45. [32] Wyllie (1840).
[33] Committee of Mexican Bondholders (1849), p. 106.
[34] Committee of Mexican Bondholders (1849), p. 107.

Mexican territory, the U.S. might gain title to the land. Given Mexico's almost assured failure to uphold the loan agreement, he argued that any pledged territory would "be suffered quietly to fall into us."[35] The U.S. government, however, rejected the idea of any loan-for-territory plan with Mexico because of debate over how to handle growing conflict in Texas.

After the 1836 war with Texas, which led to an independent Texas, the Mexican government sought to encourage colonization of the Texas territory to bring the land back under Mexican control. This plan became closely linked with the debt negotiations in April 1837 when the Mexican Congress directed the president to "proceed to make effective colonization of the lands that ought to be the property of the Republic by means of sales, long leases, or mortgages."[36] The money obtained from these public lands would be applied to "the redemption of the national debt contracted or to be contracted."[37] In the same year, interim Mexican President José Justo Corro proposed a new conversion in which the holders of bonds issued in 1824, 1825, and 1831 could exchange their bonds for titles to vacant lands in Texas, Chihuahua, New Mexico, Sonora, and the Californias. Concurrently, new 5% bonds were to be issued in London.

The London bondholders, however, strongly opposed this proposal; they had little interest in obtaining questionable Mexican territory or in emigrating to Mexico. In September 1837, the Mexican government proposed a new bond conversion instead of the bonds-for-land conversion. Instead of land, bondholders of the London debt would exchange their bonds for new active and deferred bonds. The active bonds, due to immediately accrue interest, were assigned one-sixth of the maritime custom duties at Veracruz and Tampico. These duties were to be delivered to a Mexican Commissioner and to at least one agent of the bondholders. The deferred bonds would not accrue interest until 1847. They could, however, be used to purchase titles to vacant lands in the Northern Mexican territories.

The bondholders preferred this new conversion into active and deferred bonds, but continued to reject the land offer. By contrast, the British government showed great interest in the colonization plan, perceiving the offer as an opportunity for the British to regain a territorial foothold in North America. Clearly, the interest of the British government in the debt negotiations was motivated by its own strategic interests, and not by concern for the debt problems of its nationals.

During the 1830s, a number of European powers including Britain, France, and Spain approached the Mexican government concerning lost property, damages, and forced levies inflicted upon their nationals living in Mexico. In March 1838, French King Louis-Philippe demanded a $600,000 indemnity from the Mexican government to satisfy the claims of French nationals. When Mexico did not comply, the French severed diplomatic relations and sent a fleet of 26 vessels to blockade the port of Veracruz. After taking the port and the Mexican

[35] Turlington (1930), pp. 65–66.
[36] Legislación Mexicana, vol. 3, p. 352 translated in Turlington (1930), p. 70.
[37] Legislación Mexicana, vol. 3, p. 352 translated in Turlington (1930), p. 70.

stronghold of San Juan de Ulloa, the French upped their demands to $800,000. The British-based bondholders committee, fearing that the French would receive funds that could be used for debt service, immediately petitioned Lord Palmerston of the Foreign Office to intervene. Moreover, the Committee stressed that the British ought to enter the "Pastry War" (so named because a French pastry cook claimed that during the revolution, Mexican soldiers devoured his pastries without paying), in order to open the Mexican port to commerce of all nations. Although the British sent a squadron of 13 warships to Veracruz, once again the primary motivation was their own strategic interest – gaining the upper hand over France – not concern for their bondholders. Fearing further escalation, the French withdrew from the conflict, and Louis-Philippe accepted a smaller payment from the Mexican government.[38]

In June 1839, the bondholders and Mexico agreed to the bond conversion proposed in 1837. This arrangement converted half of the bonds of 1824, 1825, and 1831 into new active bonds and the other half into deferred bonds. The land purchase offer remained open, but the bondholders continued to shun this deferred bond-for-land exchange. Although talks of the security assignment for the new bonds were still not resolved, practically all of the old bonds were converted by 1841. In February 1842, considerable pressure from the British Minister over the losses of his nationals led the Mexican government to raise the customs assignments at Veracruz and Tampico from one-sixth to one-fifth.[39]

With the terms of the bond conversion settled and the customs duties assigned, the Mexican government once again postponed much of its debt servicing. Mexico continued to pledge future revenues to debt payments to placate bondholders, but undertook little economic adjustment. The bondholders, contenting themselves with symbolic adjustment from Mexico, agreed to the conversion and again accepted customs duties assignments, which had proven an unreliable source of payments in the past.

Round three. The game matrix for this period indicates that Mexico had little ability or willingness to honor its agreements. After concluding the conversion agreement with the London debt bondholders, Mexico returned to a more important, and more dangerous, task: settling the claims of foreign nationals living in Mexico. In October 1842, the British Minister in Mexico and the Mexican Ministers of Finance and of Foreign Affairs signed a diplomatic convention. With this agreement, the Mexican government acknowledged a debt of 1,148,630 pesos to British subjects. The various claims included past advances of money to the government, sales of goods and property to the government, and other damages incurred by Mexico. This liability came to be known as the "English Convention debt."[40]

The flexing of diplomatic muscle to secure the claims of British subjects against Mexico marked an important change in the role of the British government.

[38] Meyer and Sherman (1987), pp. 328–329. [39] Payno (1862), Appendix, p. 20.
[40] Payno (1862), Appendix, pp. 67–68.

Although not directly connected to the bond debt, the British government increased its diplomatic and economic involvement in the debt issue.

In the meantime, tensions increased between the U.S. and Mexico over the Texas territory and the claims of American subjects against Mexico. In 1841, an arbitration committee awarded American claimants $2.5 million for damages incurred by the Mexican government. The U.S. hoped that the British government would release part of the customs security revenues assigned to British subjects to satisfy the debts owed to American subjects. The British government rejected this plan,[41] firmly maintaining protection of its bondholders' interests.

A different proposal enticed the British government, and more specifically the British Minister to Mexico, to enlist as a "willing intermediary." This bargain entailed the state of Texas paying the bondholders of the Mexican loan 5 million pesos in exchange for Mexico's recognition of Texas's independence. The proposal, however, was never carried out. In July 1845, Texas accepted the U.S. offer of annexation, setting the stage for future territorial conflict between the U.S. and Mexico.[42]

Earlier that year, realizing that the deferred bonds issued in the 1839–1840 conversion would soon begin drawing interest, the Mexican Congress passed a new law calling for the definitive settlement of the foreign debt. According to the law, the settlement could not include the capitalization of interest, interest rates higher than 5%, an increase in the amount of the debt, or a pledge of Mexican national property as payment. On this basis, a new debt agreement, "the Conversion of 1846," was concluded in June 1846. This agreement called for a new issue of 5% bonds worth £10,241,650 (just over 50 million pesos) to convert all existing bonds. Active bonds were converted at 90% of their face value and the deferred bonds at 60%. The remaining new bonds to be issued, worth nearly 11 million pesos, were to be sold to raise cash for Mexico. To secure these new bonds, Mexico made a general pledge of all revenues of the Republic and the special assignment of the tobacco monopoly revenue, the duties on exports of silver through all Pacific ports, and one-fifth of import and export duties at Veracruz and Tampico. With this arrangement, the Mexican government reduced its London debt by nearly 5 million pesos while adding nearly 11 million pesos to its own account. One observer believed that for Mexico, this represented, "one of the most advantageous and brilliant financial operations ever effected."[43]

At the end of this round, Mexico had again adjusted very little. The government issued new bonds to reduce the face value amount of its debt, received new bond loan cash for its public treasury, and pledged questionable future revenues to the bondholders. The lenders, by contrast, made high concessions. They agreed to reduce the amount of the debt, to float an 11 million peso bond loan to Mexico, and to accept unreliable sources of cash as security on the new bonds.

[41] Turlington (1930), pp. 86–87. [42] Bancroft (1885), vol. 5, pp. 292–293.
[43] Payno (1862), p. 16.

Summary. Throughout the first period, the Mexican government claimed it was unable to service its debts. Initially, the bondholders believed this to be true and willingly continued to make high concessions as predicted by our model. But after some time, the bondholders began to doubt Mexico's claims of poverty, and decided to investigate Mexico's financial situation. Mexican leaders, concerned about preventing foreign intervention in Mexico, symbolically concluded numerous agreements with the bondholders calling for high adjustment, but never respected its commitments – hardly a surprise to the bondholders.

Consistent with our predictions, Mexico undertook very little adjustment whereas lenders continued to make high concessions. Mexico managed to reduce the nominal amount of its debt, receive a new bond loan, and pledge only future revenues. This pledge required no painful economic adjustment by Mexico. In addition, the conversion of 1846 benefited Mexico while forcing the bondholders to make unfavorable concessions. Still, the bondholders remained optimistic that Mexico would someday service its debts.

Situational changes

The bondholders, receiving lower payoffs than they desired, and beginning to suspect Mexico's honesty, began serious efforts to change their situation soon after their first accord with Mexico. Early in the period, the lenders attempted to use norms and rules as power resources to improve their situation. The bondholders informed Mexico that all honorable, just, civilized, and decent nations of the world must fulfill their private obligations. As one might expect, such an appeal to an international meta-regime had little coercive power and Mexico remained unresponsive.

The bondholders then attempted to ally with the British government to increase its participation on their behalf. As we have seen, however, the government's isolationist tendencies were motivated by strategic concerns. But the English Convention debt changed the British government's role. The convention brought about the direct diplomatic efforts of the government to protect the property of British subjects. As we shall see, this new arrangement would prove to be hazardous for Mexico. It was one thing to string along the bondholders when they insisted on repayment; by themselves, they could exert little power. It was something else entirely to play this game with the British and French governments.

Bondholders were elated by the new British interest in their plight. The implications, however, were complicated because debt servicing is a collective good: thus the creation of the English Convention debt meant that the London debt bondholders would have to compete with the Convention debt bondholders for the scarce Mexican funds allocated to debt servicing. These actors would begin to "crowd" their interests.

Thus, the London bondholders could not automatically count on British government support. In fact, as we shall see, for the most part, the British government restricted diplomatic protection to the Convention debt, arguing that protection was purely a private good. The London debt bondholders had a difficult time in convincing the British government to extend protection to their claims. For nearly 15 years, in fact, the London debt bondholders competed with other claimants, who were privately protected by the British government, for a collective and crowded good – Mexico's debt payments.

The most dramatic development at the end of this period, however, was the outbreak of war between the U.S. and Mexico in May 1846. The war naturally became the chief priority for national expenditures, and the Mexican government quickly suspended its interest payments after only a short period of compliance.

Period two, 1848–1863: aftermath of war and civil conflict

As the U.S. waged a three-pronged military campaign to wrest the Northern territory away from Mexico, the Mexican government remained immobilized by its own domestic turmoil. Even in the face of an invasion by a foreign power, conservative and liberal Mexican leaders failed to unite. In fact, the Mexican territorial states refused to provide any money for the war effort to defend a national government they distrusted.[44] Despite defaulting on its interest payments, Mexico failed to fund an adequate defense against the U.S. As a result, U.S. forces easily claimed the Northern territories, bombarded and captured the important port city of Veracruz, and finally, on September 1847, marched into Mexico City itself.

On February 2, 1848, the U.S. and Mexico signed the Treaty of Guadalupe Hidalgo to officially end the war between the two nations. With the treaty, Mexico was forced to cede the Northern territories of Texas, New Mexico, and California to the United States. In an effort to justify its war winnings, the U.S. agreed to pay a $15 million indemnity to Mexico and to assume the $3.25 million worth of American claims against the Mexican government. The end of hostilities with the United States left the Mexican treasury bankrupt except for the indemnity it had received in exchange for the loss of its territory. This sum quickly attracted the interest of foreign creditors.

Following the war, the liberal and conservative factions remained intransigent, and local revolts plagued the national government. By 1857, Mexico found itself in the midst of a civil war that would be followed shortly thereafter by foreign invasion and the installation of Ferdinand Maximilian in 1863 by the occupying powers.

Identifying individual situations

Following the conclusion of the treaty between the U.S. and Mexico at the beginning of period two, we classify Mexico and the bondholders in similar situations to the ones they had at the beginning of period one. Mexico remains coalitionally unstable, issue weak, but overall strong (IS 4). The bondholders

[44] Meyer and Sherman (1987), pp. 344–350.

were united, but issue weak and relatively weak overall (IS 7). We begin a new period, however, because the involvement of the British government with the Convention debt in the first period significantly altered actors' calculations in the debt negotiations. In addition, because bondholders believed they were more closely allied to the British government during this period, we examine the implications of coding the lenders as "overall medium" (IS 3/7).

Mexico. Mexico continued to suffer from a high degree of political instability. During the 1830s and early 1840s, the leadership of the country often changed hands, with Santa Anna repeatedly holding the presidency for short periods. We have seen that even when faced with the possibility of war with the U.S., Mexican leaders failed to put aside their internal conflicts to unite in their country's defense. In 1846, prior to the Texas border skirmish that precipitated the war, Mexican General Mariano Parades, dispatched to the North to protect the border region, used his troops to overthrow his own president. Following the military coup, Parades installed himself as President of Mexico.[45] Before, during, and after the war, conservative and liberal factions in Mexico continued to battle for political power, with civil war breaking out in 1857.

Mexico's financial situation remained as wretched as before. In the years prior to the war, the government continued to run a deficit; the war with the U.S. drained an already depleted public treasury. The government made a number of attempts to raise new revenues, including currency changes, forced loans, property confiscations, raising taxes, and even the levy of new taxes such as one on dogs.[46] These efforts, however, failed to increase government revenues sufficiently. In addition, of the 11 million pesos' worth of bonds sold for Mexico as part of the conversion of 1846, the government received only 200,000 pesos in cash. And despite the $15 million American war indemnity, the future Mexican financial picture looked bleak. The national debt continued to grow, approaching 15 million pesos in 1846,[47] while its chief source of revenue – customs duties from foreign trade – continued to fall.[48]

Despite the war and its weak financial situation, the Mexican government maintained its sovereign powers and its overall strength. The U.S. fought the war to capture Mexico's Northern territories, but appeared disinterested in the rest of the country. In terms of military might, Mexico increased the size of its army from 50,000 men in 1828 to nearly 90,000 men after the war. In addition, Mexico remained relatively invulnerable to any possible harm from its bondholders. The Mexican government had no foreign assets, securities, or investments that could be expropriated or attached through legal measures.

Lenders. The merging of the Mexican bondholders into the Committee of Spanish-American Bondholders in 1836 strengthened their unity. The Mexican

[45] Meyer and Sherman (1987), p. 344. [46] Meyer and Sherman (1987), p. 344.
[47] Callcott (1926), pp. 160–161. [48] Meyer and Sherman (1987), p. 334.

bondholders could now pressure Mexico with the support of other Latin American creditors. Just as important, this large organization of bondholders could place greater pressure on the British government to intervene on their behalf. As the Committee wrote, "it is essential that the holders of these Bonds should unite together, for the purpose of taking more decisive measures that have not yet been adopted."[49]

On the debt issue, the bondholders remained financially weak. The bondholders, as well as their committee, lacked the reserve funds to recover any of their financial losses on the debt issue. In fact, the Committee even lacked the funds to cover its expenses or to carry out plans to improve its position vis-à-vis Mexico. When one Committee representative proposed that a permanent commissioner be appointed to represent the bondholders in Mexico, the Committee responded that:

> In regard to appointing a permanent commissioner, as strongly recommended by you [bondholder representative Robertson], I [Committee chair Robinson] can only state that such a step is out of the power of the Committee. They have neither the funds for the purpose, nor have they any authority from the Bondholders to make such an appointment.[50]

As a group, the bondholders remained relatively weak in overall capabilities; they had no power to coerce the Mexican government into maintaining its obligations or making adjustments. The creditors could not block Mexico's access to foreign capital markets or prevent new foreign investment from entering the country. Moreover, the bondholders could not influence nor affect Mexico at either diplomatic or economic levels. The bondholders, however, believed they would receive more assistance and support from the British government than before.

Although we expect the same outcome as before, it is interesting to see what, if any, effect a coding of "overall medium" capabilities for the lenders has on the game. This coding can be used to reflect the perception on the part of the bondholders that they were at least "partially allied" with the British government. Consequently, in the discussion of the game below, we code the lenders as being in a combination of individual situations 3 and 7.

Creditor governments. Despite the British government's move toward a more active diplomatic role in debt negotiations by the end of the first period, strategic self-interests continued to dictate British policymaking throughout the second period. Competition and rivalry from other creditor governments, especially France, particularly concerned the British. The British government remained reluctant, however, to intervene in their bondholders' struggles with Mexico. But with Britain now more deeply involved with debt matters after the signing of the Convention debt, the Mexicans would clearly be more responsive to any expression of concern on their part regarding debt rescheduling.

[49] Committee of Spanish-American Bondholders (hereinafter, Comm. S.A. Bond.) (1849), p. 106.
[50] Comm. S.A. Bond. (1849), pp. 73–75.

Cardinal Payoff Matrix,
Intervention Expected

Lenders IS 3/7

		HC...	MC...	LC...
	HA...	−3, 10.5	−6.5, 10.67	−9, 10.83
Mexico IS 4	MA...	1.67, 7.25	−2, 7	−5, 6.75
	LA...	**6.33, 6.5**	2.5, 5	−1, 3.5

Note: Nash equilibrium bolded; expected outcome with intervention underlined.

Ordinal Payoff Matrix,
Intervention Expected

Lenders IS 3/7

		HC...	MC...	LC...
	HA...	4, 7	2, 8	1, 9
Mexico IS 4	MA...	7, 6	5, 5	3, 4
	LA...	**9, 3**	8, 2	6, 1

Note: Nash equilibrium bolded; expected outcome with intervention underlined.

Figure 5.2. *Play phase, period two: 1848–1860*

Debt game and predicted outcome

The debt matrix for this period (Figure 5.2) reflects the modified bondholders' position, but an identical situation for Mexico as in the first period. In the two-actor game, we expect Mexico to again pursue a non-adjustment policy similar to the strategy it adopted in the first period. As in the first period, the Nash equilibrium remains at high concessions and no adjustment. But in this case, the resulting payoff in the case of the lenders for the same strategy has fallen considerably. As we shall see, this proved to be a strong motivating factor for bondholders to pursue efforts to promote situational change.

At the beginning of period two, the British government had indirectly committed itself to increased diplomatic involvement on behalf of its bondholders. British government pressure for payment of the Convention debt worried the Mexicans, and made them more responsive to settling the London debts despite the distinction between the two types of debt drawn by the government. Consequently, in view of the looming threat, we would expect more willingness on Mexico's part to make some adjustments in response to bondholders' demands. Thus, although the basic two-actor matrix predicts a little adjustment, high concessions outcome, increased British intervention, and altered Mexican perceptions of this threat should lead to an outcome of some Mexican adjustment and continued high concessions by bondholders.

The negotiations and outcome

The negotiations during this second period consisted of two rounds of game play from 1848 to 1851, and from that time until 1860, followed by a crucial game change phase, ending in 1863. Round one begins with the Treaty of Guadalupe Hidalgo and ends with the debt conversion of 1850–1851 and the new Convention debt agreements. Round two runs from the default induced by the Mexican revolution in 1853, concluding with Mexican President Benito Juárez's acceptance of temporary agreements to deal with the foreign debt in 1860. Following Mexican default in May 1861, creditor governments began to prepare for intervention, with their subsequent invasion culminating in the installation of Maximilian as the new Mexican Emperor.

Throughout these rounds, Mexico claimed that because of the war with the U.S., and a later revolution and civil war, the public treasury could not bear any debt burden. The bondholders, however, continued to question whether Mexico's situation was as dismal as claimed. Rather than relying on Mexican information sources, they decided to make their own assessment of Mexico's financial condition. Moreover, the bondholders increasingly appealed to the British government for support. These appeals helped to secure British pressure on Mexico, ensuring that the bondholders would see some Mexican adjustment in exchange for the high concessions that they would make during the first bargaining round.

Round one. The conclusion of the Treaty of Guadalupe Hidalgo compelled the Mexican government to once again address the issue of its foreign debt – in arrears since the start of the war with the United States. The London bondholders clamored for the resumption of debt servicing payments, especially after they learned of the $15 million U.S. indemnity. Meanwhile, Mexico continued to stress its sincerity. In August 1848, José María Luis Mora, the Minister Plenipotentiary of Mexico, stated:

> The government now in power is resolved honorably to fulfill the obligations contracted with respect to the foreign debt of the Republic, as far as the means of the treasury will

permit . . . (however) the possibility of payment arises from the very existence of the Government and its solidity, and neither the one nor the other could be rationally expected from an exhausted treasury, incapable of maintaining in it the vital principle and the conditions of existence.[51]

The bondholders did not believe these Mexican assertions. In August 1848, the Committee of Spanish-American Bondholders came close to accusing Mexico of willfully cheating on its debt agreements. It argued:

Your excellency speaks of the resources of the country having been exhausted by the war. It is, however, notorious, that there was in the last year a considerable increase in the amount of the coinage of the principal mints of the Republic, showing that notwithstanding the war, there had been no diminution in the mining branch of industry, nor in the means of the people to contribute to the wants of the State. It would be difficult, indeed, to point to any nation which, in proportion to its population and its internal wealth, is less burdened with debt than the Republic of Mexico; and its creditors – those who have placed confidence in its honor and good faith – have a just right to expect that it will not neglect the highest duty of a nation – the maintenance of its credit by the honorable discharge of its public finances.[52]

In 1849, Mexico accused its agent, the financial house of Messrs. John Schneider & Co., of cheating both the bondholders and Mexico itself. The government charged that after receiving sufficient funds from Mexico, Schneider only distributed three-fourths of a dividend to the bondholders instead of the full dividend on the converted bonds.[53] Schneider, however, argued that the funds were not sufficient to pay all of the bondholders:

If we had advertised the payment of a dividend in full, we could not, on any principle of law or justice, have limited it to those holders who had converted their bonds up to a certain arbitrary date, and have excluded those holders who had not converted their bonds, but who were daily coming forward to do so.[54]

In analytical terms, Schneider argued that the funds received from Mexico for the bondholders were a collective good, and as such, no bondholders could be excluded from payment out of the limited sum. Accordingly, the funds received could not fully satisfy all of the creditors.

The bondholders' committee grew weary of arrangements in which the Mexicans were forced neither to make real economic adjustments nor to pledge a reliable and adequate source of revenues to the payment of the foreign debt. With doubts about Mexico's credibility, the bondholders' committee decided to send a special representative, W.P. Robertson, to Mexico. His mission was to obtain additional information about Mexico's financial situation, and to make a claim for a portion of Mexico's U.S. indemnity. The Committee made it clear to Robertson that the primary purpose of this trip was to pressure Mexico to make high adjustments. As G.R. Robinson, chairman of the Committee, wrote to Robertson:

[51] Comm. S.A. Bond. (1848), pp. 17–19.
[52] Comm. S.A. Bond. (1848), p. 19.
[53] Comm. S.A. Bond. (1849), pp. 77–79.
[54] Comm. S.A. Bond. (1849), pp. 77–79.

It appears to the Committee, that if this compromise be carried into effect, some means should be provided by which, in the event of the assignment of revenues being insufficient at any time for meeting the dividend, there should be a resource for making up the deficiency at the moment. The Mexican Government seems always to have considered that after assigning specific portions of revenue to the payment of the interest of the debt, it had nothing further to do; not concerning itself with the question whether the funds were sufficient or not. This must be guarded against on the present occasion, or there will be no security against the recurrence of the same irregularities that have been experienced before.[55]

When Robertson arrived in Mexico in early 1849, he did find some discrepancies between the information received by the bondholders and the reality of the situation in Mexico. He wrote to London, "The question of the foreign debt of Mexico has been embarrassed by some erroneous views which have been entertained of its merits; but a simple statement of them will show that they must be considered as altogether fallacious."[56] In general, though, Robertson found Mexico's claims of an exhausted public treasury to be true. In fact, the Committee warned Robertson against publicly releasing "more unfavorable information than has been disclosed by the committee" because it might have "a very damaging effect upon the price of the stock . . . the effect of this sort of proceeding is, that the public are lead to believe that the advices are much worse than they really are."[57]

Robertson also discovered that much of the customs revenues assigned to the payment of the debt, especially the Pacific ports' silver duties, did not reach the bondholders because of smuggling and a failure to collect the duties at Mexican Customhouses. He specifically noted that even a British ship, the "H.M.S. Calypso has recently sailed from the West coast of Mexico with, it is said, about two and a half million dollars, the duty of which, for the benefit of the Bondholders, would amount to $150,000 – and I believe I am stating a fact when I say that the amount of duty recovered has been $113!"[58] The Committee proposed numerous remedies to both the British and Mexican governments – including that ships be prevented from leaving Mexican ports unless they produced certificates proving their payment of export duties. The Committee also suggested that, on British ships, commanders should receive and remit the portion of the duties from their ships pledged to the bondholders. The Mexican government, however, balked at this proposal. With these actions, the bondholders attempted to manipulate the tactical linkage between the debt issue and Mexican trade, while increasing British government involvement on their behalf. The Committee, however, agreed with Robertson that, as to the smuggling problem, "the best cure would be found in a reduction of the enormous duties [assignments], especially that on the export of silver."[59]

The bondholders were particularly interested in the $15 million war indemnity promised to the Mexican government. The Committee argued that as compensation for enduring Mexico's default during the war years, the bondholders

[55] Comm. S.A. Bond. (1849), p. 66.
[56] Comm. S.A. Bond. (1849), pp. 57–59
[57] Comm. S.A. Bond. (1849), p. 42.
[58] Comm. S.A. Bond. (1849), pp. 86–89.
[59] Comm. S.A. Bond. (1849), p. 26.

should receive a portion of the indemnity as overdue interest. On Mexico's behalf, Mora rejected this claim, arguing, "There is no right to demand, nor is it convenient to grant, the application of the said sums to the payment of the dividends, and to the amortization of the public debt."[60]

Shortly before sending Robertson to Mexico, the bondholders' committee had consulted the legal officers of the Crown. In their legal opinion, because all revenues had been pledged as collateral on the 1846 conversion, and the loss of territory to the U.S. weakened this security, the creditors were entitled to receive a fair portion of the indemnity as a payment on the debt. Armed with this legal justification, the bondholders increased their pressure on the British government for assistance. The first blow to their cause came in early 1848 when Lord Palmerston issued a circular that forbade British officials from making any "authoritative representations" in support of the bondholders. For Palmerston, British involvement in the debt negotiations was a question of discretion and by "no means of international right."[61] Palmerston declared a policy of abstention, but did hint at greater intervention in the future should the debt "become so great that it would be too high a price for the nation to pay."[62]

Still, the legal ruling proved useful to the bondholders. Because the Mexicans could not be sure of British intentions, they were reluctant to simply rebuff Robertson's overtures. In July 1849, he negotiated a new agreement which involved a $4 million debt payment predicated on the $15 million Mexico expected to receive from the United States. Mexico stipulated that the creditors had to accept this sum as a full payment for all arrears of interest up to that date.

While the Mexican Congress and the Committee of Spanish-American Bondholders considered the so-called Robertson Convention, a group of disgruntled bondholders formed the second "Committee of Mexican Bondholders."[63] These bondholders felt that the Committee of Spanish-American Bondholders had not adequately addressed the interests of the Mexican bondholders.

Robertson urged his committee to accept the convention. In his statements, Robertson held that acceptance of the convention could influence the involvement of the British government in aiding the creditors. As he put it:

> If refused here [by Mexico], I do not see how the British Government can any longer refuse effectual diplomatic assistance to the bondholders; if refused by you [the bondholders], then you will lose Lord Palmerston's sympathy, and run the risk of losing, what I have had especially in my eye to secure, the four million and a half [dollars] indemnity money.[64]

Before the bondholders had a chance to officially accept the convention, however, Mexican domestic politics undermined the agreement. The Congress overruled the Executive and reduced the payment from $4 million to only $2.5

[60] Comm. S.A. Bond. (1848), pp. 17–19. [61] Williams (1923), pp. 10–11.

[62] Williams (1923), pp. 10–11.

[63] Because this committee did not play an active role for some time, we do not code the lenders as being coalitionally unstable.

[64] Committee of Mexican Bondholders (hereinafter Comm. Mex. Bond.) (1850), p. 46.

million. Moreover, not only did Mexico offer this payment for all arrears of interest (10,241,650 pesos), but it insisted that the remaining bonds were to be converted into new bonds and the interest rate slashed from 5 to 3%.[65] For these new bonds, Mexico agreed to pledge one-quarter of all import duties, three-fourths of the export duties on the Pacific Coast, and one-twentieth of export duties on the Gulf Coast.[66] Assigned customs revenues would be delivered to designated bondholder agents.

As anticipated by the model, domestic weakness proved to be a source of strength in international negotiations. Mexico's professed inability to meet its obligations encouraged acceptance by the bondholders who had previously rejected Robertson's efforts. At this point, the question was no longer how much adjustment, but simply whether Mexico would undertake *any* adjustment (and debt servicing). The bondholders' committee wrote:

> To accept this offer in satisfaction for all arrears will, therefore inflict a loss of nearly 6,000,000 dollars on the Bondholders . . . there is, however, unfortunately, good ground for supposing that, in the present dilapidated state of the Mexican finances, this offer fairly represents the extent of the pecuniary means of the Republic to satisfy the claims of her foreign creditors for arrears . . . it will be expedient to accept that offer.[67]

The bondholders resigned themselves to accepting the new arrangement. New bonds totaling 51,208,250 pesos with a 3% interest rate were issued on the London market in 1851. Thus, after voicing concerns that Mexico was "cheating" on its debt agreements, and sending a special representative to gather more information on Mexico's ability to pay, most bondholders accepted the unfortunate truth that Mexico was unlikely to uphold its agreements.

At the end of round one, Mexico managed to reduce the size of its foreign debt, lower the interest rate from 5 to 3%, pledge only future revenues to the debt service, and make no painful immediate economic adjustment. Mexico's annual liability before the 1850–1851 arrangement was $3,327,853; after, it was only $1,674,146. As one Mexican official noted, "this financial operation is, without any doubt, the best of any hitherto made."[68] Still, Mexico did agree to give up a portion of its indemnity from the U.S., thus earning the outcome coding "some adjustment." The bondholders made high concessions by accepting a small payment for a large amount of arrears of interest, agreeing to lower the interest rate on the debt, and again accepting unreliable, future revenues as security on the debt. But as the British government began to take a more active role over the next two rounds of negotiations, Mexico would be forced to make more domestic adjustments as a counterpart to the bondholders' concessions.

In late 1851, the Mexican government turned its attention to settling the claims of foreign nationals with a series of Diplomatic Conventions. The claims of foreign nationals residing in Mexico against the government for forced loans,

[65] Legislación Mexicana, vol. 5, pp. 743–744, cited in Turlington (1930), p. 97.
[66] Legislación Mexicana, vol. 5, pp. 743–744, cited in Turlington (1930), p. 97.
[67] Comm. Mex. Bond. (1850), p. 13. [68] Payno (1862), p. 24.

advances, and damaged and seized properties had accumulated since the country's inception. In November 1851, Mexico and Spain signed a diplomatic convention in which Mexico acknowledged liability for Spanish claims. The following month, Mexico signed a similar diplomatic convention with France addressing the French claims on the Mexican internal debt. Also at that time, Great Britain and Mexico signed the Doyle Convention (named after the British Minister in Mexico, Percy Doyle, who negotiated the Convention). With the Doyle Convention, the Mexican government recognized a 5 million peso liability and debt for the various claims of British subjects. Mexico agreed to pay 5% of the entire recognized liability every year and also accepted a 3% annual interest charge on all unpaid balances. To make these stipulated payments, the Mexican government assigned a satisfactory portion of annual import duty revenues, and agreed to increase this assignment in the future.

With the Doyle Diplomatic Convention, the British government's role changed significantly (more so than with the English Convention debt because of the large amount of the new liability). The government had again used its diplomatic powers to negotiate and guarantee an arrangement for protecting the interests of British subjects against Mexico.

Round two. Despite the $15 million American indemnity paid to Mexico, the national government once again found itself in dire straits by the early 1850s. Desperate for new funds, in December 1853 Mexican President Santa Anna sold 30,000 square miles of Mexican territory in what is now Southern Arizona and New Mexico to the U.S. for $10 million. This "Gadsden Purchase" united liberal opposition to the conservative Santa Anna. One year later, the liberals overthrew Santa Anna during the Revolution of Ayulta and replaced him with a liberal president, Juan Alvarez. Before the year was out, however, Alvarez resigned and another liberal, General Ignacio Comonfort, came to power.[69]

President Comonfort, like most of his predecessors, faced a bankrupt public treasury and inadequate sources of revenues. The new administration quickly made overtures to the U.S. concerning a possible loan. U.S. Ambassador to Mexico John Forsyth saw the Mexican overture as an opportunity for the U.S. "to take advantage of the financial straits in which Mexico finds herself" and possibly acquire more Mexican territory.[70] In February 1857, Forsyth, on his own authority, signed a "Treaty of Reciprocity" and a "Treaty of Loan and Anticipation of Duties" with Mexican representatives. In the latter treaty, the U.S. would advance a $15 million loan to Mexico, $7 million of which would be repaid at an annual rate of 4%, and secured by 13% of all customs revenues. The other $8 million was an "advance made to the Mexican Republic in anticipation of its customs revenues, denominated duties on imports and exports derived from its direct trade with the U.S.," but only after Mexico instituted a 20%

69 Meyer and Sherman (1987), pp. 376–377.

70 Forsyth's no. 14, December 19, 1856, Department of State, Washington, D.C., Manuscript Despatches, Mexico, vol. 20, cited in Turlington (1930), p. 106.

reduction of import and export duties for American merchant shippers.[71] With the Forsyth deal, the link between the trade and debt issues would have become more substantive. Commercial privileges in Mexico would be exchanged for a loan, part of which would be secured by customs revenues; the commercial privileges would increase U.S.-Mexican trade and, thereby, increase Mexico's ability to pay back the loan.

This plan, however, was never implemented. The treaties were forwarded to Washington during a change of administration (President James Buchanan replaced President Franklin Pierce). Buchanan's new Secretary of State, Lewis Cass, a proponent of free and open trade, opposed the idea of exchanging commercial privileges for money and rejected the U.S. loan, even though Buchanan continued to show interest in purchasing Mexican territory.

In 1857, the liberal Mexican administration began to carry out a number of reforms aimed at destroying the power of both the church and army in the Mexican society. During this reform movement, Mexico continued to tout its inability – but good intentions – to service its debt. Comonfort declared, "It is necessary to repeat – that when the Mexican Government takes the funds from customs, it is not from a spirit of irregularity, nor from a desire to mortify the creditors, but because the imperious necessity of self-preservation obliges the Government to do so."[72]

Meanwhile, the bondholders continued their efforts to improve their bargaining position through an alliance with the British government. Appealing to the precedent set by the Diplomatic Conventions, the bondholders called on their government to extend diplomatic and active protection to their interests. Moreover, the Committee stated that without their government's assistance, there was little hope for an equitable settlement. These appeals, however, failed to generate direct intervention in the bondholders' favor.

A dispute soon arose over the Mexican liberal reforms attempted in 1856 and 1857. One of the most important reforms was the divestiture of church and ecclesiastical property to benefit the government. The bondholders' committee estimated that the sale of church property would bring in enough revenue to restore "the Mexican finances to a highly prosperous condition . . . that the Mexican government might redeem the whole of those debts, and after having done so, still retain a surplus of some consideration for the construction of roads and public works."[73]

The Mexican government, however, argued that the bondholders lacked adequate and proper information concerning the real domestic situation in the country to make such a claim. One Mexican official wrote, "The accounts which the bondholders obtained of the value of the Church-property in the Republic, were not only exaggerated, but some of them positively false."[74] Specifically, the Mexican government charged that the bondholders were misinformed as to the

[71] Forsyth's no. 14, December 19, 1856, Department of State, Washington, D.C., Manuscript Despatches, Mexico, vol. 20, cited in Turlington (1930), pp. 106–107.
[72] Payno (1862), p. 34. [73] Comm. Mex. Bond. (1856), p. 10. [74] Payno (1862), p. 39.

real value of property in Mexico and as to the portion of Mexican land owned by the church. With this response, Mexico continued to claim good intentions, but argued that it lacked the public financial resources to satisfy its foreign creditors.

The reforms of 1856 and 1857 not only fostered disputes between Mexico and its creditors, but also stirred greater civil strife and unrest. Conservatives united in their opposition to the reforms, while the liberal faction became increasingly divided. Finally, after the development of a liberal constitution in 1857, hostilities erupted between the two factions, plunging Mexico into a three-year civil war.

The conservatives, led by Félix Zuloaga, enjoyed early success in the so-called War for Reform. Zuloaga captured Mexico City, dissolved the liberal Congress, and appointed himself president of a de facto Mexican government. Benito Juárez, leader of the displaced liberal government, escaped North and established his de jure liberal government in Veracruz. Thus, Mexico had two competing political ideologies, two competing governments, and two competing leaders. Although Zuloaga held the capital, Juárez held the port city, a key source for the collection of customs revenues. In an effort to secure foreign support, Zuloaga negotiated a new Convention debt agreement with the British government in the fall of 1858 known as the Otway Convention. The conservative government agreed to raise the interest rate on the Convention bonds from 3 to 6%, and to set aside all customs revenues as security for the debt. The British sanctioned the Convention, thus giving halfhearted recognition to the Zuloaga government.

At the same time, the Juárez government entered into an agreement with the British navy. The navy assigned customs funds to protect the interests of the British bondholders. In April 1859, the British Minister issued the following circular to the British consuls:

> it would appear that Her Majesty's Government, wearied out by their fruitless exertions to obtain . . . a settlement of the outstanding claims of British subjects, . . . have determined on holding the whole country indifferently responsible for the observance of all international obligations as far as England is concerned. It is therefore the intention of Her Majesty's Government to take advantage of the presence of the fleet in the Gulf, and to hold Veracruz, by whatever party it is occupied, to be, as it were, the Treasury of Mexico, and to enforce there, as far as possible, payment of all the outstanding claims of British subjects in Mexico.[75]

The agreement between Juárez and the navy, known as the Dunlop Convention after the British naval officer involved in the negotiations, called for the constitutional government to meet its obligations to the British creditors by setting aside one-fourth of all customs revenues for the London bondholders, as well as 16% of these revenues for the Convention debt bondholders.[76] Juárez's government also agreed to allow British consuls to check all ports involved in the

[75] Comm. Mex. Bond. (1859), p. 4. [76] Turlington (1930), p. 120.

obligations. In short, the British government finally became diplomatically, economically, and militarily involved with the London bondholders' and Convention debts.

Juárez also continued to seek funds by trying to obtain a loan from the U.S. without making any treaty commitments. When this effort came to nought, his Foreign Relations Secretary, Melchor Ocampo, signed an infamous accord with new U.S. Ambassador Robert McLane. It granted the U.S. perpetual right of transit across the Isthmus of Tehuantepec, right of transit that essentially abdicated Mexican sovereignty in Northern Mexico, free trade access, and the right to U.S. intervention in case of problems. In return Mexico would receive $4 million, of which $2 million would immediately be used to compensate American property losses in Mexico. Fortunately for Mexico, the U.S. Senate failed to approve the treaty as a split developed between Northern and Southern senators over Mexico's future if it fell into American hands.

By 1860, the tide in the civil war slowly turned toward the liberal faction. The armies of the liberal government began to close in on the Mexican capital. Desperate for new funds and supplies, General Miguel Miramón (who replaced Zuloaga in 1859 as leader of the conservative government), seized 660,000 pesos that Juárez had assigned to British bondholders. In London, the bondholders protested vehemently, arguing that if the British government did not use force to protect their interests, it should compensate their loss. The Committee declared:

> if our Government, in its discretion, abstains from exercising that right, and performing that duty, either from apprehensions of the complication to which it might lead, or on account of the costs, or on whatever other grounds of national expediency, the Bondholders, in return for allegiance and for the taxes levied as probate and legacy-duty on the principal, and as income-tax on the dividends of the debt, have an equitable claim for compensation on their own Government.[77]

The British government immediately opened diplomatic talks with Juárez, promising both recognition and moral support for the liberal government if Juárez agreed to accept liability for the amount seized. He agreed to this stipulation and also acquiesced in principle to satisfy other established British claims.

By December 1860, as liberal forces were about to defeat the conservatives, Juárez entered into another arrangement with the British navy. British naval Captain Aldham negotiated this accord to address infractions on the original Dunlop arrangement. With the Aldham Convention, Juárez agreed to temporarily assign an additional 10% of import duties from Veracruz and Tampico to the London and Convention debt bondholders. In January 1861, when the liberal forces captured Mexico City, Juárez assumed the presidency of a reunited Mexican government and nation.

With the active involvement of the British government and the civil war in Mexico, the bondholders, who had made large concessions in round one,

[77] Comm. Mex. Bond. (1860), p. 13.

received a more solid promise by Mexico to undertake adjustment at the end of this round. Bondholders were encouraged because Juárez had agreed in principle to Mexican liability for all outstanding claims, and the presence of the British navy off the Mexican coast appeared to be a strong enough inducement to ensure that the pledge of 35% of customs revenues to bondholders would be honored. Juárez's action in signing the Aldham Conventions deepened the British involvement in debt matters and would prove costly for Mexico.

Summary. The most significant development of the second period was the growing involvement of creditor governments. The British government extended diplomatic protection to all British bondholders, not just to those of the Diplomatic Convention debt. The British also intervened militarily in part to protect the interests of the British creditors. Although strategic concerns of the government motivated their actions, the London bondholders managed to free-ride on the Convention debt protected by British power. As a consequence, the first round's initial outcome of some adjustment by Mexico and high concessions by bondholders was consolidated by creditor government pressure on Mexico.

Situational changes

A combination of shocks and active efforts on the part of the bondholders and governments led to significant changes in the actors' individual situations from 1861 to 1863. The civil war left Mexico in shambles. The countryside was devastated, buildings and roads were destroyed, and Mexican financial prospects appeared dimmer than ever before. The new president faced a bankrupt treasury, an unpaid army, and stagnant commercial trade. In May 1861, the Mexican Congress called for a moment of respite and declared a one-year suspension of all national debt payments except those of the Convention debts.

Facing a much reduced game payoff, in July 1861, the bondholders again called for greater assistance from the British government and for a diplomatic convention on the London debt. This time, their appeals received more support. Lord Russell of the British Foreign Office told Charles Wyke, the British Minister in Mexico, that the English bondholders' debt had "acquired a character of an international obligation" following the Dunlop and Aldham agreements.[78] Accordingly, if Mexico refused to consider redress, Wyke was to call upon the British navy to enforce creditor demands for reparation.

More ominously, as rumors circulated concerning the possible joint military intervention of British, Spanish, and French forces on behalf of their bondholders, the U.S. warned that it would defend Mexico's independence.[79] But preoccupied as it was with its own domestic affairs after the secession of several Southern states from the Union, the U.S. was not in a position to threaten military action on behalf of Mexico. As a result, the U.S. looked to non-military means to prevent European intervention and violation of the Monroe Doctrine.

[78] *Bri. For. State Papers*, vol. 52 (1861–1862), p. 238. [79] Rippy (1929/1964), pp. 227–228.

The possibility of European military intervention in Mexico became very real when the Mexican Congress passed an act in July 1861 suspending payments on *all* of the nation's obligations for two years, including payments on the Diplomatic Convention debts. Britain and France retaliated by severing all diplomatic relations with the Mexican government.

In an effort to stave off European intervention, the American Minister in Mexico, Thomas Corwin, proposed a U.S. loan of $5 to $10 million in cash or bonds to cover Mexico's foreign obligations. This loan would have been secured by Mexican territory, or negotiated as an exchange for a 50% reduction in duties on U.S. goods. In September 1861, President Lincoln and Secretary of State Seward approved Corwin's idea for a treaty in which the U.S. would assume the debt interest payments due to the London bondholders for a five-year period. For this relief, Mexico was to eventually reimburse the U.S. and pay an additional 6% interest charge. The loan was secured on a specific lien on all public lands and mineral rights in certain Mexican states. As Corwin optimistically noted, the result of this loan would probably be the end of Mexico's sovereignty and its absorption by the U.S., "the only safe guardians of the independence and true civilization of this continent."[80]

Meanwhile, on October 31, Britain, France, and Spain signed an agreement for joint military intervention into Mexico. The pact stipulated that the European powers desired only to protect the persons and property of their subjects, and sought no acquisition of territory. Moreover, the powers bound themselves to seek no special influence in Mexican internal affairs or to prejudice the Mexican people's choice in electing a new government.[81]

The U.S. continued to press forward with Corwin's idea of a loan to Mexico. But the British and French voiced serious reservations about the Corwin Plan, while the Spanish rejected it outright. Britain's Minister of Foreign Affairs, Lord Palmerston, for one, feared that the plan would greatly increase American influence over Mexico. This episode demonstrates the growing importance of strategic considerations that outweighed purely satisfying bondholders' concerns.

The British were willing to entertain some type of joint accord that concerned both debt and trade in exchange for not intervening in Mexico. Minister Wyke began to negotiate for a Mexican reduction of its import duties by 50%. Although British merchants applauded this plan, the bondholders voiced strong opposition. But Wyke argued that they had no right to cripple Mexico for the sake of clearing the debt. He did, however, also propose that British consular agents serve as commissioners at Mexican ports to control the customhouses, protecting funds assigned to the bondholders. The Mexican Congress, however, rejected this challenge to Mexican sovereignty as unacceptable. Thereafter, negotiations broke down and Wyke declared the settlement of British claims would depend upon the "employment of brute force."[82]

[80] House Executive Document, no. 100, 37th Congress, 2nd Sess, 1862, p. 15, quoted in Turlington (1930), p. 136. The next three paragraphs draw on the discussion in Turlington.

[81] Meyer and Sherman (1987), p. 388.

[82] *Bri. For. State Papers*, 52 (1861–1862), pp. 254–256.

In December 1861, Spanish troops captured the port city of Veracruz. French and British troops also arrived in Mexico in accord with the joint agreement. U.S. preoccupation with its own civil war ruled out American reprisal. In a last-minute effort to stop the intervention, the Juárez government signed an agreement with the U.S. ambassador for a $9 million loan to be used to satisfy the claims of the European powers. The Senate, however, opposed the loan to preserve U.S. neutrality in the conflict. In the end, the U.S. government did not advance the money.

Louis Napoleon III, with grandiose plans rivaling those of his more famous uncle, schemed to do more than settle outstanding French claims against Mexico. He envisioned a new French empire in North America. With French ambitions becoming clear, the English and Spanish wished to avoid a drawn-out conflict, and withdrew. He sent 7,000 French troops to Mexico, who began a march toward the capital in April 1862. Although not supported by British troops, Lord Palmerston cautiously supported French plans. He hoped that the new government would bring "order and civilization" to Mexico, making it a greater counterforce to the U.S. in North America. In addition, French involvement in North America would keep Napoleon III busy, preventing him from stirring up trouble in Europe.[83]

After more than a year of fighting, European forces defeated the Mexican army and President Juárez fled north. With the defeat of Mexican forces, the French and some conservative Mexican collaborators offered the new Mexican crown to the Austrian archduke, Ferdinand Maximilian of Hapsburg. Maximilian agreed to accept only if the Mexican people approved. After a rigged plebiscite, Maximilian accepted the Crown. He also signed the Convention of Miramar with Louis Napoleon, agreeing to pay all French expenses incurred during the intervention and assuming responsibility for the payment of all foreign claims. In exchange, Maximilian assumed full command over 20,000 French troops remaining in Mexico. Thus, through these sweeping acknowledgments, Maximilian managed to triple the foreign debt of Mexico before he even began ruling.[84]

Period three, 1863–1867: the reign of Emperor Maximilian

Period three of Mexican debt rescheduling runs from 1863 through 1867 and encompasses the entire reign of Ferdinand Maximilian as monarch of Mexico. The period outlines two important events: Maximilian's period of power that was reliant on French support, and his abrupt overthrow after the suspension of French aid and the departure of French troops. Maximilian rose to power with the aid of European governments (particularly France, and inadvertently Britain and Spain). These governments had strong alliances with their bondholders and had intervened in Mexico to protect the interests of their subjects. Now, Maximilian would have to satisfy their claims.

[83] Ridley (1970), pp. 733–734. [84] Parkes (1938/1969), p. 266.

Identifying individual situations

Maximilian's monarchy radically altered the debt situation in the 1860s. In period three Mexico is coalitionally stable, but issue and overall weak (IS 7). As for the bondholders, their complete alliance with their governments classifies them as coalitionally stable and issue and overall strong (IS 5).

Mexico. Maximilian's monarchy in Mexico was coalitionally stable. Although there were small revolts in the countryside, because Juárez remained in the north, Maximilian clearly controlled the government. He commanded a force of over 20,000 troops (mostly French), which squelched several rebellions throughout Mexico. In addition, all the major European powers recognized the monarchy as the legitimate Mexican government (the U.S. did not, for obvious strategic reasons related to the Monroe Doctrine) and dealt solely with the Crown on affairs concerning Mexico.

Even under Maximilian, however, Mexico remained financially devastated. European intervention had left the country ravaged by war. Industry, agriculture, commerce, and trade stagnated. With the addition of 20,000 French soldiers to the government's payroll, government expenditures far outstripped revenues. In addition, as noted, Maximilian had tripled Mexico's foreign debt.

As to overall capabilities, Mexico was weak. Although Maximilian possessed the powers of any sovereign monarch, these powers depended entirely upon the support of the European powers, especially France. Also, although he commanded a large army, his control over this force depended on the good graces of the French government. With respect to debt servicing, under Maximilian Mexico was clearly vulnerable to the creditor governments, which in this period increasingly supported their bondholders. The European powers who helped support Maximilian's rise to power could restrict Mexican commerce, deprive the monarchy of funds, and ultimately, withdraw their support; the Mexican Crown could do little to threaten or harm the creditors.[85]

Lenders. The bondholders were united in the second "Committee of Mexican Bondholders," formed in 1850. The Mexican bondholders had left the Spanish-American Bondholders Committee believing that the new committee better addressed their specific concerns and interests. More significantly, by the end of period two, they had managed to secure through serendipity what they had failed to secure through exhortations and protests: support from the British government, and more generally, European force to protect their interests. This alliance with the government made the bondholders both issue and overall strong. Their new muscle forced Maximilian to address their claims and interests after he took power.

Creditor governments. The British government did not directly support Maximilian, but remained involved at the highest level in the debt rescheduling

[85] Parkes (1938/1969), pp. 260–264.

issue. Although it withdrew its forces when France moved to establish the monarchy, the British government encouraged French ambitions and did not support Juárez. Immediately following the establishment of Maximilian, the British government gave diplomatic recognition and support to the new Mexican government. Palmerston assured Maximilian "of the interest that all of us in this country take in the success of the great task which your Majesty has undertaken, a success which would be beneficial for all Europe and would insure the happiness of Mexico."[86]

We would expect growing British security and military interest in Mexico to increase the government's willingness to participate in debt negotiations and to use force if necessary. In this light, bondholders' claims and the protection of nationals abroad became convenient reasons to intervene. Similarly, these claims provided all the creditor governments convenient covers for their underlying interests.

Debt game and predicted outcome

Using the theoretical model, we arrive at the debt game matrix shown in Figure 5.3 for period three. Given the matrix, we would expect bondholders to play a strategy of no concessions. Regardless of whether Mexico adjusts or not, the lenders receive their highest payoff by refusing to yield. Maximilian realized that the European governments responsible for the military intervention that brought him to power would be in no mood for concessions after years of Mexico's professing willingness yet constant inability to pay its debts. Because he recognized his issue and overall weakness, we would expect the Mexican government to initiate adjustments. The Nash equilibrium point, therefore, is at the low concessions/high adjustment outcome.

In this period, we would not expect the U.K., France, and Spain to intervene significantly beyond the existing French alliance with Maximilian. We would also expect the U.S. not to intervene – although it opposed the previous intervention of European powers. Given its civil war, we would rule out any U.S. intervention in the game until its internal problems were resolved. Only then would we expect it to take action against the other creditor governments involved with the Maximilian regime. Thus, we expect the bargaining outcome to remain unaffected.

The negotiations and outcome

We divide the Maximilian period into two short rounds of debt negotiations. The first round runs from 1863 through 1865 as Maximilian reached agreements with Mexico's creditors and obtained new bond loans. The second round runs from 1865 through 1867, ending with Maximilian's eroding power. Round one resulted in a settlement favorable to the bondholders. The second round was interrupted by the withdrawal of French support and Maximilian's execution.

[86] Ridley (1970), p. 734.

Cardinal Payoff Matrix, Intervention Expected

Lenders IS 5

		HC...	MC...	LC...
	HA...	12, −3	9, −1.33	**10, .33**
Mexico IS 7	MA...	11.67, −3.5	8, −2	7, −.5
	LA...	11.33, −3	7, −2	4, −1

Note: Nash equilibrium bolded; expected outcome with intervention underlined.

Ordinal Payoff Matrix, Intervention Expected

Lenders IS 5

		HC...	MC...	LC...
	HA...	9, 2.5	5, 6	**6, 9**
Mexico IS 7	MA...	8, 1	4, 4.5	2.5, 8
	LA...	7, 2.5	2.5, 4.5	1, 7

Note: Nash equilibrium bolded; expected outcome with intervention underlined.

Figure 5.3. *Play phase, period three: 1863–1867*

Round one. Soon after accepting the Mexican Crown, Maximilian moved quickly to obtain new loans and augment the near-empty public treasury. In 1864, he arranged a conversion and interest capitalization of the London debt bonds, negotiated a new bond loan, and created a new Mexican Finance Committee.

Maximilian agreed to convert all interest arrears from 1850 through 1863 on the London debt into new 3% bonds at the rate of £60 in old coupons for £100 in new bonds. The conversion was extremely favorable to the bondholders as £3 million in interest arrears was converted into over £5 million in new bonds.[87] At the same time, the Mexican monarch arranged the flotation of a new £8 million bond loan carrying a 6% interest rate in London. Over £1 million, however, remained unsold. After paying off other debts, the Mexican government was left with only £1.2 million for its own uses. One year later, Maximilian floated another bond loan worth FF250 million in France. The bonds were sold at 60% of their face value and the amount realized was only a fraction of the obligation incurred. Overall, by 1865 Maximilian had assumed a debt of 138 million pesos for Mexico, but received only 25 million pesos in cash.[88] Maximilian also created a new Mexican Finance Committee to monitor the nation's foreign debt situation. The Committee included one representative each from the Mexican government, the French bondholders, and the English bondholders groups.

The outcome of this round, high adjustment by Mexico and almost no concessions by the creditors, conforms with the model's predictions. In this round, Mexico made several adjustments: Maximilian accepted liability for a much larger foreign debt and agreed to convert the interest arrears on the London debt at a rate favorable to the bondholders. Moreover, the Mexican government agreed to allow representatives from the creditor groups to serve on the government's Finance Committee. For their part, the bondholders made few concessions. They only allowed Mexico to delay its overdue interest payments with the conversion and did not block Maximilian's flotation of new bond loans.

Round two. After 1865, Maximilian found it more difficult to maintain his position as the head of the Mexican government. He soon faced criticism from all sides: Conservatives disliked him for his refusal to repeal many liberal reforms; and despite his overtures, liberals simply distrusted the monarchy.

At the same time, the Juarists continued to gain strength in the Mexican countryside. Juárez's forces protested Maximilian's debt agreements and turned to the U.S. (which did not recognize Maximilian) to seek loans. The U.S. deplored the European-established monarchy in Mexico, but was too involved in its own civil war to aid Juárez. Following the defeat of the Confederacy in April 1865, however, the U.S. began making overtures to Juárez. It allowed Juárez's forces to purchase arms and supplies from the U.S. (violating U.S. neutrality laws), and made diplomatic representations to Napoleon III calling for an end to French support for Maximilian.

In 1866, Maximilian's position worsened. During that year, he agreed to a convention assigning half of all maritime customs duties to the service of the 1864 and 1865 loans. Of the other half of the customs revenues, 25% was already pledged to the service of the 1851 London debt bonds, and another 24% was pledged towards the English and Spanish Convention debts. This left only 1% of all customs revenues for the government's own use. Facing this dire situation, Maximilian resorted to new taxes and forced loans (including an 850,000

[87] Turlington (1930), p. 154. [88] Turlington (1930), pp. 153–155.

peso loan from Mexico City), but failed to significantly raise government revenues.

More ominously, with the end of the American Civil War, rumors circulated that the U.S. was considering military action to drive the French out of Mexico.[89] Americans began to call for French withdrawal in line with the Monroe Doctrine.[90] Facing his own problems with Prussia on the European continent, Napoleon III reconsidered the involvement of thousands of his troops in Mexico when the U.S. sent an army to the Mexican border and Secretary Seward demanded in February 1866 that France withdraw its troops. In November 1866 through early 1867, despite Maximilian's protests, the French government began withdrawing its forces. With Maximilian's foreign support eroding, Juárez launched an offensive against the monarchy. By May of that year, Maximilian surrendered and was subsequently shot by a firing squad; after five years of exile in the North, Juárez returned to power in Mexico City.

Summary. During this period, a rather unusual debt game took place between bondholders and Mexico. With Mexico ruled by Maximilian and the bondholders fully backed by creditor governments, negotiations inevitably favored the lenders. During the first round, as we expected, Mexico undertook a high degree of adjustment and received little in return. The second round found Mexico making still further adjustment, and in the absence of new funds from lenders, in dire financial and political straits that led to Maximilian's overthrow. During this period, then, Mexico, or rather Maximilian, played no other strategy than to reach agreements to the creditors' satisfaction, regardless of the size of the liability incurred. His goal was continued support from the European creditor governments – a goal he ultimately failed to achieve.

Situational changes

Maximilian's overthrow was the most obvious significant situational change by the end of this period. This change sharply altered Mexico's individual situation, returning Mexico to the unstable domestic political situation it had endured since its independence. For their part, the bondholders soon found themselves without the strong support they had received from the creditor governments. But as we shall see in Chapter 8, through their own efforts, the bondholders managed to increase their overall capabilities to partially compensate for this loss of support.

Conclusion

In the first period, Mexico stressed the country's inability to make any debt payments because it lacked the financial resources to do so. But in order to mollify the bondholders, Mexican officials repeatedly stated that Mexico had

[89] Ridley (1970), p. 734. [90] Vázquez and Meyer (1985), p. 70.

every intention of fulfilling its debt obligations when its financial conditions improved. This strategy also reduced the chances that the British government would intervene. The bondholders, while making high concessions, doubted that Mexico could adjust. They accepted new agreements in 1830 and 1846, however, in which the Mexican government pledged only future revenues to the debt service. Unfortunately for the bondholders, Mexico had no intention of making any adjustments, and as anticipated by the model, repeatedly failed to meet the stipulated conditions.

Although Mexico could play this strategy against the bondholders, it was a more dangerous strategy to play with the British government, which wielded real power over Mexico. In period two, Mexico negotiated the Diplomatic Convention debt agreements with the British. With these conventions, the British government moved to protect British property interests, but argued that British diplomatic protection did not extend to the London debt. Mexico, however, failed to appreciate all the nuances of this perspective. As a result, the London bondholders were able to free-ride on the Convention agreements while using the influence and threat of the British government to obtain favorable agreements from Mexico. After the Dunlop and Aldham Conventions between Juárez and the British navy, Britain granted diplomatic protection to both the London and Convention debt. Finally, when the Mexican government declared its inability to fulfill its obligations due to a traumatic civil war, the creditor governments, including Britain, intervened militarily in Mexican affairs.

With the intervention and rise of Maximilian in period three, the London and Convention debt bondholders formed a strong alliance with the creditor governments. As these governments, particularly France, created and supported his Mexican throne, Maximilian strove to please the European bondholders.

Juárez's return to power marked another significant change in the structure of the debt game. He obviously felt no compulsion to appease the same creditor governments that had forced him into exile. With Maximilian's ouster, the Mexican debt issue returned to a more typical debt game structure, a topic we will take up in Chapter 7.

6 Guano makes the world go 'round: Peruvian debt rescheduling, 1823–1850s

Peru possessed greater mineral and agricultural resources than any other region of Spanish South America, and thus represented both a political and military center for the Spanish colonial empire. The colony's wealth, combined with the benefits enjoyed by the upper classes, delayed Peru's revolt against Spanish domination compared to the revolts of other Latin American countries.

In fact, Peru's initial impetus for revolution came from outside the Andean region. General José de San Martín, an Argentine who had successfully fought for the liberation of Chile, believed that maintaining the independence of the newly formed South American republics required complete Spanish expulsion from the continent. In the early 1820s he led his forces against the Spanish royalists in Peru and fleetingly gained the upper hand. But depleted finances and suspicions concerning his plans to establish a monarchy made San Martín unpopular with Peruvians. Even though San Martín withdrew from Peru by September 1822, his agents in London, Juan García del Río and James Paroissien, continued to busily negotiate a loan to fund Peru's fight against Spanish forces. By October the two ministers had arranged Peru's first loan of £1.2 million at a 6% interest rate, floated by the London firm of Thomas Kinder. The Peruvian Congress enthusiastically endorsed the full loan, but the government only received £700,000 because the investors were pessimistic about Peru's chances for independence.[1] The final amount of the loan was also reduced because investors harbored suspicions that both ministers and Kinder had been involved in speculation related to the purchase of the Peruvian bonds.[2]

Like the fate of other Latin American loans in this epoch, these funds were spent on revolutionary war expenditures. Among other uses, the loan reimbursed numerous British merchants, paid for munitions shipped to Peru, and helped set up a mining company in Pasco.[3] As security on the loan, the Peruvian government pledged all of its revenues.[4]

This new capital notwithstanding, the Peruvian economy (based mostly on Spanish-controlled mining and agriculture) began a downward spiral due to the domestic turmoil caused by years of revolution. Ultimately, the war and the country's shattered economy stymied the government's efforts to meet obligations contracted from the first foreign loan,[5] and Peru's inability to service the

[1] See Palacios (1983) for a discussion of the initial loans undertaken by Peru. See also Mathew (1970), p. 82.
[2] Marichal (1989), p. 37 and pp. 39–40. [3] Marichal (1989), p. 33.
[4] Wynne (1951), p. 109. [5] Palacios (1983), p. 14.

loan ushered in the first epoch of its foreign debt history. After Peru contracted a second loan in 1825, it immediately defaulted, and failed to resolve its debt problems from these two initial loans for over 20 years.

I divide the analysis in this chapter into five periods. The first, from 1823 to 1839, encompassed Peru’s victory in its War of Independence, and ended with negotiations for a new loan. The second and third periods of the early 1840s opened with a dramatic change in Peru’s fortunes due to the discovery of guano, but were marked by a continued failure to resolve Peru’s default.[6] The fourth and fifth periods, from 1846 to 1851, saw increased political stability under General Ramón Castilla and the resolution of Peru’s long-standing default in 1849 with a bond conversion.

Period one, 1823–1841: debt and default

Peruvian revolutionary forces finally defeated the Spanish in 1825, which fostered the establishment of the first truly independent Peruvian state.[7] Yet after winning the War of Independence, the new government faced the equally daunting task of achieving political stability. The economy was in shambles from years of internal chaos. As a result, at the end of the war and during the first decades of Peru’s independence, the government simply failed to meet its foreign debt obligations, ruining Peru’s creditworthiness.

Identifying individual situations

Following its revolution, Peru was coalitionally unstable, issue weak, and overall weak (IS 8). The bondholders were coalitionally unstable, issue medium, and overall medium (IS 2/4).

Peru. Peru’s military and political leadership was divisive and unstable during the revolutionary period. Conservatives split with liberals, and the civilian and military segments of society were also at odds.[8] As one observer notes, “Peru experienced greater difficulty than most of its sister republics in establishing a stable political system.”[9]

During the revolution, San Martín designated himself the “Protector of Peru” granting himself dictatorial powers to fight the war and declare Peru’s independence. In the end, his authoritarian rule, combined with anti-clerical measures and an administration dominated by foreigners, led to his replacement in 1822.[10]

[6] Guano refers to the excrement of birds that was deposited on islands off the coast of Peru (and elsewhere). It had been used as a fertilizer by the Incas and became an important export commodity for Peru in the 1850s and 1860s.

[7] On this period, see Werlich (1978) and Pike (1967). The historical details below are primarily drawn from these two sources as well as Cotler (1978) and Palacios (1983).

[8] Latin American conservative ideologies represented authoritarian, centrist, mercantilist traditions based on Spanish colonial domination, whereas liberal ideologies represented egalitarian, federalist, and free trade traditions based on Enlightenment principles and the American and French revolutions. See Palmer (1980), pp. 25 and 36.

[9] Palmer (1980), p. 18. [10] Werlich (1978), pp. 61–63.

Under military pressure, however, the three-man junta that took power quickly fell in 1823, allowing Peru's first President, José de la Riva Agüero, to take office. Riva Agüero's unsuccessful expeditions against the Spaniards, who had strategically retreated into the interior of the country, combined with intrigue in the Peruvian Congress, eventually led to his impeachment. When José Bernardo Tagle, Marquis of Torre Tagle, became President, Riva Agüero immediately established an opposition government in Trujillo.

As the revolution progressed, Simón Bolívar rose to the forefront of Peru's political and military arenas. In May 1823, General Antonio José de Sucre, Bolívar's protégé, arrived in Lima, accompanied by Colombian troops, to rule on Bolívar's behalf. Both Riva Agüero and Torre Tagle grew wary of Bolívar's ulterior designs on Peru and the increasing foreign influence in the region. (Bolívar was, at the time, the chief political and military leader of Gran Colombia.)[11] Although Torre Tagle remained president of Peru, Bolívar controlled the mostly Colombian army, leaving Torre Tagle powerless. Riva Agüero attempted to drive Bolívar from the country. But after Bolívar publicized a letter in which Riva Agüero had offered to become a Spanish ally to drive Bolívar from the country, he was branded a traitor and driven out of Peru to exile in Europe. In another unsuccessful effort to defeat Bolívar, Torre Tagle joined a loyalist uprising in Lima to force the Colombians' retreat. By April 1824, however, division among the Spanish ranks opened the door for Bolívar. General José de Sucre led the revolutionary forces to victory in the Battle of Ayacucho – the decisive campaign that ultimately ended the Spanish presence in Latin America.

After liberating Peru, Simón Bolívar served for only one year as chief of state before he retired from Peru's political scene in September 1826. Political instability lasted well into the 1840s following Bolívar's departure. During this time, Peru had no fewer than 30 chief executives, many of whom were *caudillos* (the Spanish term for leaders who ruled through personalism). Needless to say, the governments of this period had brief incumbency expectations. For example, Agustin Gamarra, the only leader to last a full four-year term, had to crush 17 rebellions (including one by his vice-president) in order to stay in office.[12] In addition, leaders had to contend with a series of minor wars and confrontations with Peru's neighbors.

In the years following the War of Independence, Peru's political system, described by one scholar as an "administrative and political vacuum,"[13] failed to maintain any stable political organization, institution, or guiding principles. In addition, Peruvian leaders enacted numerous constitutions, some relatively liberal (1823, 1828, 1834), and others more authoritarian and conservative (1826, drafts in 1837, 1839).[14] In sum, after its victory against the Spanish, Peru entered a 20-year period of anarchy and instability.

[11] Werlich (1978), pp. 63–64. Gran Colombia was comprised of the states of Venezuela, Ecuador, and Colombia.

[12] Werlich (1978), p. 70. [13] Yepes del Castillo (1972), p. 33. [14] Werlich (1978), p. 67.

With regard to economic resources, the War of Independence virtually destroyed Peru's domestic economy and infrastructure. Unattended mines flooded and agricultural lands lay in ruin during the war as armies confiscated crops, livestock, and property. Foreign markets, capital, and investments disappeared, disrupting the nation's trade.[15] Even after the war, the economy remained stagnant. A lack of interest on the part of domestic financiers who possessed the necessary investment capital undermined efforts to reactivate the mines.

As a result, the national treasury remained empty as Peru's government floundered financially. Over 60% of the state's revenues went towards military expenditures, but Peru's armies and bureaucrats frequently went unpaid, resulting in mutiny and rampant graft.[16] This military spending, combined with reliance on British imports, would eventually lead to the destruction of Peru's internal production capabilities.[17] In addition, a critical specie depletion occurred during and after the revolution. British Consul Charles Ricketts estimated that British soldiers carried off 27 million pesos (£5.4 million) worth of gold and silver from Peru,[18] further exacerbating the country's morbid financial condition. According to Julio Cotler: "The expulsion and exile of thousands of peninsulars and creoles brought a massive flight of capital. The young republic encountered a deterioration of its productive apparatus with no prospect for recovery."[19]

Peru also found itself weak in overall capabilities, as indicated by its poor economic condition and lack of a strong military. Immediately following the revolution, Bolívar and thousands of Colombian troops controlled Peru. Even after they departed, Peru remained militarily weak. In subsequent wars with Gran Colombia to the north and Chile to the south, Peru – the former bastion of Spanish military power in South America – was badly beaten. As U.S. Chargé d'Affaires James C. Pickett stated: "there is not one of this official mob that would not be ready at any moment to plunge the country into civil war, if he thought he would be personally benefitted by doing so."[20] In addition, Peru had difficulty holding on to its territory. It lost land not only to Chile, but also to the creation of an independent Bolivian state. Bolivia removed all of what was once Upper Peru from the nation's dominion by 1827.

Lenders. The bondholders and bankers were divided, lacking a stable coalition to represent their interests. The banking houses did not act in concert, but instead through an intermediary, Thomas Kinder, Jr., who arranged the first loan to Peru. Kinder, however, found it difficult to get a consensus from the

[15] Werlich (1978), p. 73. [16] Werlich (1978), p. 74. [17] Cotler (1978), p. 85.
[18] Marichal (1989), p. 21. Until 1865, the exchange rate of the peso was 5 to the British pound. See McQueen (1926), pp. 2–3.
[19] Cotler (1978), p. 83.
[20] J.C. Pickett to Secretary of State John C. Calhoun, Despatch no. 110, Lima, February 8, 1845; and Pickett to Calhoun, Despatch no. 111, Lima, March 3, 1845, Record Group 59, "General Records of the Department of State, Despatches from the United States Ministers to Peru, 1826–1906" (Washington, D.C.: National Archives, Microcopy T-52, Reel 6, quoted in Werlich, 1978, p. 75).

banking houses. In one case, Kinder had to sue the bankers to fulfill their loan commitments.[21]

As for issue-specific capabilities, the relatively small size of the debt did not threaten the bondholders and bankers as much as, for example, the Mexican debt. With not much at risk, some bankers and their subscribing public resisted Kinder's efforts because their actual liability in the issue was not very large. In sum, we code the bondholders as being issue-medium in capabilities. Turning to overall capabilities, the creditors were somewhat vulnerable because they lacked significant power relative to a sovereign state. Moreover, they were not actively backed by any creditor government, and no evidence suggests that the British government wanted to intervene to support the interests of its nationals in Peru – or, for that matter, in any other Latin American country during this period. But the relatively small size of Peru's debt decreased their risk.

Creditor governments. During this age of European imperialist expansion, the Spanish retreat left the region available for the expansion of British influence and economic power. Although Britain was initially ambivalent with respect to Latin American independence, the French occupation of Spain established Britain firmly on the side of independence for the colonies. When the independence movements began to succeed, the British government quickly recognized the new republics and opened commercial trade relations. By October 1823, British Foreign Secretary George Canning had named a British Consul to Peru, and directed him to initiate negotiations with the government on commercial treaties.[22] The British government competed with the American, French, and German governments to secure strategic, diplomatic, and trade relationships with the new Latin American states. Debt negotiations, by contrast, were of relatively lower strategic significance. In particular, Britain feared that pressing the claims of the bondholders might alienate the new Peruvian government. As one observer notes: "Overly aggressive policies on behalf of the bondholders could undercut British trade relations, thereby benefiting rival French, German, and United States merchants."[23]

Debt game and predicted outcome

We arrive at the cardinal and ordinal game matrix shown in Figure 6.1 for this period. On the basis of strategic interaction, we expect the game to settle into a LA..., LC... outcome. Both actors have a dominant strategy not to cooperate. The Nash equilibrium in this game is a stable outcome according to the payoffs in the matrix. As we shall see, such an outcome is consistent with the actual events, marked by growing tension and then default. Turning to the outcome with intervention, in this instance we would not expect to see much pressure from the British or other governments. As noted, given its broader strategic objectives in Latin America, the U.K. was not interested in pressuring the Peruvians.

[21] Palacios (1983), p. 17. [22] Marichal (1989), p. 16. [23] Marichal (1989), p. 56.

Cardinal Payoff Matrix,
No Intervention Expected

		Lenders IS 2/4		
		HC...	MC...	LC...
	HA...	0, –7.5	–3.5, –3.17	–4, 1.17
Peru IS 8	MA...	4, –9	0, –5	–2, –1
	LA...	8, –8.5	3.5, –5.5	**0, –2.5**

Note: Nash equilibrium bolded.

Ordinal Payoff Matrix,
No Intervention Expected

		Lenders IS 2/4		
		HC...	MC...	LC...
	HA...	5, 3	2, 6	1, 9
Peru IS 8	MA...	8, 1	5, 5	3, 8
	LA...	9, 2	7, 4	**5, 7**

Note: Nash equilibrium bolded.

Figure 6.1. *Play phase, period one: 1823–1839*

The negotiations and outcome

This period consists of two rounds. During the first, from 1823 to 1825, Peru negotiated its second loan the same year it defeated the Spanish. Peru intended part of the loan for servicing the nation's debt. But shortly thereafter, Peru defaulted on both this and the 1822 loan. From 1826 to the late 1830s, Peru remained in default, with a change in its financial condition toward the end of this round.

Round one. Revolutionary struggle during this round impeded Peru's ability to meet its debt obligations. At the same time, it desperately needed new funds to continue the war. In 1824, Bolívar directed his consul in London, Juan Parish Robertson, to negotiate a new loan. This effort divided the banks. Banking houses led by Hodgson, Jones, Easthope, Adams, and Everett, Walker & Co. opposed the work of Kinder, and carried out an "embargo" against Peru.

The bankers' objections were eventually overcome, and Peru reached a new loan agreement with 21 bankers on January 21, 1825. The agreement called for a £600,000 bond issue for Peru, of which over £200,000 would go towards the interest arrears from the first loan.[24] Unfortunately, because the creditors and the public remained wary of new ventures in Peru, bankers disbursed less than £200,000. In fact, in an effort to avoid portraying Peru as either desperate for money or as trying to raise funds to pay off the first loan, the banks never even emitted the bonds publicly. After discovering this, many creditors questioned the propriety of the second loan as well as the "unauthorized" negotiations. In the end, the amount actually offered Peru was minimal, too little to pay back former obligations.

Peru remained in a precarious financial position. Bolívar's concern prompted him to write Finance Minister José de Larrea the following message in 1825: "As always I am thinking of Peru because of her debts, and I would recommend to the government that it should liquidate its national debt by selling all its mines and common lands . . . God save us from the debt and we shall be content."[25] In addition, Mexican, Colombian, and Argentine ambassadors in London urged their Peruvian counterparts to take advantage of the short-term loans from the French Rothschilds.[26] In the end, Peru adopted neither Bolívar's nor the ambassadors' proposals; in April 1826, Peru defaulted on both of its foreign loans, destroying its foreign creditworthiness.

The British government simply refused to help the bondholders in this case as in the case of Colombian default. When urged to make diplomatic recognition of Peru and other states contingent on these countries acknowledging their debt, Foreign Secretary Canning flatly refused.[27]

In sum, this round produced a relative stalemate in the debt game of low concessions and low adjustment. The bankers declined to lend more funds than required for Peru to maintain its debt service. Peru, for its part, focused much more on its political problems than on servicing its debt out of its own resources. Refusing to actively involve itself in the debt negotiations, Great Britain turned a deaf ear to its bondholders' pleas for help.

Round two. From 1826 through the late 1830s, Peru remained in default on its foreign loans. Peru did not repudiate the debt; it simply declared it prohibitive due to the internal distress of the country. The continuous struggles between various leaders soaked up all revenues of the new state. Lacking any means to enforce servicing, the bondholders resigned themselves to the situation.

[24] See Palacios (1983), p. 19.
[25] Pérez Vila (1979), pp. 207–208, cited in Marichal (1989), pp. 33–34.
[26] Marichal (1989), p. 53. [27] Jenks (1927/1973), p. 117.

The Peruvian government encouraged the passivity of the bondholders (and endeavored to forestall possible British intervention) by showing signs of goodwill. In 1833, it decreed that income from expropriated convent properties would be allocated to pay the public debt. Two years later, it announced that proceeds from some state monopolies would be used for the same purpose.[28] Peru's government also decreed that foreign bonds would be used in payment for import duties.[29] In the end, however, these proclamations had little effect: the bondholders received no money from these sources. Nevertheless, for the most part, relations between the British and Peruvian governments remained amicable. No evidence suggests that the British government pressed the claims of its bondholders. In fact, despite occasional entreaties to the Peruvians, British policy reflected Lord Aberdeen's warning to his own British proconsul in Lima that "The bondholders could not expect any authoritative Interference with the Government of Peru on their behalf."[30]

Summary. Both parties found themselves in a deadlock during both rounds of this period. As creditor governments refused to get involved, the bondholders continued to wait for Peru to resume its payments.

Situational changes

Although deadlocked during this period, the bondholders and Peru made several efforts to propel situational change. The most important was the bondholders' unsuccessful attempt to solicit British government assistance in securing servicing of their bonds. As anticipated from our examination of British interests, bondholders' efforts had little effect because the government had its own reasons to stay out of the debt game. For their part, the Peruvians made modest efforts to forestall a potential alliance between the British government and the bondholders by appearing conciliatory.

In 1840, however, the discovery of guano strengthened Peru's economic situation and brought a new factor into the debt negotiations. Many entrepreneurs forcefully promoted the sale of this fertilizer, rapidly improving Peru's financial situation. In November 1840, Ramón Castilla, then serving as Gamarra's Minister of the Treasury, concluded a contract for the sale of guano with Francisco de Quiros, a prominent Peruvian businessman. Quiros apparently was just a front man for British investors interested in securing access to Peruvian guano.[31] The contract gave him exclusive rights to export guano for six years at 10,000 pesos per year. Quiros paid an advance of 40,000 pesos, with an additional 10,000 to be paid at the end of the first year and 10,000 at the end of the second. Of the 40,000 pesos, 1500 was to be paid in cash and the rest in depreciated debt certificates of the Lima mint.[32] This first contract, however, did not work out as Quiros had intended. The first exports did not leave until March 1841. Although

[28] Mathew (1970), p. 84. [29] Mathew (1970), p. 84.
[30] Quoted from Foreign Office records in Mathew (1970), p. 83.
[31] See Mathew (1981), pp. 25–26 for a discussion. [32] Levin (1960), p. 51.

Peru did not formally nationalize guano until early 1842, it operated as though it were national property by late 1841.[33] Because it had control of this lucrative commodity, Peru no longer feared the bondholders. Peru's nationalization of guano is consistent with our expectation that Peru would attempt to alter its weak individual situation after receiving a low payoff in period one. On other dimensions, both Peru's and the bondholders' individual situations remained the same.

Periods two and three, 1841–1844: the guano promise

The discovery and lucrative sale of guano to Britain greatly improved Peru's financial prospects. Yet Peru remained politically unstable well into the mid-1840s, contributing to a continued impasse in the negotiations. Thus, although Peru's economic situation changed significantly, the deadlock in debt negotiations continued into the second period. At the end of 1842, the guano promise of prosperity looked somewhat empty, when the guano market collapsed due to new discoveries elsewhere. Given the continued deadlock and relatively quick change in periods, we examine both the second and third periods in this section.

Identifying individual situations

Following Peru's effort to exploit guano, I classify Peru as coalitionally unstable, issue strong, and overall strong (IS 6). The bondholders remained coalitionally unstable, issue medium, and overall medium (IS 2/4). By the end of 1842, however, Peru's economic situation quickly worsened. In period three, I code Peru coalitionally unstable, issue weak, and overall strong (IS 4), while the bondholders' position remains the same as in period two.

Peru. Guano exploitation affected both Peru's issue and overall capabilities. Political instability, however, continued to be the norm. The Peru-Bolivia Confederation, created in October 1836 under the leadership of General Andrés Santa Cruz, proved to be short-lived. Chile began efforts to end the accord almost immediately and forced its dissolution in 1839 after Chile's army defeated Santa Cruz at the Battle of Yungay. Peru's new leader imposed by Chile, General Agustín Gamarra, was not content with simply ruling Peru. In an effort to reconstruct the Confederation under his own leadership, Gamarra invaded Bolivia in 1841. His efforts were aborted when he was killed in battle. After Gamarra's death, Bolivia invaded Peru from the south as Ecuador invaded from the north. Peruvian commanders sent to resist the invasions denounced Lima, as well as each other, and a multi-sided civil war began.[34] A succession of *caudillos* followed before General Ramón Castilla took power in 1845.

In November 1841 a British ship brought word to the Peruvians that guano was fetching very high prices in England. The government immediately canceled

[33] Levin (1960), p. 52. [34] Werlich (1978), p. 72.

its contract with Quiros and negotiated a new one. The new contract with Quiros was one year with an additional four-year option. The government received 64% of profits after costs (all in cash). Quiros and his new partner, Aquilles Allier, renounced any claim to the initial 40,000 advance and advanced another 287,000 pesos against future profits.

By early 1842 the Peruvian government formally declared all guano national property. With this action, Peru significantly altered its own capabilities as well as the nature of the debt issue-area. First, Peru increased its issue capabilities with sales of guano. Second, the government gained control of the development, sale, pricing, and use of guano,[35] and thus was much less concerned about retaliation by bondholders because it now had a highly desired commodity that could be used to raise funds.

Lenders. The bondholders remained coalitionally unstable during this period. As for issue strength, the bondholders (both the original ones and speculators who had entered the market) did not face a very large Peruvian debt. I thus continue to code them as issue medium. Overall, the bondholders remained weak. Although they sought some assistance from the British government to obtain Peruvian compliance with its agreements, the British government refused to ally itself with them. Moreover, they were not in a position at this point either to threaten Peru financially or to threaten expropriation of Peru's assets.

Creditor governments. Two factors continued to motivate the British government's interest in Peru during the second and third periods: first, the discovery of guano gave Peru an important tradable commodity; second and more importantly, British developers played a key role in the development of the guano trade. For these reasons, British strategic and economic interests were potential motivations for involvement in Peru, although not necessarily on behalf of the bondholders.

The development of guano involved important British interests. The British market dominated the guano trade: more guano from Peru arrived on English shores than to all other foreign markets combined. In addition, the British firm of Anthony Gibbs & Sons dominated the guano market from 1841 through 1861.[36] British economic interest in Peru clearly focused on the continuance of productive trade relations, while British bondholders held the notes that Peru pledged to satisfy through its guano sales.

British trade had suffered during Peru's civil war, and traders felt helpless without British government intervention. As one interested party noted in a letter to the Foreign Secretary, Lord Aberdeen: Britain's "commercial interests were so intimately mixed up with her political strength, that it becomes necessary to support one in order to maintain the other."[37] The government, however, did not cooperate with the traders and refused to take action.

[35] Mathew (1977). [36] Mathew (1977), p. 339. [37] Mathew (1968), p. 565.

In spite of the enticements, several factors discouraged British government involvement. Mathew argues that it may have been due to the avoidance of "potentially complicated entanglements overseas."[38] This is quite plausible since the British government seemed very reluctant to move beyond verbal reprimand even under extreme circumstances. After the fall of Santa Cruz, Palmerston condemned the war, although sympathizing with the Confederation. But he went only so far as to instruct Lima representatives to "use their good graces to re-establish peace."[39] In addition, as a relatively small and poor country, Peru did not provide the ideal market for British export interests. Moreover, Peru's lack of an adequate transport system hampered exports. The British government also found itself cross-pressured by two groups: farmers, who wanted low guano prices, and bondholders, who wanted guano to carry a heftier price tag to finance their repayments.

Debt game and predicted outcome

From our classifications, we arrive at the game shown in Figure 6.2 for the second period. In this game, LA..., LC... continues to be the Nash equilibrium, yielding relatively high payoffs for both actors. The model suggests that Peru's increased financial resources and its use of guano as leverage to extract loans would not make Peru more willing to settle, but rather the opposite. With multiple strategic objectives, and with cross-pressures domestically, we would expect Britain to avoid direct involvement and at most signal its desire for a settlement.

The negotiations and outcome: period two

This period consists of one round of negotiations from the late 1841 capture of guano profits by the government to the collapse of the guano market at the end of 1842. In the beginning of 1842, guano profits were first tied to the debt negotiations. In January, Peru pledged to put half of the guano profits into the Bank of England to pay back the bondholders. But the Peruvian government quickly withdrew this pledge a month later to make a new "arrangement by which guano proceeds would be used to retire the debt at current market prices"[40] – prices far below the price at which the debt had been contracted. Although half of the proceeds were to be paid toward the debt, the other half of the payments from contractors could now be made in government obligations at face value, thus allowing the government to obtain a greater share of the total proceeds.[41] In addition, since the new contract was made with a variety of firms (including de Quiros-Allier and Gibbs, Crawley & Co.; the latter became the main trading house soon thereafter), Peru could obtain large amounts from the foreign guano merchants, including 200,000 pesos added to the December 1841 advance for a total of 487,000 pesos.[42]

[38] Mathew (1968), p. 565. [39] Mathew (1968), p. 567.

[40] Levin (1960), p. 55. Mathew (1977) provides a good discussion of the negotiations and particularly the role of the British government at this time.

[41] Levin (1960), p. 55. [42] Mathew (1977), p. 345.

Cardinal Payoff Matrix,
No Intervention Expected

		Lenders IS 2/4		
		HC...	MC...	LC...
	HA...	−12, −7.5	−12.5, −3.17	−12, 1.17
Peru IS 6	MA...	−7.33, −9	−8, −5	−8, −1
	LA...	−2.67, −8.5	−3.5, −5.5	**−4, −2.5**

Note: Nash equilibrium bolded.

Ordinal Payoff Matrix,
No Intervention Expected

		Lenders IS 2/4		
		HC...	MC...	LC...
	HA...	2.5, 3	1, 6	2.5, 9
Peru IS 6	MA...	6, 1	4.5, 5	4.5, 8
	LA...	9, 2	8, 4	**7, 7**

Note: Nash equilibrium bolded.

Figure 6.2. *Play phase, period two: 1841–1842*

The new contract was a major setback for the bondholders. The government "agreed to accept half of its guano receipts below 30 pesos per ton in recognized instruments of public debt – one half from the internal debt and one half from the external debt."[43] This represented a substantial savings for the Peruvian government. As predicted by the model, Peru saw little need to honor its promise to settle its foreign debt, and simply secured loans from the contractors, resulting in an outcome of LA..., LC....

[43] Levin (1960), p. 57.

Cardinal Payoff Matrix,
No Intervention Expected

		Lenders IS 2/4		
		HC...	MC...	LC...
	HA...	−3, −7.5	−6.5, −3.17	−9, 1.17
Peru IS 4	MA...	1.67, −9	−2, −5	−5, −1
	LA...	6.33, −8.5	2.5, −5.5	**−1, −2.5**

Note: Nash equilibrium bolded.

Ordinal Payoff Matrix,
No Intervention Expected

		Lenders IS 2/4		
		HC...	MC...	LC...
	HA...	4, 3	2, 6	1, 9
Peru IS 4	MA...	7, 1	5, 5	3, 8
	LA...	9, 2	8, 4	**6, 7**

Note: Nash equilibrium bolded.

Figure 6.3. *Play phase, period three: 1842–1844*

Debt game and predicted outcome

In the third period, Peru's individual situation shifted to IS 4, while bondholders remained in IS 2/4 (see Figure 6.3). As in the second period, the Nash equilibrium is still at LA..., LC.... The change in ordinal payoffs is relatively minor, with Peru securing a slightly lower payoff than in the second period but with the bondholders continuing as before. With respect to the outcome with intervention, as in the second period, we do not expect any significant pressure from the British government.

The negotiations and outcome: period three

By the end of 1842, the contractors submitted a memo to the Peruvian Finance Minister requesting that he extend their contract, warning that "short of drastic reduction in prices, there seemed no hope whatever of selling 120,000 tons by the end of 1846."[44] They also feared that if prices dropped too low, the government would not have enough profit to pay back its loans. Their fears proved to be well founded. By the end of 1842, the guano market collapsed, and prices dropped from £25–28 per ton to £12 per ton by October 1842.

The high price of £28 per ton had set off great hunts for guano in other areas, leading to the discovery of guano deposits on the island of Ichaboe off the coast of Africa. This guano, unclaimed by any government, sold for £5–7½ per ton.[45] Because the Peruvian government lost the largest share of earnings, it suffered the most, but it avoided suffering an immediate impact by continuing to secure large advances from contractors. The contractors kept lending to avoid losing their contracts and therefore their past loans. By 1846, they had advanced Peru 1,164,586 pesos.[46]

In September 1843 President Manuel Ignacio de Vivanco gave the contractors a three-year extension on their ongoing contract, providing them with rights to exploit guano until 1849. Gibbs and Myers, however, were cautious in dealing with the government, referring to the "fluctuating character" of Latin America's new governments.[47] They sought British government assistance but were unsuccessful. In 1844 Manuel Menendez took power, and quickly confirmed the contractors' fears, declaring Vivanco's deal illegal. Although no longer making large guano profits, with large advances by the contractors, Peru felt no need to undertake economic adjustments to benefit the bondholders.[48] Peru obtained funds through contractor advances, instead of being forced to seek new loans from the bondholders, leaving the outcome at LA..., LC....

Summary. As we expected from the model, during the second and third periods, we saw a continuation of the long-standing stalemate. Although Peru's financial and overall capabilities improved during the second period, it did not become more amenable to settling with the bondholders. When Peru's financial situation worsened in the third period, it simply used its overall capabilities, controlling its guano deposits, to extract additional loans from anxious guano contractors, thus avoiding adjustment.

Situational changes

After the collapse of the guano market at the end of the second period, Peru became issue weak but remained overall strong. It quickly used its capabilities to force the contractors to provide Peru with new loans. This strategy allowed

44 Mathew (1977), p. 346. 45 Levin (1960), p. 59.
46 Levin (1960), p. 59. 47 Mathew (1977), p. 346.
48 The advance accounted for a significant portion of government revenues and expenditures, which averages about 5 million pesos a year from 1845 to 1850 (McQueen, 1926, p. 5).

Peru to ignore bondholder pressure to settle because Peru could simply replace lost revenue with borrowed funds. The bondholders tried to bolster their strength by appealing to the British government, but it was not interested in their plight.

The third period came to an end with the rise to power of General Ramón Castilla in 1845. By establishing the first constitutional government in Peru, Castilla began to secure peace and order for the first time in the nation's history. As for the bondholders, because of the extended period of time that Peru remained in default, continued speculation in its bonds led to a greater concentration of their holdings. Unified by the likelihood of a settlement, the bondholders became more stable.

Periods four and five, 1845–1847 and 1848–1851: borrowing on guano and settlement

As we have seen, the discovery and development of the guano market did not spur Peru to settle its outstanding foreign debt. During the two periods examined in this section, a settlement appeared more likely after the onset of greater Peruvian political stability. Continued financial problems in Peru, and the ongoing opportunity to extract loans from guano contractors, however, made the government resistant to settling. In the end, after difficult negotiations, the 1849 settlement came as Peru began to weaken overall although its financial situation improved. I discuss both the fourth and fifth periods in this section because of their relatively short duration. The fourth period runs from 1845 to 1847 and the fifth from 1848 until 1851.

Identifying individual situations

In the fourth period, we classify Peru as coalitionally medium in stability, issue weak, and overall strong (IS 3/4). By mid-1848, however, Peru had clearly become stable and its financial situation had greatly improved. Yet Peru's overall strength diminished as its dependence on foreign contractors grew, thus making it more vulnerable to pressure from the bondholders in the fifth period (IS 1/5). The bondholders in both periods are coalitionally medium, issue medium, and overall weak (IS 1/8).

Peru. Castilla brought to Peru the hope of stability for the first time in its independent history. He began to quell opposition, vigorously suppressing revolt and rebellion, and "succeeded through effective personal autocracy in containing much of the latent conflict in the country."[49] Castilla merged liberal and conservative elements in his administration, and also allowed Congress to meet regularly, encouraged open debates, and gave greater freedoms to the press and religious groups. Overall, he "gave Peru its first 'taste' of constitutional

[49] Mathew (1968), p. 564.

government."[50] As Castilla stated before Congress in 1849, "The first of my constitutional functions is the preservation of internal order; but the same constitution obliges me to respect the rights of the citizen."[51]

During the fourth period, from 1845 to 1847, Peru's financial condition continued to flag. Competition in the guano market persisted, making it difficult for Peru's contractors to maintain their exports. In 1845, for example, Britain imported 207,679 tons of guano from Ichaboe but only 14,000 from Peru and Bolivia.[52] Estimates for the two-year 1846–1847 budget showed that only £102,685 from guano sales would be available for domestic needs.[53] To partly cope with the projected deficit of some £700,000, Peru continued to borrow, obtaining £60,000 in 1846.[54]

Peru's financial prospects began to improve rapidly by 1848, as Ichaboe's supplies were depleted. By 1847, guano from Peru and Bolivia again became the world's primary source, accounting for 57,762 tons, compared to only 1,146 tons for Ichaboe in the British market.[55] Because of the guano trade, the budget made a quick turnaround, showing a slight surplus for 1848–1849.[56]

As for overall capabilities, Castilla began to modernize the military and also implemented new public works programs, reorganized the civil service and diplomatic corps, adopted a new legal system, and developed Peru's first public education system.[57] In spite of these improvements, however, by 1847 Peru had begun to weaken overall. It had become highly dependent on loans from foreign contractors, and in the words of one analyst, "Though the contractors were exporting more guano, the government had already been paid for it and could call for no further advances."[58]

Lenders. The ongoing debt deadlock had brought speculators into the market, causing a much greater concentration of holdings. Because the number of holders was reduced and because the debt was not very significant as compared to many other countries, the bondholders were now coalitionally medium in stability, although they remained issue medium in strength. As for overall capabilities, the bondholders continued to lack direct support from the British government and were not yet in a position to block loans. When initial offers were made in 1847, additional consolidation of holdings took place in the market, and the greater eagerness on the part of most bondholders to settle put them in a more stable situation but weaker overall position.

Creditor governments. As in the last period, the British government remained interested in Peru for overall strategic reasons. With the bondholders continuing their pressure on the government, we might expect it to be somewhat more amenable to pressing for a settlement. But given the range of pressures on

[50] Werlich (1978), p. 79. [51] Werlich (1978), p. 80 (from archival sources).
[52] Levin (1960), p. 58. [53] Mathew (1970), p. 89. [54] Levin (1960), p. 60.
[55] Levin (1960), p. 59. [56] Mathew (1970), p. 94. [57] Werlich (1978), p. 89.
[58] Levin (1960), p. 60.

Cardinal Payoff Matrix,
Intervention Expected

		Lenders IS 1/8		
		HC...	MC...	LC...
	HA...	3, −1.5	−.5. .83	−3, 3.17
Peru IS 3/4	MA...	5.67, −2.75	<u>2, −1?</u>	−1, .75
	LA...	**8.33, −.5**	<u>**4.5, −.5**</u>	**1, −.5**

Note: Nash equilibria bolded; expected outcomes with intervention underlined.

Ordinal Payoff Matrix,
Intervention Expected

		Lenders IS 1/8		
		HC...	MC...	LC...
	HA...	6, 2	3, 8	1, 9
Peru IS 3/4	MA...	8, 1	<u>5, 3?</u>	2, 7
	LA...	**9, 5**	<u>**7, 5**</u>	**4, 5**

Note: Nash equilibria bolded; expected outcomes with intervention underlined.

Figure 6.4. *Play phase, period four: 1845–1847*

the government – including the fact that the interests of the contractors and bondholders continued to diverge – we would expect Britain to only signal its interest, rather than to directly intervene.

Debt game and predicted outcome

From the codings for the fourth period, we arrive at the cardinal game matrix and ordinal conversion shown in Figure 6.4. Based on the payoffs in this game, we find three equilibria: one at LA..., HC..., another at LA..., MC..., and finally a third at LA..., LC... In all cases, as we can see, Peru has little interest in adjusting, while the bondholders are indifferent among their three strategies of varying concessions. We expect somewhat more active involvement by the British government on the debt during this period, and a possible push toward an equilibrium of MA..., MC... Given the proclivities of both actors, however, this equilibrium would not likely be sustained, and thus we might expect a fall back to LA..., MC..., the more stable equilibrium.

The negotiations and outcome: period four

The fourth period runs from 1845 until the end of 1847. At the start of his reign, Castilla gave immediate attention to the debt issue. In addition to the other economic reforms already discussed, he passed a law requiring "strict compliance, in all its parts, with all contracts made with individuals either natives of Peru, or foreigners . . ."[59] Castilla also appointed a minister in London to attempt a settlement with the bondholders. Yet as we shall see, Peru's subsequent actions spoke louder than Castilla's words, and in this period Peru did not actively pursue a settlement. Because the option of seeking advances from contractors was still available, Peru was in no hurry to settle.

Following initial contacts between Peru and its bondholders, in February 1847 Peru demanded that negotiations be moved to Lima, instead of continuing in London. Despite strong protests from bondholders, Peru persisted. As one analyst put it: "One side had to give way, and in the end the bondholders decided that talks in Lima were better than no talks at all."[60]

As the bondholders became increasingly concerned about Peru's inability to repay their loans, they sought government assistance in July 1847. But Palmerston responded by simply stating his "unofficial support" for the bondholders. He noted in a message to the Peruvian government "how essential it is for the credit and interests of Peru that the Government should effect some adjustment of her Foreign Debt."[61]

At the end of 1847, despite Peru's poor financial situation, Maclean Rowe & Co. submitted a tough bondholder proposal to the government. The proposal called for the 6% interest rate to be resumed immediately, with an annual sinking fund of 1% and for arrears interest to be converted to bonds yielding 3% after June 1854, also with a 1% sinking fund.[62]

Peru simply ignored this proposal, and did not respond until almost the middle of 1848. In the end, little came of the bondholders' efforts to make some concessions in the negotiations. Given Peru's position in the debt game, at this point it was not interested in a settlement. Although the bondholders shifted away from offering no concessions to offering some negotiating concessions in the form of moving the talks to Lima, Peru refused to budge, and the outcome remained at the predicted point of LA..., MC....

[59] Mathew (1970), p. 87. [60] Mathew (1970), p. 87.
[61] Foreign Office documents quoted in Mathew (1970), p. 88. [62] Mathew (1970), p. 89.

Cardinal Payoff Matrix, Intervention Expected

Lenders IS 1/8

		HC...	MC...	LC...
	HA...	−3, −1.5	−2.75, .83	**0, 3.17**
Peru IS 1/5	MA...	−1.83, −2.75	−2, −1	−.5, .75
	LA...	**−.67, −.5**	**−1.25, −.5**	−1, −.5

Note: Nash equilibria bolded; expected outcome with intervention underlined.

Ordinal Payoff Matrix, Intervention Expected

Lenders IS 1/8

		HC...	MC...	LC...
	HA...	1, 2	2, 8	**9, 9**
Peru IS 1/5	MA...	4, 1	3, 3	8, 7
	LA...	**7, 5**	**5, 5**	6, 5

Note: Nash equilibria bolded; expected outcome with intervention underlined.

Figure 6.5. *Play phase, period five: 1848–1851*

Debt game and predicted outcome

In the fifth period, we have the game shown in Figure 6.5, with Peru in IS 1/5 and the lenders in IS 1/8. In this game, we see three equilibria, at LA..., HC..., LA..., MC..., and HA..., LC... The most likely outcome, however, would appear to be HA..., LC..., based on Zeuthen's principle. Moreover, both players receive their highest payoff at this equilibrium, making it highly stable. It may appear anomalous for Peru to be pleased with making high adjustments while the bondholders make few concessions; however, as we shall see, this prediction proves consistent with actual events.

In this case, we expect the British to reinforce the HA..., LC... outcome. But as before, we would not expect very strong pressure. In this game, with some aspects of uncertainty (as in a Chicken-type game), a simple signal from Britain should suffice to secure the game at the HA..., LC... outcome.

The negotiations and outcome: period five

This period brought a settlement to Peru's long-standing default, dating back to the revolutionary period. In May 1848, Peru finally rejected the bondholders' 1847 proposal, and issued a counter-proposal. The new proposal called for bonds to be converted to equal amounts at 3% from October 1849 to December 1854 then up 1/2% per year to 6% in December 1860. Payments in arrears were to carry no interest the first four years and then rise from 1% in December 1854 to 3% in December 1861. A sinking fund was to be established but at an unspecified time.[63]

Maclean Rowe & Co. knew that this proposed change would be rejected and asked W.P. Adams, the Chargé d'Affaires in Lima, to take over. Adams refused. But in a letter to Felipe Pardo, the Peruvian Finance Minister, Adams expressed disappointment at Peru's refusal of the bondholders' proposal. Pardo responded by noting his concern over this intervention, and the British government quickly back-stepped, stating that while "Her Majesty's government have felt it their duty to draw the attention of the Government of Peru to the great Injustice . . . Her Majesty's Government entirely agree with the Peruvian Government that the details for the arrangement" should be left to "the Peruvian Government and their British Subjects . . ."[64]

In contrast to the fourth period, however, Peru continued to seek an agreement. In September 1848, Peru suggested that negotiations move to London to expedite discussions. The evidence suggests that Peru was motivated to make this shift, not because of fear of British intervention, but rather because of domestic Peruvian pressure to settle with the bondholders. It appears that some prominent Peruvians (including the negotiators themselves!) took advantage of the opportunity to benefit by purchasing depreciated bonds in anticipation of an agreement.[65]

In January 1849, the Peruvian government and the bondholders reached a formal agreement on the defaulted loans. The agreement called for the principal of both of the defaulted loans to be converted into new active bonds, which would carry an interest rate of 4%, increasing 1/2% annually to 6%. Interest arrears would be capitalized at 75% of face value into new deferred bonds with lower interest rates (1 to 3%). In addition, the agreement called for the creation of sinking funds to protect the bonds at 1% annually for the active bonds redeemable in 1852, and at 1/2% annually for the deferred bonds redeemable in 1856. This new settlement was significantly tougher than Peru's previous offer.

[63] Mathew (1970), p. 90. [64] Mathew (1970), pp. 91–92. [65] Mathew (1970), p. 94.

The interest rate was 4–6%, up from 3%, and hypothecations increased from one-third to one-half.[66] Despite some reservations about the deal, even the normally critical paper *The Times* noted that it "appeared to exceed the expectations recently entertained."[67] As expected, Peru undertook high adjustment while the bondholders only made few concessions.

Summary. Although the final outcome of this period was asymmetrical in that Peru adjusted significantly while the bondholders did not make concessions, it still yielded a high payoff for both actors. As the model predicted, while the British government may have applied some external pressure, and may have encouraged a more rapid resolution of the debt problem, the eventual agreement cannot be attributed to British government intervention. In contrast to suggestions in work by Jonathan Levin that British intervention was central to the debt settlement, the model supports William Mathew's view that:

> the logical sequence of stages was unofficial support, diplomatic intervention, and, as a last resort, naval pressure. The British government was still operating at the first stage; it is hardly likely that it seriously intended leaping dramatically to the third.[68]

Thus, in accordance with our predictions, the 1849 settlement came about due to Peru's changed individual situation, rather than because of British pressure.

Situational changes

Despite the increased political stability under Castilla in Peru's political system, there was no formal agreement in period four. Peru was issue weak during this period because competition in the guano market persisted, but it was still able to secure loans from the guano contractors, which encouraged it to avoid adjustment. The fourth period ended with Peru holding out and the bondholders making some, but not many, concessions represented by their agreement to come to Lima despite their initial reluctance to do so.

In the fifth period, the bondholders kept up their pressure on the British government but failed to garner much support. For its part, Peru became more stable as Castilla consolidated his power. While its financial situation improved, however, its overall dependence on the contractors increased as its ability to secure loans from them declined. Although the model suggested that the Peruvians would be interested in promoting some changes in their individual situation in this period, those that took place did not appear to be the result of calculated efforts. As we have seen, the changed debt game of period five proved highly conducive to a settlement.

Aftermath

The 1849 rescheduling marked the end of a long epoch of default, but the restoration of Peruvian credit abroad proved hazardous. In the face of economic problems, the temptation to secure additional loans was irresistible. The worst

[66] Wynne (1951), pp. 110–111; Palacios (1983), p. 79.

[67] *The Times*, January 5, 1849, p. 6, cited in Mathew (1970), p. 95.

[68] Mathew (1970), p. 88.

example of this came soon after the 1849 agreement, after General José Rufino Echenique became president in 1851.

During his tenure, corruption grew as Echenique showed poor judgement in choosing his advisers.[69] During his term, the government increased its indebtedness through an improper conversion of internal debts into foreign debt bonds. Throughout its War of Independence and Caudillismo Period, Peru had accumulated a significant debt to its nationals, as well as to other South American republics. Domestic pressure mounted because the government pledged half of its guano proceeds for the debt owed to foreigners, but nothing for the debt owed to its own citizens. One year after the foreign debt agreement, the government promulgated a law consolidating the internal debt of the nation. This law called for the government to recognize all internal debts since the War of Independence and to issue a list of those who could apply for remuneration. The debt conversion began in 1850, and "turned into a gold rush" by 1853.[70] The internal debt was generously interpreted as a system of government handouts and fraud on a massive scale. The government accepted official Peruvian bonds as well as notes "scrawled" by various military chieftains.[71] As a result, the internal debt grew by a factor of six, from 4 million to nearly 24 million pesos during this time.[72] One observer stated that the Echenique regime had "placed millions of dollars in the pockets of its friends and had taken on a new external debt against which guano had been pledged in hypothecation."[73] An investigative commission in 1855 stated that 12,180,800 pesos of recognized claims were illegal.[74] One critic of the debt conversion accused the Echenique administration of "assuming through the consolidation a debt so vast that not even the guano reserves of Peru would be adequate to provide for its amortization."[75] Following this acceptance of the larger internal debt, Echenique proceeded to contract a loan in 1853 of £2.6 million, which turned a domestic obligation into a foreign one.

After 1853, Peru continued its policy of increased borrowing abroad. The creditors, however, were concerned that Peru's guano deposits were running out and that the internal debt conversion had not been legal. These fears resulted in much tougher new loan negotiations, particularly concerning stiff "sinking fund" requirements. Their skepticism about the future of the guano trade prompted the committee to seek an increase in the sinking fund on the 1853 bonds that were secured on guano reserves. Over the next 20 years, Peru would continue to use its guano to borrow for often questionable purposes. As Peru became increasingly indebted, it continued to negotiate to escape its debt quagmire.

Conclusion

As with Mexico, debt negotiations following Peru's early borrowing were long and involved. The bondholders and Peru remained locked in a standstill that

[69] Werlich (1978), p. 83. [70] Levin (1960), p. 80. [71] Werlich (1978), p. 83.
[72] See McQueen (1926), p. 5 and Werlich (1978), p. 83.
[73] Mathew (1968), p. 575. [74] Levin (1960), p. 81. [75] Pike (1967), p. 101.

lasted 16 years, without any prospects for a resolution of the outstanding default. After Peru's turn to the export market and exploitation of guano at the beginning of 1840, the bondholders appeared to be on the brink of enacting a favorable settlement. But whereas Peru could then afford a settlement, its instability did not make it particularly interested in doing so.

The changing fortunes of the guano market guided Peru's behavior. Although Peru faced a temporary problem during the third period of declining guano sales, it used its overall capabilities to press for loans from anxious guano contractors, thus helping the government to avoid any stringent economic adjustment.

Prospects for a settlement began to improve with Castilla's rise in the mid-1840s. Initially, Peru held firm in negotiations, and tried to use its capabilities to avoid an unfavorable settlement by once again turning to guano contractors. As the overborrowing continued, and as Castilla consolidated his position, however, the negotiations with the bondholders took an interesting turn in the fifth period. Peru appeared to almost bend over backward to resolve the debt problem, something we anticipated from the debt game of the period. As it turns out, Peruvian negotiators apparently benefited personally by speculating, and therefore signed on to an apparently unfavorable agreement.

Throughout the five periods we considered, the creditor governments played a relatively minor role and did little to press for a settlement different from the anticipated two-actor game. The expected equilibria from our debt games proved to be accurate for the most part for anticipating the empirical outcomes. Although our expectations of actors' efforts to promote situational changes were often accurate, most of the significant changes leading from one period to the next proved to be shocks exogenous to the model – such as the discovery of guano or a change in political leadership.

PART III

Epoch 2: 1860s–1910s

7 From stability to chaos: Mexican debt rescheduling, 1867–1914

In the mid-1860s, an important epochal shift began to take place in international debt rescheduling. Notable changes included the formation of the Council of the Corporation of Foreign Bondholders, a grouping that increased lenders' resources, giving them an opportunity to obtain better settlements.[1] In addition, France's military defeat by Prussia in 1871 left Britain as the dominant creditor government in international finance until the late 1880s, when Germany entered the competition for sovereign lending.

I divide the second epoch into five major periods. The first period is marked by the reforms of 1867–1876 that followed Maximilian's overthrow. The second begins in 1877 with the onset of the Porfiriato and concludes in 1886 with a major debt settlement. The third period, from 1888 to 1893, was a period of improved Mexican creditworthiness. During the fourth period, 1894 to 1910, lending to Mexico reached its zenith. The fifth and last period, 1911 to 1914, encompasses Díaz's fall from power in 1911, Madero's controversial succession, and Mexico's struggle with yet another revolution.

Period one, 1867–1876: conflict with creditors

After the displacement and execution of Maximilian, Juárez assumed the presidency, and along with it, an empty treasury. Because nearly all of Mexico's customs revenues had been pledged to its creditors, Juárez repudiated the obligations incurred under Maximilian soon after taking power. In particular, Juárez refused to accept Mexico's obligations on both 6% loans of 1864 and 1865, and on the 1864 conversion of arrears. His officials claimed: "The Republic neither can, nor ought, in any shape, [to] recognize the obligations which the Emperor of the French attempted to force upon her through his intervention in our domestic affairs."[2]

Juárez also denied the international characters of the Diplomatic Convention debts. Although he recognized Mexico's obligation to pay the "legitimate and recognized titles of this extinguished convention," he warned that Mexico would not be bound by "terms of payments stipulated in a no longer existing arrangement."[3] Juárez did accept liability for the principal of the London debt and indicated that his government was prepared to consider new arrangements.

[1] See Chapter 2 for details.

[2] *Foreign Relations of the United States* (1868), p. 410, cited in Turlington (1930), p. 172.

[3] Dip. Cor. U.S. (1868), vol. 2, p. 419, cited in Turlington (1930), p. 174.

Identifying individual situations

At the beginning of the first period in this epoch, Mexico was coalitionally unstable, issue weak, and overall strong (IS 4). The bondholders were coalitionally stable, issue weak, and overall strong (IS 3).

Mexico. A stable domestic coalition did not accompany Juárez's return to power. Liberals and conservatives had united behind Juárez to overthrow Maximilian, but without a common enemy, their alliance was fragile at best. Moreover, the liberals in Juárez's administration split over how to treat those who had collaborated with the Maximilian regime.[4] Juárez's victory did not curtail the use of private armies, widespread banditry, or minor rebellions in the countryside.[5] When Sebástian Lerdo de Tejada took office following Juárez's death in 1872, he managed to bring some stability to Mexico for a short time. Fraught with political conflict, Lerdo's term ended in a takeover by Porfirio Díaz in 1876.

Juárez's repudiation of the obligations incurred under Maximilian was indicative of the chaotic nature of Mexican finances. Realizing that Maximilian had already pledged most of Mexico's revenues, Juárez even repudiated the assignment of customs duties incurred *before* the foreign intervention. The wars of reform and the French-led intervention had severely hurt Mexican commerce, industry, mining, and agriculture. As a result, Mexico slid deeper into bankruptcy.

With Juárez in power, however, Mexico regained its sovereign powers and overall capabilities. No longer would the Mexican government and army be subject to the control of the European powers. Early in his term, Juárez announced his disinterest in restoring relations with the European nations that had driven him from power.[6] Although Juárez reduced his troops to 16,000 men, he still retained control of the army.[7] In addition, Juárez did not fear the bondholders or their governments. No European government cared to intervene in Mexico on behalf of their private lenders after the last period's disastrous consequences.[8] With relations severed between Mexico and most of the European creditor governments, and with the end of the U.S. Civil War, the lenders could do Mexico little economic harm.

In 1868, Juárez negotiated an important agreement with an English company (the Mexican National Railway Company) for the construction of a railroad from Veracruz to Mexico City, a project eventually completed in 1873.[9] The government agreed to pay the British firm a subsidy of 560,000 pesos for 25 years, secured on a portion of customs revenues.[10] In general, however, Juárez aimed to free the country from its dependence on foreign investments for development. Despite signs of growth from industry and commerce, they were "still

[4] Priestley (1923/1969), p. 365. [5] Parkes (1938/1969), p. 280.
[6] Turlington (1930), pp. 173–174. [7] Priestley (1923/1969), p. 365.
[8] Turlington (1930), p. 173. [9] Parkes (1938/1969), p. 279.
[10] Plumb's no. 222, November 14, 1868, Dip. Cor. U.S. (1868), vol. 2, pp. 614–616, cited in Turlington (1930), p. 185.

controlled mainly by foreigners."[11] Juárez's priorities were reforms such as the economy's revitalization and improvement of the country's educational system,[12] and he hoped that they would decrease foreign influence in Mexico's internal economy, increasing Mexico's overall capabilities.

Lenders. The bondholders remained united in their Committee of Mexican Bondholders. More significantly, the Committee began to work with the newly formed London-based Council of the Corporation of Foreign Bondholders. Although the Committee of Mexican Bondholders did not officially forge an alliance with the Council until 1876, the Council made representations to Mexico on the creditors' behalf.[13] By working with the Council, the Mexican bondholders further increased their coalitional strength while aligning themselves with other countries' lenders. Moreover, Juárez's stinging repudiation and denial of the "international character" of Mexican debts ensured that all creditors would receive the same treatment.[14]

The Committee continued to lack the financial resources to cover its expenses and its agents' salaries. With the repudiation of the two Maximilian loans and the conversion of interest arrears on the London debt, the bondholders lost a significant amount of their outstanding principal. In addition, the end of Maximilian's monarchy denied the lenders the advantage of dealing with a Mexican government solicitous of their interests. The monarchy's collapse also signaled the end of the alliance between the lenders and their governments. In its place, however, the Council was a powerful institution in both European and international financial circles, and this alliance allowed bondholders greater influence over other European creditors and capitalists.

Creditor governments. After Maximilian's fall, the British government reverted to its traditional non-intervention policy in private debt matters. Juárez's refusal of diplomatic relations with the British diminished their influence over Mexico. Local British officials in Mexico argued that only force would sway Juárez, but the British government refused to countenance such an alternative. Although still concerned about U.S. influence over Mexico, British strategists realized they could do little as long as Juárez refused to resume relations with Britain.

The French government, embroiled in conflict with Prussia, did not have the interest or the resources to get involved in the debt issue. In an effort to assuage French bondholders' complaints, the French government did, however, accept a liability for the 1864–1865 Maximilian loans that Juárez had recently repudiated, agreeing to pay one-half of the face value of the bonds to their holders.[15]

[11] Parkes (1938/1969), p. 278.
[12] Meyer and Sherman (1987), p. 404. See also Parkes (1938/1969), pp. 279–280.
[13] Wynne (1951), p. 35.
[14] Dip. Cor. U.S. (1868), vol. 2, p. 378, cited in Turlington (1930), p. 174.
[15] This paragraph draws on Turlington (1930), pp. 173–179.

Cardinal Payoff Matrix,
No Intervention Expected

		Lenders IS 3		
		HC...	MC...	LC...
	HA...	−3, 9	−6.5, 9.67	−9, 10.33
Mexico IS 4	MA...	1.67, 5.5	−2, 6	−5, 6.5
	LA...	**6.33, 3**	**2.5, 3**	**−1, 3**

Note: Nash equilibria bolded.

Ordinal Payoff Matrix,
No Intervention Expected

		Lenders IS 3		
		HC...	MC...	LC...
	HA...	4, 7	2, 8	1, 9
Mexico IS 4	MA...	7, 4	5, 5	3, 6
	LA...	**9, 2**	**8, 2**	**6, 2**

Note: Nash equilibria bolded.

Figure 7.1. *Play phase, period one: 1867–1876*

But overall, French security concerns shifted from the North American to the European continent.

Debt game and predicted outcome

From Mexico's classification as coalitionally unstable, issue weak, and overall strong (IS 4), and the bondholders' as united, issue weak, and overall strong (IS 3), we obtain the debt game shown in Figure 7.1. The game has three Nash equilibria (low adjustment by the debtor and either high, medium, or low concessions by the lender). We would, however, expect an outcome of little adjustment and few concessions because lenders have nothing to gain (and could lose) by undertaking concessions, regardless of whether Mexico adjusts. Additionally, because lenders would receive the same payoff across strategies if Mexico undertakes no adjustment, they would have no incentive to help Mexico improve its payoff.

In fact, because Juárez had repudiated Maximilian's loans and the 1864 conversion, and had even revoked customs duties pledges assigned before the European intervention and the onset of the monarchy, the bondholders could have expected Juárez to undertake no adjustments. High bondholder concessions, however, would give Mexico a higher payoff. Hence, if the bondholders were concerned for Mexico's well-being or wanted to maintain a cooperative atmosphere in debt negotiations, they would make high concessions. On the other hand, if they wanted to punish or hurt Mexico, as is the case, bondholders would make few concessions, giving Mexico a lower, unfavorable payoff. As noted, creditor governments were not interested in intervening in debt negotiations given their changing strategic interests and the end of the U.S. Civil War. Thus, we do not expect intervention in this game.

The negotiations and outcome

No satisfactory debt settlement graced the period from 1867 to 1876. As predicted by the model, during this period Mexico assumed a tough stance on its debt. Juárez's repudiation went largely unchallenged by the creditors and their governments; Mexican officials believed bondholders would grant high concessions without demanding major adjustments from Mexico. Juárez, however, miscalculated his ability to secure this favorable outcome. He presumed that since the bondholders had lost creditor government support, their position required them to make high concessions as they had earlier. In this case, however, the bondholders compensated for the loss of creditor governments' power with their own resources, drawing on the strength of their new affiliation with the Council. Frustrated by Mexico's tough stance, the bondholders resolved not to make concessions to Mexico – a scenario consistent with our theoretical expectations.

Early in 1868, the Mexican government initiated the Romero Plan (named after one of Juárez's top officials), which allowed Mexico to repurchase its foreign bonds at favorable prices. The administration allocated 50,000 pesos per month to buy the outstanding bonds at public auction, thus enabling Mexico to reduce its foreign debt. Within a few months, the Mexican government had bought over 1 million pesos' worth of outstanding bonds for only 204,995 pesos of hard cash.[16] In May 1868, Congress appropriated an additional 1 million pesos to buy the outstanding bonds. Representatives of the Committee of Mexican Bondholders, negotiating with Mexico over the resumption of interest payments, fumed at this appropriation. Nevertheless, because of the Romero Plan's success, the Mexican Minister of Finance argued against any congressional

[16] See Turlington (1930), p. 177, n. 14 for sources.

appropriation of money for interest payments. Mexico continued to resist, refusing to make any interest payments to its creditors.

In 1869, a bondholder representative proposed a new arrangement by which Mexico would pledge certain territories as collateral to the U.S. in exchange for an American guarantee to service the Mexican debt. In exchange, the bondholders would reduce the debt principal from 90 to 50 million pesos. The Mexicans immediately rejected this offer. The Minister of Foreign Affairs, Sebastián Lerdo de Tejada, expressed their fear: "Oh no! That would never do, never do, it would place us under the tutelage of Americans!"[17]

The following year, Lerdo proposed a new arrangement on the London debt.[18] This proposal called for the cancellation of almost half of the debt; in exchange, Mexico would grant a concession to the creditors on a canal construction project across the Isthmus of Tehuantepec. The 1870 proposal called for the conversion of the London debt bonds into new active bonds (which would immediately collect interest) and deferred bonds (which would collect interest in 10 years) at the rate of £100 worth of old bonds for only £50 worth of new bonds. As compensation, Lerdo proposed to increase interest on the new bonds to 6% and grant the creditors the canal concession, which they could sell. In addition, the bondholders would surrender their mortgage on a portion of Mexican customs revenues in exchange for a hypothecation on the dues charged upon the proposed canal.

Mexico hoped to use its foreign creditors to finance its ambitious public works program. Aside from the canal project, this program included the Mexican National Railway concession and other railroad construction projects by U.S. and European firms. The government thus attempted to tactically link its foreign debt and its domestic – but foreign-financed – public works program. The bondholders, however, rejected this linkage. The Committee of Mexican Bondholders stipulated that any arrangement would have to retain the original customs revenues' security until some other tangible security could be offered (unlike the hypothecation on the canal), and that the capital amount of the debt must be preserved.

In 1871, Mexico once again faced renewed political struggles. Against the advice of his advisors, Juárez decided to run for reelection against two of his former supporters, Sebástian Lerdo and Porfirio Díaz. The split election was submitted to the Congress, which reelected Juárez. In response, Díaz declared himself in open rebellion against the government. He accused Juárez of violating the Revolution's liberal principles by seeking indefinite reelection (it was Juárez's fourth term), but the government easily crushed Díaz's revolt. When Juárez died the following July, Lerdo inherited the presidency.[19] He continued Juárez's policies, including the public works program. He also proposed a new railway

[17] Rosecrans' no. 36, March 3, 1869, MS. Desp. Mex., vol. 35, cited in Turlington (1930), p. 182.
[18] The next three paragraphs draw heavily from the Corporation of Foreign Bondholders (1876), cited in Wynne (1951), pp. 31–33.
[19] Parkes (1938/1969), pp. 281–282.

to the U.S. border and granted a U.S. concern the canal concession that had been offered to the bondholders.

During this time, the bondholders began working with the Corporation of Foreign Bondholders and also appealed once again to the British government, calling on it to at least restore diplomatic relations with Mexico.[20] In addition, they also attempted to block Mexico's access to foreign capital and investment for development. In 1871, when the Mexican National Railway (an English enterprise) attempted to float a £1.2 million bond loan on the London market, the bondholders protested. They argued that no loan secured by the revenues of Mexico should be floated while the bondholders remained "unsatisfied and unpaid."[21] The bondholders made a similar protest in 1874, when the same company applied for a £260,000 bond loan,[22] but the London Stock Exchange rejected the creditors' pleas, allowing the loans to be issued.

In 1874, the Council issued a stronger warning to Mexico, saying the country would no longer be allowed to raise capital on the European markets.[23] This warning persuaded Lerdo to reopen negotiations with the bondholders; yet before the talks produced an agreement, the government once again faced political turmoil. When Lerdo sought reelection in 1876, Díaz restaged his revolt, arguing that Lerdo had "sacrificed Mexico's best interests."[24] Moreover, Díaz declared that any contract between the government and the bondholders of the English debt would be "null and void."[25] In November, Díaz's forces defeated Lerdo at Tlaxcala, and by the end of the month, Díaz captured Mexico City. The following year, Díaz assumed the presidency and informed the Mexican Congress that Mexico was about to begin a new era.[26]

Summary. As anticipated, negotiations produced no settlement of the debt problem during the first period of this epoch, leading to an outcome of LA..., LC... Mexico purchased its outstanding bonds rather than satisfying its creditors, and Juárez refused to restore diplomatic relations with the European creditor governments. In addition, the government aimed to link any debt settlement to several national public works projects.

These actions served only to alienate the bondholders. In the end, Juárez's tough strategy backfired; as the model predicted, the bondholders had little incentive to make any concessions. The bondholders instead joined with the powerful Council of the Corporation of Foreign Bondholders, which threatened to block Mexico's access to new foreign capital and investment. This threat fostered Mexican overtures for a new settlement with the bondholders, but Díaz's revolt and his rise to power stymied the negotiations.

20 Turlington (1930), pp. 186–187.
21 Committee of Mexican Bondholders (1876), Appendix III, cited in Wynne (1951), p. 34.
22 Wynne (1951), pp. 34–35.
23 Council of Foreign Bondholders (1874), p. 44, cited in Turlington (1930), p. 188.
24 Meyer and Sherman (1987), p. 414.
25 *Foreign Relations of the United States* (1877), p. 386, cited in Turlington (1930), p. 189.
26 *Foreign Relations of the United States* (1878), pp. 526–543, cited in Turlington (1930), p. 190.

Situational changes

The bondholders responded to their poor payoff from the deadlock in this period by making considerable efforts to use norms, capabilities, and allies to maintain a strong unified coalition. This effort indeed proved helpful, preventing Lerdo from taking advantage of them.

Porfirio Díaz's rise in 1877, however, would prove to be the most significant change leading to the second period. His political ascension led to a new individual situation for Mexico and its first period of sustained political stability and economic progress since its independence. His financial reforms improved Mexico's creditworthiness abroad. On the downside, Díaz's eagerness to curry favor with foreign investors made Mexico vulnerable to the bondholders' efforts to block Mexico's access to foreign capital. Thus, Mexico became weak in overall resources.

Period two, 1877–1887: Díaz settles

Porfirio Díaz's ascension to the presidency in 1877 marked a new era in Mexican history known as "the Porfiriato." Except for the period from 1880 to 1884 (when he stepped aside to allow his Vice-President, Manuel González, to take office), Díaz dominated the Mexican presidency until 1911.

Many of the policies implemented during the Porfiriato were based on reforms developed by Díaz's two predecessors, Juárez and Lerdo. As one study notes: "All of the major changes generally attributed to Díaz and his successive cabinets in the last quarter of the nineteenth century and the first decade of the twentieth are firmly rooted in the years 1867 to 1876."[27] Nevertheless, Díaz carried out these policies to their fullest. He felt that order and political stability were necessary to attract foreign capital and investment. In particular, Díaz believed that Mexico needed to settle its outstanding foreign debt to reopen foreign credit lines.

The 1886 settlement, as we shall see, marked the beginning of a sharp transition in Mexico's international debt history. Díaz channeled the infusion of foreign capital to develop the country's resources and national infrastructure, to support the national Treasury during times of fiscal crisis, and to redeem and consolidate various external and internal debts that matured during this time.

Identifying individual situations

During this period, Mexico's situation evolved to a position of high coalitional stability, but issue and overall weakness (IS 7). The bondholders remained united, issue weak, and overall strong (IS 3).

Mexico. Díaz sought to bring order to Mexico through various means. He quelled rebellion in the countryside by increasing the power, jurisdiction,

[27] Meyer and Sherman (1987), p. 414.

and appropriations for the *rurales* – the rural police force – who assumed a major peace-keeping role. Díaz did not hesitate to crush his rivals if he could not buy them off first – adhering to the dictum *pan o palo* (bread or the club).[28] During his first year, in reaction to a revolt and potential conspiracy in Veracruz, Díaz ordered the provincial governor to execute the conspirators, resulting in the death of nine people.[29]

Mexican finances were in pitiful condition when Díaz took power: he inherited an empty treasury, enormous foreign debts, and an unpaid military corps. Immediately after defeating Lerdo, Díaz requested a 500,000 peso loan from the merchants and capitalists of Mexico City. This effort was only partially successful, as he failed to raise the full amount. Díaz then enacted a 6 to 10% tax on the profits of all classes of property to increase government revenues.[30]

At the beginning of Díaz's regime, the Mexican economy remained stagnant. Mining and agriculture had not yet recovered from Mexico's many wars and rebellions. Trade suffered from a severe imbalance, with imports far outstripping exports.[31] In addition, rampant smuggling spurred Díaz to introduce harsh new punishments, including imprisonment, for smugglers caught in Mexican ports. Industry was the only hope for the country's future. Under Díaz's leadership, Mexico gradually made economic progress, industry and trade developed, and the government increased its revenues to cover expenses.

In overall capabilities, Mexico retained sovereign powers. But unlike Juárez, Díaz wanted to attract foreign – and especially European – capital and investment to Mexico. He made clear his feeling that Mexico's economic growth and well-being depended on capital from Europe and America. As a result, Díaz revealed Mexico's vulnerability to other foreign powers. As bondholders continued their efforts to block Mexico's access to foreign sources of capital and investment, Díaz got the message: Mexico would have to address the bondholders' outstanding claims before it would receive foreign capital to develop its economy.

Lenders. In this period, the bondholders remained in the same situation as before. Their affiliation with the Council of the Corporation of Foreign Bondholders had brought the Mexican bondholders into a powerful alliance. Despite the Council's status, the Committee of Mexican Bondholders and bondholders continued to remain financially weak. More importantly, however, the bondholders' association with the Council strengthened their overall capabilities. Despite their failed attempts in 1871 and 1874, during this period the creditors continued their efforts to block Mexico's access to foreign capital markets. Díaz's desire for foreign aid, capital, and cooperation enabled the bondholders to finally force Mexico to the bargaining table to meet their demands.

[28] Parkes (1938/1969), p. 286. [29] Parkes (1938/1969), p. 288.
[30] *Foreign Relations of the United States* (1877), pp. 385–395, cited in Turlington (1930), p. 190.
[31] Meyer and Sherman (1987), p. 432.

Creditor governments. During the second period, the British government continued its non-intervention policy in the debt issue. Not until 1884 were diplomatic relations restored between Mexico and Great Britain; France restored relations in 1880.

During this period, British security and strategic interests shifted from North America to Europe. Bismarck's victory in the Franco-Prussian War and Germany's subsequent rise threatened the European balance of power that had existed since the Congress of Vienna. Britain became mired in an industrial, political, and military competition with Germany that would precipitate the First World War. Thus, European security interests were the British government's first concern; its interest in Mexico and the Mexican foreign debt waned.

Debt game and predicted outcome

In this period, Mexico was coalitionally stable, issue weak, and weak in overall capabilities (IS 7), and the bondholders were coalitionally stable, issue weak, and overall strong (IS 3). The model predicts the debt game shown in Figure 7.2.

We predict the following combination of strategies based on the Nash equilibrium. We expect the bondholders to remain intransigent because regardless of whether Mexico adjusts or not, the lenders receive their higher preference by yielding no concessions. Mexico's best strategy is one of high adjustment. As in the first period, we expect a continued absence of intervention by creditor governments in the debt negotiations.

The negotiations and outcome

Period two opened with Díaz's rise to power and concluded with the settlement of both the London debt and Diplomatic Convention debts. This period consists of two negotiating rounds: the first, from 1876 until 1884, ended with a short-lived London debt agreement; the second concluded in 1887 with the definitive settlement of the outstanding debts.

Round one. In late 1878, the Mexican government proposed a London debt settlement similar to the old canal concession proposal. This arrangement called for a similar conversion and consolidation of the debt, plus 18 other obligations, at the rate of 50%. As compensation, the interest rate on the new bonds would increase from 3 to 6% and the creditors would receive a concession to build a railroad from Mexico City to the Pacific Coast. Because of its similarity to the canal plan, the bondholders disliked this arrangement. As a result, Mexico again sold the concession to an American concern. With this action, Mexico gave up its attempt to tactically link the debt issue to its public works projects.[32]

Despite this failure, Díaz remained committed to settling the debt. Accordingly, he created the Banco Nacional de México to stabilize Mexico's financial

[32] Corporation of Foreign Bondholders (1880), p. 41.

Cardinal Payoff Matrix,
No Intervention Expected

		Lenders IS 3 HC...	MC...	LC...
	HA...	12, 9	9, 9.67	**10, 10.33**
Mexico IS 7	MA...	11.67, 5.5	8, 6	7, 6.5
	LA...	11.33, 3	7, 3	4, 3

Note: Nash equilibrium bolded.

Ordinal Payoff Matrix,
No Intervention Expected

		Lenders IS 3 HC...	MC...	LC...
	HA...	9, 7	5, 8	**6, 9**
Mexico IS 7	MA...	8, 4	4, 5	2.5, 6
	LA...	7, 2	2.5, 2	1, 2

Note: Nash equilibrium bolded.

Figure 7.2. *Play phase, period two: 1877–1886*

community, instituted several measures to lower government expenditures (including cutting his salary and those of other officials), and created a committee to formulate a new debt settlement.

In 1882, the bondholders took advantage of an opportunity to realize their 1874 threat to block Mexican loans. Again, the Mexican National Railway Company (the American firm given the concession to build a railway from Mexico City to the Pacific) attempted to float a loan in London, this time for £2 million. The company was to receive a $10,000 British government subsidy per mile of track laid, secured on a portion of the customs receipts claimed by the bondholders. The Council protested loudly against the flotation; still, the London Stock Market refused to revoke the loan. Some people argued correctly that the loan would help the bondholders by fostering Mexico's economic development and by increasing its ability to satisfy creditors. *The Times* wrote, "The bondholders may rest assured that, if they are ever to witness an amelioration of their position, it will be mainly owing to the railway and the new life it may introduce."[33]

The bondholders, however, refused to recognize a substantive link between the railway loan, the development of Mexico's public works projects, and Mexico's ability to service its debt. Instead, they continued to protest the flotation. Ultimately, the loan was allowed on the market, but due to the creditors' efforts, the loan was soon withdrawn when few of the bonds were sold.

Worried about the repercussions of this successful blocking action, Mexican President Manuel González (Díaz's former Vice-President who served as a figurehead for Díaz from 1880–1884) sent a representative to London in the spring of 1883 to settle the debt. By May, the negotiators created a new agreement that would have converted the London debt into new 3% bonds totaling £15.3 million. In addition, the accord would have allowed the Mexican government to float £4.7 million in bonds for its own uses. The Mexican Congress, however, rejected this agreement. Congress passed a law on June 14, 1883, that called for the consolidation of Mexico's external debts and their conversion into a new 3% bond debt. The agreement specified that the consolidated debt must be of a purely national character (without any international status), must not include "illegitimate" debts, and must not be secured by any specific revenues.

Based in part on these conditions, Díaz, who had begun his new term in 1884, negotiated a debt settlement in September 1884. A new bond loan of £17.2 million would be floated for the conversion of the London debt bonds (at a rate of £112 worth of the new bonds for £100 worth of the old) and the bonds covering the arrears (at the rate of 52 new for 100 old). In addition, the new bonds' interest rate would increase from 2 to 3%, and would be secured by a pledge of 10% of all import duties, a violation of the Law of July 14, 1883.[34]

The bondholders accepted the agreement because it was the most favorable they had been offered for some time. No part of the debt was to be exchanged for a public works concession, and the exchange rate favored them. Moreover, the creditors believed that because "the government was more stable than it had been since the intervention, and the revenues were increasing rapidly,"[35] the Díaz Administration could make the payments due on the new bonds.

With this agreement at the end of round one, the bondholders felt they had received a favorable outcome. To their great disappointment, however, the accord proved short-lived. The Mexican press attacked the arrangement because its conversion rate hurt Mexico, and because its pledge of specific revenues

[33] July 22, 1871, cited in Wynne (1951), p. 36. [34] Wynne (1951), pp. 37–38.
[35] Turlington (1930), p. 197.

violated the July 14, 1883, law. Public opposition forced the Mexican legislature to adjourn in 1884 without even considering the agreement, which they subsequently canceled.

Round two. In 1884, Mexico and Great Britain restored diplomatic relations. As part of this accord, Mexico acknowledged liability for amounts due on the Convention debt and other claims. In return, Britain promised not to intervene in Mexican negotiations with British bondholders. On behalf of Great Britain, Sir Spenser St. John agreed "that his government would not in the future invoke in support of British subjects any Treaty, Convention, pact, or agreement between the two countries."[36]

With Díaz's return to the presidency in 1884, Mexico placed renewed emphasis on settling its foreign debt. Moreover, Díaz continued to recognize the need for continued internal economic adjustments to settle the debt and refurbish Mexico's financial image abroad. As one study noted:

> He saw clearly that to gain the confidence of investors, it would be necessary not only to settle the default on the foreign debts, but to strengthen the public finances by cutting ordinary expenditures and by reducing to an orderly basis the heterogeneous mass of unconsolidated internal debts.[37]

Díaz created a commission to prepare a comprehensive financial readjustment plan. As a part of this effort in June 1885, Díaz issued three decrees: the first temporarily reduced all salaries of civilian and military government workers above 500 pesos by 10 to 50%; the second consolidated the floating debt incurred after 1882 into new 6% Treasury bonds; and the third converted all external debts incurred before 1882 into new bonds with an interest rate gradually increasing from 1 to 3%. The new bonds were to be known as the Consolidated debt of the United Mexican States. Moreover, the debt would be secured not by any specific revenue assignments, but by funds in the Banco Nacional de Mexico – funds received directly from the customhouses at Veracruz. The Consolidated debt would be purely national.[38]

In June 1886, negotiators reached an agreement on the London debt on this basis. London debt bonds were converted at the rate of 50% of their face value into the Consolidated debt bonds, and the 1864 bonds covering arrears were to be converted at the rate of 15%. In December of that year, the Convention debt was similarly settled; the old bonds were converted at a rate of 71% of the face value into the new bonds. An important aspect of the agreement was Mexico's right to redeem these new bonds in cash at 40% of face value by 1890.

By August 1888, when the conversion offer expired, over 99% of the London debt and Convention debt bonds had been exchanged. Overall, the value of the

[36] *Brit. For. State Papers*, vol. 75, 1883–1884, pp. 908–911.
[37] Wynne (1951), p. 39. See also Parkes (1938/1969), p. 297.
[38] Wynne (1951), p. 39. The following two paragraphs' discussion of the agreements is based on Wynne (1951), pp. 39–46.

London debt shrank from £22 to £14 million of the Consolidated debt, and this was paid off two years later by £5.5 million in cash. The Convention debt's value eventually dropped down to a value of £872,000 of the new debt, and was paid off later by the sum of £350,000.

Summary. In this period, the creditors used their overall power to block Mexican access to new foreign capital and to force Mexico into making serious adjustments. Díaz, the first leader to bring significant economic stability to the country, encouraged foreign investment. His important financial reforms improved Mexico's creditworthiness abroad. After Díaz implemented strict economic adjustments, the bondholders agreed to convert their debts into a new consolidated bond issue, but still refused new loans to Mexico.

Overall, bondholders fared very well in the new agreement, considering the constant defaults, repudiations, conversions, and rescheduling agreements they had weathered in the past. The holders of the London debt bonds recovered all of their principal in 1888 with interest averaging 2.3% a year on the 1824 bond issues, and 1.1% on the 1825 bond issues.[39] The British bondholders made few concessions and did not immediately offer Mexico new loans. In fact, for a period of time after the settlement, British bankers and foreign investors were wary of any loans to Mexico, because of their familiarity with Mexico's history of offering empty promises to service its foreign debts.

Situational changes

Following the major 1886 debt settlement, Mexico continued its stabilization policies, both economically and politically. The settlement had cleared the way for new foreign borrowing by the Mexican government. Díaz's primary motivation in undertaking adjustment measures and settling the outstanding foreign debt had been reopening the European money markets to new Mexican borrowing. During period three, his strategy paid off. German capitalists, newly flush with cash from their nation's industrial development, brought lending opportunities to Mexico. Undeterred by British bondholders' problems with Mexico, the House of Bleichröder sponsored a new Mexican loan in 1888, opening a new period of foreign lending to Mexico and a new relationship with Mexico.

British lenders, however, shied away from new involvement with Mexico partially because their high payoff in the previous period discouraged them from trying to change their own or Mexico's individual situation. The entrance of new lenders into the market created a new situation for bondholders, with little leverage to block Mexico's access to foreign capital.

Period three, 1888–1893: Germany fills the vacuum

The Díaz government used new foreign capital not only for the national Treasury's immediate needs and the long-term economic development of the country,

[39] Turlington (1930), p. 6. See also Wynne (1951), p. 46.

but also to redeem, consolidate, and readjust its foreign debt. The new borrowing, in essence, allowed the government to change the terms of its outstanding debt. The new lenders' strong interest in making new loans to Mexico, combined with the latter's continued stabilization efforts, created a relatively harmonious period in Mexico's debt history.

Identifying individual situations

In this period, we classify Mexico as coalitionally stable, issue weak, and overall weak (IS 7) – the same as in the second period. We also classify the bondholders as coalitionally stable, issue weak, and overall weak (IS 7).

Mexico. Díaz's tightening grip on Mexico resulted in a long period of political stability. His harsh "pacification program" succeeded in quieting rebellion and unrest in the countryside. Throughout his rule, Díaz consolidated his power, becoming a virtual dictator. He prevented the rise of any organized opposition using a combination of adroit political maneuvers, threats, and when required, the federal army and the *rurales*. The government manipulated the periodic elections, censored the press, and harassed journalists.[40] Personally monitoring all potential rivals inside his ruling group, the president transferred ambitious men to the countryside to undermine their potential for unification and conspiracy.

Financially, the Mexican government remained in crisis. The 1886 debt settlement readjusted the nation's foreign debt, but it failed to provide immediate help for the financially strapped Mexican Treasury. During this time, government expenditures continued to outstrip revenues, despite Díaz's early efforts to control the excesses of the bureaucracy and reduce the budget. Disastrous harvests in 1891 and 1892 and a drop in the value of silver the same year prevented a quicker financial recovery.[41] Railway subsidies continued to drain revenues while the government searched for "the best possible terms" for their capitalization.[42] The financial situation did, however, improve gradually under the economic policies of the Minister of Treasury, José Limantour. He launched a series of financial reforms including a new tariff system and peso strengthening efforts that greatly improved Mexico's finances.

As for overall capabilities, Mexico continued to retain its sovereign powers, but badly needed capital and foreign technology to develop its economy and infrastructure. Mexico remained a rural country without significant industry. The nation faced poor communications (especially railways), a lack of energy sources, and a dearth of health and sanitation facilities. The government could not undertake large-scale programs without external help. In short, Mexico remained in a weak overall position.

[40] Parkes (1938/1969), pp. 194–195. [41] *The Economist*, May 4, 1895, p. 583.
[42] *The Economist*, May 10, 1890, p. 585.

Lenders. Mexico's bondholders continued to present a united position to the nation's government because of their affiliation with the Council of the Corporation of Foreign Bondholders. The 1886 settlement further cemented their unity. By consolidating and converting nearly all of the government's prior loans and foreign debts into a single bond issue, this settlement created one unified group of creditors – all of whom carried the new bonds.

In this period, however, a significant change occurred in the bondholders' overall capabilities. Prior to the 1886 agreement, bondholders successfully blocked the Mexican government's access to new foreign lending. With the debt consolidation and conversion, however, the bondholders no longer had a basis to protest the flotation of new loans and capital to the Díaz government. Moreover, although the holders of Mexican bonded debt hesitated to lend to Mexico, new lenders and investors were clearly very interested in the prospects of providing foreign capital to the country.

Creditor governments. Having just restored diplomatic relations with Mexico in 1884, Britain had no intention of alienating the new Díaz government. Moreover, the growing German challenge to British dominance in Europe focused the British Foreign Office's attention on the continent, and away from North America.

The U.S. government preferred economic penetration to direct intervention in Mexican affairs. It was extremely interested in trade liberalization and foreign investment. In addition, Díaz's changes in the old Spanish tradition of ownership and the expansion of presidential concessions discouraged U.S. intervention.

Debt game and predicted outcome

Following the conclusion of the 1886 debt settlement, we place both Mexico and the bondholders in IS 7. Our theoretical model produces the debt game matrix shown in Figure 7.3. The matrix represents a Harmony game, which gives both players their highest payoffs with a strategy combination of HA... and HC... In this case, unlike the games we have seen earlier, we expect both players to seek the "cooperative" outcome as a result of their payoff structures.

In view of the European creditor governments' focus on the continent, and American wariness of direct involvement in Mexico, we would expect no significant creditor government intervention in this debt game. Consequently, the expected outcome remains at the two-actor Nash equilibrium.

The negotiations and outcome

This third period is divided into two rounds, from 1888 to 1890, when Mexico secured a loan from Bleichröder, and from the end of 1890 to 1893, a time of growing financial problems in Mexico.

Round one. Although the 1886 debt settlement provided no new funds to Mexico, it reopened the government's access to European money markets. At

Cardinal Payoff Matrix,
No Intervention Expected

		Lenders IS 7		
		HC...	MC...	LC...
	HA...	**12, 12**	9, 11.67	10, 11.33
Mexico IS 7	MA...	11.67, 9	8, 8	7, 7
	LA...	11.33, 10	7, 7	4, 4

Note: Nash equilibrium bolded.

Ordinal Payoff Matrix,
No Intervention Expected

		Lenders IS 7		
		HC...	MC...	LC...
	HA...	**9, 9**	5, 8	6, 7
Mexico IS 7	MA...	8, 5	4, 4	2.5, 2.5
	LA...	7, 6	2.5, 2.5	1, 1

Note: Nash equilibrium bolded.

Figure 7.3. *Play phase, period three: 1888–1893*

the time, the Díaz government desperately needed new funds to meet its domestic obligations, to further railway construction throughout the country, and to meet the redemption option on the 1886 bond issues due in 1890. If the government could find the necessary funds, Mexico could redeem the whole of the 1886 outstanding debt at the advantageous rate of only 40 cents to the dollar.[43]

In December 1887, the Mexican Congress authorized the Executive to negotiate a new £10.5 million bond, 70% in cash, at a maximum interest rate of 6%. English creditors were still wary of renewed lending to Mexico, but German

[43] Turlington (1930), p. 212.

capitalists, particularly Bleichröder of Berlin, had ample new funds and were more forthcoming. In March 1888, Bleichröder and the Mexican government reached an accord on a £10.5 million loan at 6% interest and secured upon 20% of the customs receipts of the country.[44] Over one-third, £3.7 million, was floated at 70% of the bonds' face value. The flotation on European markets proved extremely successful and profitable for the Bleichröder group (the issues were nearly 20 times oversubscribed). The popularity of the bonds stemmed in large part from many capitalists' belief that Mexico was entering a period of unprecedented prosperity from which international financiers could profit.[45] Bankers took up the remainder of the loan (£6.8 million) at 85% of face value.

Some of the new funds provided a six-month advance in interest (as stipulated in the new loan agreement) and enabled the redemption of Mexico's railway bond and floating debt. But most of the new loan (nearly £6.8 million) went toward the exchange and redemption of the London debt and 1886 Conversion bonds. Because of this loan, the Díaz government engineered a major improvement in its financial picture. The Bleichröder loan conversion reduced Mexico's outstanding foreign debt from over £23 million in 1885 to only £12.1 million in 1889.[46]

Mexico achieved financial success not only because of new German investors, but also because of a continued program of strong economic adjustment under Díaz. As one financial newspaper reported, "the expenses authorized by the Budget have been met regularly and without recourse to extraordinary means." This led to a strong demand for Mexican bonds reflected in the quick rise of the price of the initial German bonds to 93.5% by April 1889.[47] Other international creditors envied Bleichröder's success. American financiers were "disgusted" that Mexico had not placed the loan in the U.S., while the English were "very much surprised" that a German banking house could provide better terms than themselves.[48]

Round two. Following the 1888 Bleichröder loan, Mexico managed to float additional loans from German financiers for railway construction. Mexico's favorable circumstances enticed others to its loan market. In September 1890, American Minister Thomas Ryan reported that a committee of English and French bankers considered providing Mexico with a new loan to consolidate the nation's entire outstanding debt. These creditors hoped to partake of the tremendous profits the Bleichröder group had enjoyed on their latest loans. Although this particular loan never materialized, the creditor group offered to advance a £6 million deposit in good faith.[49]

[44] See *The Economist*, March 3, 1888, p. 280; Wynne (1951), pp. 47–48; and Turlington (1930), p. 212 for details of the loan discussed in this paragraph.

[45] See the *New York Times*, May 22, 1888, p. 9 and *The Bullionist*, London, March 31, 1888, cited in Turlington (1930), p. 213.

[46] Turlington (1930), pp. 214–215.

[47] *The Economist*, April 27, 1889, p. 540.

[48] *New York Times*, January 7, 1888.

[49] Turlington (1930), pp. 217–220.

As expected, creditor governments maintained their non-intervention policies. Rumors circulated that French nationals holding claims on loans floated during Maximilian's reign had formed an Association of Holders of the "Petits Bleus"[50] to press the French government for redress. But the French government presented the Díaz government with a document renouncing any claims. (This abandonment of previous claims had been part of the 1880 agreement to resume diplomatic relations.) For the French government, intervention costs on behalf of these creditors outweighed the benefits. The costs would have included angering the Díaz government, diverting attention away from Europe, and alienating other legitimate foreign creditors and holders of Mexican obligations.

In the early 1890s, three bad harvests (which forced Mexico to import corn from the U.S.) and the drop in silver prices brought about a Mexican fiscal and monetary crisis.[51] These crises shook the confidence of the country's present and potential foreign creditors despite Mexico's continued efforts to improve its financial situation.

The crisis nearly brought Mexico to a default. One observer noted that "The money market continues tight . . . (while) every day it becomes more apparent that the country requires additional capital to meet the needs."[52] By early 1893, many analysts openly debated the dangers of lending to Mexico. Although some bankers foresaw better times,[53] others were less sanguine.

In May 1893, José Yves Limantour, Díaz's newly appointed Minister of Finance, sought authorization to consolidate the national debt. The liberty enabled Limantour to assist the Treasury in meeting the crises of crop failures, epidemics, and debt servicing – in the face of a declining peso which fell from 40.75 pence in 1891 to 25.14 pence in 1895.[54] His successful response to the economic crisis not only brought Mexico out of the hole but also led to the first budget surplus in Mexico's history as an independent nation in 1894 when revenues slightly exceeded expenditures.[55]

Summary. During this period's two rounds, we see the cooperative but somewhat fragile nature of debt negotiations between Mexico and its lenders. When bankers sensed risks of a Mexican default due to adverse economic conditions, they became wary of continued new lending, but resumed their lending quickly as conditions improved. Mexico, anxious to keep its credit rating, continued to make sharp adjustments. Overall, the bargaining pattern and outcomes fit well with the HA..., HC... equilibrium predicted by the model.

[50] These are the certificates that the French had received from their own government in exchange of their bonds when they renounced all further claims against their own government. See Turlington (1930), p. 217.

[51] See the discussion of the *Mexican Financial Review* in *The Economist*, October 15, 1892, pp. 1300–1301 and Wynne (1951), p. 51.

[52] *New York Times*, February 11, 1893, p. 3. [53] *New York Times*, February 11, 1893, p. 3.

[54] Turlington (1930), p. 222. [55] Parkes (1938/1969), p. 298.

Situational changes

During this period, the continued government reform program engineered by Limantour brought important results, ultimately improving Mexico's financial position by the end of the period. In addition to the power granted by Díaz, the Mexican Congress authorized Limantour to deal with the country's internal debt, to "dictate all dispositions of the debt, to realize such operations as may be considered convenient to complete the arrangement of the national debt."[56]

These reforms included:[57] internal debt consolidation into two new bond issues; reform and revision of the taxation and revenue collection system (including the abolition of the alcabala, an internal customs tax that restricted trade and commerce);[58] reduction of military expenditures (such that these expenditures accounted for only 23% of the total budget by 1900 – down from 119% in 1825);[59] and the practice of strictest efficiency and economy in the government.

We would not expect either the bondholders or Mexico to make any efforts to promote situational change as a result of the game played in this period due to the high payoffs they both received. Mexico's individual situation changed as a result of policies pursued throughout the third period by Limantour, and the discovery of oil in Mexico helped in this respect as well.

Period four, 1894–1910: from success to crisis

Limantour's 1893 and 1894 reforms bore fruit during the fourth period. His policies particularly strengthened Mexico's issue capabilities. By 1899, Mexican creditworthiness reached new heights, encouraging a loan conversion that led to considerable debt servicing savings. Still, Limantour's development strategy continued Mexico's reliance on foreign capital and technology. Although his policy of economic openness proved helpful to Mexico in its efforts to receive additional loans, the end of the period saw a startling collapse of Mexico's political stability and the end of the Porfiriato.

Identifying individual situations

In the fourth period, we classify Mexico as coalitionally stable, issue strong, and overall medium (IS 1/5). The bondholders' individual situation remains the same: coalitionally stable, issue weak, and overall weak (IS 7).

Mexico. Mexico remained politically and domestically stable under Díaz's dictatorship for many years; signs of instability appeared only after 1904. Factional divisions surfaced among the governing elites, such as the opposition of Limantour's *cientificos* to the army faction led by General Bernardo Reyes. Because politics revolved around the economy, the *cientificos* managed to

[56] *New York Times*, June 12, 1893, p. 5.
[57] For a complete account of these reforms see Wynne (1951), p. 54 and Parkes (1938/1969), p. 301.
[58] Parkes (1938/1969), p. 301. [59] Corporation of Foreign Bondholders (1890), p. 133.

maintain their advantage.[60] Outside the governing elites, opposition spurred by nationalist sentiment organized around an anti–United States position.[61] Francisco Madero led the anti-reelectionist cause, securing increasing support in his tour across the country during 1909–1910. Díaz ended Madero's campaign abruptly in June 1910, ordering his arrest and incarceration on election day in San Luis Potosí. With Madero and many of his supporters in prison, Díaz won reelection; nonetheless, his victory proved an empty one as increasing unrest brought to a close the longest stable period in Mexican history until that point.

Limantour's numerous reforms of 1893 and 1894 had strengthened Mexico's issue capabilities. Treasury receipts grew as customs collection and stamp revenues increased in the mid-1890s. In 1895, the government operated with a modest surplus, as revenues exceeded expenditures despite 40% of the annual revenues being allocated to service debt.[62] The state's surplus continued to increase, and Díaz left a Treasury in 1911 with 70 million pesos in cash reserves.[63] The Mexican economy prospered in the late 1890s because of a relatively stable foreign exchange rate and good harvests. A key contributing factor in this auspicious situation was the reduction of war expenditures to less than one-fourth of the total budget.[64] At the turn of the century, however, the decline in the value of the Mexican silver peso threatened the previous decade's prosperity as the foreign exchange denominated debt increased dramatically. Limantour reacted by proposing a national law converting the silver peso into a gold peso, on parity with the Japanese yen.[65]

In terms of overall capabilities, Mexico's position improved considerably. In addition to the healthy budget, foreign trade experienced rapid growth due to improved port facilities and tariff reforms, recording a surplus from the mid-1890s. For fiscal 1909–1910 Mexico enjoyed a 65 million peso trade surplus on total trade of 488 million pesos.[66] In addition, Mexico's discovery of oil just after the turn of the century further strengthened its overall position. Moreover, Limantour's reforms – liberal concessions and subsidies – attracted rapid foreign investment, especially in mining, oil fields, public works, manufacturing industries, and food production and distribution.[67] This continued rise of foreign investment, however, led to foreign control of vast sectors of the Mexican economy, somewhat weakening Mexico's overall position.

Lenders. The bondholders remained united by their affiliation with the Council of the Corporation of Foreign Bondholders. Financially, the bondholders and their subscribing banks remained issue weak, lacking loan loss reserves to cover potential defaults, and overall weak because of their continued inability to block new loans to Mexico. The creditors also remained overall weak because

60 Vázquez and Meyer (1985), p. 96. 61 Vázquez and Meyer (1985), p. 96.
62 Turlington (1930), p. 226. 63 Meyer and Sherman (1987), p. 441.
64 Turlington (1930), p. 232.
65 The Japanese yen was very close to a half U.S. dollar (see Turlington, 1930, p. 234).
66 Meyer and Sherman (1987), pp. 450–451. 67 Meyer and Sherman (1987), pp. 445–449.

of the increased foreign investment in many Mexican projects, particularly in the private railway developments.

Creditor governments. Although the German government openly encouraged Mexican investment, creditor governments on the whole opposed intervention in international debt matters. In fact, in 1907, 34 countries, including the European powers and the U.S., agreed "not to have recourse to armed force for the recovery of contract debts claimed from the government of one country by the government of another country as being due to its nationals."[68] This so-called "Convention Respecting the Limitation of the Employment of Force for the Recovery of Contract Debts" was signed in the Hague on October 18, 1907. The creditor governments naturally worried about Mexico's internal stability, and thus favored Díaz's regime, which safeguarded the profits of foreign investments in the country. U.S. nationals held 38% of the total foreign investment in 1911.[69] For this reason, U.S. concern with growing social unrest and strikes in the U.S.-controlled mining industries increased, but only towards the period's end.

Debt game and predicted outcome

The actors' individual situations produce the game matrix shown in Figure 7.4. From the game structure, we expect an equilibrium with the debtors making no adjustment (LA...) and the lenders making high concessions (HC...). Whereas the creditors feared mutual confrontation, Mexico did not, giving it a bargaining advantage. In view of its improving situation, Mexico could afford to play more aggressively than the bondholders.

As long as Díaz remained firmly entrenched through 1910, the end of the period, the creditor governments had no incentive to intervene in debt affairs. The Hague agreement simply reinforced this propensity, although it appeared more oriented toward preventing conflict among great powers than toward preserving the national sovereignty of weaker states. In any case, we would not expect any significant intervention in this period, and thus the equilibria should remain that of the two-actor game.

The negotiations and outcome

We divide this period into two rounds: from 1894 to 1899, when Mexico rescheduled a £22.7 million loan, and from that point to 1910, when it received its most favorable foreign loan of the second epoch – just prior to a devastating revolution at the end of the period.

Round one. During this round, foreign creditors provided new loans while Mexico managed to avoid adjustment. Limantour's fiscal reforms, combined

[68] This undertaking does not apply when the debtor state does not seek a compromise agreement. See *Treaties, Conventions, International Acts*, vol. 2, pp. 2248–2259, cited in Turlington (1930), p. 257.
[69] Vázquez and Meyer (1985), p. 97.

Cardinal Payoff Matrix,
No Intervention Expected

		Lenders IS 7		
		HC...	MC...	LC...
	HA...	−3, 12	−2.75, 11.67	0, 11.33
Mexico IS 1/5	MA...	−1.83, 9	−2, 8	−.5, 7
	LA...	**−.67, 10**	−1.25, 7	−1, 4

Note: Nash equilibrium bolded.

Ordinal Payoff Matrix,
No Intervention Expected

		Lenders IS 7		
		HC...	MC...	LC...
	HA...	1, 9	2, 8	9, 7
Mexico IS 1/5	MA...	4, 5	3, 4	8, 2.5
	LA...	**7, 6**	5, 2.5	6, 1

Note: Nash equilibrium bolded.

Figure 7.4. *Play phase, period four: 1894–1910*

with the surplus now enjoyed by thc Díaz government, led to a steady improvement in Mexican credit. In 1895, *The Economist* noted that, with the reforms in place, the improvement in trade, and the steady development of "native industry":

> American and foreign capital is reported to be flowing into the country . . . a promise of greater prosperity lies before the country, and that capital may be invested there with greater confidence . . . [as] many new opportunities for investment in Mexico will shortly be brought before the public.[70]

[70] *The Economist*, May 4, 1895, p. 583.

The dramatic improvement in Mexico's credit stimulated lucrative loan offers from financiers in the U.S., England, and Germany. Initially the banking houses, represented by Bleichröder, made floating new loans contingent upon a deposit of six months' interest in advance, as well as a claim upon the taxes of the Federal District. The Díaz government refused these conditions and negotiations were suspended.[71]

Soon thereafter, in April 1899, several banks in the U.S. expressed an interest in lending to Mexico, on extremely favorable terms. Limantour traveled to New York to discuss these financial issues before continuing to Europe to evaluate and compare the terms of potential overseas offers to consolidate Mexican debt.[72] In July 1899, Mexico and a consortium of international banks – three German institutions, the Banco Nacional de México, and J.S. Morgan and Company of London and J.P. Morgan and Company of New York – agreed on a new £22.7 million bond loan to convert Mexico's outstanding foreign debt. Sixty-two percent of the country's customs revenues secured the loan.[73]

Despite this immediate drain on revenues, Mexico benefited enormously from the agreement. First, it consolidated the entire foreign debt into one issue. Second, the security came from customs receipts only, whereas previously it had taken 44% of customs revenues plus claims on the direct taxes of the Federal District and railway gross receipts. Third, the interest rate was reduced from 6% on most of the outstanding loans (including the loans of 1888, 1890, and 1893) to only 5% for the new loan. Fourth, annual foreign debt service was reduced by £117,000. Finally, the proceeds of the bond sale allowed Mexico to redeem with cash fully one-quarter of its foreign debt.[74]

Round two. The discovery of oil in Mexico in 1901, along with its improving financial condition, encouraged foreign creditors and financiers to compete in loan offers to Mexico. Limantour selected the most favorable offers, directing new foreign capital to Mexican development. In 1904, without any specific security, the government negotiated a $40 million bond loan at 4% interest from the American firm of Speyer & Co. Despite these favorable terms for Mexico, the American company believed it achieved a major coup. As the *New York Times* put it: "The contest between the syndicate managed by Speyer & Co. of this city and the syndicate of French bankers for the new forty-million-dollar Mexican gold loan has been decided in favor of Speyer & Co."[75]

The new loan went directly to government acquisition of railways and construction of port works, rather than to general government expenditures. Following a monetary reform that stabilized and placed the peso on a gold standard (thus further improving Mexico's credit-standing), the government negotiated or

[71] Turlington (1930), p. 227. [72] Turlington (1930), pp. 227–228.
[73] Corporation of Foreign Bondholders (1898–1899), p. 258; Turlington, (1930), pp. 227–228; Wynne (1951), p. 55. For additional details, see *The Economist*, July 8, 1899, p. 978 and the *New York Times*, July 3, 1899, p. 1.
[74] Wynne (1951), p. 55. [75] *New York Times*, October 19, 1904, p. 1.

guaranteed loans for private concerns for the purpose of fostering railway construction, agriculture development, and irrigation products. Mexico's position had so improved that one observer noted:

> The Government of the country is established upon a firm basis and inspires foreign investors with a feeling of confidence, which has taken tangible shape in the huge amount of foreign capital which has found its way into the country during the past two years.[76]

By 1910, Mexico's credit soared to its zenith, allowing it to obtain a new consolidation and redemption bond loan at favorable terms. The new £22.2 million loan would have converted all outstanding 5% bonds from the 1899 issue to new 4% interest rate bonds on the same security, but Mexico chose to convert only half of the outstanding debt (a £11.1 million loan).[77] With this loan, Mexico could further reduce its interest payments, while the principal and security for the debt remained unchanged. As in the first round, Mexico took advantage of its strong credit rating to secure loans without significant concessions.

Summary. During this period, Mexico benefited greatly from its increased issue and overall capabilities. Having undertaken numerous reforms towards the end of the last period, Mexico was well positioned to dictate favorable terms in its negotiations with lenders. As predicted, the result was two rounds of highly advantageous agreements for Mexico – an outcome of LA..., HC... – without it having to make major concessions.

Situational changes

Although the debt game favored Mexico in the last two periods, after a long period of political domination, Díaz's fall in 1911 created a major change in Mexico's individual situation. The end of Díaz's reign and the ensuing jockeying for political control of the country ended Mexico's relatively long-standing period of stability. The Mexican revolution quickly depleted the government's revenue surplus, leaving it issue weak. Massive capital flight during period five also left Mexico weak in overall resources.

Period five, 1911–1914: back to chaos

Mexico had experienced steady economic growth under Díaz's politically repressive regime. In the spring of 1908, however, Díaz surprised everyone when he declared in an interview that Mexico was ready for democracy. Moreover, he expressed his willingness to relinquish control to an elected successor. But in 1910, the year Díaz himself proposed for a national election, he went back on his word and declared that the welfare of the country demanded he retain power.[78]

This reversal angered many of his upper class rivals who had been excluded from power for nearly a generation, causing them to unite against Díaz. Francisco

[76] *The Economist*, March 16, 1907, p. 453. [77] Wynne (1951), p. 57.

[78] Priestley (1923/1969), pp. 396–397 and Parkes (1938/1969), pp. 314–315.

Madero was one such dissident who wrote a popular book advocating political freedom, and criticized Díaz's exile of Bernardo Reyes, Díaz's principal opponent. Capitalizing on his influential position as a political writer, Madero organized anti-reelection clubs and ultimately gained a presidential nomination.[79] Madero's subsequent arrest and incarceration plunged the country into turmoil by late 1910.

By May 1911, Madero's united opposition forced Díaz to resign the office he had held for decades, leaving Mexico in the hands of a provisional President, Francisco León de la Barra. In June, de la Barra handed over power to the newly elected Francisco Madero. Madero's ascension to power failed, however, to restore political stability. Instead, revolts and rebellions created political and economic disarray.

Identifying individual situations

The revolution in Mexico overshadowed debt negotiations. Growing opposition to Díaz and his ensuing resignation in 1911 embroiled the country in a long power struggle. This domestic situational change explains Mexico's new classification as coalitionally unstable, issue weak, and overall weak (IS 8). We classify the bondholders and bankers as coalitionally stable, issue weak, and overall weak (IS 7).

Mexico. Díaz's forced resignation and the power struggles surrounding his succession returned Mexico to a state of domestic instability. Upon his release from prison following Díaz's reelection, Madero sought to end Díaz's dictatorship. His *Plan de San Luis Potosí* was written to accomplish this task.[80] In November 1910, military struggles began in the northern provinces, and groups of rebels rapidly defeated government forces. United under the leadership of Pascual Orozco in December, the rebels posed a significant threat to Díaz. In May 1911, rebels seized the garrison of Ciudad Juárez in "the decisive engagement for control of the north."[81] On May 25, Díaz submitted his resignation.[82] Francisco León de la Barra, a member of Díaz's government, governed as provisional President amid continuing internal chaos caused by various rebel groups vying for power.[83]

Madero's election to the presidency in October 1911 failed to improve this state of anarchy. Other "liberals," such as Emiliano Zapata in the South and Pascal Orozco in the North, as well as conservatives and the army, challenged the authority of the new President. Despite being the elected leader, Madero possessed little control over the government or the armed forces, which had previously operated under Díaz's undisputed authority.

Although the domestic situation stabilized briefly in late January 1913, a sudden coup d'état by the army overthrew Madero, leaving Mexico once again in chaos. General Huerta, commander of Madero's loyal troops, joined the

[79] Parkes (1938/1969), p. 317. [80] Priestley (1923/1969), p. 398.
[81] Meyer and Sherman (1987), p. 504. [82] Meyer and Sherman (1987), p. 504.
[83] On this period, see Smith (1972), pp. 14–22.

insurgents, assumed leadership of the anti-Madero movement, and hammered the final nail into Madero's political coffin. On February 18, 1913, the "Pact of the Embassy" proclaimed Huerta interim president.[84] But Huerta never exercised effective control over the whole country. After Madero was assassinated in late February 1913, his followers (the Constitutionalists), led by Venustiano Carranza, challenged Huerta in the North while Emiliano Zapata fought him in the South. The country thus raged in a civil war from 1913 to 1914. Huerta resigned in July 1914, forced out by decisive military successes of the Constitutionalists and financial starvation by foreign powers.

Within a few months, the revolution had exhausted the Treasury and wiped out the revenue surpluses carefully accumulated under Limantour. In addition, the revolution disrupted the government's system of revenue collection, forcing the nation into virtual bankruptcy and encouraging massive capital flight. Although Madero had declared that "not one American dollar" had helped in the triumph of his cause, he had desperately sought foreign capital to foster Mexican development and prevent his government's financial collapse.[85] When Huerta came to power, he too was in dire need of funds to finance his costly suppression of the rebellion. In addition to soliciting foreign capital, the government issued paper money without adequate hard currency reserves, causing the peso's rapid depreciation. The situation worsened when the main rebel groups issued their own currency to finance their respective campaigns. At this point, Mexico had entered a state of financial collapse.

As for overall capabilities, by this time Mexico had come to depend heavily on foreign trade, commerce, and investment. Under Huerta, the civil war depleted much of the country's work force. Plantations remained unharvested, mines were closed, cattle robbery was rampant, and many people died.[86] In the end, Mexico lacked basic food and manufactured goods. Huerta's progressive reforms in education, Indian rights, and land redistribution failed to compensate for Mexico's weak overall situation.

Lenders. Bondholders and bankers remained hierarchically organized and united but in a financially weak position. Under the Díaz regime, the bankers had extended a large number of loans to Mexico, thereby exposing themselves to possible default. Moreover, their distance from the creditor governments and inability to block investments by other lenders to Mexico contributed to their overall weakness.

Creditor governments. First and foremost, the creditor governments during this period aimed to secure the lives and properties of their nationals.

[84] Parkes (1938/1969), p. 333. This agreement was known as the "Pact of the Embassy" because it was engineered by the U.S. Ambassador to Mexico who supported the coup against Madero. But Ambassador Wilson exceeded his authority, and President Taft refused to recognize Huerta.

[85] *Commercial and Financial Chronicle*, March 11, 1911, p. 626, cited in Turlington (1930), p. 246.

[86] For a discussion of Mexico's economic problems under Huerta, see Meyer and Sherman (1987), pp. 527–528. See also Priestley (1923/1969), p. 419.

During the years of stable rule and development under Díaz, European and American creditors substantially increased their investments, assets, and ownership of Mexican property. The areas of foreign investment included railways, mining operations, private Mexican banks, and industry. American-owned property in Mexico totaled an estimated $1 billion, French investments over $1 billion, and British property nearly $800 million. Estimates suggested that the Mexicans themselves owned less than $800 million worth of property![87] Although this significant foreign interest in the Mexican economy provided creditors leverage on the Mexican government in times of stability, it proved to be a liability in times of revolution.

Debt game and predicted outcome

We arrive at the debt game matrix shown in Figure 7.5 for period five. On the basis of strategic interaction, we would expect this game to settle on the outcome LA..., HC... in the absence of any creditor government intervention. We predict Mexico will play a dominant strategy of undertaking no adjustment while the lenders will prefer to make high concessions in this situation. Should the lender withhold concessions or press for high adjustment by Mexico (the optimal outcome from the lenders' perspective), the negotiations could reach the confrontation point – the worst possible outcome in this instance for the lenders (with an ordinal payoff of 1).

For their part, the creditor governments should intervene actively in the debt game during this period to protect their nationals' large investments in Mexico threatened by the revolution. In particular, we would expect the U.S. to step in because of its proximity and substantial investment in Mexico. Moreover, we would expect the U.S. to attempt to forestall any intervention by other foreign powers who showed concern about the heavy exposure of their own nationals.

The negotiations and outcome

This period comprises two rounds. The first round occurred in the years between 1911 and 1913, when a new debt accord was concluded; the second ran from 1913 to 1914, when Huerta resigned and Mexico defaulted on its foreign debt.

Round one. To address Mexico's pressing financial needs, president-elect Francisco Madero negotiated two short-term $10 million loans in 1911 and 1912 with an American syndicate. These loans were secured on 4½% Treasury bills, maturing and due within two and one years, respectively.[88]

Yet these loans did not temper Mexico's financial crisis, and the Mexican economy remained moribund. As revenues fell, unrest and disorder spread. Mexico's problems reached their most critical stage in early 1913. Manuel Calero, the Mexican Ambassador to the U.S., admitted lying to the U.S. government for

[87] *New York Times*, April 20, 1914, p. 11. [88] McCaleb (1921), pp. 197–198.

Cardinal Payoff Matrix,
Intervention Expected

		Lenders IS 7		
		HC...	MC...	LC...
	HA...	<u>0, 12</u>	−3.5, 11.67	−4, 11.33
Mexico IS 8	MA...	4, 9	0, 8	−2, 7
	LA...	**8, 10**	3.5, 7	0, 4

Note: Nash equilibrium bolded; expected outcome with intervention underlined.

Ordinal Payoff Matrix,
Intervention Expected

		Lenders IS 7		
		HC...	MC...	LC...
	HA...	<u>5, 9</u>	2, 8	1, 7
Mexico IS 8	MA...	8, 5	5, 4	3, 2.5
	LA...	**9, 6**	7, 2.5	5, 1

Note: Nash equilibrium bolded; expected outcome with intervention underlined.

Figure 7.5. *Play phase, period five: 1911–1914*

the past year because of Mexico's desperate financial situation.[89] With Madero's government facing either bankruptcy or continued heavy borrowing, his government chose the latter. During ongoing negotiations with an international group of bankers, however, the army of General Victoriano Huerta overthrew the Madero government.

[89] *Commercial and Financial Chronicle*, February 8, 1913, pp. 385–386, cited in Turlington (1930), p. 248.

When Huerta took power in February 1913, he ignored Madero's tentative agreement. Huerta immediately began to negotiate a new loan with American and European creditors to finance his new government. Bankers in the U.S., England, and France scrambled to his assistance. American bankers were especially concerned about the $10 million short-term loans of 1911 and 1912 that were nearly due. Initially, the bankers made any new loan contingent upon U.S. recognition of Huerta. But Woodrow Wilson, elected in 1912, advocated a moral and righteous foreign diplomacy, and unexpectedly refused to recognize, finance, or legitimize the Huerta military coup. Another stumbling block to new loans arose when Venustiano Carranza, the Governor of Coahuila and Huerta's principal opponent, announced that if his forces (the Mexican Constitutionalists) came to power, he would not acknowledge any of the financial obligations assumed by the Huerta government.[90]

Despite these serious obstacles, Mexico and the bankers negotiated a new agreement in May 1913. It provided for a £16 million loan at 6% interest, secured upon the remaining 38% of customs revenues not already pledged to the service of the 1899 and 1910 loans. The government also pledged to further raise duties if their resulting revenues fell below 20% of the charges on the new issue.[91] The contract stipulated that the loan would first create a reserve fund equal to six months of interest payments, and then settle the short-term loans coming due. The bankers, however, were not simply thinking about the need to make concessions to Mexico so it could stabilize its economy and eventually pay off its debts. Instead, they had something more devious in mind. Specifically,

> [t]he loan was in essence an arrangement devised to enable the various banks which held the $20 million of matured short-term obligations . . . to rid themselves without loss of their none-too-good paper by shifting the risk to the subscribing public.[92]

This strategy became clear from ensuing events. Mexico only received 12 million pesos for the flotation of £6 million of the new loan.

In the first round, Mexico attempted to secure new loans without undertaking adjustment. Lenders were willing to oblige in this case because they saw an opportunity to transfer their risk to the subscribing public. Moreover, the bankers also worried about a possible shift in the game to mutual confrontation; thus they were willing to lend new money. But here, pressure from the U.S. government prevented the negotiation of a much larger loan, and ultimately blocked major concessions to Mexico. The final outcome was MA..., MC..., a movement indicating pressure from the creditor governments.

Round two. By mid-1913, although nearly all the European powers recognized the Huerta government, President Wilson continued his opposition. Following his new emissary's suggestion (the Lind proposal), Wilson offered to assist the U.S. creditors' extension of a loan to Mexico if Huerta agreed to resign

[90] *New York Times*, May 25, 1913, p. 1. [91] Wynne (1951), p. 60. [92] Wynne (1951), p. 61.

and not participate in future elections. Huerta rejected this proposal outright, condemning U.S. intervention in Mexican internal affairs.[93]

When Huerta dissolved the Mexican Congress and arrested over 100 government officials, Wilson invoked the duty of the U.S., as "Mexico's nearest friend," as a justification for removing Huerta for good.[94] As part of his strategy, Wilson planned to topple Huerta through financial starvation by blocking any new funds to his government. Wilson informed all European powers that the U.S. would regard any new funds or financial aid to the Huerta government as "an unfriendly act."[95] The European powers reluctantly honored this request. The German and English governments actively discouraged their financiers from providing any new funds to the Huerta government; the French government expressly forbade the flotation of bonds issued on behalf of Huerta to be quoted on the Bourse.[96]

U.S. pressure had an immediate effect. Unable to obtain funds abroad, Huerta turned to nine local Mexican banks for an 18 million peso advance. This loan was significantly delayed because foreign capitalists controlled many of the banks. Unable to obtain new funds, Huerta temporarily suspended interest payments on the nation's debt in December 1913. The *New York Times* reported that "since these bankers have refused to assist President Huerta to meet the interest, he will refuse to pay it."[97]

The suspension set off a crisis. Bondholders and bankers had withheld new funds to Huerta according to their governments' wishes; now they appealed to their governments for intervention on their behalf. Looming ahead was the outcome they feared most in the debt game: mutual confrontation, which would yield their worst payoff. With pressure on the banks not to engage in any lending or rescheduling with Huerta, the best option for the banks at this point was to pressure their governments to secure high adjustment and debt servicing from Mexico. The bondholders called for a forceful takeover of Mexican customhouses, from which nearly 100% of the revenues had been pledged to debt servicing:

> [A]s the loan of 1910 is secured by 62% of the Mexican customs and the loan of 1913 by 38%, it would be the duty and the privilege of the European Governments, whose subjects hold the bonds, to seize the Custom Houses by international landing parties and to collect the interest themselves.[98]

The bondholders even claimed that the Monroe Doctrine did not block such action. They cited President Theodore Roosevelt's 1902 claim that the doctrine "did not bar interference with a South American State by a European Power in order to enforce the just claims of its subjects."[99]

[93] Priestley (1923/1969), p. 422.
[94] *Foreign Relations of the United States* (1913), pp. 817, 821–22, cited in Turlington (1930), p. 252.
[95] American Academy of Political and Social Science (1914), p. 231.
[96] *New York Times*, November 13, 1913, cited in Turlington (1930), p. 255.
[97] *New York Times*, January 16, 1914, p. 1.
[98] *New York Times*, January 4, 1914.
[99] *The Economist*, January 17, 1914, p. 124.

Lenders failed to spur intervention.[100] Although European governments were concerned about their assets, their strategic interest in maintaining good relations with the U.S. government outweighed concern for their nationals' claims upon Mexico. The British, the most vocal advocates for the recognition of Huerta, received an important concession from the U.S. to keep them out of the debt game: equal treatment on the use of the Panama Canal.[101] The bondholders and other European creditors continued to petition the U.S. government on the matter, and to "ask President Wilson to take some action to adjust the financial position of Mexico."[102] But Secretary of State William Jennings Bryan responded by making it clear that "the failure of Mexico to pay her interest made no change in the policy of this Government."[103]

By April, desperate for financial help, Huerta announced the resumption of debt payments. According to his plans, customs revenues would be collected, but not delivered directly to the creditors. Instead, they would be deposited in the Banco Nacional de Mexico and held until the Mexican exchange rate improved. However, this "resumption" proved short-lived. As a result of the eruption of hostilities in Tampico involving a U.S. naval warship, the U.S. blocked the collection of customs revenues by the Mexican government.

Only the intervention of Argentina, Brazil, and Chile prevented the eruption of a U.S.-Mexican war over this incident. These countries' mediation persuaded Huerta to step down, handing the presidency over to Francisco Carbajal. But by October 1915, the United States and other key powers recognized Venustiano Carranza as Mexico's leader. The Mexican government remained in default on both its outstanding foreign debt, totalling £40 million, and its internal debt, totaling 135 million pesos' worth of bonds – held mostly by foreigners.

Summary. The actual outcome during this period corresponded to our prediction for only a short time, owing to Wilson's decision to overthrow Huerta. Thus, we might have expected creditor governments, including the U.S., to pressure the Mexicans to adjust and to make debt payments after the banks had been prevented from making loans. Based on our predicted game, this was a natural strategy for bondholders and bankers when faced with pressure not to lend. As expected, the European governments did push for this outcome. But Wilson's concern with overthrowing Huerta above all other objectives led to a mutual standoff between Mexico and its lenders, and a final outcome of Huerta being overthrown. The outcome, then, ended up at the point the lenders most feared: no concessions and no adjustment.

Situational changes

Mexico's political instability continued in this period as Madero was deposed by a military coup led by General Huerta and two revolutionary groups continued

[100] Turlington (1930), p. 257. [101] See Vázquez and Meyer (1985), p. 111.
[102] *New York Times*, January 25, 1914. [103] *New York Times*, January 16, 1914, p. 1.

to battle for supremacy. Wilson's interventions to rid the country of Huerta radically changed the debt game in this period. The Wilson administration's efforts to effect situational change centered around blocking Mexico's access to new foreign loans and using the tool of diplomatic recognition. This use of norms went beyond a simple legalistic formality; the U.S. was able to ensure that opponents of the U.S.-supported regime would not easily secure weapons to use against it.[104]

European bankers had expressed some willingness to extend new loans to Mexico, but when Wilson refused to allow this, they sought to increase their overall strength by appealing to their governments to intervene on their behalf. The European powers refused to buck the U.S., however, further rejecting their financiers' proposals to force Mexico to adjust its economy. Wilson held firm for the duration of the period, continuing to block Mexico's access to foreign loans until Huerta resigned.

In the transition to the next period, discussed in Chapter 9, Mexico's position continued to remain unstable and its economy remained in shambles. But with U.S. recognition in 1917, and greater control over foreign resources, Mexico managed to somewhat improve its overall capabilities. With a poor payoff in this game, the bankers made significant efforts to change their individual situation. They managed to bolster their coalitional stability by forming a new committee in 1915, and subsequently secured the U.S. as an ally.

Conclusion

This epoch saw the settlement of Mexico's first default dating back to the 1820s. In the 1870s and 1880s, following the fall of Maximilian, Porfirio Díaz steered Mexico to an accord with the London bondholders, an agreement that Juárez had failed to reach. The stability and financial reforms that Díaz introduced permitted a settlement of the long-standing default that had been repeatedly subjected to rescheduling. This new-found improvement in Mexico's financial situation allowed it to enter capital markets once again, this time with loans floated in Germany, the U.S., and other countries. Throughout much of this epoch, Mexico appeared to be a good financial risk. At times, especially in the early 1890s, Mexico began to face financial problems. But Mexican finances improved greatly following the issuance of new bonds and the surge of optimism caused by discovery of oil in 1901. Borrowing at favorable terms continued in this first decade, but domestic instability rumbled beneath the surface. In 1911, Porfirio Díaz resigned under pressure, and Mexico entered a decade of instability.

The model proved successful in predicting most of the bargaining outcomes during this epoch. During the fifth period, however, President Woodrow Wilson's active role significantly affected the debt negotiations in an unanticipated manner.

[104] See Vásquez and Meyer (1985), Chapter 7, for a discussion of the U.S. role during the Mexican Revolution.

Wilson proved to be more interested in installing a Mexican government to his liking than in forcing Mexico to adjust its economy, in contrast to the model's predictions.

At the beginning of the First World War, a major epochal transformation took place as the U.S. emerged as a significant political and financial power. As we shall see, the U.S. became the most active of all creditor governments in Mexico as the Europeans retreated to tend to their domestic problems.

8 To the victor go the spoils (and headaches): Peruvian debt rescheduling, 1875–1900s

During the 1860s, at the height of the guano boom, Peru's strong credit standing enabled it to borrow heavily. It contracted large loans throughout this decade and well into the early 1870s, but economic problems soon followed. Although the guano market weakened, Peru continued to spend wildly on the construction of railroads. By 1876, Peru, the largest debtor in Latin America, was in default.[1]

In June 1876, Peruvian negotiators concluded the so-called "Raphael contract" giving the newly formed English Peruvian Guano Company a four-year monopoly on the guano trade in exchange for help in paying off the foreign debt. This contract reestablished the important linkage between Peru's foreign debt and its guano. The Raphael contract was typical of Peru's efforts to address its foreign debt obligations during the golden age of guano. As in the 1840s and 1850s, rather than implementing stringent domestic austerity programs to meet the demands of its creditors, Peru's government granted important concessions to foreign business concerns.

Unfortunately, for all concerned, the Raphael contract also coincided with the end of the guano boom. The result, soon thereafter, was the bust of the Peruvian Guano Company. Due to Peru's weakened economy and the falling value of its guano, the Company simply could not meet its obligations to either the Peruvian government or the creditors. Both the government and the bondholder committees clamored for compensation from the Company. Accordingly, the Peruvian government looked for new national concessions that might attract foreign concerns and could ultimately be used to satisfy creditors.[2]

Along with Peru's economic problems, another crucial event influenced debt negotiations in this epoch. Despite its weak political and financial condition, Peru, allied with Bolivia, went to war against Chile in April 1879 to protect its nitrate-rich southern territories. Following a devastating defeat and loss of territory, Peru found itself under even greater pressure from bondholders and other creditors. The bondholders turned to Chile in an effort to collect on their loans

[1] Among other sources, for details on Peruvian domestic politics and the negotiation process, this chapter draws on Markham (1892), Stewart (1946/1968), Wynne (1951), Levin (1960), Pike (1967), Bonilla (1974), Cotler (1978), Werlich (1978), Palacios (1983), and Miller (1976, 1983).

[2] For example, with guano reserves petering out in the 1870s, the government looked to the development of nitrates, and, in 1876, created a national nitrate monopoly in the form of the Peruvian Nitrate Company.

from 1880 to 1886, but they had marginal success. As a result of this failed effort, in 1887 the bondholders once again attempted to satisfy their claims by returning to Peru. After a difficult set of negotiations, the creditors signed the Grace contract with Peru in 1889. The contract formed the Peruvian Corporation to run Peru's railroads for 66 years and develop Peru's other resources. In exchange, Peru was no longer responsible for its foreign debt.

Our analysis of negotiations during this epoch spans seven periods. The first, from 1875 to 1876, covers Peru's default and the negotiation of the Raphael contract in 1876. The second, 1877 to 1880, focuses on conflicts among Peru's creditors and ends with the onset of war between Peru and Chile. During the third and fourth periods, from 1880 to 1881 and 1882 to 1886, Chile occupied Peruvian territory, and Peru remained economically and politically devastated. During this time, the British bondholders settled their differences and turned to Chile to redress their claims against Peru. Periods five through seven cover the negotiations of the Grace contract from 1886 to 1889. When Andrés Cáceres passed the final version of the Grace contract in 1889, he brought to an end the second epoch of borrowing and default.

Background to rescheduling

Peru found it easy to borrow during the 1860s when the supply of guano seemed inexhaustible. From 1851 to 1860, the government had received about £18 million from its guano exports.[3] Thus, in 1862, the Peruvian government readily obtained a new 4.5% loan of £5.5 million to redeem the bonds of the 1853 loan and the 1849 settlement. When President Ramón Castilla retired in 1862, political unrest exacerbated Peruvian financial dependence. In 1865 Peru concluded a new massive bond loan of £10 million under tougher terms.

Soon thereafter, Peru began a conflict with Spain. When Peru officially declared war in 1866, the government lacked funds to mount a defense. In 1846, revenue from guano had accounted for only 5% of the national budget; by 1866, guano revenues underwrote 75% of the budget.[4] When the guano market weakened, the Peruvian government's only option to finance the war was to turn to foreign loans. As a result, Peru and its ally, Chile, contracted a $10 million bond loan in New York. Only $2 million worth of bonds were eventually offered, of which investors bought only about $1.535 million,[5] secured on the hypothecation of 500,000 tons of guano. Although the actual conflict ended relatively quickly, Spain and Peru did not sign a peace treaty until 1869.

José Balta's rise to power in 1868 returned internal stability to Peru after years of turmoil, financial crises, and war. Despite this new-found political stability, Peru's financial situation remained problematic. President Balta showed little interest in developing alternatives to revenue obtained from guano sales or

[3] McQueen (1926), p. 6. [4] McQueen (1926), p. 6 and Cotler (1978), p. 88.
[5] Award of Rapperschwyl, Desc., and Ren., pp. 213–214, cited in Wynne (1951), p. 114.

advances and customs duties. In 1869–1870, Peru faced a budget deficit of 17 million soles (equivalent to $17 million at the time).[6] Consequently, during this period, Peru's massive foreign borrowing program continued, facilitated by the general economic boom of the 1860s and 1870s in international capital markets that encouraged bankers and bondholders to speculate on new, less secure ventures and investments.

Led by Nicolás de Piérola, Peru's new Minister of the Treasury, the government indulged in additional borrowing. Once again, Peru looked for a profitable way to substantively link guano revenue to the debt issue. It achieved this goal on August 17, 1869, when the Peruvian government negotiated a contract with Dreyfus Brothers and Company of Paris. In the so-called Dreyfus contract, the Peruvian government canceled all other guano consignment agreements, giving the French Dreyfus Company exclusive rights for the sale of up to 2 million tons of guano to Europe and its colonies beginning in the early 1870s (depending on the expiration of the other contracts). In return, Dreyfus agreed to pay Peru £7.6 per ton of guano, immediately advance Peru 2.4 million soles, as well as advance an additional 700,000 soles monthly for 20 months. It also agreed to assume Peru's outstanding obligations to previous guano consignees for past loan advances – totaling some 16 million soles. Moreover, Dreyfus agreed to service the 1865 foreign debt (some 5 million soles annually).[7] Thus began a long relationship with Dreyfus that would be marked by legal squabbles, and pressure from France and other creditor governments.

Confident of an inflow of funds from the Dreyfus contract, Balta promoted a program of railway and public works. He quickly accumulated a debt of £49 million, approximately 10 times the amount he had inherited when he assumed office.[8] Balta secured all the loans necessary for the construction of the railroads by committing the sum total of the dwindling guano reserves.[9] Aided by Dreyfus, Peru floated its largest loans in 1870 and 1872, at the peak of the nation's guano age borrowing. In 1870, Peru obtained an £11,920,000 bond loan at 6% interest for railway construction. Two years later, Peru attempted to float a loan for almost £37 million, but managed to place only £22 million of the bond issue. This 5% bond – secured by the guano revenue, customs duties, and railway mortgages and revenues – was also used for the conversion of the 1865, 1866, and 1870 bond loans.[10] Speculators were wary of the 1872 bonds because of reports that the guano deposits were running out, leaving the government with no other source of revenues. In addition, financial observers distrusted Peru's ability to support the heavy load of the foreign debt, which stood at £35 million.[11] As a result, the public only subscribed to £230,000 of the £22 million bonds actually issued.[12] Dreyfus and the other associated firms took up the

[6] McQueen (1926), p. 7. The sol replaced the peso in the mid-1860s. Its value was about $1 until 1870; it then declined gradually to $.50 in 1897 (Werlich, 1978, p. 92).
[7] See Levin (1960), pp. 98–99 and Wynne (1951), pp. 115–116.
[8] Pike (1967), p. 125. [9] Pike (1967), p. 126. [10] Wynne (1951), pp. 117–118.
[11] *The Economist*, March 23, 1872, in Wynne (1951), p. 119. [12] Clarke (1877), p. 19.

remaining bonds at low rates. With this move, Dreyfus became even more important with respect to Peru. The financial agent of the nation, and solely responsible for the guano trade, Dreyfus also became Peru's most important creditor.

The net proceeds of the 1872 loan to the government totaled only £13 million, which Peru quickly spent on railroads. Given the country's sparse population and slight demand for heavy commercial transportation, these tracks, constructed under the guidance of American engineer Henry Meiggs, vastly exceeded Peru's needs.[13] As a result, this last frenzy of guano age borrowing, in which Peru poured resources into railroads as a catalyst for economic development, ended in a bust.

In 1872, when Manuel Pardo came to power at the head of Peru's first political party, the *Civilistas*, Peru's economy was moribund. The severe drop in the price of Peruvian guano on the world market was the most pressing problem. This drop resulted from an exhaustion of the richest Peruvian deposits of guano, which led Dreyfus to attempt to sell inferior guano on the world market, and from the rise of the German artificial fertilizer industry.[14] Because of this price drop, Dreyfus's minimal guano revenue was absorbed by debt servicing, leaving the company bereft of profits. By November 1873, faced with continuing financial loss, Dreyfus announced that it would no longer continue to service the foreign debt as originally agreed.

In response, the government blocked Dreyfus's right to ship guano from the country. Moreover, the government declared that the bondholders of the 1870 and 1872 loans had a preferential claim to all guano in Peru and further warned that if Dreyfus failed to meet the interest and sinking fund payments, the government would institute legal proceedings in countries where the guano was imported.

In April 1874, Peru and Dreyfus came to a new settlement. The French company agreed to continue service on the debt until July 1, 1875, and the government allowed Dreyfus to export 850,000 tons of guano, thus completing the original 2 million ton monopoly agreement.[15] In order to liquidate and balance their accounts, Dreyfus also agreed to advance the government from 400,000 to 7 million soles a month based on the gross value of the guano. However, as we will see, this new agreement did not prevent Peru from defaulting at the beginning of 1876, initiating an era of rescheduling.

Period one: the Raphael contract, 1875–1876

Peruvian President Manuel Pardo faced both political and economic problems. Despite his efforts to promote economic adjustment, and promote a peaceful succession, Peru could not avoid default. As we shall see, the economic measures

[13] See Levin (1960), pp. 99–102 and Pike (1967), p. 126.

[14] This and the next paragraph draw heavily on Wynne (1951), pp. 121–123. See also Markham (1892), p. 374.

[15] For details of this agreement, see Stewart (1946/1968), pp. 300–301.

he undertook only aggravated existing political conflict in Peru. His successor, Mariano Prado, however, managed to secure a commitment from the bondholders to fund the government's activities through the sale of guano in a highly favorable agreement for Peru.

Identifying individual situations

Peru found itself with an unstable coalition, and was issue weak and overall medium in capabilities (IS 4/8). The bondholders were coalitionally stable and issue weak in capabilities but medium in overall capabilities (IS 3/7).

Peru. President Manuel Pardo broke the political "compromise" kept by Balta. By pursuing an aggressive austerity program and promoting mass education, Pardo succeeded in alienating both the Army and the clergy, the two most powerful groups in the country.[16] He subsequently faced numerous military uprisings and assassination attempts. Another great challenge emerged after the radicalization of the conflict between Pardo and Piérola, the former minister of the treasury, which evolved into a long struggle of *Civilistas* against the *Piérolistas*. Piérola and his supporters attempted to oust the president, but Pardo crushed the insurrection, forcing Piérola into exile in Chile.

In 1876, having survived numerous military revolts, President Pardo convinced his *Civilista* party to select former military chief Mariano Prado (and dictator from 1866 to 1868) to run for office. Pardo, who had been Prado's Finance Minister during the dictatorship, hoped that Prado would end the *Piérolistas'* attempts to incite revolution. Although the elections were marred by violence, Prado assumed office in 1876.

With respect to issue-capabilities, years of unproductive spending had left Peru's economy in ruins. Guano sales barely matched the service on the huge foreign debt. Sales declined from over £4 million in 1869 to only £2.6 million in 1875, while the service on the foreign debt increased from £1 million in 1869 to £2.57 million in 1875.[17] By 1874, the government found it necessary to issue paper money inadequately backed by metallic reserves, ending the stability of the currency and marking the beginning of rapid and continuous depreciation of the sol. By 1875, the government faced a huge budget deficit.

In overall capabilities, Peru found itself heavily indebted and highly dependent on foreigners to maintain its declining guano operations. Yet Peru still retained the capability to block guano shipments and challenge private contractors if need be (as it did with Dreyfus in 1873), thus meriting coding as medium strong in overall capabilities.

Lenders. The bondholders were united under the Committee of Peruvian Bondholders. This group, based in London and led by Sir Charles Russell,

[16] See Pike (1967), pp. 132–139 for a good discussion of Pardo's regime.

[17] See Pike (1967), p. 134 and the footnote for his sources.

came into being immediately after the January 1876 default. With respect to issue capabilities, the bondholders were weak. They had exposed themselves to the threat of default through repeated lending operations, the most recent in 1872. In terms of overall capabilities, the bondholders had the ability to hinder new loan flotations by Peru, but their large overall exposure made them vulnerable to default, weakening their leverage. Thus we code them as medium in capabilities.

Creditor governments. During this period, we would not expect the creditor governments to actively involve themselves in debt negotiations. Peru had contracted with private companies and serviced its debt through guano contractors. As the importance of the guano market began to decline relative to the rise of the German fertilizer industry and the growth of the nitrate market, we would not expect Peru to figure very highly in the creditor governments' economic or political calculations.

Debt game and predicted outcome

Based on these classifications, we consider the debt game shown in Figure 8.1 for the first period. On the basis of strategic interaction, we expect the game to settle on an outcome of LA..., HC... – the Nash equilibrium of this game. Given our evaluation of creditor government interests, in this period we do not expect intervention by the creditor governments. Hence, we would expect Peru to be unwilling to make significant adjustment despite receiving high concessions from the lenders.

The negotiations and outcome

Pursuant to its 1874 agreement with Peru, Dreyfus maintained service on Peruvian debt until July 1875.[18] As this deadline for Dreyfus's last payment on the foreign debt approached, however, Peru's economic condition only worsened. The government could hardly service the foreign debt out of its own resources, because of its severe financial crunch. In September 1875, Peru obtained an 18 million sol loan from Lima banks, simply to meet the government's current expenses. As security for these internal loans, the government promised 200,000 tons of guano, commercial bills in Europe (drawn against the advances for guano sales being arranged in Europe), internal bonds worth 4 million soles, and the proceeds from the nitrate monopoly created in 1873.[19]

This action endangered the bondholders' prospects for repayment as Peru continued its policy of mortgaging guano revenues into the distant future. Although well intentioned, the Prado government's effort to remove itself from its dependence on Dreyfus as guano merchant, financial agent, and other assorted roles was a failure.[20] In an effort to secure new funds, Peru negotiated an accord in October 1875 with a company known as the Société Générale pour Favoriser

[18] The following discussion of the bargaining during this period draws heavily on Wynne (1951), pp. 122–128 and Palacios (1983), pp. 143–180.

[19] Marichal (1989), p. 108; Wynne (1951), p. 122.

[20] See Palacios (1983), pp. 143–144.

Cardinal Payoff Matrix,
No Intervention Expected

		Lenders IS 3/7		
		HC...	MC...	LC...
	HA...	−1.5, 10.5	−5, 10.67	−6.5, 10.83
Peru IS 4/8	MA...	2.83, 7.25	−1, 7	−3.5, 6.75
	LA...	**7.17, 6.5**	3, 5	−.5, 3.5

Note: Nash equilibrium bolded.

Ordinal Payoff Matrix,
No Intervention Expected

		Lenders IS 3/7		
		HC...	MC...	LC...
	HA...	4, 7	2, 8	1, 9
Peru IS 4/8	MA...	7, 6	**5, 5**	3, 4
	LA...	**9, 3**	8, 2	6, 1

Note: Nash equilibrium bolded.

Figure 8.1. *Play phase, period one: 1875–1876*

le Développement du Commerce et de l'Industrie en France. The Société agreed to pay interest and sinking fund payments on the external debt for 3½ years and to advance the government £950,000. The government, in turn, gave the Société a monopoly on the sale of guano in European and other markets. Increasingly strapped for funds, the government pressed the Société to raise the advance to £1.5 million soon after reaching this tentative agreement.[21] When the Société refused, Peru failed to ratify the accord. With no one to take over Dreyfus's safeguarding role, Peru defaulted on its foreign loans on January 1, 1876.

[21] See the discussion on this point by Bonilla (1974), p. 136.

Although the default provided a temporary solution to its foreign problems, the government's domestic needs continued. On March 31, 1876, the Peruvian government reached a new agreement with the Société Générale. The tentative agreement would have stipulated that the government would sell 1.9 million tons of guano to the Société. The Société, in turn, would provide the government with monthly installments of £700,000 per year and would continue servicing the debt.

At the same time, however, Russell negotiated similar terms for British bondholders with the Peruvian Minister in Great Britain with only one significant difference – that the bondholders select the guano contractors and consignees. These creditors objected to the fact that the Société Générale only showed interest in the Dreyfus contracts, and not their claims. Moreover, the bondholders protested against the Société Générale contract because it excluded them from having any control over guano contracting, sales, and debt servicing. Appeals to the British government for intervention on their behalf failed, but the bondholders did manage to use their overall capabilities to block the agreement.

Following this failure, the new Peruvian President-elect, General Prado, met with the bondholders' committee. Peru and the bondholders finally reached an agreement known as the Raphael contract on June 7, 1876. Entering a new agreement with the London firm Raphael and Sons enabled the formation of the Peruvian Guano Company Ltd., which would be operated by Raphael and others sanctioned by the Committee.[22] The terms of the contract granted the new company a four-year monopoly to sell a total of 1.9 million tons of guano on worldwide markets (with certain exceptions) without discriminating against existing 1869 and 1874 Dreyfus contracts. In return, the Company was to provide the government with £700,000 a year. All remaining profits were to be used to service the debt; but the interest rate on the debt itself was also reduced and provision was made for use of the profits from the operation of the Company to retire bonds on the open market.

Although many bondholders complained about this arrangement, Prado had warned the Committee that if it did not agree to furnish the money, the Peruvian government would sell the guano in Peru for export to whomsoever it chose. In essence, Peru threatened to use its capabilities – its control over guano – to get its own way.[23]

Summary. The outcome of the negotiations between the bondholders and Peru proved to be extremely lopsided. Essentially, Peru extracted the bondholders' commitment to supply the government with funds for its expenses through the sale of guano. In numerous editorials, *The Times* lambasted the agreement.[24] Thus, as anticipated by the model, Peru engaged in low adjustment and the bondholders undertook high concessions.

[22] On the terms of the agreement, see also Levin (1960), p. 107.
[23] *The Bullionist*, June 17, 1876, in Wynne (1951), p. 127. [24] See Palacios (1983), p. 192.

Situational changes

Although the bondholders' attempts to garner support from the British government failed during the first period, they did manage to use their own overall capabilities to block Peru's agreement with the Société Générale, which they considered unsavory. Peru had the last word, however, when it used its guano resources to pressure the bondholders to reluctantly accept the Peru-friendly Raphael contract.

Because they received very low payoffs from the Raphael contract in this period, we would expect the bondholders to engage in active efforts to promote situational change. In fact, because of disagreement over the contract, the bondholders' committee quickly split in period two. Bondholder James Croyle formed a separate committee, seeking to block the advances to Peru. When this new committee's legal counsel advised that it could not successfully sue Peru, the committee instigated a lawsuit against Dreyfus to force it to turn over funds from its continuing sale of guano. After considerable litigation, this lawsuit failed.

The Peruvian Guano Company also proved to be an economic failure, as discussed below, and failed to enhance Peru's position.

Period two, 1876–1880: standoff

After concluding the Raphael Contract, the government felt it had passed its debt burden to the newly created Peruvian Guano Company. But the Company suffered financially from its inception as global demand for guano declined. Possessing significant high quality guano reserves, Dreyfus continued to control the worldwide market, much to the detriment of the Company. Furthermore, the Peruvian government did not allow the Company to sell its guano at competitive prices until 1879. This restriction prevented the Company from meeting the demands of either Peru or the nation's creditors.

Problems in marketing guano soon took a back seat as Peru and Chile found themselves at war from 1879 to 1884. The conflict proved disastrous for Peru. In an attempt to overcome its lack of preparedness and to raise funds to expedite the war, the Peruvian government began negotiations with Dreyfus for new loans in return for additional guano monopoly rights. Before they could reach an agreement, however, Chilean forces captured and destroyed Peru's southern guano exporting ports, thus denying Peru its chief source of revenue. The war wrought havoc on the nation's already faltering economy, further destabilizing its political situation and leading to a crucial loss of territory. Chilean forces quickly took possession of Peru's nitrate and guano-rich Tarapacá province and the territories of Tacna and Arica. By early 1880, Chilean forces occupied Lima.

Identifying individual situations

In this period, we classify Peru as coalitionally unstable, issue weak, and overall medium (IS 4/8). The bondholders in this period had become coalitionally unstable, and continued to be issue weak but overall medium (IS 4/8).

Peru. Prado continued to face significant opposition from the *Piérolistas*. In 1877, a group of *Piérolistas* seized the Peruvian warship Huascar in Callao, and declared Piérola the President of Peru. Although Prado succeeded in suppressing these revolts, he lost the support of his *Civilistas*. Following former President Pardo's assassination in late 1878, the split between the *Civilistas* and the *Piérolistas* produced serious civil and political strife.[25]

The precarious political position of President Prado became even more unstable with the onset of the war. Taking advantage of growing popular discontent, Piérola and other prominent Peruvians refused to serve in his government. When Congress refused to commit more funds to the war effort, Prado left for Europe hoping that a direct appeal to bankers might bring new foreign loans to the financially strapped nation.

While Prado solicited funds in Europe, Piérola led a popular uprising in Lima against the absent president, denounced him as a traitor for leaving Peru, and declared himself President of Peru in December 1879. When Chilean forces took Lima, Piérola fled to Ayacucho in South Central Peru and established a government there. With Piérola and Prado simultaneously absent from Lima, a group of Peruvian notables, with the approval of the Chilean government, named Francisco Garcia Calderón President of a new Peruvian government. Thus with its capital occupied by outside forces, two separate governments ruled Peru while its duly elected President was powerless in Europe.

Financially, the country remained in crisis as Peru's economy spiraled downward. The creation of the Peruvian Guano Company had alleviated the debt burden of the National Treasury, but the Raphael contract provided only a brief respite from the nation's fiscal difficulties. Despite Prado's efforts to develop new sources of revenue and limit government spending, expenditures continued to outpace revenues at an increasing rate. In fact, after 1877, the Prado regime relied almost exclusively on unbacked paper money.[26] Peru had reached a low point economically. As Cotler states:

> [F]iscal bankruptcy, and with it that of the national economy was declared. For close to thirty years Peru had counted on sufficient resources to attain vigorous economic growth . . . but the colonial shape of society, and its political disintegration annulled any possibility (of continued growth).[27]

The War of the Pacific disrupted industry, trade, and commerce throughout the country, and the loss of valuable territory to Chile further devastated the national financial and economic condition. These difficulties left Peru desperate for funds, and thus debt-issue weak.

With respect to the bondholders, Peru continued to remain medium strong in overall capabilities. On a broader scale, however, Peru's position began to weaken. Congress refused to vote for new taxes for the war effort, and the Executive failed to secure badly needed funds from abroad. More importantly, Chile continued to threaten Peru's very sovereignty by occupying the nation's capital and

[25] Pike (1967), pp. 140–141. [26] Pike (1967), p. 141. [27] Cotler (1978), p. 112.

capturing portions of Peru's territory. The turmoil within its borders focused the energies of the country inward, rendering it powerless on the international level.

Lenders. As noted, the creditors divided into rival factions over the Raphael contract. A small group of English bondholders who organized themselves under a separate protectorate committee, the Croyle Committee, opposed the contract. The Russell Committee continued to support it.

Similar committees opposed to the contract formed among French and Belgian bondholders. These bondholders felt that the Raphael contract violated their rights because it used guano revenue to redeem advances made to the government before the revenue was applied to debt service.[28]

With large outstanding loans to Peru, the bondholders remained debt-issue weak. The British bondholders had contracted through brokerage houses and therefore, as small private investors, took the risk. Negotiations by the Peruvian government with Dreyfus in 1874 had given the French creditor rights to the country's guano, leaving the British bondholders without control over any major Peruvian assets. In addition, the bondholders lacked sufficient funds to cover litigation expenses incurred when they took their demands to their own governments' judicial systems.

As for overall capabilities, the bondholders continued to maintain their ability to block any new Peruvian bond flotations on the London market. But having contracted to develop the Peruvian Guano Company, and with a large outstanding debt, the bondholders were vulnerable to pressure from Peru. As the Company began to fail financially, the bondholders had little recourse.

Creditor governments. Both strategic and economic interests piqued the creditor governments' interest in Peru's situation. British courts refused to hear the case of the bondholders versus Dreyfus, because as an agent of the Peruvian government, he could not be sued without the presence of an official Peruvian representative. Because the principal was a foreign government, the case was outside the jurisdiction of the British courts.[29] Belgian and French lower courts heard suits against the Dreyfus brothers, but higher courts threw out the suits on similar jurisdictional grounds.[30]

The Peruvian situation, however, occasioned a particularly high level of interest on the part of British and other European governments, primarily because of the War of the Pacific. The war between the three South American republics involved important resource-rich territories in Southern Peru, Western Bolivia, and Northern Chile, which increased the involvement of the world's more powerful nations. As the war continued, creditor governments grew more interested in the situation for economic, political, and strategic reasons.

[28] *The Bullionist*, June 17, 1876, in Wynne (1951), p. 127.
[29] Wynne (1951), p. 130. [30] Wynne (1951), p. 131.

Cardinal Payoff Matrix,
Intervention Expected

		Lenders IS 4/8		
		HC...	MC...	LC...
	HA...	−1.5, −1.5	−5, 2.83	−6.5, 7.17
Peru IS 4/8	MA...	2.83, −5	−1, −1	−3.5, 3
	LA...	7.17, −6.5	3, −3.5	**−.5, −.5**

Note: Nash equilibrium bolded; expected outcome with intervention underlined.

Ordinal Payoff Matrix,
Intervention Expected

		Lenders IS 4/8		
		HC...	MC...	LC...
	HA...	4, 4	2, 7	1, 9
Peru IS 4/8	MA...	7, 2	5, 5	3, 8
	LA...	9, 1	8, 3	**6, 6**

Note: Nash equilibrium bolded; expected outcome with intervention underlined.

Figure 8.2. *Play phase, period two: 1876–1880*

Debt game and predicted outcome

From our classifications, we arrive at the debt game matrix shown in Figure 8.2. In a two-actor game, we would expect an outcome of mutual confrontation, LA..., LC.... Both players have a dominant strategy of non-cooperation, yielding a Nash equilibrium with an ordinal payoff of 6, 6. During this period, we might expect some intervention on the part of creditor governments against Peru in an effort to secure their interests in the guano and nitrate trade, leading to an outcome of MA..., LC.... But given Peru's considerably lower payoff at this point, we would also expect a need for continued pressure on the part of these actors.

The negotiations and outcome

After the Raphael contract's implementation in 1876, a number of problems concerning the actual contract stipulations developed. Dreyfus, which still controlled a monopoly of over 2 million tons of guano, posed the most important difficulty. Because Dreyfus owned thousands of tons of unsold guano, it began lowering the price, allowing the Company to dominate the market. On the other hand, with government-fixed prices, the Peruvian Guano Company was not competitive.[31]

When the Company failed to show profits, the frustrated bondholders turned again to the British government for assistance in late 1878. In this instance, the government showed greater concern, and proposed to rally other countries to pressure Peru. In response, shortly thereafter the Peruvian government agreed to give the Company £25,000 monthly out of the guano income the Raphael contract provided, and also allowed the Company to sell guano at competitive rates. Despite this move, throughout the remaining duration of the Raphael contract, the Company continued to pay the bondholders nothing and eventually even failed to meet the reduced annuity owed to the government.[32] Although the motivation for British intervention is not entirely clear,[33] the Foreign Office may have been responding to strong concern by British owners of Peruvian nitrate certificates. Both British and other companies had lost their control of the Tarapacá nitrate mines in 1875–1876 when Peru nationalized the mines to control competition in the fertilizer market.[34]

Chile's 1879 seizure of valuable Peruvian guano lands and destruction of the nation's southern ports prevented Peru from raising revenues for the war. It also brought a serious loss to the bondholders, because Peru had closely linked the debt service to the guano proceeds via the Peruvian Guano Company. The creditors realized that without the guano revenues for either Peru, the Company, or another third party with whom they might negotiate, they would never be able to secure servicing on the debts owed them.

With Peru's war effort disintegrating, President Prado attempted to secure an advance from Dreyfus. Dreyfus did not respond, however, and in October 1879 Prado sent two officials to London to obtain a loan. Although Peru signed a contract with the Société Générale that replaced the Raphael contract, events conspired to undermine this accord. This agreement, similar to previous contracts, gave the Société the right to exploit all of Peru's guano in exchange for a government royalty. It earmarked 80% of the net proceeds for payments to the

[31] Wynne (1951), p. 126. [32] Miller (1976), p. 77 and Wynne (1951), p. 126.

[33] Miller (1976), p. 77, argues that the change in policy resulted because of the replacement of Lord Derby by Lord Salisbury in the Foreign Office.

[34] See Dennis (1931/1967), pp. 68–69 and pp. 73–74 on the nitrate mines.

bondholders of the 1870 and 1872 loans.[35] Most European bondholders accepted the plan, but the British bondholders balked at the agreement. Because of Peru's relative instability, and the fact that Chile now held the important guano territories, they doubted they would ever receive a penny.

In the meantime, before the contract with Société Générale had been concluded, President Prado suddenly left Peru for Europe on December 18, 1879. Although there is disagreement as to whether Prado had simply abandoned Peru or had gone to seek aid in person, the outcome was his replacement by Nicolás de Piérola, who quickly established a de facto government. In January 1880, Piérola canceled the Société Générale contract and concluded a new one with Dreyfus. The parties agreed to annul the previous Dreyfus contract of April 14, 1874, and in exchange, the government recognized a debt of 21,083,196 soles, or £4 million, which Dreyfus would recover by exporting more guano. According to the agreement, Dreyfus would export guano to European markets except those already serviced by the Peruvian Guano Company in order to avoid ruinous competition. In fact, the parties almost reached another agreement in which Dreyfus would take over the Company's guano stocks, but in the end the Company refused.[36]

The British bondholders protested against the new Dreyfus contract, appealing to the British government to take action. The British government stated that the agreement, "if carried into effect, would deprive the bondholders of the surplus profit in the sales of guano now in the hands of the Peruvian Guano Company, to which they are both legally and justly entitled."[37] Whitehall asked the French government to join in on behalf of the French bondholders. The French, however, declined this offer because Paris favored the larger claims of its national, Dreyfus. The creditors, bondholders, and Dreyfus recognized that debt servicing based on guano represented a private good. As a result of the limited resources, the nation's creditors, already divided between the bondholders and Peru's other financiers, also split along national lines and divided the allied creditor governments as well. At the same time, realizing that Peru could hardly bargain successfully – considering the fact that many of the nation's most valuable territories were now occupied by Chile – the British bondholders looked to Chile to secure their rights to the guano.

Summary. During this period, the bondholders were frustrated by their inability to force Peru to make any concessions to them. Following the bondholders' split after the Raphael contract, we expected to see a deadlocked negotiating game, with possible intervention by the British government. In fact, the British managed to get the Peruvians to commit to turning over some of their revenue from the contract with the Peruvian Guano Company. The MA..., LC... outcome quickly fell apart, however. The war with Chile left Peru in desperate

[35] *The Bullionist*, February 7, 1880, in Wynne (1951), 138–139.
[36] See Wynne (1951), p. 135 and Dennis (1931/1967), pp. 101–106.
[37] St. John to Señor Calderón, Peru no. 1 (1882), cited in Wynne (1951), p. 136.

straits. Rapid political changes in the government, a loss of territory, and contracts being negotiated on assets of uncertain ownership helped stall the negotiations between Peru and the bondholders. In short, although we predicted an outcome of MA..., LC... with intervention, and such an outcome did take place for a short while, in the end Peru shifted back to its two-actor Nash equilibrium strategy.

With the Peruvians unable to sustain an agreement, the bondholders now turned their attention to the game with Chile. Bondholders hoped that they would be more successful with Chile than with Peru, a "bankrupt, harassed and virtually defeated state."[38]

Situational changes

Creditor governments were more involved in debt negotiations during this period than in the earlier period, but they were divided because of Peru's limited ability to satisfy all of its creditors. The British government showed a greater willingness to pressure Peru on behalf of its country's bondholders and financiers. The French government, however, was torn between supporting the claims of French bondholders and Dreyfus.

As noted, the most significant change in debt negotiations occurred when the game shifted away from Peru to a new game with Chile during the War of the Pacific, in which Chile occupied Peru's nitrate-rich northern territory. In this case, the bondholders faced a stable Chile, but one that was issue and overall weak. The divided bondholders united as a result of Chile's actions soon after the beginning of this period, but as we shall see, found themselves in competition with Dreyfus.

Periods three and four, 1880–1881 and 1882–1886: betting on Chile

From 1880 to 1886, important debt negotiations took place between the bondholders and Chile. Although the bondholders were initially pleased by this twist in their efforts to secure debt payments, they soon found Chile to be a tough bargaining opponent. Because of the primary focus on Chile in these two periods rather than on Peru, I will discuss the two periods together in this section.

Identifying individual situations

In the initial game in 1880, Chile was coalitionally stable, debt-issue weak, and overall weak (IS 7). In the third period, the bondholders were split, remaining issue weak and overall medium (IS 4/8). In the fourth period, from 1882 to 1886, Chile found itself with a stable coalition, and both issue and overall strong (IS 5). Although the bondholders became united after the end of the third period,

[38] Wynne (1951), p. 138.

the fourth period saw Dreyfus and the bondholders competing with each other for Chile's attention. We thus code the lenders as coalitionally medium. The lenders continued to be issue weak and overall medium when considered as a group (IS 3/8).

Chile. Among Latin American countries, Chile stood out in terms of political stability.[39] Following considerable conflict in the early years of its independence, the 1833 constitution greatly stabilized the domestic political situation. It gave the Executive wide-ranging powers, allowing the Congress little control over policymaking except budget approval. This budgetary control, combined with important changes in Chile's economic situation led to the civil war of 1891; however, until the late 1880s, the Executive faced little opposition. The conflict between liberals and conservatives, while at times intense, with few exceptions by and large remained contained to the political arena. In contrast to other South American countries, Chile had repeated peaceful presidential succession during the middle part of the nineteenth century.

In 1876, President Aníbal Pinto began to contend with the global economic depression that afflicted most countries after 1873 and the ensuing turmoil. In addition, he encountered growing opposition from the Church. Although Chile's vaunted political stability now seemed in jeopardy, the onset of the War of the Pacific and capture of the nitrate fields sharply stabilized Chile's political situation and created major economic improvements. In the words of one leading analyst, "The nitrate fields would provide the means to lubricate the Chilean economy and political apparatus for some years to come."[40]

President Domingo Santa María, elected in 1881, was even stronger than his predecessor. He used his power and liberal congressional support to enact many reforms including universal male suffrage, secular marriages, and other changes. His Minister of the Interior, José Manuel Balmaceda, led the reform brigade. Although these reforms antagonized the Church and conservative elements – and would eventually lead to conflict that enveloped Balmaceda – during his term, Santa María continued to successfully exercise the considerable powers of the Executive. In 1886, he engineered Balmaceda's election to the presidency.

With respect to issue-capabilities, Chile was quite weak in the initial stages of the conflict with Peru.[41] The depression had taken a major toll on its industry, causing a fall in exports and crises in industry and banking. By 1878, Chilean currency had become inconvertible. Economically, however, the war proved a boon to Chile, as the newly conquered territories bolstered their fertilizer exports and stimulated general growth in its economy. In fact, the guano export arrangement negotiated in the first period led to what a leading scholar of this period called "the strange spectacle of a government beginning a war bankrupt and

[39] This section draws on Loveman (1979), Blakemore (1974), and O'Brien (1982).

[40] Loveman (1979), p. 184.

[41] This section draws heavily on Marichal (1989), pp. 106–107 for a discussion of Chile's economic situation.

each year accumulating a surplus.'"[42] Nitrates in the captured territories led Chile's exports, accounting for over 50% of its exports from 1881 to 1890.[43] In addition, the war stimulated much more rapid industrialization, with "more factories . . . founded between 1880 and 1889 than had existed in Chile prior to the war."[44]

In terms of overall capabilities, during the first period Chile found itself in a highly vulnerable position, because it relied heavily on goodwill from the European powers. After the initial agreement with the bondholders, the structure of the game became more defined, and Chile found itself in an overall strong position. As military success stabilized its situation, Chile was in firm control of the assets on which the bondholders relied, and the prospects for a Peruvian counter-attack to retake its lost territories receded quickly.

Lenders. In the third period's negotiations, the bondholders' coalition continued to be unstable with the Russell and Croyle committees remaining estranged. But this instability quickly changed, leading to a new period as a result of Chile's offer in 1880 to provide high concessions to the bondholders as a group, an action which led to the formation of a unified bondholder front to represent their interests. In this fourth period, however, the Dreyfus and the united bondholders began to compete for a debt servicing commitment from Chile, leaving the lenders as a whole medium in stability.[45] The bondholders remained debt-issue weak because they still lacked the funds to cover any losses on the substantial Peruvian foreign debt. Moreover, unlike Dreyfus, which had guano reserves in its possession, the bondholders had no such bargaining chip to settle accounts. The bondholders could not even pay the expenses of their respective committees. Throughout the two periods, the bondholders were faced with a large outstanding debt but maintained their ability to block loans, in this case, against Chile if it sought to secure a quotation on the London market.

Creditor governments. As before, we would expect a continued active interest on the part of various creditor governments because of to the importance of the guano and nitrate-rich territories. The U.S., concerned about maintaining the Monroe Doctrine, might also be expected to involve itself in the negotiations. In addition, the French government could be expected to be solicitous of Dreyfus's interests and its contract with Peru, while the British government could be expected to support the bondholders in their dealings with Chile.

Debt game and predicted outcome: period three

From our classifications, we arrive at the debt game shown in Figure 8.3. We expect a Nash equilibrium of HA..., LC... with an outcome highly favorable to

[42] Dennis (1931/1967), p. 110. [43] O'Brien (1982), p. 129. [44] Loveman (1979), p. 192.

[45] It is somewhat difficult to code the coalition as a whole in their negotiations with Chile, and some might argue that a coding of unstable might be more appropriate. Although this changes the payoffs that the lenders receive, the equilibrium does not change (that is, for a game with Chile in IS 5 and the lenders in IS 4/8).

Cardinal Payoff Matrix,
Intervention Expected

Lenders IS 4/8

		HC...	MC...	LC...
	HA...	12, −1.5	9, 2.83	**<u>10, 7.17</u>**
Chile IS 7	MA...	11.67, −5	8, −1	7, 3
	LA...	11.33, −6.5	7, −3.5	4, −.5

Note: Nash equilibrium bolded; expected outcome with intervention underlined.

Ordinal Payoff Matrix,
Intervention Expected

Lenders IS 4/8

		HC...	MC...	LC...
	HA...	9, 4	5, 7	**<u>6, 9</u>**
Chile IS 7	MA...	8, 2	4, 5	2.5, 8
	LA...	7, 1	2.5, 3	1, 6

Note: Nash equilibrium bolded; expected outcome with intervention underlined.

Figure 8.3. *Play phase, period three: 1880 (game with Chile)*

the bondholders, who receive their highest payoff. In this case, we expect intervention favoring the lenders to reinforce the equilibrium outcome of the two-actor game.

The negotiations and outcome: period three

During period three, from November 1879 to February 1880, Peru dealt mainly with Dreyfus, while the bondholders made an arrangement with Chile. In

November 1879, the Russell bondholder committee called on the British government to protect the bondholders' interests by pressuring Chile to allow Peru's debt to be serviced. The British government responded by protesting to Chile that its wartime actions had harmed British shipping and trade interests, as well as those of Peru's creditors whose loans had been secured on that country's guano.[46] Furthermore, the British government urged Chile to allow the Peruvian Guano Company to ship guano from the southern deposits, thus respecting the rights of the bondholders. By 1880, after Chile occupied the guano and nitrate-rich province of Tarapacá, the British government once again urged it to respect the bondholders' rights to the guano through the Peruvian Guano Company.[47] The British government thereby hoped to clear British access to the fertilizer, and simultaneously pay lip service to the demands of its bondholding nationals.

The Croyle Committee had always opposed the creation of the Peruvian Guano Company, claiming it served the interests of the Peruvian government more than those of the bondholders. The Croyle Committee sent a representative, to ask Chile to cease the company's export of guano. In addition, the envoy urged Chile to allow the bondholders the rights to the guano in exchange for a substantial royalty. In response to Croyle's actions, the Russell Committee reminded Chilean government officials that only his committee could legitimately represent the bondholders.[48] In supporting the Croyle Committee, the British Minister in Lima noted that "The only plan which would prove satisfactory to the bondholders would be for them to enter into a direct arrangement with the Peruvian Government . . . [and] have the complete management of the business in their own hands . . . the interests of the [Peruvian Guano] Company are completely antagonistic to those of the bondholders."[49]

Besieged by the competing demands of the two bondholder committees, and facing an uncertain international situation including pressures from the British and the need to maintain goodwill in Europe,[50] the Chilean government proposed a guano-debt settlement based on the Croyle Committee's proposals. But Chile made the adoption of the settlement subject to majority approval of all the bondholders, to appease the Russell Committee. With this key stipulation and the prospect of an agreement with Chile, the rival bondholder committees met on February 2, 1880. They passed a resolution condemning the new Piérola-Dreyfus accord, and reconvened a new unified committee. The Committee declared that for the present, "to enter into or approve any contract with Peru would be futile."[51]

According to the settlement, Chilean Commander-in-Chief of the occupied forces at Tarapacá, General Erasmo Escala, agreed to permit the bondholders to

[46] Wynne (1951), p. 136. [47] Wynne (1951), p. 138.
[48] *The Bullionist*, February 7, 1880, cited in Wynne (1951), p. 138.
[49] St. John in Peru No. 1 (1882), No. 30, cited in Wynne (1951), p. 137.
[50] See Palacios (1983), p. 215 on Chilean interest in using this agreement to bolster its position in Europe.
[51] *The Bullionist*, February 7, 1880, cited in Wynne (1951), p. 138.

export guano from the occupied Peruvian territory. His decision was followed a day later by another decree of General J.A. Villagran. This compromise called for payment of a royalty of 30 shillings per ton. The other conditions were allowing the nomination of a committee to work with the Chilean government on this matter, and asking the bondholders to appoint a consignee, subject to the approval of the Chilean government, to carry out the guano transaction.[52]

The agreement proved highly favorable to the bondholders. As the Council of Foreign Bondholders noted:

> The assignment made by the Chilean Government to the Bondholders of Peru of the chief property forming security for their claims is a remarkable incident in the history of national indebtedness. The honourable act of that conquering Republic in preserving the rights of the creditors of its antagonist, not withstanding their repudiation of the latter, will remain an example of high national probity, and, it is hoped, will form a precedent for the future.[53]

Although the agreement sacrificed some Chilean revenues from the sale of guano and marked a high degree of concessions by the government, it proved to be a boon to Chile's economy.

Peru remained an outsider to the negotiations between Chile and the bondholders, but continued to negotiate with Dreyfus. On June 30, 1880, the Piérola government reached a settlement with Dreyfus whereby Peru agreed to consolidate its debt, to give up control of its railways for a 25-year period, to pay a 4% service on its debt, and to pay Dreyfus £3,214,388 as an adjustment of accounts dealing with the guano contract of January 1880.[54] In short by June 1880, Peru made a series of last-minute deals – using some assets that it no longer controlled – in order to sustain its war effort.[55]

The reunited bondholders had protested against the Dreyfus accord. Subsequently, Dreyfus, supported by the French government, protested the Chilean-bondholder agreement because it favored the bondholders over the other creditors of Peru who had valid claims to the hypothecated guano.

In the meantime, the U.S. had been making a number of efforts to prevent European interference in the Americas, in an attempt to enforce the Monroe Doctrine.[56] In March 1880, Secretary of State William Evarts cabled American representatives in Bolivia, Chile, and Peru asking them to be prepared to offer mediation if the Europeans took a more aggressive stance. In July 1880, the American representative in Santiago offered to mediate negotiations over ending the war, and Chile accepted this offer in August. But as Chilean battlefield successes continued, little came of a conference held aboard the U.S.S. *Lackawanna*.

52 See Palacios (1983), pp. 214–215, Dennis (1931/1967), pp. 105–108, and Wynne (1951), p. 139 for a discussion of details of this agreement.

53 Corporation of Foreign Bondholders 1880, p. 47, cited in Wynne (1951), p. 139.

54 Award of Rapperschwyl, Desc. and Ren., p. 421, cited in Wynne (1951), p. 135. Palacios (1983), p. 212.

55 Palacios (1983), p. 212.

56 This discussion of U.S. intervention draws heavily on Dennis (1931/1967), pp. 108–113. See also Millington (1948).

By January of 1881, Chilean troops had taken Lima, and Peru's defeat was assured.

Summary. In this period, we saw the bondholders attempting to negotiate with both Chile and Peru. As a result of its military success, the Chilean government gained new territory, and with it, new headaches. Pressed by the British government and the bondholders, the Chileans agreed to allow the bondholders to exploit guano in the occupied territories, leading to an outcome of HA..., LC.... This concession came at a time when Chile was deeply concerned about the British government's intentions. From the Chilean perspective, concessions to the bondholders seemed to be a reasonable strategy to prevent further British involvement and to gain support for its expansionist position. For its part, Peru agreed to major concessions because of its extreme weakness, but the deal came too late to enhance Peru's position.

Situational changes, period three

During this period, Chile used its capabilities to unite the feuding bondholders by insisting that it would deal with only one committee. It further unified them by insisting that a settlement be subject to majority approval. But although they became united as a condition of the agreement, the bondholders quickly found their stability threatened by competition with Dreyfus for debt servicing in the next period.

An additional change led to the fourth period. Chile's payoffs in period three's game indicated that it would not be very pleased with its agreement. But as Chile's financial and overall position improved – both because of the agreement and its war efforts – its situation became very strong. Its financial situation had been boosted by fertilizer exports from the new territories, and the war had stimulated general growth in the economy.

Signs of Chile's shift toward a more aggressive stance began as early as May 1880 when it began to impose new restrictions on the February 1880 agreement. The government asserted that not all of the bondholders had accepted the representative committee. Accordingly, Chile required that the bondholders register and deposit all the bonds before the agreement would take effect. Of the £33 million outstanding bonds, £26 million were registered and deposited.[57] By May 1881, the Chileans had removed the bondholders' control of funds by appointing Anthony Gibbs as their agent in London.[58]

Debt game and predicted outcome: period four

Based on the improvements in Chile's situation, we predict the game and outcome shown in Figure 8.4. In this bargaining game, we expect an equilibrium outcome of LA..., LC..., which gives the debtor a relatively high payoff. Given

[57] The balance of the bonds was most likely held outside of Britain. Peruvian Corporation, Ltd. (1891), p. 17 and Corporation of Foreign Bondholders (1881), pp. 57–58, cited in Wynne (1951), p. 140.
[58] Wynne (1951), p. 140.

Cardinal Payoff Matrix,
Intervention Expected

Lenders IS 3/8

		HC...	MC...	LC...
	HA...	−3, 4.5	−3.5, 6.83	−3, 9.17
Chile IS 5	MA...	−1.33, 1	−2, 3	−2, 5
	LA...	.33, −.5	−.5, .5	**−1, 1.5**

Note: Nash equilibrium bolded; expected outcome with intervention underlined.

Ordinal Payoff Matrix,
Intervention Expected

Lenders IS 3/8

		HC...	MC...	LC...
	HA...	2.5, 6	1, 8	2.5, 9
Chile IS 5	MA...	6, 3	4.5, 5	4.5, 7
	LA...	9, 1	8, 2	**7, 4**

Note: Nash equilibrium bolded; expected outcome with intervention underlined.

Figure 8.4. *Play phase, period four: 1882–1886 (game with Chile)*

the interest of creditor governments, however, we might expect some efforts to push Chile to undertake some adjustment. But we would not expect such intervention to be sustained, given conflicts among the creditor governments because of their differing economic and strategic interests.

The negotiations and outcome: period four

I divide period four into two rounds. The first round concludes with an agreement in February 1882. The second round examines the aftermath of the Treaty of Ancón (negotiated in 1883) until 1886, the year the bondholders turned their attention away from Chile.

Round one. After the onset of the War of the Pacific, Chile's position was greatly strengthened. Its economic situation improved rapidly, putting it in an enviable position in its negotiations with the bondholders. Moreover, its military victories gave it firm control of important resources, making it difficult for others to budge it from the new status quo.

In 1882, the bondholders' committee sent a negotiator to Santiago to conclude a new, more permanent settlement because Chile had stipulated that the 1880 guano concession would only last for the duration of the war. The Chilean government also sought an agreement that would respond to increasing pressure from the French government that Chile act to address Dreyfus's claims.[59]

Chile and the bondholders reached a new arrangement on February 9, 1882. This new agreement, which suspended the 1880 concession agreement, called for Chile to sell 1 million tons of Tarapacá guano to the highest bidder. One-half of the profit would be deposited with the Bank of England and would be paid to Peru's creditors of 1880.[60] These creditors included the bondholders, Dreyfus, and other guano shippers who had outstanding claims to the security. The agreement also established an arbitration tribunal to evaluate the validity, legitimacy, and priority of the various claims.[61] This so-called Guano Sale Agreement of 1882 recognized that Peru had numerous creditors whose claims were secured by guano. The group included Dreyfus, Peru's one-time financial agent, which would now compete with the bondholders for guano rights.

The outcome in this case appears to reflect a concern on Chile's part of possible intervention by creditor governments, and an MA..., LC... outcome. Although the agreement appears to reflect high adjustment by Chile, in fact, it is almost closer to the two-actor predicted equilibrium of LA..., LC.... The 1 million tons of guano promised in the sale probably did not exist in Tarapacá, owing to the depletion of reserves there. The agreement also excluded future guano sites, as well as the real source of potential revenue: the nitrate deposits.[62] As a result, the treaty did not initially yield the bondholders any money, which led them to complain vociferously.[63]

Round two. Following the negotiation of the 1882 agreement, the bondholders pressed the Chilean Minister in England, Blest Gana, for payments. He alluded to "delicate points" that needed to be resolved before any money could be disbursed to the bondholders, but assured them that Chile would continue to make payments to the Bank of England in an interest bearing account.

In the meantime, however, Chile worked toward a more permanent arrangement for the occupied territories. In 1883, Chile and Peru signed the Treaty of

[59] Wynne (1951), p. 146. [60] Wynne (1951), p. 146 and Palacios (1983), p. 218.
[61] These questions would not be fully settled until 1901. [62] Wynne (1951), p. 148.
[63] Palacios (1983), p. 218.

Ancón. Under its provisions, Chile permanently obtained the territory of Tarapacá and its valuable nitrate deposits, as well as the regions of Tacna and Arica for 10 years. A plebiscite would thereafter determine the future of the latter two areas.[64] A final stipulation of the treaty called for the removal of Chilean forces from Peru in 1884. Although Chile reiterated its commitment to abide by its February 1882 agreement, and promised an additional 50% of revenue it obtained from guano extracted from the territories, the bondholders still failed to receive any funds.

In December 31, 1883, the British bondholders complained to their government about Chile's actions, arguing as before that they should receive income from future deposits and demanding that their bonds should also be serviced by nitrate deposits. In this case, because Dreyfus simultaneously pressed the French government for action, they managed to evoke a response. Although the French initially considered an embargo on guano and minerals exported by Chile from the annexed territories, it backed down when the British expressed disapproval of such a dramatic move.[65] Instead, both countries joined Spain, Italy, the Netherlands, and Belgium in February 1884 in protest of the treaty, arguing that the transfer of territory also meant that the obligations of that territory (the guano and nitrate revenues) should be transferred.

The reaction from Peru and Chile was hardly what might be expected in response to the actions of such a strong group of countries. Peru denounced the foreign interference in the right of a sovereign government to make its own treaties. It stated that the debts in question involved private parties, and as such did not have an international character.[66] An occupied Peru was obviously in a weak position. Moreover, Peru wished to escape a portion of its debt service obligations, and also placed hope in the Treaty of Ancón as its best chance of recovering Tacna and Arica through a plebiscite. Chile responded similarly to the creditor governments in June 1884, but expressed a willingness to come to an accord with them. The bondholders agreed to arbitration as called for in the treaty, but Dreyfus refused. Thus, the Chileans determined that they were faced with a conflict among the creditors and simply refused to make any adjustment because of the competing claims.[67]

Faced with continued pressure from the bondholders and other creditors, on August 10, 1885, the creditor governments again asked the Chileans to accommodate the creditors.[68] Chile responded that it had already undertaken a number of actions to satisfy their claims following its occupation of Tarapacá. The Chilean government reiterated that the conflicts among the creditors prevented the satisfaction of their claims "to the injury of all."[69] It pledged to examine, but not initiate, proposals for further adjustment and settlement.

[64] A final settlement of this territory was not made until the 1920s. For a discussion, see Dennis (1931/1967).

[65] Palacios (1983), pp. 231–232.

[66] See Wynne (1951), p. 150 and Palacios (1983), pp. 229–230. [67] Wynne (1951), p. 151.

[68] Peruvian Bondholders' Committee (December 22, 1985), p. 17, cited in Wynne (1951), p. 152.

[69] Wynne (1951), p. 152.

In response to Chile's stubborn proclamation, the bondholders came to an accord with Dreyfus, whereby they agreed upon a division of proceeds from any Chilean servicing of Peru's debt.[70] In settling the dispute over the claims, the bondholders hoped to end their differences with the other creditors and thereby bring about some sort of settlement with Chile. In addition, the creditors called for greater intervention by their governments to jointly settle the amounts due from the Chilean government. The governments, however, were not as united as the creditors appeared to be. The French government accepted the plan, but the British government did not. It refused to become directly involved in a private debt servicing agreement in accord with its traditional non-intervention policy in such matters.

Despite the British government's refusal to intervene above the diplomatic level, the bondholders were encouraged by the assurance of continued official support. They decided that their best course would be to leave negotiations with Chile to the British government. Thus, in the second round of this period, the outcome can best be described as a deadlock, with Chile making no/low adjustment and the lenders offering no/low concessions.

Summary. In the first round, debt negotiations were initially deadlocked, but under pressure from creditor governments, the Chileans concluded an agreement to provide some servicing to the lenders in the talks that ended 1882. In the second round, the Chileans proved more resistant to persuasion, because ambivalence among creditor governments neutralized the pressure on Chile. The French government supported their own primary domestic economic interests in Dreyfus, while the U.K. retreated to its traditional stance of non-intervention.

Situational changes

The most significant situational change during the fourth period involved the new conflict between lenders, which created a new problem for the bondholders. As Dreyfus competed with them, and as Chile became strong across the board through the use of its capabilities, they found themselves in a highly unfavorable situation. Both the bondholders and Dreyfus turned to their creditor governments, appealing to principles and norms of international law to change their individual situation or at least to secure intervention. This alliance formation effort proved problematic. Creditor governments could not agree among themselves because of differing strategic interests, and the Chileans now played Dreyfus off against the bondholders to prevent stronger intervention. When the bondholders attempted to unify with Dreyfus by making an initial sacrifice in their servicing arrangements, their prospects improved. But the creditor governments failed to support this accord because of their own strategic and political concerns.

[70] Initially, Dreyfus would have priority over the bondholders, and then the bondholders would have priority over Dreyfus. See Wynne (1951), p. 152, n. 60 for details.

Following the deadlock of the last bargaining round and their low payoff, we would expect the bondholders to be highly motivated to promote changes in their bargaining situation. Having exhausted all avenues with both the Chilean and the British governments, the logical strategy was to rekindle negotiations with the recently stabilized Peru. It is to this negotiating arena that we now turn.

Periods five through seven, 1886–1889: negotiating the Grace contract

Our discussion of Peruvian politics in the second period ended with Piérola's assumption of power and his agreement with Dreyfus. In the third and fourth periods, the attention of the bondholders had shifted to Chile. In 1886, however, bondholders once again turned to Peru to secure debt servicing. Although I do not formally examine Peruvian politics from 1880 to 1886 because of the lenders' focus on Chile, I will make a few observations to provide background to the negotiations discussed in this section.[71]

The Chilean occupation of Lima allowed two governments to exist in Peru – Piérola in the highlands of Ayacucho and Chilean-backed Garcia Calderón in Lima. Both governments, however, ran into difficulties. One of Piérola's commanders, Lizandro Montero, turned on the dictator, overthrew him, and declared himself president. In Lima, Chilean forces arrested its erstwhile figurehead, García Calderón, for his stubborn refusal to accede to the Santiago government's territorial desires. In the North, the Congress of the northern Departments voted Miguel Iglesias new President of Peru with Chile's support, while in the South, General Andrés Cáceres laid claim to the post.

By 1882, during the War of the Pacific and the occupation of the Peruvian capital, the three military men, Montero (who later fled), Cáceres, and Iglesias, all claimed the Peruvian presidency. The Chileans recognized Iglesias's government, and concluded the Treaty of Ancón with him in 1883. When both Cáceres and Piérola's followers opposed Iglesias, he began to use heavy repression to silence his critics. Cáceres's Constitutionalist Party, formed in 1884, and Piérola's Democratic Party shared the common goal of deposing Iglesias though they were fiercely divided on other issues.

The first military attempt to oust the President in August 1884 failed, but the second succeeded a year later. Recognizing his lack of a political base, Iglesias renounced his claims and left Peru. Cáceres secured the office of the presidency with wide support in the elections of March 1886, despite the boycott by Piérola's Democratic Party.

In 1886, General Cáceres's leadership and the development of a stable government in Peru renewed the bondholders' interest in negotiating. Still, the Peruvian Congress was split on the debt issue. Many politicians called for outright

[71] The summary discussion of Peruvian politics from 1880–1886 draws heavily on Pike (1967) and Werlich (1978).

repudiation of the debt on the grounds that because the bondholders had turned to Chile, they had lost their right to recourse with Peru.[72] The majority in the Congress, however, realized that Peru needed foreign capital to rebuild the shattered economy and bring about financial rehabilitation. They understood they needed to settle any default before foreign lenders would grant new loans. With this objective in mind, Peru reopened negotiations with the bondholders.

The analysis in this section consists of three closely linked periods, which revolved around negotiation of the so-called Grace contract. As we shall see, the early negotiations proceeded smoothly, but domestic conflicts and problems among the bondholders delayed a final resolution of Peru's long-standing debt problems with the Grace contract until 1890.

Identifying individual situations

For period five, from 1886 to 1887, we classify Peru as coalitionally stable, debt-issue weak, and overall weak (IS 7). We also classify the bondholders as coalitionally stable, debt-issue weak, and overall strong (IS 3). In the sixth period, covering late 1887 to early 1889, negotiation of a tentative agreement with Grace and the bondholders led to major instability in Peru (IS 8). The bondholders also experienced some instability as delays began to hurt their unity (IS 3/4). Finally, prior to the conclusion of the Grace contract in October 1889, Peru had stabilized its domestic situation somewhat, placing it in IS 7/8, while the bondholders remained in IS 3/4.

Peru. At the outset, Cáceres enjoyed great popularity with the Peruvians. This brought Peru much needed political stability after the multiple governments of the 1880–1886 period. Piérola's supporters boycotted the election, but the support of the *Civilistas* and Constitutionalists put him in office with wide public support. The election tallied one of the largest votes in Peruvian history.[73] In short, Peru had a relatively high degree of coalitional stability at this point.

But this stability began to deteriorate after about a year, with the signing of the first contract railroad-debt swap agreement (the Grace-Anibar contract) on May 26, 1887. In addition, Piérola's supporters began to work against the coalition that had brought Cáceres to power. By September 1887, Cáceres backed away from submission of this contract to the Congress, in part because of Chilean opposition to the accord but largely because of domestic opposition. By October 1887, Cáceres could not even find any ministers who were willing to serve in his government. The problems persisted from about June of 1887 to March 1889. During this period, Peru became domestically unstable.

Finally, after April 1889, Cáceres managed to somewhat stabilize his domestic political situation by manipulating the Congress. He appointed Pedro de Solar (Grace's attorney in Peru!) as his Prime Minister, and Solar quickly

[72] McQueen (1926), p. 89.

[73] See Pike (1967), pp. 152–153 and Werlich (1973), pp. 119–120 on Cáceres.

proceeded to remove Cáceres's opponents in the Congress through special partial elections.[74] Peru's domestic situation stabilized somewhat because of these measures, and Solar helped push the Grace contract through Congress in October 1889.

Financially, throughout the three periods from 1886 to 1889, the Treasury was nearly empty after years of war and turmoil; it apparently had only about £500 in its coffers when Cáceres came to power.[75] During the war, coastal agricultural lands had been destroyed, the transportation system was incapacitated, and the mining industry had ceased to exist. Commercial establishments and banks, particularly in Lima, lacked the capital resources to resume their activities. Export agriculture was frail, and guano deposits were exhausted. The loss of these revenue bases, as well as the loss of the nitrate industry to Chile, nearly broke the national Treasury.[76] In late 1888, Peruvian newspapers reported on the desperate state of the economy, arguing that the Grace contract was the only hope for Peru.[77] Despite significant efforts to promote economic adjustment and an improvement in the economy, Peruvian finances did not improve until after 1895.

As for overall capabilities, Peru remained weak on many dimensions. The Treaty of Ancón pointed to Peru's ongoing fear of Chile. With respect to overall development prospects, the railroads that had sucked up so much guano money produced almost no revenue for Peru. In relation to the bondholders, Peru had little leverage and controlled no significant assets.

Lenders. The bondholders remained united during these periods. Cáceres's rise to power changed the negotiations arena, allowing the bondholders to abandon their strategy of competition with Dreyfus. In October 1886, the Peruvian Congress disavowed Piérola's arrangement with Dreyfus, claiming that it had been an illegitimate contract. Although the French government made a number of protests on Dreyfus's behalf, the Peruvians did not respond. Thus, in the three periods considered here, negotiations were essentially restricted to those between bondholders and Peru.[78]

With respect to debt-issue resources, the bondholders remained weak because they acted without strong financial backing. The members of the committee in particular had to rely on their leadership and often faced financial manipulation by those elected to serve them.[79]

Yet, the bondholders as a group were in a strong position throughout the periods covered here. An example of their muscle was their ability to block countries' loan flotations on the London market. This power was evident before negotiations with Peru over the Grace contract even began; the bondholders

[74] Miller (1976), p. 90. Also see Pike (1967), p. 154. [75] Miller (1976), p. 82.
[76] Cotler (1978), p. 125; Werlich (1978), p. 119. [77] Miller (1976), pp. 88–89.
[78] This would not be the case after the conclusion of the agreement in 1889, however, as I note below.
[79] Miller (1976), p. 92.

prevented Michael Grace from securing funds to complete Peru's railroads on the London market in 1885. Another factor that solidified the bondholders' strong position at this time was Peru's obvious desire to secure funds. Finally, the British government's genuine efforts to secure servicing from Chile and its assurance that it would be solicitous of the bondholders' interests allowed the bondholders to proceed more aggressively than before.[80]

Creditor governments. The creditor governments continued to hold fragmented positions. The British were more supportive of the bondholders, while the French pressed Dreyfus's case. Still, as in the Chilean negotiations, the British government remained interested in using only its diplomatic offices to help the bondholders.

Debt game and predicted outcome: period five

According to our classifications, we arrive at the game shown in Figure 8.5. In this game, we expect a Nash equilibrium of HA..., LC... The debtor receives a much lower relative payoff than the lenders, who receive the highest payoff possible in this case. Given the favorable outcome for the bondholders, we would not expect any change in the equilibrium. The creditor governments appeared disposed to pressure the Peruvians, but little intervention was necessary to secure the bondholders' demands.

The negotiations and outcome: period five[81]

About the same time as Cáceres's election, the bondholders began to work with Michael P. Grace, the Lima-based merchant. As noted earlier, Grace had initially sought to secure the right to complete Peru's railroads, attempting unsuccessfully to borrow funds in New York and London to do so. Encouraged by Peru's new political stability, the bondholders agreed to work with Grace in an effort to settle Peru's debt in exchange for railroad rights.[82]

Having reopened direct negotiations, the Peruvian government and Grace, on behalf of the bondholders, worked towards an agreement. Cáceres initially agreed to give up the railroads in exchange for cancellation of Peru's debt, but he was not entirely satisfied with the terms (which, in addition, called for the foreign leasing of coal and mercury mines, oil fields, and guano rights for 75 years).[83] Although some Peruvians rejected the notion that Peru had any debt, a commission of experts appointed by Cáceres clearly recognized the nature of the debt game, and concluded that Grace's proposal was Peru's best hope.[84]

Recognizing the need to conclude a contract that met with the bondholders' approval, Peru sent its Finance Minister, Jose Araníbar, to London to proceed

[80] Although one might argue that the bondholders should still be coded as overall medium owing to the large debt, it should be noted that this would not change any of the three equilibria in periods five through seven discussed below.

[81] The major sources for the discussion of the Grace negotiations are Wynne (1951), Miller (1976, 1983), and Palacios (1983).

[82] Miller (1976), p. 80 and Pike (1967), p. 153. [83] Miller (1976), p. 81.

[84] Miller (1976), p. 83.

Cardinal Payoff Matrix, Intervention Expected

		Lenders IS 3		
		HC...	MC...	LC...
	HA...	12, 9	9, 9.67	**<u>10, 10.33</u>**
Peru IS 7	MA...	11.67, 5.5	8, 6	7, 6.5
	LA...	11.33, 3	7, 3	4, 3

Note: Nash equilibrium bolded; expected outcome with intervention underlined.

Ordinal Payoff Matrix, Intervention Expected

		Lenders IS 3		
		HC...	MC...	LC...
	HA...	9, 7	5, 8	**<u>6, 9</u>**
Peru IS 7	MA...	8, 4	4, 5	2.5, 6
	LA...	7, 2	2.5, 2	1, 2

Note: Nash equilibrium bolded; expected outcome with intervention underlined.

Figure 8.5. *Play phase, period five: 1886–May 1887*

with the negotiations. On May 26, 1887, Araníbar and Henry Tyler, the bondholders' committee representative, signed the Grace contract. It called for the formation of the Peruvian Corporation, a company owned by and created with the capital funding of the bondholders. Peru was to cede its railroads for a term of 66 years, and the Corporation was to have the right to exploit other Peruvian economic resources as well (although oil issues no longer constituted part of the arrangement). In exchange, the Corporation would build and operate the railroads while constructing other public works projects in Peru. Finally, Peru would be released from any further responsibility for its foreign debt, and Chile would be held accountable for half of the originally contracted debt. This latter clause involving Chile, as we shall see, would later prove to be a major sore point.

Once again, as during the great guano age, the Peruvian government granted a sizable national concession to a foreign concern in return for the alleviation of the nation's foreign debt burden. In this case, however, the arrangement did not call for simply a contract on exports, but for an actual debt-equity swap that would turn over most of Peru's major sources of revenue to the bondholders. In short, the agreement was one of high adjustment for Peru and few concessions for the bondholders.

Summary. As expected, during this period of negotiations Peru was in a highly vulnerable position and thus willing to make major concessions to the bondholders. Peru clearly recognized its weakness in the debt game and acted accordingly, concluding a deal in hopes of improving its longer term financial prospects.

Situational changes

Peru signed the Grace contract in May 1887, but difficulties emerged before the Peruvian Parliament had approved it. The Chilean government attacked the contract on the grounds that Chile was not responsible for half of Peru's debt. It further claimed that the contract represented a "surrender by Peru of part of her sovereignty and economic absorption by her creditors."[85] As one scholar of this period notes, this latter concern was hardly altruistic: Chile hoped to keep Peru from improving its financial prospects because doing so might allow it to pay compensation for the Chilean-occupied territories, Tacna and Arica, if Peru won the plebiscite scheduled for 1893.[86]

Chile exerted pressure on Peruvian President Cáceres to halt submission of the Grace Plan for congressional approval. This pressure stoked the fire of domestic conflict in Peru. The new arrangement outraged the *Piérolistas*, who had unsuccessfully worked to undermine the coalition that had placed Cáceres in power. As one historian noted: "For the *Piérolistas*, the signing of the Grace contract meant – like the previous system of consignments and the auction of guano – the surrender of national resources to foreign capital and an interference in national sovereignty."[87] These conflicts resulted in the rapid deterioration of Peru's political stability; on September 7, 1887, Cáceres withdrew the Araníbar-Tyler proposal from congressional consideration.[88] Shortly thereafter, the bondholders also faced some internal unrest, bringing us to a new debt game in period six.

[85] *Anales*, XVII, Docs. 60, 62, cited in Wynne (1951), p. 155. [86] Miller (1976), p. 84.
[87] Cotler (1978), p. 125; author's translation.
[88] Although the bondholders' coalition might still be considered to be stable at this time, the equilibria for a game with Peru in IS 8 and the bondholders in IS 3 are NA by Peru and high, medium, or low concessions by the bondholders. Thus, the withdrawal of the tentative accord would be predicted accurately by the model.

Cardinal Payoff Matrix, Intervention Expected

		Lenders IS 3/4		
		HC...	MC...	LC...
	HA...	0, 3	−3.5, 5.67	−4, 8.33
Peru IS 8	MA...	4, −.5	0, 2	<u>−2, 4.5</u>
	LA...	8, −3	3.5, −1	**0, 1**

Note: Nash equilibrium bolded; expected outcome with intervention underlined.

Ordinal Payoff Matrix, Intervention Expected

		Lenders IS 3/4		
		HC...	MC...	LC...
	HA...	4, 6	2, 8	1, 9
Peru IS 8	MA...	8, 3	5, 5	<u>3, 7</u>
	LA...	9, 1	7, 2	**6, 4**

Note: Nash equilibrium bolded; expected outcome with intervention underlined.

Figure 8.6. *Play phase, period six: September 1887–March 1889*

Debt game and predicted outcome: period six

Weakened positions, for both bondholders and Peru, lead to the game shown in Figure 8.6. In the sixth period, the Nash equilibrium of the game between Peru and the lenders had shifted to one of deadlock from the high adjustment, no/low concessions outcome of period five. In this period, both actors became more unstable and less willing to make concessions. In this case, we expect intervention by the British government to pressure Peru to make adjustments. Given this solicitous attitude, we should expect some movement toward a MA..., LC... outcome, which would increase the bondholders' satisfaction but decrease Peru's payoff.

The negotiations and outcome: period six

In September 1887, members of the bondholders' committee worked toward resolving their differences with Chile. But when Chile sought a new £1.16 million loan floated by the Rothschilds on the London market for the settlement of nitrate operation claims a group of British holders of Peruvian bonds broke from the committee to block the loan quotation. Arguing that Chile had refused to assume its "just and equitable obligations" toward them, they convinced the Exchange to approve their petition in December, suspending Chile's quotation pending an agreement between the two parties.[89]

Chile initially responded by halting its negotiations with the bondholders' committee, but when the British government more actively pressured Chile to explain its intentions, Chile "hinted that the bondholders had now found a means of inducing a more conciliatory attitude on its part."[90] After further talks, Chile quickly agreed to negotiate a settlement with the bondholders aimed at smoothing out the wrinkles in the Grace contract, and the British government asked the Stock Exchange to allow Chile's loan quotation.

In an attempt to resolve its conflict with the bondholders, the Chilean government proposed a settlement to the British Minister in Santiago involving the cession to Chile of Tacna and Arica. The British were unwilling, however, to escalate their intervention in the debt affair to this level. Participating in a territorial settlement between two states for purely economic reasons would have invited heavy external criticism.

The negotiations between Peru and the bondholders appeared permanently blocked; some bondholders argued that efforts to conclude an agreement should be terminated. Nevertheless, the bondholders' committee sent the Earl of Donoughmore to meet with Antero Aspíllaga, the Peruvian Minister of Finance. The two succeeded in reaching an agreement on October 25, 1888, but made the accord contingent on Chile's approval. But opposition to the accord continued in the Peruvian Congress as well. In spite of special legislative sessions devoted to discussing the arrangement, the contract remained blocked by its vocal opponents.

Summary. Both actors suffered instability in their coalition, a weakness that contributed to a LA..., LC... outcome. We had expected that British pressure might propel the Peruvians to avoid a deadlock by making an adjustment, but because the negotiations also involved Chile, we saw Britain pressing Chile. Thus, rather than ending at the anticipated outcome of Peru making some adjustments, prospects for passage of the Grace contract looked grim at the end of period six.

[89] Wynne (1951), p. 157. [90] Wynne (1951), p. 157.

Situational changes

During this period, the British government intervened on behalf of the bondholders to pressure Chile. But when Chile tried to use British involvement to its own advantage by asking Britain to support its annexation of the northern territories, it refused.

Following the deadlock in period six, Peru faced a deteriorating financial situation. Cáceres responded by appointing Pedro de Solar as his Prime Minister. After special elections promoted by Solar replaced recalcitrant members of the Congress, the government became more stable, leading to period seven's game and set of negotiations that would result in passage of the Grace contract.

Debt game and predicted outcome: period seven

The actors' individual situations produce the game matrix shown in Figure 8.7. In this game, we return to the equilibrium of period five, with Peru playing a strategy of HA..., and the bondholders one of LC... As in the fifth period, we do not expect the creditor governments to intervene actively because the outcome should already be consistent with their overall objectives. I must note, however, that because this period's game included only Peru and the bondholders, and not Dreyfus, we expect pressure by the French to continue.

The negotiations and outcome: period seven

After changes in the Peruvian Congress engineered by Pedro de Solar, the Grace contract passed through Congress on October 25, 1889. The final version somewhat reduced Peru's mining and banking concessions. Although only slightly more favorable to Peru than in its initial form, the Grace agreement was regarded by some as imperative. In the words of one analyst, "to attract foreign capital to continue the railway construction, and to restore its own credit for wider reasons, the Peruvian government had no alternative but to come to an agreement with the bondholders."[91]

The new Grace contract included the following points:[92]

a. The agreement released Peru from absolute responsibility for its 1869, 1870, and 1872 loans, totaling some $158 million.
b. The bondholders created and organized the Peruvian Corporation in London with a capital of £16.5 million: £7.5 million in preferred shares, £9 million in ordinary shares. The bondholders would exchange their bonds for shares with the corporation at the rate of 24 preferred and 30 ordinary for £100 of 1870 bonds, and 20 preferred and 25 ordinary for £100 of 1872 bonds. The contract allowed the corporation to float new loans of up to £6 million (£5.7 million actually floated).

[91] Miller (1976), p. 324.

[92] For details see Wynne (1951), p. 171; Palmer (1984), p. 58; Marichal (1989), pp. 124–125; Pike (1967), pp. 153–154; Werlich (1978), p. 120.

Cardinal Payoff Matrix
Intervention Expected

		Lenders IS 3/4		
		HC...	MC...	LC...
	HA...	6, 3	2.75, 5.67	**3, 8.33**
Peru IS 7/8	MA....	7.83, –.5	4, 2	2.5, 4.5
	LA...	9.67, –3	5.25, –1	2, 1

Note: Nash equilibrium bolded.

Ordinal Payoff Matrix
with Possible Intervention

		Lenders IS 3/4		
		HC...	MC...	LC...
	HA...	7, 6	3, 8	**4, 9**
Peru IS 7/8	MA...	8, 3	5, 5	2, 7
	LA...	9, 1	6, 2	1, 4

Note: Nash equilibrium bolded; expected outcome with intervention underlined.

Figure 8.7. *Play phase, period seven: April–October 1889*

c. Peru ceded to the corporation a 66-year lease for the control and operation of the state railways. The railways were in poor condition, and the corporation agreed to rebuild and extend the system.
d. Peru gave up 2 million tons of guano to the corporation. The government retained the right to consume the quantity of guano required for its own agriculture.
e. Peru gave the corporation a franchise for the operation of steamers on Lake Titicaca.

f. Peru agreed to make an annual subsidy payment of £80,000 to the corporation for 30 years.
g. Finally, supplementary contracts awarded the bondholders a free grant of unappropriated land (5 million acres), as well as a concession on the Cerro de Pasco mines.

Summary. The long-delayed signing of the Grace contract ended the long saga of Peruvian guano and railroads. However, assessment of the contract varies considerably.[93] Different analysts would probably characterize the outcome as somewhere between high adjustment by Peru and medium to low concessions by the bondholders. Disagreements over how to evaluate the accord are based on whether scholars evaluate the short-term or long-term effects of the agreement, and what he or she thinks were the accord's broader implications for Peru. One scholar, Rory Miller, suggests that the bondholders made a number of sacrifices and did not secure as much as they had hoped, arguing that the real beneficiary of the accord was Michael Grace.[94]

Because of two factors, one of a subjective nature and the other more objective, I suggest that the agreement was most closely characterized by high adjustment and low concessions. In the minds of most Peruvians, the agreement was highly unfavorable, and even Miller notes that from the Peruvian perspective, "The bondholders seem to have given Peru very little in return for the cancellation of their claims."[95] From the more objective standpoint of actual behavior, Miller points out that Peru received some benefits from the corporation. However, Peru raised only a small loan in 1905, and did not borrow major amounts in foreign markets until the 1920s.[96] Peru had managed to rid itself of its debt problem, but it had also sacrificed important assets, such as the railroad, for nearly 70 years, and did not accomplish its goal of successfully returning to the credit markets in the short or medium run. Peru's relatively low equilibrium payoff is thus consistent with this empirical assessment.

Nor, over the long run, did the corporation prove very satisfactory to the bondholders. Initially the bondholders received a low return on their investment because of mismanagement of the corporation until 1907, although they were eventually able to make it more profitable until about 1930.

Aftermath. After facing problems listing its loans in London, Chile took advantage of the conciliatory mood of the Peruvian Congress by initiating negotiations with Peru over its debt obligations.[97] The two concluded the so-called Elias-Castellon protocol on January 8, 1890, whereby Chile was to cede to Peru the guano deposits in Tarapacá as they had agreed in 1880. Peru was also to receive all the money placed in the Bank of England from the revenue of the guano sale in accordance with the decree of 1882, and a few other

[93] For a discussion, see Miller (1983), particularly p. 321. [94] 1976, pp. 99–100.
[95] Miller (1983), p. 328. [96] Miller (1983), p. 329.
[97] The discussion that follows draws heavily on Wynne (1951), pp. 161–170.

concessions for the benefit of the bondholders. In return, the bondholders would cancel all Chilean obligations for the Peruvian foreign debt beyond the Treaty of Ancón, thus allowing the Grace contract to take effect.

But problems quickly surfaced with the agreements negotiated among the bondholders, Chile, and Peru. The French government protested to both Chile and Peru that the Grace contract and the Elias-Castellon protocol both benefited British bondholders while ignoring the French creditors, such as Dreyfus, to whom Peruvian guano and other revenues had been equally pledged. Moreover, the French government claimed that the English committee had no right to act on behalf of the French or other nation's creditors.

The French government then pressured the Chilean government to act on behalf of Dreyfus's interests. It demanded, among other things, that Chile assign all of the proceeds from the guano sale of 1882 to the French creditors of Peru. After considerable discussion, on July 23, 1892, the French and Chilean governments reached an agreement known as the Bacourt-Errázuriz protocol. This agreement provided for arbitration by the president of the Swiss Supreme Court to determine the rights of Peru's various creditors to the guano fund. The president assigned 20% of Chile's share of the guano proceeds under the 1882 accord to Peru's French creditors. Further objections by Peru to this accord led eventually to the Errázuriz-Eyre protocol on December 12, 1892, in which Chile guaranteed the Peruvian Corporation a minimum share of £300,000, which it paid immediately from the guano sale fund of £558,556. The Chilean government also agreed to make up the difference should the payment to the Corporation exceed the arbitration settlement. Finally, Chile agreed to give the Corporation supplementary payments totaling £630,800 in the form of 4.5% government bonds.[98]

Although Peru objected to this plan, three Swiss judges in 1901 went ahead and allocated the shares of different claimants for the Bank of England fund according to the arbitration agreement. Peru continued its refusal to settle Dreyfus's claims, until 1909 when a loan it tried to float was blocked in Paris. Peru eventually agreed to arbitration by a Hague court under the proviso that its obligations would be capped at 25 million French francs. After a ruling validated Piérola's agreement in 1880, Peru proceeded to remit 25 million francs plus interest over a four-year period from 1923 to 1926.

Conclusion

Guano was the stuff of capitalists' dreams at the beginning of this epoch. Through massive borrowing in the 1860s and 1870s, Peru attempted to promote rapid industrialization. But a combination of overspending and misallocation of resources converted guano into a massive debt – instead of a source of funding for development projects such as the railroad. After defaulting in 1876, Peru

[98] Wynne (1951), p. 160.

attempted to resolve its loan problems for some 15 years. The country's fortunes were also marred by a disastrous conflict with Chile, which resulted in the loss of a considerable amount of guano and nitrate-rich territory. As a consequence, it also shifted part of its creditors' headaches to the Chileans.

We examined seven periods of rescheduling in this chapter, five between the bondholders and Peru and two between Chile and Peru's creditors. The first period saw a continuation of Peru's strategy of postponing the inevitable need for adjustment by promising guano contracts to eager bondholders. But by the second period, the two protagonists found themselves deadlocked. Frustrated with their efforts to secure debt servicing from the Peruvians, the bondholders then turned to Chile, which had acquired rich nitrate and guano lands from Peru.

During the 1880–1882 period the bondholders had the upper hand, with a promise from Chile to allow them to exploit guano in the occupied territories. But the fourth period until 1886 proved highly disappointing for the bondholders. Although they secured assistance from the British government to press the Chileans to service part of Peru's former debt, the Chileans managed to play off the differing interests of creditor governments. Because the French and British were divided, the bondholders found themselves left out in the cold. Dim prospects in the Chilean debt repayment arena encouraged the bondholders to turn once again to a more stable Peru in 1886.

At the end of three periods of negotiations from 1886 to 1889, Peru and the bondholders came to a settlement. Although Peru was willing to make major concessions in the fifth period, subsequent internal conflicts in both Peru and among bondholders led to a deadlock by the sixth period. By the seventh and last period examined here, Peru's situation had again changed, and the bondholders secured what I consider to be a highly favorable agreement.

Throughout the periods examined here, the model was highly successful in predicting the outcomes of negotiations. In the last two periods, however, intervention by the British proved somewhat difficult to predict. With both Chile and Peru involved in the final negotiations, the locus of British pressure shifted from Peru to Chile in the sixth period, an outcome we did not anticipate. In the remainder of the cases, however, the model allowed us to anticipate both the character of the two-actor game as well as the actions of creditor governments.

PART IV
Epoch 3: 1910s–1950s

9 Riding on the storm: Mexican debt rescheduling, 1916–1942

Venustiano Carranza rose to power in 1915–1916, but Mexico's revolutionary turmoil continued sporadically until the early 1930s.[1] Still, brief interludes of stability, combined with improved finances and American pressure, led to a number of debt rescheduling agreements during this epoch. None of these agreements lasted for more than a year or two. Unlike most Latin American countries during this epoch, Mexico never received a single additional loan – although it did at times receive important concessions from bondholders on its existing debt. Throughout this epoch, as the leading creditor nation with important interests in Mexico, the American government intervened actively. In 1942, the U.S. played a key role in the negotiations leading to a major debt settlement between bondholders and Mexico. American intervention was driven largely by Mexico's role as a critical supplier of materials and goods to the Allies during the Second World War.

I divide the third epoch of Mexican debt rescheduling into eight periods. In the first and third periods, from 1916 to 1920 and 1923 to 1924, Mexico and its creditors were deadlocked. During the second period, from 1921 to 1922, however, Mexico enjoyed a brief but significant period of stability under Alvaro Obregón. At this time, the bondholders and Mexico came to an agreement that consolidated all of Mexico's debt, and Mexico made some initial payments before quickly falling into default. After Calles's election during the fourth period from 1925 to 1926, Mexico received major concessions from a revision of the failed 1922 accords. But as with the previous agreement, Mexico's worsening financial situation made it impossible for it to abide by the agreement. The fifth period, from 1927 to 1933, produced another rescheduling agreement, but this time Mexico's Congress refused to ratify the accord as the 1930s depression took its toll on the economy. During the sixth through eighth periods, from 1933 to 1936, 1937 to 1940, and 1941 to 1942, respectively, all actors made significant efforts to resolve the debt. Although an extremely favorable settlement was negotiated in both 1936 and 1938, both agreements fell through. The 1942 agreement, based on these aborted accords, eventually ended almost 60 years of debt negotiations spanning two epochs.

[1] For historical details about Mexico and U.S. policy during this time, this chapter draws on Cline (1953), Cronon (1960), Wood (1961), Gellman (1979), Vázquez and Meyer (1985), and Meyer and Sherman (1987). In addition to newspapers and archival sources, more specific secondary sources include Turlington (1930), Wynne (1951), Bazant (1968), Smith (1972), Hamilton (1982), and Collier and Collier (1991), among others.

Period one: the perils of a heavy rider, 1916–1920

Woodrow Wilson's success in ousting Victoriano Huerta in 1914 led to significant political instability in Mexico. Unresolved conflict among factions who had allied to oppose Huerta created a highly unstable situation, during which American troops in Northern Mexico lead a futile campaign to capture Pancho Villa in 1916. The U.S. became considerably more conciliatory toward Mexico soon after Germany offered to assist Mexico. Meanwhile, the bondholders began what proved to be unsuccessful negotiations with Mexico in an effort to conclude an agreement on the long-standing default.

Because of the relatively brief situational change between periods, I will discuss codings for all three periods in this section to provide continuity in the discussion. The actual bargaining in the second and third periods, however, is discussed in separate sections.

Identifying individual situations

In the first and third periods, from 1916 to 1920 and 1923 to 1924, I classify Mexico as coalitionally unstable, issue weak, and overall medium (IS 4/8). In the second period, from 1921 to 1922, Mexico was coalitionally medium in stability, issue weak, and overall weak in capabilities (IS 7/8). I classify the bondholders as coalitionally stable, issue strong, and overall strong in capabilities (IS 5) throughout the three periods.

Mexico. Carranza's rise to power failed to bring Mexico significant political stability. By late 1914, Pancho Villa and other revolutionary leaders repudiated the Carranza government at the Convention of Aguascalientes, rejecting a gradual approach to land distribution and political participation. These forces overtook Mexico City by the end of the year, forcing Carranza to flee to Veracruz. Throughout 1915, the two warring groups – the Conventionist government headed by Eulalio Gutiérrez in Mexico City and the Carranza government in Veracruz – governed different portions of Mexico. At times, factions within these two major groups claimed to control all of Mexico, and each group issued its own currency. The battle of Celaya, however, was a turning point in Carranza's consolidation of power. In April 1915, his ally Alvaro Obregón defeated Pancho Villa's troops, allowing Carranza's regime to take control of much of Mexico while securing American diplomatic recognition. Shortly thereafter, following the writing of a relatively reformist, anti-clerical constitution, Carranza won the presidential election in March 1917.

Continued violent threats came from two rebel groups, the followers of Pancho Villa in the north and those of Emiliano Zapata in the south. In April 1919, following a critical open letter written to Carranza by Zapata, Carranza had Zapata assassinated. But Zapata's demise failed to stabilize Carranza's government. When Carranza attempted to name his successor in April 1920, General

Obregón, Carranza's former ally, declared open revolt against the government.[2] Carranza had to leave Mexico City, and once again, tried to occupy Veracruz to organize a counter-move. This time, however, he was killed on the road to Veracruz by a group of rebels.

Congress declared Adolfo de la Huerta, Governor of the State of Sonora, provisional president until the December elections, when he handed the presidency to Obregón on December 1, 1920. But the United States refused to recognize Obregón's Administration, undermining his ability to deal with bondholders. Despite its lack of recognition, Obregón's government proved to be relatively stable in 1921 and 1922, and enjoyed good relations with labor and wide popular support.

In the summer of 1923, the U.S. and Mexico reestablished diplomatic relations after Mexico agreed to the creation of a joint commission to investigate financial claims resulting from the revolution. Although prospects for Mexican stability began to look more promising, the political situation quickly deteriorated when gunmen assassinated Pancho Villa in 1923. Although the true culprits were never found, the murder served to destabilize the government by providing ammunition for nationalists unhappy with the Bucareli agreement that had led to American recognition of Mexico's government. Soon thereafter, when Obregón chose Plutarco Calles to succeed him, Mexico once again erupted into conflict. Adolfo de la Huerta led the opposition. With American aid, Obregón managed to suppress the revolt. By 1924, Calles succeeded Obregón in a peaceful transfer of power.[3]

As for issue-specific resources, years of political turbulence, revolution, and civil war had impoverished the Mexican Treasury. The war consumed vast amounts of public funds, halted business and commerce throughout the country, and made revenue collection virtually impossible. Carranza believed that the best way to combat Mexico's financial crisis was to print more paper currency, despite the "disadvantages which the future might bring."[4] As a revolutionary, Carranza printed nearly 60 million pesos' worth of paper money. Upon coming to power in Mexico City, he printed another 40 million pesos, and his provisional government in Veracruz continued to print over 600 million paper pesos.[5] He persisted with this strategy, even when the newly formed Conventionist government began printing its own currency and called for the now-worthless Carranza currency to be turned in for revalidation.

By the time Carranza finally secured power, he desperately needed money as the paper peso's value plummeted dramatically. During 1916 and 1917, his government unsuccessfully approached foreign financial interests for loans on several occasions.[6] In an effort to halt the peso's downward spiral, Carranza

[2] See Meyer and Sherman (1987), pp. 548–560 for a good discussion from which this paragraph draws heavily.
[3] Meyer and Sherman (1987), p. 581.
[4] *Mexican Review* (Washington, D.C.), August 1917, cited in Turlington (1930), p. 263, n. 2.
[5] Turlington (1930), pp. 263–264. [6] Smith (1972), p. 110.

attempted to retire all paper money in circulation and issued 500 million pesos at a guaranteed gold value, but the peso's spectacular decline continued until it was virtually worthless. Reporting on Mexico's financial condition, the *New York Times* noted:

> The present state of Mexico's finances is appalling . . . The various Governments that have enjoyed brief periods of power have ruined the country's credit almost beyond repair. The Mexican paper dollar, normally worth nearly 50 cents in American money, is now selling at 5 cents. Fiat money and various issues put out without a proper basis have made people skeptical of any currency but gold. The natural sources of revenue, through the customs and other forms of taxation, have been drained, and the people generally have lost their means of livelihood.[7]

When Obregón assumed power in 1920, he attempted to remedy Mexico's dire financial situation. He pledged to develop new sources of revenue and to reduce expenditures by reducing the army by half. He established two taxes on oil, one a special export tax, and another a production tax in 1921. But the economic slump after World War I produced a sharp drop in exports. Proceeds from oil exports fell from 27,606,000 pesos in 1922 to 18,383,000 pesos in 1923, steadily declining to 5,760,000 pesos by 1927.[8] In the end, total taxes on oil yielded only 61,000,000 pesos in 1923 compared to 86,000,000 pesos the previous year.[9] Growing foreign wariness toward Mexican investment accounted for additional production declines. Lastly, the cost of quelling the 1923 de la Huerta revolt, estimated at more than 60 million pesos,[10] left the country in a financially disastrous position. Mexico's accumulated deficit for the fiscal year 1924 exceeded the debt annuity of 35 million pesos.

As for overall capabilities, the Carranza government initially found itself quite weak. When Pancho Villa's men engaged in attacks on American civilians and destruction of a U.S. border city in March 1916, the U.S. sent troops across the border who remained for nine months to pursue Villa. But the development of the Mexican Constitution in 1917, the passage of legislation potentially threatening to large foreign interests, and the subsequent inability of American interests to force a reversal of this policy earns a coding of medium overall strength. Moreover, American recognition of the Mexican government helped to prevent bondholders from pursuing retaliatory measures and to prevent opposition groups from securing weapons from the United States.

General Alvaro Obregón's rise weakened Mexican capabilities. The U.S. did not recognize his government, thus making any effort on his part to secure financial assistance bound to fail. By the latter part of his term, however, following the Bucareli agreements and American recognition, Mexico's overall capabilities improved somewhat. The importance of American support was clearly illustrated by the large role the U.S. played in suppressing revolts in Mexico.

[7] *New York Times*, February 7, 1916. [8] Wynne (1951), p. 73.
[9] Wynne (1951), p. 312. [10] Turlington (1930), p. 300.

Lenders. Following Mexico's default, bondholders and banking houses increased their coalitional unity. In October 1915, a new general committee was formed in London to represent all holders of Mexican bonds and investors in Mexican enterprises. This new committee worked closely with the Council of the Corporation of Foreign Bondholders as well as with the American, English, and French banking houses responsible for the 1899, 1910, and 1913 loan flotations.[11]

In February 1919, internal stability further improved with the creation of yet another administrative body, the International Committee of Bankers on Mexico (ICBM or International Committee). The purpose of this American-dominated committee was to represent and protect all bondholders and creditors of Mexico's foreign-held national and railway debts. Apart from American bankers, the Committee included British and French creditors. American representatives filled 50% of the seats, while the British and French creditors each had 25%. A few obstacles threatened the formation of this committee. The British raised concerns over their railroad, oil, and electrical interests, while the French were more interested in determining the percentage of their representatives on the Committee.[12] In August 1919, the entrance of Swiss and Dutch lenders, followed later by Belgian and German creditors, unified Mexico's bondholders into a single major grouping.

The lenders were especially strong in the issue-area of financial negotiations. The creation of the ICBM put this group in a very powerful position. They were not simply a group of bondholders who wished to obtain a settlement, but rather a unified group of leading financiers whose interests included more than just the bond debt.

The lenders in this period also found themselves in a strong overall position. Thomas Lamont of J.P. Morgan and Company met frequently with the State Department and had the Department's blessing and encouragement in his dealing with Mexico. State Department instructions regarding the creation of the ICBM gave the following instructions: "any group formed shall be under the leadership of American bankers and that the policy of the United States Government regarding Mexico be the dominating influence in the operations of this group."[13] Lamont referred to the ICBM as an "omnibus" committee because it dealt with all questions of Mexican finances and could block any loans to Mexico unless matters of concern to the U.S. government and financiers were settled to their satisfaction.[14]

Creditor governments. Among creditor governments, the U.S. played the most influential role in Mexico. The beginning of the First World War in Europe occupied the British and French foreign offices, forcing these countries to retreat from Mexican affairs. Other creditor governments increasingly depended

[11] See Wynne (1951), p. 60. [12] Smith (1972), p. 130.
[13] Smith (1972), pp. 128–129. [14] Smith (1972), p. 129.

on the U.S. position in Mexico because American investments dominated every sector of the Mexican economy. Given its long border with Mexico, the American government was highly concerned with Mexican stability, which provided the Mexicans with some breathing room in spite of the many economic groups in the U.S. clamoring for compensation of financial losses or protection for their Mexican assets.

Turning first to economic interests, the U.S. government was under pressure from private American economic interests throughout this first period. The government was not overly concerned with bondholders' losses or a potential threat to the financial system; rather, it acted under severe pressure from American oil, mining, and landowning interests. Total American investments in Mexico in 1914 were $853.5 million, rising to $908.9 million in 1919 and slightly over 1 billion dollars in 1924.[15] Moreover, the U.S. was the most significant actor in several key Mexican sectors including mining, cotton, fruit production, sugar, and petroleum. As a consequence, U.S. interest groups maintained pressure on the Wilson Administration.

Following Huerta's ouster, Wilson did his best to influence the process of finding a presidential successor. When it became apparent that Carranza's group was likely to gain power, Wilson decided to recognize him in 1915 – contingent upon receiving guarantees regarding American property. The most contentious element in the ensuing discussion was Article 27 of the 1917 Mexican Constitution, which asserted national control over land and subsoil rights, and which was seen as a direct threat to American and foreign oil companies operating in Mexico. In addition, the article affirmed the right to expropriate land from private owners, in exchange for compensation.

On the basis of economic factors alone, one might expect the U.S. government to have actively intervened in the debt negotiations to ensure that U.S. interests would receive adequate compensation and guarantees. Fortunately for Mexico, however, important political and strategic considerations affected American calculations – at least until 1918.

In 1914, the U.S. became highly concerned about German activity in Mexico. Secretary of State Robert Lansing summarized the problem succinctly in his private diary in 1915:

> Germany desires to keep up the turmoil in Mexico until the United States is forced to intervene; therefore, we must not intervene.
>
> Germany does not wish to have any one faction dominant in Mexico; therefore, we must recognize one faction as dominant in Mexico.
>
> When we recognize a faction as the government, Germany will undoubtedly seek to cause a quarrel between that government and ours; therefore we must avoid a quarrel regardless of criticism and complaints in Congress and the press.[16]

The famous Zimmermann telegram incident of 1917 substantiated fears of German activity. In January, German Foreign Secretary Arthur Zimmermann told his

[15] See Lewis (1938), p. 606.

[16] Lansing, Private Notes, October 10, 1915, Lansing MSS, cited in Smith (1972), p. 41.

ambassador in Mexico to be prepared to offer Mexico help in recovering the territories it had lost to the U.S. in exchange for Mexican support for Germany during the war. When the British intercepted, decoded, and publicized this message, Wilson pointed to this German act as additional justification for the U.S. to enter the war on the Allied side. The importance of supplanting German influence on Mexico was not lost on the American Ambassador to Mexico, Henry Fletcher. In 1917, following the American entry into the world war, he noted that his job was to defer consideration of the potential impact of Article 27 on American investments until after the war.[17]

The strategic concerns of the Wilson Administration were not shared by many economic lobbies and their allies in the government. Through multiple channels, they continued to pressure the Administration to intervene in Mexico. In the end, because the war made intervention politically impossible, they continued to simply demand that Mexico make guarantees for American property at every turn.[18] The administration's dismissal of the oil companies' protest of a 10% oil export tax instituted in 1917 demonstrated the government's support for Mexican political stability. As Colonel House, Wilson's key adviser, put it:

> The war had caused a phenomenal advance in the price of oil, and yet they [British and American oil companies] would have us go to war with Mexico rather than allow that government to collect a reasonable tax. The Mexican government has to live, and it cannot live without taxes.[19]

Once the war ended in 1918, however, the U.S. was no longer constrained by the fear that Germany would capitalize on political instability in Mexico.

Debt game and predicted outcome

From our classifications, we arrive at the debt game shown in Figure 9.1. Based on only the strategic interaction between Mexico and the lenders, we would expect a LA..., LC... outcome with ordinal payoffs of 6, 7. Both players have a dominant strategy, LA... for the debtor and LC... for the lender. Thus, in the absence of intervention, we would expect the parties to remain deadlocked.

Turning to potential creditor government intervention, the U.S. government was highly concerned about Germany's role in destabilizing or aiding Mexico to create a strategic problem for the U.S. in the context of World War I. Thus, at least until 1918, we would expect the U.S. to steer clear of the debt negotiations. After the war, however, we would expect the U.S. to actively pressure Mexico to satisfy the many American economic interests knocking at the State Department's door. Thus we anticipate Mexico to agree to more economic adjustment after 1918.

[17] See Smith (1972), p. 93. [18] Smith (1972), p. 100.
[19] House Diary, July 18, 1917, House MSS, cited in Smith (1972), p. 102. Parenthetical remark by Smith.

Cardinal Payoff Matrix, Intervention Expected

Lenders IS 5

		HC...	MC...	LC...
	HA...	−1.5, −3	−5, −1.33	−6.5, .33
Mexico IS 4/8	MA...	2.83, −3.5	−1, −2	<u>−3.5, −.5</u>
	LA...	7.17, −3	3, −2	**−.5, −1**

Note: Nash equilibrium bolded; expected outcome with intervention underlined.

Ordinal Payoff Matrix, Intervention Expected

Lenders IS 5

		HC...	MC...	LC...
	HA...	4, 2.5	2, 6	1, 9
Mexico IS 4/8	MA...	7, 1	5, 4.5	<u>3, 8</u>
	LA...	9, 2.5	8, 4.5	**6, 7**

Note: Nash equilibrium bolded; expected outcome with intervention underlined.

Figure 9.1. *Play phase, period one: 1916–1920*

The negotiations and outcome

In October 1915, the U.S. recognized, but did not promise financial aid to, Carranza's government, despite press reports that Washington was promoting a loan to assist the new government.[20] In 1916, responding to Mexico's economic distress, Carranza once again turned to American bankers for help. The foreign

[20] *The Economist*, August 21, 1915, p. 290.

banking houses, however, were less forthcoming than in the past. A *New York Times* article entitled "No Loans Here for Gen. Carranza" noted:

> Well-informed financiers who have gone into Mexico with capital for development work profess to see no hope for the Carranza Government . . . Bankers who have been active in Mexican affairs say that, even if the present Government were strongly entrenched, it could obtain no funds abroad, owing to its inability to obtain revenues to meet current expenses.[21]

Potential lenders stayed away from Mexico because of its political instability and the American government's "attitude of well-wishing aloofness."[22]

The U.S. attempted to prevent Mexico from turning to Germany for assistance while nudging the Mexicans to recognize U.S. demands for protection of American property. With respect to loans, the U.S. wanted to encourage a private loan to Mexico, but only if Mexico agreed to link the resolution of all economic issues to such a loan.

By 1916, the link between the bondholders' representatives and the American government had become clear. J.P. Morgan and Co., the lead bank in earlier loans to Mexico, expressed a willingness to "cooperate with the administration in Washington if so requested."[23] January 1917 saw Carranza's brother-in-law, General Zambrano, visit New York in search of a $10 million loan from J.P. Morgan. In addition, the general broached the subject of possible American financial involvement in the establishment of a National Mexican Bank.[24]

Neither the bondholders nor the bankers were excited by an opportunity to invest in Mexico's central bank. On the contrary, they angrily rejected the proposal saying it would divert funds that could be allocated to debt servicing. Thomas Lamont told the Mexicans that no new loans would be extended until Mexico resolved its internal political problems and could offer protection to foreigners and their property in Mexico.[25] As we shall see, this intimate linkage created problems for Lamont and his fellow bankers as overall American concerns began to impede a suitable debt rescheduling accord.

Aware that Mexico desperately needed financial assistance, the U.S. attempted to address several issues at once through a conditional loan: it sought to help Mexico's economy, secure resolution of outstanding economic problems (thereby taking pressure off the administration from interventionist-minded groups), and ensure that Mexico's economy would be "properly" managed. The State Department pushed the Mexicans to undertake such a loan in October 1917. Fred Kent, Deputy Governor of the New York Federal Reserve, even wanted to "send an ultimatum demanding that Mexico either join the Allies and request a loan or submit to intervention."[26] Carranza, however, refused to change Article 27; the

[21] *New York Times*, February 7, 1916.
[22] *Commercial & Financial Chronicle*, November 6, 1915, p. 517, cited in Turlington (1930), p. 265; *New York Times*, February 7, 1916.
[23] Smith (1972), p. 111. [24] Smith (1972), p. 111. [25] Smith (1972), p. 111.
[26] Smith (1972), p. 113.

U.S. was concerned about excessively pressuring Mexico during the war, and therefore did not force the issue.

But by 1918, the U.S. faced difficulties with this approach. A number of smaller banks appeared to be interested in making a loan to Mexico, an action that would undermine American government efforts to link the broader resolution of outstanding problems to a loan. In addition, the Germans and other European powers were making efforts to secure concessions from Mexico by offering loans; the U.S. had to work hard to block such initiatives.[27]

To cope with these new developments, the American government decided that the time was ripe to push for a loan from private groups, instead of directly from the government. A report by Thomas Lill and Henry Bruére, financial advisors to Carranza, catalyzed this policy change. In it, they told the State Department that "they had laid the foundation for a new approach on the financial issue."[28] In May 1918, with Carranza's blessing, Lill approached Wilson and New York bankers to reopen loan negotiations. Appealing to U.S. strategic concerns, Lill encouraged American financial involvement in Mexico to curb German influence and to place the U.S. in a position to dominate Mexico's economic development.[29]

With the end of the war in November 1918, however, pressures for intervention in Mexico began to increase.[30] At the end of 1918, General Leonard Wood pointedly "expressed the hope that the U.S. Army would not be demobilized too rapidly."[31] Meanwhile, more active discussions between investment bankers and the State Department led to the creation of the International Committee of Bankers on Mexico which came into being in February 1919. The government hoped that such a group would help it coordinate policy toward Mexico. But when the U.S. government continued to insist on a settlement of outstanding issues as part of any loan, Carranza refused to accept this linkage.

As Mexico continued to implement Article 27, cries for intervention by American oil interests grew rapidly. Rumors of intervention grew so quickly that by the middle of 1919, some U.S. officials were speculating on who would be the governor general of Mexico![32] In May 1919, the lenders hoped that an extraordinary session of the Mexican Congress would deal with the security for a new loan and resolve the conflict over Article 27 of the new constitution. Instead, growing opposition to Carranza and problems with Villista raids into the United States fostered instability and diminished prospects for an American loan.

Mexico, however, continued to take a hard line. Finance Minister Cabrera declared: "If we had the cash in our Treasury to resume payments on the national debt today we should prefer to wait. Our creditors have waited patiently and they will continue to be patient."[33] Cabrera further argued that Mexico should

[27] Smith (1972), pp. 115–117. [28] Smith (1972), p. 127. [29] Smith (1972), p. 127.
[30] See Smith (1972), Chapter 7, for a discussion of these pressures.
[31] Smith (1972), p. 132. [32] Smith (1972), p. 155.
[33] *Investigations of Mexican Affairs, Preliminary Report & Hearings* (1920), cited in Smith (1972), p. 177.

wait and see how other countries dealt with their debts before initiating any action on its own. As he put it:

> We prefer to await the outcome of adjustments of problems of world-wide importance that may affect us directly. We must know what the world in general will do with its obligations, how many nations will repudiate their debts, and how many will trim their obligations to figures compatible with their income.[34]

Finance Minister Luis Cabrera also hoped that Mexico might be able to form an alliance with other debtor nations. His declarations and efforts to resist American pressure only added fuel to the fire.

War with Mexico began to look inevitable when American Consul William Jenkins was first kidnapped in October 1919 by an anti-government group, then released, and subsequently arrested by the Mexican government on charges of collusion with the rebels. Secretary of State Lansing continued to court a diplomatic confrontation with Mexico, though he was less eager to go to war than many others. After Jenkins's release in December, the conflict still raged over the issue of drilling permits. Under continual pressure, and following an appeal by the Petroleum Producers Association in January 1920, Carranza agreed to provide provisional permits. The oil companies saw this action as an unqualified victory because they expected the permits to become permanent.

Meanwhile, the Carranza government became more amenable to new negotiations in the debt arena as well. In December 1919 Cabrera announced that Mexico would resume its debt service payments beginning January 1920.[35] The Carranza government, however, had little chance to follow upon these good intentions. In April 1920, General Obregón and his forces revolted against the Carranza government, forcing Carranza out of power within a month.

Summary. At the end of this period, Mexico and its lenders remained in a stalemate. Mexico could not afford the price of internal adjustments, and the lenders were powerful but tightly constrained by American policy goals. As expected, after 1918 the U.S. did exert pressure on Mexico, resulting in a Mexican promise to resume debt servicing. Despite this move toward a "no concessions, medium adjustment" outcome, however, Mexico failed to shift its policies. The final outcome, then, was the Nash outcome of the two-actor game, (LA, LC), rather than the intervention outcome, (MA, LC), we expected.

Situational changes

During this period, the bondholders continued to increase their coalitional stability by developing the ICBM in 1919. The Carranza government's actions also helped to bolster Mexico's bargaining position. In the end, as we have seen, the game ended in stalemate, leaving both actors relatively dissatisfied.

[34] Turlington (1930), p. 279.

[35] *New York Times*, December 24, 1919. See also an article in the *New York Times* of March 29, 1920.

Following the breakdown of negotiations, we would expect Mexico to attempt situational change. In fact, Mexico did try to improve its financial situation by seeking loans from various private sources, but emerged empty-handed because its continued unrest made lenders wary. Meanwhile, General Alvaro Obregón brought some stability to Mexico but faced a situation of overall weakness as the incoming Harding Administration refused to recognize him.

We would expect the bondholders to also be somewhat motivated to change the game because they would receive higher payoffs if Mexico adjusted. But although they failed to change their situation, they did manage to delink their negotiations from the many items on the American government's agenda, thus allowing them to use their capabilities on their own. The most decisive efforts to change situations in this period, however, came from the United States. The Harding Administration again used the instrument of recognition, this time to pressure Obregón to come to terms with the U.S. on outstanding bilateral issues. This action proved important in weakening Obregón and in impeding Mexico's efforts to improve its financial capabilities.

Period two: don't stand so close to me, 1921–1922

The bondholders, led by Thomas Lamont of the ICBM, failed to secure a settlement during the first period of negotiations. Strong American government support had proved to be a case of "heavy riding" – with the bondholders saddled by excessive issue linkage among the issues of oil, property rights, reparations, and bonds. Frustration among the bondholders began to set in by 1920. Lamont began to feel pressure to move forward – particularly from other foreign creditors who did not share the American government's overall political and economic objectives. When the British suggested in August 1920 that the Mexicans should seek advice on how to reorganize their finances, they expressly noted that *anyone* but an American should be the contact person. Lamont had to move quickly to hold his bankers' coalition together.[36] As he said to the State Department, "My private opinion to you is that we ought, within a reasonable time, find a *modus vivendi* or else we shall not be able to hold our five-power team in hand to the end."[37]

Debt game and predicted outcome

In this period (see Figure 9.2), we code Mexico as coalitionally medium in domestic stability, issue weak, and overall weak in capabilities (IS 7/8). The bondholders are stable and strong across the board, as during the first period (IS 5). We expect an equilibrium outcome for this game of high adjustment by Mexico and no concessions by the lenders. This outcome provides the highest possible payoff to the lenders. In this case, the two-actor game's Nash equilibrium should

[36] See Smith (1972), p. 187. [37] Cited in Smith (1972), p. 187.

Cardinal Payoff Matrix, Intervention Expected

Lenders IS 5

		HC...	MC...	LC...
	HA...	6, −3	2.75, −1.33	**3, .33**
Mexico IS 7/8	MA...	7.83, −3.5	4, −2	2.5, −.5
	LA...	9.67, −3	5.25, −2	2, −1

Note: Nash equilibrium bolded; expected outcome with intervention underlined.

Ordinal Payoff Matrix, Intervention Expected

Lenders IS 5

		HC...	MC...	LC...
	HA...	7, 2.5	3, 6	**4, 9**
Mexico IS 7/8	MA...	8, 1	5, 4.5	2, 8
	LA...	9, 2.5	6, 4.5	1, 7

Note: Nash equilibrium bolded; expected outcome with intervention underlined.

Figure 9.2. *Play phase, period two: 1921–1922*

not be affected by intervention, because U.S. intervention will only encourage greater adjustment by Mexico, already an outcome of the two-actor game.

The negotiations and outcome

Indeed, movement in the stalled debt negotiations began to appear on two fronts during this period. First, on Mexico's behalf, Obregón issued a reassuring statement:

First, we will take care of Mexico's foreign obligations . . . we will attack the foreign debt. The principal will be paid in full as it comes due, of course, if we can possibly pay; otherwise we will make arrangements for extension which will satisfy our creditors. As for interest overdue, we will do what good business men would naturally do – we will try to reach a satisfactory compromise . . .

When that is done, we will talk about borrowing more money for the rehabilitation . . . In other words, we propose to establish a credit in just the same way that the individual merchant establishes a credit, and that is by paying our debts.[38]

At the same time, Obregón promised to make a number of internal reforms to improve the country's economy. To reduce government expenditures, he pledged to cut his 50,000-man army in half. He also guaranteed that any new loans would be used for the development of the country, vowing that "not one penny of borrowed money [would] be spent for the current expenses of the Government." Moreover, the new government declared it would pay what was owed "in conformity with all recognized principles of international law" (although Obregón considered the loans obtained under de la Huerta to be illegal).[39]

Meanwhile, following pressure from other countries' lenders, the ICBM sent William Wiseman of the British delegation to Mexico to discuss debt matters with the new government. Initially, Lamont intended to accompany Wiseman on the trip, but the State Department advised against it. It was concerned that independent efforts would undermine the general American strategy of linking all issues. Wiseman returned with a letter from the finance minister indicating Mexico's desire to resume negotiations.[40]

The U.S. government, however, continued to prioritize protecting American property from confiscation over settling Mexico's debt. In 1921, Secretary of State designate Charles Evans Hughes, a lawyer and jurist representing the incoming Harding Administration, made the safeguarding of property rights, and not the payment of the foreign debt, the key condition for American recognition of the Obregón government.[41] Under pressure from various lobbying groups, the U.S. continued to withhold recognition of Obregón until 1923, which delayed resolution of the debt problem.

By March 1921, "Lamont and other committee members believed that making any debt negotiations contingent upon the settlement of the article 27 controversy . . . created a major problem for continued unified action of all the banking interests."[42] Facing the danger that J.P. Morgan might lose the bondholders' support, Lamont pressed the new secretary of state to allow him to pursue negotiations with Mexico. Lamont was finally given the go-ahead in July 1921, which led to two rounds of negotiations that finally resulted in a 1922 settlement.[43]

Round one. During the fall of 1921, debt negotiations resumed between Obregón government officials and the ICBM's Thomas Lamont. Simultaneously,

[38] *Mexican Review*, September 1920, cited in the *New York Times*, September 10, 1920.
[39] *New York Times*, September 10, 1920. [40] Smith (1972), p. 188.
[41] Turlington (1930), p. 283. [42] Smith (1972), p. 204. [43] Smith (1972), p. 205.

an important set of parallel negotiations took place between oil companies and Mexico. In an attempt to break out of the previous debt negotiations deadlock, the Obregón government made efforts to increase its financial solvency. In June 1921, Mexico imposed a heavy oil export tax, directing the proceeds to resuming the country's foreign debt service. The American-owned oil companies vehemently protested, but eventually negotiated a compromise with the Mexican government. Reaching a consensus in September 1921, the companies agreed to a bond redemption plan that would link the tax to refunding the debt. The oil companies would pay the tax in cash at 40% of the amount decreed or by purchasing Mexican government bonds issued before 1910 at market rates (then less than 40 cents on the dollar in face value).[44] The oil companies then asked Lamont to form a bankers' syndicate that would buy all outstanding bonds, but he refused to support this strategy.

In defense of the proposal, and in an effort to appease the ICBM, Finance Minister Adolfo de la Huerta pointed out that the plan was not unprecedented; previous contracts had allowed governments to repurchase their foreign debt bonds at market rates. He noted that the bankers could profit from the transaction by floating the bonds to the oil companies. The Finance Minister ultimately hoped to split the coalition formed between the bankers and their subscribing bondholders by providing incentives for the bankers to participate in the plan.

Lamont, however, firmly refused to budge, and eventually killed the proposed bond buy-back plan. He viewed it as unethical – and potentially scandalous – for the banks to profit twice by reselling Mexico's debt bond to the detriment of their bondholding clients who had initially purchased the bonds at par. According to Lamont, it was illegal for the Mexican government to use revenues pledged to the service of debt interest and principal arrears to retire bonds at low rates.

The Mexicans then pursued another strategy to play bankers off one another. In Mexico City, de la Huerta notified Lamont that Speyer and Company, with whom the Mexicans had engaged in preliminary discussions earlier in the year, had discussed a debt rescheduling program with the Mexicans.[45] Lamont quickly countered this effort to weaken his coalition by encouraging Speyer to participate in the ICBM, a move Lamont had previously avoided because of Speyer's German connections. Shortly thereafter, Speyer informed the Mexicans that he was withdrawing his proposal. By October 1921, it became clear that negotiations were deadlocked, and Lamont returned to New York.

Round two. Negotiations between de la Huerta and the ICBM resumed during the first half of 1922 at meetings in both New York and Mexico City. A number of issues hampered these negotiations. The Mexican government insisted that any debt settlement include a new loan. Obregón claimed that without new funds, Mexico would probably be unable to live up to any agreement.

[44] *Commercial and Financial Chronicle*, February 25, 1922, pp. 802–803, cited in Turlington (1930), p. 283; Smith (1972), p. 206.
[45] See Turlington (1930), p. 281.

Members of the ICBM stipulated, however, that no new loan would be granted without a debt agreement and official American recognition of the Obregón government.

The State Department's continued concern over Article 27 of the new Mexican Constitution lessened the likelihood of American recognition. Furthermore, many argued that the State Department "should, in view of possible national interests, have the opportunity of indicating any objection which it might perceive to the flotation of any issue of the bonds of any foreign country in the U.S."[46]

In May 1922, Obregón sent Finance Minister de la Huerta to New York to meet with Lamont and negotiate two issues: a consolidation of the foreign and railway debts and new loans for the creation of the National Bank and agricultural projects. Initially, de la Huerta reported to Obregón that negotiations appeared fruitless. Obregón instructed his finance minister that no agreement was better than an onerous one as "[t]he only power in the hands of a weak people is given them by their own dignity, and we should be very unwise if we renounced this power."[47]

By mid-June, however, de la Huerta believed that negotiations had improved to the point that a debt accord could soon be reached. At Obregón's insistence that any new debt settlement must include new loans, de la Huerta approached the creditors about possible funding for the establishment of the Banco Unico. French bankers showed initial interest in funding the National Bank, until Mexico demanded controlling interest in the bank. The French balked, and the other Committee members also quickly rebuffed the minister. They informed him that any discussions of new loans would have to wait until there was a definitive settlement of the outstanding debt then in default. Instead, the Committee members offered to insert a preamble into any agreement on debt consolidation, stating the creditors' desire to cooperate and ensure prosperity throughout the country.[48] On this basis, de la Huerta signed a new debt accord on June 16, 1922, consolidating Mexico's foreign and railway debts, and certain internal obligations held by foreigners. This tentative accord awaited ratification from Obregón.

Despite the lack of a new loan in the accord, de la Huerta assured Obregón that obtaining new loans would be simple after the agreement's ratification, judging from his previous negotiations with the bankers. In addition, the preamble of the accord stated that the ICBM recognized the "difficulties with which Mexico has had to contend and the limitations upon her capacity for the immediate payment." It desired to cooperate "with the Mexican government in the solution of its problems and in the upbuilding of its credit."[49]

Obregón, however, refused to ratify the agreement, stating that he was skeptical of the "good faith and sincerity" of the Committee.[50] Instead he directed de la

[46] *U.S. Daily* (Washington), October 15, 1927, cited in Turlington (1930), p. 285.
[47] Turlington (1930), p. 287. [48] Turlington (1930), p. 288.
[49] *The Economist*, July 1, 1922, p. 15 and Turlington (1930), p. 289.
[50] Turlington (1930), p. 294.

Huerta to immediately open negotiations for a new loan. Lamont reminded de la Huerta that no loan was possible until the U.S. recognized the Obregón government, stating that "the American government during the past year often explained that it did not encourage its citizens to make loans to governments not recognized by the White House."[51]

Realizing that recognition from the U.S. would not be forthcoming without a debt agreement,[52] Obregón reluctantly signed the de la Huerta–Lamont debt accord in August 1922; the Mexican Congress ratified it on September 29.

The provisions of the 1922 agreement called for the full resumption of debt service by 1928. Defaulted interest arrears up to 1923 were to be paid at par, without interest, over a period of 40 years beginning in 1928. Interest accumulated from 1923 through 1927 would be paid in two phases: first, the government would set aside 30 million gold pesos in 1923, adding 5 million gold pesos annually to reach a payment of 50 million in 1927; and second, the balance would be paid after 1927 at 3% interest over 20 years. All of the oil export taxes plus a tax on 10% of the gross receipts of the railways and operating revenues secured the readjusted debt. All the sinking funds were to be postponed for a period not to exceed five years, and all matured obligations would be extended for a "reasonable length of time." In addition, the Mexican government agreed to return the railways to private management, while at the same time endorsing and assuming the railways' debts.[53] The $30 million that Mexico pledged to pay for four years came to about one-quarter of Mexico's annual income at the time.[54]

Summary. The 1922 de la Huerta–Lamont debt agreement ended the previous stalemate greatly in favor of the lenders. The lenders secured a promise of high adjustment from Mexico while offering almost nothing in return, corresponding to the predicted HA..., LC... outcome. In the first round of negotiations, we saw considerable maneuvering on Mexico's part to restructure the debt negotiations to its liking. These efforts failed to bring about the desired changes and left the outcome deadlocked. By the end of the second round, with continued pressure from the lenders, and additional support from the creditor governments, Mexico essentially capitulated and agreed to a severely unfavorable agreement as expected from our situational analysis.

Situational changes

Drawing on norms of repayment, Mexico likened its position to that of a business firm with problems and sought a satisfactory compromise at the beginning of this period. This call for compromise had little direct effect in altering Mexico's

[51] Wynne (1951), p. 71 and Official Documents Relating to the de la Huerta-Lamont Agreement, #70, cited in Turlington (1930), p. 294.
[52] See *The Economist*, July 1, 1922, p. 16.
[53] *The Economist*, June 24, 1922, p. 1290 and September 9, 1922, p. 425.
[54] Vásquez and Meyer (1985), p. 130.

situation, but it did stimulate new negotiations. Mexico also attempted to use its capabilities to foster favorable changes in its individual situation. The government pushed internal economic reforms, and then attempted to improve its financial situation by taxing oil corporations, but these efforts came to nought. A similar fate befell Mexico's bid to play the bankers off each other.

Bankers used a variety of power resources as well. Drawing on norms of repayment, they argued it was illegal and immoral for Mexico to use its funds to buy back bonds at sharply reduced prices. In addition, they refused to make additional loans, and successfully tested their internal cohesion when Mexico attempted to obtain a loan from Speyer and Company. Finally, the bankers succeeded in redefining the issue-area of negotiations by delinking the debt issue from the larger American government agenda, to avoid being saddled with the entire agenda of issues that the Administration sought to resolve. The banks were able to obtain permission to proceed with negotiations while maintaining a cohesive alliance with the U.S. government.

Turning now to situational changes leading to a new period, as at the end of two rounds of negotiations, the banks had received a high payoff and Mexico a poor one. The Mexicans tried to improve their bargaining strength. To secure American recognition following the debt settlement, Obregón attempted to settle several outstanding issues with the United States. Recognition not only increased the possibility of securing additional loans to improve Mexico's financial situation, it also helped to prevent Americans from giving aid to potential opponents of the Mexican regime.[55] Obregón was helped by several Mexican Supreme Court decisions to uphold the right of oil companies to full rights to the oil fields if they had performed some "positive" act to exploit the oil prior to May 1, 1917, the date Article 27 of the Constitution came into effect.[56]

Soon thereafter, following discussions during the winter of 1922–1923, both parties attempted to clear up their differences through the intermediary of James A. Ryan, a retired American general with interests in Mexico. On April 9, Obregón suggested an agenda for future negotiations. President Harding accepted the proposal and a bilateral meeting, known as the Bucareli Conference, began on May 14. Three months later, the conference produced two treaties: a Special Claims Convention covering losses sustained between November 10, 1910, and May 31, 1920; and a General Claims Convention covering the other losses from 1868 onwards. The conference also produced a third category agreement, a so-called "unofficial pact" that addressed the impact of future oil and land legislation on American interests. The principal result of the Bucareli Conference, however, was a period of detente between the U.S. and Mexico: on August 31, 1923, Washington finally extended formal recognition to the Obregón government.

But problems in the Mexican economy led to a number of undesirable changes. A few months after the Bucareli accords, Mexico made its first debt service

[55] See Vázquez and Meyer (1985), p. 128. [56] Meyer and Sherman (1987), p. 578.

payment since the onset of revolutionary turmoil. This payment was made "only with great difficulty";[57] Obregón had correctly predicted that Mexico could not live up to the conditions of an agreement without new loans. The Mexican Treasury, under new Finance Minister Alberto Pani, was "marching toward disaster"[58] with expenditures outstripping revenues. In the first nine months of 1923, the government accumulated a 37 million peso deficit.[59] Obregón placed the blame of Mexico's financial mess squarely on the "systematic pilferage" of his outgoing Finance Minister, Adolfo de la Huerta, with whom he had been at odds ever since the ratification of the 1922 debt accord. Furthermore, Obregón claimed he would have never ratified the debt accord without the assurances from de la Huerta that new loans (which had yet to materialize), were virtually guaranteed.[60] These conflicts set the stage for the next period of negotiations.

In summary, toward the end of 1923, situational changes had left Mexico in the same position (IS 4/8) as that of the earlier period from 1916 to 1920. The government now faced growing instability and continuing financial problems. Still, U.S. recognition had increased Mexico's overall capabilities somewhat and would prove a valuable asset.

Period three: return to deadlock, late 1923–1924

The bankers were pleased with Mexico's resumption of debt servicing after the long hiatus. For its part, having secured some satisfaction by concluding the Bucareli agreements, the U.S. now showed little interest in undermining the Mexican government.

But opposition to Obregón was triggered by the assassination of Pancho Villa in the summer of 1923. Although the assassins were not found, many called Villa's death a politically motivated murder. Adolfo de la Huerta, Obregón's previous Finance Minister, mobilized the opposition. De la Huerta had opposed concessions to the U.S. in exchange for recognition. At the same time, he had been attacked by Obregón for failing to secure a loan.

Obregón successfully repressed the rebellion, aided in large part by arms from the U.S. as well as de la Huerta's inability to secure American assistance. U.S. Secretary of State Hughes also resisted pressure from various American interest groups to intervene in the conflict, arguing that "the United States could not interfere with the action of government forces to defeat the rebels."[61] Obregón also received support from the ICBM, which refused to aid de la Huerta with funds. Although successful, the cost to Obregón's government proved to be on the order of 60 million pesos.[62] During this period, Mexico found itself in IS 4/8. The bankers' situation remained relatively constant (IS 5). (Since the matrix is identical to the one in period one of this chapter, I show only the ordinal matrix.)

[57] Turlington (1930), p. 299. [58] Turlington (1930), p. 300. [59] Wynne (1951), p. 72.
[60] Wynne (1951), p. 72. [61] Smith (1972), p. 224. [62] Turlington (1930), p. 300.

Ordinal Payoff Matrix,
No Intervention Expected

		Lenders IS 5		
		HC...	MC...	LC...
	HA...	4, 2.5	2, 6	1, 9
Mexico IS 4/8	MA...	7, 1	5, 4.5	3, 8
	LA...	9, 2.5	8, 4.5	**6, 7**

Note: Nash equilibrium bolded.

Figure 9.3. *Play phase, period three: 1923–1924*

Debt game and predicted outcome

From our classifications, we arrive at the game shown in Figure 9.3 for period three. Without intervention, we expect a stalemate. Given that the United States had achieved most of its goals through the Bucareli agreement, we would not expect it to intervene in debt negotiations at this point, thus leaving an outcome of low adjustment and concessions.

The negotiations and outcome

With the national treasury deeper into crisis, in large part due to costs associated with quelling the rebellion, Mexican officials cut back the amounts going toward debt repayment, and sought immediate financial relief from foreign bankers. The bankers refused, however, to make any new concessions or to forward any funds to the government. Obregón gained some relief from American oil companies in Mexico via a 20 million peso advance on the country's oil taxes,[63] but this proved insufficient.

In April 1924, the Mexican government approached the ICBM with a proposal for a new loan. Mexican officials requested $15 million, to be secured on oil *production* tax revenues (as opposed to the oil *export* tax revenues already pledged to debt service). The bankers, however, rejected this proposal because of falling oil production in the country, wariness of a new Mexican venture, and most importantly, the opposition of American oil companies to the tax. If the bankers had accepted the proposal, it would have put them at odds with other foreign investors in Mexico (primarily American oil interests). In fact, Mexican officials blamed American oil companies for their failure to get the bankers to

[63] *New York Times*, January 17, 1924 and March 27, 1924.

cooperate.[64] When Lamont complained to Secretary Hughes that the Mexicans were not abiding by the terms of their agreement with the ICBM, Hughes displayed little interest in these problems.[65]

With the Mexican Treasury virtually bankrupt, Obregón suspended the 1922 debt agreement on June 30, 1924 – less than one year after its ratification. As Obregón had warned, it was impossible for Mexico to maintain its debt servicing obligations without new loans. Unable to obtain a new loan from the ICBM, Mexican officials turned to other sources of foreign capital. By September 1924, Secretary of Finance Pani tentatively negotiated a $50 million loan at 6% interest, secured on the oil production tax, from J.L. Arlitt of Austin, Texas. The loan was to be used to meet the obligations of the 1922 agreement, reduce the floating debt, and fund general government expenses. In the end, the loan never materialized because Arlitt failed to come up with the necessary funds. The State Department, however, did nothing to block this loan effort.[66]

Summary. As anticipated, the bondholders and Mexico once again fell into a deadlock in 1923–1924. The change in Mexico's individual situation left the debt game in a position similar to the first period. In this period, however, the American government failed to show much concern about Mexico's lack of cooperation and the resulting deadlock with the banks because it had satisfied the most important American pressure groups with the Bucareli agreement. Thus, despite Lamont's appeals to his close ally, Secretary of State Hughes, the U.S. government failed to pressure Mexico to break the stalemate.

Situational changes

Mexico and the bankers made a few efforts to promote situational changes during period three. Mexico tried to play the bankers off against the oil companies, but was unsuccessful. The bankers sought to enlist the U.S. government on its behalf, but it became apparent that the American government would only promote the bankers' objectives if they closely mirrored the government's broader agenda. When the U.S. solved what it perceived as its most crucial problems, the government's waning interest weakened the bankers' position.

Facing a lack of new funds and a deadlocked game, toward the end of the period, Obregón implemented severe austerity measures in government spending. Through a variety of economic reforms, administrative reorganization, and tax reforms, Obregón and General Plutarco Calles (Obregón's handpicked successor elected to the presidency at the end of 1924) were able to wipe out the Mexican government's deficit by the end of 1925.[67] This amazing budget turnaround occurred partly at the creditors' expense. The Mexican government used all its revenue sources to meet its pressing expenses, including those pledged for debt service by the 1922 agreement. When Calles entered office in December

[64] *New York Times*, July 2, 1924, cited in Turlington (1930), p. 301.
[65] Smith (1972), p. 227. [66] Smith (1972), p. 227. [67] Wynne (1951), p. 74.

1924, this event marked the first peaceful transition in Mexico since 1884. For 40 years, succession had been marked by the assassination or forced exile of the chief executive.[68]

With the successful transfer of power from Obregón to Calles, Mexico's polity and economy appeared to be developing a sounder footing. Although Calles would remain the key player in Mexican politics for nearly a decade, Mexico's domestic political stability and financial stability only persisted for a couple of years, from 1925 through 1926.

The bondholders' position began to change, with their issue and overall strength eroding somewhat. Lamont was under pressure to conclude some type of arrangement to secure payments, while at the same time, the ICBM could no longer count on much direct support from the United States government.

Period four: toward the Pani-Lamont agreement, 1925–1926

The bankers and their bondholders had been disappointed by the aborted rescheduling arrangement negotiated in 1922. With the situation again temporarily stable in Mexico, optimism grew about a new arrangement to resume payments. But as we shall see, hope for a beneficial agreement would be unfulfilled during this period, as Mexico ignored the bondholders and pursued its own economic objectives. Relations with the U.S. once again soured during this time, as Calles pressed on with efforts to restrict the oil companies' activities in Mexico.

Identifying individual situations

In this period, Mexico was more stable, issue strong, and overall medium (IS 2/5). The bondholders, by contrast, were weaker than in earlier periods, with high stability but only medium overall and issue capabilities (IS 5/7).

Mexico. Calles served officially as president only from November 30, 1924, until December 1928, but in fact reigned over the country from behind the scenes until November 1934. He was the real power behind his three handpicked provisional presidents: Emilio Portes Gil, Pascual Ortiz Rubio, and Abelardo Rodríguez. Calles continued Obregón's political stabilization policies. He intensified the incorporation of the labor sector into the government by appointing as his Secretary of Labor Luis Morones, leader of the Confederación Regional Obrera Mexicana (the country's largest labor organization).[69] Morones later became Calles's intimate confidant. But political opposition continued, and Calles resorted to traditional repressive measures such as jailing and torture. Although Calles enjoyed considerable political stability initially, his July 1926 decree suppressing all public worship by priests created political instability. Fervent Catholics resorted to violence to defend the rights of their Church, beginning an

[68] Meyer and Sherman (1987), p. 581.

[69] See Collier and Collier (1991), pp. 202–250 on labor incorporation in Mexico during the 1920s and 1930s.

insurgency movement that would continue for several years. The Church protested Calles's action as state persecution and called for a "liga de resistencia" – an economic boycott to put financial pressure on the government. As a result, the government was forced to devote considerable resources to fighting the Cristeros (the Catholic opposition).

Calles strengthened the nation's financial system by creating a national bank, by reforming and consolidating private banks, and by reorganizing the taxation system.[70] These efforts, along with domestic peace and the end of a global economic slump, wiped out the budget deficit in 1925 – albeit for only a relatively brief period.

Under Calles, the government gained strength. He improved the state of education nationally by creating 2,000 additional rural schools and began vaccination campaigns. The government increased land redistribution, launched irrigation projects, and allocated large funds for the construction and development of communications. Still, the economy remained reliant on foreign capital, thus making Calles somewhat vulnerable to pressure. With respect to the bankers, Mexico was on more solid footing, in part because the American government made it clear it would not intervene and force Mexico to service its debt.

Lenders. The ICBM continued to be the focal point for debt negotiations, unifying the international group of bondholders who had made loans to Mexico. Thomas Lamont continued to serve as the group's leader, and he acted to bolster the coalition in the face of fissiparous tendencies.

Having secured a settlement in 1922, which yielded few payments from Mexico, however, the Committee found itself under increasing pressure from bondholders to ensure that the default of 1924 would not continue. Although the bankers still maintained considerable financial strength, pressure to make some further arrangement guided their behavior, leading us to classify their issue capabilities as medium rather than strong.

In overall capabilities, the bankers no longer found themselves in a tight alliance with the U.S. government. Although the government did not prevent bankers from generally controlling Mexico's ability to secure foreign loans, compared to the State Department's earlier guidance and encouragement, the bondholders were weaker. As the last two periods had already witnessed, the objectives of the U.S. government and the bankers were beginning to diverge, a tendency that accelerated in this and the next period of negotiations.

Creditor governments. Following the Bucareli agreements, the U.S. appeared to have sufficiently stabilized its relationship with Mexico to lose interest in continuing to pressure the Mexicans. Mexico's hope on this score proved to be short-lived. Just one year after coming to power, Calles passed the Petroleum Law and the Alien Land Law, giving teeth to Article 27 of the

[70] See Smith (1972), p. 230.

Constitution. The Alien Land Law restricted foreigners' land holdings; the Petroleum Law took control of the oil fields by substituting the rights of companies to long-term concessions for outright ownership to the fields. These changes quickly led to the renewal of pressure on the U.S. government by various interest groups and to a sharp deterioration in American-Mexican relations.[71]

Debt game and predicted outcome

Mexico's improved situation, in contrast to the bondholders', is reflected in period four's debt game (Figure 9.4). Based on the actors' individual situations, we expect the bankers to be willing to make high concessions and Mexico to be unwilling to undertake adjustment. Based on the bankers' previous problematic experience of being constrained by close ties to the American government, we should expect them to resist trying to secure aid from the United States. Thus, we expect some American intervention in these negotiations to prevent the bankers from undermining American policy objectives by making a large loan to Mexico without strings attached. In short, the likely final outcome should be no adjustment by Mexico and medium concessions by the bankers.

The negotiations and outcome

Following Calles's rise to power at the end of 1924, Finance Minister Pani attempted to secure a large loan from the bankers, calling for a revision of the 1922 agreement. Pani claimed that both contracting parties caused the suspension of the 1922 agreement. He said the Mexican government had ratified the agreement based on de la Huerta's assurances of new funds and on incorrect estimates of Mexico's financial situation. He pointed out that despite pledging in the 1922 agreement's preamble to cooperate and ensure Mexico's prosperity, the ICBM refused to provide new loans. Pani warned that the bankers' refusal

> had made [the] sacrifices of the government and people seem wholly fruitless; and an intense public opinion, which could not be disregarded without danger to the stability of the national political institutions, had compelled the government to suspend the execution of the agreement.[72]

He proposed that negotiators modify the 1922 accord to restore the railway debt as a separate issue. Pani also suggested an extension of the five-year debt service transition period, to be supplemented by the oil production tax. In addition, he called for the establishment of a national bank, the Banco Unico, and for a new $60 million loan to make interest payments on the existing debt.[73]

The Committee members agreed to suspend payments until 1928, but argued that they were bound by the bondholders to the 1922 agreement. In addition, because the Committee believed the Banco Unico was not urgently needed, Lamont claimed that a $20 million loan would suffice to meet Mexico's needs.

These initial efforts to force each other to adjust masked the underlying

[71] See Vázquez and Meyer (1985), pp. 134–136 for a discussion.

[72] Turlington (1930), p. 303. [73] Turlington (1930), p. 304.

Cardinal Payoff Matrix,
Intervention Expected

		Lenders IS 5/7		
		HC...	MC...	LC...
	HA...	−7.5, 4.5	−7.5, 5.17	−5.5, 5.83
Mexico IS 2/5	MA...	−4.67, 2.75	−5, 3	−4, 3.25
	LA...	**−1.83, 3.5**	<u>−2.5, 2.5</u>	−2.5, 1.5

Note: Nash equilibrium bolded; expected outcome with intervention underlined.

Ordinal Payoff Matrix,
Intervention Expected

		Lenders IS 5/7		
		HC...	MC...	LC...
	HA...	1.5, 7	1.5, 8	3, 9
Mexico IS 2/5	MA...	5, 3	4, 4	6, 5
	LA...	**9, 6**	<u>7.5, 2</u>	7.5, 1

Note: Nash equilibrium bolded; expected outcome with intervention underlined.

Figure 9.4. *Play phase, period four: 1925–1926*

motivations on both sides, which quickly became evident. As one analyst notes, "The bankers desperately wanted to preserve the debt agreement and avoid repudiation."[74] The bankers were indeed willing to offer a loan to Mexico. Yet with an improving financial situation and with Mexican officials dissatisfied with the 1922 agreement, the Mexican government had little interest in proceeding unless it could secure much better terms. In fact, soon thereafter, Calles and

[74] Smith (1972), p. 241.

Pani sought to create the Banco Unico solely from Mexican funds. The bankers remained skeptical. As *The Economist* wrote:

> Mexican politicians and officials remain incurable optimists, and although the Treasury is at present practically bare, the project for the establishment of a State bank with a monopoly of the right of issue is talked of as being on the eve of consummation.[75]

Yet the Mexicans successfully raised the needed funds and then announced the formation of a new bank as well as a plan for a sharp modification of the 1922 agreement. But in the meantime, the U.S. had decided to take a hard line with the Calles government and released a note to the press in June 1925 noting that "The government of Mexico is now on trial before the world."[76] Aware that the controversy would likely threaten the formation of the new bank, Mexico withdrew its demand for a large loan. Still, the Committee responded to the bank announcement by launching a series of protests. Lamont claimed that, whereas the government had previously suspended the debt service to meet pressing needs, Mexico had now "simply taken revenues pledged to the bondholders and diverted them to a wholly new purpose."[77] He warned that if the Mexican government went ahead with the bank, the bankers would declare Mexico to be in default and seek recourse with the U.S. State Department and other foreign offices. Although concerned about the U.S. position, the Mexicans did not budge, sticking to their proposals for the Banco Unico and the new debt arrangement.

Although the bankers continued their protests, they quickly capitulated when one ICBM representative, E.R. Jones, declared that Pani would not negotiate further unless he was "'practically assured' that his plan would be accepted."[78] Moreover, Pani had also threatened to "use all of the oil taxes for irrigation purposes unless a new arrangement was formulated."[79] Lamont recognized the ICBM's weakness vis-à-vis Mexico, later telling an associate that some bankers, such as Millhauser of Speyer and Co., "talk glibly about wielding the big stick or kicking them in the stomach. There is no big stick to wield and we have no boot that could possibly reach their remote and very tough stomach."[80]

In December 1925, Pani and Lamont reached an agreement. The Pani-Lamont agreement separated the railway and the direct foreign debts. The foreign debt was secured on the entire oil export tax, and on the other $5 million in gold delivered annually to the Committee from the oil production tax proceeds. Arrears from the suspension of service in 1924 and 1925 (amounting to $37.5 million) were to be liquidated over eight years beginning in 1928 at 3% interest. Finally, the railway debt became the responsibility of the railways. After a return to private management, all revenues from railway operations were to be delivered to the Committee debt service.[81]

As a result of the agreement, Mexico reduced its liabilities (with a new public

[75] *The Economist*, December 6, 1924, p. 913. [76] See sources in Smith (1972), p. 234, n. 12.
[77] Turlington (1930), p. 305. [78] Smith (1972), p. 243. [79] Smith (1972), p. 243.
[80] Quoted in Smith (1972), pp. 246–247.
[81] *The Economist*, October 31, 1925, p. 702; Wynne (1951), pp. 75–76; Turlington (1930), p. 307.

debt of $499 million),[82] such that annual service was reduced from $25.5 to $10.7 million in 1926, and from $25 to $11 million in 1927.[83] The Mexican Congress ratified and enacted the new debt agreement in January 1925. Despite the 1925 readjustment, many remained justifiably skeptical of Mexico's abilities to uphold the agreement. *The Economist* wrote:

We assume that Mexico really means business this time. But, as Mexican bondholders have so often learnt, there is many a slip 'twixt the cup and the lip. In view of recent history in this respect, and of the present financial difficulties of the Mexican Government, premature jubilation should be discouraged.[84]

Summary. During this period, Mexico's increased strength and the banks' anxiety to secure an agreement led to a highly favorable rescheduling accord for Mexico. Although the agreement initially appeared to reflect medium adjustments and medium concessions, it quickly became evident that the agreement was much closer to very few adjustments by Mexico and medium concessions, as the model predicted. When Mexico encountered problems in paying the debt as a result of declining oil tax revenues, the Committee advanced Mexico part of the money (with the rest being borrowed from the newly formed Bank of Mexico). Although under pressure from the U.S. government on a host of issues relating to petroleum and land laws, the Mexican government successfully took a tough line with the bankers and did not make significant concessions.

Situational changes

Following the debt game that led to the 1925 agreement, the bankers should have been highly motivated to alter their individual situation, given their poor payoff. Instead, they soon found that their failure to secure a good outcome had weakened their coalition. Even worse, they soon found themselves without U.S. government support, despite their best efforts to secure such assistance.

We would not expect Mexico, on the other hand, to have an interest in promoting changes given its high payoff. But shocks put Mexico in quite a different individual situation as major domestic conflicts erupted, leading to both domestic instability and financial problems. Declining oil revenues coupled with the depletion of reserves and the difficulty of tax collection during a series of rebellions once again drove the country to the brink of default.

Period five: et tu, Morrow, 1927–1933

Although Mexico quickly fell into default following the 1925 agreement, the ICBM became more optimistic about the resumption of debt payments when President Coolidge appointed Dwight Morrow (a fellow banker) as the new American Ambassador to Mexico in 1927. In the end, they were sorely disappointed.

[82] Vázquez and Meyer (1985), p. 134. [83] Wynne (1951), pp. 75–76.
[84] *The Economist*, October 31, 1925, p. 702.

Morrow was willing to help the bankers, but he had a much broader vision of Mexico's problems, particularly after a special committee of experts investigated Mexico's financial situation. Mexico, meanwhile, fell into serious political and financial problems, which caused it to resist the resumption of debt servicing.

Identifying individual situations

In this period, Mexico became coalitionally unstable, issue weak, but remained overall medium strong (IS 4/8). The bondholders were now coalitionally medium, issue medium, and overall weak in capabilities (IS 1/8).

Mexico. Mexico's domestic stability rapidly deteriorated by the beginning of 1927. A series of crises beset both the Calles reign and that of his puppet successors. In 1928, after Obregón was reelected as Calles's successor, two opposition candidates, General Francisco Serrano and General Arnulfo Gómez, claimed the election had been fraudulent, and they launched an attack against the government. Within a few months, the government quashed the rebellion, ordering the execution of both men. The same year, a Catholic militant murdered Obregón at a garden banquet. The Cristeros Rebellion then spread terror throughout Mexico until 1929 when the State and Church agreed on a settlement. Further unrest took place in 1929, when half of the army attempted to overthrow provisional President Emilio Gil in the so-called Escobar Rebellion. In this case, weapons support from the American government as well as denial of sanctuary enabled loyalists to crush the uprising and quiet the political scene.

The National Revolutionary Party (PNR), created in 1929 to mediate differences between the various interest groups of the new regime, began promoting peaceful and orderly power transitions. The party failed to become a significant instrument of stability during this period, however, because of Calles's continuous maneuvering behind the scenes, and his use of the party as a personal instrument of power.

With respect to financial strength, in 1928 Mexico's economic situation rapidly worsened. Declining oil revenues coupled with the difficulty of tax collection during the Cristeros Rebellion once again drove the country to the brink of default. The 1929 Escobar Rebellion further depleted the Treasury, which in 1930 had only 30 million pesos in cash reserves.[85] When the Great Depression hit Mexico in 1931 and 1932, the peso depreciated from 2 pesos to 1 dollar to 3.5 to 1 dollar in 1932.[86] Balancing the deficit consumed the entire Treasury.

On a more general economic level, Mexico's economy continued its downward slide throughout the 1920s. From a peak of 182 million barrels in 1922, oil production fell to only 50 million barrels by 1928. The uncertainty generated by disagreement between the oil companies and the Mexican government over Article 27 accounted for most of this drop.[87] As a result, government revenues

[85] Meyer and Sherman (1987), p. 593. [86] Meyer and Sherman (1987), p. 593.
[87] For a discussion, see *The Economist*, May 5, 1928, p. 915.

from the oil production and export taxes fell from 86 million pesos to only 11 million pesos during the same period of time.[88] As these vital revenues fell, the government deficit reappeared only a short time after the budget turnaround in 1925.

In overall capability terms, Mexico continued to be medium strong. Its relations with the United States continued to improve in 1927 with the appointment of Morrow as ambassador and because the U.S. increasingly recognized Mexico as a fully sovereign state in whose affairs it would not intervene.

Lenders. The ICBM continued to represent the bondholders but began to experience difficulties in maintaining internal cohesion. In fact, a so-called "International Protective Association" was formed to deal with the Mexican debt in 1929 as ICBM competitors. Although this group was never taken seriously, it did help foster discontent with the ICBM. In 1930, the Association went so far as to write to the American Secretary of State, criticizing the ICBM's activities.[89] Dissatisfaction began to grow with Lamont's leadership, which had accomplished little; he himself warned Morrow that "his own influence as head of the International Committee was declining and that the group itself was showing signs of disintegration."[90] Although this was partially an exaggeration in an effort to secure Morrow's support for a debt settlement, the bondholder group's internal cohesion can best be characterized as medium in overall stability.

In issue-specific terms, little changed from the previous period when the bondholders were issue medium. Pressure continued to increase as the bondholders found their efforts to secure an agreement met by only short payments. No long-term arrangement had been successfully made, however, despite significant concessions by the ICBM to Mexico in the revision of the 1922 agreement.

Finally, in overall terms, the bankers' group was weaker as their alliance with the oil companies collapsed and direct support from the American government was now history.

Creditor governments. The U.S. continued to play the crucial role in Mexico's foreign relations. With Morrow as Ambassador, the Americans became more conciliatory on a host of issues. When Calles passed a new petroleum law that granted oil companies much greater security for their oil properties, while maintaining Mexican sovereignty over the fields, the State Department regarded this as a victory for the U.S. although the oil companies continued to complain. Following this settlement of the oil question, we would expect the U.S. government to have little interest in participating in the debt negotiations.

Debt game and predicted outcome

From our classifications, we arrive at the debt game shown in Figure 9.5. Based on the debt game, and the Nash equilibrium, any one of three possible equilibria

88 Wynne (1951), p. 74 and Turlington (1930), p. 310.
89 United States Department of State archives (hereinafter SD) 812.51/1578.
90 Smith (1972), p. 262.

Cardinal Payoff Matrix,
No Intervention Expected

		Lenders IS 1/8		
		HC...	MC...	LC...
	HA...	−1.5, −1.5	−5, .83	−6.5, 3.17
Mexico IS 4/8	MA...	2.83, −2.75	−1, −1	−3.5, .75
	LA...	**7.17, −.5**	**3, −.5**	**−.5, −.5**

Note: Nash equilibrium bolded.

Ordinal Payoff Matrix,
No Intervention Expected

		Lenders IS 1/8		
		HC...	MC...	LC...
	HA...	4, 2	2, 8	1, 9
Mexico IS 4/8	MA...	7, 1	5, 3	3, 7
	LA...	**9, 5**	**8, 5**	**6, 5**

Note: Nash equilibrium bolded.

Figure 9.5. *Play phase, period five: 1927–1934*

are likely. Although Mexico would benefit if the lenders made high concessions, the latter would not be particularly motivated to play such a strategy. Given our analysis of U.S. interests, we would expect little official intervention during this period. But with Morrow's background as a banker, we might expect him to personally play an active role in arranging a debt settlement. Thus, a focus on creditor government intervention in this case does not allow us to choose among the possible equilibria. Instead, we are likely to see movement among the lenders between the extremes of high and no concessions during the negotiations.

The negotiations and outcome

Following the suspension of the debt agreement at the end of 1927, preliminary negotiations began again between Mexico and the ICBM. In the meantime, there were important developments in the struggle to settle conflict over oil land in connection with Article 27. After extensive discussion, the parties agreed that Mexico would maintain ownership of lands and deposits as of January 1928. However, drilling rights acquired before 1917 would be protected and foreign companies would be allowed to work those sites indefinitely. Although some oil companies found this settlement objectionable, they realized they now had little support from the State Department.[91] With this major problem out of the way, the U.S. began to show even less interest in pressuring Mexico.

Morrow, however, decided to involve himself in creditors' attempts to resolve the debt problem. After Mexican officials held a preliminary conference with the ICBM, the Committee accepted Mexico's current inability to meet its debt service, contingent on an investigation of Mexico's economic and fiscal conditions in the country. Morrow strongly endorsed this idea, and he initially convinced both sides that this was the optimal way to proceed. Negotiators agreed that two American financial and economic experts, Joseph E. Sterrett and Joseph S. Davis, would travel to Mexico on the creditors' behalf and at the invitation of the Mexican government, to conduct a study of Mexico's financial problems.

After three months of research, these analysts concluded their study. The Sterrett-Davis Report argued that Mexico's immediate capacity to service its debt was abnormally low due to the years of revolution and the depressed economy, particularly in the oil industry. This report convinced Morrow that Mexico was indeed virtually bankrupt. More optimistically, the study also noted that many of Mexico's difficulties were created by controversies surrounding the state's land policy, oil policy, and Church conflict, and if the country could resolve these issues, it would be able to satisfy its internal and external obligations in the near future.[92] In addition, the report admonished Mexican officials, stressing the need for Mexico to control spending and pay its debt to improve its credit rating. Based on their findings, Sterrett and Davis estimated that the Mexican government could afford to pledge 30 million pesos annually to the debt service. If the economy improved as expected, this amount could be raised to 70 million pesos in three years and 90 million pesos within five years.[93]

The report concluded that any debt settlement must be comprehensive, taking into account all of Mexico's incurred obligations. There was "little hope of permanent success for any plan of settlement that [did] not envisage the debt as a whole."[94] As it warned:

> There are advantages enjoyed by the holders of some obligations that are not shared by others, yet even in the case of the best secured of the debts the holders have no absolutely effective means of enforcing their preferences over other creditors.[95]

[91] Vázquez and Meyer (1987), p. 138.
[92] Wynne (1951), pp. 77–78 and Turlington (1930), p. 314. [93] Wynne (1951), pp. 77–78.
[94] Wynne (1951), pp. 77–78. [95] Sterrett-Davis Report, p. 236, cited in Wynne (1951), p. 78.

But the U.S. had always been more concerned with protecting American property in Mexico than with the rights of its creditors. Morrow's actions reflected this view. In the words of *The Economist*:

> silly are the stories that the new Ambassador came to Mexico, and sacrificed the oil interests for the financial interests. The fact is that the bondholders are no longer receiving interest, while the Ambassador's efforts have secured to the oil companies all the rights they possessed before 1917.[96]

Differences between Morrow and the ICBM became readily apparent in reaction to the report. Whereas Morrow thought that Mexico "should be handled as a bankrupt corporation,"[97] and should be allowed to function without undue debt pressure in the eventual hope that all creditors would be repaid, the members of the ICBM became restless. They worried that with other governments negotiating agreements with Mexico, they would be left out in the cold. Apparently at Morrow's suggestion, Secretary of State Kellogg "formally instructed Ambassador Morrow to register the objections of the State Department to any new agreement between the International Committee and the Mexican government."[98] Despite this warning, the ICBM decided to press on. After some further discussions, it secured Morrow's commitment to help convince the Mexicans to resume their debt service. But Morrow had little success in this effort. As divisions grew within the ICBM, Lamont took over the effort to secure an agreement.[99]

Negotiations between the ICBM and Mexico resumed in October 1928. As these negotiations proceeded, the Mexican Congress passed a law in January 1929 that set the basis for any future agreements. The law authorized the Executive to conclude agreements with foreign governments regarding claims accumulated during the revolution. It also established an Internal Debt Commission. Under this law, the president could conclude an agreement with the Committee on the consolidation of the debt into a single issue. The debt was made redeemable in no less than 45 years, bearing an interest rate of no more than 5%, and within the government's capacity to service annually.[100] But after having suppressed yet another financially draining uprising (the Escobar Revolt of 1929), the Mexican government had to suspend negotiations, reaching an agreement only in 1930.

The Lamont–Montes de Oca accord was signed in July 1930. The tentative agreement consolidated all of the government's direct debt issues, totaling some $267.5 million, into a new 45-year refunding issue divided into two series, A and B. The A series bonds were derived from secured loans, receiving greater

[96] *The Economist*, May 19, 1928, p. 1018. [97] Smith (1972), p. 260.

[98] Smith (1972), p. 261. The remainder of this paragraph draws heavily on Smith (1972), pp. 262–263.

[99] Lamont's break with Morrow became clearer when, in an effort to discredit Morrow, Lamont apparently called attention to a gaffe by one of Morrow's aides. Colonel Alexander MacNab said in a speech that his boss had taught the Secretary of Finance about finance. When Morrow subsequently tried to block an agreement that Lamont had concluded, he was rebuffed by the Mexican President.

[100] Wynne (1951), p. 79.

priority on security revenues than the B series bonds derived from unsecured loans. Interest varied on the two series, ranging from 3 to 5%. The entire refunding issue was secured on 10% of all customs revenues. Mexico was required to pay a debt service of $12.5 million in 1931, increasing $500,000 annually to $15 million in 1936 and thereafter. Overall, more than $211 million in interest arrears was liquidated by $11.75 million in service, as the entire debt was reduced to three-fifths of the total of the 1925 adjustment accord.

A separate agreement covered the railways debt. This debt, totaling $225 million, was refunded into another 45-year issue at varying interest rates below 5%. The net revenues of the railways were meant to finance debt servicing, but the debt was guaranteed by the government with its 65% of the stock in the reorganized Mexican National Railways.

By and large, this agreement reflected medium to high concessions by the bondholders and little adjustment by Mexico. But the accord never saw the light of day. Official enactment of the agreement required ratification from the Mexican Congress. With the advancing tide of the world depression, ratification appeared dubious in late 1930. In fact, four deputies from Chihuahua proposed a 10-year debt moratorium in November 1930 to redirect funds toward constructive domestic expenditures. Other senators attacked the agreement because the negotiations with the bankers had been conducted in secrecy, unmonitored by Congress. In December, Congress voted to put a 15 million peso appropriation for the 1931 debt service on reserve until ratification. Congress later adjourned for the year without any action on the agreement.

Meanwhile, the Mexican economy soon felt the effects of the world depression. Business activity halted, foreign trade collapsed, and prices fell dramatically. In addition, the silver peso's value fell against gold dollars. This proved to be a significant problem because most of the government's revenues were collected in silver pesos, and converted to gold dollars to pay creditors.

The Mexican government petitioned the International Committee for relief on this matter. The Committee recognized that:

> the decline in exchange on Mexico has increased so greatly the amount of silver pesos which would be required in order to provide for the remittances in U.S. gold dollars called for by the July agreement, that it is a fact that the Government's capacity to pay has been so decreased that it cannot within the limits of its budget revenue and requirements provide such amounts of silver pesos.[101]

As a sign of goodwill, the Committee allowed Mexico to make the stipulated annuities payments in silver pesos deposited to the Committee's credit in a Mexico City bank. The Committee agreed to suspend any conversion and transfer of funds until the value of the silver peso had increased to an acceptable level.

Despite this supplementary agreement reached in January 1931, Mexico failed to make any of the stipulated monthly silver payment deposits. Anticipating a

[101] Wynne (1951), p. 83.

potential default, the International Committee called for an interim agreement suspending all previous agreements and returning the $5 million previously deposited with the Committee. If the deposit was restored by July 1933, the 1930 agreement would be revived. The creditors hoped that by unilaterally suspending the debt agreements, they could avoid a complete default on Mexico's foreign debt.

In January 1932, the Mexican Congress approved this innocuous interim agreement, but at the same time declared void the 1930 and 1932 agreements. In 1933, Mexico failed to make the $5 million redeposit, fully defaulting on the country's foreign debt. Mexican leaders were quick to denounce the previous debt accords. In September 1933, the new Mexican President, Abelardo Rodríquez, announced that the government had allowed the agreements to lapse because the terms were too onerous, and that the present and future financial policy of the government did not call for renewing service on the foreign debt. Instead, the government would now favor a policy of amortizing the internal debt to keep funds in the country, to reincorporate them into national wealth.[102]

Summary. The model suggested that this period would see little adjustment by Mexico, while the bondholders could follow any one of three strategies ranging from low to high concessions. The 1930 Lamont–Montes de Oca agreement fit this prediction. As we expected, Morrow played an active role, but in the end, despite his many repeated efforts, without the backing of the U.S. government he had little influence. Although at one point an agreement with the bondholders making high concessions seemed likely, because of a severely worsening economic situation, the Mexican government quashed even this highly favorable agreement. In short, the exigencies of domestic politics, combined with a financially disastrous situation, forced the equilibrium to settle on no adjustments and no concessions.

Situational changes

At the beginning of this period, Calles's continued efforts to strengthen his coalition sharply backfired. Beginning in mid-1926, his struggle with the Cristeros undermined his political stability, and his continued efforts to manipulate Mexican politics behind the scenes did little to stabilize the country's political situation. This domestic instability also eroded Mexico's financial position, which was also severely weakened by the onset of the Great Depression in 1931. Mexico's only saving grace in preventing major domestic political turmoil was the government's ability to secure weapons from the United States to suppress rebellions.

As noted earlier, the bankers fell flat in their efforts to improve their situation in this period. Their coalitional stability was tested as many foreign bankers grew tired of the U.S. promoting its own objectives. American bankers held on

[102] Council of Foreign Bondholders (1933), p. 39.

to their alliance with the U.S. government, but the U.S. lost most of its interest in helping them secure a debt accord – even as Morrow became the American Ambassador to Mexico. This weakened the bankers' coalition, as well as further diminished their overall capabilities. Unlike earlier bondholders, the bankers had failed to significantly develop their own overall capabilities to bolster their negotiating position.

Following the deadlocked outcome of the 1927–1934 debt game (ordinal payoffs of 6 for Mexico and 5 for the lenders), both Mexico and the bankers were somewhat motivated to alter their situations. Mexico's domestic coalition stabilized as a result of Cárdenas's popularity and policies, while its economy began to pull out of its depression in 1934. The lenders faced an increasingly weakening financial position.

Periods six and seven: working toward a final resolution, 1934–1936 and 1937–1940

After Cárdenas became president in 1934, Mexico followed a more radical policy both domestically and toward foreigners. Many scholars have argued that his regime should be seen as a second Mexican revolution. This dramatic comparison refers to Cárdenas's willingness to break with past policies as well as confront the oil companies, ending a problem that had long impeded U.S.-Mexican relations. Cárdenas was also willing to resolve the ongoing debt problems, but only on terms that would strongly favor Mexico.

With the approach of the Second World War, interaction between the U.S. and Mexico increased dramatically. The Mexican economy benefited from the war boom after the onset of the war, and throughout the early 1940s as the U.S. looked to its neighbor for important materials and supplies. These important changes would lead to a final resolution in 1942 of debt problems dating back to the turn of the century.

I divide my analysis of the 1934 to 1942 time span that led to the final resolution of outstanding debt problems into three periods. The sixth period, from 1934 to 1936, took place during the beginning of the Cárdenas regime. The seventh period covers a time of growing financial difficulties for Mexico from 1937 to 1940. The eighth period, which follows the withdrawal of a Mexican offer after the sudden oil company nationalizations in March 1938, spans 1941 to 1942. I will discuss period eight's negotiations and outcome in a separate section. Because of the ongoing nature of the negotiations, and with lenders remaining in the same position throughout, however, I discuss the codings for all three periods in this section to avoid repetition.

Identifying individual situations

During the first period, from 1934 to 1936, I classify Mexico as coalitionally medium in stability, issue strong, and overall medium (IS 2/5). Throughout the three periods, the lenders were coalitionally medium, issue weak, and overall weak (IS 7/8). By 1937, Mexico's financial position dramatically weakened, although its domestic stability and overall strength improved, placing it in IS 3. With the war boom after 1940, however, Mexico's position rapidly strengthened and remained highly favorable through the eighth period (IS 5).

Mexico. Calles's support and the backing of his newly developed PNR ensured Lázaro Cárdenas's presidential election in July 1934. Unlike previous presidents, however, the new leader was unwilling to let Calles remain in power behind the scenes. Instead, Cárdenas worked quickly to secure the support of the army and mass organizations. He cultivated promising junior officers and undertook important reforms in the army. More directly, he raised salaries and benefits, improved the system of education within the army, and reformed the entire military structure. By 1935, Cárdenas had gained sufficient control over the army to remove former Calles supporters from important jobs in the government and military.[103]

As Calles grew unhappy with the new administration, he attacked Cárdenas's policies. The latter responded by arresting Calles and deporting him to the United States in 1936. Thereafter, Cárdenas began to enjoy enormous power in the country. He benefited from the army's loyalty and that of the PNR (in 1938, renamed the PRM – Partido Revolucionario Mexicano). He also gained support from newly created unions and peasant organizations, such as the Confederación de Trabajadores de México (CTM) (which replaced the corrupt CROM).[104] Lázaro Cárdenas became one of the most popular presidents in Mexican history and was able to easily suppress the single rebellion during his term (led by Saturnino Cedillo).

In 1939, Cárdenas supported the PRM's nomination of his Secretary of War, Avila Camacho, for President. Camacho, elected in November 1940, was a more traditional Roman Catholic. He slowed the pace of his predecessor's reforms and worked to keep a balance between the leftist remnants of Cardenism and the conservative factions gaining power in the country. He was careful not to lose control over the CTM, and replaced its Marxist leader Vicente Lombardo Toledano with the more conservative Fidel Velásquez. Camacho successfully used fears of an external threat to maintain political stability and limit strikes and protest.[105]

In sum, in the first period, Mexico enjoyed growing political stability, followed by two periods including a smooth transition of power. Internal factions failed to seriously threaten Cárdenas after 1936. In addition, the Mexican Congress began to assert itself as a more significant political institution, further stabilizing Mexico's political apparatus.

Turning next to Mexico's financial situation, throughout the early and middle 1930s, the nation experienced an economic downturn, along with the rest of the

[103] See, among others, Hamilton (1982), Chapters 4 and 5; Collier and Collier (1991), pp. 232–250; Meyer and Sherman (1987), p. 597 for a discussion of Cárdenas's regime.
[104] Vázquez and Meyer (1985), p. 146.
[105] See Vázquez and Meyer (1987), p. 155 for a discussion.

world. By 1934–1935, economic conditions began to improve considerably, however, as export demand for Mexican raw materials increased, and as Mexican exporters encountered greater success in the sale of manufactures.[106] Moreover, as revenues increased, the Treasury appeared to be in considerably better shape.[107] Unfortunately, these hopeful signs began to disappear by 1937. Mexican exports began to fall, and revenue from oil drilling decreased as Mexican relations with the oil companies began to sour. Mexico turned to its central bank to borrow, but this source of income proved problematic as the government exceeded its limits. Moreover, the bank itself experienced a dramatic fall in foreign exchange reserves. By 1938, following the March oil nationalizations, the Mexican economy entered into a serious economic crisis, forcing the government to devalue the peso. Problems with running PEMEX, the newly created state-owned oil company, coupled with the huge costs of land redistribution, education programs, and distribution of benefits for labor depleted the Treasury and fueled inflation.

By late 1940, however, Mexico's economy again took a turn for the better as war demand from the U.S. and other countries provided a strong impetus to industrial development. From 1939 to 1943, industrial production boomed, increasing by 46%. Output for foreign markets grew by 600%.[108] In aggregate terms, exports doubled from 1941 to 1945.[109]

As for overall capabilities, Mexico began to increase its strength under both Cárdenas and Camacho. In addition to an increasingly powerful government, the country was more self-sufficient, and for the first time could decide on the disposal of its economic resources. Land redistribution and oil nationalization ended American control of investment, providing Mexico with more autonomy. Mexico's new overall strength was reflected in Cárdenas's intransigence on the issue of compensation for nationalized oil fields, and his eventual imposition of a solution. Mexico was not at the mercy of foreign investors or their creditor governments. When he came to office, President Camacho not only benefited from this new overall strength but took advantage of American strategic concerns during the Second World War.

Lenders. The bondholders and bankers remained united behind their committee of banking houses, although as in the prior period, they faced some internal conflicts. Financially, the ICBM, the most influential group negotiating Mexico's debt, came under increasing pressure to secure a financial settlement. It had been operating for over two decades and despite a series of agreements had little to show by way of renewed Mexican payments.

As for overall capabilities, the lenders remained weak. They lacked the power to influence international trade with Mexico, to discourage foreign investments in the country, or to block new American financial aid to the government. In

[106] For a discussion of Mexico's financial situation under Cárdenas, see Hamilton (1982), pp. 190–194 from which this section draws.
[107] See SD 812.51/2476, 1934 letter, and SD 812.51/2110.
[108] See Hansen (1971), p. 72 for data on this period. [109] Vázquez and Meyer (1985), p. 154.

part, this situation stemmed from Mexico's settlement of nearly all of its other outstanding foreign claims throughout the late 1930s and early 1940s, thus leaving the bondholders with little leverage.

Creditor governments. President Franklin Roosevelt pursued new priorities in American policy toward Mexico and Latin America.[110] The U.S. administration was still concerned with protecting the property of its nationals, but it also focused on ensuring that the U.S. would not be threatened by European activities in Latin America as fascist movements began to gather strength. This concern found expression in the "Good Neighbor" policy that promised to end unilateral American intervention in Latin America, and was embodied in Mexico with the appointment of Josephus Daniels as Ambassador. Moreover, the U.S. preferred to support Cárdenas, a nationalist but also a strong antifascist, rather than another regime that was more tolerant of the fascist groups.[111] Mexican nationalization of the oil companies in 1938, however, suddenly increased the probability of an active U.S. government role, because of fears that this action would set a precedent throughout the world.

The outbreak of World War II again altered American security interests, establishing a new relationship between Mexico and the United States. The U.S. needed oil, rubber, metals, and other strategic materials and supplies from Mexico. Mexico, now cut off from other trading areas, became increasingly dependent on the U.S. market. The war fostered a close and interdependent relationship between the neighboring countries.

In addition, Mexico's formal entry into the war in June of 1942 furthered economic cooperation between the two nations. Allied with Mexico, the American government promised it additional financial aid, trade agreements, and an assortment of other benefits.[112] By contrast, American concerns with helping the bondholders – never a primary objective to begin with – quickly diminished. Given Mexico's importance at this time, the U.S. was eager to see the debt problem go away.

In sum, we would expect the U.S. to be relatively neutral during the first period, until the oil nationalizations at the end of the second period provoked active involvement of the U.S. government. After 1940, we would expect the U.S. to actively favor Mexico in debt negotiations because of its strategic interests in the region.

Debt game and predicted outcome: period six

From our classifications, we arrive at the debt game shown in Figure 9.6 for the sixth period, with Mexico in IS 2/5 and the lenders in IS 7/8. In this game, I predict an equilibrium of low adjustment by Mexico and high concessions by the lenders. Such an outcome would provide the highest possible payoff for Mexico

[110] For good discussions of U.S. policy during this period, see in particular Cronon (1960), Wood (1961), Gellman (1979), and Vázquez and Meyer (1985).

[111] Vázquez and Meyer (1985), p. 151. [112] Wynne (1951), p. 95.

Cardinal Payoff Matrix,
No Intervention Expected

		Lenders IS 7/8		
		HC...	MC...	LC...
	HA...	−7.5, 6	−7.5, 7.83	−5.5, 9.67
Mexico IS 2/5	MA...	−4.67, 2.75	−5, 4	−4, 5.25
	LA...	**−1.83, 3**	−2.5, 2.5	−2.5, 2

Note: Nash equilibrium bolded.

Ordinal Payoff Matrix,
No Intervention Expected

		Lenders IS 7/8		
		HC...	MC...	LC...
	HA...	1.5, 7	1.5, 8	3, 9
Mexico IS 2/5	MA...	5, 3	4, 5	6, 6
	LA...	**9, 4**	7.5, 2	7.5, 1

Note: Nash equilibrium bolded.

Figure 9.6. *Play phase, period six: 1935–1936*

and a relatively low payoff for the lenders. As noted, we do not expect any significant pressure from creditor governments because the U.S. does not have any compelling reason to intervene. Therefore the equilibrium point should be stable.

The negotiations and outcome: period six

Negotiations in the sixth period began with Lamont's initial query to the Mexican government in 1934, asking if the Mexicans would be interested in undertaking debt negotiations. In August 1935 George Rublee and John Laylin, representing the ICBM, traveled to Mexico to begin informal discussions on the stalled debt situation. Meeting with Mexican Finance Minister Eduardo Suárez, Rublee offered a major concession by calling for an exchange of the original dollar debt for its equivalent in pesos, an action that would considerably reduce the debt because the exchange rate was 3.6 pesos to the dollar. At the same time, Rublee insisted that the $7 million held by the Committee since the aborted 1931 agreement should be used to service the outstanding debt.[113] The money was supposed to have been part of the foreign debt payment to bondholders. Suárez, however, argued that Mexico had a right to $7 million because it had not been distributed to the bondholders as promised when Mexico had made this initial payment. In extended conversations between Rublee and Suárez, the sticking point continued to be the linkage between a possible agreement and the funds held by the Committee. When the Minister proposed a compromise of splitting the funds, Rublee rejected this proposal, and pressed for a final settlement on the outstanding debt.

Rublee then inquired about the prospects of solving the railway debt. Minister Suárez attempted to increase Mexico's leverage by linking the $7 million fund with a solution to the railway debt.[114] According to a memorandum of conversation, the minister stated, "Yes, that is possible; but we cannot do anything about the railroad debt so long as the Committee will do nothing about the funds in its hands."[115] After informal talks came to nought, Rublee took a more concessionary stance: the Committee would credit the $7 million to the Mexican government in a New York–based bank if Mexico promised to use the money to make the first payments called for in the accord.[116]

Mexico and the International Committee concluded a draft agreement in October 1935. In addition to accepting the terms of the $7 million fund, the proposal stipulated that the Committee would return approximately $1 million of that sum. Finally, if the Mexican Congress did not ratify the agreement by April 1, 1937, the Committee could use the funds as they saw fit.[117]

When Rublee and Laylin returned to Mexico in March 1936, they learned that Cárdenas had failed to approve the accord.[118] Mexican officials informed Rublee that negotiations had been delayed because "the Mexican Government was making every effort to continue its large construction program and did not have funds for the beginning of payments at this time."[119] Rublee and his associates at the International Committee were thus unable to secure the necessary concessions from Mexico, and the game became deadlocked.

In March 1936, Rublee asked the State Department to intervene on behalf of the ICBM, but as we expected, American officials showed little inclination to do so. On April 1, Ambassador Daniels wrote to the Secretary of State that he did not "think it wise to act on the proposals made by Mr. Rublee or Mr. Laylin" because of the other pending claims against Mexico involving land expropriation

[113] SD 812.51/2110. [114] SD 812.51/2110. [115] SD 812.51/2110. [116] SD 812.51/2110.
[117] SD 812.51/2117. [118] SD 812.51/2149. [119] SD 812.51/2192.

and other general concerns. He went on to say that "it would seem to me unwise and would do no good to take up the old external debt which Mr. Rublee and Mr. Laylin are pressing until more progress has been made in the three matters to which we are committed."[120] In response to this last point, Herbert Feis, Economic Adviser to the State Department, dryly noted in a handwritten parenthetical comment: "Unless Mexico seeks new loans."[121]

Summary. Although a final agreement was not reached in 1936, the very high concessions offered by the lenders and relatively little adjustment promised by Mexico are consistent with the model's predictions. Yet in the end, the game ended in deadlock, rather than at the predicted outcome. Indeed, the agreement was very favorable to Mexico and yet Cárdenas refused to sign the accord at the last moment. How might we explain this anomaly?

The explanation for why Cárdenas did not sign the agreement initialed by Suárez appears to lie with American actions, rather than any drastic change in Mexico's individual situation. The U.S. Ambassador to Mexico, Josephus Daniels, apparently had a long-standing animosity toward helping U.S. business when it got into political trouble. He had told a group of Americans who had fled Mexico, "You went there to get rich quick; and now you want the whole country to protect you, and you wouldn't pay a cent to support it there."[122] As noted above, Daniels was also reluctant to support American bondholders.

Yet Daniels may have gone beyond his lack of interest in helping the bankers to actively opposing them. In a private conversation with Undersecretary of State Welles in 1939, Mexican Ambassador Castillo Nájera claimed to know that Daniels had told Finance Minister Suárez that "the Government of the United States was not interested in the agreement inasmuch as a large percentage of the bondholders were not American citizens . . ." Nájera said that "as soon as this information was given to President Cárdenas by Señor Suarez [sic] the instructions previously given to sign the agreement were revoked . . ."[123]

Although we cannot be sure if Daniels took this extraordinary action,[124] it would clearly account for Cárdenas's last-minute change of heart about the agreement. As the game payoffs show, Mexico did not have much to lose in a continued deadlock, and it had reason to expect additional concessions from the ICBM in the future, with the U.S. showing little inclination to come to the bankers' aid.

[120] SD 812.51/2149. [121] SD 812.51/2149.

[122] Quoted from the *Chicago Tribune*, May 8, 1914, cited in Cronon (1960), p. 11.

[123] *Foreign Relations of the United States* (1957), pp. 711–712 (refers to 1939 discussions).

[124] Commenting on this report, David Cronon, in a study of Josephus Daniels, argues that although "This was certainly Daniels' view, and he may well have stated it to Mexican officials . . . it is unlikely that he went out of his way to block the agreement, as Castillo Nájera implied. The latter occasionally sought to ingratiate himself with State Department officials at Daniels' expense." Cronon (1960), p. 120.

Situational changes

The deadlocked outcome of this period left Mexico with a relatively high payoff, but the bondholders with the worst possible outcome. Mexico's financial position deteriorated, however, with a fall in exports. As discussed in my coding of the next period above, Mexico's nationalization of the oil companies further exacerbated its financial problems. Yet this action served at the same time to bolster Cardenas's political position, and also increased Mexican control of key resources. Mexico's overall capabilities also benefited from a steady growth in industrial production.

For their part, the disappointed bankers could do little. Having failed to interest the U.S. government in intervening in their favor, and having endured a longstanding default, they had few options but to continue negotiations in hope of an eventual settlement.

Debt game and predicted outcome: period seven

By 1937, as discussed above, Mexico's financial position had weakened, placing it in IS 3, while the lenders remained in IS 7/8. The resulting game is shown in Figure 9.7. On the basis of strategic interaction and no intervention, we would expect this game to settle into one of three potential outcomes: LA..., HC...; HA..., LC...; or MA..., LC.... For the most part, the game resembles one of "Chicken." If the lenders believe that Mexico will undertake only little adjustment, then the creditors' best strategy is to play high concessions, resulting in a LA..., HC... outcome. By contrast, with either medium or high adjustments, the optimal lender response is high concessions. In such a game, a LA..., LC... outcome leaving both players in their worst possible outcomes becomes likely as each tries to secure their favored equilibrium.

With the American government becoming concerned about the oil expropriations, we might expect it to pressure Mexico to make adjustments. But in general, given what we know about U.S. overall interests, and its relatively low concern with the lenders, we would not expect a very decisive move by the U.S. until after March 1938. In this game, even with intervention, we would expect much posturing before a final agreement would be reached and a real danger of the game ending in deadlock.

The negotiations and outcome: period seven

In early 1937, the International Committee agreed to repayments based on the Mexican peso instead of the American dollar, and promised to cut the interest rate from 5 to 4%.[125] But two points caused particular difficulty. The first was the lack of a provision to protect the bondholders in case the Mexican peso declined in value.[126] The second obstacle involved 20 million pesos of bonds "to be issued five years hence to take care of accrued interest on the foreign debt and preferred stock."[127] According to Minister Suárez, the bondholders should

[125] SD 812.51/2192. [126] SD 812.51/2196. [127] SD 812.51/2196.

Cardinal Payoff Matrix, Intervention Expected

		Lenders IS 7/8		
		HC...	MC...	LC...
	HA...	9, 6	5.5, 7.83	**3, 9.67**
Mexico IS 3	MA...	9.67, 2.75	6, 4	**3, 5.25**
	LA...	**10.33, 3**	6.5, 2.5	3, 2

Note: Nash equilibria bolded; expected outcomes with intervention underlined.

Ordinal Payoff Matrix, Intervention Expected

		Lenders IS 7/8		
		HC...	MC...	LC...
	HA...	7, 7	4, 8	**2, 9**
Mexico IS 3	MA...	8, 3	5, 5	**2, 6**
	LA...	**9, 4**	6, 2	2, 1

Note: Nash equilibria bolded; expected outcomes with intervention underlined.

Figure 9.7. *Play phase, period seven: 1937–1940*

absorb this sum "as part of the 275,000,000 peso bond issue settlement."[128] Rublee said the bondholders would not accept such terms.

After nearly three years of proposals and counterproposals, Mexico and the ICBM came to a tentative agreement in 1938. The accord essentially proposed to substitute 275 million pesos of peso bonds for $250 million of direct government

[128] SD 812.651/2196.

debt and about $250 million of past-due interest. The accumulated interest and principal of the peso bonds would be paid at a rate of 3.6 pesos per dollar. Furthermore, the agreement called for "annual payments of 13,000,000 pesos plus 10% of Mexican budgetary revenues in excess of 280,000,000 pesos."[129]

Finance Minister Suárez did not submit the draft agreement for congressional ratification, arguing that he was unable to do so because of Mexico's oil nationalization.[130] In October 1938, Chairman Lamont wrote the finance minister in an attempt to save the agreement, but failed to revive the accord. In fact, no negotiations took place between Mexico and the bankers as Mexican and American concerns shifted to settling the dispute over Cárdenas's nationalization of the international oil companies.[131]

Summary. In the game during period seven, both parties attempted to force an outcome in their favor, but Mexico quickly took the harder line in the game of "Chicken." It followed a tough policy, especially when it became clear that the lenders would not receive support from the U.S. government. Toward the end of the seventh period of negotiations, an asymmetrical outcome strongly favoring Mexico seemed all but certain but failed to materialize.

Why would the Mexicans once again fail to accept such a favorable agreement where almost all concessions in the negotiations were made by the lenders? The most plausible explanation for Mexican withdrawal of the agreement appears to be consistent with Suárez's reference to the oil nationalizations. It seems likely that Suárez would have faced intense pressure had any payments been made to the bankers because Mexico was arguing at the same time that compensation would only be paid to the oil companies after thorough study. To agree to pay the banks at this point – no matter how small the sum and how advantageous the agreement – seemed out of the question. Thus, in this case, even "a little adjustment" was not a good agreement in the broader context of the oil game with the United States.

Situational changes

Following the abrupt end to the debt negotiations in 1938, and despite a highly favorable agreement, Mexico and the bankers found themselves in a deadlock that continued without any negotiations until early 1941.

The most significant event leading to change in Mexico's individual situation was the Second World War. Growing demand for Mexico's products, combined with an end to the problems created by the oil nationalizations, led to sharp growth and financial well-being for Mexico in the seventh period.

The bankers continued to be marginalized from central U.S. government concerns. After the U.S. concluded several agreements with Mexico only a month before the Pearl Harbor attack, the U.S. had little interest in assisting the

[129] SD 812.51/2543. [130] SD 812.51/2526.

[131] For an excellent discussion of this time period, see Hamilton (1982), Chapter 7, and the citations therein.

bankers, and wished for a quick settlement in line with its broad strategic concerns. In sum, despite significant efforts, the bankers failed to alter their individual situation.

Period eight: toward the Lamont-Suarez agreement, 1941–1942

After the beginning of the Second World War, and the subsequent involvement of both the United States and Mexico as allies, resolution on many outstanding claims became a high American priority. By 1942, in addition to a number of general agreements between the two countries, they had reached an accord to settle Mexico's default, which dated back to before the First World War.

Debt game and predicted outcome

In this period (see Figure 9.8), we code Mexico as coalitionally stable, issue strong, and overall strong (IS 5). As noted earlier, the lenders remained in IS 7/8. With changes in Mexico's financial situation, the game now shifted to a strongly asymmetrical one favoring Mexico. Having emerged from the uncertainty of a Chicken game, Mexico could now confidently pursue a strategy of making very few adjustments, while securing high concessions from the lenders – the Nash equilibrium of this game.

As noted in the previous section, the U.S. actively sought to eliminate remaining thorns in its relationship with Mexico. With strategic concerns as the highest priority, we would expect the U.S. to support a resolution to the debt problems that favored the Mexicans. Given that the two-actor equilibrium was already to Mexico's advantage, however, we would not anticipate a change in the outcome as a result of U.S. efforts.

The negotiations and outcome

Following preliminary feelers in early 1940, the U.S. began to negotiate a settlement of outstanding issues with Mexico. By late 1940, the U.S. had proposed a draft agreement addressing outstanding claims involving agricultural claims and oil claims. The draft of October 7, 1940, called for these and other claims to be settled but also included a U.S. call for a debt settlement including railroad debts.[132] The Mexicans were reluctant to discuss a debt settlement as part of a general agreement, and the U.S. did not press the Mexicans on this issue. Meanwhile, in early 1941, Mexican officials called for new negotiations with the ICBM based on the 1938 debt proposal. Specifically, on January 24, 1941, soon after Avila Camacho assumed the presidency, Finance Minister Eduardo Suárez wrote to ICBM Chairman Lamont suggesting that negotiations be resumed.[133] The Mexican negotiators wished to see a reduction in principal using a peso equivalent at the rate of 5 pesos to the dollar. In addition, they called

[132] *Foreign Relations of the United States* (1940), vol. 5, p. 1050. [133] SD 812.51/2488.

Cardinal Payoff Matrix,
Intervention Expected

Lenders IS 7/8

		HC...	MC...	LC...
	HA...	−3, 6	−3.5, 7.83	−3, 9.67
Mexico IS 5	MA...	−1.33, 2.75	−2, 4	−2, 5.25
	LA...	**.33, 3**	−.5, 2.5	−1, 2

Note: Nash equilibrium bolded; expected outcome with intervention underlined.

Ordinal Payoff Matrix,
Intervention Expected

Lenders IS 7/8

		HC...	MC...	LC...
	HA...	2, 7	1, 8	3, 9
Mexico IS 5	MA...	6, 3	4, 5	5, 6
	LA...	**9, 4**	8, 2	7, 1

Note: Nash equilibrium bolded; expected outcome with intervention underlined.

Figure 9.8. *Play phase, period eight: 1941–1942*

for eliminating a clause in the 1938 proposal requiring higher debt service if Mexico's budgetary revenues exceeded 280 million pesos.[134]

Eager to come to an agreement with Mexico, the ICBM clearly recognized Mexico's stronger bargaining position. In a February 27 confidential communication to the State Department, Committee member Laylin made clear his

[134] For details, see SD 812.51/2526.

willingness to entertain a reduction in the debt on a peso-to-dollar equivalence, even though the exchange rate had fallen to around 5 pesos to the dollar. As a State Department report noted, "Mr. Laylin stated that it was his personal opinion that the Bankers' Committee should accept what it could and not hold out, as does the Foreign Bondholders Protective Council, for some unrealistic figure."[135]

In March 1941, Lamont attempted to secure a better deal for the bankers by suggesting that the old exchange rate provision of 3.6 pesos to the dollar be used to reduce Mexico's principal payment obligations. Mexico did not respond to this memorandum; with no response forthcoming, the Committee sent Mexico a second aide-mémoire in June.[136] This time, the Committee agreed to the 5 pesos to the dollar rate, but used a different set of calculations on which debts would be included in the restructuring to reduce the approximately $500 million to $75 million (versus the $50 million that the Mexicans were willing to accept). Again, Mexico took no action on the ICBM's proposal for some time.

In late August 1941, the Committee received a memorandum from Luis Legorreta, head of the Mexican Banco Nacional. In his message, Legorreta persisted with the Mexican demand that the new exchange rate should be the basis for principal reduction. The ICBM sent a letter accompanying an aide-mémoire to the State Department, complaining that Suárez had been following a two-pronged strategy that was undermining the Committee's efforts. First, the Mexican government had apparently been purchasing its bonds on the open market at low prices – a strategy that many debtors, Mexico included, had pursued in the past. Second, the Committee complained that Suárez "has simply been delaying the discussions in regard to the existing draft proposal for the handling of the debt in order to delay the matter until the projected agreement with the American Government was consummated."[137]

The reference to projected agreements concerned the ongoing negotiations between the Mexican and American governments over agrarian claims going back to the Revolution and the oil conflict. In fact, Mexican-American governmental level relations fundamentally improved with the signing of an agreement on November 19, 1941.[138] The accords included a promise by Mexico to pay $40 million in compensation for agrarian claims and the establishment of a joint commission to determine the amount of compensation owed the oil companies. The U.S. also agreed to a trade treaty, a commitment to purchase silver to back the Mexican peso, and another to make loans to Mexico through the Export-Import Bank. America's interest in deferring to Mexico because of its broader objectives is reflected in the pressure it put on the oil companies to take the $23 million or so settlement for the expropriation. When the companies objected, the State Department told them to either take it or accept nothing. The oil companies relented.[139]

[135] SD 812.51/2501. [136] SD 812.51/2526. [137] SD 812.51/2539.

[138] For a good discussion of the terms of the United States–Mexico agreement, see Cline (1953), pp. 248–249. For other discussions, see Cronon (1960) and Wood (1961).

[139] For discussion of these negotiations, see Cronon (1960), Wood (1961), and Krasner (1978).

With these arrangements in the works, the U.S. government had no interest in helping the lenders in their negotiations with Mexico over its debt. In an internal memorandum, E.G. Collado, the Special Assistant to the Undersecretary of State, revealed his sympathy for the Mexican position, commenting on the contending ICBM and Mexican proposals:

> It is my own personal opinion without reference to the equities of the situation that the position of the Mexican Government is almost as far as that Government could properly go in view of the economic effects on the Mexican economy and balance of payments of the entire program which it is proposed to enter into, including the claims settlement, the petroleum settlement, and the stabilization and highway programs.[140]

The State Department's refusal to get involved in helping the ICBM in any way was made clear in a circular dated February 9, 1942:

> The Department has on various occasions, and at least as recently as November, informally discussed the question of the Mexican Foreign Debt with the Mexican Minister of Finance with a view to lending its friendly offices towards expediting a settlement . . . the Department does not contemplate any further action except possible renewal of its good offices at some appropriate time in the future.[141]

Meanwhile, negotiations proceeded along the lines of Mexican demands. After more proposals and counterproposals, on November 5, 1942, a new agreement was reached on Mexico's direct foreign debt. The Chamber of Deputies of the Congress of the United States of Mexico unanimously approved the accord on December 22.[142] Under the agreement, the bondholders would present their bonds for registration of new assenting government bonds. These new bonds would be retired either by purchase or by drawings at the rate of 1 peso per dollar of nominal principal. The offer would commence in 1948 and end in 1968, retiring at least $5 million annually. Secured bonds would be retired before unsecured bonds. Accrued interest arrears from 1923 through 1943 would be liquidated at 1% of face value, while arrears accumulated prior to 1923 would be liquidated at 0.1 to 0.2%. The government would resume payment of interest in 1943 with an annuity not exceeding 10 million pesos (approximately $2.062 million).[143]

Overall, the Mexican government would pay 23.7 cents on every dollar of secured debt bonds, and only 14.2 cents on every dollar of unsecured debt bonds. Over $500 million in direct government debt (principal and interest) would be paid by $50 million in debt service.[144]

Commenting on Mexico's policies after the agreement, *The Economist* wrote:

> having escaped liability to redeem at anything like the full price, and presumably, having effected a parallel saving in interest, on the ground of inability to meet such heavy demands, Mexico proceeds to devote large sums to buying up the bonds at the depreciated levels produced by her default.[145]

[140] SD 812.51/2543. [141] SD 812.51/2578. [142] SD 812.51/2653.
[143] Wynne (1951), pp. 97–98; *The Economist*, December 5, 1942, p. 709.
[144] Wynne (1951), pp. 97–98; *The Economist*, December 5, 1942, p. 709.
[145] *The Economist*, December 5, 1942, p. 709.

Despite the negative impact of the agreement, however, the very same article urged, "it may be the wisest course to cut past losses and take the reduced amount now offered rather than hope that an obviously unwilling debtor will continue to implement a bargain over a quarter of a century."[146] In any event, by August 1949 nearly 92% of all eligible bonds had been turned in and converted to the assenting bonds.[147]

It should be noted that at least some bondholders did fare well with this agreement. In some cases, the original bondholders had long sold out to speculators who would benefit from almost any agreement. But on the whole, this agreement, as well as the agreement on the some $500 million in railway debt along the same lines in 1946, did represent major concessions by the ICBM and little adjustment for Mexico.[148]

Summary. Mexico clearly gained the upper hand during this period of negotiations. The government took a hard line in the debt negotiations, refusing to budge from its demand that the approximately $500 million accumulated debt be written down to $50 million. Signals by the U.S. government that it was willing to help Mexico and was not planning to pressure the Mexicans in any way further reinforced Mexico's hard line. In the end, the agreement reached by Mexico and the bankers strongly favored the Mexicans.

Situational changes

At the beginning of this period, the onset of the Second World War had the most profound effect on negotiations. The war strongly encouraged the U.S. to come to terms with the Mexicans and to avoid putting pressure on them to agree to an unfavorable deal with the lenders. In addition, and most significantly, the ongoing demand for goods and raw materials as a result of the conflict led to a major improvement in Mexico's financial situation. For their part, the bondholders failed to secure any significant assistance from the American government.

During the negotiations and toward the end of the period, the most effective use of capabilities was in Mexico's strategy of buying up its bonds at discounted prices. The lenders found it hard to prevent this, and thus needed an agreement as quickly as possible to prevent the Mexicans from simply refusing to undertake any negotiations whatsoever once they had secured the bulk of the bonds through intermediaries. The bondholders blocked the disbursement of the $7 million held by them until the agreement was concluded, but this proved to be a less significant source of leverage than they might have anticipated.

Conclusion

During most of the eight periods in this epoch, the United States played a very active role in the debt games between Mexico and the lenders. By granting and

[146] *The Economist*, December 5, 1942, p. 709.
[147] Council of Foreign Bondholders, 1949, p. 41, cited in Wynne (1951), p. 99.
[148] For details of the railway agreement, see Wynne (1951), pp. 100–105.

withholding both financial aid and diplomatic recognition, the U.S. pursued its own objectives in the various negotiations.

During the first three periods, Mexico's coalitional stability changed due to external and internal pressures. In the first and third periods, the deadlocks I expected from the model occurred. The exception was my expectation that U.S. intervention would shift the equilibrium away from a deadlock in the first period; although such a shift did occur, it proved only temporary and the game slipped back into the two-actor game's Nash equilibrium. The second period saw a Mexican commitment to high adjustment, despite a lack of concessions by the bondholders; but the strain on Mexico's economy proved to be quite great, and growing political instability quickly put an end to these payments.

The fourth period once again found Mexico in a relatively favorable game. The bondholders' position began to weaken as the U.S. pursued its own interests and the ICBM began to face problems. Despite U.S. pressure, the Mexicans resisted making any major adjustments and did secure a favorable reduction in their debt burden. In the fifth period, facing both a deepening political crisis and economic problems, Mexico was in no position to make significant adjustments. The debt game for this period suggested the possibility of three equilibria with different ranges of concessions by the lenders. In fact, we saw movement among different equilibria during this period until the final deadlock outcome.

The sixth through eighth periods saw a game wherein Mexico had the upper hand. Although an agreement favorable to Mexico seemed assured by the end of 1938, Mexico's oil nationalizations threw off my debt game-based prediction. Despite the offer of a very favorable agreement, Mexico chose to withdraw from any agreement, because of domestic pressure to take an extremely hard line with foreigners. Only in the eighth period, when the U.S. took a clear interest in ending Mexico's long-standing debt problems, did the strong Mexican government produce a final agreement with a weak group of lenders that met almost all of Mexico's demands for massive debt reduction.

Throughout the time span analyzed here, we saw many efforts at situational change. The Second World War brought about the most important changes in Mexico's situation and in American interest to promote a resolution to the debt conflict.

10 Years of false hope: Peruvian debt negotiations, 1930–1953

The formation of the Peruvian Corporation, the result of the 1887 Grace contract, ended Peru's debacle with the massive debts it accrued in the 1860s and 1870s. Yet contrary to the expectations of Peruvian policymakers, this settlement did not allow Peru to restore its international credit or facilitate new borrowing on a large scale. As we saw in Chapter 1, the hiatus in lending was mainly driven by international factors, accompanied by a shift from British and French lenders to American creditors in the 1920s. Thus, despite some outstanding problems that may have hurt Peru's ability to borrow, including conflict with French creditors, Peru was not alone in its failure to secure significant loans in the years before the First World War.[1]

In the immediate post–World War I period, however, Peru's economy showed strong growth, led by exports of raw materials. Just as Balta and Pierola had attempted to turn guano into railroads in the 1860s, President Augusto Leguía decided to use foreign lending to promote the development of the Peruvian infrastructure. Taking advantage of the banks' eagerness to lend, especially American banks, Peru went on a major borrowing spree in the 1920s, securing just over $100 million in loans. By 1931, the Great Depression had thrown a heavily indebted Peru into default. Negotiations to resolve these problems continued off and on for over 20 years, until a final settlement was reached in 1953.

We consider seven periods of negotiations during this epoch. The first, from 1930 to 1936, examines efforts by creditors and Peru to cope with default. The second period, covering the second part of President Benavides's regime from 1936 to 1939, saw continued stalemate between Peru and its creditors. During the third period, from 1939 to 1943, it appeared as if a settlement was imminent, but an agreement failed to emerge. The fourth period, from 1944 to 1946, saw a commitment by the bondholders to make high concessions, but even this offer did not lead to a final accord. Peru entered the fifth period with high domestic instability, and weakening of both its issue and overall capabilities (1946–1947). In period six, from 1948 to 1950, Peru negotiated directly with the bondholders, rather than with their representatives. Although this strategy did not successfully split the bondholders into separate committees, it spurred two sets of negotiations, one in which Peru prevailed and the other in which it found itself deadlocked. Resolution of its long-standing debt problem finally occurred during the seventh period, from 1951 to 1953, when the lenders benefited from sustained support from creditor governments and international organizations.

[1] See Miller (1983), p. 329 for an excellent discussion of this point.

Background to rescheduling

In 1919, incumbent President José Pardo faced domestic unrest and a major national strike on the eve of the presidential election. The president soon renounced his nomination and reluctantly endorsed conservative candidate Antero Aspíllaga. Returning from exile in Europe, former President Augusto Leguía entered the presidential race in February. Denouncing Pardo's oligarchy and promising a new fatherland, Leguía immediately won popular support and the election in May. Although Aspíllaga and the Supreme Election Tribunal challenged his victory and invalidated thousands of Leguía's votes, pro-Leguía factions in the army organized a coup, arrested Pardo, and installed Leguía as president in July.

The onset of Leguía's 11-year rule (the "*Oncenio*") ushered in a period of immense foreign borrowing to fund ambitious domestic projects.[2] The domestic economy began to encounter problems, however, when export revenues fell. In 1921 and 1922, the budget deficit reached 3 million Peruvian pounds.[3] In response, Leguía negotiated two foreign loans in 1922. U.S. bankers lent $2.5 million at 8% interest based on the security of Peru's petroleum reserves in July.[4] Within a month Leguía had spent all the proceeds and requested additional funds. An American bank, Guaranty Trust, which held an option on any future loans guaranteed by the customs revenue, balked at lending new money. The U.S. State Department, alerted by its chargé d'affaires in Lima, intervened to prevent Leguía from turning to Britain. Guaranty Trust relinquished its option, and the State Department paved the way for the Wall Street firm of White Weld to enter negotiations.[5] Despite this intervention, the second loan issued in 1922 was British, a £1.25 million loan at 7.5% interest rate, secured on the guano tax.[6]

Following these initial loans, further borrowing came considerably more rapidly and easily. In October 1924, White Weld negotiated a $7 million loan at 8%, followed by another a year later for $7.5 million at 7.5% interest.[7] This loan, based on the security of petroleum revenues, partly retired the Guaranty Trust Loan of 1922 and other loans based on oil reserves. Additional loans followed, culminating in two loans underwritten by J. & W. Seligman and the National City Bank of New York, two institutions that dominated lending to Peru.[8]

These two banks together floated three substantial loans. The first (known as the tobacco loan) represented a $15 million loan at 7% secured on the tobacco revenue.[9] The second and third loans completed the so-called Peruvian 6% National Loan – consisting of two series of bond issues.[10] The first series of $50

[2] Werlich (1978), p. 158.
[3] United States Department of State Archives (hereinafter, SD) 823.51/655, p. 5.
[4] Wynne (1951), p. 183.
[5] Stallings (1987), p. 256. This is the best single source on this period of debt negotiations.
[6] Wynne (1951), p. 183. [7] Wynne (1951), p. 185. [8] Stallings (1987), p. 259.
[9] Wynne (1951), p. 185. [10] SD 823.51/655, p. 6 and Wynne (1951), p. 186.

million was issued in 1927, followed a year later by the second of $25 million, plus a sterling tranche of 2 million pounds.[11] With the National Loan, Peru aimed to retire all previous external loans except the guano loan of 1922 and tobacco loan of 1927.[12] To compensate for the loan's insecurity, an agency known as the Caja de Depósitos y Consignaciones was established to manage the debt payments.

In 1929, the worldwide depression hit Peru. The drastic fall in world prices slashed the value of Peru's chief exports, strangling Peru's foreign exchange situation, which reverberated throughout its economy. Inflation and other monetary difficulties also increased the government's financial woes. Both social and political discontent ensued. In contrast to the previous period's easy access to foreign capital, American financial houses began limiting foreign loans to Peru, signalling the end of the "U.S. dollar decade."

Relations between Peru and its bankers began to sour.[13] In November 1929, bankers refused additional credit extensions. Leguía's attempt to use the currency stabilization funds to revalue the Peruvian pound without first pursuing fiscal reforms increased conflict between the bankers and the government. In December 1929, Seligman's fiscal agents proposed a renewal of existing credits for three months if authorized by the Peruvian Congress to dispose of the National Loan's remaining $15 million par value at the best available price. The agreement was contingent on three conditions: a balanced budget, control over the appointment of the Director of the Budget and the Comptroller General, and control over the Reserve Bank and its loan policy. In addition, the agents requested that Peru deposit all funds on deposit abroad with them and the Reserve Bank.[14] Leguía characterized this proposal as "outrageous," and promptly refused the offer. The American Chargé in Lima warned that Seligman's agents' attitude was "implacably hostile."[15]

On January 13, 1930, foreign and local banks in Lima agreed to loan 1 million Peruvian pounds to the government.[16] This loan, however, still did not permit the government to meet its obligations. The Congress then authorized a series of bills that called for the government to issue internal bonds or to borrow from local banks for a total of about $17 million – an amount roughly equal to Peru's total estimated floating debt.[17]

The fiscal agents remained cautious and reluctant to lend on a large scale but did provide short-term renewable credit. In May, they advanced $1.5 million on six months' credit.[18] This measure did not, however, prevent the country's economic difficulties from escalating further during the summer of 1930, as the prices of its main commodity exports rapidly declined. The economic crunch spurred social and political unrest. These events combined with serious dissension over the settlement of two boundary disputes, leading to Leguía's overthrow in

[11] Wynne (1951), p. 186. [12] SD 823.51/655, p. 6
[13] This and the next paragraph draw heavily on SD 823.51/469, pp. 1–3.
[14] SD 823.51/469, p. 7. [15] SD 823.51/469, p. 7. [16] SD 823.51/469, p. 8.
[17] SD 823.51/469, pp. 11 and 18. [18] SD 823.51/521, p. 4.

August 1930. A new government formed under the rule of Colonel Luis Sánchez Cerro. Within seven months, the Peruvian government began taking its first steps toward declaring a default that would not be resolved for over 20 years.

Period one, 1930–1936: depression and default

Our analysis in this section consists of two rounds of debt rescheduling efforts: the first ran until 1933, and the second culminated in a deadlock between Peru and the lenders that lasted until 1936.

Identifying individual situations

Throughout this period, we classify Peru as coalitionally unstable, and issue and overall weak (IS 8). The lenders were unstable, issue weak, and overall medium in capabilities (IS 4/8). Although Peru's individual situation had changed slightly by the second round to IS 2/8 after some improvement in its financial condition (issue medium), given the relatively minor change which does not affect the game outcome, I consider the 1933–1936 period a second round rather than a separate period.

Peru. From 1930 to 1936, Peru experienced considerable domestic instability and several changes in leadership. Despite many domestic economic successes, funded in large part by foreign loans, President Leguía's popularity plummeted because of the onset of the 1929–1930 depression and because he signed an unpopular treaty (the Salomón-Lozano agreement) with Colombia. By mid-1930, disenchanted students and workers considered Leguía an enemy, and by August, he was overthrown in a military coup.

His successor, Luis M. Sánchez Cerro, was not as successful in his efforts to stabilize Peru as Leguia had been for 11 years. Within a short period, Sánchez Cerro found himself embroiled in both economic and political difficulties. A series of strikes, particularly in the mining sector, soon paralyzed the country. In November 1930, the Cerro de Pasco mining district suffered particularly serious labor disturbances.[19] Soon thereafter, the transportation workers staged a general strike. By February 1931, as the government failed to meet its domestic financial obligations, the army went into open rebellion. Charles Cunningham, the American commercial attaché in Lima, described Peru as "a football being kicked about by military leaders."[20] Open revolt plagued most of the south and the city of Piura in the north. Col. Sánchez Cerro appeared to have Lima and Callao under control but, as Cunningham put it, only by means of an iron hand: "a state of siege declared and soldiers with guns on all corners."[21] By March, facing serious opposition, Sánchez Cerro resigned and left for what would be only a temporary exile in France.

[19] SD 823.51/533 1/2, p. 2. [20] SD (State letter, weekly report no. 26, February 26, 1931).
[21] SD (State letter weekly report no. 26, February 26, 1931).

The new provisional President, David Samánez Ocampo, was not particularly popular. The election campaign before the October vote soon became a contest between Víctor Raúl Haya de la Torre of the APRA party (formed in 1924) and the recently returned Sánchez Cerro and his Revolutionary Union. The hotly contested election was won by Sánchez Cerro, but APRA did not readily accept electoral defeat. Following sharp protests and growing domestic conflict, the government began a campaign to subdue APRA. When it sought to arrest Haya de la Torre, however, an Aprista loyalist retaliated by shooting and wounding Sánchez Cerro. The conflict soon escalated and gave birth to a failed APRA-led coup attempt in July 1932. Although a new constitution banning the Communist Party and preventing APRA from contesting elections was promulgated in 1933, stability did not follow. In April 1933, Sánchez Cerro was assassinated by another Aprista, throwing the country into turmoil again.

Peru's next President, General Oscar Benavides, inherited a host of problems along with stewardship of the country. In addition to financial difficulties inherent to the depression, he was charged with resolving a border conflict with Colombia and reconciling political conflicts between various groups and APRA. He resolved the Colombian problem by agreeing to abide by the Salomón-Lozano treaty, but this action, combined with his conciliatory approach, provoked attacks from the Revolutionary Union and other right-wing groups. When Benavides refused to give in to all of APRA's demands for amnesty for political prisoners and to grant the installation of Apristas who had been ejected from Congress, he found himself caught between the right and the left. Benavides's choice of José de la Riva Aguero as his new Prime Minister created new domestic battles as Riva Aguero attempted to suppress APRA completely. APRA retaliated on November 26, 1934, by launching a new coup attempt, but this effort failed, and many Apristas were arrested. Although Benavides attempted once again to be conciliatory, an Aprista assassination of a major newspaper publisher in May 1935 created political problems. In the fall of 1936, Benavides backed Jorge Prado as his successor and leader of the multiparty National Front. APRA responded by convincing a Social Democratic leader, Luis Antonio Eguiguren, to run against Prado. The election in October 1936 apparently gave Eguiguren a plurality, but Benavides had the election invalidated and managed to get the national assembly to endorse his presidency for an additional three years.[22]

Turning to Peru's financial situation, after the 1929 stock market crash, the country's financial difficulties multiplied. The drastic decline in the value of Peru's leading exports cut the nation's purchasing power, limiting its ability to import, and shrinking government revenues from import taxes.[23] Between 1929 and 1932, the value of Peru's exports fell from 335 million soles to less than 180 million soles, decreasing the government's income by 45%.[24] U.S. Commercial

[22] For a discussion, see Werlich (1978), pp. 209–210. [23] SD 823.51/619, p. 1.
[24] Werlich (1978), p. 211.

Attaché Charles Cunningham reported that, "one day last week [February 1931] Callao customs collections dropped to 850 soles. The average collections under Leguía were about 70,000 soles."[25]

The government fought to keep monetary difficulties under control. Analysts evaluated the cost of maintaining the exchange rate of the Peruvian pound at $4.00 at $7 million during 1929.[26] Despite the Peruvian government's new tax measures, especially a tax on government employees' salaries, and its increased scrutiny of expenditures through the newly created Office of Controller General, its budget problems increased. But intervention by the Sánchez Cerro Administration prevented the collapse of some industries, improved the institutional framework of the republic's financial system, and initiated a trend toward economic nationalism. The government slashed its budget to stay within the meager limits of the state's revenue.

The situation improved somewhat between 1933 and 1936 as mineral prices rose, and the positive effect of a stabilized sol increased the value of foreign commerce between 1933 and 1936. As a result, government revenue from foreign commerce taxes rose from 24 to 54 million soles during the same period.[27] While government revenue increased, the balance of trade surplus with the U.S. remained very low. During this period, it continued to average only $611,000, compared with $6,896,000 from 1926 to 1930. Foreign trade stagnated.

As for overall capabilities, Peru was weak. In the sphere of foreign relations, for example, it could not afford to antagonize Colombia; Benavides's decision to abide by the Salomón–Lozano agreement demonstrated Peru's overall weakness. Peru's economy also remained highly dependent on the world economy, and it could not afford to have its raw materials closed off from world markets – particularly the lucrative American market. Foreigners also held large foreign assets in Peru – some $400 million worth of investment by the end of Leguia's term.[28] Although under some circumstances Peru was able to use foreign investment to its own advantage, the fact that Peru's overall economy was highly dependent on foreign markets weakened its overall position.

Lenders. The bondholders had not been organized before the 1931–1932 defaults, but following it, they formed four committees, leading to an unstable coalition. In addition to creating committees for each of the three dollar loans, they formed a fourth independent committee that proceeded to take legal actions against Peru, disrupting unity among the four groups. In 1934, the bondholders created a new committee of a more general nature, but the other committees continued their operations. The Foreign Bondholders Protective Council (FBPC) also began negotiations of its own with Peru.[29]

[25] SD weekly report no. 26, February 26, 1931. [26] SD 823.51/469, p. 12.

[27] Pike (1967), p. 272 (at that time 1 sol equaled $0.23–$0.25 U.S.).

[28] Werlich (1978), p. 157. See Carey (1964), Chapter 4, for a discussion of U.S. investment in Peru in the 1920s.

[29] SD archive document dealing with information sent by the Foreign Bondholders Protective Council on November 16, 1943 to Mr. Lee Orton in Rio de Janeiro, p. 1a.

Financially, the lenders were weak due to the wide distribution of the holders of various bonds. Although the banks had floated the various loans, individuals had actually purchased the majority of Peruvian bonds. These bonds were widely distributed and individual holdings averaged less than $3,000.[30]

In overall capabilities, we code the lenders as overall medium. The lenders had the power to create problems for Peru if it tried to secure additional funds internationally. At the same time, however, the bondholders as a group had made large loans to Peru and thus were vulnerable to default. By the end of the 1920s, Peru's foreign debt amounted to some $116 million.[31] Moreover, the wide dispersal of their holders also made it more difficult for them to act as a group against Peru.

Creditor governments. Throughout the time period considered here, the U.S. had few strategic interests in Peru. This view changed toward the late 1930s as the U.S. became more concerned about possible German and Japanese influence. But in the early 1930s, U.S. policy was mainly concerned with its economic interests in Peru, based on the relatively large investments made by American firms who held the bulk of the large foreign investment made during Leguia's regime.

We would expect the U.S. to be relatively disinterested in sharply pressuring Peru, given its competing interests in supporting bondholders and also in preventing the climate for American investment from becoming hostile.

Debt game and predicted outcome

We arrive at the debt game shown in Figure 10.1 for this period. In the two-actor game, we expect the debtor to play its dominant strategy of LA... and the lender to play LC... (the Nash equilibrium). Although we might expect some minor efforts by the U.S. to push the Peruvians and bondholders to a situation of MA..., MC..., I do not expect this to be sustainable. In sum, in spite of the U.S.'s competing interests that might prompt it to help both actors, because of the absence of a strategic imperative, we would not expect any change between the two-actor bargaining outcome and the outcome with intervention.

The negotiations and outcome

Prelude to default and round one, 1930–1933. President Sánchez Cerro was much less receptive to American interests than Leguía had been, and immediately demonstrated his unwillingness to meet the financial obligations contracted by the former administration. At the same time, the bankers were in no mood for compromise, cabling this message to their agent in Peru: "before present Government can expect foreign financial assistance it must demonstrate intention to use every effort to meet country's external financial obligations of which

[30] SD 823.51/11–2945, pp. 1–3. [31] SD 823.51/521, p. 1.

Cardinal Payoff Matrix, No Intervention Expected

Lenders IS 4/8

		HC...	MC...	LC...
	HA...	0, −1.5	−3.5, 2.83	−4, 7.17
Peru IS 8	MA...	4, −5	0, −1	−2, 3
	LA...	8, −6.5	3.5, −3.5	**0, −.5**

Note: Nash equilibrium bolded.

Ordinal Payoff Matrix, No Intervention Expected

Lenders IS 4/8

		HC...	MC...	LC...
	HA...	5, 4	2, 7	1, 9
Peru IS 8	MA...	8, 2	5, 5	3, 8
	LA...	9, 1	7, 3	**5, 6**

Note: Nash equilibrium bolded.

Figure 10.1. *Play phase, period one: 1930–1936*

most immediate is October 1st loan service."[32] At the beginning of October 1930, Sánchez made the first hostile move: he canceled a contract between Peru and the Foundation Company and ordered the accounts liquidated.[33] The new government was unwilling to spend as much as 31% of its total revenues for debt service,[34] especially on the foreign debt, arguing that such an amount was disproportionately large in a depression era both at home and abroad.

[32] SD 823.51/503, p. 1. [33] Carey (1964), p. 62.

[34] SD 823.51/516, pp. 3–4. This document provides a good financial picture of the Peruvian government for 1930.

The fiscal agents were less than conciliatory. They were reluctant to follow through with the renewal of a $1.5 million credit to Peru's Reserve Bank issued in May. U.S. Ambassador Fred Dearing wrote the State Department his view of the factors accounting for bankers' reluctance to make concessions: fear of what the future held politically, suspicion regarding the Peruvian government's motives and expenditures, lack of confidence in the competence of financial officials, and fear of graft in Peru.[35] But the ambassador also noted that he thought the bankers were being "less conciliatory and helpful than they should be . . ."[36]

The bankers refused to make any major advances to Peru. Their only charitable move was to offer a monthly advance of $115,000 for the continuation of the Callao Portworks. In response, the Peruvian government assumed a tough attitude by declaring its unwillingness to commit to paying arrears due for the Callao Portworks. Evidently, the situation was ripe for confrontation.

On October 11, the Cerro Administration published a decree permitting the Banco del Peru y Londres to suspend payment for six days, to buy time for concocting a rescue plan for the bank. The difficulties of the Banco del Peru y Londres dealt a serious blow to Peru's financial stability. This institution was responsible for virtually all the banking business in the country with the exception of transactions made in foreign institutions. For this reason, failure to save the bank would have been disastrous: It could have caused the closing of all types of businesses and increased unemployment. Local and foreign bank representatives agreed on a rescue loan to enable the government to pay off small savings accounts of the Banco del Peru y Londres. The bankers also agreed on a 30-day debt servicing moratorium.[37] Unfortunately, this plan only took care of small savings account holders. The plan's failure to address the personal and business accounts left an urgent need to reorganize the nation's entire financial system.

The American government began to play a more active mediating role in the conflict between the bankers and Peru. The U.S. supported Lionel Stahl's suggestion (Stahl represented the fiscal agents in Lima) that Peru's financial situation be investigated by Edwin W. Kemmerer, a well-known economics professor who had led financial commissions in other countries. But the U.S. was wary of being perceived by the bankers as too openly involved in Peru's affairs. As Secretary Stimson of the State Department warned Ambassador Dearing in a telegram:

> While the Department would welcome Kemmerer's going to Peru as probably the best means of stabilizing the Peruvian financial position, it does not feel that it can make this recommendation. If the Peruvian government does not suggest Kemmerer's coming of its own volition, the suggestion, if it comes from an outside source, should come from the bankers rather than from the Department.[38]

Both Ambassador Dearing and Lionel Stahl felt strongly that Kemmerer's proposals represented Peru's only chance to break off its present course down the

[35] SD 823.51/516, pp. 6–8. [36] SD 823.51/516, p. 5. [37] SD 823.51/514, p. 3.
[38] SD 823.51/516, Stimson telegram, p. 4.

road to default. The Ambassador told the Peruvians that the bankers would accept Kemmerer's recommendation – whether he supported a moratorium or felt that Peru should avoid default on its public debt service obligations.[39] In November 1930, the Peruvian government cabled Kemmerer, asking for his advice on complete financial reform and reorganization of the Reserve Bank.[40] Kemmerer accepted the offer to advise Peru.

At this point, with Kemmerer's mission due to arrive in a month or so, the Peruvian government still hoped to secure assistance from the U.S. by demonstrating its cooperation. The government secured local money for the December 1 installment of the national loan and wrote a balanced budget for 1931 by sharply cutting public expenditures.[41] But even before Kemmerer arrived, Cerro's government began to experience strong domestic unrest. As conflict and financial difficulties grew in Peru, its interest in cooperating with the international community quickly diminished. Kemmerer arrived in January 1931, but as early as February, he was "disgusted," expressing his certainty that the Peruvian government was "determined to secure postponement of service on foreign debt."[42] Peru's financial situation continued to worsen, and deteriorated from mid-February figures, with Callao customs collections dropping to almost zero on some days. It seemed impossible for the government to meet the March 1 service deadline on the tobacco loan (roughly $600,000), and Sánchez Cerro threatened but did not declare a moratorium even before Kemmerer had completed his mission.[43]

The Kemmerer mission released its first report at the end of February. In addition to various recommendations for economic adjustment, the report called for the government to continue making payments on its foreign debt to avoid having problems borrowing on international markets. But at the same time, Kemmerer's report noted that if the government decided not to continue all of its servicing, it should suspend amortization before interest and make at least a partial payment on its debt service. Commenting on the contents of Kemmerer's study, in a confidential report to the State Department, American Commercial Attaché in Lima Charles Cunningham criticized the Mission's report:

> [This advice] does not seem to adequately meet the situation and would appear to be impractical of realization for the most part. The best recommendation in the lot is the feeling as set forth by the Mission that Peru should not pass its public debt service.[44]

Immediately after the report was issued, Peruvian Minister of Finance Manuel Vinelli told the bankers that Peru would not pledge customs revenues, that it planned to institute a five-year moratorium, and that it would only make payments if a budget surplus permitted.[45] Thus, the Peruvians used Kemmerer's report as a cover for a policy that they were already well on the path to following – even though the report recommended avoiding a moratorium at this point. But

[39] SD 823.51/530, pp. 4–6. [40] SD 823.51/531.
[41] See SD 823.51/541 and 823.51/538 for details. [42] SD 823.51/570, p. 1.
[43] SD 823.51/591, p. 2. [44] SD 823.51/619, p. 4. [45] SD 823.51/602, p. 2.

by encouraging the mission in hopes of improving their positions, the bankers were now trapped into negotiations over a moratorium because of Peru's interpretation of the mission's preliminary conclusions.

Peru continued to press its position in the negotiations. On March 20, 1931, following Cerro's resignation, the new Peruvian government pressured the Caja to break an agreement to service the national loan. The government "ordered the Caja to pay to the treasury the amount required for the service of the national loan instead of turning it over to the fiscal agents."[46] The fiscal agents naturally attempted to stop the bank from redirecting funds in an effort to keep Peru from suspending service on its foreign debt. Lacking significant power resources, the bankers searched in vain for allies. The American government's sympathy for Peru's plight is clear from a private conversation between an official of the Grace Company and the Assistant Secretary of State:

> The members of the Peruvian Government are actuated by political motives and will naturally first look out for their internal situation and where the votes and support that will keep them in office come from just as politicians in this country do not take into consideration foreign relations or how they hurt foreign interests by the tariff, but act according to the votes in this country. We cannot expect the Peruvians to be less selfish than our politicians.[47]

To maintain good relations with the U.S., Finance Minister Vinelli announced the government's willingness to follow the final recommendations of the Kemmerer mission regarding stringent budget economies.[48] On May 29, however, the government issued a decree suspending payment on the interest until December 31, and diverting funds due on the national loan for the "purpose of paying off all arrears of salaries and pay of all Government employees and forces."[49]

Peru's strategy of seeking goodwill and discouraging intervention by the U.S. paid off. Ambassador Dearing clearly illustrated the lenient American attitude:

> [T]his temporary but complete default on all obligations of the Government has necessarily dealt another serious blow to Peruvian credit, and yet I believe consideration will show the Department that the issuance of the Decree is a step in the right direction.[50]

Peru's unilateral action increased Peru's advantage over the lenders, but such a situation could not last in the long run. The country desperately needed funds; commandeering money earmarked for debt service would not by itself stabilize Peru's financial situation. The budget for the second half of 1931 showed a deficit, even without the cost of foreign debt service.[51] Facing continued financial problems, Peru searched for new sources of money. It attempted to get a loan from French creditors by selling the Callao Portworks for a period of 100 years.[52] But these efforts ultimately failed, proving that Peru could rely only on the creditor governments' sympathy – not their money.

[46] Wynne (1951), p. 188. [47] SD 823.51/654, p. 3. [48] SD 823.51/695.
[49] SD 823.51/677. [50] SD 823.51/689, p. 2. [51] SD 823.51/713.
[52] For details see SD 823.51/762, p. 2.

In January 1932, the Peruvian government passed a law indefinitely extending the moratorium on the entire external debt service. It justified the extension in part by pointing to the findings in the 1931–1932 U.S. Senate hearing about the corruption involved in lending to Peru. At the time, the defaulted Peruvian foreign debt stood at $114 million originating from three dollar issues: the tobacco loan of 1927, the sterling guano issue of 1922, and the National Loans of 1927 and 1928. In response, the bondholders formed the previously mentioned committees, but failed for some time to create one stable overarching committee. The Foreign Bondholders Protective Council, a committee developed and promoted by the U.S. government, came into being in October 1933 and would eventually be the key focus of the negotiations. In the interim, however, conflict among the bondholders prevented a unified position, and negotiations between Peru and its lenders stalled.

In April 1932, Ambassador Dearing cabled the State Department the following message:

> [T]here is not the faintest chance of getting any money out of this government at the present time and but very little of getting any better commitments than is constituted by the contracts now in existence.[53]

The negotiation process reached a turning point with Peru's complete and indefinite default at LA..., LC... From then on, bargaining focused on the conditions necessary for Peru to resume payments instead of the conditions for it to continue them. No progress was made in 1933 toward resolving the default.

Round two, 1934–1936. These years saw a continuation of Peruvian intransigence and American frustration. Peru responded to all entreaties for debt service by claiming that it could not spare the money, despite the fact that its financial situation was improving somewhat. During the very heart of the Great Depression, it is hardly surprising that lack of funds was Peru's standard defense. Furthermore, the new President considered his most pressing problem to be maintaining domestic stability, rather than his country's international creditworthiness.

This round of negotiations featured repeated attempts on the part of the Peruvian government to link American market access to its renewal of loan payments. Throughout the 1930s, one of the thorniest issues between Peru and the U.S. was not only the default on the dollar loans, but also what the U.S. considered Peruvian discrimination against U.S. bondholders, after Peru resumed payments on only the British Sterling Guano Loan. The U.S. commercial attaché speculated in August 1934 that Peru's Finance Minister, Benjamín Roca, "is an Agrarian and he may have been influenced in this matter by the attitude of British bankers, who may have increased pressure through threats to obstruct guano, sugar or cotton sales in the British market, which is of such transcendental importance for Peruvian products . . ."[54]

[53] SD 823.51/820, p. 2. [54] SD 823.51/1048, p. 2.

The Peruvians hinted that the U.S. could obtain similar results by increasing imports of Peruvian products. In March 1934, Ambassador Dearing issued a report:

> The Government here is somewhat bewitched by the easy arithmetic of a great increase in Government revenues resulting from an increase in oil production . . . what I feel certain is in the back of the minds of the President and of the Minister of Finance – that if the bait of some possible payment to American holders of Peruvian external bonds is held out, our Government will find a way to assist the bondholders and to assist Peruvian credit and recovery by conveying a hint to the Standard Oil interests which will cause them to curtail production elsewhere and increase production in Peru to the desired figure.[55]

The following day, Roca asked the U.S. ambassador to let the Bondholders' Council know the conditions for Peru's repayment of its external loans. He replied: "First; the International Petroleum Company must export annually thirty million barrels. Second; reduction and revision of loans. Third; the United States must give Peru a quota in the petroleum market."[56]

In the same vein, in early 1934, Roca asked Secretary of State Hull for a U.S. import quota in Peruvian cotton, sugar, and wine.[57] Just over a year later, the finance minister noted with displeasure that Cuba was dumping sugar in England and Cuba, two of Peru's principal markets, but Ambassador Dearing argued that "to increase the Peruvian quota [in the U.S. market] would establish a precedent which it would be impossible to live up to and in conflict with [American] policy."[58]

In November 1935, the finance minister noted that when the original loans in question were negotiated, there were no U.S. tariffs against Peruvian exports nor was there preferential treatment for Cuban sugar. "The Minister said that he thought the [Foreign Bondholders Protective] Council could use its influence in order to have 200,000 tons of Peruvian sugar admitted annually to the United States under the same conditions as Cuba."[59]

The Peruvian government clearly viewed the U.S. government as a tool to pressure American producers to increase access for Peruvian exports, whose revenues would serve as the basis for repayment to bondholders. In the same manner, it saw its foreign creditors as a means by which to pry open the U.S. market for Peruvian goods. The American government, for its part, rejected this substantive linkage, having no intention of intervening in this way on Peru's behalf. The bondholders continued to fight against Peru's default with little more than State Department rhetoric to strengthen their position. Thus, the Peruvian debt issue remained hopelessly stalemated.

Summary. As predicted by the model, Peru and its lenders failed to come to terms during this period. Selectively drawing on the Kemmerer report that dealt with Peruvian finances, the government instituted a moratorium on

[55] SD 823.51/1018, pp. 3–4. [56] SD 823.51/1016. [57] SD 823.51/1014.
[58] SD 823.51/1075. [59] SD 823.51/1126.

debt payments. Although the U.S. government made some efforts to encourage payments, by and large, it clearly recognized Peru's financial problems and was not eager to unduly pressure Peru. On the other hand, the U.S. did not respond favorably to Peru's efforts to link debt servicing with increased exports and access to the U.S. market. In the end, then, with both the bondholders and Peru intransigent, the negotiations remained deadlocked at LA..., LC....

Situational changes

Both Peru and the banks used the full panoply of power resources available to them in an effort to alter their bargaining situation. For example, Peru appealed to norms and rules in implementing its moratorium by referring to the U.S. Senate hearing held by the Finance Committee on lending to Latin America. In 1933, the Peruvian government wrote to Ambassador Dearing, questioning the discrepancy between testimony by an official for J. & W. Seligman & Co., in which he reported that the bank had made a profit of about $600,000, and financial records that the Peruvian government interpreted as stating that the bank had in fact made over $5 million. The Peruvians then suggested that the bank submit to an investigation under U.S. income tax law.[60] In addition, the Peruvians attempted to draw a distinction between obligations incurred by a "state" and those incurred by a "regime," arguing that their constitutional government should not be responsible for loans undertaken by the earlier dictatorship.[61] These efforts did not, however, help Peru change its fundamental position, but they did elicit a small degree of sympathy from the U.S. government.

In addition to norms and rules, Peru also turned to capabilities and allies. Most directly, it attempted to improve its financial position with some quiet purchases of its bonds on the open market, but this does not appear to have been a very significant success.[62] More aggressively, as we saw in the second round of negotiations, Peru attempted to alter the contours of the issue-area by linking exports to debt servicing. Although this effort appears to have paid off in the case of Peruvian negotiations with British bondholders and their government, the U.S. resisted this linkage. Instead, the U.S. appears to have seen this attempt purely in tactical terms, rather than as a serious substantive connection.

For their part, the bondholders' and bankers' efforts to enlist the U.S. State Department on their side failed to bear much fruit, as we have seen, leaving their bargaining position relatively unchanged.

The one active change by bondholders was somewhat greater stability as the bondholders joined together in the General Advisory Committee of Peruvian Bondholders. More significant were the efforts by the new Peruvian leader to stabilize his domestic situation. Specifically, Peru's financial and overall situation improved greatly before the Second World War as demands for its exports increased.

[60] SD 823.51/968. [61] SD 823.51/781. [62] SD 823.51/1334.

Period two, 1936–1939: the stalemate continues

Negotiations continued between Peru and the bondholders during this period, but despite Peru's improving financial situation, little came of the talks. The Peruvians agreed to begin debt service on a small British loan, but the deadlock continued on the vast bulk of the American-held debt.

Identifying individual situations

In this period, we classify Peru as coalitionally medium in stability, and issue strong and overall medium in capabilities (IS 1/6). We classify the bondholders as coalitionally medium, issue weak, and overall medium (IS 3/8).

Peru. Benavides's second term from 1936 to 1939 was a more stable time for Peru.[63] Still, after short-circuiting the electoral process by declaring Eguiguren's victory in the 1936 election invalid, Benavides found himself opposed by both the right and the left. But through repressive measures, and by exiling Aprista leaders, Benavides managed to undercut both APRA and Flores's Revolutionary Union. Despite partially stabilizing the political situation through these actions, Benavides still faced opposition. In 1939, a joint plot by APRA and the Revolutionary Union headed by his minister of government, General Antonio Rodríguez, nearly led to Benavides's ouster. Enlisting help from his security contingent (who assassinated Rodríguez), Benavides managed to hold onto power. Because of the uneven stability of the era, we code Benavides's years as one of medium coalitional stability.

Benavides's rule coincided with a significant economic recovery from the years of the Great Depression. By 1936, Peru's exports equaled pre-depression levels; by 1939, they exceeded 1929 exports by 35%.[64] In this period, Peru's trade with the U.S. initially remained in balance (compared to a large surplus in the 1926–1930 period), but by 1939, Peru again showed a large surplus of about $7.5 million. By 1936 Peru's budget equaled its 1930 budget,[65] and remained relatively balanced with a sharp rise in both expenditures and income over the previous three years.[66]

In overall terms, the administration undertook ambitious projects such as the expansion of Peru's irrigation systems, the building of modern water systems, and the construction of modern highways to unite Peru's different regions. Benavides also began a major program to improve the efficacy of the nation's military establishment. Although still highly reliant on export markets and under continued pressure to resolve its external debt, Peru now relied more on domestic resources for its development.

Lenders. The lenders remained somewhat divided during this period. Although the groups joined together in the General Advisory Committee of Peruvian Bondholders during this time, independent committees continued to

[63] This section draws mainly on Werlich (1978) and Pike (1967). [64] Werlich (1978), p. 213.
[65] SD 823.51/1102. [66] SD 823.51/1451, tables 1 and 2.

exist. The Foreign Bondholders Protective Council also began to take a more active and central role.

As for issue capabilities, the bondholders did not hold the financial assets to survive a Peruvian default. As a nonprofit organization, the Council possessed no financial resources beyond its operating expenses. Until December 1945, the Council depended entirely on its members' voluntary contributions of $1.25 per $1,000 bond in connection with permanent settlements. (After this date, the Council required contributions of $1.25 per $1,000 bond in permanent settlements, and mandatory contributions of $0.50 per $1,000 bond in temporary settlements.)[67]

As for overall capabilities, the bondholders continued to be medium strong. The bondholders benefited from the indirect support of the American government for the Foreign Protective Council. At the same time, the relatively large debt and the dim prospects for repayment put the bondholders in a somewhat vulnerable position.

Creditor governments. As Europe teetered on the verge of conflict in the late 1930s, the U.S. was interested in securing its Latin American flank. But in the absence of direct involvement in conflict, the U.S. was not overly conciliatory toward Peru. At the same time, although inclined to support the bondholders, the U.S. government was concerned about its overall economic interests and stability in Peru, and not simply with the question of financial interests.

Debt game and predicted outcome

Based on Peru's classification as 1/6 and the lenders' as 3/8, we predict the game and outcome shown in Figure 10.2. In this period's debt game, the two-actor outcome is once again a deadlock. However, in this case, the lenders' payoff for LA..., LC... is relatively worse than in period 1, whereas Peru's is considerably better. As we can see from the bondholders' payoffs, they would be willing to make concessions, but only in the unlikely event that Peru made some adjustments. With intervention, we might expect some pressure toward a compromise of MA..., MC..., although given the many competing interests the U.S. had at stake, it is unlikely that the U.S. would be willing to intervene forcefully enough to break the deadlock.

The negotiations and actual outcome

As Peru's financial situation improved after 1936, J. Rafael Oreamuno, representative of the General Advisory Committee, began to press for more serious negotiations to resolve the outstanding debt problem. In response, Peru merely continued its strategy of preventing direct involvement by the U.S. The Peruvian government allocated a small amount, 4 million soles, for partial service on the national and tobacco loans in its 1936 budget. Of the 4 million, one-half was to go toward interest payments, while the other half was for amortization or the

[67] SD 823.51/12–2645, pp. 1–4.

Cardinal Payoff Matrix,
No Intervention Expected

		Lenders IS 3/8		
		HC...	MC...	LC...
	HA...	−7.5, 4.5	−7.25, 6.83	−4.5, 9.17
Peru IS 1/6	MA...	−4.83, 1	−5, 3	−3.5, 5
	LA...	−2.17, −.5	−2.75, .5	**−2.5, 1.5**

Note: Nash equilibrium bolded.

Ordinal Payoff Matrix,
No Intervention Expected

		Lenders IS 3/8		
		HC...	MC...	LC...
	HA...	1, 6	2, 8	5, 9
Peru IS 1/6	MA...	4, 3	3, 5	6, 7
	LA...	9, 1	7, 2	**8, 4**

Note: Nash equilibrium bolded.

Figure 10.2. *Play phase, period two: 1936–1939*

purchase of bonds in the market. Although the Advisory Committee was not unduly upset by this arrangement, the Foreign Protective Council considered the amount grossly insufficient. It worried that Peru would simply repurchase bonds at low prices on the open market. The Council requested that Peru devote the 4 million soles to interest payments alone, but Peru rejected this demand, and continued to divide the allocated 4 million soles in two parts in its budget until 1940.[68] Because the bondholders refused to accept this division, Peru made only a minimal payment on its bonds from these budgeted allocations.

[68] SD 823.51/1334, report, p. 5.

Negotiations continued throughout 1937, with little progress. After some effort in March of that year, Oreamuno managed to secure a promise that Peru would continue to allocate another 4 million soles in its budget for 1937. As promised, but with considerable delay, Peru finally transferred $500,000 (2 million soles) to New York for debt service. It purchased the 1931 coupons of the National Loan for an interest yield of only 1/2 of 1%. Beyond this token amount, Peru failed to advance any new proposals to resume debt servicing until 1938. In that year, influenced by Finance Minister Roca, in May the Peruvian government proposed a definitive readjustment based on a maximum $2,500,000 annual service. The proposal also called for the following:

> a reduction of the principal face amount of the total indebtedness by roughly fifty percent; interest to be resumed at the rate of 3% per annum on the reduced face amount; the balance of the two and one-half million dollars to be applied to the amortization of the reduced debt over a period of twenty-five years by calling bonds by lot at par.[69]

The proposal was deemed unsatisfactory by the Bondholders' Council, which argued that Peru could do better in view of its improved financial situation. The American government tried to avoid a definitive refusal from the bondholders for fear of alienating the Peruvians. As Ambassador Steinhardt characterized the situation:

> The most recent proposal made by Roca is substantially the best that can be obtained and . . . if it is not accepted, the members of the Committee or Council who may cause its rejection must be prepared for a return to the status of total default with virtually no prospect of any payments to the bondholders for many years to come, and a grave doubt that any terms arrived at years hence will be of any greater advantage to the bondholders.[70]

Ongoing negotiations with the bondholders failed to produce an accord. Following a counterproposal from the Advisory Committee, in October, Minister Roca made a new offer. According to his plan, interest payments for the first five years would be at 1.5% on the national loan, 2% on the tobacco loan, and 3% on both thereafter.[71] The Protective Council considered these proposed payments also too low, and refused Roca's last offer. Herbert Feis of the State Department was not pleased by the Council's action, and he suggested at one point to Council President Francis White that it might be better if they withdrew from participating in the negotiations between the bondholders and Peru.[72] The Council refused to drop out. As the U.S. Ambassador to Peru had earlier predicted, Roca, in ill health, resigned immediately following this refusal on December 3, 1938.

Negotiations resumed in January with conversations between the new finance minister, Manuel Ugarteche, and the Advisory Committee representative Oreamuno. Ugarteche appeared less eager than Roca to conclude an agreement, concerned as he was that the government would criticize him for agreeing to

[69] SD 823.51/1210. [70] SD 823.51/1210.
[71] SD 823.51/1234, Telegram in *Foreign Relations of the United States* (1938), vol. 5, p. 886.
[72] SD 823.51/1231, p. 2.

service Peru's debt prior to the October 1939 elections.[73] The U.S. government continued to press for a solution to the debt problem, this time by pressuring Peru. The State Department refused to grant Peru $600,000 worth of credits to order hospital supplies, and the American Ambassador concurred in this decision. This U.S. pressure, however, failed to have an immediate effect. By late April, Oreamuno reported that his negotiations with Ugarteche had broken down, and the embassy criticized the bondholders' groups for not being more forthcoming in October 1938 when an agreement appeared possible. By September 1939, as the war progressed in Europe and Peru continued to lose important markets, Peru's economy began to rapidly deteriorate.

The situation was very different with respect to the 1922 £1,250,000 guano loan. Through Henry Schroder Co. and the Baring Bros. Co. of London, the Peruvian government made an offer for a permanent settlement in November 1938. The plan called for a reduction of £239,000 in principal, a reduction of the interest rate from 7.5% to 4%, and an increase in the sinking fund from 1.5% to 2%.[74] In addition, all arrears of interest up to that date were to be canceled. After failing to obtain a higher interest rate, most of the bondholders of this British loan accepted the offer as the best possible settlement under the circumstances. The Foreign Bondholders Protective Council immediately alerted the U.S. State Department to Peru's policy of discrimination against the dollar bondholders, who were paid nothing while the holders of the British-held sterling guano bonds were offered a permanent settlement. Peru justified its discrimination claiming that the guano loan had a strong security based on guano and that the amount of the outstanding bonds was much lower than for the National and tobacco loans. It contended that the settlement did not discriminate in favor of British bondholders because both British and American holders of the National Loan were receiving the same treatment.

Summary. During this period, Peru and the bondholders appeared to move toward a settlement. Still, despite some willingness on Peru's part to service its debt, and considerable eagerness on the part of some bondholders to agree to a settlement, differences between the two parties could not be resolved. The U.S. played a relatively even-handed role in this period, reminding Peru of the need for a settlement while at the same time cajoling the bondholders' groups to make some accommodation. In the absence of very strong pressures by the U.S., due to its relatively moderate interest in a settlement at this time, the game fell back into the deadlock that had characterized Peruvian rescheduling for nearly a decade.

Situational changes

As a result of the deadlock in this period, the bondholders received a relatively poor payoff compared to Peru. We would therefore logically expect the bondholders to be more eager to promote situational changes.

[73] SD 823.51/1266. [74] SD 823.51/1334, report, p. 6.

The bondholders managed to stabilize their coalition as the FBPC took the leading role in debt negotiations. Disgruntled bondholders had given up on their individual committees following the failure of Oreamuno's efforts. In other respects, however, the bondholders failed to improve their individual situation.

The changes that led to Peru's new individual situation are largely external to our analysis. In 1939, Benavides finally succeeded where he had failed three years earlier: he secured the election of his chosen successor, Manuel Prado, giving Peru a succession with a degree of stability it had not enjoyed since the *Oncenio*. At the same time, however, Peru's loss of markets and deteriorating financial situation made it more willing to accommodate the interests of the bondholders.

Periods three and four, 1939–1943 and 1944–1945: wartime negotiations

Following on the heels of the failed negotiations of the late 1930s, prospects for a debt settlement appeared slim. But with the onset of the Second World War, and as the U.S. interest in the debt negotiations grew as a result of its overall strategic wartime concerns, the odds for an accord improved. But in this instance, unlike in the case of many other Latin American countries who resolved their debt problems during this time period, Peru failed to come to terms with its lenders. During the time span covered in this section, Peru's financial and overall position changed as the war progressed. Because of this shift, I divide the bargaining into two distinct periods; however, because the factors that came to bear on the wartime period as a whole remain similar, I consider both periods together in this section.

Identifying individual situations

During the third period from 1939 to 1943, Peru was coalitionally stable, issue weak, and overall medium (IS 3/7). From 1944 to 1945, however, Peru's financial situation improved and its overall strength also increased: it was stable, issue medium, and overall strong (IS 3/5). Throughout the two periods, the lenders were in IS 3/7 with a stable coalition, but remained weak in issue capabilities and overall medium.

Peru. Manuel Prado's election in 1939 ushered in a period of considerable political stability,[75] with Peru remaining "calm, tranquil, and orderly."[76] Moreover, Prado managed to complete his term and was replaced with a relatively peaceful election. The stable period can be attributed to the relatively conciliatory position Prado took toward his opponents, the moderate stance

[75] This discussion of Peruvian domestic politics draws heavily on Pike (1967), pp. 276–281 and Werlich (1978), pp. 221–230.

[76] Pike (1967), p. 276.

assumed by APRA, and the collapse of the far right. Concerned about fascism and encouraged by Roosevelt's "Good Neighbor" policy, APRA found it more palatable to support the Prado regime. More practically, under the Benavides period, Peru had begun to enjoy an economic recovery, and a radical strategy would have politically isolated APRA. Although APRA was formally banned, it was able to hold political conventions and its leaders were not unduly harassed by the government. It even allowed the APRA paper, *La Tribuna*, to be published.

Toward the end of Prado's term, as former President Oscar Benavides returned from an ambassadorship in Argentina, many elites worried that either of the two politicians might try to strong-arm a continuing leadership role. But the development of the Frente Democrática National (FDN) or National Democratic Front helped to defuse a potentially tense situation. Promoted by a group of Peruvians interested in broadening the political circle of power, this party promoted the candidacy of professor and former attorney José Luis Bustamante. Both Benavides and Prado decided to cooperate with the FDN's strategy, and Prado granted Bustamante's demand to legalize the APRA. In June 1945, supported by the Partido del Pueblo (the newly renamed APRA party), Bustamante secured a solid victory, swelling hopes that Peru had entered a new period of political stability. As we shall see in the next section, these expectations would prove to be overly optimistic.

During the third period, from 1939 to 1943, Peru was financially weak. Most other countries benefited from a sharply rising wartime demand for their products, but Peru did not enjoy such benefits until the closing years of the war. It ran a considerable budget deficit until 1944, totaling 93 million soles.[77] With respect to foreign exchange holdings, by the end of 1941 Peru had less than $5 million in reserves. In an examination of Peru's financial situation, the Department of State's Financial Division concluded that although the government could conceivably service part of its debt, its financial situation was considerably worse than what the Foreign Bondholders Protective Council had claimed.[78] In particular, the study noted that statistics on Peru's improving export trade were misleading because these figures included large exports by American firms. Thus the foreign exchange that appeared available was not, in fact, controlled by the Peruvian government. At the same time, Peru had been exporting a large amount of gold but did not appear to be likely to sustain this over a longer run. Finally, the study stated that in dollar terms rather than in soles, the 1942 budget was quite small, amounting to about the same as the budget in 1930.

By early 1944, the beginning of the fourth period, Peru's financial situation had improved considerably with a foreign exchange surplus estimated at $15 to $20 million.[79] In addition, in November 1944, a new 2% tax on most imports increased government revenues by 10 to 12 million soles.[80] At the same time, however, the trade surplus had begun to decline and was estimated at only about

[77] SD 823.51/8–2045, p. 5. [78] SD 823.51/1451. [79] SD 823.51/1544, p. 2.
[80] SD 823.51/11–2844, p. 1.

$14 million by November. Because of these changes, during this fourth period we code Peru as issue medium in capabilities.

During the third period, Peru was medium in overall capabilities. It had successfully defeated Ecuador in battle over a border issue in 1941. By 1942, following talks related to American efforts to persuade Latin American countries to break diplomatic relations with the Axis powers, Peru settled with Ecuador on terms favorable to Peru. Still, Peru encountered important economic difficulties as a result of the war, and relied on the United States for Lend-Lease aid as well as loans for foreign exchange stabilization.

By the end of the war, in 1944–1945, Peruvian exports boomed. Domestically, the development of many industries progressed steadily, and Peru had attained complete or near self-sufficiency for key products such as cement, coal, hulled rice, canned milk, and glassware, thus reducing its dependence on imports and promoting its overall capabilities.[81]

Lenders. With the exception of the improvement in the bondholders' coalitional stability, their position remained the same in terms of capabilities. As mentioned earlier, while potentially competitive bondholders' committees closed their operations, the Foreign Bondholders Protective Council became the single unified actor with whom Peru negotiated. The lenders' position remained the same throughout both the third and fourth periods.

Creditor governments. The United States became highly interested in Peruvian debt negotiations with the onset of the Second World War. It was very concerned about maintaining Peru's allegiance during the war for strategic reasons. Moreover, the U.S. laid claim to key Peruvian exports; by 1940, the U.S. was the principal buyer of its exports.[82] Peru supplied the U.S. with raw materials crucial to a wartime economy – metals, rubber, and flax. At the same time, the government continued to face pressure from the lenders to help them negotiate a satisfactory settlement with Peru. But on balance, it appears that for the U.S. overall strategic and political-economic concerns outweighed pressure from the bondholders' group.

Debt games and predicted outcomes

From the codings for the third period, we arrive at the cardinal game matrix and ordinal conversion shown in Figure 10.3. In this game, we encounter a classic Chicken situation. Both players want to avoid the disastrous outcome of LA..., LC... with the worst possible payoffs. At the same time, given the payoff structure, the HA..., HC... outcome would be hard to achieve because the Nash equilibria rest at LA..., HC... and HA..., LC.... In such a case, if one player can

[81] SD 823.51/1544, p. 3.

[82] In 1944 while Peru's balance of trade with all foreign nations was favorable up to an amount of 10,951,458 Peruvian soles, the positive balance was up to 100 million Peruvian soles with the U.S.; SD 823.51/1544, p. 2.

Cardinal Payoff Matrix, Intervention Expected

		Lenders IS 3/7		
		HC...	MC...	LC...
	HA...	10.5, 10.5	7.25, 10.67	6.5, 10.83
Peru IS 3/7	MA...	10.67, 7.25	<u>7, 7</u>	5, 6.75
	LA...	**10.83, 6.5**	6.75, 5	3.5, 3.5

Note: Nash equilibrium bolded; expected outcome with intervention underlined.

Ordinal Payoff Matrix, Intervention Expected

		Lenders IS 3/7		
		HC...	MC...	LC...
	HA...	7, 7	6, 8	**3, 9**
Peru IS 3/7	MA...	8, 6	<u>5, 5</u>	2, 4
	LA...	**9, 3**	4, 2	1, 1

Note: Nash equilibrium bolded; expected outcome with intervention underlined.

Figure 10.3. *Play phase, period three: 1939–1943*

successfully convince the other that it would risk disaster, then the player could significantly improve its outcome at the cost of its opponent. In sum, we would expect the outcome to be one of the two equilibria, but a poor payoff for both actors is not out of the question – at least for a short period of time.

With respect to the outcome including third-party intervention, given what we know about the United States' objectives during this period, we might expect a middle compromise outcome of MA..., MC.... This outcome would suit the U.S.,

Cardinal Payoff Matrix, No Intervention Expected

		Lenders IS 3/7		
		HC...	MC...	LC...
	HA...	3, 10.5	1, 10.67	0, 10.83
Peru IS 3/5	MA...	4.17, 7.25	2, 7	.5, 6.75
	LA...	**5.33, 6.5**	3, 5	1, 3.5

Note: Nash equilibrium bolded.

Ordinal Payoff Matrix, No Intervention Expected

		Lenders IS 3/7		
		HC...	MC...	LC...
	HA...	6.5, 7	3.5, 8	1, 9
Peru IS 3/5	MA...	8, 6	5, 5	2, 4
	LA...	**9, 3**	6.5, 2	3.5, 1

Note: Nash equilibrium bolded.

Figure 10.4. *Play phase, period four: 1944–1945*

because it would serve to stabilize Peru while at the same time soothe its domestic groups. But in view of the U.S. preoccupation with security issues, it might not wish to become too deeply involved in debt negotiation beyond attempting to broker an agreement. Still, given the uncertainties involved in intervention in a Chicken game, we cannot confidently predict American actions in this case.

Peru's improved overall and financial capabilities lead to period four's game and outcome (see Figure 10.4). According to the model, the game shifts to one of Called Bluff in the fourth period. In this case, Peru can play a strategy of LA..., to capture it its highest payoff, and confidentially expect a high degree of concessions from the lenders. In the game with intervention, we might expect the U.S. government to push the Peruvians to be more conciliatory toward the bondholders because of domestic pressures. But given its overriding security concerns nurtured by the ongoing conflict with Japan and Germany, we would not expect the U.S. to make very strong efforts to force the Peruvians to change their policy.

The negotiations and outcome

Period three. Prado's election to the presidency in 1939 gave the bondholders fresh hope that the new government would resolve the outstanding debt default. In March 1940, the government discussed the possibility of including 21 million soles in the national budget for both internal and external debt repayment. The Acting Finance Minister described the limitations of its conciliatory stance: "[C]onsolidation of internal [debt] is a preferential matter but . . . the government also believes it essential to arrive at an agreement with the bondholders regarding the external debt 'without sacrificing the vital necessities of the country.' "[83] Thus, although willing to cooperate, Peru had no desire to unilaterally make concessions. During 1940, no serious negotiations took place. In March 1941, however, the Peruvian government authorized a permanent settlement on the outstanding bonds with an interest rate rising from 1 to 2%.

The U.S., for its part, seemed unwilling to dramatically push either Peru or the bondholders. As Warren Lee Pierson, President of the Export-Import Bank, put it:

> [T]here is no inclination on the part of the United States to be unreasonable or to expect the impossible . . . there is no inclination on the part of the United States to drive a hard bargain, but it is equally impossible to acquiesce in an attitude which sought to ignore the fact that the debts had been incurred.[84]

With an eye on its overall security concerns, the U.S. was reluctant to push the Peruvians very hard. In fact, the Export-Import Bank agreed to a loan of $10 million for Peruvian purchases from the U.S. Shortly thereafter, Peru expropriated planes from the German airline Lufthansa; in March 1941, it closed Transocean, a German shipping group.[85] The U.S. government continued to encourage negotiations between the Council and Peru, but its primary motivation for involvement was clear.

Prospects for a settlement looked especially bleak in October 1941, after talks between Peruvian Finance Minister Dasso and Bondholders' Council representative White. Minister Dasso bluntly stated, "[T]here is no sense in entering into an agreement at present when there is no tangible means of complying with it. Peru cannot make the service payments at this time. Consequently a promise to do so should not be given."[86] White suggested that temporary service on a modest

[83] SD 823.51/1330, p. 2. [84] SD 823.51/1372, p. 3.
[85] Carey (1964), pp. 106–107. [86] SD 823.51/1423, p. 1.

scale would be greatly appreciated as a sign of goodwill. Failing to receive any positive response, the bondholders appealed to the American government for help. The U.S., however, was unwilling to do more than provide neutral territory for negotiations, especially because it appeared to perceive the Peruvian attitude as sincere.[87]

Dasso and White resumed their talks on the scale and amount of payment in April 1942. Dasso immediately pleaded a lack of foreign exchange and informally proposed a 1% interest payment,[88] a drop from White's 3% request.[89] The Council argued that Peru could now service its debt at a higher rate because of positive trade results in 1941,[90] and thus rejected Dasso's proposal as unfair.

The U.S. government reacted negatively to the Council's refusal to accept Peru's offer. Although the State Department continued to prod the Peruvians to address the issue of debt repayment, the Department was hardly sympathetic to the bondholders. In internal discussions, Frederick Livesey, Chief of the Financial Division, wrote to Emilio Collado, Special Assistant to Undersecretary of State Welles:

> if the Finance Minister [Dasso] today with conditions of today wants to make a certain payment on a strictly provisional basis, some responsibility is incurred in thwarting him. The Council has been an effective thwarter of various payments to bondholders for years at a time. Need the Department join in this unless it has specific reasons in its own field for doing so?[91]

Although Collado suggested that the undersecretary press the Peruvians to make repayments, in a memo to Welles he noted that "I agree with Mr. Livesey that the Department should not do anything to keep Dasso from going ahead with his intention to resume at least some small temporary payments."[92] In the end, responding to the Council's demand for active U.S. pressure on Peru, Welles wrote to Francis White, President of the Council, in connection with Dasso's offer:

> These should be good auspices for assuring some payment to the bondholders whether on the provisional and empirical basis Mr. Dasso has in mind or on any other practical basis you may work out. I hope some early payment can be made. Defeat of such a display of will to pay would be unfortunate.[93]

Ignoring the continued impasse on debt negotiations, the U.S. concluded a trade treaty with Peru in May 1942.

Dasso failed to propose a final settlement offer. After he became ill in June 1942, negotiations stalled, and the Council tried to improve its bargaining position by appealing to the State Department in September. Appealing to the norm of equity, the Council asked the American government to press Peru into remedying its practice of discriminating between dollar bond holders and sterling bondholders.[94] The Department of State considered this request but would not take action, remarking only that there was a "gap between the Peruvian ideas

[87] SD 823.51/1423, p. 2. [88] SD 823.51/1443, p. 2. [89] SD 823.51/1439, p. 1.
[90] SD 823.51/1448, pp. 1–2. [91] SD FW 823/51/1439. [92] SD FW 823.51/1439.
[93] SD 823.51/1448. [94] SD 823.51/1465, pp. 3–4.

and the Council's ideas."[95] Not everyone in the State Department agreed on this strategy. Considerably more sympathetic to the Peruvians than most, Livesey hoped the problem would simply go away. He noted ironically in an internal memo:

> After reading Mr. White's letter of September 11, I judge the Peruvian bond situation is in a bad way and is not likely to improve soon unless the Peruvians, like sensible fellows, decide to take such funds as they have available, buy up bonds in the market and retire them. Such a procedure would of course be lamentable and is commended only by its good sense.[96]

The Chief of the Division of the American Republics, on the other hand, complained that "I do not feel that the Peruvians have been as cooperative as they might have been in this matter."[97] Meanwhile, following along the lines of Livesey's suggestion, in November 1942, Nelson Rockefeller suggested that the U.S. government buy Peruvian bonds and convert the total amount to Peruvian soles, which Peru would pay on low interest.[98] Such an action, however, would have antagonized the Council and other financial groups, and thus was rejected by the State Department.

The Council appealed to the U.S. for help again in March 1943 when no accord had been reached. Some Department of State officials began to ask more of Peru, as reflected by advisor Laurence Duggan's message: "[W]hat we really want from the Peruvians is an offer. Once we got an offer and have an expression from the Council, the Department then . . . could be instrumental in bargaining these two positions into focus."[99]

The Council's persistence succeeded in persuading the Department to reexamine its attitude. It considered linking debt to economic facilities to propel cooperation, but such a strategy appeared too risky while the world war raged. In fact, the State Department could not act against Peru without running the risk that Peru might limit its raw material supplies. An issue-linkage strategy on Peru's part would have endangered the American priorities as defined by Ambassador Norweb: "Cooperation in our economic warfare program and in continental defense had been my two major preoccupations in Peru. Next in importance had come the settlement of various debts and claims."[100] Replying to Norweb's query as to how much pressure should be put on Peru, Undersecretary of State Sumner Welles summarized the U.S. position as follows:

> It seems to me that it would be a serious mistake for us to tie any specific foreign debt settlement to any specific measures of economic cooperation. For a variety of reasons, including that of political expediency, I think we wish to avoid any semblance of a clear cut bargain. On the other hand, we are prepared to make it clear that the whole trend of our economic policy toward Peru is by no means independent of and is, in fact, highly sensitive to the trend of Peru's policy toward the interests of our citizens.[101]

[95] SD 823.51/1465, p. 4. [96] SD 823.51/1465, p. 1. [97] SD 823.51/1465, Bonsal to Livesey.
[98] SD 823.51/1470, pp. 1–3. [99] SD 823.51/1486, p. 2.
[100] SD 823.51/1477, p. 1 of Norweb letter to Welles.
[101] SD 823.51/1477, p. 1 of Welles letter to Norweb.

The Council once again failed to change the Department of State's Peruvian strategy.

The Council insisted on at least a 3% servicing of the debt, while Peru held out at a maximum of 1%. Thus negotiations ended up at the LA..., LC... point. As the Peruvian economy began to improve, however, the actors now entered a new period of negotiations.

Period four. In February 1944, hopes for a settlement reemerged as Peruvian Finance Minister East declared that his government considered an agreement on the service and amortization of the debt imperative.[102] But progress remained impossible because Peru did not make a new offer to the bondholders. By the end of March, East declared that Peru could only afford a settlement on the most reduced scale of payment, and that Peru would be unable to repay even part of the small postal debt it owed.[103]

Faced with this never-ending problem, the U.S. embassy in Lima showed signs of impatience, as illustrated by Ambassador White's comments:

> Mr. East's attitude seems to suggest little more than a desire to reiterate, as he and his predecessors have in past years, Peru's expression of an intention to come to a "friendly settlement of the debt problem within Peru's economic capacity to pay," with special emphasis on our side under the "Good Neighbor" policy and no stress on Peru's. Presumably this method of procedure will continue so long as we rely chiefly on oral persuasion based on debating figures covering Peru's budget, foreign trade and balance of payments.[104]

Yet despite its annoyance, the U.S. did not change its stance. As the war continued, and aware of American eagerness to secure its position in Latin America, the Peruvians did not fear strong intervention. The American Chargé in Peru put it succinctly:

> The continuously generous, even if meritorious from a political or social standpoint, expenditure of funds in Peru by other agencies of the United States Government naturally encourages the belief among Peruvians that our Government is really more interested in contributing to Peru's welfare than in pressing for the payment of Peruvian obligations to the United States.[105]

Peru resumed talks with the Foreign Council in the beginning of May, but discussions stumbled over the nation's financial situation. Both parties tried to strengthen their stance, and Peru resorted to tactics along the lines of "why agree now if we cannot fulfill obligations later?"[106] At the same time, Peru attempted to link any debt solution to trade advantages, arguing that "any agreement as to the percentage of interest or of amortization would have to be conditional on the continuance of such [American] purchases . . ." But U.S. officials rejected such a link.[107]

The two parties failed to reach a bilateral agreement, and on May 9, Peru submitted a unilateral offer. Its proposal consisted of a reduction of the principal

[102] SD 823.51/1534, p. 1. [103] *Foreign Relations of the United States* (1944), vol. 7, p. 1571.
[104] SD 823.51/1544, p. 2. [105] *Foreign Relations of the United States* (1944), vol. 7, p. 1572.
[106] For more details see SD 823.51/1549. [107] SD 823.51/1549, p. 5.

amount by dividing the total by 6.5 (the exchange rate of soles for one dollar) and the cancellation of all arrears of interest. Such terms would yield less than 0.75% interest on the principal.[108] This proposal caused another breakdown in negotiations as reported by Ambassador White: "[T]he gap between Peru's insincerely supported proposal and anything deserving consideration is too great to be bridged by continued negotiations now and any practicable settlement requires a new start."[109] The Council formally refused the proposal in June – even after Finance Minister East tried to jump start cooperation by agreeing to immediately pay the postal debt. Negotiations were adjourned, and renewed efforts for a settlement were hampered by a lack of exchange availability and upcoming elections in Peru.

In November 1945, Peru included a provision of $3,500,000 in its 1946 budget for debt service – not a significant increase.[110] In December, Peru was back to Roca's original proposal:

- Interest payments would begin at 1% and reach 3% by the fifth year and thereafter;
- Peru would make no payment of arrears of interest; and
- Payments would be inconvertible if the country faced exchange difficulties.[111]

This proposal was incompatible with the Council's former conditions,[112] which, among other requirements, insisted on the payment of interest arrears. But as our bargaining game predicted, the Council gave in to Peru's request, agreeing to allow no payment toward interest arrears,[113] leading to an asymmetrical outcome with all the concessions coming from the bondholders.

Summary. Using the opportunity presented by World War II, Peru continued to reject any significant concessions to the bondholders. In the third period, this strategy led to an extended deadlock in negotiations. During the fourth period, as financial and overall conditions in Peru improved, we expected it to continue to play tough, but for the bondholders to be highly conciliatory. In fact, this is what happened. The bondholders agreed to cancel all interest arrears – a major concession on their part, but this success did not prompt Peruvian reciprocation.

Situational changes

Both Peru and the bondholders experienced a situational shift during periods three and four. Peru's economy initially suffered at the onset of the Second World War, but by 1944, it was able to export larger quantities of materials and

108 SD 823.51/1548.
109 SD 823.51/1548, in *Foreign Relations of the United States* (1944), vol. 7, p. 1577.
110 SD 823.51/11–1045, p. 3. 111 SD 823.51/12–545, p. 1.
112 For details of these conditions see SD 823.51/11–1045, p. 1.
113 SD 823.51/12–1245, p. 1.

become considerably more self-sufficient. As we saw, the Council became more stable, but remained the same on other dimensions.

At the end of the Second World War, Peru's new-found strength changed the terms of the negotiation. It prompted the lenders to pursue high concessions, but a final accord still eluded them. Despite their unhappiness with their payoffs, the bondholders failed to change their situation on their own. By 1946, however, Peru's situation took a turn for the worse, both economically and politically, as growing domestic unrest destabilized the government. After Bustamante took office in 1945, the discontented Apristas urged political and guerilla warfare against the administration, throwing the country into chaos. At the same time, Peru's exports decreased dramatically after the war, hurting Peru financially.

Periods five and six, 1946–1947 and 1948–1950: direct offer

These two periods saw Peru's development of an unconventional direct offer to the bondholders, one that changed the latter's individual situation by splitting the lenders and that greatly benefited Peru – at least in the short run. The Peruvians hoped to gain the upper hand by bypassing the Council. Peru's unique strategy of undercutting the bondholders gave the Peruvians a partial victory. In the end, however, this strategy failed to yield a lasting solution. Given the relatively short time frame involved, we examine both periods in this section.

Identifying individual situations

During period five, we classify Peru as coalitionally unstable, issue weak, and overall medium (IS 4/8). The lenders, represented by the Council, were stable, issue weak, and overall strong (IS 3). During the sixth period, Peru became more stable domestically, shifting it to IS 4/7. The lenders split completely in this period, creating two separate games with Peru. The bondholders were stable coalitionally, but issue and overall weak (IS 7). The Council can be coded as stable, issue medium, and overall strong (IS 3/5).

Peru. Peruvians' hopes for a stable coalition government led by President José Luis Bustamante were quickly dashed by events following his inauguration in July 1945. Now functioning under the label of the Partido del Pueblo, APRA immediately began jostling for control over policymaking. Partido del Pueblo members assumed that Bustamante would simply concede some control – rather than expend energy on reconciling competing political forces in the country. Unwilling to simply be a puppet, however, Bustamante soon showed his independence by choosing a non-Aprista prime minister – a move that alienated the Apristas. Holding a majority in Parliament, the Apristas led a constitutional fight to reduce the powers of the president and to transfer them to the Parliament. Outside the government, the Apristas infiltrated labor and student organizations, used censorship against hostile newspapers (*La Prensa* and *El Comercio*), and killed political opponents. The country descended into political chaos – despite attempts at conciliation by Bustamante. The right-wing factions took this situation as proof that cooperating with APRA was impossible, and they succeeded in suspending sessions of Parliament with their one-third blocking minority. Although Bustamante could have governed by decree, he attempted to cooperate with APRA. But when the Apristas were accused of having assassinated a prominent publisher, tensions increased dramatically.

Despite Bustamante's efforts to mollify his opponents, both APRA and conservative factions began to scheme to overthrow him. After suppressing an Aprista coup attempt on October 3, 1948, Bustamante declared APRA illegal. This action failed to stabilize the political situation. On October 27, senior conservative military officers led a "Restorative Revolution" in Arequipa that forced Bustamante to resign two days later. General Manuel Odría, installed by the coup leaders, succeeded in restoring political stability by about 1950 through authoritarian methods. Aprista leaders such as Haya de la Torre were jailed; others were forced into hiding. The government made all decisions by presidential decrees until 1950. In that year, it called an election, and managed to increase its stability by legitimating the military junta.

Turning to Peru's financial situation, immediately following World War II, the United States cut down on Peruvian import commodities, leading to a precipitous decline in export tax revenues for Peru. Copper, cotton, lead, and wool did not regain their 1945 export levels until 1951, coffee until 1952, sugar until 1953, and petroleum until 1960.[114] Peru faced a decline in per capita income during the period after the war, and inflation increased rapidly.

With respect to overall capabilities, Peru no longer enjoyed as favorable a position. It still maintained its overall military capabilities, but no longer was as self-sufficient as before. The government was forced to import food from abroad, but still could not meet domestic demand. The need for financial resources drove the government to seek an agreement with the International Petroleum Company, a subsidiary of Standard Oil. This effort was blocked by a Congress concerned that Peru was now willing to give away the national patrimony.[115]

Lenders. In the fifth period, the Council continued to represent the bondholders and maintain a secure and stable position. Although the lenders as a whole remained issue weak, they secured a strong alliance with the United States that greatly improved their overall capabilities.

By 1948, however, a sharp split developed between the Council and the bondholders it represented. Because Peru offered a deal directly to the bondholders, while negotiating unsuccessfully with the Council at the same time, we treat the lenders as two groups. The bondholders were stable in the sense that there were no repercussions from the rest of the group for individuals who took up Peru's offer. At the same time, individual bondholders were issue and overall weak, lacking large financial resources or the power to coerce or block Peru in its trade or borrowing efforts. The Council also survived the split in stable condition, and acted strongly in concert with British bondholders. In terms of

[114] Pike (1967), p. 285. [115] See Pike (1967), p. 285 for details.

capabilities, we code the Council as issue medium, because those who backed the Council were presumably not financially desperate and could afford to hold out for a better deal. In terms of overall capabilities, although the Council was unable to prevent the U.S. from offering an Export-Import Bank loan to Peru, it did have the ability to block quotations of Peru's new bonds on the New York Stock Exchange. In addition, it also continued to have the support of the U.S. government soon after the split, thus leading us to code the Council as overall strong.

Creditor governments. With the end of war, U.S. concern about pressuring Peru unduly could be expected to diminish. Peru could no longer use its participation in the war effort as an excuse to avoid servicing its debt. At the same time, the U.S. continued to face demands from bondholders to help them secure debt servicing.

Debt games and predicted outcome

The actors' situations produce the games shown in Figure 10.5 for both periods five and six.

The game between Peru and the bondholders (see Figure 10.6) yields three equilibria, with Peru choosing a strategy of LA... and the bondholders responding to the choice between high and low concessions with indifference. Given the altered political environment – the U.S. no longer worried about Peru's wartime allegiance – we would expect the U.S. to be more willing to push for a more favorable outcome for the bondholders. We have already taken into account U.S. pressure in our coding of the bondholders as overall strong. We would not expect pressure beyond this support. We would, however, expect the two equilibria involving higher levels of concessions by the lenders to be unlikely in this case, given the U.S. government's concerns for its lenders.

In the sixth period's game with the bondholders, the Nash equilibrium is at LA..., HC..., resulting in an asymmetrical outcome favoring Peru. Although the U.S. should be interested in helping the lenders, we would not expect it to very actively intervene to help the disparate group of bondholders, in contrast to the more organized Council (see Figure 10.7). In this Prisoner's Dilemma game, in which the Council negotiates with Peru, we would expect pressure from the U.S. government to encourage some Peruvian adjustment. But since we have already accounted for this likely pressure in part by coding the Council as strong based on its alliance with the U.S. government, we would not expect enough additional pressure to shift the equilibrium outcome from a deadlock.

The negotiations and outcome

Period five. As we have seen, at the end of period four, creditors' high hopes for a debt settlement with the Bustamante government were dashed. Peru became unstable shortly after Bustamente's 1945 election, which led to domestic political conflict that hampered rescheduling. Although the Peruvian government was initially backed by APRA, this backing soon proved to be a handicap.

Cardinal Payoff Matrix, Intervention Expected

		Lenders IS 3		
		HC...	MC...	LC...
	HA...	−1.5, 9	−5, 9.67	−6.5, 10.33
Peru IS 4/8	MA...	2.83, 5.5	−1, 6	−3.5, 6.5
	LA...	**7.17, 3**	**3, 3**	<u>**−.5, 3**</u>

Note: Nash equilibria bolded; expected outcome with intervention underlined.

Ordinal Payoff Matrix, Intervention Expected

		Lenders IS 3		
		HC...	MC...	LC...
	HA...	4, 7	2, 8	1, 9
Peru IS 4/8	MA...	7, 4	5, 5	3, 6
	LA...	**9, 2**	**8, 2**	<u>**6, 2**</u>

Note: Nash equilibria bolded; expected outcome with intervention underlined.

Figure 10.5. *Play phase, period five: 1946–1947*

Because he had APRA's backing, traditional government supporters turned away from supporting Bustamante in debt negotiations. Staunch opponents of APRA preferred to kill any debt agreement – even those resembling proposals they had made when they had been in power – rather than help APRA. Commenting on the source of conservative opposition to a debt accord, led by Pedro Beltrán, former Peruvian Ambassador to the U.S., the American Ambassador in Peru noted

Cardinal Payoff Matrix,
No Intervention Expected

		Lenders IS 7		
		HC...	MC...	LC...
	HA...	4.5, 12	1.25, 11.67	.5, 11.33
Peru IS 4/7	MA...	6.67, 9	3, 8	1, 7
	LA...	**8.83, 10**	4.75, 7	1.5, 4

Note: Nash equilibrium bolded.

Ordinal Payoff Matrix,
No Intervention Expected

		Lenders IS 7		
		HC...	MC...	LC...
	HA...	6, 9	3, 8	1, 7
Peru IS 4/7	MA...	8, 5	5, 4	2, 2.5
	LA...	**9, 6**	7, 2.5	4, 1

Note: Nash equilibrium bolded.

Figure 10.6. *Play phase, period six: 1948–1950 (game with bondholders)*

it may be stated that Beltrán has an axe to grind. He does not really wish the resumption of service on the foreign debt on a sound basis for *both* parties; such a resumption of service means added taxes and export duties for years to come on products, chiefly agricultural, owned and produced by the conservatives who for generations have directed politics in Peru. Such a measure affects adversely their pocket book and *his*.[116]

Debate in the Peruvian Congress paralyzed the government and the negotiations. Hoping to push the negotiations onto a more expeditious course, the American government exerted considerable pressure in support of the Council. In January

[116] SD 823.51/2–1946, p. 4.

Cardinal Payoff Matrix,
Intervention Expected

		Lenders IS 3/5		
		HC...	MC...	LC...
	HA...	4.5, 3	1.25, 4.17	.5, 5.33
Peru IS 4/7	MA...	6.67, 1	3, 2	1, 3
	LA...	8.83, 0	4.75, .5	**1.5, 1**

Note: Nash equilibrium bolded; expected outcome with intervention underlined.

Ordinal Payoff Matrix,
Intervention Expected

		Lenders IS 3/5		
		HC...	MC...	LC...
	HA...	6, 6.5	3, 8	1, 9
Peru IS 4/7	MA...	8, 3.5	5, 5	2, 6.5
	LA...	9, 1	7, 2	**4, 3.5**

Note: Nash equilibrium bolded; expected outcome with intervention underlined.

Figure 10.7. *Play phase, period six: 1948–1950 (game with Council)*

1946, the U.S. Ambassador in Peru, supported by the State Department, threatened that "the Export-Import Bank could consider no additional credit so long as the present default on Peru's bonded indebtedness continues unchanged."[117]

In April, the Peruvian government, pressed by its domestic political opponents, pushed for additional concessions from the bondholders. It was quickly

[117] SD 823.51/1–347, p. 1. For Acting Secretary of State Acheson's concurrence with this view, see SD 823.151/11–1146.

rebuffed by the Council with the full support of the U.S. government.[118] Trapped by both internal and external pressure, the Peruvian government tried to escape its uncomfortable position by approaching American merchants in distressed securities.[119] The Peruvians hoped that by circumventing the Foreign Protective Council, they could secure better conditions and improve their bargaining leverage. But in this case, the U.S. intervened to prevent any divisions between the lenders, warning merchants in distressed securities not to interfere with the Council negotiations.[120]

Faced with a worsening financial situation in December 1946, and in desperate need of money to keep its industry running, Peru made a new offer. It proposed a maximum 2.5% interest payment instead of the 3% requested by the Council. The U.S. Ambassador encouraged the Council to seriously consider this offer, arguing that if Peru agreed to compensate for the low interest rate with a rate of 3 or 4% for good years, the offer would not be so bad.[121] But when Peru attempted to capitalize on the Council's conciliatory attitude on this matter by making an even weaker offer to the American Attaché in Lima, the U.S. government rejected this suggestion. In the end, Peru formally proposed a 2.5% maximum on interest payments (to be reached after five years). In addition, it called for a 0.5% amortization payment and a non-interest bearing scrip of 0.5% payable at the termination of the amortization schedule.[122]

An agreement now appeared forthcoming. Both sides began making offers and counter-offers with respect to the maximum level of annuities and on the division between interest and amortization payments. But by the end of 1946, these efforts resulted in a deadlock. Peru was unwilling to offer more than 3% in total annuities with a maximum of 2.5% on interest payments, whereas the Council would not accept less than 3% on interest payments.[123] The bondholders then rescinded their informal acceptance of the 2.5% maximum interest payment when Peru refused to agree to make higher payments during financially better years.

On February 28, 1947, the Peruvian Congress passed a law overwhelmingly that enabled the government to resume service on major defaulted loans (tobacco, National, Lima Municipal of 1911, and Callao Municipal) with the following conditions:

- Interest arrears earned before December 31, 1946, would be canceled;
- Interest payments would start at 1% in 1947 and reach 2.5% in 1953; and
- A 0.5% amortization payment would be applicable.[124]

At the beginning of March, the Bondholders' Council condemned Peru's unilateral move. It found the proposed service obligations "disproportionately low"

[118] SD 823.51/4–346. [119] SD 823.51/7–3146.
[120] SD 823.51/8–846, p. 2; see also SD 823.51/8–1546. [121] SD 823.51/12–1746.
[122] SD 823.51/12–2146. [123] SD 823.51/2–2547.
[124] SD 823.51/Bondholders 2–147, p. 1; see also 823.51/3–1347.

and "the ultimate interest rate (2.5% reached in the seventh year)" below standard.[125] On the basis of these complaints, the Council refused to recommend Peru's offer to the individual bondholders.

In April and May, American businessmen and some officials including U.S. Ambassador Cooper worked actively toward an agreement. This effort failed to produce substantive change, even though the Council believed that President Bustamante was not trying to cheat them but rather was acting in good faith. With no agreement in sight, Peru threatened to approach the bondholders directly in an attempt to organize a new committee. It contacted the Central Hanover National Bank to act as its agent. This move provoked a divided response among the bondholders, but the U.S. government prevented a coalitional split by refusing to introduce a new committee to the Peruvian government, arguing that "one voice is better than several."[126]

The Peruvian government persisted and in June 1947 proposed the so-called Exchange Offer to the bondholders. It offered to resume service on the dollar bonds of the tobacco and National loans on terms specified in the February 28, 1947, domestic legislation. The offer proposed canceling interest arrears accumulated under the 16-year default. The old bonds would be replaced by new unsecured bonds, maturing within 50 years and bearing a variable interest rate that would grow from 1 to 2.5%. The proposal also stipulated that the amount allotted in the Peruvian budget for service of the debt would be deposited in the Central Reserve Bank of Peru as a safeguard against the country's persisting dollar exchange stringency.[127] The Foreign Bondholders Protective Council maintained the same attitude it held prior to Peru's February 28 legislation, recommending that the bondholders reject Peru's offer, leading to an outcome of LA..., LC... in this case.

The Council's rejection of Peru's offer did not stop the Peruvian government from making direct offers to individual bondholders, offers that remained open until June 30, 1948. Peru's action resulted in a sharp split among the lenders, which initiated the next period of negotiations and the two separate games, the first between Peru and the bondholders, and the second involving Peru and the Council.

Period six. The Peruvian Exchange offer temporarily disrupted negotiations. Although the U.S. government was willing to consider Export-Import Bank loans to Peru, it still did not endorse Peru's unilateral action with respect to the Council.[128] Unsanctioned by the U.S., two games went into effect.

In the first game involving the bondholders and Peru, many bondholders were willing to accept Peru's offer, even though it was described by a high U.S. official as "a source of disappointment to many American bondholders."[129] By

[125] SD 823.51/3–1347 in *Foreign Relations of the United States* (1947), vol. 8, pp. 1006–1007.
[126] SD 823.51/6–347. [127] See Wynne (1951), p. 194.
[128] SD 711.23/7–947 in *Foreign Relations of the United States* (1947), vol. 8, pp. 1011–1013.
[129] SD 823.51 Bondholders/11–2047, p. 4.

December 31, 1947, holders of only $5,493,000 of old bonds (face amount) had accepted the Peruvian offer on a total of $76.5 million foreign debt bond.[130] By August 1949, however, the rate of acceptance had risen to nearly half or $36.4 million of the outstanding total.[131] Peru eventually extended its offer to the bondholders through June 1952, with the number of acceptances eventually peaking at 65%.[132] This game, then, resulted in an asymmetrical outcome of LA..., HC... favoring Peru.

By contrast, the outcome of the second game involving Peru and the Council, benefited no one: the negotiations remained deadlocked at LA..., LC... No progress was made on negotiations between the two parties through 1949.

Summary. Negotiations between Peru and the Council were deadlocked in the fifth period. Although close to an agreement, as predicted by our model, neither side budged. In an effort to reestablish its credit, Peru made a unilateral offer to the individual bondholders, causing a split among the lenders in the sixth period. From 1948 to 1950, the bondholders and Peru played an asymmetric game, as over half of the bondholders accepted Peru's unilateral offer of no interest and a maximum rate of 2.5% interest. The distinct second game with the Council during this period, by contrast, remained deadlocked.

Situational changes

The most radical change in period six was Peru's unusual strategy of direct negotiations with the bondholders. Although Peru received high payoffs from its gamble of bargaining directly with the bondholders in period six, it subsequently faced problems with the Council. Bargaining directly with the Council, Peru received a very low payoff, as did the Council.

Peru also made an effort to further split the creditors by encouraging British bondholders to accept its offer, but the British government blocked this effort. It simply refused to let Peru appoint an agent whose duties would be to accept Peruvian bonds for exchange. When Peru attempted contact with the British Council of Foreign Bondholders asking about terms, it was rebuffed by the Council's President, Lord Bessbrough. He noted simply that "the two Councils work closely together, that the Peruvian situation had been left to be handled by the American Council, and that the British Council was still willing to leave it that way."[133]

But as we shall see, Peru could not simply allow matters to rest with the deadlock. Its access to credit by the World Bank was blocked. As the President of the American Council reported with respect to his conversation with Bank officials, "They said they had told the Peruvians that they should reach satisfactory agreements with the Councils before asking the Bank to extend credit to Peru."[134]

[130] SD 823.51 Bondholders/11–2047. [131] Wynne (1951), pp. 194–195.
[132] SD 823.10/8–151, p. 1 of Enc. No. 1. [133] SD 823.11/10–1150, p. 2.
[134] SD 823.11/10–1150, p. 2.

To get back into the good graces of the financial community, Peru needed to begin playing by the book.

Peru's attempts to gain the Council's approval of its unorthodox strategy failed, and its efforts to change its situation or the Council's eventually came to nought. The Council continued to curry U.S. approval and assistance, and as a result it was able to maintain its strong position.

Period seven, 1951–1953: to the final agreements

After years of negotiations, this period brought an end to Peru's outstanding default. Pursuing an open economic strategy based on major efforts to encourage an inflow of capital, Peru needed to settle with the Council to gain access to loans. The Council, for its part, pushed for an arrangement that was satisfactory to its remaining constituents, using its favorable situation to drive a relatively hard bargain.

Identifying individual situations

During this period, Peru became more stable, and its financial situation improved greatly. At the same time, however, because of its liberal economic policies, it became overall weak as it became highly reliant on foreign investment and more generally on foreign funds. In short, it was in IS 1. The Council remained in the same situation as before, with a stable coalition, medium issue capabilities, and overall strength (IS 3/5).

Peru. Having purged much of his opposition, Odría held elections in 1950. After banning APRA and the communists, Odría faced little opposition, but did not take any chances. Shortly before the election, he disqualified Ernesto Montagne, his only opponent. As a result, the vote stood only as an affirmation or rejection of Odría. The government claimed that the July polls gave him over 80% approval. Odría subsequently made an effort to gain both working class and middle class support, and at least until about 1953, proved highly successful in doing so.

Part of Odría's popularity was the result of a radical improvement in Peru's economy. With the onset of the Korean War, its export prices surged upward. The three years of wartime trade surpluses noticeably improved Peru's general economic situation. During these years, Peru experienced a high rate of economic growth and large gains in its manufacturing output.[135] Much of its growth was driven by burgeoning foreign investments that stimulated both the manufacturing and mining sectors of the economy.

With respect to overall capabilities, the Odría Administration concentrated on programs designed to end the nation's postwar economic slump. To lure foreign investment, Odría made the country attractive by reducing state controls. But as

[135] See Werlich (1978), pp. 250–251.

U.S. investment more than doubled between 1950 and 1955, and as foreign investments grew to $800 million by the end of Odría's term, Peru's dependence on external funds and markets to finance its development made it vulnerable to potential retaliation.

Lenders. The FBPC remained stable, without any obvious weaknesses Peru might exploit. The American and British councils worked together. The FBPC continued to remain issue medium because of the exodus of the eager bondholders, who had accepted Peru's direct offer, and was overall strong because of the strong support of the World Bank.

Creditor governments. With growing leverage over Peru as its major source of investment, the U.S. government was in a good position to influence Peru's decisions. As Odría blocked the communists and APRA, the U.S. had little to fear from a security perspective and was thus willing to help the Council apply pressure on the Peruvians.

Debt game and predicted outcome

The debt matrix (Figure 10.8) reflects Peru's modified position, but an identical situation for the lenders. In this game, we predict that Peru will willingly undertake high adjustment even though the lenders will provide few concessions. This predicted outcome should not be surprising in view of Peru's strong desire to receive funds from the World Bank and other agencies, and its effort to worm its way into the good graces of the United States. With Peru undertaking high adjustment after so many years of default, and finally coming to terms with the Council, we would not expect any further intervention by creditor governments. Their objectives are not incongruous with the two actors' equilibrium position.

The negotiations and outcome

In July 1951, Peru began to make overtures to the Council for a settlement of its outstanding debt. As expected, the Council's block of its credit strongly encouraged Peru to be more forthcoming. In April, when Peru had sought a World Bank loan to develop its Port of Callao facilities, it asked the bank if it "would be willing to make such a loan without waiting for a final settlement of Peru's eternal debt." In response, the President of the Bank, Eugene Black, wrote back to Peru:

> if the President [Peru's] would indicate to the Bank that Peru was prepared to negotiate with the Bondholders' representatives, and, if a reasonable settlement could be negotiated, to recommend its approval by Congress, the Bank would consider making such a loan before final settlement had been reached.[136]

In response to this direct linkage, Peru moved quickly to accommodate the Council's demands. By July, President Black announced that the Bank would be

[136] SD 823.10/7–3151, Annex C, p. 1 for this and previous quote.

Cardinal Payoff Matrix,
No Intervention Expected

Lenders IS 3/5

		HC...	MC...	LC...
	HA...	−3, 3	−2, 4.17	**3, 5.33**
Peru IS 1	MA...	−2.33, 1	−2, 2	1, 3
	LA...	−1.67, 0	−2, .5	−1, 1

Note: Nash equilibrium bolded.

Ordinal Payoff Matrix,
No Intervention Expected

Lenders IS 3/5

		HC...	MC...	LC...
	HA...	1, 6	4, 8	**9, 9**
Peru IS 1	MA...	2, 3.5	4, 5	8, 7
	LA...	6, 1	4, 2	7, 3.5

Note: Nash equilibrium bolded.

Figure 10.8. *Play phase, period seven: 1950–1953*

willing to negotiate with Peru to conclude the Callao Port loan, but still insisted that "Before concluding the negotiations, however, I would expect to receive confirmation that the President is prepared to make a recommendation to Congress . . ."[137]

In discussions with U.S. government officials, Peruvian Ambassador Fernando Berckemeyer clearly recognized the direct linkage of successfully signing an accord to receiving a fresh supply of World Bank loans. After discussing the

[137] SD 823.10/7–3151, Annex C, p. 1.

various projects for which Peru sought financing from the World Bank, the U.S. embassy acknowledged Berckemeyer's perspective:

> the only hindrance to the immediate establishment of these credits is the lack of a satisfactory settlement for the Peruvian foreign debt . . . and he feels optimistic that with the proposed offer for settlement that he hopes to get from his Government, this hindrance will be eliminated.[138]

By August, Peru was willing to address the objections the Council had raised with regard to Peru's 1947 offer. Peru offered to pay 3% interest on the outstanding bonds, and back interest in the form of $70 cash for each $1,000 of bonds plus $10 in scrip, starting in 1954.[139] The Foreign Protective Council agreed to the 3% interest payment, but wanted it to begin in 1953. In addition, it wanted $200 cash per $1,000 bond for past due interest. Close to a consensus, both parties seemed capable of eliminating the remaining difficulties. The British, however, were taking no chances. When the World Bank appeared to consider making Peru a small loan, the British took "violent exception to the loan," warning that "'the city' [London financial interests] will have nothing further to do with the Bank if the Bank pursues such a course."[140]

Soon thereafter, Peru came very close to an agreement with the U.S. Council based on a 3% interest payment from 1953, and a back interest of a non-interest bearing scrip in the amount of $100 per $1,000 bond (payment equivalent to 10% of interest arrears).[141] The Peruvians also began discussions to resolve the outstanding default on sterling loans. Although some minor obstacles involving the question of succession of rights on the new bonds (whether payment of arrears went to present owners or to owners who did the exchange), and the base for revision of the 1947 offer,[142] the Peruvians essentially acquiesced to the bulk of the Council's demands. By April 1952, Peru and the Council reached a final agreement for dollar bonds, formally announced in January 1953, with the following conditions:

- Payment of interest at a rate of 3% per annum from January 1, 1952;
- Payment of one-tenth of the total arrears of interest due up to December 31, 1946 over a period of 15 years commencing in 1953; and
- Payment of arrears of interest for the period January 1, 1947 to December 31, 1952 at rate of: 1% for 1947–1948, 1.5% for 1949–1950, and 2% for 1951–1952.[143]

The Peruvian debt had not yet been entirely settled because provisions regarding the sterling bonds were still pending. In particular, a conflict developed between Peru and the British Council over the conversion rate in dollars of the sterling bonds. At issue, each holder clearly had the option to convert its bond in dollars at a rate of $4.80 per pound. The British Council requested this old rate because the sterling pound had lost almost one-half of its value against the

[138] SD 823.10/8–151, p. 1 of Enc. 1. [139] SD 823.10/8–1351. [140] SD 823.10/9–1351.
[141] SD 823.10/10–2651. [142] SD 823.10/12–1851. [143] SD 823.10/6–2752.

dollar. By contrast, a conversion at the nominal face amount would represent considerable losses to the bondholders.[144]

Once again, as in the American case, the World Bank's strong support for the British Council facilitated an agreement. The Bank refused to make additional loans to Peru until it settled with the British.[145] Peru reacted by quickly accepting the British demands and agreeing to convert sterling bonds at the original dollar rate, thus closing to a final agreement on December 16, 1953.[146]

Summary. During this period, the bargaining game strongly favored the lenders. We expected to see an asymmetrical outcome with Peru undertaking the bulk of concessions, while the lenders enjoyed wielding the upper hand. In both cases of rescheduling, the Peruvians gave in to the demands of the American and British councils in an effort to end its default and open the way for new funding.

Conclusion

Peru along with many other countries borrowed in the U.S. market during the 1920s. The onset of the depression of the 1930s threw almost all these countries into default. During the 1930s and early 1940s, negotiations dragged on without an end in sight despite the changing individual situations of the actors.

By the mid-1940s, significant movement in the negotiations began. But at the end of the Second World War, the Peruvians could no longer count on receiving highly sympathetic treatment from the United States. Although the 1944–1945 negotiations found the bondholders willing to make high concessions, a final agreement still evaded the negotiators. Following a deadlocked game in 1946–1947, the Peruvians created a split among the lenders that we modeled as two different games. In the first game with the bondholders, they accepted Peru's unilateral offer, which proved quite favorable to Peru. But negotiations with the Council were more complicated. Both the American and British Councils continued to rebuff Peru's overtures, and by securing the strong and continued support of their creditor governments, they were able to force Peru into making high levels of adjustment by the early 1950s. In the end, in contrast to the debt rescheduling case of Mexico in the 1940s, Peru ended up with a considerably less favorable agreement, in which it agreed to repay the full principal on its loans and back interest as well.

[144] SD 823.10/5–1652. [145] SD 823.10/1–1453, p. 2.
[146] For details on the terms of the British accord, see SD 823.10/12–1853.

PART V
Epoch 4: 1970s–1990s

11 The good guys get tired: Mexican debt rescheduling in the 1980s and 1990s

Since the 1970s, two key factors have shaped Mexico's economic performance and bargaining capabilities. First, the internal political stability of the country at the beginning of the debt crisis allowed the government to have a longer-term outlook. Second, a special rapport with the U.S. government gave Mexico a powerful ally. In addition, the discovery of large oil reserves in the 1970s permitted Mexico to maintain steady growth in this decade. These factors distinguished Mexico's position from those of other Latin American debtors in the rescheduling negotiations in the 1980s and 1990s.

Mexican debt rescheduling is particularly important because of its precedent-setting arrangements. In the wake of the 1982 payments crisis, Mexico's agreement with the IMF required bankers and creditor governments to co-lend to Mexico – a phenomenon that came to be known as "involuntary lending." In return, Mexico agreed to adopt an IMF austerity program. Signs of rapid economic growth in 1984 prompted IMF claims of success.[1] By 1985, however, declining oil prices and increasing imports produced new financial difficulties and the need for a new and innovative agreement on Mexico's foreign debt.

After 1985, bargaining between Mexico and its lenders became harsher; agreements were increasingly difficult to reach. In September 1985, two earthquakes devastated Mexico City and oil prices dropped dramatically.[2] After these events, Mexico desperately needed a new inflow of capital but lacked the political stability to undertake stringent economic adjustments. Unable to stomach a strictly financial solution to the debt problem, Mexico attempted to link its debt servicing with open Northern markets.

In the 1986–1987 negotiations, Mexico faced a large group of disunified banks. The less-exposed banks were willing to suffer immediate losses and withdraw from Mexico altogether. But the core group of large over-exposed banks, fearing free-riding by their counterparts, assumed a tougher bargaining stance. Moreover, all the banks feared that granting all of Mexico's requests

[1] *Financial Times*, September 15, 1983.

[2] Beginning in June 1985, oil exports dropped to 800,000 barrels a day, half the volume of previous years. Prices fell from $30 a barrel in 1982 to $26.25 with a $2 freight charge per barrel for European customers and $26.75 with a $0.40 freight charge per barrel for Americans in 1985. In 1983, Mexico earned $16.6 billion in oil exports. Earnings from these oil exports fell from $8.4 billion in the first half of 1983, to $7.1 billion in the first half of 1984 (*Financial Times*, July 30, 1984, p. 4). Every $1 drop in oil crude prices represents an estimated $550 million annual loss in export earnings (*Boston Globe*, December 15, 1985, p. A85).

would set a precedent of leniency. Consequently, an agreement was not signed until March 20, 1987. Only strong intervention by the IMF and creditor governments succeeded in breaking the deadlock.

The March 1987 agreement did not alleviate Mexico's debt servicing problems. Soon thereafter, banks increased loan-loss reserves, enhancing their bargaining strength, but Mexico deteriorated both economically and politically. They maintained an uneasy stalemate, underlaid with high potential for confrontation. The prevailing system of debt negotiations seemed to offer little hope for a solution.

Taking a bold step, in December 1987, J.P. Morgan proposed that Mexico swap discounted loans against bonds. This proposal represented the first alternative approach to simply muddling through debt rescheduling. Such a novel strategy promised to rejuvenate negotiations after five years of rescheduling efforts that had done little to alleviate Mexico's crushing debt burden, but failed to dramatically change the terms of debt rescheduling in the short run.

The presidential elections in July 1988 tempered this new-found optimism. Charges that the election of the Partido Revolucionario Institucional (PRI) candidate, Carlos Salinas de Gortari, was fraudulent dramatically split the nation. His victory fueled both anti-PRI and anti-U.S. sentiment. Attempting to rally domestic support with a show of rejection of U.S. and European pressure, the new government refused to comply with the lenders' demands.

In March 1989, growing concern about Mexico's political and financial problems, and growing problems in other debtor countries, prompted the U.S. Treasury to announce the so-called Brady Plan.[3] This effort departed significantly from previous efforts in that it accepted the notion that principal and interest reductions should form a part of debt rescheduling accords. After considerable effort, Mexico became the first country to sign an accord under the auspices of this plan in February 1990.

To analyze the events following the post-1982 crisis, I divide the Mexican rescheduling process into five bargaining periods. The first bargaining period commenced in August 1982 with Mexico's cash shortage and subsequent call for financial rescue and ended in March 1983 after the signing of the first jumbo loan agreement. The second period ran from that agreement to the completion of the multi-year rescheduling in August 1985. The third bargaining period, marked by both geological and political earthquakes in Mexico, lasted until the final signing of the March 1987 agreement, followed by major situational changes in the fall of that year. The fourth period began in December 1987 and ran until August 1988. During this period, the U.S. had little incentive to intervene in debt negotiations as the threat to the financial system abated as a result of increasing bank loan-loss reserves. The chapter concludes with a fifth period of negotiations after Mexico signed a debt accord under the auspices of the Brady Plan in February 1990.

[3] See Chapter 1 for a discussion of the Brady Plan.

Background to rescheduling

Mexico's debt problems surprised much of the financial community. In the mid-1970s, Mexico had undergone a "crisis of confidence" that shook its financial system, stimulating massive capital flight and a dramatic devaluation of the peso in 1976. But by the end of the decade, many observers declared Mexico well on the way to recovery. With huge oil reserves and a strong credit rating at the end of the 1970s, the country seemed to be in excellent financial health. Although it had concluded an agreement with the IMF after the 1976 crisis, economic growth came mainly after Mexico engaged in massive spending and after oil sales grew rapidly.

Because of its apparently healthy economy, spreads on its loans from bankers fell rapidly after 1979.[4] Mexico also moved toward shorter-term financing (three years was now typical), relying on banks' acknowledgement of its good performance to get the loans renewed.[5] By 1980, Mexico's credit rating had improved to the extent that it could successfully raise $125 million at fixed rates for Pemex on the Eurobond market – a source of funding usually inaccessible to developing country borrowers.[6] Flush with petrodollars to lend, bankers found Mexico a good place to unload these new assets. As one banker said, "maybe no one's making a fortune here any longer, but you've got to be in Mexico. This is where the action is."[7]

Mexico's troubles began soon after the price of oil fell in the spring of 1981. Export earnings dropped as a worldwide recession took hold, and Mexico borrowed to cover the shortfall. In 1981 alone, Mexican debt grew from $55 billion to $80 billion. More importantly, maturities were shortened even further. At the beginning of 1981, only 5% of Mexico's loans had maturities of less than one year. By the end of the year, 22% were of this type, with most of these due in either February or August 1982.

In February 1982, the Mexican government recognized its impending crisis. An overvalued currency had made dollars and American assets attractive for wealthy Mexicans, and had made the external debt seem lighter than it really was. In an effort to stem the massive capital outflow that had transpired during the previous six months, and amid calls for exchange controls, the government devalued the peso by 30%.[8]

Mexico's negotiations for a $2.5 billion loan from private banks foreshadowed a larger impending crisis. Although the loan was finally signed in July 1982, it did not come easily. Many smaller banks refused to participate altogether; the largest agreed only after personal appeals from Mexico's finance minister.[9] Six weeks later, Mexico's cash shortage became even more apparent when the

[4] As Angel Gurria, then director of foreign financing for the Finance Ministry put it, "we have been able to raise more and more external credit on cheaper spreads." *Euromoney*, January 1980.
[5] *Financial Times*, January 18, 1979. [6] *Institutional Investor*, December 1980, p. 158.
[7] *Institutional Investor*, December 1980, p. 158.
[8] *Journal of Commerce*, February 18, 1982 and *New York Times*, February 19, 1982.
[9] *Wall Street Journal*, July 9, 1982.

country had to resort to raising a $150 million Eurodollar loan. This was to be the last unforced loan to Mexico for almost a decade and it came at a steep price – 18.5% interest.[10]

High interest rates and personal appeals were not the only factors that encouraged bankers to make these last two loans in spite of Mexico's increasing difficulties. Some observers felt the bankers were operating on the assumption that the U.S. could not afford to let Mexico go broke. Just as important, bankers later admitted that they were unaware of the size of Mexico's short-term debt.[11]

Three trends merit particular attention in the subsequent rescheduling efforts: the emerging cooperation among banks, which paved the way for a unified bankers' cartel in subsequent periods; the active role played by the IMF and the U.S. government; and Mexico's efforts to pursue linkage strategies to elicit U.S. action on its behalf. Mexico linked debt repayment to trade flows, immigration, and U.S. economic prosperity. Fortunately for Mexico, these links coincided with American economic, political, and foreign policy objectives. Consequently, the U.S. and the IMF pushed lenders to make loan concessions to ensure that Mexico would be able to continue with its adjustment efforts.

Period one, August 1982–March 1983: crisis and the jumbo loan

The first major rescheduling effort of the fourth epoch began when the Mexican Finance Minister, Jesus Silva Herzog, came to the United States and warned of the impending danger of Mexican bankruptcy and a domino effect on the banks on August 13–15, 1982. In the negotiations that followed, Mexico appealed to the IMF and the U.S. government for financial assistance. The banks, for their part, faced a collective action problem and continued to retrench. They wished to avoid a further commitment of funds to Mexico, but this very action was contributing to the outcome that they most feared: Mexican default.

Identifying individual situations

During the first period, we classify Mexico as coalitionally stable, deficient in debt rescheduling resources, and weak in overall capabilities (IS 7). The banks were coalitionally unstable, as well as lacking in both debt-related and overall capabilities (IS 8).

Mexico. At the onset of the debt crisis, Mexico's political system appeared to be one of the most stable in Latin America. President José López Portillo, whose term ran from 1976–1982, benefited from Mexico's strongly executive-based system, and entrenched as the party was in Mexico's political system, the PRI was able to establish a degree of popular legitimacy without resorting to directly repressive measures. The government's corporatist structures

[10] *International Herald Tribune*, August 11, 1982. [11] *The Economist*, December 11, 1982.

also supported stability. For decades, the PRI had officially integrated labor unions and peasants into the ruling coalition, and used its instruments of co-optation to keep potential dissenters in line. As such, the "revolutionary family," as the PRI's ruling core came to be known, had the capacity to implement stringent measures and defuse resulting political discontent. By the early 1970s, however, this system showed some signs of weakening, which was made evident by the student rebellions of 1968 and an increased level of political agitation during the Echeverría *sexenio*. Yet if we measure political stability in terms of the incumbency expectations of the ruling officials, Mexico remained stable; the PRI faced little opposition at this time, and as in all post-revolutionary elections, there was little doubt that the party's nominee would easily assume the presidency. López Portillo chose Miguel de la Madrid as the PRI's nominee in September 1981, and as expected, de la Madrid won the election in December 1982.

Throughout this period Mexico lacked the necessary financial capabilities to maintain debt servicing obligations. Massive capital flight, as much as $250 million a day at times, nearly drained Mexico's cash reserves by early August 1982.[12] When Mexico's Finance Minister, Silva Herzog, arrived in Washington, D.C. on Friday, August 13, 1982, Mexican cash reserves were under $200 million. Mexico risked bankruptcy by the end of the weekend if no solution was reached.[13]

Mexico was relatively weak in overall capabilities. It relied heavily on imports and recognized that economic autarky was not a feasible option. Silva Herzog recognized these structural constraints in the following way:

> On the part of Mexico it was very important to . . . have the necessary money to import essential products that we need to import, for instance, corn, which is the basic staple of the Mexican population. We need to import about 30 percent of our total consumption.[14]

In addition, in 1982, 52% of Mexican exports went to the U.S., reinforcing Mexico's dependence on open U.S. trade.[15] Mexico needed to maintain good relations with the U.S. and the American financial community.

Lenders. Throughout 1982 and early 1983, coalitional fissures split Mexico's 1,400 commercial creditors. Differences arose as a consequence of varying loan exposures among banks, coupled with disparate fiscal regulations among host countries. The large money-center banks with heavy exposures had stronger incentives to continue lending, in the hope that debt servicing would continue to maintain their profits and lead to eventual repayment of their loans. Less exposed smaller banks meanwhile were more willing to cut their losses. A clear division also developed between American and European banks; the latter

[12] Interview with Jesus Silva Herzog, IIS (1987), p. 2.
[13] Kraft (1984), p. 13. [14] IIS (1987), p. 3.
[15] IMF Direction of Trade, cited in Economist Intelligence Unit, *Quarterly Economic Review of Mexico* (hereinafter *QER*) (1985), p. 21. In 1983, the U.S. accounted for 58.2% of Mexico's exports.

were less enthusiastic about providing Mexico with new loans. Greater loan-loss provisions taken by banks in Europe and different foreign policy objectives account for this regional divergence.[16] Additional reasons for favoring non-participation included the following: insufficient interest rates, legal lending limitations, and uncertainty as to whether Mexico would honor its private sector debts. Fear of free-riding also discouraged many large banks from making significant concessions to Mexico and encouraged smaller banks not to participate.

The banks, like Mexico, lacked issue-specific resources. Their large loans made them highly reliant on servicing from Mexico. On September 30, 1982, for example, the 10 largest American banks had a total exposure in Mexico of about $14 billion for both public and and private lending.[17]

With respect to overall capabilities, a Mexican default would have bankrupted many lenders. Extremely high exposure, exceeding 40% of capital in 9 of the 12 largest American banks,[18] left the banks vulnerable. The 10 largest American banks possessed loan-loss provisions of only $3.6 billion for the entirety of their loans.[19] In addition, creditor governments showed no inclination to use force to help banks recover their money. Even the U.S., which had substantial interests in Mexico's markets, would not intervene with military force. In many cases, the banks had indiscriminately over-lent, and had few options but to reschedule loans in the hope of recouping their investments or simply cutting their losses.

Creditor governments and international organizations. During this period, strong incentives existed for both the American government and the IMF to mediate negotiations and push for a mutually satisfactory agreement. The U.S. and IMF were poised to intervene because of their fear of the possible repercussions a Mexican default could have on the international financial system. Moreover, given the long border the U.S. shares with Mexico, American calculations were influenced by a concern that a massive immigration problem might erupt in response to an economic crisis in Mexico. In addition, because Mexico was an important market for the U.S., trade interests would be damaged by a collapsing Mexican economy. As Paul Volcker, Chairman of the U.S. Federal Reserve, summarized American sentiment: "[F]ailure to deal successfully with the immediate international pressures could only jeopardize prospects for *our* jobs, for *our* export markets and for *our* financial markets."[20] In sum, this situation was ripe for active participation by both the U.S. and the IMF in this period.

Debt game and predicted outcome

The actors' individual situations resulted in the game matrix shown in Figure 11.1. On the basis of strategic interaction and in the absence of intervention,

[16] Aggarwal (1987), p. 20. [17] *Financial Times*, December 9, 1982.
[18] Cohen (1986), p. 213. [19] Cohen (1986), p. 37.
[20] Statement before the Committee on Banking, Finance and Urban Affairs, U.S. House of Representatives, February 2, 1983.

Cardinal Payoff Matrix,
Intervention Expected

		Lenders IS 8 HC...	MC...	LC...
	HA...	12, 0	9, 4	**10, 8**
Mexico IS 7	MA...	11.67, –3.5	8, 0	7, 3.5
	LA...	11.33, –4	7, –2	4, 0

Note: Nash equilibrium bolded; expected outcome with intervention underlined.

Ordinal Payoff Matrix,
Intervention Expected

		Lenders IS 8 HC...	MC...	LC...
	HA...	9, 5	5, 8	**6, 9**
Mexico IS 7	MA...	8, 2	4, 5	2.5, 7
	LA...	7, 1	2.5, 3	1, 5

Note: Nash equilibrium bolded; expected outcome with intervention underlined.

Figure 11.1. *Play phase, period one: August 1982–March 1983*

we expect Mexico and the banks to settle into an asymmetric outcome of HA..., LC..., the Nash equilibrium favoring the banks. The banks' dominant no-concessions strategy determines this outcome. Thus, in the two-actor game, we would expect Mexico to make the bulk of concessions in the negotiations. Turning to the outcome with intervention, given IMF interests, we would expect it to extract concessions from the banks in order to stave off Mexican bankruptcy. Similarly, American interests in Mexico should lead the U.S. government to pressure the banks. We would not, however, expect the U.S. to encourage Mexico to undertake less adjustment. On the contrary, both the U.S. and IMF will be inclined to promote standard macroeconomic programs involving strong adjustment measures. In sum, we would expect the outcome after intervention to be HA..., MC... rather than the two-player game equilibrium of HA..., LC....

The negotiations and outcome

The story of Mexican debt negotiations has by now become part of debt rescheduling lore.[21] Unlike most cases we have seen in earlier epochs, creditor governments and the IMF did not wait to intervene in the debt game after a period of time, but jumped in immediately. These actors' rapid involvement was driven by their concern over the implications of a deadlocked bargaining outcome for both the banks' solvency and Mexico's economy.

On August 13, 1982, Mexican Finance Minister Silva Herzog met with U.S. Deputy Treasury Secretary R.T. McNamar, Managing Director of the IMF Jacques de Larosière, Chairman of the Federal Reserve Paul Volcker, and then Secretary of the Treasury Donald Regan in quick succession. His message was that Mexico could no longer meet its obligations and needed immediate help.[22]

Although sympathetic, de Larosière insisted that Mexico would have to acknowledge any help provided by the IMF, and insisted that Silva immediately begin work toward developing an economic adjustment program.[23] For his part, Volcker telephoned the major central banks about an impending $1.5 billion loan, of which the Fed had agreed to put up half. Meanwhile, the Mexicans called the heads of Chase, Citibank, Morgan, and Bank of America. A meeting was arranged for the following week.[24]

Silva then turned to Regan directly to solve the cash flow problem. After tough negotiations, the U.S. Treasury agreed to provide $2 billion in cash: $1 billion as prepayment for Mexican oil and $1 billion in credit toward U.S. food exports to Mexico.[25] Taking advantage of Mexico's vulnerability, the U.S. government drove a hard bargain, securing a $50 million negotiation fee and 20% discount on the oil.[26]

On August 18, 1982, the Federal Reserve called a group of central bank deputies to an emergency meeting at the Bank for International Settlements (BIS) in Basel. The central bankers decided to give Mexico a $1.85 billion credit, of which the U.S. agreed to contribute $925 million. The bridge loan was to be released in three tranches with disbursement of the first third hinging on the negotiation results between Mexico and the IMF over austerity measures.[27]

The U.S. government and the IMF also pressured commercial banks to participate in a loan to Mexico. On August 20, Silva Herzog met with an advisory committee of Mexico's bankers and then with over 800 bankers in New York,

[21] The best published source on the negotiations is Kraft (1984). The discussion of the first period's negotiations relies heavily on this work.
[22] Delamaide (1983), p. 1. [23] Kraft (1984), p. 7. [24] Delamaide (1983), p. 3.
[25] *Washington Post*, August 15, 1982. [26] Kraft (1984), pp. 15–16. [27] Kraft (1984), p. 18.

requesting a 90-day moratorium on principal repayments; Anthony Solomon, head of the New York Fed, pressured the banks to cooperate with the Mexican financing program.[28]

Although many bankers had doubts about Mexico's efforts, the advisory committee quickly began to work toward ensuring that the moratorium would not create havoc. With Mexico's cooperation, the committee urged all banks who were involved to roll over their debts, arranged to keep interbank lines open, and worked with the Federal Reserve to keep open the Pemex $4 billion line of credit. Meanwhile, Mexico continued to negotiate with the IMF and appeared to be on the verge of concluding an agreement by the end of August when President López Portillo suddenly threw a wrench into the negotiations.

On September 1, with his eye on the history books, Portillo nationalized all Mexican banks, and imposed exchange controls. He also appointed Carlos Tello Macías, an opponent of the IMF's programs, as director of Mexico's Central Bank. Tello replaced Miguel Mancera, who had shared Silva Herzog's support for an austerity program.[29] These announcements immediately undermined depositors' confidence in Mexico's financial stability, and led to a run on New York branches of Mexican banks. Soon out of cash, these branches turned to the American banks that represented them at the New York clearinghouse. The whole clearinghouse system was soon jeopardized, and the Fed had to step in to avoid a major crisis. Paul Volcker and other central bankers immediately pressured the Mexican government to ask Mexican banks to refuse to honor their obligations in the interbank market, in order to prevent money advanced to Mexico through the BIS deal from leaking out through interbank channels. Moreover, the central bankers halted their credit to pressure Mexico to settle with the IMF.[30]

In a conciliatory move toward its creditors, in mid-September Mexico rejected an opportunity to bolster its ties with OPEC. Saudi Arabia approached Mexico toward the end of August offering to lend $12 billion at a concessionary interest rate – in exchange for a commitment on Mexico's part to control its oil output and raise prices. But by early October, Mexico had rejected this overture. As one source reported, in addition to fears of losing its independence, Mexico had decided not to pursue this course because it did not want to "fall foul of the U.S. by joining OPEC at the very moment when it needs all the trade and financial concessions it can extract from Washington."[31]

Negotiations with the IMF resumed in October. Tello pressed for exchange controls, low interest rates, wage increases, and higher government spending,[32] but the IMF stood firm and isolated Tello from President-elect Salinas and Silva, the other main figures on the Mexican negotiating team. De Larosière met

[28] See Kraft (1984), pp. 21–22 for details.
[29] *Wall Street Journal*, September 3, 1982 and September 7, 1982.
[30] *Financial Times*, September 9, 1982.
[31] *Financial Times*, October 4, 1982. On the proposed loan, see also the September 18, 1982 issue.
[32] Kraft (1984), p. 45.

with each separately, assuring them that the IMF would not consent to Tello's demands.[33]

The meetings proved to be effective: on November 10, 1982, the IMF and Mexico reached an agreement. In return for a $3.92 billion credit, Mexico agreed to five concessions: (1) to reduce the budget deficit from 16.5% of GDP in 1982 to 8.5% in 1983, 5.5% in 1984, 3.5% in 1985, and near 0% in 1986; (2) to phase out the triple exchange rate system and allow interest rates to rise; (3) to increase the trade surplus to $8–10 billion; (4) to reduce inflation; and (5) to cut the current account deficit.[34]

Armed with this agreement, Mexico asked the banks to extend the 90-day moratorium. The banks initially balked. Large banks were upset because Mexico had been paying off smaller banks at their expense in the interbank market.[35] Moreover, the banks expressed concern that private companies in Mexico were unable to secure the foreign exchange they needed for their own debt servicing to a number of these creditor banks.

Mexico promised to address both of these issues. Aware of the pressure from banks on Mexico, the IMF feared that its funds would be diverted to the banks as they had been in a 1979 rescheduling arrangement with Turkey.[36] To prevent such a recurrence, de Larosière chose to impose the equivalent of a conditionality program on the banks: on November 16, he told the banks' advisory committee that if they did not commit to providing $5 billion in additional loans by December 15, he would not ask the directors of the IMF to accept the Mexican accords.[37] During the next few days the Fed joined the IMF's efforts. It stressed "the strongest kind of community of interest among borrowers and lenders,"[38] and hinted at possible catastrophic consequences if bankers refused to cooperate. With the stick dangled a carrot: Volcker indicated that new loans would not be "subject to supervisory criticism" – thus removing bankers' fear that regulators would come after them if they agreed to new lending.[39]

On December 8, the advisory committee and Mexico agreed to a new package. It called for a new $5 billion jumbo loan, to be repaid in six years, with a three-year grace period, at an interest rate of 2.125% over the U.S. prime rate or 2.25% over the London Interbank Offered Rate (LIBOR), topped by a 1.25% fee.[40] Twenty billion dollars of debt owed by Mexico from August 1982 to the end of 1984 would be rescheduled and repaid over eight years with a grace period of four years at an interest rate of 1.875% over LIBOR and a fee of 1%.[41]

[33] Kraft (1984), pp. 45–46.
[34] *Euromoney*, March 1983 and July 1983; *The Economist*, July 16, 1983.
[35] *Financial Times*, September 8, 1982 and Kraft (1984), p. 47.
[36] For a discussion of this problem, see Aggarwal (1987), p. 40.
[37] Although this IMF strategy was unprecedented, the notion of a bank-government joint effort to bail out a debtor was something that de Larosière was familiar with. In his previous role as head of the French Treasury, he had successfully developed such programs with French companies who faced bankruptcy. Interview with a French government official.
[38] Kraft (1984), p. 49. [39] *Euromoney*, January 1983, p. 39.
[40] *Wall Street Journal*, February 25, 1983.
[41] *International Herald Tribune*, December 15, 1982.

Even though the proposed agreement was to involve slightly higher interest rates, such meager increases did not in themselves secure participation from the reluctant smaller banks. In fact, avoiding the free-rider problem and ensuring active lending from all banks proved to be difficult. In the end, the IMF and creditor governments stepped up the pressure to secure contributions from all of the banks involved.

The $5 billion loan was an additional 7% of each bank's outstanding loan(s) to Mexico. Pressure on recalcitrant banks came from several sources. In the U.S., for example, the Federal Reserve pushed a number of bankers to lend, even though technically it did not have the legal authority to force contributions. But as one U.S. Federal Reserve official summarized the issue: "Whatever their legal rights, banks don't want to annoy Federal Reserve. It pays to maintain good relations with the Fed."[42] Similar pressure was exerted by the Bank of England and other European central bankers on their banks. Moreover, the larger banks themselves were able to pressure regional banks, which in turn exerted pressure on the smaller banks.[43]

Through steady work and pressure by central bankers, the IMF, and Mexico, about $4.3 of the $5 billion was raised by the middle of December 1982. On this basis, in December the IMF approved the adjustment program it had negotiated with Mexico. By the end of February 1983, prospects for an agreement improved following a bridge loan of $433 million by the large banks. The final agreement, signed on March 3, 1983, involved 530 banks.

In sum, by the end of the first period of negotiations, the outcome was one of high adjustment by Mexico and some concessions by the banks. The banks did not forgive any of their loans to Mexico nor did they reduce interest rates. In fact, they even managed to secure additional rescheduling fees, a move creditor governments and the IMF would strongly criticize in subsequent negotiations. But they did extend a large loan to Mexico at a time when no one else was willing to lend.

Summary. Mexico faced a crisis of major proportions by August 1982. As capital flight accelerated, the Central Bank found itself on the verge of bankruptcy. Rather than seeking negotiations directly with the banks, the Mexican government immediately turned to the U.S. to secure a bridge loan and then a funding agreement from the IMF. Normally, banks choose whether and how to reschedule a country's loans after that country signs an IMF agreement. But in this case, the IMF turned the tables on the recalcitrant banks. Concerned about the implications of a possible Mexican default, and aware that the banks were likely to attempt to free-ride on the IMF by pressing for debt servicing without any further loan advances of their own, de Larosière threatened not to

[42] Interview with a U.S. Federal Reserve official.

[43] For a discussion of this process, see Kraft (1984), pp. 52–54; Lipson (1985), Aggarwal (1987), Chapter 3.

proceed with an IMF program in the absence of a guaranteed loan of $5 billion from the banks.

Taking the likelihood of intervention into account, the model led us to expect an outcome of high adjustment by Mexico and some concessions from the banks. As we expected, the Mexicans did indeed agree to a high degree of adjustment in their IMF program. The banks, forced by the creditor governments and the IMF, also made real concessions to Mexico in the form of loans they were otherwise reluctant to make.

Situational changes

Mexico's lack of financial resources, reliance on food imports, and general overall weakness severely limited its bargaining power. At the same time, the PRI's strong coalitional base enabled Mexico to adjust its economy – as long as banks continued to allocate new funds. Because the U.S. and the IMF were both concerned about the stability of the financial system, and because the U.S. worried about the broader repercussions of Mexican political instability, these actors were highly receptive to requests for aid by the Mexican government. This appeal to allies did not directly change Mexico's individual situation but constituted Mexico's main effort to improve its individual situation during the period. The cost of this tentative alliance was a severe austerity plan with deep budget reductions. The Mexicans would, of course, have preferred less economic adjustment and more concessions from the banks, but the U.S. and IMF strongly believed that no funds should be forthcoming without major adjustment efforts by debtors. They promised additional lending to ease Mexico's adjustment burden.

With respect to lenders, the banks unified and moved toward greater coalitional strength toward the end of the period. Through appeals to norms, threats to cut off correspondent relationships with recalcitrant banks, and an alliance with the IMF and creditor governments, the 13-member advisory committee of large banks cajoled and coerced the smaller banks into supporting the rescheduling agreements negotiated by the committee with Mexico. The banks as a group fared fairly well in this period, but financially, they continued to be at risk and were unable to alter their overall capabilities. As we shall see, however, the Mexicans were particularly interested in altering their individual situation because of their mediocre payoff. These efforts focused particularly on cartel formation with other debtors, as we shall see in the next period.

Period two, March 1983–August 1985: the roller-coaster recovery

Following the successful negotiation of the $5 billion jumbo loan, Mexico continued to try to reschedule the principal payments it owed. At the same time, it pursued the adjustment program while managing to greatly increase its export surplus. By May 1983, Mexico had received the IMF's seal of approval that it was complying with the terms of the standby agreement. Optimism about the success of the rescheduling effort proved to be premature, however, as oil prices fell and capital flight increased. In 1985, after mid-term senatorial elections brought disputed PRI victories, Mexico's economic and political problems became more severe. For their part, having become more unified through the actions of the advisory committee of leading banks and its allies, the banks became less fearful of free-riders. Moreover, intervention by the IMF and the U.S. stabilized the bargaining process to prevent both actors from balking to gain an advantage.

The negotiations in the second period consist of two rounds. The first lasted from March through December 1983 and the second from then until August 1985.

Identifying individual situations

During this period Mexico remained coalitionally stable, deficient in debt-related resources, and weak in overall capabilities (IS 7). The actions of the advisory committee of leading banks toward the end of the last period had stabilized the banks' coalition, but they still lacked debt rescheduling resources and overall capabilities (IS 7).

Mexico. Although most observers of Mexico's political system considered it stable, many expected some degree of political unrest as Mexico attempted to adjust its economy under IMF auspices. As Jesus Silva Herzog put it, "everybody thought when [Mexico] launched the austerity program in 1983 and when [it] maintained it in 1984 that [it was] going to be facing serious political and social problems."[44] Yet as Silva noted, "probably my biggest surprise has been the degree of political and social solidarity of the Mexican people."[45]

This stability was rooted not only in the PRI's "tentacular hold on every last corner of Mexican society,"[46] but also in the generally cooperative attitude of organized Mexican labor.[47] In the words of President de la Madrid, their attitude was "exceptionally responsible and mature in the great economic crisis."[48] The key actor in this labor stability was Fidel Velásquez, leader of the large labor central, Confederación de Trabajadores Mexicanos (CTM). In the past, he had proven to be compliant with respect to government demands for wage restraint. In this case, however, although the CTM initially supported austerity measures, the tiny increase in wages compared to the high levels of inflation and unemployment spurred large protests and a call for a strike on June 5, 1983. In an effort to dilute the CTM's power by decentralizing organized labor, President Miguel de la Madrid changed the registration rules, permitting rival groups such as the Revolutionary Confederation of Workers and Peasants (CROC) and the Mexican Regional Labor Confederation (CROM) to organize legally. As a result,

[44] IIS, p. 7. [45] IIS, p. 7. [46] *Financial Times*, May 24, 1983.
[47] On the relationship of labor to the PRI, see Collier (1992).
[48] *Business Week*, October 1, 1984, p. 79.

the CTM was unable to forge a consensus on an appropriate wage rates policy at the Labor Congress (CT, the labor sector's umbrella organization). Thus organized labor failed to present a unified front against the government, and ultimately the CTM resigned itself to austerity, continuing as a source of political stability for the PRI.[49] Velásquez stated, "we're still trying [to get salaries raised] but it's not possible in current circumstances. The economic crisis doesn't allow greater increases."[50]

After the mid-term elections of July 1985, however, the stability of Mexico's political coalition began to wane. Accused of fraud, the PRI suffered a loss of legitimacy in the eyes of many Mexicans despite an overwhelming victory. Moreover, the mishandling of the reconstruction following two devastating earthquakes in Mexico City further damaged the PRI. Combined with the persistent economic crisis, these factors would lead ultimately to an important situational shift by late 1985.[51] During the years analyzed in this period, however, we continue coding Mexico as politically stable.

Mexico still lacked debt-related resources – even though its cash shortage was less acute than in the first period. Primary international reserves increased from $1.8 billion at the end of 1982 to $3.5 billion by the close of August 1983.[52] At the same time, estimates of capital flight from the 1982 crisis to mid-1984 ran as high as $18 billion.[53] To complicate matters further, oil prices were falling, thus threatening Mexico's hard-won trade surplus. In early 1983, oil exports accounted for 82% of Mexico exports, making it highly vulnerable to shifts in the market.[54] Mexico's general financial situation remained extremely fragile.

With respect to overall power, Mexico's situation had only worsened. Though its special relationship with the U.S. provided Mexico with direct aid, trade credits, food, oil purchases, and a safety valve for unemployment, it had become increasingly dependent upon its Northern neighbor.[55] Not only did Mexico have to rely upon the U.S. for a bail-out, but urgently needed to run a trade surplus. Thus, Mexico had become dependent upon economic revival in its export markets. As we saw in the negotiations of the last period, Mexico refused financial assistance from Saudi Arabia because of its concerns about alienating the U.S.

Lenders. Banks successfully created a unified front by the end of the first period. Despite numerous differences in their national origin, exposure, and size, this cartel survived the jumbo loan of 1983 and operated effectively throughout the second period. Even if the agreements did not include every small bank, the effects of non-participation seemed to be contained.[56] This situational change reduced the banks' fear of free-riders.

[49] See Middlebrook (1989) for a discussion of labor's response to austerity measures during this period.
[50] *Business Week*, October 1, 1984, p. 86.
[51] The change in Mexico's individual situation (loss of political stability), ushered in a new period of negotiations, to be examined below in the third period.
[52] *Financial Times*, September 15, 1983. [53] *Business Week*, October 1, 1984, p. 75.
[54] *Euromoney*, July 1983, p. 44. [55] *Business Week*, October 1, 1984, p. 75.
[56] Lipson (1985), p. 224.

With respect to debt-related resources, the banks remained weak. The huge exposures, especially of the American banks, created severe liquidity problems.[57] Consequently, most banks increased their loan-loss reserves, and some began to take insurance policies against default (though some failed to adjust and went bankrupt). However, in the initial stages, these moves were insufficient to counter a potential Mexican default.

In terms of overall capabilities, although the banks had managed to secure the IMF's participation in encouraging Mexico to maintain its debt servicing, they remained highly vulnerable to a Mexican default. While the U.S. and IMF actively involved themselves in the negotiations, the banks were not given any financial guarantees against Mexican non-payment.

Creditor governments and international organizations. The smooth functioning of the international financial system remained the primary concern of the IMF, which ensured that Mexico would pursue an austerity plan. At the same time, the U.S. remained concerned over Mexico's economic and political situation. Negotiations emphasized the interdependence of the two countries. One foreign banker said, "I am sure the U.S. would do everything in its power to keep Mexico stable. And it can do a great deal."[58]

Debt game and predicted outcome

From our classifications, we arrive at the game shown in Figure 11.2 for the second period. In the two-actor game, both actors find themselves in a game resembling one of harmony. Both actors have a strong incentive to make concessions to each other, resulting in a Nash equilibrium of HA... and HC.... Taking into account the possibility of intervention as depicted in the second game, given the interests of the IMF and the U.S., we would not expect to see any efforts to discourage cooperative play. Rather, we would expect both actors to strongly approve of the strategies of the debtor and bankers in the two-player game.

The negotiations and outcome

Round one. After the jumbo agreement was signed in March 1983, efforts to reschedule principal on the loans due from August 1982 to the end of 1984 moved to the top of the negotiating agenda. In general, Mexico acted quite conciliatory, but did initially attempt to pressure the banks to reciprocate by talking about an alliance with other debtors. In April 1983, President de la Madrid put pressure on the banks by discussing a contingency plan "whereby the two countries [Mexico and Brazil] would join forces into pressing the IMF and the world's banks into accepting their own, more favorable terms of repayment of their vast foreign debts."[59]

[57] *New York Times*, December 2, 1983.
[58] *Euromoney*, July 1983, p. 44.
[59] *The Times* (London), April 27, 1983.

Cardinal Payoff Matrix, Intervention Expected

		Lenders IS 7		
		HC...	MC...	LC...
	HA...	<u>**12, 12**</u>	9, 11.67	10, 11.33
Mexico IS 7	MA...	11.67, 9	8, 8	7, 7
	LA...	11.33, 10	7, 7	4, 4

Note: Nash equilibrium bolded; expected outcome with intervention underlined.

Ordinal Payoff Matrix, Intervention Expected

		Lenders IS 7		
		HC...	MC...	LC...
	HA...	<u>**9, 9**</u>	5, 8	6, 7
Mexico IS 7	MA...	8, 5	4, 4	2.5, 2.5
	LA...	7, 6	2.5, 2.5	1, 1

Note: Nash equilibrium bolded; expected outcome with intervention underlined.

Figure 11.2. *Play phase, period two: April 1983–August 1985*

On the positive side, Mexico met its IMF targets in May 1983; moreover, due to an unexpectedly large trade surplus, it delayed borrowing the second portion of the $5 billion jumbo loan. In addition, by September 1983, Mexico had repaid all of a $925 million bridge loan and half of the $1.85 billion BIS loan.[60]

Lenders reciprocated by granting important concessions. In August 1983, the international banks agreed to postpone $11.4 billion of the $20 billion principal

[60] *International Herald Tribune*, August 25, 1983; *The Times*, September 9, 1983.

due between 1982 and December 1984 on Nafinsa and Pemex loans.[61] The agreement also delayed principal payments until 1987 and restructured the loans with eight-year maturities. In September 1983, another $8.3 billion from these public-sector banks and two state agencies were restructured.[62]

In December, the Mexicans broached the idea of rewriting the recently signed rescheduling arrangements with a lower interest rate. Though the bankers reacted unfavorably to this idea, Federal Reserve Chairman Volcker apparently pressured the banks to provide Mexico with an additional loan at a lower interest rate.[63] Ultimately, the banks agreed to $3.8 billion in new loans with interest reduced by an entire percentage point and lower general and origination fees.[64]

Encouragement for the banks to continue making concessions came not only from Volcker but from the IMF and the New York Federal Reserve as well. De Larosière argued that banks should provide credit "on reasonable terms in order not to compound unduly the balance of payments and indebtedness problems." Anthony Solomon of the New York Fed asked banks to "reduce the spreads on rescheduling to levels more in accord with the debtor countries' near-term ability to repay."[65]

By the end of the first round, then, Mexico continued to undertake high adjustment while the banks made medium to high concessions. Bankers still appeared to be reluctant to conclude more than a single-year's rescheduling. The game they were playing appears consistent with our expectation of a Harmony game, although there was some reluctance on the part of banks. This indicates less unity than our coding might suggest, some possible misperception of the nature of the game by the banks, or simply bargaining efforts to bluff Mexico. It might also result from anticipated pressure by creditor governments on Mexico, which would make the banks less concerned about being conciliatory toward Mexico.

Round two. By 1984, Mexico had secured two jumbo loans (the first for $5 billion and the second for $3.8 billion), and had managed to reschedule about $20 billion in principal repayments. But it paid heavily in terms of domestic economic costs. In 1983, GDP fell by 5.3%, industrial output by 10%, and real wages by over 30%.[66] While Mexico's immediate balance of payments crisis was at least temporarily under control, Mexico attempted to pursue a longer-run strategy to cope with the debt. In its efforts, it enjoyed the support of the IMF and the U.S. government. The large banks continued to work for maintaining the servicing of debt, thereby allowing them to avoid taking a loss on their earnings. For the most part, they were willing to participate in additional

[61] *Wall Street Journal*, August 29, 1983.
[62] *Wall Street Journal*, September 30, 1983; *New York Times*, September 30, 1983.
[63] *Wall Street Journal*, December 20, 1983, p. 2.
[64] *Financial Times*, December 20, 1983; *Wall Street Journal*, January 4, 1984, p. 26.
[65] Both quotes from *Wall Street Journal*, January 4, 1984, p. 26.
[66] *Euromoney*, March 1984, p. 38.

loans to Mexico as long as they were assured that Mexico would continue to pursue stringent adjustment measures.

Mexico continued its conciliatory efforts. In March 1984, it organized a $500 million bail-out package for Argentina to help it clear up its interest arrears to the banks. At the end of March, U.S. banks would have been forced to list Argentine loans as non-performing.[67] Such positive intervention by Mexico helped the lenders in two ways: first, it prevented the spread of serious domestic dissatisfaction among other debtor countries by encouraging good behavior on Argentina's part;[68] second, it enabled the banks to avoid reporting some losses in the first quarter. Some also saw this as a strategy for Mexico to achieve better terms in its own negotiations by assuming the role of regional leader, and in doing so influence the U.S. government to help Mexico negotiate its own debt.[69]

The IMF and the U.S. government did in fact pressure the banks to go beyond a single year's rescheduling and to provide Mexico with better terms on its loans.[70] In June 1984, the banks agreed to Mexico's proposal to reopen rescheduling talks. As one banker put it: "We still think [a cartel is] a danger, and we ought to be ready to do something. Those countries that comply with the terms of [austerity programs] . . . should be rewarded with better terms."[71] By September 1984, Mexico and the banks' steering committee reached an accord on a multi-year rescheduling agreement over Mexico's $48.7 billion commercial debt. The accord provided an extension of maturities up to 14 years, no rescheduling fees, and an end to the banks' control over the reference interest rate. In addition, the agreement softened the provisions of the 1982–1984 restructuring accord, spread out repayments on the 1982 jumbo loan, and included a currency-conversion clause to protect the loans of non-American banks against the rising dollar.[72]

The accord, however, had been signed only by the bankers' advisory committee. The package still had to be sold to Mexico's 550 or so creditor banks. In an effort to lock in Mexico's adjustment program, the banks secured the IMF as a monitor. The banks requested semi-annual rather than annual IMF reviews, and insisted that the results be reported to them.[73]

Because the Mexican government had proceeded with earlier adjustment policies, it won over the other bankers by reassuring them of its intent. Mexico made a "good faith" payment of $250 million in principal on the $5 billion loan, even though they were not obligated to pay until banks ratified the agreement.[74] Moreover, in February 1985, the Mexican government made new budget cuts,

[67] For details, see the chapter on Argentina. Mexico had also discreetly bailed out Costa Rica with a $50 million credit earlier on. See the *Wall Street Journal*, April 5, 1984.
[68] *Wall Street Journal*, April 4, 1984. [69] *Wall Street Journal*, April 10, 1984.
[70] For a discussion of this pressure, see *Wall Street Journal*, June 6, 1984.
[71] *Wall Street Journal*, June 6, 1984. Quoted as in original including parenthetical remarks.
[72] *Wall Street Journal*, September 10, 1984; *The Economist*, September 15, 1984, p. 85.
[73] This was an unprecedented move. IMF reports had customarily been restricted and available only to the government of the country under review. *Wall Street Journal*, October 10, 1984.
[74] *Wall Street Journal*, January 4, 1985.

including the sale, transfer, or liquidation of 236 state-run companies. Creditors of these firms were also permitted to trade debt for equity positions, thus fostering goodwill with financiers.[75]

On March 25, 1985, Mexico and the IMF agreed on the terms for the third year of the austerity plan. The IMF requirements were the most severe ever, calling for sharp domestic budget cuts. The last impediment to the multi-year rescheduling of $48.7 billion had thus been removed, causing Mexico's 550 creditor banks to sign the first part of the agreement on March 29, 1985. Rather than retreating, Mexico actually accelerated the adjustment process. In July it announced trade liberalization, cut the size of the public sector, and devalued the peso.[76] The banks agreed to sign the second part of the multi-year agreement on August 29, 1985.[77]

Summary. Consistent with our expectations, Mexico and the banks undertook relatively high adjustment and high concessions, respectively. In this Harmony game, the IMF and the U.S. government encouraged the final cooperative outcome. But on the whole, both the lenders and Mexico appeared quite conciliatory, although each made some aggressive moves during the first round of this period.

Situational changes

Following its relatively mediocre payoff in the first period of negotiations, Mexico was particularly active in trying to alter its individual situation during the second period. It sought to develop a debtors' cartel to counter the banks' unity. Success in such an effort would have contributed to greater issue and overall strength for Mexico. Although debtors held numerous meetings in 1983 and 1984, they failed to organize effective collective action.[78]

Banks quickly responded to this perceived danger by making some additional concessions to Mexico, thereby reducing Mexican incentives to play a leadership role in this issue. In this counter-cartel effort, the banks and the U.S. government were in accord. In the words of one adviser connected to these efforts, the banks and U.S. government "are dissuading the Latin nations from collaborating by promising more rapid treatment if they act alone."[79]

The banks attempted to increase their overall strength, enlisting the IMF as an ally in ensuring more stringent economic surveillance of Mexico. To secure this agreement, however, they had to reduce interest rates and lower renegotiation fees with Mexico.

[75] *Wall Street Journal*, February 8, 1985 and March 15, 1985.
[76] *Financial Times*, July 30, 1985.
[77] *Financial Times*, August 30, 1985; *Wall Street Journal*, August 30, 1985.
[78] Multilateral discussions took place March 1983 in Panama, September 1983 in Caracas, January 1984 in Quito, June 1984 in Cartagena, and September 1984 in Mar del Plata. See Aggarwal (1987), Chapter 4, for a discussion of why a debtors' cartel proved unsuccessful.
[79] *Institutional Investor*, July 1984, p. 233.

With respect to promoting efforts at situational change at the end of the game in period two, we would not expect Mexico or the banks to be motivated to change their situations because both fared well in this period. But Mexico faced a number of important shocks shortly before and after the beginning of the next period that altered its individual situation. Most important politically were electoral fraud allegations related to the mid-term senatorial elections in July 1985. Two additional unanticipated shocks dwarfed the election results: the September 1985 earthquakes in Mexico City and the sharp plunge in oil prices beginning in January 1986 (following a year-long softening of the oil market). The earthquakes not only increased the government's financial burden, but popular perceptions of its inadequate response further discredited the PRI.[80] The second shock, meanwhile, crippled the country's ability to meet its payments obligations.

In spite of the banks' high payoff in the period two debt game, renewed conflict among banks created a somewhat weaker coalition, thus setting up a markedly different bargaining game in period three. Some banks began to reduce their relative exposure and set aside loan-loss reserves. By accumulating primary capital while continually seeking to reduce or stabilize their foreign lending, these banks increased their capacity to weather a major repudiation. Yet in this period, the different pace at which banks took such actions began to destabilize their coalition without significantly improving the banks' issue capabilities as a whole.

Period three, September 1985–November 1987: confrontation

As important changes took place in both Mexico's and the banks individual situations, period two's outcome of high concessions and adjustments gave way to confrontation. Although the IMF and the creditor governments intervened to break the deadlock, they could not restore the cooperative attitude that prevailed during the second period.

Identifying individual situations

Mexico during this period was coalitionally medium in stability, deficient in debt-related resources, and weak in overall capabilities (IS 7/8). The banks were more unstable than previously as a coalition, and remained weak in both debt-related resources and overall capabilities (IS 7/8).

Mexico. After two and a half years of austerity programs, elections in July 1985 were a political litmus test for the government. The PRI hoped for a victory to reaffirm the electorate's loyalty to the Party and government; in fact, it became clear that in many parts of Mexico the PRI lacked popular support. The PRI's biggest challenge emerged in the Northern ranch and industrial states

[80] Examples of the PRI's inadequate response include the failure to deliver sufficient emergency aid or to provide temporary shelter. See Davis (1990), pp. 343–367.

of Nuevo Leon and Sonora. The main opposition party, the center-right Partido de Acción National (PAN), had strong grass-roots support in these border states.[81] In addition, the election drew much foreign press coverage.[82] Reports of abuses and electoral manipulations abounded[83] as citizens blamed domestic economic problems on the one-party rule and began to clamor for democracy.[84] In fact, many observers felt these irregularities discredited the PRI, foreshadowing the end of 55 years of "democratic" rule.[85]

The earthquake increased the PRI's political woes. As one observer put it, "As soon as the ground stopped shaking, Mexico's political system started to tremble."[86] In the aftermath of the earthquake, the government was slow to respond, and individuals took matters into their own hands, setting up community efforts to deal with the disaster. Organizing without the PRI for the first time, many realized the extent of the PRI's inefficacy: the loss of legitimacy for the party this occasioned was paralleled only by the PRI's problems after it ordered the 1968 military attack on students and workers. Moreover, many buildings collapsed as a result of shoddy construction which was blamed on endemic corruption of the system and further reinforced the public's disillusionment with the PRI. Finally, de la Madrid's failure to actively and publicly manage the emergency also undermined the PRI's political base.[87]

There was fierce opposition to the PRI in the July 1986 gubernatorial elections in the Northern state of Chihuahua as the PAN and other groups coalesced around the "clean-vote" issue. In addition to the PAN, four parties from the fragmented independent left, the Catholic Church, a large part of the private sector, and a raft of civic, professional, student, and peasant organizations joined the movement.[88] Once again, the PRI tampered with the votes to win the elections.[89] In response, the opposition attempted to spread this "clean vote" movement to other parts of the country.

These developments undermined the PRI's credibility and led to an accelerated rise in opposition movements, culminating in pressure from the PAN on the right and an organized challenge to the PRI on the left with the merger of the PSUM (Partido Socialista Unificado de México) and PMS (Partido Méxicano Socialista).[90] In short, despite winning resounding victories in the mid-term

[81] *The Times*, June 5, 1985 and *Los Angeles Times*, July 11, 1985.
[82] *New York Times*, July 16, 1985; *The Times*, July 16, 1985; *Boston Globe*, July 12, 1985; *Wall Street Journal*, August 1, 1985.
[83] See, e.g., *Los Angeles Times*, August 21, 1985. [84] *Wall Street Journal*, February 20, 1986.
[85] A commentary in the *Wall Street Journal* bore the headline "Mexico's Rigged Elections Hurt Its Image and Its Credit Rating" (July 12, 1985).
[86] *Wall Street Journal*, October 15, 1985, pp. 1 and 24.
[87] See the *New York Times*, October 4, 1985, p. 3 for a discussion of the PRI's problems in the aftermath of the quake. See also Collier (1992) and Davis (1990) for a discussion of the quake's effect on Mexico's political stability.
[88] *Financial Times*, September 8, 1986.
[89] *Wall Street Journal*, July 24, 1986; *Los Angeles Times*, August 13, 1986; *Financial Times*, September 8, 1986.
[90] Collier (1992), p. 110.

elections, the overt fraud it employed contributed to growing Mexican political instability,[91] leading us to code Mexico as being coalitionally medium in strength.

Financially, Mexico's condition began to worsen as its reserves fell and as the costs of reconstruction after the earthquake continued to climb. Mexico's reserves fell in large part due to a plunge in export revenues, but also because of import growth. The private sector imported capital goods to increase its production capabilities: this led to a 42% decrease in the trade surplus compared to the previous year.[92] Moreover, after the earthquake, massive capital flight to the U.S. occurred in anticipation of a probable peso devaluation and expropriation of empty apartments in Mexico City.

From an overall capability perspective, Mexico still depended heavily on world markets for its oil sales and on the American market for other exports. The price of oil dropped from an average price of $30 a barrel in 1982 to around $24 in December 1985. At that point, "a plunge below an average of $20 would have left Mexico close to default."[93] Such a plunge occurred in February 1986. For two weeks the price dipped to around $15 a barrel.[94] Because oil accounted for 68% of Mexico's total exports in 1985,[95] this drop posed a severe threat to its economic stability.

Lenders. The unified bankers' cartel began to face some internal divisions as well. In particular, decreasing loan exposures of some banks led to coalitional fissures, because these banks preferred to write off their loans rather than continue throwing "good money after bad." In October 1985, Mexico asked for a postponement of its repayments, but regional banks in the U.S. with low levels of exposure, and most European banks, opposed future involvement that included lending new money.[96] Banks disagreed whether to allow interest capitalization or continue making additional loans.[97] In July 1986, with these issues still in dispute, the large Swiss banks (particularly Mexican advisory committee member Swiss Bank Corporation) balked at an agreement. As differences based on banks' loan portfolios became more apparent, tension among the banks increased. One banker put it colorfully: "Why should we put up more money so . . . those other clowns can get paid out?"[98]

The decrease in loan exposures coupled with the increase in loan-loss provisions seemed to imply that banks had grown stronger with regard to debt rescheduling and thus could survive a Mexican default. But in fact, the increased strength was far from uniform. Swiss banks had taken loan-loss provisions equalling more than one-third of their exposures, whereas U.S. banks set aside

[91] For a good discussion of the repercussions of the 1985 and 1986 elections, see Collier (1992).
[92] *Financial Times*, May 22, 1985. [93] *Boston Globe*, December 15, 1985.
[94] *New York Times*, March 11, 1986. [95] *The Economist*, June 7, 1986.
[96] *New York Times*, July 23, 1986; *Wall Street Journal*, July 25, 1986.
[97] Interest capitalization refers to converting interest payments which are due to the principal amount owed by debtors.
[98] *Wall Street Journal*, July 23, 1986.

only less than 5%. Other European banks' loan-loss coverage was estimated to be somewhere in the middle.[99] In sum, banks essentially remained issue weak.

As in the previous periods, the banks' weakness in overall capabilities stemmed from their inability to persuade the creditor governments to force Mexico to pay its debt. However, other factors exacerbated their weakness. Falling oil prices necessitated renewed funding, increasing the size of the debt.[100] Faced with the disturbing news of a payments moratorium by Brazil, bankers scrambled to strike deals with other countries in order to avert the possibility of a domino effect.[101]

Creditor governments and international organizations. The U.S. government continued to show concern for Mexico's stability and its implications for trade, immigration, and drug trafficking. Yet, for the most part, the voices calling for a large-scale effort to help Mexico were outside the Bush Administration. For example, the Governor of Arizona, Bruce Babbitt, was an advocate of giving Mexico greater support, warning that Mexico was "the ultimate domino." He went on to complain that the Administration was placing too much pressure on Mexico and that Republican assistance to the PAN could endanger the PRI's willingness to promote a more open Mexican political system.[102] Others argued for more active American government intervention to ensure that the banks made additional concessions to Mexico to tackle the problems created by the earthquake. On the whole, the U.S. appeared willing to nudge the banks and Mexico toward continued cooperation, but remained unwilling to actively promote major reduction in debt.

For its part, the IMF continued to insist on Mexican adherence to an adjustment program. It still saw itself as the stabilizer of the international financial system and the arbiter of debt negotiations between banks and debtor countries.

Debt game and predicted outcome

We arrive at the game shown in Figure 11.3 for the third period. On the basis of strategic interaction, Mexico and the banks find themselves in a game of Chicken, with Nash equilibria at LA..., HC..., and HA..., LC.... In such a game, there is a danger of the outcome ending up as LA..., LC... if both parties play too aggressively. In view of U.S. concerns in the debt rescheduling process as well as the IMF's interests, we would expect both actors to promote a solution that avoided such a disastrous outcome. As long as it appeared that both parties might head toward some mutually beneficial accord, and that neither the banks nor Mexico were in imminent danger, we would not anticipate that the U.S.

[99] Such differences were fostered in part by varied national regulatory procedures. See *The Economist*, March 6, 1987.

[100] The plunge in oil prices led Mexico to request an additional $4 billion, that is, $8 billion in foreign capital. See *The Economist*, February 6, 1986.

[101] *The Economist*, March 3, 1987.

[102] *Los Angeles Times*, May 28, 1985, Part II, p. 5, op-ed article.

Cardinal Payoff Matrix, Intervention Expected

Lenders IS 7/8

		HC...	MC...	LC...
	HA...	6, 6	2.75, 7.83	**3, 9.67**
Mexico IS 7/8	MA...	7.83, 2.75	**4, 4**	2.5, 5.25
	LA...	**9.67, 3**	5.25, 2.5	2, 2

Note: Nash equilibria bolded; expected outcome with intervention underlined.

Ordinal Payoff Matrix, Intervention Expected

Lenders IS 7/8

		HC...	MC...	LC...
	HA...	7, 7	3, 8	**4, 9**
Mexico IS 7/8	MA...	8, 3	5, 5	2, 6
	LA...	**9, 4**	6, 2	1, 1

Note: Nash equilibria bolded; expected outcome with intervention underlined.

Figure 11.3. *Play phase, period three: September 1985–March 1987*

would pursue major innovations in the handling of the debt. We would expect more radical measures only if Mexican problems became more severe; pushing the outcome to one of high adjustments and high concessions could entail undesirably high costs for the U.S. if such an action destabilized either the banks or Mexico. In sum, then, given relatively balanced concerns on the part of the U.S. and the IMF and their desire to see continued rescheduling, a MA..., MC... outcome appears the most likely one.

The negotiations and outcome

Even as he signed the final part of the major rescheduling package in August 1985, Silva Herzog initiated a more aggressive approach to debt rescheduling. At the formal signing, he asked international bank regulators to be more "flexible" and warned that without bank loans, "countries cannot be expected to pay their full interest bill."[103] Moreover, he warned that "cooperation between banks and debtors will no longer be enough" and went on to call for interest capitalization and additional funds from international agencies.[104]

On September 1, President de la Madrid echoed his Finance Minister's more assertive stance in his state of the union address, calling for a "search for new formulas that satisfy, fairly and pragmatically, the real interests of the parties of the international economic system, making it clear that to pay it is necessary to grow."[105] In a separate statement, de la Madrid argued that "The domino theory must be kept in mind."[106]

These statements were clearly interpreted by the banks as an aggressive move. One banker commented that these statements were intended to "scare the bankers into living up to their side of the compromise" by increasing lending to Mexico.[107]

Meanwhile, the bankers also took a hard line. Before the earthquake, U.S. bankers warned that they were unlikely to meet Mexico's demands for new loans the following year.[108] But the Chicken-like nature of the game became evident in the real concern expressed by some bankers as Mexico allowed its budget deficit to grow. One said, referring to renewed discussions about a cartel, "Now Mexico is going to be the leader again, but in the opposite direction. The whole game plan is blown out of the water."[109]

The conflict soon intensified. With unfortunate timing, on September 19 (the day of the first earthquake), the IMF suspended the remaining $900 million scheduled to be disbursed as part of the $3.4 billion specified in the 1983 accord. It claimed that Mexico had failed to meet austerity conditions, including budget deficit and inflation targets.[110] This suspension, coupled with the earthquake and the anticipated cost of reconstruction, prompted Mexican demands for an interruption of debt payments and increased pressure on Mexican government officials to secure concessions from the banks. The Foreign Minister, Bernardo Sepulveda, in a U.N. General Assembly speech argued that "Latin America's foreign debt problem could not be definitively solved through a rescheduling that granted only temporary relief to the debtors . . ."[111]

[103] *Wall Street Journal*, August 30, 1985. [104] *Financial Times*, August 30, 1985, p. 1.

[105] *New York Times*, September 2, 1985, p. 21.

[106] *Wall Street Journal*, September 26, 1985 referring to an interview with de la Madrid before the earthquake.

[107] *New York Times*, September 2, 1985, p. 21. [108] *Washington Post*, September 16, 1985, p. 1.

[109] *Washington Post*, September 16, 1985, p. 1.

[110] *Wall Street Journal*, September 20, 1985; *New York Times*, September 21, 1985. See also *Los Angeles Times*, August 11, 1985.

[111] *Financial Times*, September 26, 1985, p. 4.

As growing sentiment emerged among many Latin Americans for a complete debt moratorium, banks realized that it would be difficult to secure an IMF austerity program as a precondition for new loans. The dangerous situation provoked a meeting between Mexican representatives and the 13-bank advisory committee on September 30, 1985. The Mexicans requested an extension on the $950 million principal payment due the following week.[112] The banks accepted this request only after both Treasury Secretary Baker and Fed Chairman Volcker appealed to the banks to cooperate.[113] But such cooperative behavior did not last long. After reluctantly agreeing to defer principal repayments, the creditors rapidly resumed an intransigent position and refused additional loans. Meanwhile, Mexico revised and increased its estimated needs for new loans from $2–3 billion to $4.6–4.8 billion.[114]

From the point of view of both the IMF and the U.S. government, the continued stalemate posed a danger to the financial health of many banks, as well as for Mexican economic and political stability. In Mexico, labor unions, student groups, and the Catholic Church called for a moratorium on debt and a "continental day of action against the external debt."[115] Strong intervention proved necessary to move both the banks and Mexico toward a more concessionary stance.

In an effort to push the parties to an agreement, the IMF reversed its plans to suspend the $900 million payment and resumed its talks with Mexico. Discussions addressed both the earthquake and the proposal of a new austerity plan.[116] Meanwhile, the IMF cleared the way for Mexico to receive $300 million under a disaster relief program, while the U.S. government disbursed disaster aid and declared that it was ready to provide substantial economic aid if Mexico requested it.[117] These actions not only demonstrated lenience toward Mexico, but they also reassured the bankers that they would not have to foot the whole bill for Mexico's misfortune. The next American initiative, a plan proposed by U.S. Treasury Secretary Baker, addressed the 15 largest debtors.[118] But as one source reported, "Baker had Mexico very much in mind"[119] when he presented his plan during the annual IMF meeting on October 8 in Seoul. Although Mexico and the banks perceived it as a positive move, the plan hardly affected the negotiation process. For more than two months after the presentation in Seoul, not a single bank made a loan offer.[120] The banks desired a firmer commitment from the multilateral organizations and continued to resist the U.S. government's lobbying efforts to convince them to contribute additional loans. Moreover, led by the World Bank, other international organizations opposed such a commitment before the IMF secured adjustments from the debtors.

[112] *International Herald Tribune*, September 30, 1985. [113] *New York Times*, October 2, 1985.
[114] *Wall Street Journal*, October 7, 1985.
[115] *Latin America Weekly Report* (hereinafter *LAWR*), WR-85-40, October 11, 1985.
[116] *Wall Street Journal*, October 9, 1985; *New York Times*, October 31, 1985.
[117] *Wall Street Journal*, September 23, 1985.
[118] See Chapter 1 for a more detailed discussion of the Baker Plan.
[119] *LAWR*, October 18, 1985.
[120] *Washington Post*, December 19, 1985. This paragraph draws heavily on this article.

Already seriously affected by declining oil prices, Mexico complained that the new loans would be insufficient. Mexico was in a crisis due to increased capital flight as well as the government's loss of credibility. Mexican officials speculated that as much as $15 billion might be required over the next three years, a figure that represented half the funding proposed for all debtor countries combined.[121]

Talks with the banks resumed in mid-January 1986, but were inconclusive pending negotiations between Mexico and the IMF. The banks only agreed to give Mexico more time to repay a $500 million bridge loan.[122] These developments further diminished confidence in Mexico's economic future, triggering further capital flight.[123] The Mexican government desperately needed financial help. Raising the ante, President de la Madrid presented a proposal for the negotiation of debt service based "on capacity to pay."[124]

When negotiations resumed in the beginning of March, Mexico demanded "unorthodox" financial methods to lower the repayment burden, while banks insisted that serious discussions still depended on an IMF agreement.[125] The U.S. government also made an IMF agreement the prerequisite for any emergency loan it might offer.[126] Consequently, talks between Mexico and the IMF assumed center stage. The parties reached a tentative agreement in July 1986. The IMF agreed to provide an emergency loan package of $1.6 billion in credits over the next 18 months. Contingent upon the proposed agreement, Mexico announced its intention to broaden its initiatives toward privatization and opening the economy in the spirit of the Baker Plan. The agreement called for lower levels of austerity and included a plan for additional funding if oil prices were to fall.[127]

The IMF's $1.6 billion loan was only the capstone of the intricate 18-month plan. Contributions from the World Bank and the U.S. – who came up with $4.4 billion – and commercial banks, who provided half of the proposed $12 billion in total funding, were also key. De Larosière viewed bank involvement as essential to the success of this package, and he applied increased pressure to force concessions.[128]

Still, an agreement between Mexico and the banks proved elusive. Extending a $500 million bridge loan, aimed at providing short-term liquidity to Mexico, became the first obstacle in negotiations. It was overcome when creditor governments and large American banks successfully coerced some large foreign banks, particularly the Swiss, to participate.[129] The talks stalled again over the spread of interest rates over LIBOR.[130] Only strong intervention by de Larosière and Volcker broke the potential collapse of negotiations.[131] In the meantime, short-term emergency credits kept Mexico afloat through August and September.[132]

121 *New York Times*, December 30, 1985. 122 *Wall Street Journal*, January 30, 1986.
123 *International Herald Tribune*, February 12, 1986, p. 6.
124 *Wall Street Journal*, February 24, 1986; *Financial Times*, February 24, 1986.
125 *New York Times*, March 4, 1986. 126 *New York Times*, March 6, 1986.
127 *New York Times*, July 22, 1986. 128 *New York Times*, July 25, 1986.
129 *New York Times*, August 14, 1986. 130 *New York Times*, September 26, 1986.
131 *Financial Times*, September 30, 1986.
132 *Wall Street Journal*, August 19, 1986; *New York Times*, September 18, 1986.

Nearly two months of intense bargaining transpired before the parties reached an agreement on September 30, 1986. The accord provided Mexico with the $6 billion from commercial banks, part of it linked to co-financing with the World Bank; the average interest rate was 13/16 of a point over LIBOR; and repayments of $43.7 billion were stretched from 14 years to a 20-year period (with a seven-year grace period on principal repayments). In addition, the agreement called for an additional $1.7 billion in a contingency fund should Mexico's economy falter.[133] The struggle, however, was not over. The banks had until October 31 to subscribe to the $6 billion loan. They failed to meet this first deadline, which postponed the IMF contribution.[134] On November 19, after 90% of Mexico's creditors had finally agreed to subscribe, the IMF began disbursing $1.68 billion in loans.[135] On March 20, 1987, 434 banks signed the final agreement. Some regional banks stated that these new loans would be "the last to any other Latin American debtor."[136]

Summary. At the end of this play phase, Mexico and the banks came to an agreement – but only after the U.S. and the IMF applied considerable pressure and offered incentives to prevent a possible collapse. The resulting outcome was quite consistent with our expectation of medium concessions by the banks and medium adjustment by Mexico. Although some analysts might argue that the outcome was closer to high concessions by the banks, aside from a small contingency fund, the banks did not make any special concessions to Mexico. More important, the banks secured guarantees from the World Bank and much greater involvement by international organizations. Mexico, for its part, came away with a much less stringent IMF accord and provisions for funding in case its economy faltered.

Situational changes

Mexico made efforts to change its individual situation during the third play period. One change was its decision to join the GATT in November 1985. Entry required lowering domestic subsidies, and reducing non-tariff barriers – moves that would eventually improve Mexico's long-run economic competitiveness. In the short run, the Mexicans hoped to improve their standing with the U.S., which had been pressing Mexico to join the GATT for several years. But these moves did not directly change Mexico's individual situation. In addition to this effort, Mexico stepped up cooperation with other Latin American debtors. The debtor group, Consensus of Cartagena, met in Montevideo. The communiqué that resulted from the meeting warned creditors that debtor nations would unilaterally reduce debt servicing burdens.[137] But as with earlier debtor cartel efforts, this group was unable to collectively carry out its threats.

133 *New York Times*, October 1, 1986; *Wall Street Journal*, October 1, 1986.

134 *Washington Post*, November 13, 1986.

135 *Wall Street Journal*, November 20, 1986; *New York Times*, November 20, 1986.

136 *The Economist*, April 11, 1986, p. 84.

137 *Washington Post*, February 4, 1986.

The most significant event that led from this period to the next took place during the change phase. Citicorp and other large banks began to accumulate significant loan-loss reserves after April 1987. Although these efforts exacerbated coalitional problems, they also gave rise to a change in the banks' individual situation by increasing their debt-related capabilities and decreasing their overall vulnerability. The banks no longer had to live in terror of a Mexican default.

Period four also brought an important domestic political change for Mexico. For the first time in the epoch, Mexico became coalitionally unstable as the ruling PRI party suffered an unprecedented loss of support and credibility. Opposition candidates gained an unusually large following in both state and national elections. Dissatisfaction with the PRI reached a zenith in the 1988 presidential election, which many people claimed the PRI won only through electoral fraud.

Periods 4 and 5, December 1987–July 1988 and August 1988–February 1990: a radically different approach to debt

The emergence of new approaches to debt rescheduling dominated the fourth and fifth periods. "Muddling through" had led to a dangerous game of Chicken and would lead to a deadlock in the fourth period as a result of Mexico and the banks' changing individual situations. The first innovative step toward coping with the debt problem came in December 1987 with Mexico and J.P. Morgan's announcement of a plan to retire up to $20 billion of Mexico's $105 billion debt through the exchange of loans for government bonds at a 50% discount. This move paved the way for consideration of alternative solutions to the banks' standard approach that had been pursued since 1982: granting jumbo loans and principal rollovers. Other banks, the IMF, and creditor governments slowly began to work in the same direction, but would only be motivated to significantly intervene in response to the growing crisis in Mexico.

Growing opposition to the PRI was the most important characteristic of the fourth and fifth period. The PRI's candidate, Carlos Salinas de Gortari, was seriously challenged during the July 1988 presidential elections. Many asserted that the PRI had cheated to secure Salinas's victory, a charge that fueled dissatisfaction and unrest. As Mexico's internal problems continued and the austerity program took its economic and political toll, domestic pressure to take a tougher stance toward the banks increased.

As the deadlock persisted, the U.S. became highly concerned about potential instability in Mexico and was thus strongly motivated to intervene forcefully in the debt negotiations. The Brady Plan, announced in March 1989, proved to be a major effort to change the pattern of debt negotiations, and led to an important agreement between the banks and Mexico. I consider both periods in this section in view of the relatively short fourth period of bargaining.

Identifying individual situations

Mexico became coalitionally unstable, but increased its debt-related resources to issue medium, and weak in overall capabilities (IS 2/8). It weakened financially by the latter part of 1988, leaving it coalitionally unstable, and issue and overall weak in capabilities (IS 8). Although the banks remained coalitionally unstable, they were now issue strong, and medium in overall capabilities (IS 2/6) throughout the two periods of negotiations.

Mexico. Without exception, the chosen PRI candidate has always ascended to power. The 1988 election was the first in which a PRI candidate was seriously challenged. The campaign, which began in March 1987, illustrated the PRI's continuing problems. The Democratic Current was a reformist faction within the PRI led by Cuautémoc Cárdenas, former governor of the state of Michoacan and son of the popular former President Lázaro Cárdenas. The faction advocated open, democratic elections. Outside the PRI, the opposition strove to achieve unity. By the mid-1980s, the PAN leadership had shifted from traditional conservatism to pro-business advocacy of an economically liberal policy. Led by this group of "neo-panistas," the right demonstrated electoral strength in several northern states during 1985 and 1986.[138] As we saw in the previous period, in two of these states – Nuevo Leon in 1985 and Chihuahua in 1986 – the PAN in fact claimed to have won governorships, but apparently lost as a result of PRI fraud. Increasingly organized and active, the right began preparations to challenge the PRI for the presidency with its neo-panista candidate Manuel Clouthier.

At the same time, unable to reform the PRI from the inside, Cárdenas led the Democratic Current's withdrawal from the PRI. The PRI defectors joined with the Unified Socialist Party, the Mexican Workers' Party, and three smaller groups (all of which had already merged into the New Socialist Party) to form the leftist National Democratic Front with Cárdenas as its presidential candidate. By the early part of 1988, signs of significant opposition began to appear, as Cárdenas was greeted with huge numbers of supporters and his campaign became the focal point for opposition to the PRI.[139]

As a result of the new alliances, three major candidates, Salinas, Cárdenas, and Clouthier, ran in the fiercely competitive 1988 elections. The PRI lost its overwhelming majority in Parliament and apparently clung to the presidency by resorting to ballot manipulations. Official results were abruptly postponed because of an alleged computer breakdown. In fact, it was not the technical system that failed, but rather the entire system of the PRI. Cárdenas, who officially won 31.2% of the votes (compared to 50.36% for Salinas and 17.07% for Clouthier), described Salinas's ascent to the presidency in December 1988 as a "technical coup d'état."[140] Thus, the 1988 elections further weakened the PRI's control.[141]

[138] For a discussion, see Story (1987) and the discussion in period three.

[139] See Collier (1992), pp. 111–117 on Mexico's elections.

[140] *Newsweek*, July 18, 1988 and July 25, 1988.

[141] For a discussion of the implications of the election, see Collier (1992).

Following the elections, the PRI stumbled in its attempts to regain support. As electoral opposition continued, the PRI recognized a PAN gubernatorial victory in Baja Norte, but refused to recognize victories in Michoacan of the PRD (the leftist party that emerged from the National Democratic Front with Cárdenas as its leader). In sum, the PRI lacked both the stability it had previously enjoyed because of its political dominance, as well as the legitimacy of a fairly contested presidency.

In terms of Mexico's financial situation, the worldwide stock market crash of October 1987 severely hurt its economy. The crash indirectly led to high inflation, a peso devaluation, and finally, the creation of a tripartite pact between state, business, and labor (PSE, Pacto de Solidaridad Económica). It did not, however, prevent Mexico from steadily increasing its foreign exchange reserves, which peaked at an estimated $15 billion in June 1988, thus leading me to code it as issue medium in the fourth period.

By the fall of 1988, after a drop in oil prices, a 60% increase in imports, and increased capital flight, serious balance-of-payments problems reappeared.[142] Toward the beginning of the fifth period of negotiations, Mexico managed to drastically reduce inflation (from 200% in 1987, to 99% in 1988, to a projected annual rate of 25% by March 1989). It decreased the fiscal deficit through spending cuts and the continued sale of state enterprises, and maintained a more realistic exchange rate with steady devaluations.[143] But by early 1989 Mexican foreign exchange reserves were estimated at between $4 and $5.5 billion, less than the expanding current account deficit expected to reach between $5 and $8 billion that year.[144] In order to alleviate this drain on the economy and realize 4% GDP growth (the amount considered necessary to create enough jobs for the expanding population), Mexico needed a reduction of net transfers from 6% of GDP to less than 2%.[145]

Because economic recovery depended on trade and foreign investment, Mexico could not afford to isolate itself from the world economy by calling for a moratorium. Mexico's overall position was further weakened by its dependence upon maintaining amicable relations with the international financial community. These relations were a means to repatriate much of the capital that had fled the country during the previous 15 years. Thus, as in the previous period, Mexico needed to negotiate to adjust its debt. Yet the once-quiescent, now-mobilized left clamored for a tougher stance.

Lenders. During both periods, past rivalries reemerged after five years of forced cooperation. In December 1987, Morgan's swap proposal exacerbated earlier divisions and eventually broke the core of the creditor cartel. The fierce rivalry among the large banks sharply reduced cooperation among the bankers' group.[146] Citicorp, for example, preferred to swap discounted debt for equity

[142] *New York Times*, November 8, 1988, p. A15. [143] *The Economist*, April 15, 1989, p. 89.
[144] *Financial Times*, March 14, 1989, pp. 1–2. [145] *The Economist*, April 15, 1989, p. 89.
[146] *Washington Post*, January 10, 1988.

rather than accept greater debt reduction in exchange for bonds for which interest was still not guaranteed.[147]

Despite their loss of unity, many banks increased their debt-related resources. Although some banks began setting aside reserves against their sovereign loans in 1983, most – especially American banks – waited until 1987 to boost these reserves.[148] At this point, banks could have survived a Mexican default; the cost, however, would have still been high. Citicorp chairman John Reed began a trend of increasing loan-loss provisions against third world debt when he decided to set aside an additional $3 billion, raising the bank's reserves to 25% of developing country debt. According to an official bank statement "the bank is now in a stronger position to resist pressure from Washington for a deal along Mexican lines."[149] Other banks slowly followed suit with Security Pacific leading the pack with 54% of its third world debt ($980 million) covered.

Banks had also become stronger overall, with a declining fear of default. The market has begun to react positively to the accumulation of reserves, and thus the banks became overall medium in capabilities.

Creditor governments and international organizations. Increasing bank set-asides for potential loan-losses reduced the systemic financial risk of the debt crisis. As late as January 1989, three bank regulators testified to the U.S. Congress that American banks could absorb the suspension of interest payments by debtors. Although these regulators would not explicitly endorse debt reduction, they agreed that the debt crisis had abated for the U.S. banking industry.[150]

By the fifth period, with growing instability in Mexico, the creditor governments' concern shifted from maintaining the stability of the international financial system to disarming potentially confrontational nationalist-populist movements in debtor countries.[151] The experience of Mexico's 1988 elections (in which Cárdenas's nationalist economic platform had featured a unilateral moratorium) heightened U.S. concern for keeping non-cooperative leaders out of power in Latin America. Cárdenas was particularly threatening because similar nationalist-populist campaign platforms were garnering strength in Argentina and Brazil as those countries prepared for presidential elections in 1989.

Debt game and predicted outcome: period four

Our theoretical model produces the debt game and matrix shown in Figure 11.4. In the two-actor game, we expect a deadlocked outcome at LA..., LC.... We do not expect significant intervention by either the U.S. or the IMF in this period, as the danger of a collapse of the financial system abated with the banks' considerably stronger position.

[147] *The Economist*, March 12, 1988, pp. 74–76. [148] *Washington Post*, January 10, 1988.
[149] *The Economist*, January 16, 1988, p. 82. [150] *New York Times*, January 6, 1989, p. C1.
[151] *Los Angeles Times*, April 2, 1989, Part IV, p. 2.

Cardinal Payoff Matrix,
No Intervention Expected

		Lenders IS 2/6		
		HC...	MC...	LC...
	HA...	–6, –12	–7.5, –7.67	–6, –3.33
Mexico IS 2/8	MA...	–2, –12	–4, –8	–4, –4
	LA...	2, –10	–.5, –7	**–2, –4**

Note: Nash equilibrium bolded.

Ordinal Payoff Matrix,
No Intervention Expected

		Lenders IS 2/6		
		HC...	MC...	LC...
	HA...	2.5, 1.5	1, 5	2.5, 9
Mexico IS 2/8	MA...	6.5, 1.5	4.5, 4	4.5, 7.5
	LA...	9, 3	8, 6	**6.5, 7.5**

Note: Nash equilibrium bolded.

Figure 11.4. *Play phase, period four: December 1987–August 1988*

The negotiations and outcome: period four

After Mexico and the banks signed the jumbo package in March 1987, little direct bargaining took place as the banks altered their individual situation. In December, J.P. Morgan ventured a new proposal. It proposed that banks exchange up to $10 billion of Mexican debt in return for 20-year Mexican government securities, whose principal would be guaranteed by U.S. Treasury zero-coupon bonds. Aiming for a discount rate of 50%, Mexico had hoped to retire $20 billion worth of debt. Though the new bonds would pay a higher interest rate (15/8% over LIBOR instead of 13/16% over LIBOR), the structure of the deal made it virtually impossible to realize as large a reduction as Mexico had hoped for. Under the proposal, banks were to submit offers individually, and the Mexican finance ministry would then decide which offers to accept.

U.S. government actions did little to encourage the plan. According to a ruling by the Securities and Exchange Commission (SEC), even if the institution's bid was denied, the mere act of offering the debt for exchange required American banks to either write off the difference between the face value of the loans and their bid price or increase their reserves to reflect this difference.[152]

The SEC's ruling made large banks especially reluctant to participate. Mexico had not missed a single interest payment, and upon completion of this deal it would be in an even better position to continue meeting its debt-servicing obligations. Thus, larger banks encouraged smaller banks that wished to cut their ties with Latin American debtors to participate. Without facing a loss of value of the debt they themselves carried, the larger banks could therefore reap the benefits of this reduction in Mexico's payment burden.[153] In addition, between the arrangement of the deal in late 1987 and the actual offer in March 1988, Brazil ended its moratorium and returned to the negotiating table. Thus, the debt crisis began to appear slightly more under control, and banks became less inclined to accept losses on the Mexican debt.[154]

Indeed, the debt auction on March 3 fell flat as the banks failed to seize this opportunity without arm-twisting. Only 139 of Mexico's 500 creditor banks placed bids. Of these, 95 were accepted at an average price of 69.77 cents on the dollar, retiring just $3.67 billion of debt in exchange for $2.56 billion in bonds.[155] Despite this disappointing outcome, Finance Minister Aspe pointed out that the agreement marked the first formal recognition on the part of bankers that a difference exists between the book value and market value of debt. He proclaimed that the deal "constitutes an important step in finding new mechanisms that will contribute to a fundamental solution to the debt problem."[156] Yet it was clear that regulation by outside actors would be necessary for future proposals to produce large-scale results.

Yet the U.S., for one, showed no inclination to pursue a new strategy on debt. Rejecting a proposal by James Robinson of American Express for a more global debt solution, Treasury Secretary James Baker warned that "It puts the solution squarely on the backs of the taxpayers in the creditor countries."[157] Following the Morgan debt auction, the IMF proposed a plan to reduce the debt burden of many IMF members (involving the IMF, debtor, and creditor banks) that called for the purchase of a portion of a country's debt at an agreed discount. The Fund would then give its own bonds to the banks.[158] Serious pursuit of major economic

[152] *Wall Street Journal*, January 8, 1988, p. 2. [153] *Wall Street Journal*, January 8, 1988, p. 2.
[154] *Financial Times*, March 5–6, 1988.
[155] *International Herald Tribune*, March 7, 1988. In fact, Mexico accepted all bids up to 74.99% of face value, dangerously close to the margin of 77% beyond which Mexico would get no savings at all. *Financial Times*, March 5–6, 1988, pp. 1–2.
[156] *Financial Times*, March 5–6, 1988, p. 1. [157] *Financial Times*, March 5–6, 1988.
[158] *New York Times*, March 8, 1988.

adjustment by debtors, monitored by the Fund, would be the price for this partial write-off. Opposition to this plan by powerful actors stymied any real progress in negotiations. In particular, the U.S. argued that the plan demanded too much help from Fund members.

In mid-1988, the U.S. government began to show signs of concern about Mexico, encouraging discussions between the banks and Mexico over a new proposal based on the guidelines of the December 1987 version. The tentative goal was to reduce Mexican debt by about $10 billion before December 1988.[159] But these talks failed, and the U.S. did not take any significant action to foster an agreement.

Summary. At the end of this period, the banks and Mexico remained deadlocked. As the threat to the financial system diminished, the U.S. refused to take any action to facilitate negotiations between the banks and Mexico as I anticipated. Toward the end of the period, however, the U.S. began to express some concern. This set the stage for more dramatic action as Mexico's financial position worsened and instability in Mexico continued, leading to the fifth period of negotiations.

Debt game and predicted outcome: period five

In the fifth period, we have the game shown in Figure 11.5. On the basis of strategic interaction, we expect Mexico and the banks to settle in a position of mutual intransigence. Each has a dominant strategy of no concessions: the Nash equilibrium of LA..., LC....

As Mexico's political system grew more unstable and its economy worsened, I expect the U.S. to focus increasingly on Mexico's plight. Moreover, as Japan's role increases, the U.S. might be expected to show concern about overall strategic matters. As a consequence, we might expect the U.S. to actively push the banks into high concessions to aid Mexico. I also expect the IMF to continue showing concern about the success of negotiations with its "ideal" debtor, Mexico, setting a precedent of aiding those countries that continue to follow through on their adjustment programs.

In short, we expect creditors' governments and the IMF to intervene to press Mexico into making high adjustments because of general concerns about debt repudiation. The emphasis in this case, however, should be on pressing the banks (whose payoff would decline dramatically with a HA..., HC... outcome), rather than on pressing Mexico, because its payoff would remain the same. Thus, we predict that the outcome will be one of high adjustment and high concessions, instead of the deadlock that is more likely to occur in the absence of such active intervention.

The negotiations and outcome: period five

Signs of a new U.S. attitude came in October 1988. As oil prices fell, and concern grew about Mexico's political and financial problems, the U.S. cobbled

[159] *Los Angeles Times*, July 2, 1988.

Cardinal Payoff Matrix, Intervention Expected

		Lenders IS 2/6		
		HC...	MC...	LC...
	HA...	<u>0, −12</u>	−3.5, −7.67	−4, −3.33
Mexico IS 8	MA...	4, −12	0, −8	−2, −4
	LA...	8, −10	3.5, −7	**0, −4**

Note: Nash equilibrium bolded; expected outcome with intervention underlined.

Ordinal Payoff Matrix, Intervention Expected

		Lenders IS 2/6		
		HC...	MC...	LC...
	HA...	<u>5, 1.5</u>	2, 5	1, 9
Mexico IS 8	MA...	8, 1.5	5, 4	3, 7.5
	LA...	9, 3	7, 6	**5, 7.5**

Note: Nash equilibrium bolded; expected outcome with intervention underlined.

Figure 11.5. *Play phase, period five: September 1988–February 1990*

together a $3.5 billion bridge loan to Mexico in the hope that this offer would give President-elect Carlos Salinas some breathing room.[160] Still, Mexico's problems continued to worsen.

Following discussions of debt reduction schemes in the latter part of 1988, Treasury Secretary Brady proposed a new approach to handle the debt crisis.

[160] *The Economist*, October 22, 1988, p. 70.

Following his March 10, 1989 speech, Mexico's Finance Minister, Pedro Aspe, met with U.S. officials.[161] Next Mexico submitted a letter of intent to the IMF, requesting $3.6 billion through the Extended Fund Facility. The request also included specific proposals for debt and debt-service reduction on its $57 billion commercial debt. Mexican officials argued that Mexico's economy had remained stagnant, despite seven years of adjustment and excellent fiscal performance in the previous extended arrangement, extensive trade liberalization,[162] reduction of inflation, and export diversification.[163] They noted that real GDP growth had remained close to zero. Like others, they felt that in order to complement successful balance-of-payments adjustment with growth, Mexico would need to reduce its debt overhang.[164]

The Fund concurred with the Mexican proposal, and in May 1989 the two parties agreed to a three-year extended arrangement including an immediate disbursement of funds from the Compensatory and Contingency Financing Facility (CCFF).[165] Most importantly, this unprecedented arrangement included debt reduction. Thirty percent of each purchase under the EFF was to be set aside for debt and debt service reduction, and pending agreement with its creditor banks, Mexico would be allocated up to 40% of its quota to support reduction. The Fund displayed its support of debt reduction by disbursing the cash to Mexico before the debtor had reached an agreement with its creditors.[166]

The World Bank became more deeply embroiled as well. In June, also before Mexico and the banks had reached any agreements, the Bank announced three Structural Adjustment Loans, each for $500 million, directed toward Mexico's financial, industrial, and public sectors to support economic liberalization reforms. By issuing the loans, the Bank aimed to continue the trend toward privatization of state enterprises and to improve efficiency in non-privatized public enterprises among other goals.[167] The Bank emulated the Fund's policies by allowing a portion of the loans to be put toward debt reduction.[168] We would expect such strong support from international institutions to bolster Mexico's

[161] *Financial Times*, March 14, 1989, pp. 1–2.

[162] In 1982 virtually all imports were subject to non-tariff barriers. As of April 1989, less than 20% of the value of all imports were subject to any form of restrictions.

[163] In 1982, oil exports accounted for 75% of the value of all exports earnings. For 1989, oil was projected to account for less than 33%.

[164] *LAWR*, April 27, 1989, p. 10. See also *IMF Survey*, April 17, 1989, pp. 114–115. For a transcript of the Mexican letter of intent, see *Comercio Exterior* (Mexico City), April 1989, pp. 355–359.

[165] Of the SDR3250.7 million package, SDR2797.2 million was from the Extended Fund Facility (EFF) and SDR453.3 million was from the CCFF. The CCFF was created in August 1988 to expand the utility of the Contingency Financing Facility. The CCFF portion in this case was more compensatory than contingent. In 1988, the decrease in prices for petroleum, coffee, and tomatoes, combined with damaged crops, necessitated more imports of Mexico's main cereal imports and increased prices of these same imports, causing serious damage to the trade balance. See *IMF Survey*, May 29, 1989, p. 175.

[166] *The Economist*, April 29, 1989, pp. 15–16.

[167] *LAWR*, June 30, 1989, p. 7.

[168] According to Bank guidelines, up to 25% of Structural Adjustment loans may be used for debt reduction. As such, $125 million of each loan was to be used in support of reduction. See *IMF Survey*, July 10, 1989, p. 211.

bargaining position in its negotiations. Yet the parties remained deadlocked through late July. In order to reduce its net resource transfer, Mexico originally requested a 45% reduction of either principal or interest on existing loans plus $4 to $4.5 billion annually in new loans for six years. Based upon overly pessimistic estimates of oil prices at $12 per barrel, the bankers thought this request too high. Their counter-offer included a discount of just 15%.[169]

Rather than easing the way toward agreement between debtors and creditors, then, the Brady Plan initially caused both sides to become more intransigent.[170] Mexico argued that to meet pressing balance-of-payments needs, it required a net savings of $6 billion a year through either new loans or lower servicing costs. The banks countered that only $2 billion in savings was necessary. Mexico sought a discount of 55%, while the banks offered only a 15% reduction.[171] In short, the banks rejected any diagnosis that made debt reduction a prerequisite for renewed economic growth. The key to recovery, they argued, was more extensive economic reforms on the part of debtors.[172] Advocating continued market-based, voluntary debt reduction, increased official financing, and domestic structural reforms as the appropriate debt management strategy, the bankers' position had not changed despite their improved capital stocks. It was further suggested that if debt reduction became mandatory, development capital would have to come from multilateral agencies or equity markets – not banks.[173]

Debt-equity swaps were another area of disagreement. Mexico regarded them as inflationary and inappropriately beneficial to foreign capital rather than domestic capital. It had proscribed such transactions in April 1988 and wanted to keep them out of the new package. The banks, meanwhile, made it clear that a reopening of the swap window would be a prerequisite for their participation.[174] All in all, by raising expectations without offering details, Brady's announcement had driven both sides into "sulky solidarity," making cooperation unlikely.[175]

By late July 1989 the stalemate was finally broken. That month Secretary Brady was scheduled to accompany President Bush to the G-7's annual economic summit. French President Mitterrand, who had proposed alternative strategies for resolving the debt crisis and consistently clashed with the U.S. over the proper handling of the situation, was to be the host of the summit. Bush Administration officials worried that Mitterrand would attempt to embarrass the U.S. over the debt issue.[176] Earlier, with an eye toward the summit, Secretary Brady personally telephoned the chairmen of the largest New York banks urging them toward settlement. The U.S. government thus accelerated its efforts to produce an agreement prior to the Paris summit to deflect criticism on its new approach.[177]

[169] *International Herald Tribune*, May 8, 1989, p. 11.
[170] *The Economist*, June 24, 1989, pp. 16–17.
[171] Economist Intelligence Unit, *Country Report: Mexico* (1989), p. 9.
[172] Institute of International Finance (1989), pp. 7–11, and passim. See also Horst Schulman's testimony in U.S. House of Representatives, *Third World Debt: Public Reactions to the Brady Plan.*
[173] *The Economist*, April 29, 1989, pp. 15–16.
[174] *The Economist*, June 10, 1989, p. 82.
[175] *The Economist*, June 24, 1989, pp. 16–17.
[176] *Wall Street Journal*, July 7, 1989, p. A8.
[177] *Wall Street Journal*, July 7, 1989, p. A8.

Strong intervention by the U.S. Treasury Department finally brought results. After four months of talks between Mexico and the 15-bank steering committee, Brady convened a meeting with both sides in Washington, and produced an agreement.[178] The July package presented Mexico's creditors with three options. The first option was to reduce the principal of the debt by 35%. This entailed exchanging loans for 30-year bonds at 65% of the face value of the loans. These bonds would pay interest at 13/16% over LIBOR (the same rate as before the discount). The second option was interest-rate reduction. Here banks would exchange their loans for 30-year government bonds with the same face value, but with a fixed interest rate of 6.25%. The final option on the menu was the extension of new loans in proportion to outstanding exposure. Except for the amount reduced, banks were to offer new loans worth 25% of their outstanding exposure, with a 15-year payback period (beginning after a seven-year grace period), at an interest rate of 7/8ths over LIBOR.

In both the principal and interest reduction plans, the principal on the exit bonds was guaranteed with U.S. Treasury zero-coupon bonds. In order to finance a guarantee on interest payments for at least 18 months, the IMF, the World Bank, Japan, and Mexico itself set aside a total of $7 billion.[179] The arrangement addressed the problem of free-riding banks by leaving banks that refused to participate in the plan to collect interest under the old rescheduling agreement, where they assumed the lowest priority for servicing. In the meantime, the U.S. offered to provide up to $2 billion to tide Mexico over until the deal was formally accepted by the individual banks and the agreement became operational.[180]

Two aspects of this deal are worth noting. First, the agreement stipulated that if after July 1996 the inflation-adjusted price of oil was higher than $14 a barrel, banks could charge up to 3% higher interest than the "fixed" rate. If the price fell below $14 a barrel, however, interest rates would be unaffected. In this case Mexico would receive compensatory financing from a selected group of banks and the IMF. Second, Mexico did agree to the resumption of debt-equity swaps. Under the agreement, up to $1 billion per year of debt could be converted over a 42-month period. Though this was less than the $3 billion ceiling the banks had hoped for, its reintroduction was nonetheless a triumph for the creditors (along with the allowance that banks capture up to 18% of the interest in privatized companies).[181]

Predicting that 60% of participant banks would opt for interest-rate reduction, 20% would choose the principal reduction option, and 20% would extend new loans, Aspe anticipated approximately $2.5 billion in new bank loans for Mexico during the subsequent four years. He also expected to receive a cut in principal and interest payments between $3.5 and $4 billion during the same period.[182]

[178] *The Economist*, July 29, 1989, pp. 65–66. For a discussion of the Mexican agreement, see Aggarwal (1990).

[179] *The Economist*, July 29, 1989, pp. 65–66.

[180] *Wall Street Journal*, July 24, 1989.

[181] *The Economist*, July 29, 1989, pp. 65–66.

[182] *Wall Street Journal*, July 24, 1989.

Yet such expectations would prove to be overly optimistic. At least 20% of debt-holders needed to give new money for there to be enough guarantee funds to make the plan work. The success of the Brady Plan depended on debtor countries having their interest payments reduced, while receiving additional capital inflows to finance the exchange operation.[183] In fact, $7 billion was set aside to purchase the zero-coupon bonds and guarantee interest payments on the exit bonds ($1.7 billion from IMF, $1.3 billion from Mexico itself). Mexico, however, could only make these guarantees according to how much capital it had. Because the provisions from the Fund, World Bank, and creditor governments were fixed, Mexico depended upon a sufficient number of banks indicating a preference for the new money option to "enhance" the exit-bond options. Although Aspe expected 20% of the banks to offer new loans, by October 31 – the initial deadline for bankers to submit their offers – only 7–8% of the more than 500 creditor banks agreed to lend more money,[184] and only Citibank had opted exclusively for this option. One reason for the reluctance to choose the new money option was that U.S. bank regulators had ruled that exit bonds would not require new provisions (while new money would). Thus, despite Mexico's offer of a bonus fee for banks that opted to provide new money by October 31, it found few takers.[185] By late 1989 all parties feared that official enhancements would not be sufficient to guarantee the bonds,[186] and they delayed signing the final deal until 1990 while making arrangements to find the necessary financing for the guarantees.[187]

Ultimately, in order to make up the shortfall of $300 million, Mexico agreed to put up another $100 million and the banks agreed to let interest earned over the first 18 months on the bonds count toward the total guarantee (with the assurance that after 18 months, interest would be guaranteed).[188] In late March 1990, the deal was finally concluded as $44 billion of loans were exchanged for bonds.[189] Angel Gurria, Mexico's key debt negotiator, said this was the first time in eight years that Mexico could think beyond the debt crisis. The U.S. Treasury viewed the deal as a way of preventing Mexico's debt from rising further (as earlier deals had done) and replacing commercial lending with increased direct foreign investments.[190]

Of the $48.5 billion of medium- and long-term debt covered by participating banks, 41% chose the principal reduction option. This cut the face value of $20 billion worth of loans by 35%, yielding a savings of $625 million annually, assuming then-current interest rates of 9%. Forty-nine percent of the banks chose interest reduction, meaning that nearly $24 billion of the debt would pay 6.25% interest, yielding an annual savings of approximately $700 million for

[183] *The Economist,* August 12, 1989, pp. 63–64. [184] *The Economist*, November 4, 1989, p. 15.
[185] *New York Times*, November 13, 1989, p. C1.
[186] *New York Times*, November 13, 1989, p. C1; and *Financial Times*, December 6, 1989, p. 7.
[187] *Financial Times*, December 20, 1989, p. 6. [188] *The Economist*, January 13, 1990, p. 78.
[189] *Financial Times*, April 5, 1990, p. 18.
[190] *Wall Street Journal*, February 2–3, 1990, pp. 9 and 11.

Mexico. However, to purchase the U.S. zero-coupon bonds used to guarantee the exit bonds, Mexico borrowed $5.8 billion from the World Bank, the Japanese Export-Import Bank, and the IMF. Since these are held in trust, Mexico's net debt does not rise – but they do not yield any income either. Furthermore, the costs of the borrowing alone are about $300 million annually.

Summary. Noting that the Brady Plan deal for Mexico was the first formal recognition by creditors as a group of the need for debt reduction, the deal was hailed as a landmark event.[191] Although some argue that the banks failed to make significant concessions to Mexico, in view of their unprecedented acceptance of significant debt reduction, a coding of high concessions would seem appropriate. For its part, Mexico's commitment to continue adjusting its economy and the need for it to borrow from international financial institutions reflect a decision to pursue high adjustment.

As we anticipated, in this period, the U.S. and IMF became more willing to press for a more enduring solution to the debt crisis. Responding to Japanese and French criticism of the way the debt crisis was handled, the Treasury developed the Brady Plan, which acknowledged that principal and interest reductions were now necessary. They saw that additional jumbo loans and rollovers without significant financial concessions would simply not do the trick. Under this plan, Mexico and the banks signed an accord in early 1990, thus breaking the deadlock that had dominated the period as a result of their changing situational positions.

Situational changes

During this period, Mexico continued its efforts to form a cartel to improve its bargaining power. In 1987, Mexico met with Argentina, Brazil, Colombia, Panama, Peru, Uruguay, and Venezuela to discuss new proposals to ease the debt burden. The eight countries pledged joint action to secure better terms of payment and quicker results from discussions with the banks and creditor governments. They decided to pursue three goals: (1) to unlink new commercial bank credits from adherence to an IMF austerity plan, (2) to link repayment to export-market access, and (3) to create mechanisms whereby the benefits from secondary-market discounts on debts are transferred to the respective debtors.[192]

Once more the communiqué failed to produce effective results. This prompted the meeting of seven of these countries in Punta del Este the following year to discuss the same problems. They complained of the lack of goodwill in the industrialized countries and the unfair attitude of the commercial banks.[193] They failed, however, to propose an original scheme for immediate implementation. Again the American government proved to be Mexico's most effective supporter: the U.S. promoted new initiatives and gave Mexico the financial capacity to sustain long, seemingly fruitless talks without slipping into default.

[191] *Financial Times*, July 25, 1989, p. 14. [192] *New York Times*, November 30, 1987.
[193] *Newsweek*, November 7, 1988.

Conclusion

Mexico became the first major victim of a triple whammy that included rising interest rates, falling oil prices, and a recession in the developed countries in 1982. It quickly sought to reschedule its debt as it neared bankruptcy in August. In the four periods of rescheduling examined in this chapter, the debt bargaining model proved successful in predicting bargaining outcomes. In all four periods, in contrast to negotiations in earlier epochs, we saw a consistent pattern of heavy involvement by the U.S. and the IMF.

During the first period that ended in March 1983, in the absence of U.S. and IMF intervention, we would have expected Mexico to make high adjustments and the banks to refrain from making any concessions, primarily because of their unstable coalition. The intervening actors helped a group of leading banks raise a large loan for Mexico and successfully brought the immediate crisis to a quick conclusion.

The second period of negotiations, from April 1983 to the end of August 1985, distinguished itself from the first by the presence of a stable bankers' coalition. This change altered the debt game to a Harmony-type game, with high adjustments and concessions the preferred outcome for both actors. In this case, although the IMF and the U.S. engaged in active monitoring of Mexico and cajoling of the banks during the first round of this period, they participated much less actively in the negotiation of the multi-year debt rescheduling agreement concluded by August 1985.

Prospects for cooperative behavior dimmed, however, by the third period of negotiations. The mild political crisis of the July 1985 midterm elections was followed by a catastrophic economic and political crisis arising from two earthquakes in Mexico City in September 1985. The PRI lost legitimacy by bungling the post-earthquake management of Mexico City, and Mexico's financial crisis continued to worsen after a precipitous fall in oil prices. Banks also became more unstable as differing debt management strategies, based on their varying national and financial positions, led to divisions on the debt issue. As a result of these situational changes, we expected to see a game of Chicken where both actors would aggressively try to pursue a unilaterally favorable outcome at the others' expense, with the danger that both might find themselves deadlocked in an outcome harmful to both. But fearing serious unrest in Mexico, the U.S. and the IMF pushed both actors into making concessions under the auspices of the Baker Plan, thus preventing a potential collapse of the negotiations. The resulting agreement with the banks involved large sums of new money, but it became quite clear to all concerned that the era of additional jumbo loans was nearing an end as bankers became more reluctant to continue lending. In short, the Baker Plan proved to be more of the same debt management strategy.

By the fourth period, from December 1987 to February 1990, important innovations by the U.S., based on a number of extant proposals on better debt management, led to a Mexican agreement under the auspices of the new Brady

Plan. Important situational shifts had made the prospects of continued rescheduling along old lines problematic. These included worsening political instability in Mexico and growing financial problems, and efforts by the banks to take loan-loss reserves to protect themselves. The resulting debt game proved to be an even stronger deadlock than in the third period. Following a relatively unsuccessful loan/bond swap proposed by J.P. Morgan, the March 1989 Brady Plan broke new ground in calling for principal and interest reductions as a debt management strategy. Mexico quickly began negotiations under the auspices of this plan, and after considerable difficulty with recalcitrant bankers, secured an agreement in February 1990.

In terms of situational change, a number of planned efforts proved at least partially successful. Although Mexico never succeeded in altering its overall capabilities through the formation of a debtors' cartel, its moves in that direction stimulated more concessionary behavior on the part of banks and active intervention by the U.S. and IMF. The changes in Mexican stability came about as a result of growing dissatisfaction with the PRI, but did not result from active situational change strategies by either Mexico or the banks. The banks made two significant efforts at situational change, the first being the development of a unified coalition by the beginning of period two as a result of concerted efforts by large banks. A second major change took place as a consequence of the decision by many large American banks to increase their loan-loss reserves in the fourth period, thus increasing their issue-strength and protecting them against a Mexican default.

By 1990, then, Mexican debt rescheduling had moved considerably away from the initial jumbo loan approach. With a growing recognition all around that banks would need to start taking losses on their loans instead of simply rolling them over, debt rescheduling in the late twentieth century now became more akin to the resolution of Mexico's other debt crises over the last 170 years.

12 The politics of confrontation: Peruvian debt rescheduling in the 1980s and 1990s

In this epoch, Peru was one of the first countries in Latin America to develop extensive ties with private commercial banks.[1] The Peruvian case highlights difficulties facing small countries in the international financial system. In 1954 Peru became the first country to sign an IMF-designed standby agreement.[2] Peruvian policymakers' coping strategies have varied dramatically, from orthodox "shock" treatment to cautious rebellion against the international monetary system.[3]

In August 1983 President Fernando Belaúnde Terry, whose term in office began in 1980 and ended in 1985, began a quiet moratorium on the debt.[4] He carefully maintained the front of a compliant debtor by negotiating with the banks and promising but not delivering orthodox adjustment. By contrast, Belaúnde's successor, President Alan García Pérez, in office between 1985 and 1990, condemned the IMF outright as a "modern system of imperialism." In an unprecedented move, García suspended payments to the IMF and unilaterally declared that Peru would pay commercial banks no more than 10% of its export earnings. By 1990 Peru was the world's "worst" debtor: it owed $950 million to the IMF, roughly half the Fund's total bad debts.[5]

We divide our analysis of Peruvian rescheduling in the 1980s into four periods. The first began in March 1983 when negotiations over a jumbo loan began, and ended in June 1983 with an agreement with the banks. Growing instability in Peru led to a changed bargaining game, with the second period encompassing the major rescheduling in February 1984 and the remainder of the Belaúnde Administration until the inauguration of President García in July 1985. The third period covers the announcement of García's "10% solution" in July 1985 and the IMF's declaration of Peru's ineligibility to borrow in August 1986. The final period runs from the deadlock between Peru and the banks from August 1986 to the beginning of Alberto Fujimori's presidency in 1990. A postscript examines Fujimori's efforts to "reinsert" Peru into the international financial system.

Background to rescheduling

Peru in the immediate post-war period has been described as "unique in Latin America for the enthusiasm with which export-led growth, economic liberalism,

This chapter was co-authored with Maxwell Cameron.

[1] Devlin and de la Piedra (1985), p. 383. [2] Scheetz (1986), p. 91. [3] Wise (1989).
[4] Webb (1988), p. 248. [5] *The Andean Report*, October 1990, p. 175.

foreign investment, and the general reintegration of Peru with the U.S. economy were welcomed and encouraged by policy measures."[6] During the first of two separated terms of office, President Fernando Belaúnde Terry (1963–1968) sharply reversed this pattern through expansion of public sector expenditure and the promotion of import-substitution industrialization to fuel local entrepreneurship.[7] Congressional opposition to reforming the narrow and inelastic tax base, however, resulted in a fiscal deficit that was financed by foreign borrowing.[8] By 1968 the government had attempted to implement several stabilization programs to rectify Peru's critical balance of payments situation. Throughout the crisis, private banks continued to provide credit, although always in line with the tough terms of the IMF standby agreement.

To reduce Peru's dependence on the international economic system, the military government of General Juan Velasco Alvarado (1968–1975) expropriated basic industries and mining to channel their surpluses into domestic industrial growth.[9] A major land reform reorganized agricultural production into cooperatives and destroyed the agro-exporting oligarchy. Worker participation in the management, ownership, and investment decisions of firms was encouraged through the formation of "industrial communities."

Initially, the attitude of commercial banks toward the Velasco government was cautious. One reason for this stance was Peru's nationalization of U.S.-based multi-national corporations and the subsequent U.S. economic blockade.[10] The blockade also stopped multilateral aid to Peru. Another factor that concerned the banking community was Peru's refusal to renew its standby agreement with the IMF – an organization that Velasco said had "trafficked in the misery of the poor."[11] Despite these actions, the banks continued to refinance past loans to avoid a default.

But the lenders' timidity of the early 1970s vanished after 1972 when surplus liquidity in international banking coincided with strong domestic demand in Peru. Responding to the emerging Eurodollar market, banks competed to expand their portfolios in developing regions. This development, along with the discovery of petroleum, suddenly made Peru an increasingly attractive investment site: as Devlin and de la Piedra put it, "The euphoria in banking circles was such that a former pariah became the darling of international banks."[12]

Less than one-third of the credit was invested productively.[13] Arms spending consumed a large percentage of the new loans.[14] Reforms in industry and agriculture did not produce the expected surge of domestic investment. An investment strike crippled the government's program. The deteriorating tax base forced it to continue heavy borrowing from commercial lenders to sustain costly development projects and the domestic consumption that was the linchpin of its popular support.

[6] Thorp and Bertram (1978), p. 147. [7] Scheetz (1986), pp. 106–107.
[8] Devlin and de la Piedra (1985), pp. 386–387. [9] Becker (1982, 1983), passim.
[10] Stallings (1987), pp. 270–275. [11] Velasco (1972), p. 91.
[12] Devlin and de la Piedra (1985), p. 391. [13] Webb (1988), p. 243. [14] Ugarteche (1986).

In 1975, Peru's financial outlook was increasingly grim due to the erosion of international commodity terms of trade, the overestimation of petroleum reserves, and the destruction of Peru's lucrative fish-meal industry. As the government lurched to the right, groups within the armed forces attempted to align with organized labor, unorganized shantytown and slum dwellers, and the peasantry. These social tensions weakened the governing coalition; in the end, an internal coup against Velasco installed General Francisco Morales Bermúdez.

To buy off opposition from within the Armed Forces, the Morales Bermúdez government (1975–1980) spent record shares of the national budget on the military. Fearing domestic opposition, Morales Bermúdez refused to go to the IMF and sign a letter of intent. Instead, he sought a balance of payments loan from commercial bankers without a prior agreement with the IMF. The bankers agreed to cooperate with Morales Bermúdez as a bulwark against the "military radicals" of the earlier period. The banks welcomed the opportunity to monitor the Peruvian economy. In the end, this effort at private negotiation failed, and Peru was forced to undergo a typical IMF adjustment program. Massive labor protest erupted, followed in 1977 and 1978 by major general strikes. Increasingly isolated and faced with mounting labor opposition and internal divisions, the military rulers set a timetable for the transition to democracy by 1980.

Between 1976 and 1978, the Peruvian economy adjusted under austerity measures initiated by Morales Bermúdez. But the renewal of economic activity after 1978 had more to do with the recovery of traditional Peruvian exports and new output in mining and oil in 1979 and 1980. By 1982 the international economy fell into recession, interest rates rose, and Peruvian exports slumped, throwing Peru into crisis once again.

Period one, March 1983–January 1984: rescheduling from weakness

The year 1982 represents the transition between the exuberant expansion and lending of 1979–1981 and the harsh rescheduling of 1983–1984. Peru repeatedly met with the IMF in early 1982 and finally agreed to an Extended Fund Facility (EFF) in June. In this agreement Peru adopted a set of economic targets recommended by the IMF in exchange for a $960 million three-year loan.[15] The EFF disbursement depended upon Peru's success in meeting the economic targets. Peru's reputation as an orthodox debtor, the support of the World Bank, and the persuasive ability of President Belaúnde's young team of technocrats soothed commercial bankers' fears concerning Peru's ability to implement austerity policies and stick to adjustment targets.[16] These strengths bolstered Peru's successful negotiation of a $320 million loan to Confide, a public financial development corporation, to pay off public debts and develop the country's infrastructure.

[15] *Latin American Weekly Report* (hereinafter *LAWR*), August 20, 1982.
[16] *LAWR*, June 5, 1981.

When the creditors were convinced that the government was willing to adjust, price became the main bargaining issue: Peru had to pay 1.375% over LIBOR (up from 0.875% paid to Morgan Guaranty for a loan earlier in the year).[17] The government wanted cheaper credit, but at the same time wished to remain on good terms with the banks and to distance itself from other debtors petitioning for debt rescheduling.

Even though Peru had secured an IMF loan in 1982, it still continued to experience difficulties. It had a total external debt of over $11 billion in 1982.[18] Peru's most pressing concerns were implementing the IMF-mandated austerity measures and finding the funds to roll over its commercial debt in 1983. The scene was thus set for negotiations with the commercial banks at the beginning of 1983.

Identifying individual situations

The Peruvian government had a stable domestic coalition, but was both issue and overall weak (IS 7). The banks, by contrast, were unified and strong overall, but were weak in issue capabilities (IS 3).

Peru. The democratically elected Belaúnde government was stable between 1980 and 1983. It succeeded in systematically dismantling many of the major reforms of the previous 12 years of military rule with little opposition from either the military or the Congress. The labor movement was "demobilized" under the Belaúnde government by the dramatic effects of the crisis.[19] The government's stability was also reflected in the regime's ability to enact monetarist policies that elsewhere in Latin America were part and parcel of repressive authoritarian rule.[20] A majority in Congress – assured by the alliance between Belaúnde's party, Acción Popular (AP), and the Partido Popular Cristiano (PPC) – enabled Belaúnde to pass important budgets and legislation. The president also controlled the political opposition within his coalition, led by Alva Orlandini, whose efforts to build a political challenge to Belaúnde were confined to behind the scenes maneuvering until the end of this period.

Peru found itself weak in issue capabilities during this period. Efforts to prepay old debts had used up two-thirds of Peru's $1.28 billion foreign exchange reserves since 1981. This effort proved ill-timed, because it coincided with a deterioration of Peru's balance of payments, the onset of the world recession, and the Mexican collapse. By June 1983, net international reserves equalled about $500 million – barely worth two months of exports.[21] Peru's financial straits were further exacerbated by the loss of one-third of the government's tax revenues after 1975, and $600 million in capital flight. Peru also ran a massive budget deficit of 10% of GDP. The financial system was thrown into chaos as

[17] *LAWR*, June 4, 1982. [18] Devlin and de la Piedra (1985), p. 390.
[19] Parodi (1986). [20] Cotler (1981). [21] *LAWR*, June 17, 1983.

exports shrank, investment fell off, and economic activity contracted.[22] Prime Minister Fernando Schwab blamed Peru's pessimistic economic prospects for 1983 on three factors: (1) low prices for Peru's exports, (2) unfavorable trends in financial markets, and (3) continuing disorder in public finance.[23]

In overall terms, Peru was also weak. Its GDP contracted by a catastrophic 12% in 1983.[24] The deterioration in Peru's terms of trade led to a commercial deficit that severely reduced its ability to generate revenue for debt repayment.[25] International terms of trade declined by 25% between 1980 and 1982; falling mineral prices alone generated $500 million in export losses. At the same time, Peru faced a dramatic decline in domestic agricultural production in 1983 because of natural disasters. Peru desperately needed international bank credits, trade credits, and access to markets for its exports.

Lenders. The bankers had a stable coalition during the rescheduling negotiations with Peru. However, they did not have a unified steering committee to present a common front in negotiations prior to March 1983. In early 1983, small regional U.S. and Japanese banks began to close down lines of credit to Peru. They were succumbing to the temptation of "taking a hit" rather than getting drawn into a collapsing economy.[26] Citicorp and Chase Manhattan quickly counseled the Peruvian government to "declare a unilateral moratorium on debt payments so that retreating institutions would be 'locked into' the country's fate."[27] The government suspended payments from March 7, 1983 until an agreement was reached between the Banco de la Nación (Peru's state bank) and 287 creditor banks led by Citicorp on June 30, 1983.[28] With this action, Peru helped create a stable coalition of bankers in order to guarantee that the banks would not defect from the rescheduling negotiations.

The banks were issue weak; they were concerned about their assets because competition in the 1970s had created a high level of exposure. By the end of the 1980s the banks had dramatically reduced their exposure, but at the outset they were still vulnerable to default. Many banks had competed for shares of the

[22] The April 15, 1983 collapse of Banco Regional Sur Medio y Callao, the seventh largest private national bank, became the third in a series of bank collapses beginning with the December 1981 state liquidation of Luis Leon Ripp's Banco de la Industria de la Construcción (BIC). This trend continued with the liquidation of Banco Commercial (Bancoper), Peru's third largest private commercial bank, after the chairman of the board, Luis Bertello, was discovered to have indulged in over $100 million in irrecoverable loans – 80% to Bertello's personal investment interests (*LAWR*, April 15, 1983). These bank collapses and the subsequent increasing state involvement in this sector illustrate Peru's issue weakness.

[23] *LAWR*, February 23, 1983.

[24] Economist Intelligence Unit, *Country Report: Peru, Bolivia*, no. 1, 1987, p. 2.

[25] Economist Intelligence Unit, *Country Report: Peru, Bolivia*, no. 1, 1987, p. 2; Banco Central de Reserva (1985), p. 6.

[26] *Los Angeles Times*, December 31, 1984.

[27] Devlin and de la Piedra (1985), p. 410. Interview with Javier Abugattas, August 17, 1988. Many small creditors resented being "locked into Peru by their big brothers on the steering committee." *LAWR*, May 13, 1983.

[28] Banco Central de Reserva (1985), p. 21.

Peruvian market because it had not already been captured by the large banks. For example, Wells Fargo and some small consortiums used Peru to expand their international portfolios and thus faced relatively high exposures.[29]

As competition diminished in the 1980s the banks became more concerned about their exposure to risk.[30] They realized they had not set aside sufficient reserves to protect their capital base from a potential loss of bad loans. This was especially troublesome in countries like Peru which had heavily "overborrowed"; Peru owed far more than could be repaid by internal savings and investment.[31] Yet, in overall terms the Peruvian debt was small in comparison with Brazil, Argentina, or Mexico. Peru owed the commercial banks only $5.2 billion in 1982, compared with Brazil's $56.1 billion, Argentina's $22.2 billion, or Mexico's $59.0 billion debt.[32] The small size of the Peruvian debt gave banks the flexibility to bear the loss if negotiations failed to resolve in their favor or if Peru ever attempted default.

Creditor governments and international organizations. At this early stage of debt negotiations, the IMF and the U.S. were particularly concerned about the stability of the international financial system and the potential threat to banks of en masse default by debtors. Although Peru by itself was not a direct threat to the banks, it could set a precedent for other debtors. At the same time, during Belaúnde's regime, the U.S. was somewhat concerned about the maintenance of domestic political stability and the consolidation of democracy in Peru. For their part, Peruvian government officials felt that support from the IMF and World Bank would ensure bank involvement.[33] At the beginning of the period analyzed here, the IMF remained well-disposed toward Peru.[34]

Debt game and predicted outcome

In the first period, Peru's situation was IS 7 while the lenders' was IS 3. These situations lead to the debt game and matrix shown in Figure 12.1. The game has a structure akin to a Called-Bluff situation, giving the lenders a more advantageous bargaining position. It has one equilibrium, at HA..., LC..., with high adjustment by Peru and few concessions by the banks. Turning to the likely outcome with intervention, given U.S. government and IMF concern about Peru setting a precedent that would undermine the financial system, we might expect the U.S. to simply reinforce the equilibrium outcome of HA..., LC... as this would meet U.S. and IMF goals.

The negotiations and outcome

Peru demonstrated considerable willingness to adjust its economy. Under the financial leadership of Carlos Rodríguez-Pastor, Peru promised to pursue austerity in order to secure the IMF's "stamp of approval" in an effort to win agreement

[29] Stallings (1987), p. 278. [30] Devlin and de la Piedra (1985), passim.
[31] Devlin and de la Piedra (1985), p. 383. [32] Devlin (1987), p. 36.
[33] *LAWR*, March 4, 1983.
[34] See the discussion by Richard Webb, President of the Banco Central de Reserva del Perú, in *LAWR*, March 4, 1983.

Cardinal Payoff Matrix, Intervention Expected

Peru IS 7 \ Lenders IS 3	HC...	MC...	LC...
HA...	12, 9	9, 9.67	<u>**10, 10.33**</u>
MA...	11.67, 5.5	8, 6	7, 6.5
LA...	11.33, 3	7, 3	4, 3

Note: Nash equilibrium bolded; expected outcome with intervention underlined.

Ordinal Payoff Matrix, Intervention Expected

Peru IS 7 \ Lenders IS 3	HC...	MC...	LC...
HA...	9, 7	5, 8	<u>**6, 9**</u>
MA...	8, 4	4, 5	2.5, 6
LA...	7, 2	2.5, 2	1, 2

Note: Nash equilibrium bolded; expected outcome with intervention underlined.

Figure 12.1. *Play phase, period one: March–June 1983*

with its creditors.[35] Rodríguez-Pastor's stewardship reassured the bankers, who considered him "more rigorous than his predecessor in applying the IMF's stabilization policy."[36]

[35] Rodríguez-Pastor, a banker from Wells Fargo and principal negotiator of the Cofide loan for the lenders in 1982, had replaced the previous Minister of Economy and Finance, Manuel Ulloa. Brian Jenson of the Banco Central de Reserva del Perú, who also participated in the negotiations, was a vice-president in Wells Fargo.

[36] *LAWR*, January 14, 1983.

Beginning in March 1983, the Peruvian negotiating team focused on obtaining more credit and ensuring foreign bank acceptance of a new agreement.[37] Peru faced no short-term alternative to large-scale foreign borrowing because it held only $500 million in international reserves.[38] Peru had requested an $800 million jumbo loan from its commercial creditors to avoid a forced rescheduling. Peru also opened negotiations with the Paris Club to reschedule the debt it owed government creditors. To strengthen its bargaining position in both sets of negotiations, Peru announced a $400 million crack-down on government spending to demonstrate its commitment to the new austerity program.[39]

Peru's commercial bank creditors stalled during May. The discrepancy between the economic assumptions for 1983 declared by Peru's financial ministry in early March and those made by the IMF disturbed the banks. Still, the IMF urged commercial banks to cooperate with the rescheduling of the jumbo loan. Rodríguez-Pastor told the banks that unless they cooperated with Peru's request, the IMF would cease to back Peru, and everybody would be "in the soup."[40] This pressure proved effective because IMF withdrawal from the collective bailout would jeopardize the over-exposed banks as well as Peru.

In June 1983, the IMF granted Peru new credits and negotiations with the commercial banks were proclaimed successful. In what amounted to an elaborate recycling of Peruvian debt, the commercial banks, led by Citicorp, agreed to stretch out payments on $320 million in loans over eight years and to provide $450 million in new loans. Interest on both portions was at 2.25% over LIBOR or 2% over the U.S. prime rate, at the lender's option.[41] Peru paid all the costs of the rescheduling, which was not a trivial sum.[42] Two analysts who have examined three periods of debt negotiations between 1965 and 1984 argue that the terms of the agreement "were extremely stiff." They were "equal to the most onerous borrowing conditions recorded" in previous borrowing cycles.[43]

The terms were onerous because the banks had little incentive to make concessions beyond those necessary to cover a short-term liquidity crisis, and Peru had great incentive not to default. There were almost no concessions by banks because they were mainly concerned with quickly recovering their assets. Moreover, Peru's need for borrowing and willingness to adjust encouraged the conclusion of such a deal.

Summary. The equilibrium outcome proved to be the one we expected, and was consistent with the stronger position of the lenders in the negotiations.

[37] Interviews with negotiators Ismael Noya, Lima, August 12, 1988 and Adela Lerner, Lima, August 17, 1988.

[38] *LAWR*, January 8, 1982 and June 17, 1983. [39] *Journal of Commerce*, March 4, 1983.

[40] *LAWR*, March 4, 1983.

[41] In negotiations concluded later in the year with the Paris Club, an agreement was reached to reschedule over 90% of the principal and interest on Peru's official debt maturing that year, with an advance agreement to consider extending the maturities again in 1984.

[42] The two sources used to ascertain the terms of the agreement were Banco Central de Reserva (Lima, 1985) and Devlin (1987). See also *LAWR*, June 17, 1983.

[43] Devlin and de la Piedra (1985), p. 410.

Peru committed itself to undertake high adjustment, and the banks refused to make any serious concessions to Peru. As expected, the IMF supported the outcome that we saw.

Situational changes

Despite Belaúnde's best efforts, external factors made it difficult for him to implement an austerity program. Peru failed to meet the economic targets agreed upon in its IMF program. The fiscal deficit rose to 9% of GDP by the end of 1983, over twice the IMF targeted 4.2%. The main cause of the deficit growth was not excessive expenditure but falling revenue – due to a combination of natural disasters, a massive recession, and the disappearance of new lines of foreign credit. In 1983, as GDP shrank by 12%, underemployment and unemployment rose to over 50% of the work force, and real wages declined to 84% of their 1980–1982 plateau.

Political problems quickly accompanied economic ones. Belaúnde was unable to prevent extravagant arms purchases by a disgruntled military.[44] Arms spending led the IMF, the World Bank, and the commercial banks to threaten to halt their loans in August. During the same month, Belaúnde confronted growing opposition within his party. Opposition within AP tied to Alva Orlandini called for a price freeze, as well as a slow-down in the subsidies removal program. Demonstrating his still considerable power, Belaúnde crushed the parliamentary opposition after Rodríguez-Pastor threatened to resign.[45]

By late October 1983, however, unable to comply with the original targets, the Belaúnde government requested a new IMF program, and announced its intention to reschedule the following year's debt. On October 14, at Peru's request, the IMF relaxed previously set target ceilings on the condition that Peru increase taxes. The IMF immediately offered new, adjusted deficit and domestic credit ceiling targets. With continued political problems, this IMF effort looked increasingly unrealistic. A top official of the Banco Central de Reserva del Perú said Peru had no intention of complying with IMF targets, but would continue to negotiate with the Fund for more lenient targets.

The IMF continued to object to Peru's "substantial deviations" from its objectives into the end of 1983, and Peru continued to face difficulties in complying with the accord. In November 1983, Belaúnde's party suffered a humiliating defeat in municipal elections. The populist Alianza Popular Revolucionaria Americana (APRA) secured 33% of the vote, Izquierda Unida (IU) won 29%, and Belaúnde's AP trailed with about 17%. Even worse for Belaúnde, however, was the victory of the IU in Lima, and the inauguration of their candidate, Alfonso Barrantes, as the first Marxist mayor of Lima.[46] The decisive victory of the left in the preliminaries raised the prospect of a strong electoral challenge by APRA, led by Alan García, for the presidency in 1985. The potential threat of a radical municipal government in Lima and growing civil unrest caused Belaúnde

[44] *LAWR*, October 14, 1983. [45] *LAWR*, August 26, 1983, p. 1. [46] See Wise (1989), p. 170.

to waver in his commitment to orthodox rescheduling. Arguing that the IMF was "excessively severe," Belaúnde replaced Finance Minister Rodríguez-Pastor and refused to increase gasoline prices. Despite such measures, he failed to restore his 17–18% loss of popular support.

In addition to serious electoral vulnerability, Belaúnde was unable to stop the terrorist attacks of the Sendero Luminoso, the Maoist terrorist movement responsible for an average of six disappearances daily.[47] In certain regions of the countryside, violations of human rights went unchecked. Toward the end of 1983, Sendero Luminoso's attacks increased, and it managed to create a region of guerilla control that threatened democratic rule and exposed the growing instability of the Belaúnde government.

U.S. Ambassador Jordan offered Belaúnde a U.S. Treasury/USAID $60 million loan in an effort to prevent Belaúnde from openly breaking with the banks and the IMF. Following the American lead, the steering committee of major banks continued disbursing their loans even though Peru had fallen out of compliance with IMF targets. Bank exposure in Peru increased by 12% in accord with the June agreement, accounting in part for their heightened concern for Peruvian assets.

After a month in Peru checking figures, the IMF evaluating committee left without signing a letter of intent. This lack of confidence in Peru's ability or willingness to lower its public deficit from 10.3% of GDP to under 4% in 1984 stemmed from the fact that Belaúnde's economic policies were rejected and tax collection was virtually impossible. In January 1984, the IMF suspended its standby loan while Belaúnde continued his pre-election spending spree despite the 11% public deficit.[48]

The IMF eased performance targets, overlooking Peru's failure to manage its deficit, and drew up a new adjustment package to buy time for further rescheduling in 1984. Peru used this grace period to build up international reserves and strengthen its bargaining position. The Bank Advisory Committee led by Citicorp then came through with an emergency rescue operation to lend Peru $100 million for 90 days since no comprehensive restructuring was expected until the new president assumed power in July 1985.[49]

In the following period, these shock-induced and policy-promoted situational changes produced a new bargaining context and hence a new negotiating game.

Period 2, February 1984–July 1985: manipulating the banks?

In this period Peru attempted to use its reputation as an honest but hard-pressed player to extract further concessions for the banks. As we shall see, and as predicted by the model, Peru did not intend to undertake serious economic adjustment. Based on the bargaining situation, the banks had little to lose by being concessionary in the hope that Peru's situation might change enough to

[47] *LAWR*, September 23, 1983. [48] *LAWR*, January 4, 1985. [49] *LAWR*, January 4, 1985.

encourage it to reciprocate. By the second round of negotiations, however, the banks saw little purpose in helping Peru and began to pursue a more confrontational policy.

Identifying individual situations

In this period, the Peruvian government was unstable, issue medium in debt resources, but overall weak (IS 2/8). The banks remained unified and strong overall, but weak in issue capabilities (IS 3).

Peru. For reasons discussed in the section on situational change above, Peru's domestic coalition was clearly unstable by early 1984. In addition to strong outside opposition, the government also faced internal conflict involving Richard Webb, the Director of the Banco Central de Reserva del Perú, and President Belaúnde, because of Webb's advocacy of tight monetary policy. Conversations between Webb and Belaúnde illustrate this conflict. Belaúnde claimed,

> I was never satisfied with the leadership of Webb. I have expressed this in words and in writing. It [the chair of the Banco Central de Reserva] is a position that has a certain autonomy. Of course, appointed by the president, but it has some autonomy. Naturally, when there are differences of opinion what is done, in the good manners of politics, is that the functionary resigns. This did not happen in the case of Webb.[50]

Webb refused to allow the Banco Central de Reserva to release foreign exchange in order to prevent the government from embarking on a course of excessive spending.[51] In an interview, asked whether he wanted to increase government spending at the time of the resignation of Rodríguez-Pastor to help secure political support, Belaúnde acknowledged that there were a "series of government projects that were being detained."[52] These conflicts within the Belaúnde Administration prevented the implementation of any coherent strategy.

Ironically, this domestic weakness proved to be a source of some issue strength. Javier Abugattas, one of the principal negotiators for Peru, noted that the Banco de la Nación, which negotiates directly with the international banks, did not have hard currency to repay the commercial banks, despite the fact that foreign reserves increased to $1 billion early in this period. Foreign reserves were controlled by Webb of the Banco Central de Reserva del Perú, who opposed using Peru's reserves toward debt servicing. He thus restricted the emission of hard currency in compliance with the IMF limits on the size of the deficit. By refusing to transfer foreign reserves to the Banco de la Nación to pay off the commercial banks, Webb and the Banco Central de Reserva del Perú pitted the IMF against the commercial banks and helped to improve Peru's financial situation.[53]

[50] Interview with Belaúnde, November 9, 1987.

[51] Webb also made this argument in writing: "Fresh money from banks was conditioned on an IMF agreement, and this was ruled out by the size of the deficit. The central bank refused to lend. Additional fiscal measures were ruled out by the government. Starting in August, the shortfall was made up by postponing debt payments." Webb (1988), p. 248.

[52] Interview with Belaúnde, November 9, 1987. [53] Interview, Lima, August 17, 1988.

In overall capabilities Peru remained weak. The unprecedented 12% decline in Peru's GDP for 1983 was double that of any other Latin American nation that year.[54] The lethal combination of contraction and inflation continued into 1984. Peru's dependence on foreign imports, even food, effectively eliminated the possibility of withdrawal from the international systems of trade and finance. In the end, Peru had little alternative but to accept IMF help and implement austerity measures.

Lenders. There is no change in our coding of the banks in this period. The banks were clearly preoccupied by the big debtors during this period.[55] Peru's relatively small debt allowed the banks to choose between taking an immediate "hit" on interest arrears or allowing Peru to drift along until a new administration took office. This meant the banks could either refuse new loans which eventually would cause them to declare their outstanding loans value-impaired, or provide emergency credit in the hopes that Alan García's administration would take debt servicing more seriously.

Creditor governments and international organizations. Both the U.S. government and the IMF showed limited interest in Peru because of its relatively small debt compared to the other debtors in the region. The main concern at this time was that lenience toward Peru in terms of rescheduling and emergency aid would provoke resentment and similar demands among other debtors.

Democracy and the successful transfer of power from one administration to another at the end of Belaúnde's term were the principal U.S. concerns. The decision in 1986 to double military aid to Peru made it the largest recipient of U.S. aid in South America, and demonstrated clear U.S. interest.[56] The U.S. argued that such extensive military support was to ensure the political stability necessary to facilitate a democratic transfer of power. The U.S., however, denied serious strategic interest in Peru, and claimed indifference to the presence of Soviet advisors and influence.[57]

The IMF, on the other hand, was interested in maintaining a reputation for toughness. It refused to allow Peru to get by without making appropriate adjustment for two reasons: (1) the desire to maintain its credibility and (2) concern that a Peruvian default could inspire other debtor countries to do likewise.[58] From a country with a large debt, such a move would be disastrous. For these reasons, the Fund delayed a standby agreement with Peru in January 1984.

Debt game and predicted outcome

We predict the cardinal and ordinal game matrix shown in Figure 12.2 for this period. In this game, there are three Nash equilibria, each with little/no adjustment by the debtor and with the lenders undertaking either high, medium, or no/

[54] *LAWR*, January 13, 1984. [55] *Financial Times*, November 27, 1984, p. 19.
[56] *LAWR*, January 14, 1985. [57] *Financial Times*, November 27, 1984.
[58] *LAWR*, January 27, 1984.

Cardinal Payoff Matrix, Intervention Expected

		Lenders IS 3		
		HC...	MC...	LC...
	HA...	−6, 9	−7.5, 9.67	−6, 10.33
Peru IS 2/8	MA...	−2, 5.5	−4, 6	−4, 6.5
	LA...	**2, 3**	**−5, 3**	**−2, 3**

Note: Nash equilibria bolded; expected outcome with intervention underlined.

Ordinal Payoff Matrix, Intervention Expected

		Lenders IS 3		
		HC...	MC...	LC...
	HA...	2.5, 7	1, 8	2.5, 9
Peru IS 2/8	MA...	6.5, 4	4.5, 5	4.5, 6
	LA...	**9, 2**	**8, 2**	**6.5, 2**

Note: Nash equilibria bolded; expected outcome with intervention underlined.

Figure 12.2. *Play phase, period two: February 1984–July 1985*

low concessions. Unlike in the previous game, Peru's dominant strategy is now no adjustment. The banks face a difficult situation. No matter which strategy they undertake, they receive a very low payoff if Peru successfully refuses to adjust. Although the banks are indifferent among different levels of concessions, they could improve their payoff if Peru undertook at least some adjustment. For its part, Peru would receive a higher payoff with higher rather than lower concessions from the banks. Thus, Peru has a strong interest in misrepresenting its situation to encourage concessions by the banks; and the banks would be interested in promoting some adjustment by Peru.

The U.S. and the IMF had different interests in this case. Whereas the U.S. might encourage some concessionary behavior on the banks part to help stabilize the Peruvian political situation, the IMF would undoubtedly oppose concessions to Peru without reciprocal adjustment on its part. Thus, in this case, we do not expect intervention to have much effect on the game.

The negotiations and outcome

The second period consists of two rounds, the first from February 1984 until about mid-1984, when the banks' strategy shifted from conciliatory to confrontational. The second ran from that time until June 1985.

Round one. Following the provisional approval of an IMF adjustment package in January 1984, Peru began negotiations to reschedule $2.6 billion in old loans with a 12-bank advisory group representing 270 commercial banks. The whole package depended upon prior completion of an IMF agreement. The government agreed to adopt austerity measures in exchange for $350 million in IMF loans so Peru could conclude an agreement with commercial banks and government creditors. The agreement was scheduled to be signed in early April 1984, but the IMF expressed concern about Peru's economic policy intentions and registered complaints about its lack of compliance with several preconditions to an agreement. Still, after assurances from Peru, and despite domestic opposition to austerity, an agreement with the IMF was ultimately signed.

Peru made superficial attempts at orthodox rescheduling, but began to use its difficulties in policy implementation as an excuse to avoid adjustment. The measures it took to boost its balance of payments included changing tax rebates on exports, lowering sales taxes, and altering some restrictions on imports. But economic analysts at the time noted that to pursue serious adjustment, Peru needed to devalue its currency or sharply raise interest rates.[59] With domestic instability ruling out serious adjustment efforts, the President continued negotiations to avoid a rupture with international creditors. Belaúnde begged off on adjustment as "inconvenient."[60] Instead Peru adhered to the IMF agreement long enough to conclude its agreement with the banks in April 1984 and secure about $130 million in funds from the IMF and banks.[61] The Peruvian government played the role of orthodox debtor so well that one Peruvian banker suggested it deserved an Oscar.[62]

[59] *LAWR*, May 25, 1984.

[60] As President Belaúnde put it: "The Monetary Fund was too stringent, and a sovereign country can accept advice or reject it. At one point we more or less arrived at an agreement. But in the second part when the agreement was to be perfected at the end, there we could not reach an agreement because the accord was inconvenient for the country. So, like any sovereign country we can choose not to agree." Interview, Lima, November 9, 1987.

[61] Webb (1988), p. 247. [62] *LAWR*, January 13, 1984.

The commercial bank agreement technically included no new loans, but it did allow for the renewal of $880 million in trade credits and the disbursement of the remaining $200 million in tranches from the previous year's agreement. More importantly, Peru managed to significantly improve its repayment terms: interest rates were lowered half a percentage point (from 2.25 to 1.75 over LIBOR); the maturity of 90% of the loans was extended to nine years (in comparison to the eight-year maturity on loans rescheduled in 1983); and the grace period was extended from three to five years.[63] Payments on the remaining loans were deferred until December 31, 1985. The total amount rescheduled, $1.045 billion, exceeded bankers' original intentions to reschedule Peru's debt by some $280 million.

The banks made some concessions to Peru in order to help stabilize the government and protect their increasingly damaged and precarious loans. The banks' willingness to "carry" Peru in the hope of stabilizing its situation or possible uncertainty as to Peru's "real" strategy may account for why they opted to provide Peru with some concessions. Given Peru's economic situation, the bankers tolerated Peru's position as the best alternative to open default. By mid-1984, however, it was clear that the Belaúnde government had failed to impose the negotiated measures, and it was obvious significant emergency aid would be necessary to keep Peru solvent until the election of a new president. The banks now realized that their efforts would not suffice to encourage Peruvian economic adjustment.

Round two. By August 1984, Peru had stopped meeting its debt obligations. The IMF suspended its 18-month standby agreement with Peru because the government's deficit continued to exceed the agreed upon target of 4.2% and remained at 9.4%.[64]

Indifferent to Peru's large public deficit of 11% of GDP in 1984, Belaúnde squandered precious funds on his reelection campaign.[65] The government resorted to using money allocated for repayment to commercial banks to finance the deficit. In addition, reports that Peru was secretly spending millions of dollars in scarce foreign reserves on French Mirage jets annoyed bankers. Even more upsetting to them was that Peru had fallen into arrears while the Banco Central de Reserva del Perú amassed over a billion dollars in international reserves. Belaúnde continued to claim that the Banco Central de Reserva del Perú not only denied him access to these funds[66] but also refused to release the funds destined for his development projects.[67]

Belaúnde criticized the banks for not cooperating; the banks responded by tightening their credit lines. Credit available to Peru fell from $880 million in

[63] Devlin (1987), p. 44. Peru also won improved terms in its agreement with the Paris Club.
[64] *South*, February 1985, p. 23. [65] *LAWR*, January 4, 1985.
[66] *South*, February 1985; *Los Angeles Times*, December 12, 1984.
[67] This interpretation came from Drago Kisic, Director of Macroconsult. Interview, August 12, 1988.

June to $310 million in mid-November. From August 1984 through July 1985 the government failed to meet payments on a timely basis.

Interestingly, in April 1984, the *LAWR* had suggested:

> Last week would probably have been ideal, politically, for Belaúnde to have taken Webb at his word (in the sense that Peru has enough reserves to face a break with the IMF) and to have launched Peru on a radically different supply-side oriented populist course. A well-timed editorial in the *Wall Street Journal* of 3 April ('Opportunity in Peru') along these lines appeared to set the scenes for precisely this option.[68]

Although Belaúnde has said he could not remember this option being discussed, Webb has confirmed it: "a policy debate within the government had questioned the advisability of an IMF program, citing the standard objections – the primacy of output recovery, the role of credit as a productive input, and the feedback from devaluation and energy prices to inflation. In the end, these objections were overruled and negotiations with the fund were completed."[69] This discussion of dropping the IMF program was based on Peru's increase in issue-specific capabilities; it ignored Peru's lack of the coalitional stability necessary to break from the IMF. According to Webb, "a go-it-alone course would have meant the loss of official and commercial bank loans as well as [the creation of] difficult-to-foresee diplomatic waves during President Belaúnde's last year in office."[70]

In the final months of office, the Belaúnde team had a difficult time maintaining even the appearance of orthodoxy. The military had spent $650 million on 20 Mirage jets, perhaps a necessary palliative from the government to prevent potential regime opposition by the military.

By 1985, to avoid a complete break with the bankers, Peru had made three "goodwill payments" worth between $16 and $52 million, which prevented its U.S. regulatory status from falling into the "value-impaired" category. Belaúnde admitted to a delay in loan payments, "but a delay with dialogue; it was not a unilateral moratorium but a negotiated delay." Peruvian debt negotiators acknowledged that the government was merely trying to "keep appearances" in order to "remain part of the game." In the last year in office, "a 'best effort' policy was followed, with the government making ad hoc payments according to its monthly cash position, maintaining an ongoing dialogue with the Fund and other creditors, and taking additional fiscal measures. By maintaining a low profile and, again, keeping-up appearances, Peru gained a considerable measure of de facto acceptance of its inability to pay."[71]

Strong U.S. support prevented Peruvian loans from becoming value-impaired "for political considerations"; the U.S. sought to avoid antagonizing the next government.[72] The banks rewarded Peru's apparently "conciliatory" gestures by granting a one-month freeze on loans maturing in late 1984. Peruvian Finance Minister Guillermo Garrido Lecca led a mission to Washington. He told creditors

[68] April 13, 1984. [69] Webb (1988), p. 247. [70] Webb (1988), p. 247.
[71] Webb (1988), p. 248. [72] *LAWR*, February 22, 1985.

that Peru's improved treasury balance was due to increased tax revenues from such unpopular adjustment measures as increased fuel prices. In fact, the government was borrowing this money from the state-run Banco de la Nación. Meanwhile, Webb claimed that there were not enough funds for typewriters in the Ministry of Finance.[73] In effect, the banks believed Peru was making a good-faith effort to service its debts, but abandoned hope for any real progress from the "lame-duck" government and allowed the country to drift along until a new government was inaugurated in July 1985.[74]

Belaúnde walked a fine line to avoid angering either the banks or domestic interest groups. By making random payments he avoided a major cutoff of credit and by eschewing adjustment he prevented the rise of labor opposition that would have resulted from further austerity. As the *Financial Times* reported:

> Close associates of President Belaúnde believe he will avoid further austerity measures which would prejudice the slim chances of the ruling Acción Popular (Popular Action) retaining the presidency, but also threaten serious social unrest. That could cause the military to intervene . . . one achievement he wants to be noted for is a democratic transfer of authority.[75]

Belaúnde was to be disappointed by the new government that closed the lines of credit he had so assiduously kept open. He did, however, accomplish his major aim: the successful transfer of power from one civilian government to another. July 1985 marked the first such peaceful transfer in nearly half a century.

Summary. In this period, Peru became both domestically unstable and financially stronger. According to the model, the resulting game with the banks made it likely that Peru would follow a strategy of little adjustment, no matter what strategy the bankers followed. In the initial stages of negotiations, it appears that the bankers were conciliatory for a combination of reasons: they did not fully recognize the new situation and expected Peru to adjust; and they may have been concessionary toward Peru in the hope of stabilizing the government and encouraging Peru to respond with its own conciliatory behavior. In any case, given their payoff structure, the banks had little to lose by initially playing a more conciliatory strategy. Once it became clear what the structure of the game was, however, the banks lost interest in being "nice guys," leading to an outcome of no adjustment and no concessions.

Situational changes

During this period, Peru's government appeared to be more concerned about its fragile political stability than coming to an agreement on debt. The banks used their capabilities to make some initial concessions to Peru, possibly in the hope of stabilizing the government and encouraging a situational change that would

[73] *LAWR*, February 22, 1985. [74] *Los Angeles Times*, December 31, 1984.

[75] November 27, 1984. Belaúnde mildly disagreed with this report, saying "a fundamental aim of any government is to survive, this is elemental, it is the first duty of a government. But that was not our first priority. The first priority was to develop the country." Interview, Lima, November 9, 1987.

lead to a more favorable rescheduling outcome. In the end, however, this effort came to nought and the banks simply retrenched and bided their time, waiting for a change in government.

With García's election, Peru would once again become stable as in the first period of negotiations. In contrast to the first period, however, the events of the second period and Peru's economic strategy in the early part of the next period to bolster its reserves and withdraw assets that might possibly be attached made Peru both issue and overall strong. For their part, as part of a general strategy to protect themselves and in response to U.S. regulatory policy, the banks increased their issue strength.

Period 3, July 1985–August 1986: Garcia confronts the banks

In his inaugural speech, President García declared that for a period of 12 months, Peru would dedicate no more than 10% of its export earnings to servicing the medium- and long-term public debt.[76] Priority would be given to servicing Peru's obligations with multilateral agencies and creditor governments; the commercial banks would receive no money until January 1986. Under García, Peru never normalized relations with the banks. Its confrontation with the international financial system led the IMF to declare that Peru would be "ineligible" for further IMF funds. At the end of the García administration, Peru was at risk of outright expulsion from the IMF. President García began with a promising debt initiative, yet by the end of his term in office Peru was the most financially isolated country in Latin America. Why did Peru's debt strategy go so badly awry? The analysis of García's negotiations with the banks is divided into two periods, the first until August 1986 and the second until his term ended in 1990.

Identifying individual situations

The Peruvian government had a stable domestic coalition, and also became both issue and overall strong (IS 5). The banks, by contrast, were unified and strong overall, and had bolstered their issue capabilities to some extent (IS 3/5).

Peru. For its first year in power the García coalition was stable. Peru's new leader won the presidential elections of July 1985 with a decisive margin of victory. No previous candidate had ever captured over half the votes cast in a fair Peruvian presidential election. García represented an alliance of young, reform-oriented sectors of APRA. He had the acquiescence of the military, substantial campaign funds from big business, strong support among workers, the middle sectors, and the provinces, and control over both houses of Congress.[77] García enhanced the stability of his coalition by attacking the IMF. The election results

[76] For an overview of the debt policies of the García government see Ugarteche (1988) and Kisic (1987).
[77] Wise (1989), p. 172.

repudiated Belaúnde's economic policies; the popularity of "anti-imperialist" rhetoric reflected the dissatisfaction of groups that had seen the erosion of real wages and declining employment opportunities. As García noted, "All successful revolutions require a foreign enemy. The [International Monetary] Fund is my enemy."[78]

Under García, Peru further increased its issue strength. Although it faced $2.734 billion in debt arrears, of which $1.924 billion was owed to the commercial banks,[79] the new administration had roughly $1 billion in reserves.[80] These reserves represented a significant source of issue strength, and they grew to over $1.5 billion by the end of the year as the result of a positive trade balance, "de-dollarization" of the economy, and the moratorium on the debt.[81]

The government's quiet removal of Peru's foreign assets from the U.S. in anticipation of a disruption of relations with the banks also further increased Peru's overall capabilities.[82] Peru removed a total of $500 million in gold and $200 million in silver.[83] The Peruvian government also warned local banks to remove their assets from U.S. banks and place them in safe Swiss and London accounts.[84] In sum, Peru had fewer attachable assets in the U.S. and increased gold and silver reserves at home. In addition, the García administration's heterodox strategy led to two years of the fastest economic growth in Latin America – 9.5% in 1986, and 7.8% in 1987.[85] For a while Peru was able to stimulate rapid growth with the foreign exchange it was no longer paying the banks. By August 1987, Peru had been living without fresh bank credit and surviving on trade financing and barter for approximately two years.[86] Although trade lines decreased to about $250 million from nearly $900 million in 1984, Peru still managed.[87] The significant increase in reserves fostered the belief in Peru's ability to survive on its own:

> García and his top aides have reached the judgement that unless the rest of the world agrees to its terms, Peru will go it alone. The country already has nearly $1.5 billion in foreign exchange reserves and will accumulate more by squeezing Peruvians with dollar-denominated accounts and forcing them to convert dollars into soles.[88]

One reason for the conviction that Peru could "go it alone" was the fact that Peru's industry was running far below capacity, relieving the immediate need for large quantities of foreign cash for expansion. This was an important source of overall strength; Peru's economic team believed that reserves they held from not paying the debt, plus a trade surplus in 1985–1986, could provide the cash to buy imports to fuel a major domestic economic expansion.[89]

[78] *Los Angeles Times*, March 3, 1986. [79] *LAWR*, September 6, 1985, p. 7.
[80] Kisic (1987), p. 183. [81] *LAWR*, November 29, 1985, p. 5.
[82] *Los Angeles Times*, February 25, 1986. [83] *The Economist*, March 15, 1986.
[84] *LAWR*, November 1, 1985, p. 7.
[85] Economist Intelligence Unit, *Country Report: Peru, Bolivia*, no. 4, 1990, p. 3.
[86] *Wall Street Journal*, August 2, 1985. [87] *Wall Street Journal*, August 2, 1985.
[88] *Washington Post*, November, 3, 1985. [89] *Washington Post*, November, 3, 1985.

Lenders. The bankers' coalition remained stable. They increased their issue strength as a result of actions by U.S. federal banking regulators (the Inter-Agency Country Exposure Review Committee – ICERC) in October 1985, only a few months after García came to power. This body forced U.S. banks to set aside reserves on their Peruvian loans equal to 15% of their total value.[90] This was the first such move against a Latin American debtor, and it increased the issue strength of the banks somewhat.[91]

The bankers were overall strong due to the size of Peru's debt. One banker summarized the attitude of the banks saying, "Peru's debt is small, and no one is interested in setting precedents useful to other debtors."[92] Peru's debt was small enough to write off and banks did not believe Peru's intransigence would set a precedent.[93] In sum, banks would be scathed but could ultimately survive a Peruvian default.

Creditor governments and international organizations. The aspect of Peru's maverick behavior that most concerned the U.S. and IMF was its potential to stir up interest in a united regional debtors' cartel. Alone, Peru did not represent a substantial threat. As a promoter of novel approaches to the debt problem – such as linking debt repayment to export receipts or ending payments entirely – however, Peru was a potential problem for both the IMF and the U.S. government. The Reagan Administration was unhappy with the "rhetoric" of Peruvian public officials, and it stopped military aid as well as USAID disbursements for new projects.[94] The United States was also concerned about the negotiations between Peru and the U.S.-based oil companies Occidental Petroleum and Belco Petroleum. The latter, owned by the American firm Encron Corporation, was expropriated in December 1985.[95] Bankers feared getting caught in a larger confrontation between Peru and the U.S. "It is very worrying," said one banker, "that there'll be a confrontation, not with the banks directly, but with the U.S. government, or via the oil companies, but the banks will be pulled in."[96]

Debt game and predicted outcome

Strong situations for both Peru and its lenders lead to the game shown in Figure 12.3. The Nash equilibrium in this game is the lower right-hand cell (7, 3.5). Thus, the predicted outcome is no/low concessions by the banks and no/low adjustment by Peru. Peru would diminish its payoff by granting any concessions to the banks. The banks in such a case have little choice but to take a hard line, although the resulting payoff for them is considerably lower than Peru's. In short, in such a game we would expect much posturing and little actual negotiation. Taking into account possible intervention, we should expect the banks

[90] *Wall Street Journal*, October, 29, 1985. [91] *Wall Street Journal*, November 29, 1985.
[92] *New York Times*, September 1, 1986.
[93] *South*, June 1985 and *Wall Street Journal*, September, 25, 1985.
[94] *LAWR*, November 29, 1985, p. 5. [95] Asheshov (1988), p. 264.
[96] *LAWR*, November 29, 1985, p. 5.

Cardinal Payoff Matrix,
No Intervention Expected

		Lenders IS 3/5		
		HC...	MC...	LC...
	HA...	−3, 3	−3.5, 4.17	−3, 5.33
Peru IS 5	MA...	−1.33, 1	−2, 2	−2, 3
	LA...	.33, 0	−.5, .5	**−1, 1**

Note: Nash equilibrium bolded.

Ordinal Payoff Matrix,
No Intervention Expected

		Lenders IS 3/5		
		HC...	MC...	LC...
	HA...	2.5, 6.5	1, 8	2.5, 9
Peru IS 5	MA...	6, 3.5	4.5, 5	4.5, 6.5
	LA...	9, 1	8, 2	**7, 3.5**

Note: Nash equilibrium bolded.

Figure 12.3. *Play phase, period three: July 1985–August 1986*

to be highly motivated to appeal to creditor governments and the IMF for help in pressuring Peru to adjust. But although we might see some movement by Peru in this direction, its strong incentive to pursue a strategy of little adjustment would make this outcome difficult for the IMF to sustain.

The negotiations and outcome

At no point under García did Peru and the banks formally agree to reschedule the debt. Rhetoric replaced serious negotiation. Although the banks consistently sought to coax Peru into adjusting, they had little real leverage over the new president. Likewise, García gave little priority to the commercial bankers and in return was unable to extract any concessions from them.

At first, President García attempted to assuage the fears of the bankers. He told them he would take a tough stance in his inaugural address, but that the banks ought not to assume this was a true confrontational approach.[97] In September he praised the bankers for being "prudent and intelligent" in their response to his announcement of a "10% solution." The banks clearly hoped to encourage at least some payments from Peru. This strategy would save Peru $450 million annually, or 2% of GDP, which the government argued would be used to reactivate the economy.[98] García claimed the revenue generated by the economic recovery would ultimately be used to pay back part of the debt.

At the same time, however, it was clear that the "10% solution" would not be viable in the medium term unless the debt was massively restructured. Prime Minister Luis Alva Castro acknowledged that "the foreign debt problem will not be solved by paying US$300–350 million a year, which is what 10% of our income from exports will amount to . . . We must not forget that our debt will increase at a rate of US$1 billion per year through the accumulation of interest alone." Attempting to foster fear of a debtors' cartel, he argued that Peru's proposal was "none other than a common proposal with other Third World countries, especially those in Latin America, for the handling of the foreign debt."[99] Shortly after taking office, García announced that Peru would unilaterally roll over interest due on short-term working capital debt of $960 million coming due between September 1985 and the end of January 1986.[100] The head of the bankers' steering committee complained that Peru was paying "next to no money" to the commercial banks. They pressed for some interest payments at the very least. In October and November 1985, the bankers' steering committee insistently telexed Peru to request a meeting "as soon as possible" to discuss the debt. The government repeatedly refused to consider such a meeting: "we are preparing our medium term economic program and there is no point in talking before it is ready" said the Vice-Minister of Public Finance, Leonel Figueroa.[101] Figueroa noted that the "10% solution" did not necessarily mean the commercial banks would get no money. But help from multilateral agencies to help Peru repay the banks was being held up by delays in projects already financed.[102]

Pressure on Peru to adjust came mainly from the IMF and to a lesser extent from the U.S. The Peruvian government wanted to downplay its concern over having its loans declared "value impaired" by the U.S. government's ICERC.[103] But they were obviously upset about the ICERC's decision in October to declare Peruvian medium- and long-term loans "value impaired."[104] Furthermore, the ICERC's ruling that U.S. banks, collectively holding $2.5 billion in loans to Peru, had to set aside reserves of 15% of their total exposure made fresh credit

[97] *Los Angeles Times*, August 9, 1985, p. 24. [98] *LAWR*, November 29, 1985, p. 5.
[99] *LAWR*, September 6, 1985, p. 7. [100] *LAWR*, January 17, 1986.
[101] *LAWR*, October 11, 1985, p. 3. [102] *LAWR*, October 11, 1985, p. 3.
[103] *LAWR*, September 6, 1985, p. 7. [104] *LAWR*, November 29, 1985, p. 5.

to Peru extremely unlikely. The reaction in Peru was more anti-imperialist rhetoric from García, a decision to keep dollar-denominated bank deposits frozen to protect foreign reserves, and a cancellation of the token interest payment demanded by the commercial banks.

Informal talks with the commercial banks took place in mid-January 1986, but Peru continued to insist that no formal rescheduling process could begin until the "medium-term" economic plan was prepared. Peru told the banks at that time that the unilateral roll over of interest payments would be extended.

After Peru rebuffed the bankers, the IMF began to exert pressure on García to adopt a more cooperative strategy – although with little effect. Executive Director Jacques de Larosière told Alva Castro to pay $75 million in arrears by mid-April, or face ineligibility for further funds. García's haughty response was "we will pay when Peru decides to."[105] The leader of Peru's debt team, Deputy Economy Minister Gustavo Saberbeín, said "Paying those arrears would blow our 10% of exports ceiling for servicing the public (medium- and long-term) debt."[106] Peru expelled the IMF mission in Lima just prior to the deadline, but offered $33.7 million as a "goodwill gesture" and received an extension of the deadline until August 1986. Peru agreed to file a proposal detailing how it would pay off its debts to the IMF by the August deadline.[107] It also made a $15.8 million payment to the U.S. government for USAID and military assistance as a symbol of its "less confrontational" approach. These payments generated the expectation among bankers that they would be next in line.[108]

In March and April 1986, Peru floated a number of proposals with its creditor banks involving a rescheduling of the debt over an extremely long 25-year period, with five years grace and a 3 or 4% interest rate. Saberbeín, president of Peru's external debt team and Deputy Economy Minister, said Peru was willing to make a "modest but symbolic payment" to demonstrate its willingness to honor commitments to the banks as much as it could.[109] Such proposals were clearly unrealistic. The bankers had no incentive to listen as long as Peru obviously did not intend to pay.

In his annual speech to Congress in July 28, 1986, García announced that Peru would continue to unilaterally roll over the principal on short-term working capital debt, service its interest, and default on both the interest and principal of the medium- and long-term debt. The President added that payments on the private debt would also be restricted, increasing the confrontation between Peru and the creditors as well as damaging foreign investments in Peru. He deplored the $1.3 billion that had left the country in the form of private remittances, profits, and royalty payments abroad in the previous year.

The next month Peru defied the IMF by paying only $35 million of its $180 million arrears. The Prime Minister emphasized Peru's challenge to IMF by saying it was irrelevant whether the Fund declared Peru ineligible.[110] The IMF

[105] *LAWR*, February 21, 1986, p. 7. [106] *LAWR*, February 21, 1986, pp. 8–9.
[107] *LAWR*, May 16, 1985, p. 7. [108] *LAWR*, April 25, 1986, pp. 7, 11.
[109] *LAWR*, March 21, 1986, p. 7. [110] *LAWR*, August 21, 1986, p. 7.

promptly did declare Peru ineligible, damaging Peru's relationship with the World Bank and the Inter-American Development Bank (IDB) as well. By August 1986 it was clear that García's debt strategy had failed to extract concessions from the international financial community, although it had served to increase his domestic popularity. The banks had not succumbed to the temptation to make concessions because they had no expectation that Peru would adjust, and the Peruvian government reinforced that perception repeatedly.[111] Peru was on its own. On August 16, 1986, García made a speech from the balcony of the government palace announcing that Peru would go it alone – without international creditors.[112]

Summary. As expected from my model, Peru and its bankers faced a deadlocked situation. Neither was willing to make concessions to the other, and the rhetoric simply increased over time. Although the IMF pressured the Peruvians to undertake some adjustment, the game matrix shows that García had great incentive to resist any such efforts. In the end, an issue and overall strong Peru refused to budge, leaving a game deadlocked at LA, LC.

Situational changes

During this period, Peru pursued a number of measures to bolster its position. It appealed to the idea of a sustainable level of interest payments by advocating a "10% solution." Peru also increased its issue and overall strength in early 1986 by withdrawing assets that might possibly be attached by creditor banks. Finally, Peru sought to improve its bargaining position by securing allies. Following his inaugural speech in which he called for Peru to assert its role as the Latin American leader of the non-aligned movement, in March 1986, García made a direct overture to Argentina to form a debtors' cartel. This effort proved fruitless, however, as Argentine authorities "cold-shouldered" García.[113] On the whole, however, Peru's efforts reinforced its preferred strategy of avoiding any economic adjustment.

As negotiations with the banks stalled, however, Garcia found himself facing growing domestic political unrest and financial difficulties. The first major political blow to García had occurred in June 1986 when a coordinated prison uprising in three jails in Lima resulted in a massacre of several hundred inmates. The mutiny sparked a period of spiraling violence, social discontent, internal divisions in the governing party, and political opposition. Financially and overall as well, Peru's position began to rapidly deteriorate, leading to yet another period of unsatisfactory negotiations with increasingly powerful banks.

[111] It is reported, for example, that the Peruvian debt team refused to answer telexes from the banks, and at one point even told a banker on the advisory committee that "the check is in the mail" – as if debt payments were disbursed through the notoriously irregular Peruvian postal service! Interview with Adela Lerner, Lima, August 17, 1988.

[112] *LAWR*, August 28, 1986, p. 2.

[113] *LAWR*, March 21, 1986, p. 7.

Period 4, August 1986–July 1990: endgame with the banks

From August 1986 until the government changeover in June 1990, Peru entered a period of intense political instability. García had called for a "resistance economy" to face "imperialism" and the "dire days ahead." Trade and short-term working credit was reduced to a trickle, and Peru faced increasing isolation. The banks maintained a tough line with Peru. They threatened court action, demanded interest payments, set aside reserves against bad Peruvian loans, and refused to make new loans. In such an atmosphere, a deadlock appeared inevitable.

Identifying individual situations

Faced with growing economic problems, Peru in this period was unstable, issue weak, and overall weak (IS 8), while the banks were stable, issue and overall strong (IS 5).

Peru. Peru's domestic situation once again became unstable. A major general strike and a police rebellion by 1,000 of the civil guard in Lima in May 1987 underscored massive discontent with the cost of living. The resignation of the Prime Minister, Luis Alva Castro, and a cabinet shuffle highlighted major differences within the García administration concerning economic strategy. The Congress elected Luis Alva Castro to be president of the Chamber of Deputies. García's decision to nationalize the banks fostered strong resistance from the right. Business, intellectuals, and the middle class coalesced in a new movement called Libertad, catapulting writer Mario Vargas Llosa into the role of opposition to the president. García backed down from nationalization in the face of a court challenge to its constitutionality, a move that further eroded his support within the APRA party, especially in the youth wing.

Peru also became issue weak. Public spending quickly used up much of the foreign reserves, creating a serious foreign exchange squeeze. Net reserves fell from about $1.49 billion in 1985 to under $40 million by the fourth quarter of 1987. During 1988, net reserves were negative; although they rose to a peak of about $650 million in 1989, they again became negative by 1990.[114] Throughout 1986–1987 the Peruvian government desperately sought to promote local investment and generate export earnings. Trade credits became a source of leverage for the bankers over the administration (these credits were unaffected by the "value-impaired" status of loans to Peru). By mid-1986 the reactivation of the economy cost more than the country was saving by not servicing the debt. The cash situation of the central government deteriorated so quickly the government began to sell off gold reserves. Tax cuts to stimulate investment and price controls limited public revenue, yet they failed to prompt a surge of investment.[115] When the government took more coercive measures and finally nationalized the banks, business confidence collapsed. Between 1988–1990 the economy contracted by 23%.[116]

[114] Larraín and Sachs (1991), p. 232. [115] *LAWR*, November 23, 1986.

[116] The economy contracted by 6.7% in 1988; 12.9% in 1989; and 2.1% in 1990. *Cuanto*, vol. 3, no. 25 (February 1991), p. 33.

Peru became overall weak. A negative commercial balance was created by declining oil and mineral prices as well as the anti-export bias of government policies. The Peruvian government was isolated internationally. But bankers feared support for the Peruvian initiative. To their relief, García received little concrete regional or international support. The president referred to himself as a "solitary gladiator" against the IMF. He noted that officials of Argentina and Brazil only visited Peru when negotiating with the IMF to put pressure on the Fund. Other debtors sought negotiating leverage on the banks by threatening to follow Peru's example.[117] As we saw, however, Argentina rejected President García's call for a united front among Latin American debtors, and Mexico did likewise during García's visit in March 1987.

Lenders. The key change in the individual situation of the banks in this period was that they became issue strong. Most banks had written off large parts of their Peruvian loans, and steadily increased their capital base. In October, after Peru was declared ineligible for further loans from the IMF, the banks were ordered by the ICERC to increase provisions against bad loans to 30% of total exposure.[118] By 1989, it had ordered the banks to make provisions equivalent to 75%.[119] Moreover, no new medium- or long-term loans were made to Peru, a point that enhanced the bankers' overall strength.[120] By 1990 Peru could default without having much impact on the banks.

Creditor governments and international organizations. As the world's worst debtor, Peru presented a singular problem for the international financial system. It had been declared ineligible for further funding. Yet the strategy of autarkic economic reactivation ultimately led to an unprecedented economic collapse. Under such conditions, a government with the best intentions would have difficulty generating the foreign exchange necessary to clear its arrears with multilateral agencies. Yet no credit would become available from other sources as long as such outstanding obligations made it "ineligible." The outcome of the "deadlock" game seemed to be the possibility of medium- to long-term isolation from the international financial community. Creditor governments and multilateral agencies would be expected to search for solutions that would make "reintegration" into the international system possible yet punish Peru's failure to comply with demands for adjustment.

Debt game and predicted outcome

Based on Peru's classification (IS 8), we predict the game and outcome shown in Figure 12.4. In this game, the ordinal Nash equilibrium is no concessions/no adjustment, the lower right-hand cell (**5, 7**). This equilibrium indicates a continuing deadlock between Peru and the banks. As compared to the previous

[117] *LAWR*, July 28, 1988. [118] *LAWR*, October 2, 1986, p. 10; September 25, 1986, p. 10.
[119] *LAWR*, June 22, 1989, p. 7. [120] *LAWR*, September 25, 1986, p. 7.

Cardinal Payoff Matrix,
No Intervention Expected

		Lenders IS 5		
		HC...	MC...	LC...
	HA...	0, –3	–3.5, –1.33	–4, .33
Peru IS 8	MA...	4, –3.5	0, –2	–2, –.5
	LA...	8, –3	3.5, –2	**0, –1**

Note: Nash equilibrium bolded.

Ordinal Payoff Matrix,
No Intervention Expected

		Lenders IS 5		
		HC...	MC...	LC...
	HA...	5, 2.5	2, 6	1, 9
Peru IS 8	MA...	8, 1	5, 4.5	3, 8
	LA...	9, 2.5	7, 4.5	**5, 7**

Note: Nash equilibrium bolded.

Figure 12.4. *Play phase, period four: August 1986–July 1990*

equilibrium outcome, Peru's ordinal payoff has worsened while the banks' has increased considerably. Bankers are less concerned about their assets, and thus improve their payoff. Peru on the other hand is no longer refusing to adjust because it can afford to buck the IMF, but rather because political instability will not allow it to. Thus, we may expect the bargaining posture, rhetoric, and goodwill of the debtor to change, even though the outcome predicted is the same as the last period. In addition, in this case, we would not expect the U.S. or the IMF to have much success in pushing the equilibrium away from a deadlock.

The negotiations and outcome

In this period all parties concerned made various efforts to engineer a rapprochement between Peru and the banks, yet every one was clouded by a deep pessimism about the feasibility of breaking the deadlock. Over time, the IMF became more active in searching for a way to reintegrate Peru into the international financial community. Peruvian negotiators met with commercial bankers in autumn of 1986. The García government became increasingly weak. Forced to increase reserves by 15 to 30% to cover their Peru loans, bankers were in no mood to make concessions. They negotiated aggressively and even declined to send a mission to Lima – Peru had to go to New York.

Peruvian negotiators formally proposed a plan that had been proposed earlier in the year that involved a stretching out of the loans over 20 years with a five-year grace period and 3 or 4% interest rates. They received a flat no. "We don't even give that to countries which maintain themselves current," said one banker. After failing to reach an agreement on September 26, 1986, the banks issued a statement saying that rescheduling negotiations would resume only after Peru made a "meaningful" effort to pay its $630 million in interest arrears. Indeed, the banks threatened to dissolve the advisory committee – formed with Peru's help in a more cooperative round of the bargaining – and leave the some 270 banks free to try to attach Peruvian assets, including exports, through the courts. Such measures could include embargoes and nuisance suits. "You don't even have to harass the government; just other people dealing with Peru," said a banker on the committee.[121]

In response Peru offered to pay the creditor banks a maximum $20 million over the next year in order to persuade the banks to send an information-gathering mission to Peru. Peru also offered to pay up to $140 million in kind. The steering committee rejected the offer as inadequate to justify a mission, and demanded a minimum of $60 million in cash. Peru had sufficient funds to pay this at this time, but balked because of increasingly troublesome signs that the economic recovery would falter.

President García met frequently during 1986 and 1987 with members of big business (called the 12 Apostles) in an effort to convince them to invest in Peruvian projects. Having reduced taxes and stimulated consumption to encourage further economic recovery, the president was dissatisfied with the response by business. In April he confirmed the fear that his government was "both anti-business and inconsistent by making a forced issue of valueless inti bonds."[122] All companies with sales of over $100,000 in 1986 had to purchase these government bonds of between 20 and 30% of their gross profits.[123] The result was to destroy the relatively cooperative relationship between President García and business that had prevailed to that date. Entrepreneurs were reluctant to invest

[121] *LAWR*, September 25, 1986, p. 10. [122] Asheshov (1988), p. 253.
[123] *LAWR*, April 23, 1987, p. 2.

after these bonds were issued because they had no guarantee that the rewards of their investments would not be similarly confiscated in the future.[124]

Despite this dismal situation García appeared eager to reach an agreement with international creditors, pushing a range of exotic schemes to make payments in kind. The new policy was to pay in accordance with the "capacity to pay," using methods that did not deplete foreign exchange. In fact, two banks – the Midland Bank and the First Interstate Bank of California – actually accepted these solutions, to the dismay of the banks' advisory committee.[125]

When reserves fell down to $454 million in October 1987, Peru instructed the newly appointed Minister of the Economy, Saberbeín, to talk with the World Bank, the Paris Club, and the commercial banks. Government officials also began to speak more favorably about the IMF.[126] But the proposal required even greater concessions from the banks than those already discussed and rejected – Peru offered payment in kind in exchange for the banks' accepting 25-year zero-coupon bonds.

Public officials soon reversed their positions in response to political pressures. Following public opposition to the devaluation of the inti in December 1987 and January 1988, García began to backtrack. Peru simply avoided any meetings with the banks. It became obvious that World Bank money would come too little and too late to ward off a balance-of-payments crisis. Rapprochement became "a fifth-rate consideration" once again.[127] Instead, the government began to sell off the country's gold reserves.[128] Yet with net reserves in February valued at only between $400–500 million, Peru had little room to maneuver.[129] Saberbeín insisted that the reserves were "there to be used," and it was "normal" to sell them.[130]

A stabilization plan in September 1988 which included a massive devaluation of the inti and a major increase in prices, especially petroleum, led to riots and looting in Lima's market areas. Annualized inflation in 1988 reached 1,722%, up from 115% in 1987.[131] Bowing to pressure from within his party, President García sent the Minister of the Economy, Abel Salinas, to Berlin to mend fences with the IMF.[132] Salinas conferred with IMF executive manager Michel Camdessus, and subsequently announced that the IMF would send a mission to Lima. But he denied that Peru had signed a letter of intent.[133] Hopes of obtaining fresh credits quickly evaporated. The Fund sent a team to Lima, but took a hard-line stance, warning that if Peru did not stick to its apparent intention to normalize relations, it should be expelled. Peru realized that it did not stand to gain fresh credit from restoring relations with the Fund because the Fund's

[124] See the poll conducted by Apoyo and reported in *LAWR*, October 1, 1987, p. 5.
[125] *LAWR*, September 24, 1987, p. 2; and October 1, 1987, p. 7.
[126] *LAWR*, November 26, 1987, p. 7. [127] *LAWR*, February 4, 1988, p. 9.
[128] *LAWR*, February 25, 1988, p. 1.
[129] *The Andean Report*, vol. 15, no. 3 (March 1988), p. 83.
[130] *LAWR*, May 12, 1988, p. 7. [131] Dornbusch and Edwards (1990), p. 158.
[132] *LAWR*, October 20, 1988, p. 2. [133] *LAWR*, October 13, 1988, pp. 2, 7.

contribution would be limited to Peru's quota, the loss of its reserves over the previous year.[134]

Carlos Rivas Dávilas, who replaced Minister of the Economy Salinas after Salinas resigned in November in the wake of a second economic shock package, had no better luck reestablishing contact with the IMF. Dávilas visited Washington in late January 1989 and arranged for Peru to make a "symbolic" payment. He returned to Lima to discover that García was "unconvinced" by the IMF's position; the president refused to pay even the token $30 million negotiated by Dávilas.[135]

In a new turn of events, in early 1989 the IMF informed Peru that it would give it a $1 billion bridge loan to cover its arrears with other countries and organizations. Another mission was sent to Peru in April. The IMF, according to Dávilas, had adopted a new attitude. Observers suggested, however, that far from any serious effort to reschedule Peru's international debt, the IMF only sought to prevent the further deterioration of relations as creditors waited for the change of government in 1990. The President also remained cynical about the IMF's goodwill: "it is . . . nearly impossible for us to obtain [from them] more than we have to pay."[136]

In late August the Fund threatened to expel Peru by declaring the government in "non-compliance" with IMF regulations. This action was not taken, and in October Peru reached an agreement with the Fund to "negotiate the securing of the resources necessary to pay Peru's arrears with multilateral organizations and to negotiate the securing and payment of the resources necessary to support the medium-term programme." The IMF was to help Peru normalize financial relations with official creditors. Peru promised to make a number of small symbolic payments before turning the government over to the next administration in July 1990, which it did with regularity.

The agreement with Peru presaged the outcome of negotiations between Peru and the IMF under the new government of Alberto Kenyo Fujimori, who took office in July 1990. Multilateral lending organizations asked Fujimori to agree to the terms of a standby loan without receiving new credit. The payoff for compliance would be that the IMF, the World Bank, and the IDB would use their influence to broker a huge bridge loan by OECD countries to pay for Peru's arrears to multilateral lending organizations. This strengthened arrears strategy would provide no new funds for Peru in the immediate run, but would clear up $2 billion in obligations with multilateral agencies, thereby going a long way toward normalizing Peru's relations with the international financial community. The IMF informed Fujimori that his only other option was to have Peru's membership suspended. This new "cooperative" strategy was aimed at helping countries like Peru that were unable to break the deadlock created by the strategy of playing "bad debtor."[137]

134 *The Andean Report*, vol. 15, no. 11 (November 1988), p. 282.
135 *LAWR*, February 9, 1989, p. 10. 136 *LAWR*, May 4, 1989, p. 3.
137 *The Andean Report*, vol. 18, no. 9 (October 1990), p. 175.

Conclusion

As a relatively weak debtor in the international financial system in this epoch, Peru's options were relatively limited. In this chapter, we have seen both conciliatory and confrontational behavior by Peru, but neither led to a significant accord that enabled Peru to emerge with a favorable debt agreement. The model predicted both types of behavior based on the changing individual situation of Peru and the banks.

Despite the generally negative assessments of the Belaúnde government, we argue that in terms of international debt negotiations it was not so inadequate. The Belaúnde government avoided the costs of direct confrontation with the banks by assiduously courting international lending institutions, both public and private. At the same time, it paid very little beyond what was necessary to "keep up appearances." In this manner, Peru preserved its reputation of being an orthodox debtor and avoided the stigma of having its debt declared "value impaired."

In 1985 and 1986 García made debt payments comparable to those made under the Belaúnde Administration – they were more than 10% of export earnings – yet Peru's debt was declared "value impaired" and no concessions were extracted from the banks.[138] The Fujimori government that followed García inherited international reserves so low it was unable to make even the symbolic payments on its multilateral debt necessary to recover its credit worthiness among the developed market economies.

In the end, Peru's efforts to challenge the banks produced only misery and further crises. Reintegration into the financial system, the only option for countries who do not have great strategic importance for major creditor governments, was the only option left for Peru.

Postscript

In July 1990 Alberto Fujimori was inaugurated President of Peru. He immediately began "reinserting" Peru into the international financial system. It took until February 1993 to clear arrears with the IMF and World Bank, and thus become eligible for new multilateral loans. Only then did Peru seriously consider mending fences with the commercial banks.

Fujimori sought to normalize relations with the international financial community. The first task was to create a "Support Group" of creditor nations to help Peru clear arrears with the multilateral institutions. In April 1991 the United States and Japan agreed to form a Support Group, and by August Peru convinced five European nations to join. Finally, in September 11 members of the Club of Paris agreed to make donations and concessional loans to help Peru clear its arrears with the multilateral institutions. The IMF agreed to Peru's

[138] Economist Intelligence Unit, *Country Report: Peru, Bolivia*, no. 1, 1987, p. 2, and no. 4, 1990, p. 3.

economic program for 1991–1992, and a schedule of payments that gave Peru a period of grace ending in late 1992.[139]

In the case of the World Bank, Peru designed a similar program. Peru was allowed to gradually acquire the right to obtain loans up to the amount in arrears until the end of 1992.[140] Debts to the Inter-American Development Bank were cleared with a loan from the Fondo Latinoamericano de Reservas.

As soon as Peru reached an agreement with the IMF it also renegotiated the public external debt with the Paris Club. The goal was to minimize payments in 1991–1992, and then renegotiate in 1993. Peru was granted favorable terms in the Paris Club. In September 1991, the Paris Club rescheduled Peru's debt over extended periods. Short-term payments were also reduced.

The "reinsertion" of Peru was placed in doubt when Fujimori closed Congress and suspended the constitution on April 5, 1992. A loan from the IDB was postponed until new elections were held for a new congress to rewrite the constitution on November 20, 1992. After the elections Peru and the IMF reached a new agreement. By February 1993 it had cleared arrears with both the Fund and the Bank, thus becoming eligible for fresh credit from them.

In May 1993 Peru rescheduled its Paris Club debt again, substantially reducing the amount it needed to pay in 1993–1995. The relief amounted to 60% of the amount Peru was scheduled to pay – more than the publicly stated goal of the Peruvian negotiators.

Only after Peru had mended fences with the multilateral agencies and creditor governments did it begin to talk, and get reacquainted, with the Citicorp-led steering committee. In July Peru sent a letter to the banks proposing a meeting to discuss restructuring the debt and resuming interest payments. Peru was under pressure from at least 10 pending lawsuits by the creditors.

Optimism about the normalization of relations between Peru and the banks led to a dramatic rise in the value of Peruvian debt paper on the secondary market – the mere formality of negotiations resulted in a doubling over its value at the start of 1993 to slightly over 40%. With interest arrears worth 90% of the principal, many bankers hoped for a lucrative settlement. But there were major disagreements over the amount owed. Peru put the number at around $6 billion, but the banks claimed they were owed $8.5 billion.

Peru met with the banks in 1993, in a preliminary meeting at which representatives of the IMF and World Bank were also present. Peru sought to have creditor lawsuits dropped in return for agreeing to resume interest payments and permitting debt-equity swaps. In 1994, U.S. and foreign banks stopped their litigation against Peru in anticipation of concluding a final deal along Brady Plan lines.

Following Alberto Fujimori's reelection in April 1995, debt negotiations moved to a faster track, with repeated rounds of talks continuing through August of 1995. Peru pursued efforts to buy back its debt at reduced prices as it had done

[139] Boloña Behr (1993), p. 136. [140] Boloña Behr (1993), p. 137.

historically – a strategy which the banks strongly criticized. Meanwhile, Peruvian debt increased in value to nearly 60 cents on the dollar in anticipation of an agreement. As of this writing, Peru and the banks had still not settled, but could be expected to come to terms on a more or less standard Brady Plan accord.

13 Collision course: Argentine debt rescheduling in the 1980s and 1990s

High interest rates and the global recession of the early 1980s crippled Argentina's ability to service its mounting debt along with virtually all the third world borrowers. Unlike other debtors, however, the Argentine economy also staggered under the burden of a $3 billion war waged in the South Atlantic against Great Britain in 1982. Apart from its cost, the conflict subsequently pitted Argentina against its creditors, casting a shadow over the first period of debt negotiations, and politicizing Argentina's debt issue in a way that those of Mexico and Brazil were not.

I divide Argentina's external bank debt negotiations into seven periods, beginning with initial bargaining in late 1982 and ending with a Brady Plan agreement in 1992. The first period, from October 1982 to July 1984, encompasses several stop-gap agreements between Argentina and the banks, as well as an accord with the IMF. The next period, from August 1984 to March 1985, found Argentina in negotiations with a somewhat more stable coalition of bankers. Although the game headed for an outcome of medium adjustment and high concessions, in the end the IMF's intervention threw the game into deadlock.

Period three, from April 1985 to December 1985, found Argentina with a short-lived increase in coalitional stability and some adjustment on both the bankers and Argentina's part. The fourth period from January 1986 to August 1987 – marked by bankers' fear of a spreading moratorium – ended with considerable concessions by the bankers but little adjustment by Argentina. By contrast, the fifth period from September 1987 to June 1989 was marked by deadlock between an unstable and weak Argentina facing a financially strong but now unstable group of banks. The sixth and seventh periods, from August 1989 to August 1991, and from then until the end of 1992 brought a decade of rescheduling efforts to a close. The U.S. actively intervened with the Brady Plan, and the banks and a considerably more stable Argentina reached an agreement under its auspices.

Background to rescheduling

One of many victims, Argentina suffered from the 1980s recession and the high interest rates that accompanied it. These international factors diminished Argentina's ability to service its mounting debt. In addition, debt problems festered with poorly applied neoclassical policies of José Martínez de Hoz (Finance Minister under the military government from 1976 to 1981). By pushing up domestic interest rates, by initiating forward crawling-peg exchange rate adjustment, Martínez de Hoz generated an overvalued currency and a troubled economy. As the overvalued currency encouraged consumption of imports and free-spending trips abroad by rich Argentines, the government resorted to foreign borrowing to finance its escalating deficit. Beyond this, military rulers funded many expensive and questionable projects favored by their cronies.[1] The war with Great Britain only worsened Argentina's problems.[2]

Argentina needed to reschedule its debts even before the war began. The country's debt had more than doubled in the two years before 1981.[3] By June of that year Hugo Lamonica, Undersecretary of Finance and Foreign Investment, had traveled to New York, his goal to refinance part of the $13.8 billion in principal and interest due that year.[4] War simply aggravated matters. Following the conflict, Argentina had stopped debt service on all credits from British banks; in response, the U.K. froze Argentine assets. By September the bankers refused to extend new credits until Great Britain released the $1.45 billion of frozen assets.[5] Argentina found itself saddled with a handicap unique among Latin American debtors: it had just lost a bitter war with a country whose banks were among its major creditors.

The loss to Britain discredited and ultimately ended military rule, and the Argentines felt betrayed by American support of Britain. Any government, particularly the one democratically brought to power in 1983, would have to delicately handle the talks with the foreign bankers.

Period one, October 1982–July 1984: an unstable brew

Argentina's interest arrears had reached $2.3 billion by the end of June 1982 (with a total of $12.7 billion in principal and interest payments due by the end of the year)[6] when the government announced that it would attempt to reschedule $36 billion of foreign debt.[7] Yet, at the same time, a wave of protests and strikes over the country's deteriorating economy prompted the Minister of Economy, Jose Dagnino Pastore, to resign after only seven weeks in office.[8] His replacement, Jorge Wehbe, affirmed in early September that Argentina would have to adopt a stabilization program to meet its obligations. Attending the annual IMF meeting in Toronto, Wehbe initiated discussions about rescheduling the part of the $15 billion debt that would fall due over the next four months.[9] At the Toronto meetings, U.S. Deputy Treasury Secretary Timothy McNamar shuttled between the Argentine and British delegations to promote Argentina's eligibility for further loans.[10] The following month, the Argentines sought a

[1] *The Banker*, April 1984. [2] Cost estimate from Congressional Research Service, 1984.
[3] *International Herald Tribune*, June 19, 1981. [4] *International Herald Tribune*, June 19, 1981.
[5] *Business Week*, August 13, 1982. [6] *Financial Times*, September 30, 1982.
[7] *International Herald Tribune*, July 3, 1982. [8] *Financial Times*, September 30, 1982.
[9] *Financial Times*, September 3, 1982. [10] Delamaide (1984), pp. 114–115.

short-term commercial bank loan for $1 billion. These efforts set the stage for a decade of rescheduling negotiations.

Identifying individual situations

After the Falklands/Malvinas War with Britain, in this period Argentina can be classified as coalitionally unstable, issue weak, and overall medium in capabilities (IS 4/8). The banks were coalitionally unstable, and also deficient in both debt-related resources and overall capabilities (IS 8).

Argentina. After its bloody war, in the early part of this period, Argentina's military government teetered on the brink of collapse. General Reynaldo Bignone, selected by the military as president on the basis of his obscurity and distance from the war, had popular support; he thus found it difficult to resist public pressure to end austerity. Bignone feared that continuing foreign debt servicing or other unpopular policies would make his government susceptible to another military takeover. Subsequently, the government chose to yield to popular demand in order to maintain power. With civilian elections scheduled for late 1983, Argentina remained coalitionally unstable throughout the first period.

By 1982, Argentina's total reserves – including gold – had dropped to less than $4 billion from about $10 billion in 1980.[11] With non-gold foreign exchange reserves below $3 billion, and interest arrears of nearly $3 billion, the country badly needed new financing. Thus I code Argentina as weak in issue-specific capabilities.

Under military rule, the Argentine economy suffered from poor growth rates and rampant inflation. In 1982, the economy underwent a 5.1% contraction with inflation at an annual rate of 165%.[12] The Argentines could, however, claim some degree of independence from foreign creditors and trading partners. In contrast to many other debtors, Argentina had a large reservoir of natural resources and was less vulnerable to interruptions in trade and capital flows. Thus, in the event of a debt impasse the nation could potentially survive a cutoff of short-term credits. Moreover, in agricultural goods, Argentina was a net exporter. Because Argentina was not dependent upon imported food, threats of becoming self-sufficient were more credible. In overall terms, then, Argentina is coded as medium.

Lenders

In 1982 Argentina's creditors did not form a united front primarily because of the varying levels of exposure among the 325 commercial banks.[13] Large banks favored policies that continued to supply Argentina with new cash, hoping that fresh money, complemented by IMF-monitored economic reforms, would enable Argentina to regularly service its debt. By contrast, lower levels of exposure

[11] Economist Intelligence Unit, no. 3, 1983. [12] Kaufman (1988), p. 28.
[13] *Financial Times*, December 16, 1982.

gave smaller banks a different outlook. They preferred refusing new funding and writing off outstanding loans. The lenders' coalition was also split because of the British banks' continued hostility toward Argentina. Because the banking community was divided along these two fault lines, I code the lender's coalition as unstable throughout the whole period. Unlike the bargaining involving Mexico and Brazil, the banks failed to unify for a considerable length of time because of the conflict between Argentina and Britain.

The banks' high levels of exposure to Argentina placed them in a precarious position. For example, in the first quarter of 1983 alone, Argentina accounted for an estimated $650 million in interest payments on a total of $8.6 billion borrowed from U.S. lenders.[14] For other banks, Argentina contributed as much as 40% of their earnings.[15] Because of the extent of its exposure, the creditors were in a vulnerable position in terms of a possible "Black Thursday" stock market collapse.[16] Thus, on issues related specifically to debt rescheduling, the lenders were weak.

With respect to overall capabilities, because they were unable to enforce debt servicing or recoup outstanding loans, the banks were weak. Moreover, with the huge amount of debt outstanding to Argentina and other major debtors, the banks' very existence would be endangered by default. Although they hoped to secure assistance from the IMF or the creditor governments, the banks could never be certain of their support.

Creditor governments and international organizations. Against the backdrop of the Falklands/Malvinas war, the attitudes of the largest creditors, the U.S. and Britain, obviously differed in this period. The Americans were concerned about improving relations with Argentina, a by-product of American support for British efforts in the Falklands War.[17] In addition, the U.S. was solicitous of Argentina's interests as a newly emerging democracy. Washington was also worried about the health of the international financial system: Its greatest fear was that an Argentine moratorium could inspire similar actions in other countries. With the high level of U.S. banks' exposure in almost every Latin American country, American officials clearly recognized the threat posed by an "en masse" default on Latin American debt. As one senior Federal Reserve official remarked, "Argentina was not a risk per se; it did not threaten a collapse of the system. [The problem was that] if they took an unorthodox approach, others would as well."[18]

In contrast, the British had little reason to assist Argentina. The war had caused Argentina to impose financial sanctions against UK companies. Though British officials were concerned with the stability of the international financial system, unlike the U.S., they focused on protecting British lenders – rather than aiding Argentina in its democratic transition.

[14] *Los Angeles Times*, March 30, 1984. [15] *Los Angeles Times*, March 30, 1984.
[16] *The Economist*, October 22, 1983. [17] *International Herald Tribune*, July 3, 1982.
[18] Interview, 1985.

Cardinal Payoff Matrix,
Intervention Expected

		Lenders IS 8		
		HC...	MC...	LC...
	HA...	−1.5, 0	−5, 4	−6.5, 8
Argentina IS 4/8	MA...	2.83, −3.5	−1, 0	−3.5, 3.5
	LA...	7.17, −4	3, −2	**−.5, 0**

Note: Nash equilibrium bolded; expected outcome with intervention underlined.

Ordinal Payoff Matrix,
Intervention Expected

		Lenders IS 8		
		HC...	MC...	LC...
	HA...	4, 5	2, 8	1, 9
Argentina IS 4/8	MA...	7, 2	5, 5	3, 7
	LA...	9, 1	8, 3	**6, 5**

Note: Nash equilibrium bolded; expected outcome with intervention underlined.

Figure 13.1. *Play phase, period one: October 1982–July 1984*

The IMF's predominant concern was the stability of the international financial system. Therefore, keeping Argentina both cooperative and current on its payments was the IMF's preoccupation in this period.

Debt game and predicted outcome

We arrive at the cardinal game matrix and ordinal conversion shown in Figure 13.1 for the first period. If we examine the outcomes based solely on strategic interaction among the banks and Argentina, the outcome would be LA..., LC.... This is the Nash equilibrium yielded by the banks' dominant strategy of no concessions, and the debtor's dominant strategy of no adjustments.

In view of U.S. concerns, we expect intervention to lead to a different outcome than the one in the two-actor game. Specifically, we expect an outcome of LA..., MC... as the U.S. pushes the banks to help Argentina. We might also expect the IMF to press the Argentines to adjust and the banks to contribute new money, but given the primacy of U.S. concerns for helping Argentina, we expect it to resist adjustment.

The negotiations and outcome

Three rounds of talks marked the first period of negotiations. The first, from October to December 1982, focused on a bridge loan; the second, from January to October 1983, involved discussion of a bank loan and interest arrears; and the third, from November 1983 to July 1984, involved a "rescue" package for Argentina and the banks.

Round one. In October 1982, already in negotiations with the IMF, Argentina sought a $1 billion short-term credit from commercial banks. As noted above, the banks appealed to traditional norms of balance of payment adjustment, insisting that Argentina adopt austerity measures before receiving any new credits. Thus, the banks required Argentina to reach an agreement with the IMF before they would consider a new agreement on their own.

By the end of the year Argentina had reached a preliminary accord with the Fund for a $1.95 billion standby credit. As in the Mexican case, the IMF made disbursement of the money contingent upon new commercial bank loans, thus effectively coercing the banks into providing new capital. The head of the IMF, Jacques de Larosière, met with Argentina's creditors on November 16. He instructed them that Argentina would need $2.6 billion in new loans – a $1.1 billion bridge loan from January 1983 to March 1984, and a $1.5 billion five-year loan.[19]

As usual, the large banks, worried about their huge existing exposure in Argentina, favored extending new funds and were receptive toward the Argentine proposal. On the other hand, smaller banks with limited exposures preferred immediate capital losses to the idea of throwing good money after bad.[20]

Given the similar balance-of-payments crises in other Latin American countries, Argentina found itself jockeying with the other debtors for a limited amount of money from the same sources.[21] Concerned that cutting off Latin American countries completely from international finance would end any hopes of their

[19] *Wall Street Journal*, December 30, 1982.

[20] The Argentine government attempted to enhance its offer by offering smaller banks a way to cut their losses. Argentina would exchange promissory notes and dollar-denominated bonds for approximately $5 billion in private debts to foreign banks. *International Herald Tribune*, November 19, 1982.

[21] *Wall Street Journal*, December 30, 1982.

economic recovery (let alone renewed debt servicing), the Federal Reserve stepped in to pressure the banks into continued lending.[22] Compared with other debtors, Argentina's volatile domestic situation following the South Atlantic War provided a more compelling incentive for the international organizations to intervene on its behalf. Though the British impeded the negotiations' progress by freezing assets and by refusing to finance new loans, U.S. and IMF intervention facilitated agreements through increased bank lending and debtor cooperation. Both the IMF and the Fed worked under the assumption that future debt servicing depended on new funding from U.S. and European banks, and they worked to secure this outcome.

De Larosière continued to pressure the banks, warning that without assurances from the banks that they would participate in a jumbo loan, he would not ask the executive board of the Fund for an Argentine standby agreement.[23] In the end, the banks backed down. The $1.1 billion bridge loan was signed on December 31, 1982, but the lenders made clear that they were not willing to make further long-term commitments to the uncooperative debtor.

In this first round of negotiations, as we expected, the U.S. government was the critical actor. At the onset of negotiations the banks made an immediate appeal to the traditional norms of balance of payments adjustment, whereby debtors receive emergency financing from the IMF while undergoing domestic economic reform. Yet the banks failed to find a ready ally in the U.S. government. Sympathetic to Britain during the Falklands/Malvinas War, the U.S. sought to repair damaged U.S.-Argentine relations. Argentina's efforts to install a democratic regime also touched a nerve where U.S. foreign policy was concerned. Thus the U.S. favored Argentina over the banks, coercing new bank lending before a solid IMF agreement had been reached. Argentina's domestic problems and inability to continue debt servicing had attracted allies. Without demanding harsh adjustment policies that might risk domestic upheaval, the U.S. and the IMF saw to it that the necessary emergency funds were provided. Thus, rather than a deadlock, after intervention this round ended in LA..., MC... as we predicted.

The larger problem of long-term balance-of-payments financing still remained unresolved. Negotiations over a more significant bank loan would await a second round of talks.

Round two. In January 1983, the IMF formally approved a $1.95 billion standby credit to be disbursed over a 15-month period. By contrast, negotiations with commercial banks (over the $1.5 billion loan from the previous year) remained unresolved.[24] The second round of bargaining reflects Argentine efforts to secure new loans to repay its debts without further depleting its reserves, despite bankers' hopes that Argentina would first resume interest payments as a sign of good faith. Once again, negotiations between the banks and Argentina

[22] See Aggarwal (1987) for a discussion of this effort.
[23] *Wall Street Journal*, December 30, 1982. [24] *IMF Survey*, February 7, 1983.

headed toward a stalemate. As in the first round, Argentina's transition to democracy attracted allies, leading to helpful intervention on the part of the U.S. government.

Although they did not involve the banks directly, negotiations for a $750 million loan from the BIS illustrated the solicitous attitude of the United States and problems with the British. Argentina's refusal to pledge its gold reserves as security limited the BIS loan to only $500 million. In fact, this reluctance could have scuttled the entire BIS loan had the U.S. not stepped in to complete the agreement. The U.S. contributed more than half the funds for the January 1983 loan whereas the Bank of England refused to participate.[25]

Throughout the first half of 1983, Argentina pressed for completion of a new $1.5 billion loan from the banks, but they refused to release the credit until Argentina resumed its interest payments. The banks also withheld the final $300 million tranche of the $1.1 billion bridge loan granted at the end of 1982, pending IMF confirmation of Argentina's adherence to its first quarter austerity targets.

By July 1983, still behind on interest payments on its public sector debt it had promised to resume, Argentina claimed that domestic conflicts were tying its hands. It again attempted to obtain new loans before resuming payments on interest arrears. This strategy met with some success as banks stopped citing overdue interest as a reason for delaying the loan, and decided to target August 5, 1983 to dispense the loan.[26]

In this case, however, Britain intervened to try to force Argentina to release $10 million in British profit remittances. It also warned lenders under its jurisdiction against contributing to the $1.5 billion loan. Subsequently, British banks stalled on dispensing the loan because Argentina had failed to abolish its sanctions over the movement of British funds.[27] Regarding the frozen assets, the Argentine government quietly approved the release of an estimated $10 million of British profit remittances frozen at the outbreak of the war.[28] Two days after Argentina leaked the news that it would release the funds, the British government then cleared its banks' participation in the $1.5 billion commercial loan.[29] Finally, in October the banks announced they would disburse $500 million of the new $1.5 billion loan. In return, Argentina agreed to pay $130 million in arrears, promising to bring interest payments up to date through September 1983. In this case, then, active British government involvement helped to shift Argentina toward more adjustment than in the first round, although the banks once again made relatively more concessions than Argentina.

Round three. Despite its promises, Argentina's actual economic performance failed to satisfy the IMF. By the end of 1983, the Fund had suspended its 15-month agreement. In response, after initially disbursing $500 million in

[25] *Financial Times*, January 26, 1983 and *Wall Street Journal*, January 28, 1983.
[26] *Wall Street Journal*, August 8, 1983. [27] *Wall Street Journal*, August 8, 1983.
[28] *Financial Times*, August 16, 1983. [29] *The Times*, August 16, 1983.

October, the banks withheld the remaining $1 billion of the promised commercial loan. A stalemate once again ensued, plunging the negotiations back into crisis.[30]

As the end of 1983 approached, Argentine arrears were estimated at $2.9 billion – nearly $1 billion more than first projected. Moreover, in 1984, $14 billion in principal and another $5 billion in interest would come due. Even with a large trade surplus, estimated at $3.5 billion, Argentina was going to need external assistance.[31] To further complicate matters, following on the heels of nearly two decades of military rule,[32] the new civilian government of Raúl Alfonsín faced enormous popular pressure to disavow the debt accumulated by the military regime. Thus, Alfonsín could not count upon any public support – either for the resumption of interest payments or for the imposition of austerity measures.[33] Yet given its weak balance-of-payments position, the Argentine government could not afford to completely alienate the international financial community.

Given this situation, not surprisingly, the Alfonsín government sought to elicit creditor government sympathy by expanding the issue-area to include the needs of its infant democracy.[34] The government argued that without assistance Argentina could not possibly make the payments that were coming due. Further, to expect the new government to implement difficult adjustment measures would be unreasonable, given popular expectations of a better life under democratic rule. By pleading hardship, Alfonsín attempted to simultaneously assuage the bankers' fears that his government would repudiate the military's debt, and to demand their assistance.

Immediately after taking power in December 1983, the Alfonsín government requested a six-month moratorium on interest payments, a rescheduling of outstanding debt, and extension of new loans. The linkage of debt and democracy evoked concern from Washington; news reports noted that "U.S. banks have been asked by the U.S. administration to be flexible as a gesture of goodwill toward the new democratic authorities."[35] Yet such requests fell upon deaf ears. Bankers generally agreed a delay in interest payments was unacceptable. One banker complained, "we expected to get facts and figures [during the talks with Argentina]. All we got were platitudes about Argentina's new democracy."[36] In the end, the banks refused to grant the interest moratorium.

Both the banks and Argentina were treading in dangerous waters at this point. If Argentina did not resume interest payments by March 31, the banks would be forced to declare their loans "non-performing." If a stalemate were to force the

[30] Economist Intelligence Unit, *Quarterly Economic Report* (hereinafter *QER*), no. 2, 1984.
[31] *QER*, no. 1, 1984.
[32] From 1966–1983, with the exception of three years of a Peronist government from 1973–1976, Argentina was under military rule.
[33] *Wall Street Journal*, November 7, 1983.
[34] *Financial Times*, December 15, 1983; *Wall Street Journal*, April 23, 1984.
[35] *QER*, no. 1, 1984. See also *Financial Times*, December 15, 1983.
[36] *Financial Times*, February 1, 1984.

lenders into such a move, the bankers would have a very difficult time justifying new loans they wanted to float in the future.

The Argentines continued to cover all their bases as the deadline approached. On the one hand, confident that the country's special political situation would garner intervention on its behalf, and unwilling to risk the domestic repercussions of submission to the IMF, Economy Minister Bernardo Grinspun blustered, "deadlines . . . are simply deadlines for banks and not for Argentina."[37] At the same time, however, Argentina sent a confidential letter of intent to the IMF outlining its plans to qualify for a revised standby loan.[38]

During this period other Latin American debtors took an interest in Argentine negotiations for fear of the negative effects a default could have on the international financial system and their own situations. Mexico's Treasury Secretary, Silva Herzog, warned, "If one Latin country gets into trouble, it affects the willingness of the banks to lend to other Latin countries."[39]

At the last moment, Mexico, Venezuela, Brazil, and Colombia made a loan of $300 million to Argentina.[40] Supplemented by $100 million from creditor banks[41] and another $100 million from Argentina's own foreign currency reserves, the government essentially acquired a $500 million emergency bridge loan to make long-overdue interest payments. As a key part of this rescue arrangement, the U.S. Treasury offered a $300 million bridge loan to Argentina to pay back its Latin American creditors, pending Argentine agreement on an IMF adjustment package.[42] The package gave Argentina three months' worth of breathing room to reach a new agreement with the IMF. The agreement stipulated that if the Argentines had not signed an accord with the Fund by the new deadline of June 30, they would not receive the U.S. Treasury loan and would thus be obliged to pay back both their Latin American and private creditors out of their own reserves.

Yet Argentina failed to reach an agreement with the IMF team in Buenos Aires. Six months into his term, the precarious coalitional position of the Alfonsín government made it difficult for Argentina to adopt an IMF stabilization program. As talks between Argentina and the IMF stalled, the deadlines for repayment had to be postponed. In a conciliatory gesture, in April 1984, the 11-bank committee recommended a two-month extension on a $750 million payment due that month.[43] In addition, the U.S. Treasury extended its offer of $300 million for two consecutive months.[44] Finally, in an address to the nation calling for shared sacrifice in the fight against inflation, an exasperated Alfonsín proposed

[37] *Wall Street Journal*, March 29, 1984. [38] *QER*, no. 2, 1984.

[39] *New York Times*, April 2, 1984.

[40] Mexico and Venezuela each extended $100 million, while Colombia and Brazil each contributed $50 million. *Wall Street Journal*, April 2, 1984.

[41] This $100 million came from the remaining $1 billion that was never disbursed out of the 1983 loan.

[42] *New York Times*, May 1, 1984. [43] *Wall Street Journal*, April 19, 1984.

[44] *New York Times*, May 1, 1984 and June 11, 1984.

a new adjustment program in June. But the Argentine proposal, spelled out in a letter of intent submitted directly to the Managing Director of the IMF, did not meet Fund standards regarding wage policy.[45]

As the June 30 deadline rapidly approached, another rescue package was put together. The banks loaned another $125 million, supplemented by $225 million from Argentina's reserves. Additionally, the deadline for repaying the $300 million loan from Mexico, Venezuela, Brazil, and Colombia was extended for a month, and the banks agreed once again to defer the payment of $750 million owed to them. With this arrangement, Argentina would be able to repay the Latin American creditors by the end of July and to make sufficient payments to prevent the reclassification of its loans as "non-performing." As in previous rounds, for the most part only the bankers and creditor governments made significant concessions, without much reciprocity on Argentina's part, leading to an outcome of LA..., MC....

Summary. As expected, in all three rounds of period one, Argentina and the lenders gravitated toward stalemate over the terms and disbursement of new money: a $1.1 billion bridge loan in 1982, a difficult $1.5 billion loan in 1983 and 1984. But in each round, concerns for the fragile Argentine political situation attracted outside intervention that broke the stalemate in favor of the debtor. As the Argentine government continued to blame its inability to implement adjustment measures on political instability, it managed to continue to avert crisis with minimal adjustment.[46] Instead creditor and fellow debtor governments that feared the repercussions of both Argentina's adjustment and possible default propped it up. The banks, however, declared that the rescue arrangement would be the last one; they refused to be party to another lending arrangement until Argentina reached an agreement with the IMF.

Situational changes

Judging from the outcome of the first round after intervention, the banks were clearly highly motivated to alter their individual situation. In particular, the banks' attempts centered on improving their coalitional stability. The formation of an advisory group, comprised of the largest lenders, created a hierarchical structure within the lenders' coalition. This, in turn, gave the larger banks the means for coercing the smaller regional banks into sharing rescheduling costs. In fact, in all of the other cases of negotiations in the 1980s and 1990s examined in this book, the creation of a bank advisory committee mended the rift between small and large banks and thus created a stable lenders' coalition. But in the

[45] *New York Times*, June 11, 1984.

[46] The brief exception to this would be in 1983 when Argentina's former antagonist, Britain, intervened to realize its own interests. Whereas in 1982 the bridge loan was produced with minimal debtor adjustment, in the following year Argentina pledged to clear up its arrears and satisfy the conditions of the IMF.

Argentine case, the banks remained divided along a second fault line. In the aftermath of the Falklands War, the large British banks could not be counted on to cooperate. Though these banks ultimately contributed to the new Argentine loans, they did so only after receiving the "political endorsement" of the British government. Thus in the wake of the war, the banks remained coalitionally unstable throughout the first period.

With respect to situational changes leading to the next period, as British banks continued to lend despite Whitehall's grumbling, the coalition of bankers stabilized. But the banks never really achieved very strong stability. In June 1984, the U.S. Federal Reserve and the Office of the Controller of the Currency issued a "clarification" of policy on classifying non-performing loans. This policy obliged banks to put loans on non-accrual status when payments were more than 90 days overdue, previously it had been done at the end of the quarter. In response, the big money-center banks changed their accounting procedures and took losses at the end of June 1984.[47] Differences in how banks reported their losses and the underlying divisions among banks undermined their potentially strong cohesion.

For its part, Argentina's instability continued, and it remained issue weak. In both periods two and three, Argentina continued to seek an advantage by linking debt with U.S. concern for Argentine democracy. But in this case, though still concerned, neither the U.S. nor the IMF was willing to demand too much from the banks without being able to guarantee Argentine compliance with IMF austerity guidelines. As Argentina grew more dependent on foreign markets, and as the U.S. began to lose interest in its plight, it became overall weak as well.

Periods two and three, August 1984–March 1985 and April 1985–December 1985: a major rescheduling agreement

The second and third periods both encompass a bargaining series that led to a major rescheduling of Argentine debt. Because Argentina's individual situation changed only slightly and the banks' remained constant during these periods, they are analyzed together in this section. Although the parties reached an agreement in late 1984 in which Argentina consented to meet IMF economic targets, the government almost immediately afterwards ignored its requirements. Consequently, another period of bargaining took place the following year, marked by the most thorough Argentine attack on inflation up to that time. Negotiations eventually culminated in the signing of a rescheduling accord in August 1985.

Identifying individual situations

During the second period, Argentina became coalitionally unstable, issue weak, and overall weak (IS 8). The creditors' position changed to one of medium coalitional stability, and issue weakness, but continued overall weakness (IS 7/8). In the third period, Argentina's political situation stabilized somewhat, while

[47] Congressional Research Service, 1984; *Institutional Investor*, August 8, 1984, pp. 189–194.

remaining the same on other dimensions, leading us to code it as coalitionally medium (IS 7/8). The banks remained in IS 7/8.

Argentina. Domestic instability accompanied Argentina's transition to democracy. Attempting to promote significant economic changes, President Alfonsín faced the difficult challenge of retaining popular support while pursuing economic policies aimed at maintaining relations with the international financial community. In particular, the labor movement applied a large amount of pressure. Highly organized and linked to the opposition Peronist Party, labor resisted the sorts of wage restraint inherent in IMF stabilization and proved itself capable of carrying out disruptive strikes. Furthermore, efforts to prosecute high-ranking officials of the military regime for human rights abuses further charged an already tense domestic situation. Combined with an economy in dire straits and a populace expecting an improved standard of living, the Alfonsín government was forced "to tread a delicate path between introducing policies which will bring the economy back on course on the one hand and, on the other, avoiding a degree of austerity which would endanger its very existence."[48] Constrained by its precarious domestic situation, the government could not easily implement a harsh adjustment program – no matter how favorable in the eyes of the international financial community or how useful over the long run. By the third period, Argentina's political situation stabilized slightly. Toward the end of the second period, the replacement of Minister of the Economy Bernardo Grinspun and Central Bank President Enrique Garcia Vasquez with Juan Sourrouille and Alfredo Concepcion, respectively, created new-found harmony in Alfonsín's cabinet. Alfonsín then gained additional room to maneuver to implement the Austral Plan, an effort that significantly improved his popularity for some time.

Argentina remained weak in debt-related and overall resources. By the fourth quarter of 1984, Argentina's reserve situation had reached a critical juncture. Foreign exchange holdings continued to drop; the first quarter of 1985 saw reserves of only $800 million. Although this quarter marked the nadir of Argentina's reserve situation, even by the first quarter of 1986 reserves remained at only $2.5 billion. The economic growth rate in 1984 fell by 2.4% from 1983, and again by 4.4% in 1985. Moreover, inflation in 1984 raged at 626.7%, almost double the rate of the previous year.[49]

With respect to overall capabilities, Argentina had attained a trade surplus of about $3.5 billion in 1984 and about $4.5 billion in 1985.[50] However, a penetrating look at this figure reveals the trade surplus as a consequence of Argentina's trade with markets under the control of creditor governments, demonstrating Argentina's growing reliance on foreign markets. In March 1985, President Alfonsín visited the United States, seeking improved trade as well as political ties between the two countries.[51] This visit was strongly motivated by continued

[48] *QER*, no. 2, 1984. [49] See Kaufman (1988), p. 28, table 3.
[50] Kaufman (1988), p. 28, table 3. [51] *Wall Street Journal*, March 18, 1985.

protectionism by the EEC, and the loss of the Soviet market to Brazil, both of which pushed Argentina to look elsewhere for market access for its meat exports,[52] making it more vulnerable to trade disruption.

Lenders. As it became clear that British banks would continue to lend to Argentina despite animosity between the two governments, the lenders' coalition stabilized. But the downgrading of Argentine loans created strain among Argentina's bankers, leading one source to note that "Banks had been worried that a decision to downgrade Argentina's debts might provide many small creditors with just the excuse they have been looking for to back away from putting up any new loans."[53] Financially, the banks continued to face difficulties with the debt crisis continuing in full force in many countries. The lenders remained weak in overall resources, with enough exposure to remain vulnerable to an Argentine default but without the ability to force a sovereign government to fulfill its obligations.

Creditor governments and the IMF. As before, concerned with the fragility of Argentine democracy, the U.S. and IMF demonstrated a willingness to accept less orthodox stabilization measures. At the same time, as suggested by the new banking regulations discussed above, the U.S. became increasingly concerned about the solvency of the money-center banks and the stability of the international financial system. Moreover, although sympathetic to Argentina's situation, the U.S. feared the repercussions of rewarding non-cooperative behavior on other Latin American nations. Having gone out on a limb to bail out Argentina in early 1984, the U.S. could be expected to be less sympathetic the second time around. In addition, while Argentina faced problems domestically, it was no longer unique, and had after all made the transition successfully from military rule to democracy.

Debt game and predicted outcome

The debt matrix for this period (see Figure 13.2) reflects the lenders' weak situation (IS 7/8). The Nash equilibrium of the two-party negotiations without intervention would be no adjustment, high concessions (LA..., HC...), with Argentina receiving its highest payoff.

In view of changing creditor government interests and the IMF's desire to secure adjustment programs, however, we would expect to see a somewhat different outcome than that of the two-actor game. Though Argentine negotiators will likely continue linking their payments crisis with Argentina's fledgling democracy to excuse minimal adjustment, we would expect this strategy to be less successful than in the first period. Given American concerns not only for Argentine political stability but also for the international financial system, we expect the U.S. to support IMF efforts to pressure Argentina to adjust.

[52] *Wall Street Journal*, March 18, 1985. [53] *Financial Times*, November 7, 1984.

Cardinal Payoff Matrix,
Intervention Expected

		Lenders IS 7/8		
		HC...	MC...	LC...
	HA...	0, 6	–3.5, 7.83	–4, 9.67
Argentina IS 8	MA...	<u>4, 2.75</u>	0, 4	–2, 5.25
	LA...	**8, 3**	3.5, 2.5	0, 2

Note: Nash equilibrium bolded; expected outcome with intervention underlined.

Ordinal Payoff Matrix,
Intervention Expected

		Lenders IS 7/8		
		HC...	MC...	LC...
	HA...	5, 7	2, 8	1, 9
Argentina IS 8	MA...	<u>8, 3</u>	5, 5	3, 6
	LA...	**9, 4**	7, 2	5, 1

Note: Nash equilibrium bolded; expected outcome with intervention underlined.

Figure 13.2. *Play phase, period two: August 1984–March 1985*

The negotiations and outcome: period two

By the end of September 1984, Argentina and the IMF reached an agreement on a 15-month $1.4 billion standby loan. In addition to setting June 1985 as the deadline for an agreement between Argentina and the banks on rescheduling, and calling for Argentina to remove its arrears, the new arrangement included difficult policy reforms. Inflation, which ran at an annual rate of 680% as of September 1984, was to be reduced to 300% within 12 months' time, and to

150% by the end of 1985. The public sector deficit, which had peaked at 16.5% in the final quarter of 1983 and reduced to 8.1% in 1984, was to be held down to 5.4% in 1985.[54] With the economy in such terrible shape, it appeared that the public was more willing to initially endure more austere policy reforms. Yet given the Union Civica Radical's (UCR) (Alfonsín's party) lack of control over Argentine labor unions, it would be increasingly difficult for his administration to meet even these targets – no matter what it was willing to promise.

In the meantime, Argentina and the bank advisory group began negotiations in late October on the extension of new loans and a comprehensive rescheduling agreement. These talks produced an agreement calling for the banks to extend $4.2 billion in new money and reschedule payments on another $13.4 billion worth of debt. The Argentines, in return, agreed to pay $750 million in overdue interest by the end of 1984, to repay the $750 million principal outstanding on the 1982 $1.1 billion bridge loan by early 1985, and to try to remove its arrears during the first half of 1985.[55] Because Argentina had signed an agreement with the IMF and was proceeding in a cooperative manner with the banks, the U.S. Treasury was prepared to lend $500 million to tide Argentina over, provided the banks agreed with the package presented to them by the advisory committee.[56]

By the end of 1984, the arrangements appeared to be solidified, marking an episode of apparent debtor-creditor cooperation unprecedented in this period of Argentine negotiations. On December 28, after 90% of the banks had agreed to make contributions to the $4.2 billion loan, the IMF's directors gave their approval to the $1.42 billion standby loan; the $500 million bridge loan from the U.S. Treasury immediately followed.

Juan Sourrouille and Alfredo Concepcion's new economic positions sent the positive message to Argentina's international creditors that the government was indeed serious about economic stabilization. Sourrouille's economic views – he supported export-oriented policies and attacking inflation – closely resembled those of the IMF and the banks. But while these personnel changes increased the cohesion of Alfonsín's Radical Party and allowed it to implement the Austral Plan in the short run, cabinet changes alone could not enhance Argentina's ability to implement a tough austerity program. Argentina continued to face difficulty in pursuing austerity measures despite its international promises. Asserting that workers would not "pay for the cost of the foreign debt," the Confederación General de Trabajadores (CGT) protested and refused to participate in the effort ("*concertación*") called for by Alfonsín.[57]

Facing declining business and labor support, Alfonsín's government acceded to domestic pressures to relax monetary restrictions in early 1985. As inflation raged out of control, a displeased IMF announced the suspension of the standby

[54] *QER*, no. 4, 1984.

[55] The $750 million payment was actually due in late 1984, but the banks agreed to defer until January. *Washington Post*, December 3, 1984; *Financial Times*, December 4, 1984; *Wall Street Journal*, December 4, 1984.

[56] *Washington Post*, December 3, 1984. [57] *QER*, no. 1, 1985.

loan in late March. De Larosière stated that though negotiations for setting new performance targets would follow, further credits were unlikely until July, despite Argentina's "substantial effort" to comply with the IMF program.[58] In the meantime, following the Fund lead, the banks also refused to release new funds. In essence, the entire 1984 deal was undermined by Argentina's failure to adjust, which led to the subsequent fallout with the IMF. The IMF refused to accept a no adjustment, high concessions outcome. It made its position clear: in order to qualify for a resumption of disbursements, Argentina would have to agree to a new IMF stabilization program.

In sum, rather than the expected outcome of MA..., HC..., in the short run, intervention failed to produce such an outcome. Instead, the IMF's actions threw the game into a deadlock, with poor payoffs for both Argentina and even worse payoffs for the banks. But as Argentina's domestic coalition stabilized, the game began to shift to a less conflictive one, which we analyze in the third period.

Debt game and predicted outcome

In the third period, Argentina shifted slightly to 7/8, while the lenders remained at 7/8 (see Figure 13.3). Argentina and its bankers now found themselves in a game of Chicken with two Nash equilibria in pure strategies, one at LA..., HC... and the other at HA..., LC.... Given creditor government and the IMF's interests, we would expect the outcome to move to one of MA..., MC... or possibly even to the even more cooperative HA..., HC.... As noted, both these potentially intervening actors wanted to encourage adjustment on Argentina's part, while maintaining continued concessions from the banks to keep their debt strategy going. In this case, it would not take much of an effort to push the two actors into a more cooperative stance in view of the payoff structure.

The negotiations and outcome: period three

In mid-March of 1985, Alfonsín visited the U.S. to secure the previously promised $500 million bridge loan and to defend his country's recent economic performance. The U.S. government ignored Argentina's attempts to link debt to trade and political issues, insisting that the bridge loan would not be granted until Argentina and the IMF had resolved their differences regarding economic targets.[59] Thus while intervention in the first period broke the stalemate to the benefit of the debtor, in this period the U.S., like the IMF, would not allow Argentina to escape adjustment.

On June 11, 1985, Argentina and the IMF reached a revised agreement, clearing the way for resumption of disbursements from the suspended 1984 standby agreement. The new agreement called for a reduction of the budget deficit by 6% of GDP, and a 30% devaluation of the peso. But Fund disbursement would be withheld pending actual implementation of adjustment measures. This required Argentina to secure funds for immediate interest payments to forestall

[58] *Financial Times*, March 26, 1985. [59] *Financial Times*, March 27, 1985.

Cardinal Payoff Matrix, Intervention Expected

		Lenders IS 7/8		
		HC...	MC...	LC...
	HA...	6, 6?	2.75, 7.83	**3, 9.67**
Argentina IS 7/8	MA...	7.83, 2.75	4, 4	2.5, 5.25
	LA...	**9.67, 3**	5.25, 2.5	2, 2

Note: Nash equilibria bolded; expected outcomes with intervention underlined.

Ordinal Payoff Matrix, Intervention Expected

		Lenders IS 7/8		
		HC...	MC...	LC...
	HA...	7, 7?	3, 8	**4, 9**
Argentina IS 7/8	MA...	8, 3	5, 5	2, 6
	LA...	**9, 4**	6, 2	1, 1

Note: Nash equilibria bolded; expected outcomes with intervention underlined.

Figure 13.3. *Play phase, period three: April–December 1985*

American regulators from downgrading its debt. In this case, the U.S. Treasury, impressed with the revised Fund arrangement, arranged a 12-country short-term bridge loan of $483 million to help with interest payments.[60]

Less than a week after the details of the revised IMF agreement were made public, the Argentine government announced its own even more extensive

[60] *IMF Survey*, June 24, 1985.

adjustment package. Aiming to finally curb the inflationary tendencies that had been plaguing the Argentine economy for years, the Austral Plan included freezes on both prices and wages, and replacement of the peso with the austral, fixed at a value of $1.25.[61]

Based on implementation of economic reforms, the Fund resumed disbursements on the suspended 1984 standby loan in August. Likewise, with Argentina again in good standing with the IMF, the banks signed the $4.2 billion loan; and the first $2.2 billion was drawn in September followed by another $800 million in November. In fact, Argentina quickly became touted as a prime candidate for new loans under the Baker Plan (announced by the U.S. Secretary of the Treasury in September 1985 at the annual IMF meeting in South Korea).

Summary. During this period, Argentina actually undertook significant adjustment. In addition to signing the formal plan, 1985 was marked by a significant payment of interest arrears. In contrast to the accumulation of previous years, it actually reduced what it owed by $1.3 billion, working to catch up on previous arrears.[62] For their part, the banks extended significant amounts of new funds with encouragement from the IMF and U.S. government, thus resolving a potentially deadlocked Chicken game. Because the Austral Plan was not a completely orthodox stabilization package, but more a price and wage freeze plan designed to break inflationary expectations, and because the rescheduling arrangement did not offer significant debt relief, the outcome is best seen as one of medium adjustment and concessions (MA..., MC...).

Situational changes

In this period, Alfonsín tried to link debt not only to economic issues such as trade and investment policies, but also to broader political issues concerning democracy in Latin America. In a speech to the U.S. Congress, he warned that the debt crisis threatened peace and stability throughout the region.[63] He noted, "to achieve security it is necessary to have the desire to defend something that one already has. But what meaning can there be for the majority of a population in defending a freedom that it does not enjoy or a prosperity it does not have?"[64] Still, the U.S. held firm, rejecting this mainly tactical linkage strategy in favor of the economic adjustment Argentina finally effected.

The Austral Plan experienced some initial success. Inflation fell from 31% per month in June to 1.9% in October, and new taxes and budget cuts moved the government toward fiscal balance.[65] This early success of the Austral Plan created a surge in Alfonsín's popularity, and in November the UCR defeated the Peronists in mid-term elections.[66] Seeking to capitalize on the immediate success

[61] The plan aimed to bring inflation down to 8% per month for the remainder of 1985, thus breaking the cycle of inflationary expectations.

[62] World Bank (1990–1991). [63] *Financial Times*, March 26, 1985.

[64] *New York Times*, March 22, 1985. [65] *Wall Street Journal*, December 4, 1985.

[66] The UCR received 43% of the votes, as opposed to 34% for the Peronists. *QER*, no. 1, 1986.

of the plan, Alfonsín attempted to consolidate domestic support, especially from labor unions and business, by pursuing a path of tripartite bargaining. Calling for a "democratic pact," Alfonsín went so far as to bring Peronists into the governing team.[67] But labor proved unwilling to acquiesce to real wage reductions, and business proved equally reluctant to implement a price freeze. As opposition to the austerity measures increased and underlying political divisions persisted, Argentina quickly returned to an unstable political situation.

Period four, January 1986–August 1987: toughing it out

This period saw the resumption of Argentina's hard-line stance toward the banks. As domestic political instability once again rose and opposition to austerity began to increase, Argentina took a much firmer stance in the negotiations. When Brazil began an interest moratorium in February 1987, Argentina quickly took advantage of the banks' fear of a domino effect by pressing for substantial concessions.

Identifying individual situations

During this period, Argentina returned to a situation of coalitional instability, and issue and overall weakness in capabilities (IS 8). The banks remained coalitionally medium, and weak in both debt-related resources and overall capabilities (IS 7/8).

Argentina. The first and slightest sign of economic trouble turned teamwork into conflict, destabilizing Alfonsín's government. Inflation during the first half-year of the Austral Plan dropped from 30.6% in June to less than 3% by the end of the year, but the Argentine recession lingered on: unemployment increased to a decade high of 13%, real wages fell by 30%, and weakened wage and price controls diminished some of the positive effects of the program.[68] Because the anti-inflation strategy translated into a reduction in real wages, organized labor resisted the plan. For example, when the government raised wages by 5% on January 1, 1986, the CGT responded to this meager increase by calling for a one-day general strike later that month. The CGT went on to four nationwide general strikes in 1986 to protest economic policy and continued debt servicing, and sectoral work stoppages were common. In November the union held its first national congress in over 10 years, confirming the goals and strategies of the labor movement. In short, despite the UCR's electoral gains and Alfonsín's efforts to solidify the coalition, the organization and political alignment of the labor movement obliged the government to tread lightly on dangerously thin ice.

Argentina remained weak in debt-related resources and overall resources. With respect to foreign exchange reserves, Argentina experienced some improvement in 1986, with second quarter reserves of slightly over $4 billion. But

[67] *QER*, no. 1, 1986. [68] *QER*, no. 1, 1986.

the reserve situation worsened throughout the period, falling to a low of about $1 billion by the third quarter of 1987. Although inflation dropped to less than 80% in 1986, Argentina's $2.7 billion trade surplus could hardly keep up with its estimated interest payments of $4.8 billion for 1987.

Lenders. The same advisory committee represented the banks during this period. The coalition faced a significant degree of conflict, but still managed to stay together through the leadership of large banks. In terms of capabilities, the banks remained issue and overall weak, a problem exacerbated by Brazil's announcement of an indefinite moratorium on interest payments in February 1987. The curtailment of payments on the part of Latin America's largest debtor further weakened the position of the lenders. In particular, the banks remained weak in overall resources, vulnerable to an Argentine default and without the means to enforce the debtor to honor its debt servicing obligations. Although the banks began to take significant steps to write off their debts, which led to a significantly changed situation for them, this process did not have a significant impact on this period's negotiations.

Creditor governments and international organizations. As Mexico's problems worsened during 1986 and 1987, and the shock of Brazil's moratorium reverberated in February 1987, the U.S. and IMF became more concerned about keeping Argentina in the debt rescheduling game. Worried about the stability of the Argentine democracy, the U.S. was willing to accept less than orthodox stabilization on the part of Alfonsín's government.

Debt game and predicted outcome

Argentina's shift back to IS 8 is reflected in the game shown in Figure 13.4. In this game, without intervention, the Nash equilibrium of the negotiations would be no/little adjustment and high concessions (LA..., HC...), with Argentina receiving its highest payoff at this point. In this case, we might expect intervention on the part of the IMF and the U.S. to pressure Argentina to make some adjustment. However, in view of their concerns with other major debtors, we would not expect a very strong push by these actors that would sustain a different outcome.

The negotiations and outcome

I divide negotiations in this period into two rounds. The first, from January to August 1986, covers the second phase of the Austral Plan and Argentina's effort to secure the promised funds from the IMF and the banks. The second round began in September 1986 when the government initiated discussions with the IMF and creditor banks to obtain a new standby loan, a new commercial bank loan, and further rescheduling. After an initial postponement, in early 1987 Argentina received highly favorable terms from the banks on a multi-year rescheduling arrangement and $1.95 billion in fresh funds.

Cardinal Payoff Matrix,
No Intervention Expected

		Lenders IS 7/8		
		HC...	MC...	LC...
	HA...	0, 6	–3.5, 7.83	–4, 9.67
Argentina IS 8	MA...	4, 2.75	0, 4	–2, 5.25
	LA...	**8, 3**	3.5, 2.5	0, 2

Note: Nash equilibrium bolded.

Ordinal Payoff Matrix,
No Intervention Expected

		Lenders IS 7/8		
		HC...	MC...	LC...
	HA...	5, 7	2, 8	1, 9
Argentina IS 8	MA...	8, 3	5, 5	3, 6
	LA...	**9, 4**	7, 2	5, 1

Note: Nash equilibrium bolded.

Figure 13.4. *Play phase, period four: January 1986–May 1987*

Round one. The cooperative resolution of the "Chicken" game of the previous period quickly broke down at the beginning of 1986. As Argentina failed to meet the stipulated performance targets, the IMF deferred payment on the standby loan. As before, the banks interpreted the IMF's disapproval as a sign to withhold the next disbursement of the $4.2 billion loan. Furthermore, as indicated above, the Argentine domestic situation made compliance with IMF guidelines increasingly difficult. The January 24 general strike succeeded in paralyzing the country and mobilizing widespread opposition to continued debt servicing.[69]

[69] *QER*, no. 2, 1986.

In televised speeches in early February, President Alfonsín and Economy Minister Sourrouille attempted to regain the upper hand. Labeling a moratorium irresponsible and counter-productive, Alfonsín maintained that his government would seek to improve relations with the country's creditors. Sourrouille announced phase two of the Austral Plan to complement the continuing anti-inflation package with additional measures specifically designed to stimulate economic growth.[70] The speeches were followed by a revised letter of intent to the IMF, offered in the place of actual economic results. By mid-March, the IMF disbursed the $240 million tranche deferred in January. As expected, the IMF payment unblocked disbursement of a $600 million payment from the banks.

The government's modifications of the Austral Plan did little to allay opposition. In late March the CGT engineered another general strike, and the Peronists continued to openly advocate a payments moratorium.[71] This time, the government responded with further changes in the Austral Plan, permitting an increase in some prices, the beginning of regularized mini-devaluations, and a loosening of wage controls. When the CGT withdrew from tripartite talks in disagreement with the government over wage rates, the government decided to set new levels unilaterally. Unimpressed, the CGT planned another general strike for June.

In late June, the IMF released the final tranche from the oft-suspended 15-month standby loan formalized in December 1984. In this instance, however, the Fund released the credits despite Argentina's failure to meet performance targets. Overwhelmed by the worsening crisis in Mexico, the Fund decided to release the final payment – even if that meant letting Argentina off the hook undeservingly. Consistent with the pattern established in this period, disbursal by the IMF was followed by final payment from the banks of the $1.2 billion loan. In this round, then, the Argentines were allowed to revert to their preferred strategy of little or no adjustment, and the banks made loans despite this behavior.

Round two. In September 1986, Argentina began formal discussions in Washington on a new $1.2 billion IMF standby loan. It sought $2 billion in new money from the banks for the remainder of 1986 and 1987 at a lower interest rate than the present rate of 1.6% above LIBOR. Additionally, the government pressed for a Multi-Year Rescheduling Arrangement (MYRA) covering $9.5 billion due between 1986 and 1990. In the rescheduling negotiations, the Argentines requested the same long maturity and very low spread as that obtained by Mexico (0.81% over LIBOR).[72] Lastly, in order to insulate Argentina from future declines in world agricultural prices, Argentina attempted to link the IMF loan to farm prices.[73] Mario Brodersohn, Argentina's Treasury Minister,

[70] Phase two included export incentives, incentives for agricultural production, more accessible credit for industry, housebuilding programs, and outlines of a privatization program. *QER*, no. 2, 1986.

[71] During this period Peruvian President Alan Garcia, in Buenos Aires on a state visit, was received as a hero by masses of Argentineans.

[72] *Latin American Weekly Report*, December 11, 1986 (hereinafter *LAWR).*

[73] Due to subsidy wars between the U.S. and the E.E.C., Argentine food exports (equal to 80% of total exports) had decreased 40% in value since 1980. *New York Times*, September 5, 1986.

sought a commodity price linkage similar to the oil price linkage the IMF conceded to Mexico in its $1.6 billion July agreement.

The banks granted Argentina another six months' stay on its obligation to make some $7.5 billion in principal repayments on its $50 billion foreign debt, thus assuring its solvency until 1987. They also extended short-term trade credits until the year's end. Rolling over $10 billion worth of medium- and long-term debt due in September, the banks set March 1987 as the new deadline for negotiating a 10–12 year rescheduling arrangement.[74] In January 1987, Argentina and the IMF agreed on a 15-month standby loan, worth $1.35 million. But the Fund set rigorous conditionality targets of a 3% monthly inflation rate (half of the average monthly rate through 1986), further reductions in the budget deficit, and an increased rate of mini-devaluations. Still, in its favor, Argentina did qualify for an additional $480 million in case its agricultural export revenues should decline.

After reaching an agreement with the IMF, Argentina resumed negotiations with the banks for new loans. By February 1987, the government found itself in dire need of new funds to continue debt servicing; the rescheduling postponement had failed to generate any new money. With the Brazilian moratorium lurking over the heads of the bankers, the banks' advisory committee met with Treasury Minister Brodersohn in New York. The Argentines insisted on $2.15 billion in new money ($1.85 billion from private banks and $300 million from government sources). Brodersohn warned that the government would be unable to meet its servicing obligations without this concession. He argued that Argentina had made great efforts (if not progress) toward lowering inflation while restoring positive economic growth rates. Growth, the Argentines insisted, was not negotiable, and the country could not support further sacrifices in economic growth in order to service the foreign debt. They said that without receiving the $2.15 billion Argentina would be forced to suspend interest payments.[75]

As to the rescheduling arrangement, coveting the lower interest rates included in Mexico's recent rescheduling accord, Argentina sought a reduction in interest on its $32 billion commercial bank debt.[76] Yet, despite the bankers' favorable view of the Argentines as reliable debtors compared to the Brazilians, little progress was made on the rescheduling arrangement. Disputing the relevance of the Mexican accord, the banks insisted that such reduced interest rates were unique to the Mexican package and could not be replicated in Argentina's case. In this instance, the U.S. stepped in to promise Argentina a $500 million bridge loan, making clear its interest in preventing Argentina from following in Brazil's footsteps.

By April 1987 Argentina and the bankers' advisory committee reached an agreement in principle. In view of Argentina's political instability and poor

[74] *Financial Times*, September 22, 1986.

[75] *New York Times*, February 24, 1987. *Wall Street Journal*, February 26, 1987.

[76] Also, Argentina sought an end to foreign banks' influence over the distribution of money to the private sector within Argentina. *New York Times*, February 24, 1987.

financial condition, the banks clearly worried about another moratorium. The agreement concerned a multi-year rescheduling arrangement covering $32.8 billion worth of Argentine commercial debt, and the extension of $1.95 billion in new money. The disputed interest rates were finally set at the same low rates as those in Mexico's 1986 package.

The April agreement required all countries' creditor banks to contribute sums equal to 90% of their medium- and long-term Argentine loans outstanding as of June 1982. Small banks, however, increasingly balked at participating as the two largest commercial banks admitted that many of their Latin American loans could no longer be valued at their full amount.[77] Argentina offered exit and new money bonds to encourage lending by banks reluctant to contribute new money. In addition, to seal the agreement quickly, Argentina offered fees on a declining scale.[78]

While Argentina was getting a good deal in the rescheduling arrangement with the banks, the IMF pressed for some adjustment from Argentina. In fact, when the Argentines failed to meet the January standby targets, the IMF refused to disburse any funds during the first half of the year. In July, when Argentina submitted a revised letter of intent, the IMF agreed to its first disbursement. Finally, in late August of 1987, with the debtor in good standing with the IMF and all of the banks participating in one form or another, the favorable MYRA and the $1.95 billion loan were signed.

In the end, the agreement came closer to little/medium adjustment by Argentina, and the medium to high concessions by the banks. Although the deal was approximately the same as Mexico's, given the clear desire of the banks not to repeat such an accord, their caving in to Argentina's demands can best be seen as a considerable degree of concession.

Summary. In this period, Argentina's aggressive stance, a product of its individual situation as well as knowledge that the bankers feared a Brazil-type moratorium, served the country well. In both rounds, Argentina offered to undertake only slight adjustment but received significant concessions from the banks. In the first round, the IMF attempted to intervene in the negotiations, but was unable to push Argentina to undertake significant adjustment in the first round. In the second round, however, it had greater success, and Argentina wrote a new letter of intent.

Situational changes

Having repeatedly secured low payoffs in its rescheduling game with Argentina, and responding to the Brazilian moratorium, Citicorp began to take significant loan-loss reserves in May 1987.[79] Its move encouraged similar actions by many other major banks. Like Citicorp, which would lose about $1 billion in 1987, it

[77] *Wall Street Journal*, May 29, 1987. [78] *The Economist*, April 25, 1987, pp. 77–78.
[79] For details, see *Wall Street Journal*, May 19, 1988.

appeared initially that banks would become more vulnerable overall by taking the reserves. Yet this action actually served to improve the banks' overall position as well, as financial markets reacted by assuming that the worst was now behind the banks.

In debt issue capabilities, it gave the banks considerable strength. Indeed, one source noted that "by accepting that some of its loans may not be repaid, Citicorp is now in a stronger position to bargain with debtor countries over the terms of their repayments."[80] At the same time, however, the banks became more sharply split by differences in loan-loss reserves and the continuing problems with Brazil.

For its part, the Alfonsín government faced an increasingly turbulent domestic situation. Its stabilization policies had produced a decline in real wages of 20% over 18 months, just as mid-term elections approached in September 1987. Thus, despite the relatively high payoffs it enjoyed in the last period, even the small amount of adjustment it agreed to undertake because of IMF pressure in the last rescheduling episode proved too much. Alfonsín replaced Labor Minister Hugo Barrionuevo with Carlos Alderete, the top official of the influential Power Workers' Union. Alderete represented a faction of the labor movement that had distanced itself from the hard-line approach of the CGT's Secretary General, Saúl Ubaldini. By appointing a Peronist to this important cabinet position, Alfonsín hoped to divide the opposition and attract some Peronist supporters in the September elections. The following section illustrates, however, that like Alfonsín's previous attempts to bolster the debtor's coalitional strength, the change in labor minister did little to improve his Radical Party's fortunes.

Period five, September 1987–June 1989: deadlocked

This period covers the end of Alfonsín's term and has the dubious distinction of marking the lowest point in Argentine-creditor relations. As the Argentine economy continued to deteriorate, bargaining focused upon continued disbursement of the $1.95 billion loan signed in August 1987, as well as on new loans. With Argentina in arrears on its interest payments, it found itself unable to secure any significant funding from the international financial system.

Identifying individual situations

We continue to code Argentina as coalitionally weak, issue weak, and overall weak (IS 8). In this period, the lenders were coalitionally unstable, issue strong, and overall medium (IS 2/6).

Argentina. Although Alfonsín made immediate concessions to the Peronist Labor Minister Carlos Alderete by granting wage increases and repealing some labor laws introduced by the military, Alderete and his supporters remained dissatisfied. In July and August before the elections, a wave of strikes broke out.

[80] *The Times*, May 25, 1987.

The September polls demonstrated that the political experiment had been a resolute failure, when the Radicales lost control of the Chamber of Deputies to the Peronists.[81] For the remainder of his term, Alfonsín's popularity continued to decline, as he presided over a country in economic crisis with both houses of Congress controlled by the opposition party. Compounding these problems, an aborted military rebellion in January 1988 demonstrated just how precarious civil-military relations were.

Argentina also remained weak in debt and overall resources. A sharp decline in world commodity prices hindered its ability to continue running large enough trade surpluses to meet its debt servicing requirements. In early 1988, with debt servicing on Argentina's $52 billion foreign debt projected at $4.7 billion, the country's foreign reserves were only $1.5 billion. With only a $2 billion trade surplus expected for the year, Argentina faced a foreign exchange crisis. Thus even with a $1 billion loan from the World Bank (conditional upon policy reforms), and $500 million in expected revenues from debt-equity swaps, Argentina would fall well short of meeting its capital needs. Argentina attempted to cement an alliance with Brazil, but this effort failed to produce a significant increase in power.

Lenders. As discussed in an earlier section, the increase in loan-loss reserves set aside by Citicorp and other major banks bolstered the lenders' issue strength. Fortunately for the banks, the markets' positive reaction and the end of the Brazilian moratorium helped the banks' overall position. But as banks engaged in write-offs, conflict among the banks grew because they set aside very different amounts of reserves.

Creditor governments and international organizations. In this period the IMF continued its alliance with the banks, insisting that debtors reciprocate lender concessions by making adjustment. U.S. interests could be expected to vary considerably during the period. In the initial stages, with it fearing another Brazilian moratorium, we would expect it to be sympathetic to Argentina. As banks continued to bolster their reserves, however, the U.S. could be expected to be considerably less interested in intervening in the negotiations. Toward the end of 1988, with problems worsening in Mexico, the U.S., in view of its own elections, could be expected to take more significant action.

Debt game and predicted outcome

In period five, we have the game matrix shown in Figure 13.5. Both players have dominant strategies in this game, creating a Nash equilibrium of little adjustment and concessions. As before, we expect IMF intervention preventing banks from extending new money without being assured of debtor adjustment. Moreover, although we should expect to see signs of pressure by both the U.S. and IMF

[81] Not surprisingly, Alderete was replaced after the elections by a UCR appointee.

Cardinal Payoff Matrix,
No Intervention Expected

		Lenders IS 2/6		
		HC...	MC...	LC...
	HA...	0, −12	−3.5, 7.67	−4, −3.33
Argentina IS 8	MA...	4, −12	0, −8	−2, −4
	LA...	8, −10	3.5, −7	**0, −4**

Note: Nash equilibrium bolded.

Ordinal Payoff Matrix,
No Intervention Expected

		Lenders IS 2/6		
		HC...	MC...	LC...
	HA...	5, 1.5	2, 6	1, 9
Argentina IS 8	MA...	8, 1.5	5, 4	3, 7.5
	LA...	9, 3	7, 5	**5, 7.5**

Note: Nash equilibrium bolded.

Figure 13.5. *Play phase, period five: September 1987–May 1989*

to move the parties away from stalemate, for the most part this effort seems unlikely to prove sufficient to ensure a more cooperative outcome in view of the very strong deadlock in this game.

The negotiations and outcome

The negotiations during this period comprise three rounds of bargaining. The first two short rounds run from September to November 1987 and from then until March 1988. The bulk of conflict was concentrated in the third round, which lasted until June 1989.

Round one. The period began with strained relations between Argentina on one side and the IMF and commercial banks on the other. As we noted earlier, the economic targets agreed upon in January 1987 were never met. They were revised in July, and subsequently the IMF and Argentina signed an August accord. Still, the IMF remained dissatisfied, insisting on more stringent economic reforms.

Based on a set of reforms announced in October, the Argentines proposed yet another revised set of targets in a new letter of intent in August. The new economic reform package aimed to reduce the fiscal deficit by 3–4% of GDP and to attain a trade surplus of $2.5–3 billion for 1988. The adjustment package included wage and price freezes and the introduction of a two-tier exchange rate system that allowed the austral to be devalued without significant inflationary repercussions.[82] Argentine negotiators made it known that if the Fund and banks withheld disbursements, Argentina would be forced to stop payments because the government's depleted reserves were on the verge of running out.

In the past, the Argentine government had used threats of default as tranquilizers for domestic consumption, rather than as credible declarations of intent. In fact, the government frequently offered bankers and creditor governments confidential assurances that it would not repudiate its obligations no matter what it proclaimed publicly. After the 1987 elections, however, the Alfonsín government took a much more confrontational stance toward the commercial banks and the international financial community.

In October 1987, Sourrouille traveled to Brazil to discuss a multilateral decision to halt payments with Brazilian and Mexican officials.[83] Fearing a joint moratorium, the U.S. Treasury pressed the IMF to accept the new Argentine proposal and disburse the second $225 million tranche. The Fund relented and released the money, further triggering the disbursement of $500 million from the banks (the second tranche of the $1.95 billion loan). The first round of negotiations thus ended with an outcome close to MA..., MC.... Still, it remained unclear whether Argentina could genuinely undertake any adjustment in view of its troubled domestic political situation.

Round two. Though the price and wage freeze included in the November 1987 letter of intent brought inflation down to under 5% for the month of December, the policy quickly met strong business and labor opposition. In early January 1988, the government announced an "orderly departure," allowing public sector wage increases and opened negotiations on the return of collective bargaining. A number of other measures included in the November letter of intent, such as tax reform, were also relaxed in early 1988.

Despite the Fund and bank disbursements of late 1987, Argentina's balance-of-payments crisis persisted. At the same time that the debtor resisted significant adjustment, the government once again found itself dependent upon external

[82] *QER*, no. 1, 1988. [83] *QER*, no. 4, 1987.

financing. In 1988, $4.65 billion in interest payments would come due, in addition to Argentina's $490 million in arrears. In short, faced with a grim financial situation, Alfonsín's negotiators began a desperate search for an infusion of capital.

In January and February Argentine officials made the rounds in Washington, D.C. and New York to meet with officials from the U.S. Treasury, Federal Reserve, the IMF, and the commercial banks. The Argentines had both an immediate and a longer term goal. The government's most pressing need was for the IMF to unblock disbursement of the third tranche of $225 million from the standby loan, a move that would also trigger payment of $541 million from the banks. It also sought major concessions on its huge debt for the longer term.

Argentina maintained that the debt overhang was wreaking havoc with the economy, but Fund officials had tired of Argentina's perennial inability to meet agreed-upon targets. Showing little sympathy, they insisted that the government needed to more aggressively pursue economic adjustment.[84] In February 1988 the government again revised its letter of intent to the IMF – the fourth time since the $1.4 billion standby facility was approved in January 1987. Having lost the last mid-term elections and with two years left to turn the economy around before the 1989 presidential elections, the Radicales attempted to follow the orthodoxy prescribed by the Fund. The new targets included a budget deficit of 2.7% of GDP, the elimination of all price and wage freezes, and a 4% monthly inflation rate. This effort marked an abandonment of the heterodox efforts to stabilize the economy that had been begun with the Austral Plan in June 1985. With few viable options left, Alfonsín turned to the market.[85]

At the same time, the U.S. Treasury offered to join with other creditor governments to provide a $550 million bridge loan to help tide the debtor over. This was the third time in 18 months, and the second time since November 1987, that the U.S. made such an offer. In March 1988, the IMF endorsed Argentina's new letter of intent, thus freeing up the needed capital from the Fund and the banks.

This brief episode follows the course of events we expected in this period: to the best of its ability, the IMF saw to it that the debtor promised to adjust, while the U.S. showed some willingness to intervene to elicit greater flexibility on the part of the IMF. This round thus ended with Argentina committing to medium to high adjustment as the creditors offered medium concessions.

Round three. Once again, the Argentine government's coalitional weakness imperiled its attempts at adjustment. In April 1988, the CGT called a one-day general strike, the eleventh such work stoppage in Alfonsín's presidency. Far from the 4% inflation rate called for in the February letter of intent, the monthly rates in March, April, and May were 14.7%, 17.2%, and 15.7%, respectively. Although the government denied a conscious decision to return to heterodoxy, it was clear that the orthodox experiment had failed.

[84] *Financial Times*, January 25, 1988. [85] *QER*, no. 2, 1988.

In May, Alfonsín met with IMF Managing Director Michel Camdessus, World Bank President Barber Conable, and the heads of several large U.S. banks to explain his country's difficult situation. Championing the increased trade surplus and reduced budget deficit, Alfonsín argued that the Argentine economy had undergone substantial reform. Still, rampant inflation and contraction of production had hindered Argentina's ability to meet interest payments without outside help.[86] Argentina had managed to cover its arrears through March of that year, but its negotiators warned that April and May payments would likely be stalled without $2 billion in new lending.[87]

At his meetings in the U.S., Alfonsín presented Argentina's latest proposal. Arguing that interest rates had risen since 1982 because of the tight monetary policy pursued by creditor governments, he called for restoration of "historic" interest rates – specifically he asked that interest on debt contracted prior to 1982 be rescheduled at pre-1982 rates of 4%.[88] Argentine negotiators estimated that this scheme, which had been called for by other debtors in the region throughout the decade, would reduce Argentina's annual interest payments from $4.5 to $2 billion. In order to attract support for the proposal, Alfonsín agreed to extend the controversial debt-conversion program and to continue with structural reform of the Argentine economy.

Reactions to the plan were mixed, though mostly critical. The bankers considered interest-rate concessions a hand-out Argentina did not deserve in view of its lack of success in putting its own house in order. The U.S. Treasury, in fact, did not even recognize the proposal, maintaining only that it would support Argentina's request for further standby credits from the IMF. By June, Argentine Foreign Minister Dante Caputo began to back off from its position, noting at the UN that Alfonsín's proposal was "not a take-it-or-leave-it initiative, but something to discuss."[89]

Despite some conciliatory moves on both sides, negotiations continued without resolution. Although Argentina made a payment of between $50 and $70 million on arrears in late June, it was still a half-billion dollars short of becoming current on interest payments.[90] By mid-1988, further economic deterioration had left Argentina in no position to make such payments. Argentina's June and July negotiations with the IMF and the banks accomplished nothing. It now appeared that the debtor was unlikely to receive the new standby loan it had hoped to pick up when the current standby expired in September. Even worse, Argentine negotiators were forced to face the fact that they were never going to receive the final $450 million from the current loan; the banks made it clear the

[86] *Wall Street Journal*, May 27, 1988. [87] *LAWR*, June 9, 1988.

[88] This reduction was to be realized with a sliding-scale mechanism that would ultimately put half of the Argentine debt at "historic" 4% interest, while the remaining half would be at market rates. According to this scheme, for four years 90% of Argentine's debt would be serviced at 4%, gradually descending to 50% of total debt after eight years. At the same time, the remaining 10% of Argentina's debt being serviced at market rates would increase to 50% after eight years. *LAWR*, June 16, 1988.

[89] *LAWR*, June 16, 1988. [90] *Wall Street Journal*, July 1, 1988.

$2 billion the country had requested remained out of the question. The U.S. once again offered to lead a bridge loan, but none of the other industrialized countries would participate.

On August 4, 1988, Alfonsín announced yet another new economic reform package. The Spring Plan (*Plan Primavera*) included a devaluation of the commercial exchange rate accompanied by an overvalued official rate, a government-industry pact to restrain prices, and a 30% increase in energy, petroleum, and telephone prices. The bankers, meanwhile, upset over the consistent accumulation of arrears and the imminent need to put their loans on a non-accrual basis, remained unimpressed. Although the Spring Plan also attempted to combat hyperinflation, it did not include the measures that the international financial community considered the most essential. In particular, the IMF and the bankers complained that the package failed to address the most serious problem in the Argentine economy – the seemingly out of control budget deficit.[91]

The month of August marked the most contentious point of the stalemate between Argentina and its creditors. Despite intermittent payments, the government had accumulated as much as $1 billion in arrears by skipping regular payments. Alfonsín sought a $1.2 billion standby agreement with the IMF, but talks floundered and the current standby loan was suspended indefinitely. Negotiations with the 300 creditor banks were also stalled, pending an IMF agreement that was nowhere in sight. The IMF awaited a firm proposal from Argentina to reduce the budget deficit, and the Spring Plan failed to satisfy either the IMF or the bankers in that regard.[92] Additionally, Argentina could not present a revised letter of intent to the Fund until it worked out a budget for 1989. But a new budget would not pass through Congress until September at the earliest; in any case, passage seemed unlikely because the Congress was controlled by the opposition.

The Argentine economy remained in shambles: inflation raged at an annual rate of 400% and the budget deficit ballooned to nearly 10% of the GDP. Not eager to increase their losses and skeptical about economic reform in the near future, the banks refused to consider granting additional loans.[93] Furthermore, as the Argentine crisis worsened, the Brazilian situation began to improve, strengthening the banks' resolve in proportion to their growing capabilities.

In September the U.S. again assumed the role of the mediator. It pushed the World Bank to agree to a $1.25 billion loan package in exchange for a commitment by Argentina to reduce the budget deficit to 2.4% of GDP (as promised earlier in the Spring Plan). This effort marked a significant departure from the Bank's normal operating procedures. Customarily, the World Bank only lent to countries that had already agreed to IMF programs. Though Bank officials denied that there was any conflict between the Bank and the IMF, the IMF's stubbornness had produced a stalemate that the U.S. considered unhealthy in

[91] *The Economist*, August 8, 1988. [92] *Financial Times*, September 12, 1988.
[93] *Financial Times*, September 22, 1988.

view of its concerns about both the fragility of Argentine democracy and the outcome of its own domestic election.[94] The World Bank loan failed to break the stalemate, however. Although the symbolic and unprecedented agreement encouraged several industrialized countries to collectively extend a $500 million bridge loan they had previously resisted issuing, it failed to produce a significant inflow of new funds.

An IMF mission arrived in Buenos Aires in September 1988, and Sourrouille optimistically announced that Argentina's revised letter of intent was complete. Yet the IMF took an even harder line toward Argentina than it had in the past, holding out for evidence that the budget deficit would be reduced. For their part, the banks remained reluctant to lend more to a country with such extensive arrears, estimated at $1.6 billion by the end of 1988. The banks warned that if the impasse continued past the May 1989 elections, no agreement could be reached until the transfer of power in December 1989.[95]

As negotiations continued, both sides remained stubborn. The banks requested large provisions of debt to be converted via debt-equity swaps, onlending, and relending – provisions that would benefit large banks with operations in Argentina. The government resisted, however, fearing the inflationary consequences of onlending as large amounts of local currency entered circulation.[96] As the talks dragged on, the Argentines recalculated their borrowing needs for 1989, insisting that a total of $4.7 billion in new capital would be needed. Thus, in addition to the $1.2 billion standby loan it requested from the IMF, the government now called for $3.5 billion from the banks.

By early 1989, despite Argentina's conflict with the international financial community and its desperate external accounts, the Spring Plan surprisingly appeared to be working. Inflation for the last three months of 1988 and the first month of 1989 had been reduced to 9%, 5.7%, 6.8%, and 8.9%, respectively. Yet by mid-February, the plan had failed. Fearing a devaluation, in the first week of February Argentine banks and finance houses had bought dollars. The run on the austral had effectively brought down the plan's two-tier exchange rate system, depleting the Central Bank's foreign reserve holdings.

With the Spring Plan in ruins, February's inflation rate rose above 9% for the first time since September 1988, followed in March by a rate of 17%. In March, with arrears estimated to have reached $2.5 billion, loss of confidence in the Argentine economy appeared complete. Even the World Bank, the lone international creditor to side with the troubled debtor in late 1988, deferred payment on $700 million of structural adjustment loans because of Argentina's poor economic performance.

[94] *Financial Times*, September 26, 1988. According to *The Economist* (March 11, 1989), the Reagan Administration badly wanted progress to be made on Latin American debt prior to the November 1988 elections, and thus applied a great deal of pressure on the World Bank to make these loans.

[95] *Wall Street Journal*, December 21, 1988.

[96] Onlending allows banks to direct their new lending in local currency. Relending allows banks to redirect principal payments from former loans to other borrowers in local currency. *Wall Street Journal*, November 3, 1988.

The Alfonsín government appeared completely incapable of preventing further economic deterioration. On March 31, six weeks before the election, the cabinet resigned en masse. Highlighting his promises of change, Peronist candidate Carlos Menem announced immediately prior to the elections that if he were to win the presidency, he would demand that bankers accept suspension of interest payments to allow for restructuring of the economy.[97] In other circumstances, this warning might have confirmed the bankers' fears about a Peronist resurgence, promoting quick concessions on their part. But because Argentina's interest arrears had been accumulating for over a year, this threat evoked little concern.

On the eve of elections, the Argentine economy had reached a low point. In the previous year, Argentina had been cut off from the IMF and then from the World Bank; its arrears surpassed $2.5 billion. With an annual inflation rate of between 13,000% and 28,000%, *The Economist* exclaimed, "This is Weimar."[98] Menem's election victory returned the Peronists to power. Yet because Alfonsín had decided to schedule the elections as early as possible, hoping to ride a wave of popularity from the short-lived success of the Spring Plan,[99] the interim period between the May election and the December inauguration was quite long. Not surprisingly, Argentina's economic situation only worsened after the election.

After the initial success of the Austral Plan in 1985, each new package had been less successful than the previous one. Although the government announced a major new initiative nearly every two weeks, by May 1989 they were virtually ignored by the markets. The economy deteriorated and inflation raged out of control. By early June, as one observer noted, Argentines had

> little money in their pockets, . . . with the money they did have disappearing by the hour. They had a lame-duck president whose economic plans had failed, and an incoming president who said that he had new ideas but would not get a chance to test them until the scheduled transfer of power in December. No one could trade australes, no one could get dollars, and nothing in the stores cost what it had cost the day before.[100]

Not surprisingly, citizens responded to the uncertain political and economic future of the country according to the resources at their disposal: those with access to hard currency wasted little time in depositing it abroad in safer havens; those without this option turned to rioting and looting in the streets of Buenos Aires and Rosario. Still months short of the transfer of power and with the economy in absolute chaos, this round ended in complete stalemate at LA..., LC....

Summary. Throughout the three rounds examined in this period, Argentina found itself in severe conflict with the international financial community.

[97] *LAWR*, May 11, 1989. [98] *The Economist*, April 29, 1989.

[99] The Spring Plan was launched in August 1988, yet by February the Central Bank was experiencing a severe foreign exchange shortage as exporters were hording their dollars in fear of a devaluation.

[100] *Washington Post*, June 4, 1989.

U.S. pressure initially pushed the parties away from deadlock in the first two rounds – at least on paper. But the underlying reality of Argentina's political instability, combined with the increasing unwillingness of banks to advance additional funds, could not prevent an inexorable slide toward a total standoff between Argentina and its creditors. As expected, the bulk of negotiations in this period were marked by empty promises and finally collapsed.

Situational changes

In each of the previous periods, we have seen that as long as organized labor was linked to the opposition party, Argentina remained coalitionally unstable. This was especially true for the beginning of this period when the opposition Peronists controlled both houses of Congress. But when Menem, a Peronist, was elected President in 1989, labor became part of the supporting political coalition of the government in power. Although this alone did not assure a changed outcome, this shift in Argentine politics meant that when the government did attempt significant economic adjustment, primary opposition to such policies would come from within its own ranks. As we shall see, the government was able to defuse such opposition.[101]

Regarding the lenders' situation, they had not received interest payments on commercial loans for more than a year. Classifying loans to Argentina as "value-impaired," in June, U.S. regulators ordered a 20% write-down on outstanding Argentine loans.[102] This action forced banks to set aside additional reserves, which bolstered the lenders' issue-strength. Meanwhile, the banks also continued to raise primary capital, thus strengthening their overall position. At the same time, increasing similarity in their financial positions also increased their coalitional stability in the fall of 1989, although the Brady Plan continued to create some disagreement among the banks.

Period six, July 1989–August 1991: Peronist adjustment

The May 1989 elections proved to be the critical turning point in this epoch of Argentine debt negotiations. When Carlos Menem, a Peronist who publicly advocated declaring a moratorium, won the presidency, many observers expected a further deterioration of debtor-creditor relations.[103] Yet the bottom line was that timely interest payments had not been made for almost a year, and in spite of this non-payment the economy remained an horrific mess. In his inaugural speech of July 8, the President recognized that he had inherited a country that, in his own words, was "broken, devastated, destroyed, [and] razed."[104] Peronist or not, the new President of the country found himself constrained by

[101] This coalitional situation is similar to that of the Mexican government from 1982 to 1988.

[102] The ruling was made by the Interagency Country Exposure Review Committee, a body consisting of officials from the Federal Reserve, the Comptroller's office, and the Federal Deposit Insurance Corporation, FDIC. *Wall Street Journal*, June 12, 1989.

[103] For *The Economist*'s reaction, see my discussion in the conclusion.

[104] *QER*, no. 4, 1989.

a difficult situation and banks empowered by their lack of concern over provoking a confrontation. The model accurately predicts what on the surface appears to be a significant paradox for the conventional wisdom: a Peronist government guiding Argentina through difficult economic reforms required by the international financial community.

Identifying individual situations

In the sixth period, Argentina was coalitionally medium, issue weak, and overall weak (IS 7/8). The banks were issuestrong, overall medium, and became coalitionally medium toward the end of 1989 (IS 1/6).

Argentina. Argentina remained weak in overall and debt-related resources, with the economic crisis peaking as Menem prepared to assume the presidency in July 1989. But as a new President, Menem was immediately afforded a degree of political support that Alfonsín had lacked in his final years. Though the honeymoon had ended by the end of 1989, as workers and business resisted austere economic policies and accused his administration of corruption, the government remained relatively stable throughout the period. For example, even as Menem's popularity fell in early 1990, the UCR, Alfonsín's party, offered him its support.[105]

Turning to issue-resources, by late June 1989, just weeks before Menem became president, foreign reserves were as low as $140 million, and the Central Bank was compelled to place a $1,000 limit on foreign currency purchases. Unable to pay interest for over a year, as arrears approached $3 billion, Argentina was clearly issue weak. Although Argentina managed to run a trade surplus of slightly over $5 billion in 1989, its arrears by early 1990 had risen to nearly $5.5 billion. Reserves at the end of 1989 were less than $1.5 billion. In overall terms, Argentina faced a contracting economy. GDP dropped by 2.7% in 1988 and by another 4.5% in 1989.

Lenders. After the conflict among banks stemming from the write-offs of 1987, the lenders' coalition began to stabilize somewhat. As the number of banks taking write-offs increased, particularly with the forced write-down of 20% on Argentine loans, the coalition became more stable. Still, the Brady Plan created some conflicts among the banks because they disagreed over the terms of possible concessions to Argentina. Moreover, as Argentina proceeded with its privatization program, banks involved in this effort did not see eye to eye with others who had not pursued this course. In short, the banks had a medium stable coalition.

As banks took additional reserves against possible losses in Argentina, their position continued to strengthen. In terms of overall capabilities, over this time period, the banks continued to gain in strength as they raised primary capital and reduced their exposure to third world debt.

105 *LAWR*, January 11, 1990, p. 10.

Creditor governments and international organizations. As in the Mexican case, the late 1980s witnessed a fundamental reorientation of the American government's strategy toward dealing with third world debt. Driven by the 1987 Brazilian moratorium and the deadlocked negotiations in both the Mexican and Argentine cases, the U.S. threw its support behind debt relief in the form of the Brady Plan. The IMF and World Bank soon offered support of this approach, but were willing to do so only after inflation had been brought down to "international levels." Moreover, we would expect the U.S. and IMF to be reluctant to help an avowed Peronist.

Debt game and predicted outcome

Using the theoretical model, we predict the game shown in Figure 13.6 for period six. Based on strategic interaction, assuming no intervention by outside actors, we would expect a high adjustment, low concessions outcome (HA..., LC...). Despite a willingness by Argentina to undertake economic adjustment, we expect the banks to refrain from further lending. As noted, given their concerns, and Argentine economic performance, the creditor governments and the IMF had little interest in intervening at this point in the negotiations.

The negotiations and outcome

Argentina's willingness to implement difficult adjustment measures quickly became evident. As a first step to getting back into the good graces of the international financial community, Argentina made a token payment of $40 million to the IMF almost immediately. Menem also appointed Miguel Roig, from the large Argentine multinational company Bunge y Born (historically a target of Peronist criticism), as his Economy Minister. Demonstrating his markedly free-market orientation, Roig quickly announced his desire to resume negotiations with creditor banks.[106] The government also announced an "Economic Emergency Act," including dramatic public sector reform, a 54% devaluation of the austral (from 300 australes per dollar to 650), tariff reductions, price increases on public services, and price controls on private sector goods. When Roig became ill and died suddenly after less than a week in office, Menem turned again to Bunge y Born, appointing Nestor Rapanelli as Roig's successor. Though the Argentines were ready to cooperate, as the model predicts, the bankers maintained a hard-line approach, warning that any new loans would only follow an IMF endorsement.[107]

The stabilization package appeared to have an immediate effect, as the monthly inflation rate dropped from 196% in July to 38% in August and 9.4% by September. The reform program also included a three-month agreement with labor and business to freeze wages and prices. The administration's commitment to fiscal austerity and economic liberalization quickly began winning the respect of bankers and conservative opponents within Argentina, and the IMF ultimately

[106] *LAWR*, July 13, 1989. [107] *LAWR*, July 13, 1989.

Cardinal Payoff Matrix,
No Intervention Expected

		Lenders IS 1/6		
		HC...	MC...	LC...
	HA...	6, −7.5	2.75, −4.83	**3, −2.17**
Argentina IS 7/8	MA...	7.83, −7.25	4, −5	2.5, −2.75
	LA...	9.67, −4.5	5.25, −3.5	2, −2.5

Note: Nash equilibrium bolded.

Ordinal Payoff Matrix,
No Intervention Expected

		Lenders IS 1/6		
		HC...	MC...	LC...
	HA...	7, 1	3, 4	**4, 9**
Argentina IS 7/8	MA...	8, 2	5, 3	2, 7
	LA...	9, 5	6, 6	1, 8

Note: Nash equilibrium bolded.

Figure 13.6. *Play phase, period six: August 1989–August 1991*

agreed to a $1.4 billion standby facility for the following year.[108] Soon thereafter, Argentina and the Paris Club reached an agreement on a $2.8 billion rescheduling of official debt.

Though the monthly inflation rate dropped to 5.6% in October and November, trouble quickly returned in December as prices rose rapidly and the value of the austral fell on unofficial markets. The adjustment effort was redoubled in December, with announcement of a further devaluation of 34.8%, fixing the parity of the austral at 1,000 per dollar (it had been 300 per dollar prior to the Roig

[108] *IMF Survey*, November 23, 1989; *The Economist*, November 11, 1989.

July devaluation). Despite this intervention, the value of the austral continued to drop in unofficial markets to 1,600 per dollar. The government's inability to protect the currency, and consequent fears of the return of hyper-inflation, prompted divisions within the Menem cabinet.

Bunge y Born argued for a fixed exchange rate, but Menem favored a floating austral. When Menem won this battle, the partnership between the Peronists and Bunge y Born finally came to an end. Economy Minister Rapanelli resigned and the Health Minister, Antonio Erman González, replaced him in December.[109] Because González was a close political associate from Menem's home province, many feared that this ministerial change would result in a "Peronization" of the economy. Yet in his first official proclamation, in a speech publicized nationwide from the Casa Rosada with the President, cabinet members, and business and union leaders present, Minister González announced that he intended to remove all price and exchange controls and to further liberalize the economy. The new Economy Minister appeared to be even more "neo-liberal" than his Bunge y Born predecessors.[110]

By early 1990, Menem's troubles with the economy deepened as he faced renewed economic problems. Inflation rates of 40% in December 1989, and 80% in January 1990, coupled with the introduction of three new economic packages within three weeks, and incessant cabinet reshuffling reminiscent of the Alfonsín Administration,[111] all undermined the new President's popularity. Moreover, splits developed within the Peronist coalition itself. In particular, in late 1989 the CGT had split into two factions. One group of unions, *menemistas*, led by the Labor Minister continued to support the President. The *ubaldinistas*, however, opposed Menem's policies as vehemently as they had opposed Alfonsín's.

In a two-day CGT congress, the *menemistas* attempted to remove Saúl Ubaldini from his position as general secretary and to place their own leadership in charge of the confederation. Accusing their rivals of rigging the vote, the *ubaldinistas* abandoned the congress, forming its own independent organization with its own general secretary. The situation was very dangerous from the government's point of view, especially because immediately after the split there was a series of strikes. In fact, in January 1990, there were 75 industrial disputes (the highest monthly figure in a decade), and Menem risked losing the support of both wings of the CGT. By February, when a wave of riots and looting broke out, Menem's approval rating fell to 48% (from 80% in September), and the government's approval rating fell to just 11%.

Argentina struggled on the foreign lending front as well. In the IMF standby accord signed in October 1989, the budget deficit had been targeted at 1.5% of

[109] *International Herald Tribune*, December 20, 1989. [110] *LAWR*, January 11, 1990.

[111] In addition to the change at the Economy Ministry, at the end of October 1989 Treasury Secretary Rodolfo Frigeri resigned. In November, Central Bank President Javier González Fraga resigned, criticizing Rapanelli's exchange rate policy. Fraga's replacement, Egidio Ianella, who had been Central Bank president under the military regimes and was much more to Rapanelli's liking, left within two weeks, however. His replacement, in turn, was gone by the end of January 1990.

GDP. Noting a 12% deficit, the IMF suspended the agreement, refusing to disburse the $230 million tranche due in February 1990. With reserves falling below $1 billion and owing another $6 billion in interest payments coming due in 1990, the Argentines still desperately needed assistance from the international financial community. The IMF argued that Argentina had no one to blame but itself for its isolated state, because it had cut itself off from external sources of credit by failing to meet conditionality targets and by accumulating massive arrears. The Fund's prescription was a deepening of the adjustment process including revamping the tax system.[112]

In late March the government sent a revised letter of intent to the IMF, setting ambitious targets of an average 4% monthly inflation rate for the rest of the year, an enormous trade surplus, and large cuts in public spending. The banks, meanwhile, refused to make any new loans. The Argentine behavior was clearly heavy on the adjustment, but concessions on the part of the creditors was not forthcoming. The outcome was HA..., LC..., as the model predicted, and the biggest question remained whether or not the debtor government's domestic situation would allow it to continue to pursue the high adjustment path.

Not surprisingly, Menem's popularity was tied to the rate of inflation. When prices increased at a rate of 96%, as they did in the month of March 1990, the governing party showed signs of disunity, and relations with the IMF were strained. The new government's domestic situation appeared no better than the previous administration's had been. Yet the two situations were indeed distinct; even when his approval ratings were low, Menem's position was in little political danger.

The Peronists' chief electoral rival, the Radicales, were split into four factions. The labor movement was not effectively united against Menem either. In late March, the Ubaldini-led wing of the CGT called a general strike against the government's policies. However, the strike failed because Ubaldini failed to elicit the support of some of the nation's largest unions. In response, Menem became more resolved, ordering an acceleration of plans to reduce spending and challenging dissidents to join the opposition if they were not content.[113] Weeks later, the number of Argentines who attended a rally to express support for the Menem government was more than double those who had struck.

The achievement that had eluded Alfonsín for six years – controlling enough of organized labor to implement painful economic reforms without committing political suicide – served the Peronist President well. Thus, even though Menem's approval rating had dropped below 50%, he and his brother Eduardo demonstrated their control of the leadership of the Peronist Party by defeating their intra-party rivals.[114] Moreover, the party as a whole did not face a serious electoral challenge.

[112] *LAWR*, February 1, 1990. [113] *LAWR*, March 22, 1990.

[114] Menem's chief rival, Antonio Cafiero, resigned as president of the party after losing a referendum to change the constitution on August 5, 1990.

When Argentina resumed negotiations with the bankers in June 1990, it again exhibited its willingness to adjust – even in the absence of concessions. The government made a $40 million interest payment, its first in over two years, and announced that as negotiations continued $40 million would be paid each month as a "gesture of goodwill."[115] In July, the IMF warned that inflation was still too high, and that new lower targets could be negotiated. In late August Economy Minister Gonzalez declared that austerity would be continued regardless of the costs, announcing the dismissal or compulsory retirement of approximatcly 30,000 public employees, and proscriptions on the workers' right to strike.[116]

Despite a worsening domestic crisis, the Menem government continued with its economic reforms. This was done in an even less hospitable international environment than the one the Alfonsín government faced. The lenders refused to make any new loans, but increased oil prices because of the Persian Gulf War sent inflationary impulses through the Argentine economy. By 1990, much of the industrialized world, including Argentina, found itself again in recession.

As Argentina continued to make the monthly payments throughout the year and persisted in its stabilization efforts (inflation was brought below 8% for each of the last three months of the year), the IMF disbursed a long-awaited tranche of $267 million by the end of 1990. By this point the debtor was benefiting from American support. In their fourth meeting since the Peronist was inaugurated in July 1989, U.S. President George Bush hinted that Argentine progress on stabilization and privatization would be rewarded by a bank deal, but little came of this promise in the short run.[117]

In late January 1991 the economy appeared poised to take another nosedive, presenting Argentina with its greatest challenge. A run on the austral prompted González's resignation as Economy Minister and a devaluation of the currency. On a previous occasion in Menem's presidency, the economy had appeared to stabilize only to explode into another bout of hyper-inflation. Many Argentines feared that the scenario would repeat itself. Despite these severe economic difficulties, Argentina actually increased its monthly payments of interest from $40 to $60 million.

Inflation shot up to 27% in February, but the new Economy Minister, Domingo Cavallo, quickly declared that the austral would be supported. In March, Cavallo announced that the austral would be fixed at 10,000 australes per dollar, that the government would guarantee the availability of dollars by refraining from printing more money, and that it would back the entire monetary base with dollars and gold.[118] The ambitious Cavallo Plan appeared to work, with inflation falling to 5.5% in April. By July 1991, with mid-term elections around the corner, interest and inflation rates were both falling. As fears of devaluation faded, Argentines appeared to regain confidence in the economy, while the Central Bank was able to live up to its promises of free convertibility. That month the IMF approved a $1 billion standby loan, for which negotiations had begun in April.

[115] *Wall Street Journal*, June 8, 1990. [116] *LAWR*, September 6, 1990.
[117] *QER*, no. 1, 1991. [118] *QER*, no. 2, 1991.

Summary. Throughout this period, Menem's actions surprised most analysts. Despite significant domestic opposition and a difficult international economic situation, Argentina persisted with a harsh economic adjustment program. Yet in return the bankers offered little, although the IMF showed its approval by concluding a standby loan. In short, as the model predicted, Argentina and the banks propelled the asymmetrical outcome of HA..., LC....

Situational changes

Throughout this period, despite a lack of allies, Argentina pursued economic adjustment and improved its issue capabilities. Menem's successful implementation of austerity measures paid a political dividend in the first set of mid-term elections in August 1991. President Menem had doggedly led the country into a deep depression with an economic program that violated the promises of the campaign. Moreover, many had bitterly accused the Menem Administration of corruption and scandal. Yet the Peronists won throughout the country, and Peronist candidates continued to strongly support Menem. By late 1991, as the economy picked up, the government had weathered the wave of discontent and had significantly increased its coalitional strength. With inflation under control, it now appeared to be only a matter of time before Argentina would be able to secure a Brady Plan of its own.

During this period, additional write-offs by the banks (in April 1991) contributed to their growing overall strength as they continued to raise primary capital. These changes lead us to the final period of Argentine debt rescheduling in this epoch.

Period 7, September 1991–December 1992: Brady Plan accord for Argentina

Although the public continued to despise harsh adjustment measures, by the middle of 1991, the government's success in controlling inflation and restoring some degree of normality in the economy helped the Peronists. Menem's mid-term election successes further bolstered his political stability. Indeed, by the end of the seventh period, Argentina had concluded a Brady Plan rescheduling accord.

Identifying individual situations

By the seventh period, Argentina improved its issue capabilities, but remained overall weak. Menem's coalitional support increased, putting Argentina in IS 1/7. The banks continued to raise primary capital. As their Latin American portfolio diminished in importance, they became considerably stronger, both issue specifically and overall, leading us to code them in IS 5/6.

Argentina. Following the Cavallo Plan's success in early and mid-1991, Menem was victorious in the mid-term elections. Having largely patched up civil-military relations, and without a viable electoral challenger, Menem's and the Peronists' incumbency expectations were never seriously threatened. By 1992, politicians began discussing the possibility of amending the constitution to allow Menem to succeed himself as his popularity soared.

With respect to issue capabilities, by 1991 Argentina showed important signs of economic recovery. Its reserves rose to nearly $7 billion by the end of 1991, and it continued to run a trade surplus. Inflation dropped to an annual rate of 170%.

In overall terms, Argentina remained overall weak. Although the economy showed signs of recovery and grew rapidly in 1991 and 1992, Argentina's strategy of privatizing its state-owned enterprises made it highly dependent on foreign capital. Moreover, with an economy that had just begun a fragile recovery, Argentina remained extremely vulnerable to any economic shocks.

Lenders. The banks' coalition continued to be medium in stability and they remained issue strong. In mid-April 1991, U.S. regulators told banks to write down another 10% of their loans to Argentina as losses, bringing their write-downs to 70%.[119] Thus the banks found themselves overwhelmingly strong in debt-related resources with little to fear from Argentina. By the seventh period, the banks were overall strong. American banks were especially robust, having only $19.6 billion in loans outstanding at the end of 1991 compared to $66.3 billion at the end of 1987.[120]

Creditor governments and international organizations. As the U.S. and IMF continued to encourage debtors and lenders to conclude Brady Plan agreements, and Argentina followed through on "good debtor" policies, the U.S. and IMF could be expected to press for a final resolution to the long-standing debt problems.

Debt game and predicted outcome

In the seventh period, we have the debt game and outcome shown in Figure 13.7. In the two-actor game, we expect another asymmetrical equilibrium outcome. In effect, we expect Argentina to continue undertaking its adjustment policies despite coaxing few concessions from bankers. Taking into account intervention, however, we would expect pressure by the U.S. and international institutions to encourage banks to respond to Menem's adjustment efforts by making concessions to Argentina.

The negotiations and outcome

After receiving his mid-term vote of confidence, Menem pressed on with domestic reforms and international negotiations. In September 1991, the government

[119] *New York Times*, April 20, 1991 and *Wall Street Journal*, April 22, 1991.
[120] *New York Times*, April 8, 1992.

Cardinal Payoff Matrix,
Intervention Expected

		Lenders IS 5/6		
		HC...	MC...	LC...
	HA...	4.5, −7.5	3.5, −4.33	**6.5, −1.17**
Argentina IS 1/7	MA...	4.67, −8	3, −5	4, −2
	LA...	4.83, −7.5	2.5, −5	1.5, −2.5

Note: Nash equilibrium bolded; expected outcome with intervention underlined.

Ordinal Payoff Matrix,
Intervention Expected

		Lenders IS 5/6		
		HC...	MC...	LC...
	HA...	6, 2.5	4, 6	**9, 9**
Argentina IS 1/7	MA...	7, 1	3, 4.5	5, 8
	LA...	8, 2.5	2, 4.5	1, 7

Note: Nash equilibrium bolded; expected outcome with intervention underlined.

Figure 13.7. *Play phase, period seven: August 1991–December 1992*

concluded a rescheduling agreement with the Paris Club covering about $6.5 billion worth of debt.[121] Domestically, Menem announced a major deregulation effort to promote Argentine competitiveness. With Argentina's currency tightly linked to the dollar, and devaluation out of the question, all efforts were oriented toward maintaining economic competitiveness. The Cavallo Plan continued to be successful, and monthly inflation fell to less than 1%.

[121] *Wall Street Journal*, September 20, 1991.

Movement toward a Brady agreement on Argentina's outstanding debt to private bankers began with Menem's visit to the United States in November 1991. The president sought private investment as well as an accord with the IMF that would spur the conclusion of a Brady Plan agreement. Specifically, Menem sought a $3 billion loan from the IMF, part of which he planned to use for guarantees on new bonds that would be exchanged for Argentina's existing debt.

By January 1992, success on the international front was in sight. The government managed to produce a budget surplus of $1.74 billion in the final quarter of 1991, beating an IMF target of $1.43 billion.[122] While Argentina continued negotiations with the IMF, it proceeded to hold simultaneous talks with creditor banks on a possible deal under the auspices of the Brady Plan. The banks continued to play hard ball, insisting that Argentina pay a portion of its $8 billion interest arrears in cash before they would agree to any type of accord. In response, Argentina again made conciliatory moves, expressing a willingness to pay a portion of the arrears in cash, but arguing that it needed to maintain a sufficient level of reserves to retain its fixed exchange rate vis-à-vis the dollar.

As negotiations continued in February, the banks rejected Argentina's initial request for a 40% debt reduction, offering instead a 30% cut and insisting on cash payment of at least $1 billion on interest arrears. By March, Argentina had secured a $3 billion extended fund facility from the IMF in exchange for agreeing to produce a fiscal surplus of $275 million a month.[123] Domestically, things were not rosy, however, as the CGT factions agreed to unite in demonstrating their dissatisfaction with a drop in wages. Still, this move did little to undermine Menem's popularity, and he pressed on with the international negotiations.

By the first week of April, Argentina came to a tentative agreement with private bankers on $23 billion of its short- and medium term debt and $8 billion worth of interest arrears.[124] As in the Mexican case, both parties agreed on two alternative methods for exchanging debt for bonds: (1) banks could agree to a 35% principal reduction with the new 30-year bonds paying 13/16% over LIBOR and interest collateralized for 12 months by U.S. Treasury bonds (discounted bonds), or (2) they could take a lower interest rate of 4% in the first year rising to 6% after seven years with the principal collateralized by U.S. bonds (par bonds). A third option was for the banks to swap loans for shares in Argentine firms. On arrears, Argentina agreed to $400 million up front in cash, another $300 million in collateralized bonds, and the rest in 12-year Argentine bonds at 13/16% over LIBOR. Funds of some $3.2 billion were needed to purchase the zero-coupon bonds providing "loan enhancements" on the new bonds. In this case, these funds were to be furnished by the IMF, World Bank, IDB, and Japan.

The deal was very attractive to the banks. Despite having to write down a portion of the principal, they had much to gain. The market price of Argentine debt was about 41 cents on the dollar before the agreement, but banks had

122 *Financial Times*, January 16, 1992. 123 *LAWR*, March 19, 1992.

124 For details, see *LAWR*, April 23, 1992, and *New York Times*, April 8, 1992.

already written off 70% of the loans. And although the interest rate was lower than the Mexican case's 6.25%, global interest rates had fallen considerably, making a 4–6% rate very attractive. In fact, the guaranteed rate proved to be an important incentive for the creditor banks to sign the final agreement by the year's end.

By August 1992, Argentina had secured a final Paris Club rescheduling agreement with official creditors on favorable 16-year repayment terms – the longest for any debtor to this point. In negotiations with commercial banks, however, Argentina encountered problems. The government had hoped for a 50–50 balance between par bonds and discounted bonds. But the fixed rates on par bonds were attractive because of declining interest rates, which enticed creditors to choose par bonds 4 to 1 over discounted bonds. This ratio meant that Argentina would need additional funds to collateralize the bonds, but creditor governments and international institutions were unwilling to come forth with such financing. After the steering committee of 13 banks applied pressure, however, in the end, Argentina's approximately 500 creditor banks agreed to take more discounted bonds in exchange for their debt, finally tallying 68% par bonds to 32% discounted bonds. The actual signing of the agreement, begun in December 1992, was concluded on April 7, 1993 when Argentina transferred $3.8 billion to fund the enhancements and $1 billion to cover arrears.[125]

Summary. The final agreement fits well with our prediction of HA..., MC.... Although the banks did agree to reductions in principal and interest rate, compared to their situation during the past several years, and in view of the strong guarantees due to the enhancements, the agreement was favorable to them. Argentina, for its part, committed itself to continued adjustment, and exchanged part of its private debt for loans from public institutions.

Although the model predicts the correct outcome in terms of adjustment and concessions, the payoffs that Argentina and the banks received as a result of the accord appear to be odd. The game suggests that Argentina's payoffs would go *down* if banks made higher concessions. Under normal circumstances, if Argentina was worried about maintaining the banks' goodwill, this would be more plausible. Under the Brady Plan, I expected actors' payoffs to be strongly affected by what I have characterized as a meta-regime and partial regime. From my model's perspective, Argentina would now be less concerned about goodwill from the banks, and more concerned about creditor governments' and international organizations' views. Moreover, with the greater certainty that these actors will provide sustained intervention, Argentina would also be more willing to undertake adjustment and more concerned about securing financial assistance from public actors. As a consequence, the new multi-actor game would leave Argentina with better payoffs if banks made higher concessions. This example illustrates the influence that international regimes are likely to have on actors'

[125] *LAWR*, April 29, 1983.

assessments of different policy choices, and demonstrates the problem of using my model under such circumstances.

Conclusion

Negotiations between Argentina and the banks has been marked by intense conflict. Unlike Mexico, Argentina generally took a highly aggressive stance toward the bankers. Although this approach initially benefited it to some extent, Argentina's final agreement in 1992, which marked the end to its debt rescheduling in this epoch, came about in large part because Argentina had undertaken significant adjustment. In sharp contrast to the expectations of most observers, the Peronist Menem brought about a Brady Plan rescheduling accord through the pursuit of traditional economic stringency.

Period one found Argentina and the banks struggling to gain the upper hand until the deadlock was resolved through intervention by the U.S. and the IMF which pushed banks to make some concessions to Argentina. Faced with poor payoffs, the banks attempted to alter their individual situation, but had little success. The second period found the banks more motivated to make concessions to Argentina, but the latter once again resisted adjustment. In this instance, the IMF refused to countenance such behavior from Argentina, but in refusing to approve an IMF adjustment program, it threw the game into a deadlock.

By April 1985, as political stability in Argentina increased, the debt game in the third period shifted to one of Chicken. Given our expectation of continued intervention by the U.S. government and the IMF, we predicted concessions from both actors, and in the end both Argentina and the banks did indeed undertake significant concessions and adjustment (MA..., MC...). But this agreement to pursue adjustment on Argentina's part undermined Alfonsín's political stability. Because the bankers feared a Brazilian-type moratorium, and because Argentina was in no mood to undertake adjustment, the IMF and U.S. only managed to extract a promise of low adjustment by Argentina – despite medium to high concessions by the bankers.

By the fifth period, which began in 1987, the bankers began to tire of the debt game with Argentina and other major debtors. Key money-center banks, led by Citicorp, began to sharply increase their loan loss reserves, strengthening their individual situation. At the same time, other banks dragged their feet. The ensuing unstable coalition of significantly stronger banks faced an unstable Argentina. Once again, the protagonists found themselves in a game of deadlock. In this case, however, efforts by the U.S. and the IMF ultimately failed to budge the banks or Argentina.

By 1989, the U.S. responded to ongoing conflict in debt rescheduling by sponsoring the Brady Plan. When Menem came to power in mid-1989, most observers expected the effectiveness of the negotiations to take a nosedive in view of the Peronist's strong calls for a moratorium or some other form of aggressive behavior. Yet my model predicted that a more stable Argentina, interacting with a more stable group of stronger banks, would undertake high adjustment despite a lack of corresponding concessions by the banks. In actuality, this prediction proved to be correct: the "Peronist" Menem pursued sharp economic adjustment. Despite his fiery campaign rhetoric, when Menem came to office he immediately sought to improve relations with creditor banks and institutions. On the one hand, analysts have argued that the economy had so deteriorated that he had no choice: apparently foreign reserves were so low that by the end of June hardly a week's worth of imports were covered. Yet where the threshold of deterioration lies is relative. Alfonsín maintained a hard-line position despite unprecedented economic deterioration during his presidency. The weakness of the Argentine economy alone is an insufficient explanation of Menem's course of high adjustment. More relevant is the fact that he arrived in office as the first democratically elected head of state to succeed a democratically elected president in Argentina in over a hundred years. Menem took office five months early with a mandate to repair the broken-down Argentine economy, and with considerable coalitional stability. Thus, he was able to swiftly break the stalemate that had plagued debtor-creditor relations towards the end of the Alfonsín Administration.

The Peronists did not have an easy time implementing the austerity measures. Menem's reforms came crashing down by the end of his first five months in office, and he too was confronted with hyper-inflation, strikes, and food riots throughout the country. In fact, by April 1990 the mayor of Buenos Aires declared the capital in a "state of health, food, and social assistance emergency."[126] But the Peronists were able to maintain adjustment measures by forging a coalition of loyal Peronist supporters and pro-stabilization business interests. Furthermore, they could not have done so without having links to organized labor, whose split ultimately forced the Peronists to broaden their bases of support and effectively precluded the rise of any viable opposition.

During the last period, as Argentina's economic situation led to a moderate improvement in its individual situation and the banks continued to increase their overall capabilities, once again Argentina was willing to undertake significant adjustment despite relatively few concessions from the banks. Thus, ironically, the ultra-nationalist Peronists paved the way for Argentina to qualify for the Brady Plan and the apparent conclusion of a decade of rescheduling efforts.

[126] *LAWR*, April 12, 1990.

14 The search for independence: Brazilian debt rescheduling in the 1980s and 1990s

Brazil's debt strategy during the 1980s and early 1990s has been characterized by attempts to maintain as much policy independence as possible from its foreign creditors, be they commercial banks or the International Monetary Fund. Its strong economic position during part of the decade allowed it to adopt a particularly intransigent stance vis-à-vis its creditors.

Brazil's ability to successfully remove foreign creditors from a say in its policies varied considerably during the course of the nine periods of bargaining examined here. The first bargaining period began in August 1982 as banks sharply cut back credit to Brazil, and ended in May 1983 when the banks and Brazil failed to implement "Phase I" of the rescheduling agreement signed in February 1983. By the second period, from June 1983 to January 1984, the larger banks had managed to unify their coalition by coercing smaller lenders to participate in joint action. In the third period, from February 1984 to August 1985, an increase in worldwide demand for Brazil's exports in combination with the nation's shrinking supply of imports created a considerable trade surplus. Brazil's greater supply of debt bargaining resources – and concern for political fallout from austerity measures – encouraged Brazil to secure significant concessions from the banks and IMF even thought it failed to comply with most of its IMF-approved measures during 1984.

The fourth period, composed of two rounds, began in September 1985 with the election of Tancredo Neves, Brazil's first civilian President in 21 years. After Neves's untimely death, his replacement, José Sarney, managed to capitalize on Brazil's strengthened bargaining capabilities and secure important concessions from the financial community. Sarney's populist government assumed a confrontational attitude toward the IMF. Announcing that Brazil would ignore IMF prescriptions, Sarney implemented pro-growth heterodox economic programs rather than orthodox austerity packages. In 1986, for example, Sarney initiated the anti-inflation "Cruzado Plan," which was popular with Brazilian consumers yet ultimately devastating to Brazil's trade and foreign exchange accounts. Still, Brazil continued to receive additional concessions from the banks.

By November 1986, however, the Cruzado Plan had failed to restore Brazil's economic health. As its economy continued to deteriorate, Brazilian officials responded by attempting to radically alter the terms of debt negotiations in early 1987 by declaring a moratorium on its interest payments. The banks responded by taking large loan-loss reserves, and the fifth period ended with a deadlock, marking a failure of Brazil's strategy. Following the deadlock, in the sixth period from December 1987 to December 1988, a chastened Brazil reentered the fold of traditional debt negotiations, but continued to assert its individuality by reversing the usual protocol of signing an IMF accord before securing an agreement with its creditors. Despite the efforts of the international financial community, Brazil again fell out with its creditors in the seventh period, unsuccessfully attempting to use the threat of a moratorium to encourage leniency on the part of the bankers.

The election of Fernando Collor de Mello to the Brazilian presidency in December 1989, and his subsequent adoption of an unorthodox readjustment plan, raised hopes in Brazil. But after alienating private bankers by ignoring their claims, a politically unstable and economically limp Brazil returned to the negotiating table. It reached agreement on interest arrears during the eighth period from July 1990 to July 1991. Following this accord, Brazil concluded a Brady Plan agreement in principle in the ninth period in 1992, but this agreement was only finalized with great difficulty after two years of negotiations. In the end, the agreement proved unique among Brady Plan accords in that Brazil used its own reserves to back the agreement with the banks.

Background to rescheduling

Brazil's contentious relationship with foreign creditors, and particularly the IMF, goes back to the 1950s (and to earlier epochs as well). In October 1958, President Juscelino Kubitschek first began negotiations with the IMF for a loan. Because of Brazil's high inflation rate, however, the IMF made its lending conditional on Brazil's commitment to slash public spending. Private creditors also waited for IMF approval before committing new funds. But instead of making the commitment, Kubitschek denounced the IMF's conditions, and broke with the Fund. Economic growth coupled with rapid inflation characterized the remainder of his tenure.

In early 1961, President Janio da Silva Quadros adopted a tough stabilization program. However, political opposition to its stringency forced him to resign during August of the same year. Quadros's successor, Joao Goulart, also abandoned stabilization efforts because of protests against his wage and credit restrictions. In 1964, a military coup ousted Goulart from power as inflation skyrocketed and Brazil's balance of payments deficit worsened.[1]

The orthodox economic policies of the military government led by Castello Branco reduced inflation from 86.6% in 1964 to 24% in 1967. This achievement still fell short of announced goals and contributed to stagnant per capita economic growth.[2] In 1967 Castello Branco's successor, General Artur da Costa e Silva, shifted to a successful heterodox economic policy, which attempted to control inflation without clamping down on money supply. Brazil's economic

[1] Skidmore (1977), p. 171. [2] Skidmore (1977).

boom began as the government sustained rapid economic growth,[3] convincing Brazilians that their economy could be managed without following orthodox IMF policies.

Brazil's economy grew at an impressive rate throughout the 1960s and early 1970s, encouraging foreign lenders to recycle petrodollars to Brazil. Its debt stabilized at around $3 billion during the 1960s, but jumped to $12 billion in 1974, and soared to five times that amount by the turn of the decade. The first quadrupling of the foreign debt, from $3 to $12 billion, helped finance Brazil's "economic miracle" from 1968 to 1974. During those years, growth rates averaged 10% annually. In 1974, incoming President Ernesto Geisel made a decision to cope with the first oil shock by borrowing rather than by economic retrenchment. Foreign loans launched ambitious investment projects in infrastructure and basic industries such as electricity and petrochemicals. To encourage bank lending, Brazil paid higher than average spreads after 1979.[4] Following self-imposed adjustment in 1980 that included tight monetary policy, Brazil managed to achieve a trade surplus by mid-1981. Pleased by Brazilian policies, bankers found lending attractive at the high rates they received. In October 1981, Walter Wriston, chairman of Citicorp, predicted, "In the near future, Brazil's airports will be full again with international bankers interested in the country."[5] Wriston's prophecy came true: however, the bankers who arrived during the following year were more interested in rescheduling huge debts than in making new loans.

Period 1: August 1982–May 1983: the biggest jumbo

The bankers' unwillingness to provide fresh loans to Latin American countries following Mexico's August 1982 crisis caused serious debt servicing problems for Brazil. To restore short-term liquidity, Brazil began negotiations with its creditors to restructure its $100 billion external debt. Concerned about the enormous size of Brazil's debt, both the U.S. government and the IMF promoted an agreement. Still, the agreement was inherently fragile because neither Brazil nor the banks were able to achieve a stable coalition during this period.

Identifying individual situations

During the first period, we classify Brazil as coalitionally unstable, weak in debt rescheduling resources, and weak in overall capabilities (IS 8). The banks were in the same boat, coalitionally unstable and lacking in both debt-related and overall capabilities (IS 8).

Brazil. Throughout 1982, a military government maintained tight control in Brazil. General João Baptista Figueiredo's regime dominated the electoral

[3] Fishlow (1973).
[4] On the spreads, see *The Banker*, December 1981, and Delamaide (1984), p. 118.
[5] *Business Week*, October 26, 1981, p. 66.

college, ensuring control of presidential succession. However, following long-standing discussion of electoral reform, in 1982 free and open gubernatorial elections were allowed. Opposition party candidates of the Partido Movimento Democrático Brasileiro won the governor's office in 10 out of 23 states, which accounted for more than half of all Brazilians and three-quarters of Brazil's gross national product. Popular support for a more open political system came from such disparate groups as business, Roman Catholic episcopates, the bar association, and the press.[6] The growing opposition to the military regime had the effect of seriously limiting the government's ability to implement austerity measures.

Brazil's lack of financial resources exacerbated its political instability. With regard to debt-specific resources, Brazil's reserves dropped from a $7.5 billion at the end of 1981 to $3.2 billion by December 1982. Even worse, about half of the remaining reserves were actually uncollectible debts owed by Poland.[7]

Brazil's overall capabilities were no better. It relied primarily on trade revenues to generate foreign exchange, yet its trade surplus was a mere $800 million in 1982.[8] Moreover, the country was becoming increasingly dependent on the United States for markets. In 1981, it exported 17% of its total exports to American markets. That share rose to 20% in 1982, and to 23% in 1983.[9] Fear of U.S. trade retaliation increasingly limited Brazil's bargaining latitude in debt issues. Brazil's weak financial position prevented the country from ignoring international creditors in favor of an autarkic economic course. These conditions forced Brazil to maintain the goodwill of its creditors.

Lenders. As discussed in the Mexico chapter, throughout 1982 and early 1983, the banks faced coalitional instability because of differing exposures to major debtors. In Brazil, as in other countries, smaller U.S. regional banks, as well as European banks, were much less heavily exposed. Swiss banks, for example, had virtually no loan exposure in Brazil. As might be expected, the banks with the largest stake in Brazil led the rescheduling effort, attempting with varying success to induce smaller regional banks and European banks to follow suit. Although many large banks were in accord, as they confronted the possibility of serious financial losses stemming from high exposure to Brazilian debt, divisions within the greater lending community were heightened by variations in the maturity and types of outstanding loans made to Brazil. This led to disagreements over the formula the banks used to calculate the amount each bank would be expected to contribute to Brazil's loan package. For example, American banks had a high proportion of short-term loans to Brazil. During debt rescheduling negotiations, Japanese bankers were dismayed to learn that the negotiating committee had calculated required contributions to the Brazilian jumbo loan on

[6] *New York Times*, December 20, 1982.

[7] The Economist Intelligence Unit, *Quarterly Economic Review* (hereinafter *QER*), no. 1, 1983, p. 15.

[8] IMF (1990). [9] Confidential documents.

the basis of outstanding medium- and long-term loans. Japanese bankers argued that they were being pressured to contribute a higher proportion of total exposure than their American counterparts.[10] Similarly, banks disagreed about the date that should be used as the basis for determining the amounts each bank should contribute. For instance, France had increased its exposure in Brazil during 1982–1983, and thus favored an early base date to minimize its total contribution to the Brazilian jumbo loan. American banks, whose lending to Brazil had begun much earlier, vehemently opposed this move.[11]

With respect to debt and overall resources, U.S. money-center banks had the largest exposures in Brazil and Latin America. At the end of 1982, the nine largest American banks had $13.3 billion of loans in Brazil alone, an exposure amounting to 46% of their capital.[12] Their need for debt servicing made U.S. banks extremely vulnerable to threats of a Brazilian default. The banks had no resources to enforce the contracts into which they had entered. As we shall see, while governments actively intervened in negotiations, the United States and other creditor governments were not tightly aligned with the banks. Given their high degree of exposures, the banks were left with two choices: to continue rescheduling in the hope of eventually collecting the debts or to simply write off the loans and minimize additional commitments. It fell to the money-center banks to persuade less heavily committed banks to choose the first rather than the second option.

Creditor governments and international organizations.[13] The U.S. government and the IMF took an active interest in the progress of Brazilian debt negotiations during this period. Creditor governments, especially the U.S. government, were well aware that a Brazilian default could have a devastating effect on the international financial system. The U.S. government was also highly concerned about the maintenance of political stability in Brazil – not only because Brazil was making the difficult transition from a dictatorship to a democracy, but also because political instability would decrease the likelihood of continued debt servicing.

Debt game and predicted outcome

From these classifications, we arrived at the game matrix shown in Figure 14.1 for period one. In the absence of intervention, we expected Brazil and the banks to retreat into a position of mutual intransigence – LA..., LC.... However, because of the interests of the U.S. and the IMF in preserving the financial system as well as in preventing Brazilian political instability, we predict that both the IMF and the United States government will try to push Brazil and the banks to a position of medium adjustment and concessions (MA, MC).

[10] Ibid. [11] Interview in Brazil with an international commercial banker, May 10, 1985.

[12] *The Economist*, July 16, 1983, p. 65.

[13] The major focus in the bulk of this chapter is on the role of the International Monetary Fund, although other organizations did at times actively participate.

Cardinal Payoff Matrix, Intervention Expected

Lenders IS 8

		HC...	MC...	LC...
	HA...	0, 0	−3.5, 4	−4, 8
Brazil IS 8	MA...	4, −3.5	<u>0, 0</u>	−2, 3.5
	LA...	8, −4	3.5, −2	**0, 0**

Note: Nash equilibrium bolded; expected outcome with intervention underlined.

Ordinal Payoff Matrix, Intervention Expected

Lenders IS 8

		HC...	MC...	LC...
	HA...	5, 5	2, 8	1, 9
Brazil IS 8	MA...	8, 2	<u>5, 5</u>	3, 7
	LA...	9, 1	7, 3	**5, 5**

Note: Nash equilibrium bolded; expected outcome with intervention underlined.

Figure 14.1. *Play phase, period one: August 1982–February* 1983

The negotiations and outcome

Brazil faced grave financial problems in late 1982. The "lessons" that bankers learned from the Mexican debt crisis were applied to Latin American debtors generally, resulting in a sharp contraction of credit flows to the region's largest country. For example, money market lines to Brazil dropped by $3.2 billion during the period from June 1982 to May 1983. The reluctance of bankers to send new money into Latin America made any rescheduling agreements difficult at best. Without active intervention, the negotiations appeared to be deadlocked.

In October 1982, Brazilian Finance Minister Ernane Galveas met with U.S. Deputy Treasury Secretary Timothy McNamar at the GATT ministerial conference in Geneva. They worked out a plan for the U.S. Treasury to lend Brazil $1.23 billion from its Exchange Stabilization Fund. The money was disbursed in November but not publicized until President Ronald Reagan visited Brazil in December.[14] The U.S. Treasury increased its $1.23 billion loan by $300 million in December 1982 and by $400 million in February 1983.[15] Similarly, on December 23 the Bank for International Settlements agreed to provide Brazil with a $1.2 billion bridging loan.[16]

The U.S. government also took steps to encourage private creditors to take interim measures while the rescheduling negotiations were being held. To this end, Washington guaranteed a $600 million bridging loan granted by Citibank, Chase Manhattan, Bank of America, Banker's Trust, Manufacturer's Hanover, and Morgan's in November 1982.[17]

At the same time that creditor governments were intervening on behalf of Brazil, the country was negotiating an agreement with the IMF. On December 5, 1982, in return for $4.86 billion from the Fund's standby facility and $1.08 billion from its Compensatory Finance Facility, Brazil agreed to implement an IMF austerity package. The package, signed on February 23, 1983, contained targets for exports, domestic inflation, and the public internal deficit.[18] A particularly controversial provision canceled a 10% wage adjustment for the lowest paid Brazilian workers.[19] Choosing to please the international financial community, Brazilian negotiators reluctantly accepted the terms of adjustment despite vehement protests from the Brazilian business and labor communities.

In return for its agreement to IMF adjustment measures, Brazil obtained not only an IMF loan commitment, but also benefited from the Fund's leverage against banks that resisted efforts to package a new jumbo loan. Under pressure from the IMF and creditor governments, lenders signed an agreement to assemble a jumbo loan package, which included $8.8 billion in trade credits, and commitments to restore interbank deposits to their June 1982 level of $9 billion, reschedule $4 billion worth of principal repayments due in 1983, and extend new monies worth $4.4 billion.[20]

Yet what initially appeared to be a successful outcome of medium to high adjustment by Brazil and some concessions by the banks began to crumble

[14] Delamaide (1984), p. 119. [15] *International Herald Tribune*, December 24, 1982.

[16] *International Herald Tribune*, December 24, 1982. An additional $250 million contribution from Saudi Arabia, which was originally kept secret, brought the actual total of the loan to $1.45 billion. See *International Herald Tribune*, June 8, 1983.

[17] *International Herald Tribune*, December 16, 1982; Delamaide (1984), p. 119; interview with a U.S. central banker. *Financial Times*, November 25, 1982.

[18] *The Banker*, January 1983.

[19] *Latin American Weekly Report* (hereinafter *LAWR*), January 28, 1983, and March 4, 1983.

[20] *Wall Street Journal*, August 30, 1983.

almost immediately. Under pressure from the IMF and creditor governments, the banks had made promises they could not keep. Heavily exposed money-center banks, concerned with gaining Brazil's goodwill, attempted to package the jumbo loan but encountered resistance from smaller banks who balked at increasing their own exposures. Large lenders were unwilling to assume the entire cost and risk of assembling the package, but they were also unable to get many smaller banks to restore their interbank deposits.[21]

As economic conditions rapidly deteriorated, Brazil was not in a good position to keep the promises it had made to the IMF either. By May 1983, Brazil's public sector debt was running twice as high as expected, and inflation floated between 120 and 150% (significantly above the 90% ceiling).[22] Although the severity of Brazil's financial crisis gave the country a strong incentive to respect the agreement, the political fragmentation of the country made it virtually impossible to implement the austerity measures. The Brazilian government indicated that it was unable – not unwilling – to adjust, claiming that its cash crisis severely hindered its ability to implement austerity measures. Brazilian spokesmen said creditor countries were at least partially responsible for Brazil's continued difficulties with implementing economic reforms. They pointed, for example, to the rupture in money market lines of short-term credit by smaller regional banks in the United States and Europe. They argued, furthermore, that private creditors had issued an inadequate amount of fresh funds – and on such unfavorable terms that Brazil had little chance of successfully implementing reforms.[23]

As banks were increasingly unable to hold their coalition together, Brazil fell out of compliance with the IMF agreement, and the IMF responded by suspending disbursements at the end of May.[24] The private creditors quickly followed, halting implementation of the jumbo loan package.

Summary. The initial outcome of the debt game was some adjustment and some concessions (the predicted equilibrium with intervention). But under pressure from the IMF and the United States, both Brazil and the private lenders promised more than they could deliver. Brazil promised to implement IMF austerity measures; the banks put together a comprehensive jumbo loan package. The IMF had intervened to preserve the stability of the international financial system, paying little attention to the ability of individual banks to fulfill their promises. Moreover, because its policy toward Brazil was to treat the adjustment problem as a purely technical economic one, the IMF was not particularly worried about Brazil's ability to service in spite of its rocky political situation. But, without sustained pressure from the IMF and U.S. government, the agreement disintegrated. Instead, the banks and Brazil ended up at the predicted two-actor Nash equilibrium of LA, LC by the end of the period.

[21] *The Banker*, June 1983, p. 71; *Wall Street Journal*, August 30, 1983.
[22] *The Banker*, June 1983, p. 71. [23] *Washington Post*, May 25, 1983.
[24] At that point, the IMF had disbursed $230 million. It suspended disbursement of a second tranche of $411 million (*Wall Street Journal*, July 18, 1983).

Situational changes

Because both players received relatively poor payoffs and were deadlocked in late 1982, both Brazil and the banks had incentives to alter their individual situations. Large banks faced the problems created by the disagreements among factions of private banks, smaller regional banks, European banks, Japanese banks, and the advisory committee led by U.S. money-center banks. Even after Phase I of the rescheduling package was signed in February 1983, 200 out of 455 of Brazil's private creditors refused to cooperate for the sake of restoring Brazil's interbank deposits to $9 billion. Instead the deposits leveled off at $6 billion.[25]

When Citibank's William Rhodes replaced Morgan Guaranty's Antonio Gebauer as chairman of the advisory committee, he began to restructure the committee in an attempt to increase the participation of smaller lenders. Rhodes reorganized the banking coalition into a pyramid structure that placed eight regional banks in the advisory committee.[26] This restructuring enabled larger regional banks to pressure recalcitrant banks to contribute their share to the jumbo loan. This new structure also increased the lead banks' ability to monitor the cooperation of smaller banks.

The IMF also took action to strengthen the lending coalition. Not only did the Fund make its $4.6 billion loan conditional on further bank lending, but it also assisted the lenders' efforts by preparing a list of 1,400 banks that had made loans to Brazil and the amount of their contribution. Using this information, the IMF calculated the amount it expected each bank to contribute to the next jumbo loan.[27] The Fund put its information facilities at the disposal of the large advisory banks and the Brazilian government in order to improve their monitoring of the other lenders.

In an effort to secure additional funds, even Brazil attempted to strengthen the coalitional unity of the lenders. Brazil's Central Bank Chairman Carlos Langoni helped organize the banker advisory groups and facilitated information flows to the lead banks.[28] For example, when Banker's Trust (the bank in charge of restoring interbank deposits) ran into resistance from smaller banks, the Brazil Central Bank helped Banker's Trust compile information on who had restored interbank lines and who had not.

Moreover, on December 19, 1982, Brazil itself tried to equalize incentives for banks to contribute to the jumbo loan package by blocking payment on medium- and long-term loans due by the end of January 1983. The banks with a higher proportion of their loan exposure monopolized by outstanding medium- and long-term loans were thus prevented from receiving debt servicing payments. This awarded their share of the remaining rescheduling costs to the banks with a higher proportion of loan exposures in short-term loans.

[25] *Washington Post*, May 25, 1983.
[26] For details on lead bank actions in this connection, see Lipson (1985) and Aggarwal (1987).
[27] Aggarwal (1987), p. 29. [28] Interview with a Brazilian central banker, May 1985.

Period 2: June 1983–January 1984, the banks unite

By the beginning of this period, the large banks had managed, with Brazil and the IMF's help, to unify their lending coalition as large, heavily exposed banks devised ways to deal more effectively with recalcitrant banks. Brazil's individual situation remained unchanged. Suffering from a shortage of currency reserves, it continued to go through the motions of submitting to IMF conditions.

Identifying individual situations

In the second period, Brazil remained coalitionally unstable, issue weak, and overall weak (IS 8). Lenders managed to solidify their coalition, but remained issue weak and overall weak (IS 7).

Brazil. Brazil was coalitionally unstable during this period, and in terms of financial resources, its position deteriorated. After the May 1983 suspension of IMF and private credit flows, Brazil faced a severe liquidity crunch. Consequently, it struggled during most of this period to avoid default. Without new loans, Brazil was unable to meet its payments on existing loans to the Bank of International Settlements and private creditors; by September it was over $2 billion in arrears on its loan payments.

Lenders. After considerable efforts by the large banks, the banks had forged a much more unified coalition by the beginning of this period. Lead bankers realized that creditor banks had to speak with a unified voice if they were to be effective in negotiating with debtors. Large U.S. banks took the initiative in forging cooperation – ensuring that Japanese and European banks would jump on the bandwagon early and display a commitment to remaining with the coalition. Smaller and regional banks were another matter. They continued to have little incentive to contribute new money or make other concessions to problem debtors like Brazil. However, William Rhodes's decision to include regional banks on the Brazil advisory committee established a hierarchical chain of command. Regional banks were now given more responsibility to ensure that smaller banks participated in the rescheduling. In this case, threatening a loss of future business was decisive in convincing the smaller banks to participate in the coalition. In terms of debt and overall resources, the banks continued to be as weak on both dimensions as in the previous period.

Creditor governments and international organizations. As in the first period, creditor governments and the IMF had little choice but to continue their active involvement in the Brazil debt situation. As the largest debtor in Latin America, Brazil had the potential to destabilize the international financial system by defaulting.

Cardinal Payoff Matrix,
Intervention Expected

		Lenders IS 7		
		HC...	MC...	LC...
	HA...	0, 12	–3.5, 11.67	–4, 11.33
Brazil IS 8	MA...	4, 9	0, 8	–2, 7
	LA...	**8, 10**	3.5, 7	0, 4

Note: Nash equilibrium bolded; expected outcome with intervention underlined.

Ordinal Payoff Matrix,
Intervention Expected

		Lenders IS 7		
		HC...	MC...	LC...
	HA...	5, 9	2, 8	1, 7
Brazil IS 8	MA...	8, 5	5, 4	3, 2.5
	LA...	**9, 6**	7, 2.5	5, 1

Note: Nash equilibrium bolded; expected outcome with intervention underlined.

Figure 14.2. *Play phase, period two: June–November 1983*

Debt game and predicted outcome

Given Brazil's weak situation, we predict the game shown in Figure 14.2 for period two. On the basis of two-party interaction, we expect that Brazil will not adjust, while the lenders – aware of their vulnerability to Brazilian retaliation – will make high concessions. When we include the role of creditor governments and international organizations, we predict a different outcome. Given the IMF's perspective on balance of payments adjustments, we expect it to push Brazil toward accepting adjustment measures. At the same time, we expect the U.S. to support efforts by the banks to conclude a successful agreement with Brazil. Therefore, we predict an outcome of high concessions by banks, and some adjustment by Brazil.

The negotiations and outcome

Soon after the IMF halted its loan disbursements, Brazil faced a liquidity crunch and was unable to make a $411 million payment to the BIS in May 1983. The BIS extended the deadline until the end of June, but Brazil also missed this target.[29] In an attempt to push the Brazilians to settle with the IMF, Swiss National Bank Governor and BIS President Fritz Leutwiler announced on July 11 that the BIS would not roll over the $400 million bridging payment again.[30]

The U.S. government was concerned, however, about the consequences of pushing a coalitionally fragile Brazil to undertake more adjustment than the country could handle.[31] Its fears were exacerbated on July 6, 1983, when production at Brazil's largest oil refinery was stopped for the first time in 20 years as workers struck to protest existing austerity measures.[32] Consequently, in early July the U.S. Treasury and the Federal Reserve agreed to extend Brazil a $600 million loan if an agreement with the IMF did not appear quickly forthcoming.[33] By the same token, the Fed supported the U.S. banks' involvement in Brazil; Fed Chairman Paul Volcker gave the U.S. banks specific assurances that bank supervisors would not require the banks to reclassify these loans – as would normally happen when banks rescheduled debt on more favorable terms.[34]

Under pressure from the IMF and the BIS, on July 18 Brazil agreed to adopt new austerity measures in return for the release of its second IMF tranche. Brasilia promised to bring inflation down from roughly 150% in 1983 to an average 55–60% by December 1984; to eliminate the public sector deficit by the end of 1984; to cut the current account deficit to between $6 and $6.5 billion (down from the 1982 level of $14.7 billion); and to increase its trade surplus to a target $9 billion by 1984.[35] The key component of the agreement, however, was a change in Brazil's wage law. Under this provision, Brazil agreed to adjust its indexation system. The new system called for raising wages by only 80% of the inflation rate and increasing public sector wages only once a year.[36] Brazil's agreement with the IMF also induced the BIS to roll over the July payment at the last minute.[37]

Naturally, the adjustment package heightened domestic political tensions in

[29] *International Herald Tribune*, June 8, 1983. [30] *The Times*, July 16, 1983.
[31] *The Economist*, July 16, 1983, p. 65. [32] *Wall Street Journal*, July 21, 1983.
[33] *The Economist*, July 9, 1983, p. 75.
[34] *Financial Times*, October 13, 1983.
[35] See *Financial Times*, September 6, 1983 and *The Times*, September 3, 1983.
[36] *The Economist*, July 23, 1983, p. 70.
[37] When, in August, Brazil again missed the payment deadline, the Bank for International Settlements (BIS) announced that it would not demand repayment "for the time being," due to the "improved prospects for a resumption" of IMF funds. *Wall Street Journal*, August 30, 1983.

Brazil. On July 21, in a salient manifestation of Brazil's fragile domestic situation, labor leaders called a 24-hour nationwide general strike in response to the austerity measures.[38] Opposition parties also joined in the protest over the new wage provisions. But in September, Congress voted down the changes in the wage laws, prompting President Figueiredo to invoke emergency powers and to decree the law into immediate effect.[39] Also in September, Central Bank Governor Carlos Langoni resigned on the grounds that the austerity targets were unrealistic and would cause too much social havoc.[40]

In spite of the conflict it provoked, the austerity package gave private creditors a green light for a new agreement. The IMF attempted to coordinate the effort at the annual IMF/World Bank meetings in September when it organized a secret meeting with 20 of Brazil's major creditors. Under terms not immediately disclosed to the public, the banks agreed to provide Brazil with $6.5 billion in new loans.[41] Predictably, the banks disagreed on how the financial burden should be divided, but money-center banks still pressed the private coalition to raise more than 90% of the $6.5 billion. This all took place even before the IMF voted on Brazil's new austerity program at its subsequent meeting.[42]

The IMF approved the program on November 22, a move that unlocked more than $11 billion in new funds. In addition to the banks' $6.5 billion loan, creditor governments contributed $2.5 billion in trade credits, and the IMF released the remaining $2 billion of "Phase I" money that had been frozen. On November 23, the Paris Club agreed to reschedule more than 85% of Brazil's $3.8 billion debt owed to creditor governments that would come due by the end of 1984.[43]

Summary. Despite increasing numbers of strikes and public demonstrations, Brazil bowed to IMF pressure to implement some austerity measures. It even managed to meet the IMF targets during this period. By the end of 1983, Brazil's trade surplus reached $6.5 billion, surpassing the original $6 billion target that had been set in January, although it continued to run a balance of payments deficit. In addition, the operational public sector deficit was brought down to 2.5% of GDP, below the revised 2.7% target set in September 1983.[44]

At the same time, bankers made relatively high concessions. Although bankers had hoped to keep the loan limited to $5 billion[45] (as with the Mexican jumbo loan), they agreed to a $6.5 billion package, putting together the largest Euromarket loan ever raised for a sovereign nation.[46] In October, the banks even agreed to soften the terms of the new loans. The loan period was for nine years

[38] *Wall Street Journal*, July 21, 1983. [39] *Los Angeles Times*, October 23, 1983.

[40] *Financial Times*, September 6, 1983. Interview with a Brazilian banker.

[41] *New York Times*, September 30, 1983; *International Herald Tribune*, September 28, 1983; *Financial Times*, September 22, 1983.

[42] *Financial Times*, November 24, 1983. [43] *Financial Times*, November 24, 1983.

[44] Data on performance from confidential materials. [45] *The Economist*, October 1, 1983.

[46] *Financial Times*, September 28, 1983. While the $6.5 billion figure was unprecedented, it was nonetheless smaller than the $8.5–9 billion that Brazilian policymakers had asked for. See *The Times*, October 6, 1983.

(compared to the eight-year period in the 1982 loan package), had a five-year grace period (compared to the 30-month grace period in the previous package), and had an interest rate of two points (instead of 2 1/8 points) over LIBOR.[47] The number of banks that participated in the package was also high. When the agreement was signed in January 1984, between 560 and 700 banks were reported to have taken part. Only 11 out of 144 U.S. banks with outstanding credits to Brazil refused.[48]

Situational changes

Brazil's domestic dispute over economic policies came to a head when Carlos Langoni resigned as Central Bank governor in September 1983. The resignation was an indication of the coalitional fissures in the country, but it strengthened the position of Planning Minister Antonio Delfim Netto. Netto and Langoni had battled for months over issues of domestic economic policy and strategies to handle foreign debt. When Langoni resigned, President Figueiredo delegated full authority over issues of economic policy to Netto, but coalitional stability would continue to elude Brazil.

The most significant development leading to the next period of negotiations was the government's successful efforts to increase its financial strength through an export drive. As a result, Brazil was able to considerably increase its foreign reserves, thus decreasing its immediate need for loans. For their part, the banks continued to cooperate with Brazil, as the large banks led the battle to maintain stability among the lenders.

Period 3, January 1984–September 1985: breaking away from the IMF

This period is divided into two rounds, the first from January 1984 to February 1985, the second from March until August 1985. The first round opened as Brazil experienced a surge in its exports. This expansion of Brazil's financial resources strengthened its bargaining power with its private creditors and the IMF. Still, under strong IMF pressure, Brazil initially agreed to some adjustment of its economy in exchange for a multi-year rescheduling package. But when Brazil failed to meet its targets, the IMF blocked the accord and threw the negotiations into deadlock. During the second round, however, Brazil stuck with a hard-line position, as the debt game predicts, and the bankers in this instance were willing to make significant concessions.

Identifying individual situations

In the third period, Brazil became issue strong, but remained coalitionally unstable and overall weak (IS 2). The individual situation of the lenders remained

[47] *International Herald Tribune*, October 8–9, 1983.
[48] *New York Times*, January 28, 1984.

the same as in period two: coalitionally stable, issue weak, and overall weak (IS 7).

Brazil. During this period, Brazil's domestic situation remained highly uncertain. The country was undergoing a transition from military to democratic rule; consequently, it suffered a leadership vacuum at the national level. The Figueiredo government continued to negotiate with the IMF and private creditors, but the lenders feared that the civilian government to be elected in January 1985 might not support similar policies.

As the specter of elections loomed on the horizon, the domestic political climate was shaky. The five parties that had existed when the military left office had broken into squabbling factions, leading to the creation of 25 new and invariably minuscule parties. These parties tended to represent the ambitions of individual politicians rather than political ideals or voter interests. On a community level, thousands of neighborhood associations and church-linked "base communities" attempted to mobilize poor and middle-class people to participate in Brazil's newly competitive political system.[49]

The victorious candidate, Tancredo Neves, managed the transition from military to civilian rule, but in March 1985, before he had even formally taken office, Neves died. His running mate Jose Sarney inherited the presidency, finding himself in a delicate position. He lacked the active support of either the military's old guard (PDS) or the reformers (PMDB). Neves had left behind only an uneasy alliance with the military. The new civilian regime had pledged not to carry out any witch hunts within the military and to avoid any drastic departures from the broad policies of the Figueiredo government. In return, the military had agreed to allow the process of constitutional reform and democratization to occur unimpeded. Nonetheless, political divisions plagued the government. Soon after Sarney assumed office, the Congress authorized direct presidential elections – a move that threatened Sarney's ability to remain in office let alone shape policy.

Political uncertainties notwithstanding, Brazil enjoyed a surge in material resources during the period, an asset it used as leverage in the bargaining process. Brazil's trade surplus improved substantially by the end of the first quarter of 1984. Its exports increased 21% from the previous year and imports fell by 16% – leaving a quarterly trade surplus of $2.5 billion. By the end of 1984, the surplus had reached $13 billion, and the 1985 surplus was about $12.5 billion. Moreover, Brazil's position regarding foreign exchange reserves was enviable; in February 1985, the country had an impressive $9.9 billion in reserves. The domestic economic picture was also bright.

Nonetheless, the limits of Brazil's bargaining latitude were clear. Brazil's improved trade balance was largely the result of increased access to American markets. Thirty percent of Brazilian exports were directed to the U.S. during the first half of 1984, compared to just 17% in 1981.[50]

[49] *New York Times*, September 25, 1985.

[50] *The World Today*, March 1985, p. 62.

Lenders. As in the second period, the lenders enjoyed a relatively stable coalition, but had very little bargaining latitude. In terms of debt-related resources, the enormous exposure of money-center banks made them highly vulnerable to Brazilian threats of default. Bankers were also overall weak because they had no guarantees of government intervention on their behalf; indeed, they found that favorable creditor government intervention was scarce during this period, although the IMF's goals were in concert with their own.

Creditor governments and international organizations. Creditor governments and the IMF continued to desire a viable settlement. Because of the size of Brazil's debt and the continued vulnerability of commercial banks to a default, the governments and the IMF were highly motivated to facilitate an agreement between Brazil and its private creditors. Additionally, Sarney's eloquent pro-democracy arguments seemed to have brought U.S. concerns for the successful consolidation of Brazil's democratic reform to the forefront. But because of its mandate, the IMF, on the other hand, was more sympathetic to the bankers' desire to see Brazil stick to an adjustment program.

Debt game and predicted outcome

Brazil's improved situation leads to the cardinal matrix and ordinal conversion shown in Figure 14.3. In the two-actor game without intervention, we expect an outcome of high concessions and no adjustment. Given the pro-democracy concerns of the U.S. Administration, we expect intervention to be minimal. We would expect the U.S. government to show patience with Brazil by not pushing it too quickly to solve its domestic economic problems. By contrast, in keeping with its financial mandate, we expect the IMF to be more concerned about strict adherence to its austerity programs. To the extent that the U.S. government intervenes, it will likely be in favor of Brazil – and therefore will reinforce the Nash equilibrium outcome. Given our expectation that the IMF will continue to remain active in the negotiations, we would expect conflict between these third-party intervenors, and thus only little movement on Brazil's part to make economic adjustments.

The negotiations and outcome

Round one. Although Brazil attempted to comply with IMF performance criteria during much of 1984, by the end of the first round, it was unwilling to pursue any further adjustment. In fact, Brazil adopted an increasingly confrontational attitude as debt negotiations progressed.

Brazilian officials stressed the improvement in their country's economic performance during this period, suggesting that lenders would no longer be able to use the availability of new loans as a bargaining chip during negotiations. In April 1984, for example, Finance Minister Galveas said that as far as he was

Cardinal Payoff Matrix, Intervention Expected

		Lenders IS 7		
		HC...	MC...	LC...
	HA...	−12, 12	−11.5, 11.67	−8, 11.33
Brazil IS 2	MA...	−8, 9	−8, 8	−6, 7
	LA...	<u>**−4, −10**</u>	−4.5, 7	−4, 4

Note: Nash equilibrium bolded; expected outcome with intervention underlined.

Ordinal Payoff Matrix, Intervention Expected

		Lenders IS 7		
		HC...	MC...	LC...
	HA...	1, 9	2, 8	4, 7
Brazil IS 2	MA...	4, 5	4, 4	6, 2.5
	LA...	<u>**8.5, 6**</u>	7, 2.5	8.5, 1

Note: Nash equilibrium bolded; expected outcome with intervention underlined.

Figure 14.3. *Play phase, period three: January 1984–August 1985*

concerned, 1984 would be "entirely closed" with regard to new loans, although many bankers and economists had predicted Brazil would need more bank loans.[51] Galveas also suggested that Brazil might not need new bank money for as long as three or four years.[52]

[51] *Wall Street Journal*, April 10, 1984.

[52] This continued to be Brazil's official stance throughout the period; in January 1985, Central Bank President Pastore reemphasized that new loans were not needed.

In addition to stressing Brazil's increasing financial independence, Brazilian officials began to suggest that lenders might not get repaid in full. Removing his diplomatic gloves for a moment, in July 1984 Galveas declared:

> We're not going to pay off our debt. The bankers know it, the official financial institutions know it, and the governments know it. We're going to pay off our interest to the extent of our possibilities, and when we cannot, the bankers will lend us the money and then we will.[53]

However, even as Brazil became more verbally intransigent, it took some actions to comply with IMF performance criteria. The IMF had been withholding a $380 million tranche until the final details on the country's 1984 third quarter performance became available.[54] On November 30, 1984, the IMF found Brazil in compliance with third quarter austerity targets and released the $380 million tranche.[55] Moreover, in the same month, the Brazilians unveiled a plan to cut annual inflation to 120–150% in 1985.[56]

In December, Brazil and the IMF reached a tentative agreement on a new austerity program for 1985. Negotiations had been somewhat difficult, especially regarding the issue of public sector surplus targets. The IMF pressured Brazil to accept a target of 4% of gross domestic product; the Figueiredo government held out for a lower 1.2–1.5% of GDP.[57] Brazil's December 1984 letter of intent to the IMF included a compromise public sector surplus target of 3% of GDP (still much higher than the 0.3% target in 1984). The agreement also limited money supply growth to 60% (as compared to 152% in 1984). This agreement with the IMF enabled commercial debt negotiations for a multi-year rescheduling agreement to resume on December 17.[58]

Brazilian negotiators argued during the talks that, in exchange for Brazil's commitment not to request new loans, bankers should improve the rescheduling terms on existing debt. In particular, the Brazilians wanted a five- or six-year grace period on principal repayments.[59] The bankers and Brazil reached an initial agreement in January 1985. Under the agreement, the lenders made considerable concessions, although they were not as generous as Brazil had hoped. On the one hand, the banks provided Brazil with favorable new terms. They rescheduled about half of the country's $100.2 billion debt, the bulk of which was loans that would fall due from 1985 through 1991. They also agreed to spread out over 16 years the $5 billion in principal repayment due during this period and to resume the policy of automatically renewing interbank lines to Brazilian banks.

On the other hand, bankers limited their concessions by denying Brazil a grace period for making the $5 billion principal repayment. Brazilian policymakers

[53] *New York Times*, July 30, 1984.

[54] *Washington Post*, October 1, 1984; *Financial Times*, November 12, 1984.

[55] This figure contrasts with the $400 million figure reported above (*Journal of Commerce*, November 26, 1984).

[56] *Financial Times*, November 12, 1984. [57] *Financial Times*, November 11, 1984.

[58] *Financial Times*, December 13, 1984; *Wall Street Journal*, December 13, 1984.

[59] *Journal of Commerce*, November 26, 1984.

were also especially disappointed by the interest spread of 1.75% over LIBOR. Negotiators had hoped to get interest rates comparable to the interest rate given to Mexico in its multi-year agreement, but the bankers refused.[60]

Brazil's relationship with the IMF became extremely rocky soon after Neves was elected in January 1985, when the Fund withheld approval of Brazil's December letter of intent. The IMF insisted that Brazil devise ways to keep the public sector deficit and money supply within specified targets before it would approve the letter of intent. This brought negotiations with bankers to a standstill – despite the fact that the terms of the rescheduling arrangement had just been concluded.[61]

In summary, bankers displayed a willingness to make medium to high concessions during this round by concluding a multi-year agreement – even though they could not count on Brazil's political stability in the short term or on the goodwill of the incoming civilian government. Brazilian policymakers also agreed, under heavy IMF pressure, to undertake some adjustment. As Brazil failed to adhere to adjustment targets, however, the IMF toughened its bargaining stance. Its decision not to approve the December letter of intent prompted Brazil to refuse further adjustment. Finally, the banks followed the IMF's lead in refusing concessions, which resulted in a bargaining impasse (LA..., LC...).

Round two. During this round, continued issue strength gave Brazil significant credibility in withstanding a credit cutoff. Furthermore, the installment of a populist civilian regime made the government less willing to accept controversial austerity measures. Consequently, Brazil secured its favored outcome of no adjustment, while the more cohesive bankers' group offered significant concessions.

Sarney faced a difficult situation when he took office in March 1985. Although Brazil's trade surplus and financial reserves situation were strong, other problems plagued the country. For example, the public sector deficit continued to be very high. Inflation was running at roughly 230% annually. To complicate things further, popular expectations about the new civilian government were unrealistically high. In other words, Sarney faced strong domestic pressure not to implement unpopular austerity measures at exactly the same time that the IMF was increasing pressure on Brazil to embrace those kinds of policies.

From April through August, a public debate over economic policy pitted the monetarists in the Finance Ministry and Central Bank against the neo-Keynesians at the Planning Ministry. Monetarists favored deep cuts in public spending at the risk of initiating a recession, whereas the neo-Keynesians advocated economic growth as the cure for inflation and external debt. On August 26, 1985, it became evident that the neo-Keynesians had gained the upper hand, when a dozen of Brazil's senior financial officials resigned.[62] Most significantly, Dílson

[60] *Financial Times*, January 17, 1985. [61] *The Banker*, April 1985.
[62] *The Economist*, August 31, 1985.

Funaro replaced Francisco Dornelles as Finance Minister. Dornelles had favored negotiating with the IMF, but Funaro took a hard-line stance against IMF participation in negotiations and against its monitoring Brazil's economy.

Funaro's anti-IMF views had an immediate effect on Sarney's policy. In August, Sarney announced that Brazil might delay entering into a new IMF agreement. Sarney said his country needed time and flexibility to restructure the economy, which made a postponement of an IMF program seem appropriate.[63]

At the same time, Brazil adopted a more confrontational attitude toward its creditors. In August 1985, Luis Paulo Rosenberg, the President's adviser on the economy, responded to a reporter's question of whether or not Brazil needed new outside funding by asserting "not only do I not need it . . . I don't want it."[64]

To the surprise of most analysts, on August 21, the worried advisory committee of Brazil's large private creditors decided to urge other banks to extend a freeze on repayments of principal due in 1985 until January 17, 1986 – despite Brazil's refusal to settle with the IMF. The committee also decided to propose a third extension of $16 billion in interbank lines and trade facilities that ended on August 31.[65] They made this decision despite Brazil's rising public-sector deficit, totaling $5.6 billion, almost 140% higher (after adjusting for inflation) than the previous year, which they considered a sign of the country's failure to adjust its economy.[66] In effect, the banks had buckled to Brazil's intransigence to avoid a Brazilian default.

Summary. In the first round of this period, Brazil agreed to an austerity program in return for significant concessions. But as its economic position continued to improve, Brazilian negotiators took a much harder line and refused to adjust. By the end of the second round, as predicted, the banks gave in and agreed to significant concessions despite the lack of any commitment on Brazil's part to continue with its adjustment program for an outcome of LA..., HC....

Situational changes

Brazilian policymakers attempted to capitalize on the country's stronger position in issue-specific resources during this period by drawing substantive linkages between debt and other economic issues. To this end, Brasilia criticized Washington, saying it should reevaluate its economic policies in terms of the ability of debtor countries to repay their creditors. Specifically, Brazil attempted to tie the issues of U.S. interest rates and trade into the debt rescheduling issue-area, claiming that high U.S. interest rates and protectionist legislation hindered Brazil's ability to service its debt.

In February 1984, Brasilia vehemently protested the U.S. decision to impose a 27.7% tariff on plate and sheet steel. Brazilian officials argued that the tariff would remove Brazil's competitive edge in the U.S. market. Because steel

[63] *New York Times*, August 12, 1985. [64] *Financial Times*, August 20, 1985.
[65] *The Economist*, August 31, 1985. [66] *The Economist*, August 31, 1985.

exports brought $1.3 billion a year to the Brazilian economy, they claimed, those sales were crucial to keeping Brazil's pledge to achieve a $9 billion a year trade surplus to the IMF.[67] In May, Brazil's Industry and Commerce Minister, João Camilo Penna, suggested that if the U.S. did not buy a satisfactory amount of Brazilian steel, Brazil's U.S. creditors would not be paid.[68] In September, he warned that Brazil might decrease its debt payments if the International Coffee Organization and the International Sugar Organization failed to increase international coffee and sugar prices.[69]

With regard to U.S. economic policy, Brazilian Finance Minister Galveas warned in April 1984 that increases in U.S. interest rates threatened to further constrict the ability of developing countries to service their foreign debts.[70] Later in the year, Galveas pointed out that every percentage point rise in international interest rates cost his Brazil a further $650 million annually.[71]

Brazil's attempt to link U.S. economic policy and debt rescheduling questions was largely unsuccessful in this period; U.S. policymakers continued to ignore Brazil's pleas for greater trade access. In June, under the threat of U.S. quotas on carbon-steel products, Brasilia imposed "voluntary" restraints on exports of plate coil and rolled steel to the U.S. The U.S. Senate had meanwhile increased tariffs on Brazilian-made fuel alcohol by 15%.[72]

Following the asymmetrical outcome of this period in Brazil's favor in August, Brazil's financial position began to weaken as its export success began to wane. For their part, the banks coalition began to face growing internal conflicts. The lenders had failed to secure any Brazilian adjustment, despite having made significant concessions. Moreover, the U.S.-promoted Baker Plan in October 1985 created dissension among banks by once again urging "voluntary" lending as a means to resolve the debt crisis.

Period 4, October 1985–May 1987: the road to deadlock

In this period, a domestically developed economic reform plan kept the creditors on board with favorable rescheduling terms.[73] But Brazil's financial situation deteriorated during the year and a half in spite of additional concessions by the financial community toward the end of 1986. Faced with a worsening situation, Brazil attempted to radically alter the context of negotiations in February 1987, following the 1986 end of the play phase of the game.

Identifying individual situations

During the fourth period, we classify Brazil as coalitionally unstable, medium in debt rescheduling resources, and weak in overall capabilities (IS 2/8). The

[67] *International Herald Tribune*, February 22, 1984. [68] *Wall Street Journal*, May 14, 1984.
[69] *International Herald Tribune*, September 26, 1983.
[70] *Wall Street Journal*, April 10, 1984. [71] *Wall Street Journal*, September 10, 1984.
[72] *Wall Street Journal*, June 22, 1984.
[73] Because the coding of the variables remains quite similar throughout this time period, I analyze the negotiations as one period with two rounds rather than as two separate periods.

banks became less stable than in the previous period as conflicts developed in response to Brazil's aggressive stance (IS 7/8). In round two, after mid-1986, Brazil's economic situation deteriorated further, putting it closer to IS 8, while the banks remained in IS 7/8. Because this change for Brazil from medium to weak in issue resources does not significantly affect the game, I present only one game with a medium coding for Brazil's issue capabilities for the entire period.

Brazil. The political fragility of Brazil's first democratic government in over 20 years, combined with persistent economic frustration, kept the country coalitionally weak throughout the period. In particular, the mayoral elections of November 15, 1985, in which both the left and right made sharp gains, demonstrated the fragility of Sarney's position. In early and mid-1986, following a heterodox adjustment program, Sarney enjoyed a short-term increase in popularity. By year's end, however, the domestic political situation was grave, as Brazilians staged massive protests against the adjustment program.

Large foreign exchange reserves and a strong trade balance gave Brazil significant debt-related resources, but a skyrocketing public deficit and growing inflation weakened Brazil's economic strength compared to the previous period. By the end of 1985, inflation climbed to over 200% and the value of the cruzeiro plummeted to nearly 10,000 to the dollar. Brazil's economy continued to deteriorate, especially in the latter part of 1986. Whereas Brazil had enjoyed monthly trade surpluses of over $1 billion in mid-1986, by the end of the year the surplus had dropped dramatically. In January 1987, the surplus was just $129 million, the lowest it had been in four years.[74] For 1986, the trade surplus was $9.5 billion, narrowing from approximately $12 billion in 1985.[75]

Brazil continued to be weak overall. With a major export drive in place to improve its trade balance, Brazil continued to be highly dependent on Western markets, despite overtures to the Eastern bloc.

Lenders. During this period, the lenders coalition began to weaken following the advent of the Baker Plan in October 1985. The plan called for banks to lend $20 billion over three years, with substantial funding coming from official creditors as well. But because of the ongoing debt crisis and the banks' different levels of exposure, this approach simply exacerbated tensions among the bankers. Although they still maintained coherence with their advisory committees, signs of strain were evident. Throughout the time period, the banks continued to be issue and overall weak, with large exposure to Brazil and other major debtors.

Creditor governments and international organizations. U.S. Treasury Secretary James Baker's October 1985 proposal for additional bank lending and official assistance reflected the U.S. concern about the ongoing debt crisis. This plan, which addressed the fate of banks as well as of democratic reform in Latin

[74] *New York Times*, February 21, 1987. [75] *Wall Street Journal*, January 25, 1987.

America, marked a modest break between the U.S. and the IMF. Although the U.S. pressed for significant economic adjustment as part of the Baker Plan, as one U.S. Treasury official noted, the plan carried "no requirement of an IMF role."[76] For its part, the IMF was concerned about its role as an enforcer of adjustment programs and was thus skeptical of any adjustment efforts that did not have its imprimatur.

The debt game and predicted outcome

The debt matrix for this period reflects the actors' individual situations (see Figure 14.4). Without intervention, the Nash equilibrium of the game in the fourth period is one of high concessions and no adjustment. Given the U.S. interest in promoting the Baker Plan, however, we would expect it to encourage at least some adjustment on Brazil's part to justify the U.S. program of encouraging the banks to lend to the debtors. Thus, we expect continued pressure from the U.S. for some adjustment, and considerable pressure from the IMF for a significant adjustment program. But given the payoff matrix, we would expect Brazil to strongly resist high adjustment.

The negotiations and outcome

Round one. Following the bankers' cave-in in August 1985 when Brazil received substantial loan concessions while failing to undertake adjustment, the country continued to take a tough stance toward the banks. In October, Finance Minister Dílson Funaro stated that Brazil was not in any hurry to reach an accord with the IMF. Brazilian financial officials added that because the country had no need for IMF cash or new money from the banks, the government would not accept harsh IMF austerity measures that might jeopardize its nascent democracy. One senior financial official warned that Brazil expected U.S. Federal Reserve Chairman Paul Volcker to press recalcitrant banks to maintain credit lines. If they refused, Brazil would be forced to trim the annual $12 billion in interest payments it owed to international banks.[77]

Meanwhile, the economic situation in Brazil began to worsen. Sarney's policy of encouraging high growth rates through deficit spending only increased the internal public deficit, further fueling inflationary pressures. In the first half of 1985, federal borrowing had surged from 1.7 to 48.9 trillion cruzeiros ($8.8 billion), as the Sarney government's failure to confront the need for dismantling the system of indexation increased the debts of public sector enterprises and the need for borrowing to cover those burgeoning debts. This policy also eroded his standing with both business leaders and Brazilian consumers.

As a result of the economic crisis, Sarney's centrist party lost ground both to right-wing and to left-wing forces in the mayoral elections of November 15, 1985.[78] President Sarney needed to confront the seemingly intractable problems

[76] *Washington Post*, November 28, 1985. [77] *Wall Street Journal*, October 8, 1985.
[78] *Wall Street Journal*, December 5, 1985.

Cardinal Payoff Matrix, Intervention Expected

		Lenders IS 7/8		
		HC...	MC...	LC...
	HA...	–6, 6	–7.5, 7.83	–6, 9.67
Brazil IS 2/8	MA...	<u>–2, 2.75</u>	–4, 4	–4, 5.25
	LA...	**2, 3**	–5, 2.5	–2, 2

Note: Nash equilibrium bolded; expected outcome with intervention underlined.

Ordinal Payoff Matrix, Intervention Expected

		Lenders IS 7/8		
		HC...	MC...	LC...
	HA...	2.5, 7	1, 8	2.5, 9
Brazil IS 2/8	MA...	<u>6, 3</u>	4.5, 5	4.5, 6
	LA...	**9, 4**	8, 2	7, 1

Note: Nash equilibrium bolded; expected outcome with intervention underlined.

Figure 14.4. *Play phase, period four: October 1985–December 1986*

of skyrocketing inflation and the erosion of confidence in the policies of his government.[79]

On February 18, 1986, in an attempt to address these issues using an alternative approach to the one advocated by the IMF, President Sarney unveiled a heterodox adjustment scheme to control inflation. The plan, dubbed the Cruzado

[79] *The Economist* reported that Brazil had a trade surplus of $12.5 billion in 1985 and had increased its foreign-exchange reserves to $9 billion in January 1986 (January 25, 1986).

Plan, knocked three zeros off the value of Brazil's fast-depreciating cruzeiro and renamed it the cruzado. The plan also froze prices, implemented across-the-board wage increases, and set up a trigger mechanism so that when inflation reached 20%, wage increases would automatically go into effect. After this program began in March 1986, inflation fell from 300–400% a year to a rate of approximately 2–3% a month.[80]

This plan bolstered Sarney's credibility and popularity for a short time. Because the plan led to increased wages, the benefits to labor came in the form of increased real purchasing power. Business also approved of the Cruzado Plan because it allowed for longer-term planning, and its price freeze provided a much-needed incentive to improve productivity.[81]

In July 1986, President Sarney followed up on the Cruzado Plan by unveiling an economic package designed to create a multibillion-dollar development fund, a package financed through a set of "harsh, reimbursable levies" on auto purchases and sales of gasoline and gasohol. Under the new measures, Brazilians would pay a tax of 30% on new cars, 20% on a car as much as two years old, and 10% on a three- or four-year-old car. A 28% tax was to be levied on gasoline and gasohol as well.[82] This package represented a different approach to achieving high growth – one, according to Brazil's deputy planning minister, Henri Reichstuhl, "aimed at ensuring the investment necessary to maintain 7% annual economic growth."[83]

The initial reaction from the international financial community was favorable. For example, the Morgan Guaranty Trust Company suggested in August that "the [Cruzado] Plan has worked wonders for the inflation so far . . . These economic achievements, plus the successful transition from military to a democracy with stable policy prospects, provided Brazil [with an] opportunity . . . to be the first Latin American country to recover normal access to the international capital markets."[84]

The banks were sensitive to the fragility of Brazil's economy and to their own coalitional and economic fragility as well. The banks needed the Brazilian loans to at least appear to be performing. They could not afford the mandatory interest profit write-offs required by the government if loan servicing were disrupted for more than 90 days.[85] Therefore, they responded almost immediately to Brazil's Cruzado initiative: on July 26, 1986, the banks rescheduled $6 billion of its debts due in 1985 over seven years with a five-year grace period and a spread of only 1.125% over LIBOR (one percentage point below the original spread). The banks also agreed to roll over $9.5 billion originally due in 1986 until 1987 when the multi-year rescheduling agreement would be negotiated. In addition, the banks agreed to maintain the current level of short-term and interbank deposits at $15.5 billion.[86] By September, Brazil and the banks completed an

[80] *The Economist*, November 22, 1986. [81] *Wall Street Journal*, June 3, 1986.
[82] *Wall Street Journal*, July 25, 1986. [83] *Wall Street Journal*, July 25, 1986.
[84] See Lehman and McCoy (1992), p. 614. [85] *New York Times*, February 21, 1987.
[86] *Wall Street Journal*, July 28, 1986.

agreement in which approximately 750 of Brazil's private creditors were committed to restructuring part of its foreign debt.[87]

Round two. Ironically, the Cruzado Plan's success in holding down prices proved to be its undoing. As early as June 1986, many Brazilians were convinced that the price freeze established by the plan would lead to prompt price distortions, as well as to a flood of consumer imports into the country. The price freeze also discouraged investors from making the investments needed to maintain business growth.[88] By November, these fears were becoming realities. The trade surplus was down to $200 million (from $1.3 billion in May) and inflation was spiraling out of control.[89]

After the legislative elections in late November, Sarney announced a new economic package that came to be known as Cruzado II. He acknowledged the problems with the first Cruzado Plan. In an attempt to redress these, the special package included price hikes, increased interest rates, elimination of some state companies, abolition of Treasury bonds indexed to inflation, and the return to a policy of "mini-devaluations" designed to maintain export competitiveness. Although the package left the wage trigger mechanism untouched, the announcement of austerity measures so soon after the election created a public uproar. Labor unions threatened to strike if workers' pay did not keep pace with inflation.[90] In fact, on November 18, violent protests organized by the Confederation of Trade Unions broke out on the streets of Brasilia. On a national level, the two main labor confederations called for a nationwide strike on December 12 to protest government economic policies.[91] Business executives accused the government of draining resources from the private sector, and civilians expressed a general sense of feeling betrayed by the new government.[92] Brasilia was plagued by street riots in the worst violence in the capital city's history.[93]

Concerned with growing unrest in Brazil, both creditor governments and the international financial community made concessions. In December, the U.S. government said it would drop its customary demand that a debtor country agree to a formal IMF belt-tightening program before it rescheduled overdue payments on existing loans. U.S. officials justified this exception by their desire to avoid undermining Sarney's government.[94]

On December 10, the IMF's executive board told the Paris Club group of creditor nations that a new economic restructuring program was feasible for Brazil,[95] but the assembled creditor government representatives refused to pressure Brazil. Instead, the following week Brazil's creditor governments began negotiations on rescheduling about $3.2 billion in overdue Brazilian loan payments without requiring the country to sign an accord with the IMF.[96] This

[87] *Wall Street Journal*, September 8, 1986. [88] *Wall Street Journal*, June 3, 1986.
[89] *Wall Street Journal*, February 23, 1987. [90] *Wall Street Journal*, November 24, 1986.
[91] *LAWR*, December 11, 1986. [92] *Wall Street Journal*, November 24, 1986.
[93] *Wall Street Journal*, December 1, 1986. [94] *Wall Street Journal*, December 10, 1986.
[95] *Wall Street Journal*, December 11, 1986. [96] *Wall Street Journal*, December 19, 1986.

amount was increased to $4.1 billion in mid-January 1987. The only stipulation was that Brazil's balance-of-payments policies receive a favorable report from the IMF during the July annual consultations.[97] This major concession paved the way for the country to start talks on a new loan package from commercial banks.

Summary. Initially bargaining from a position of strength, Brazil adopted a confrontational attitude toward the IMF during this period. The strategy appeared to work, at least in the short run, as private creditors made high concessions in their negotiations with Brazil. Even as Brazil's individual situation weakened through the course of the period, the creditors continued to make concessions as we predicted.

Sarney's government did undertake some adjustment, but the adjustment was more a response to domestic than international pressures. Clearly an adjustment written on Brazil's own terms, the Cruzado Plan was very different from standard IMF prescriptions. It did, however, suffice to instill private creditors with enough confidence to make significant concessions in rescheduling part of Brazil's debt – despite the absence of an IMF accord. Further austerity in the second phase of the Cruzado Plan resulted in such sudden political instability that both the U.S. and the IMF agreed to provide rescheduling concessions and the all-important "stamp of economic approval" without more belt-tightening. In summary, then, the outcome of MA..., HC... in both negotiating rounds proved consistent with our expectations.

Situational changes

By the end of 1986, Brazil was at a crossroads. Its worsening financial situation meant that it continued to need a large inflow of additional funds, but its deteriorating domestic situation made adopting any sort of unpopular adjustment measures impossible. Brazil had moved from negotiating from a position of strength to reacting defensively to economic events from a position of weakness. Brazil's only advantage was that the banks were also weak.[98] Partly because they had few alternatives and partly because they thought that the strategy might lead to a still more generous rescheduling agreement, Brazilian policymakers began to discuss the possibility of a payments moratorium.

On February 20, 1987, Finance Minister Dílson Funaro embarked on a dramatic situational change effort, announcing that Brazil would suspend payments on $67 billion of its commercial debt. Shortly thereafter, Brazilian authorities froze payments on approximately $15 billion of trade credits and money-market deposits, bringing the total moratorium value to $83 billion. In addition, Funaro attempted to divide the "creditors cartel" by approaching the banks in separate groups. He sought to exploit fissures created by the differing regulations among the banks' host countries, as well as the banks' varying levels of reserves and

[97] *Wall Street Journal*, January 22, 1987.
[98] See the discussion of banks' balance sheets. *Wall Street Journal*, February 23, 1987.

exposures. In particular, Funaro attacked the American banks, which had a 50% voice in the committee despite the fact that they held only 35% of Brazilian debts.[99]

The banks responded to the moratorium by strengthening their balance sheets: they took large loan-loss reserves so that other Latin American countries could not threaten similar strong-arm tactics.[100] However, the differences in bank provisioning created some instability in the bankers' coalition. As we shall see, this change, combined with continued political instability in an economically troubled Brazil, would spur a complete deadlock in the negotiations.

Period 5, May 1987–November 1987: "May God help us"

Brazil's dramatic bid to change the context of debt negotiations during this period grabbed the attention of the international financial community. Although Brazil did not directly benefit from its drastic actions in the short run, it was a wake-up call to the U.S. government and other creditor governments that the Baker Plan was insufficient to end the debt crisis. As a consequence, this action, along with increasing political unrest in Mexico, would help in stimulating the development of the Brady Plan.

Identifying individual situations

In this period, Brazil remained coalitionally unstable, issue weak, and overall weak (IS 8). By contrast, the banks' position changed considerably from the previous period. Although they remained coalitionally unstable, they were now both issue and overall medium in strength (IS 6/8).

Brazil. The second Cruzado Plan had drawn harsh and widespread criticism of Sarney's Administration. This growing widespread disillusionment with the Sarney Administration represented a critical weakening of his faction's position in the PMDB ruling coalition. Moreover, Brazil's constitutional assembly, which was in the process of drafting a constitution for the civilian government, was considering including a number of clauses that would undercut Sarney's power. One of these was a clause to reduce the president's term of office; another would set up a parliamentary rather than presidential system of government.[101] The May 28, 1987 vote was close, but Sarney prevailed. Still, during this period Sarney remained under considerable political pressure, facing growing criticism from the military.

Economically, Brazil remained in serious trouble. As of February 1987, inflation in Brazil had hit an annual rate of 700%.[102] By May, inflation had reached an annual rate of 1,000% and, despite debt payment savings, its foreign exchange

[99] *New York Times*, March 4, 1987.
[100] This process had actually begun earlier, but Brazil's action accelerated the trend.
[101] *Wall Street Journal*, April 9, 1987. [102] *New York Times*, February 21, 1987.

position had not improved. In fact, Brazil's foreign exchange reserves had fallen to less than $4 billion by February 1987.[103] The first few months of the year also saw interest rates reach 750%, capital flight increase, and wages fall. The government had little room to maneuver, because public salaries accounted for 60% of federal spending.[104]

In overall terms, Brazil was highly vulnerable to a trade embargo. In fact, to cope with this potential threat, the government began to stockpile essential imports such as wheat and oil.[105]

Lenders. The fragile unity that the banks had achieved in earlier periods was derailed by Brazil's moratorium and the subsequent increase in loan-loss provisioning by the banks. In particular, the sharply higher levels of provisioning by European banks compared to American, Japanese, and British banks created rifts in the coalition. European banks also favored interest capitalization over lending additional funds.[106] The American banks were also divided, evidenced by Manufacturers Hanover's cool reaction to the tough position taken by Citicorp.[107] Moreover, smaller and regional banks became more interested in exiting the rescheduling business.[108]

With respect to issue strength, Citicorp had taken the lead by nearly quadrupling its 1985 loan-loss reserves to $4.7 billion.[109] The large European banks increased their reserves by much larger percentages.[110] The increase in reserves led the banks to take a big hit in total earnings: the 26 largest U.S. banks lost $342 million in profits (16%) during the first quarter of 1987.[111]

While we might expect financial losses to hurt the banks' overall position, as noted in the Argentina chapter, there was instead a parallel growth in the overall strength of the banks. As banks took increased reserves, the financial markets reacted positively. Moreover, the banks assuaged fears of the possible contagion of the Brazilian moratorium by reaching rescheduling agreements with Venezuela and Chile. Bankers also gave Mexico a $7.7 billion loan package and Argentina a $500 million temporary bridge loan.[112] Thus, in overall terms we code the banks as medium in strength as well.

[103] *New York Times*, February 21, 1987. [104] *Financial Times*, February 4, 1988.
[105] *New York Times*, February 23, 1987, p. D1. [106] *New York Times*, September 28, 1987.
[107] *Wall Street Journal*, February 4, 1987. [108] *Wall Street Journal*, March 3, 1987, p. 1.
[109] *American Banker Yearbook*, p. 34.
[110] Several reports argued that this increase in loan-loss provisions had actually weakened the banks' financial position. According to the *Wall Street Journal* (July 29, 1987), "the reserve additions have eroded the major banks' equity capital, and some have been so weakened that they face intense pressure to sell assets or issue new shares." But my measure of the banks' issue-strength is based on their ability to cope with a cutoff of payments from the debtor country. Therefore, coding them as issue medium seems to be justified despite the fact that the banks paid a high price for these increased provisions. The key point is that by this time, a default or suspension of interest payments would not likely cripple the banks – an event that was highly feared after the Mexican threat in August 1982.
[111] *New York Times*, May 22, 1987.
[112] *Wall Street Journal*, March 3, 1987. See also *San Francisco Examiner*, March 2, 1987.

Creditor governments and international organizations. In this period, although the creditor governments and the IMF remained concerned about the implications of a deadlock in Brazilian debt negotiations, the banks' increase in their provisions diminished their worries of a possible collapse of major international banks. At the same time, while the U.S. was also concerned about Brazil, it interpreted the moratorium as a sharp challenge toward the American approach to coping with the debt crisis. Thus, the U.S. in this instance had little motivation to encourage or aid Brazil, despite the domestic unrest in that country. Likewise, the IMF could be expected to sharply oppose giving any concessions to Brazil under these circumstances.

Debt game and predicted outcome

The shift in the lenders' situation leads to our prediction of the game shown in Figure 14.5. In this game, in the absence of intervention, we expect Brazil and the banks to retreat into a position of mutual intransigence – LA..., LC.... In the game with possible intervention, we would expect the U.S. and IMF to be much less concerned with pushing the parties out of a deadlock than in the previous period as their fears about an imminent risk to the financial system diminished. Therefore, the model predicts the game will remain deadlocked at LA..., LC....

The negotiations and outcome

President Sarney had originally planned to announce a suspension of interest payments for 90 days, but his financial advisors persuaded him to make the moratorium "open-ended" so that banks would have an incentive to cut a deal before the banks would have to declare their loans non-performing.[113] Yet as bankers took reserves, they were not easily pressured by Brazil. Nor was the U.S. government willing to intervene. As one U.S. official put it, "The banks can take the hit, so we can afford to show the patience of Job."[114] In May 1987, facing the bankers' hard-line stance, Sarney chose to return to the negotiating table.

Brazil's strategy was to first try to entice creditor governments into making loans, in hopes that private banks would follow. In July, Brazil's request for $7.2 billion in interest-free loans was rejected by the Reagan Administration, which advised Brazil to deal directly with the private banks.[115]

Having failed to enlist creditor government cooperation, Brazil turned its attention back to the private sector. On September 25, Brazil resumed negotiations with the 14-bank advisory committee. During this round of talks, Brazil asked for a $10.4 billion loan to cover interest payments from 1987 to 1989. It also requested that the banks restructure all medium- and long-term loans with a 0% spread. Finally, Brazil proposed to issue debt-conversion bonds, which would eventually be converted to equity.[116] The banks reacted to Brazil's proposal

[113] *New York Times*, February 21, 1987. [114] *Wall Street Journal*, April 9, 1987.
[115] *Wall Street Journal*, February 27, 1986, p. 38. [116] *New York Times*, September 26, 1987.

Cardinal Payoff Matrix,
No Intervention Expected

		Lenders IS 6/8		
		HC...	MC...	LC...
	HA...	0, −6	−3.5, −1.67	−4, 2.67
Brazil IS 8	MA...	4, −8	0, −4	−2, 0
	LA...	8, −8	3.5, −5	**0, −2**

Note: Nash equilibrium bolded.

Ordinal Payoff Matrix,
No Intervention Expected

		Lenders IS 6/8		
		HC...	MC...	LC...
	HA...	5, 3	2, 7	1, 9
Brazil IS 8	MA...	8, 1.5	5, 5	3, 8
	LA...	9, 1.5	7, 4	**5, 6**

Note: Nash equilibrium bolded.

Figure 14.5. *Play phase, period five: May–November 1987*

differently. American banks were more eager to reach an agreement so that they could resume receiving interest payments, but European banks, which had increased their loan-loss reserves to a much greater extent, were less willing to cut a deal. In the end, the advisory committee rejected the proposal, which U.S. Treasury Secretary Baker called a "non-starter."[117]

In November 1987, Brasilia and the banks reached a provisional agreement to cover Brazilian arrears. Under the agreement Brazil was to contribute $500 million and the banks were to lend $1 billion to cover the interest payments that

[117] *New York Times*, September 9, 1987, p. 25.

had fallen due during the final quarter of 1987. Moreover, Brazil would still need to come up with another $1 billion and the banks with another $2 billion by mid-1988 to cover remaining interest arrears for 1987.[118]

The agreement was not to be, however. Creditor instability made the agreement difficult for the banks, and Brazilian domestic instability made political acceptance of this plan equally as difficult. His credibility already severely weakened by economic problems, Sarney's ability to reach agreement with international creditors became further restricted by the debate within the Brazilian Congress over the length of the President's term.[119] The period ended in November in stalemate between Brazil and the banks.

Summary. The model correctly predicted that because of the significant changes in the banks' position in this period, the game would end in deadlock. Although Brazil made consistent efforts to secure a favorable accord, and some banks were willing to go along with Brazil's proposal, the negotiations failed to yield an agreement.

Situational changes

Toward the end of the period, the most significant development was an increase in Brazil's coalitional stability. Even as Brazil remained economically weak, its Congress came together to reject the constitutional reforms that would have curtailed Sarney's power. The banks, for their part, continued to strengthen their position by increasing their loan-loss reserves. The net effect of these changes was a game that was considerably more favorable to the banks.

Period 6, December 1987–December 1988: "A new beginning?"[120]

Almost one year after Brazil suspended its interest payments, it backed down and resumed negotiations with the banks. The worsening economic situation in Brazil had prompted policymakers to rethink the confrontational debt strategy. In particular, President Sarney, who was originally supportive of Funaro's hard-line stance toward the IMF and creditor banks, seemed to change his outlook. Recognizing his country's economic dependence, in early 1988 Sarney noted, "the fact is that we can't destroy the international financial system . . . We can scratch it, but it can destroy us."[121]

Finance Minister Maílson Ferrera da Nóbrega similarly recognized, "Confrontation is not the best way to work out our problems . . . We lost business and opportunities."[122] In fact, shortly after he took over the Finance Ministry in February 1988, Nóbrega announced budget reduction measures, trade liberalization, and policies aimed at eliminating costly subsidies. At the same time, he

[118] *New York Times*, November 9, 1987. [119] *New York Times*, November 9, 1987.
[120] "A new beginning" statement by Maílson Ferrera da Nóbrega, quoted from *New York Times*, February 22, 1988.
[121] *New York Times*, February 15, 1988. [122] *New York Times*, September 23, 1988.

reiterated the administration's desire to restore amicable relations between Brazil and the IMF.[123]

Identifying individual situations

In this period, we code Brazil as medium stable coalitionally, issue weak, and overall weak (IS 7/8). The banks continued to be issue strong, but remained coalitionally unstable and overall medium (IS 2/6).

Brazil. Sarney's regime remained under pressure from political opponents. However, the resignation of the politically unpopular Bresser Pereira as Finance Minister – and the selection of Nóbrega as his replacement – helped to shore up the regime. Moreover, in March 1988, the Brazilian Congress voted to maintain the presidential system of government rather than to switch to a parliamentary system; the Congress also opted to give the President a five-year term, significantly increasing Sarney's power. Not only was the decision a vote of confidence for the current system, it meant that Sarney could remain in office until 1990.[124]

With respect to issue capabilities, Brazil's moratorium had effectively isolated it from international financial markets. Banks and creditor government had responded to the moratorium by holding up lending to Brazil, as well as by cutting it off from trade credit lines. Brazilian officials estimated that the moratorium actually resulted in a loss of $1–2 billion for Brazil because of these actions.[125] Despite the expected savings from the payments moratorium and an $11.2 billion trade surplus, Brazil's level of foreign reserves increased only slightly in 1987 from $3.9 to $4.4 billion. As a result, Brazil's economic situation deteriorated further. Inflation reached nearly 20% a month, and increased even more sharply toward the end of 1988, totaling 933% for that year. As a result, domestic investment declined and capital flight increased. By March 1988, the federal deficit was 7% of GDP.

In overall terms, Brazil was as weak as in previous periods because of high dependence on industrialized country markets and trade credits. Finance Minister Nóbrega recognized Brazil's dependence when he warned other cabinet ministers that the country desperately needed foreign investment to achieve economic growth.[126]

Lenders. The bankers coalition remained divided mostly because of the large number of banks from different countries involved in negotiations, as well as variation in their overall financial exposure. As many more banks increased their loan-loss provisions, however, the coalition as a whole moved from a position of issue medium to issue strong. American and British banks, for example, increased their loan-loss reserves by more than $23 billion from early

[123] *Washington Post*, May 24, 1988. [124] *Christian Science Monitor*, March 31, 1988.
[125] *New York Times*, February 22, 1988. [126] *Financial Times*, February 4, 1988.

1987.[127] The banks also continued to increase the size of their capital base, which made them less vulnerable to possible default.[128]

Creditor governments and international organizations. As creditor governments continued to hope for stability and democracy in Brazil, and as Brazil backed away from its moratorium, the U.S. and IMF became more favorably disposed toward Brazil. They wished to prevent a recurrence of the moratorium, and would be willing to reward good behavior with help for Brazil's democratic reform.

Debt game and predicted outcome

We predict the cardinal and ordinal game matrix shown in Figure 14.6 for this period. In the two-actor game, we expect an outcome of HA..., LC.... With intervention, however, the model suggests that U.S. concern about Brazilian political stability and desire to encourage continued orthodox adjustment will prompt the U.S. to press for some concessions by the bankers.

The negotiations and outcome

Brazil entered negotiations on a multibillion-dollar loan with the 14-bank advisory committee in December 1987, well before Brazil had officially renounced the moratorium.[129] By early 1988 it was clear that the moratorium had failed. Over the course of the previous year, the banks had begun to charge higher interest rates on the short-term loans used to finance trade, and Brazil was forced to move its foreign reserves holdings from interest bearing accounts to non-interest but protected Swiss accounts.

An article in the *Financial Times* summed up the shifting power relations between Brazil and the banks: "When the foreign bankers called Brazil's bluff by refusing to negotiate a medium-term rescheduling without a January payment, the country could only stay out in the cold or concede."[130] Brazilian officials first showed signs of conceding in early February. Finance Minister Nóbrega stated "It's time to return to normal," and announced that Brazil intended to make unconditional payment of the $350 million in interest it owed to banks.[131] Brazil's conciliatory behavior included a mid-February visit by Nóbrega to Washington to meet IMF Managing Director Michel Camdessus, World Bank President Barber Conable, and U.S. Treasury Secretary James Baker. Nóbrega's meeting with Camdessus marked a particularly significant step because it ended Brazil's three-year boycott of the IMF.[132] The Finance Minister then met with the steering committee of Brazil's top creditors in New York. For their part, the banks refused to budge from their requirement that any agreement be subject to IMF approval.[133]

[127] *Wall Street Journal*, February 5, 1988, p. 12.
[128] For a discussion, see *Financial Times*, June 14, 1988.
[129] *New York Times*, February 29, 1988. [130] *Financial Times*, February 4, 1988.
[131] *Los Angeles Times*, February 5, 1988. [132] *New York Times*, February 19, 1988.
[133] *Financial Times*, February 25, 1988.

Cardinal Payoff Matrix,
Intervention Expected

Lenders IS 2/6

		HC...	MC...	LC...
	HA...	6, −12	<u>2.75, −7.67</u>	**3, −3.33**
Brazil IS 7/8	MA...	7.83, −12	4, −8	2.5, −4
	LA...	9.67, −10	5.25, −7	2, −4

Note: Nash equilibrium bolded; expected outcome with intervention underlined.

Ordinal Payoff Matrix,
Intervention Expected

Lenders IS 2/6

		HC...	MC...	LC...
	HA...	7, 1.5	<u>3, 5</u>	**4, 9**
Brazil IS 7/8	MA...	8, 1.5	5, 4	2, 7.5
	LA...	9, 3	6, 6	1. 7.5

Note: Nash equilibrium bolded; expected outcome with intervention underlined.

Figure 14.6. *Play phase, period six: December 1987–September 1988*

On February 28, 1988, Brazil and the banks reached a preliminary agreement. The banks agreed to provide Brazil with a total of $5.8 billion in new loans to help cover interest payments from 1987–1989, as well as to reschedule $61 billion of long- and medium-term debt. In return, Brazilian authorities announced that they would make payments of approximately $700 million to cover the interest that had fallen due in January and February 1988, a larger amount than most observers had expected.[134] Although Brazil tried to achieve a better LIBOR rate than other Latin American countries, it also conceded to a spread of 13/16 of 1% (the same rate being paid by Mexico and Argentina). Out of worry that the unstable coalition of bankers might not be able to put together the negotiated package, Brazil also agreed to pay an "early participation fee" of up to 3/8 of 1% as an incentive for other creditor banks to participate in the loan package.[135] Not only did these concessions assist in restoring Brazil's credibility, they helped pave the way for reaching the official accord later that year.

Although Brazil appeared to be conciliatory, the banks' negotiations with Brazil did not proceed smoothly as bankers pursued an extremely hard line. Disagreements between the banks and Brazil over Brasilia's debt-equity auctions impeded agreement on the new loan package.[136] Brazil also fought against other provisions including the attachment of IMF conditionality to the disbursement of the new money, and the right of creditors to seize Brazilian reserves held abroad in case of another moratorium.[137] From the Brazilian perspective, such demands were excessive and would be unworkable, in view of its delicate domestic political situation. Brazilian officials stressed that the government was implementing its own stabilization plan, and did not wish to be perceived domestically as slavishly following IMF directives.[138] When Brazil temporarily halted negotiations in May, the U.S. stepped in to pressure the banks to make concessions.[139]

After Brazil agreed to cut its budget deficit by $2.8 billion, a projected reduction from 7 to 4% of its GNP, an agreement was reached in June. The package stipulated that the banks would provide $5.8 billion in new funds. Of this sum, two loans (one worth $4.6 billion and the other $600 million) were to be disbursed in the second half of 1988. The remaining $600 million would be disbursed in the first quarter of 1989, contingent upon Brazil's fulfillment of IMF targets.[140] At the same time, Brazil would pay $350 million, out of its existing currency reserves, to cover interest payments that had fallen due in March 1988, and an additional $1 billion on June 30 to meet interest payments for April and May.[141]

In addition to the new money provided by commercial banks and co-financing with the World Bank, the restructuring package included lower interest rates, continuation of the debt-equity program, and a spreading of principal repayment over a 10-year period beginning in 1995, a provision that allowed banks to purchase up to $15 million in 25-year tradeable exit bonds (at 6%).

After Brazil and the banks signed the agreement, in August 1988 the IMF approved $1.4 billion in standby credits.[142] Except for its unusual timing (instead of preceding the agreement between debtor and creditors, the loan followed it),

[134] *New York Times*, February 29, 1988. [135] *New York Times*, February 29, 1988.
[136] *Wall Street Journal*, April 26, 1988. [137] *New York Times*, May 19, 1988.
[138] *New York Times*, May 19, 1988. [139] *Washington Post*, May 24, 1988.
[140] *LAWR*, June 30, 1988. [141] *New York Times*, June 23, 1988.
[142] *Wall Street Journal*, August 25, 1988.

by most appearances this was a standard IMF loan. It was to be issued in installments through February 1990, it subjected Brazil to traditional conditions such as the reduction of public spending, and it maintained the Fund's right to curtail disbursements in the absence of adequate Brazilian economic performance.[143]

On September 23, the package was officially signed in New York. The IMF released its first disbursement, totaling $4 billion, in November 1988. At the same time, Brazilian interest payments in excess of $1.35 billion provided evidence of Brazil's goodwill (Brazilian authorities did not officially renounce the moratorium until the day of the signing). By early November, after making large payments to the banks, Brazil was no longer in arrears on its interest.

Summary. Facing off against the financially and overall stronger banks, the more stable Brazilian government saw few alternatives to traditional negotiations for coping with its growing economic difficulties, which were brought on in part by the moratorium. As expected, then, the Brazilian government during this period was considerably more willing than before to engage in debt negotiations with the banks and IMF, which led to a HA..., MC... outcome. Given Brazil's self-imposed adjustment program, the agreement to engage in debt-for-equity swaps (a program staunchly opposed by Brazil under the financial leadership of Dílson Funaro), and the resumption of orderly debt-servicing, major creditors considered the agreement "the return to orthodox debt management of the eighth-largest economy in the West."[144]

Situational changes

By the beginning of this period, Brazil had recognized that its dire financial condition would not allow it to continue on its defiantly independent course. When Sarney somewhat successfully consolidated his political power, Brazil began pursuing a strategy of cooperation rather than confrontation to improve its financial position. For their part, the banks continued to decrease their exposure and overall vulnerability, which helped the banks force a more pliable Brazil to the bargaining table.

Brazil received a poor payoff in this debt game. But instead of changing its individual situation for the better, Brazil was unable to prevent its problems from quickly worsening. The September agreement immediately came under attack in Brazil because of a deteriorating economic climate. Sarney's political stability began to dissipate once again. Meanwhile, the banks continued to strengthen their financial positions.

Period 7, January 1989–June 1990: back to square one

By late 1988 hyper-inflation was again a major headache for Brazilian leaders. In early November, Sarney announced a social pact calling for a set of price

[143] *New York Times*, August 24, 1988. [144] *New York Times*, February 29, 1988.

freezes to combat inflation, which was expected to surpass 700%.[145] Sarney proposed controlling wages as well, but without changing the procedure for implementing such controls.[146] The government was under constant criticism from the local press for ceding too much to creditors while imposing too much austerity upon Brazilians (including a series of front page editorials by the influential Rio daily *O Globo*), and it was only a matter of time before the Brazilians once again began challenging their foreign creditors. Critics targeted debt-equity swaps as the alleged cause of hyper-inflation, calling for their termination or at least reduction from the $150 million monthly level. Yet the recently signed package guaranteed three years of such debt auctions, and abrogation of this clause would have had serious implications for debtor-creditor relations.[147] In fact, the auctions (also referred to as debt conversions) continued throughout the year.

The breaking point came in January 1989, and deadlock would continue throughout the play phase. By the year's end, Fernando Collor de Mello had been elected President and attempted extensive efforts to alter Brazil's individual situation in the first few months of 1990.

Identifying individual situations

Brazil was coalitionally unstable in this period. It was also both issue and overall weak (IS 8). The banks remained coalitionally unstable, issue strong, and overall medium in capabilities (IS 2/6).

Brazil. The moderately stable political situation Sarney had managed to attain earlier in 1988 began to crumble by early 1989. The Brazilian populace saw the social pact signed in early November as a deal put together by large industrialists and union leaders, and it failed to garner widespread support. Responding to worsening economic conditions, and a debt agreement that many saw as draconian, Brazilians took to the streets. Public worker strikes, in which tens of thousands of oil workers and transportation workers participated, led to clashes with the military. Strikes in both the public and private sectors continued through 1989, proliferating especially as the election approached. Amid political uncertainty, exacerbated by the possibility that the military might disallow an open election at the end of 1989, Brazil faced a highly unstable political situation.

As Brazil continued to service its debt by paying off its interest arrears, its foreign reserves reached dangerously low levels despite the record trade surplus in 1988 of $18 billion. In part because January was historically a weak export month for Brazil, reserves had fallen to $4 billion by early 1989.[148] By mid-1990, Brazil suffered falling industrial production as its Summer Plan adjustment program failed. In addition to its large external debt, Brazil also saw its internal debt grow to over $100 billion (nearly as large as its $109 billion debt at the end

[145] For details on the pact, see Economist Intelligence Unit, *Country Report: Brazil*, no. 4, 1988.
[146] *Wall Street Journal*, November 7, 1988. [147] *Wall Street Journal*, November 22, 1988.
[148] *LAWR*, February 2, 1989.

of 1989), which further decreased the government's ability to maneuver.[149] Toward the end of 1989, inflation had increased to over 40% a month, for an annualized increase of over 1000%. Brazil remained highly dependent on overseas markets. To service its debt and maintain domestic economic stability, it needed to run a trade surplus. But the banks controlled trade credit lines and could easily block them. Moreover, Brazil continued to be vulnerable to U.S. pressure. Although not directly related to debt negotiations, in June 1989, Brazil was cited as engaging in unfair trade practices because of its use of import restrictions and licensing.[150]

Lenders. As noted in the chapter on Argentina, during this period the banks continued to remain divided. The introduction of the Brady Plan in March 1989 further created conflict among the banks as a menu of options were developed and banks in the Mexican negotiations divided over the provision of new money and debt relief.

Creditor governments and international organizations. In March 1989, reacting mainly to growing political and financial problems in Mexico, the U.S. developed the Brady Plan. Although the plan held out the prospect of debt relief, it clearly specified that only countries that had demonstrated a commitment to adjustment and which had controlled inflation and state spending would be eligible for the plan.

Debt game and predicted outcome

In the seventh period, Brazil's situation shifted slightly to produce the game and outcome shown in Figure 14.7. In the game that involves only Brazil and the banks, we expect a return to a deadlock. We might expect the U.S. to show some interest in helping Brazil, but not a sustained effort until the debtor had met the criteria for a full Brady Plan. With the strong deadlocked game, more than mild efforts would be required to move the parties away from deadlock.

The negotiations and outcome

In January 1989, with Brazil's economy worsening and creditor banks and multilateral agencies refusing to disburse approximately $1 billion in payments, Finance Minister Nóbrega called for halving Brazil's interest payments and threatened a new moratorium. According to Nóbrega, "What was bad about [the first moratorium] was that it was not accompanied by a negotiating proposal, which is what one must do with a moratorium. It did not arise from a negotiating stance but from one of confrontation."[151] Brazil expressed its new interest reduction demands, by delaying for one week a $530 million interest payment. Though the official explanation was "operational problems" (a computer malfunction in the Central Bank), observers understood the implicit threat of another moratorium.[152]

[149] *LAWR*, September 29, 1989. [150] *LAWR*, June 8, 1989. [151] *LAWR*, January 19, 1989.
[152] *Financial Times*, January 20, 1989.

Cardinal Payoff Matrix,
No Intervention Expected

		Lenders IS 2/6		
		HC...	MC...	LC...
	HA...	0, −12	−3.5, −7.67	−4, −3.33
Brazil IS 8	MA...	4, −12	0, −8	−2, −4
	LA...	8, −10	3.5, −7	**0, −4**

Note: Nash equilibrium bolded.

Ordinal Payoff Matrix,
No Intervention Expected

		Lenders IS 2/6		
		HC...	MC...	LC...
	HA...	5, 1.5	2, 6	1, 9
Brazil IS 8	MA...	8, 1.5	5, 4	3, 7.5
	LA...	9, 3	7, 5	**5, 7.5**

Note: Nash equilibrium bolded.

Figure 14.7. *Play phase, period seven: January–December 1989*

Making the threat of a moratorium explicit, in an interview with *Gazeta Mercantil*, President Sarney noted that if foreign reserves were to drop too far, interest payments would be suspended.

At the same time, in an effort to stabilize its economic situation, combat rising inflation, and possibly improve its bargaining position with the banks, in January 1989, Sarney announced the "Summer Plan." This program included an indefinite price freeze, the end of inflation-linked monthly pay raises, more fiscal austerity, and a 17% devaluation of the cruzado.[153]

[153] *Wall Street Journal*, January 17, 1989. See also *LAWR*, January 26, 1989.

Yet given the political instability and the uncertainty stemming from the elections scheduled for 1989, the Sarney government managed to maintain pressure on its international creditors. To convey the message that Brazilians alone could not be expected to sacrifice, immediately after Sarney's proclamation of the Summer Plan, Nóbrega announced a series of radical measures. These measures included an indefinite suspension of the monthly debt-equity swaps, centralization of all foreign exchange operations, and a 25% reduction of the Banco do Brasil's relending program, in which commercial banks were permitted to lend locally part of their frozen assets.[154]

Brazil subsequently made a $530 million quarterly interest payment due in January, and by the end of the month it was announced that debt auctions would resume in February, though with certain changes.[155] By late February 1989, however, it appeared once again that the previous year's deal would fall apart. Sarney notified the Brazilian Congress that without additional capital the March interest payments would not be made.[156] A key impediment to Brazil's continued debt servicing was the co-financing arrangement with the World Bank. The final loan of $600 million was tied to IMF approval and a World Bank loan to the Brazilian energy sector. However, it was indefinitely postponed because of environmental concerns and Brazil's non-participation in the Nuclear Non-proliferation Treaty. Without this capital, Brazil would have had a great deal of difficulty meeting the March servicing obligations. But changing the conditions for disbursement of the $600 million would not have been easy either, because it would have required a full waiver from all of the lenders. Yet the pending crisis was resolved. In order to help Brazil make its March payment of $550 million, the $600 million originally tied to the World Bank's energy loan was reconditioned and tied instead to an alternative basket of World Bank project loans.[157] At the same time, the Summer Plan met with IMF approval, which triggered the disbursement of the necessary funds.

The pattern established in March continued throughout the year. Facing continuing inflation, presidential elections on the horizon, political unrest caused by the failure of the Summer Plan, and successive foreign exchange shortfalls, Brazil continued to delay or skip parts of interest payments. But the banks refused to make additional concessions, with some arguing that "creditor banks [are] reluctant to make any commitments until they are sure of the country's political direction."[158] By late May, Brazil's financial situation worsened as the Summer Plan was now universally considered as "dead and buried."[159]

As Brazil's economic woes grew, in July, Armin Lore, the operations director

[154] *Wall Street Journal*, January 17, 1989. *Financial Times*, January 11, 1989.

[155] The changes were that the monthly amount of debt to be auctioned would be reduced to $100 million from $150 million, that the auctions would occur every two months (rather than every month), and, in accordance with the recent foreign exchange decree, the Central Bank would be in charge of the disbursement of all cruzados purchased through debt conversion. *Wall Street Journal*, January 26, 1989.

[156] *Financial Times*, February 21, 1989. [157] *Wall Street Journal*, March 6, 1989.

[158] *LAWR*, May 4, 1989. [159] *LAWR*, June 1, 1989.

of Brazil's central bank, angrily warned the banks, "If creditors insist on holding up money until the next government takes office, they will not be paid until next year."[160] By July 20, having received no concessions from the banks, Brazil had begun a "white moratorium," warning that interest payments would only be paid if reserves did not fall further.[161] It expanded its hard-line strategy in August, when Sarney announced that Brazil would hold no further negotiations with creditors until after his successor took office in March 1990.

In September an interest payment of $1.6 billion fell due. However, claiming that Brazil was suffering from a "negative Marshall Plan" by paying out 4% of its GDP to creditors, Sarney declared that Brazil would postpone payment until the IMF lent it the capital to tide it over. The Brazilians claimed this move was not a moratorium, but rather a postponement.[162] Still, Brazil was now nearly $4 billion in arrears. This time the IMF showed no mercy, declaring that because Brazil had failed to meet previous inflation and deficit targets, it would demand further austerity measures before reaching any new agreement.[163] By October, Brazil faced a sharp contraction in trade credit lines from $15 to $10 billion, with smaller banks suspending operations altogether.[164]

Summary. In this period, both Brazil and the banks stubbornly pursued defiant strategies. Because Brazil was concerned about the reaction of international financial organizations and the U.S. to the moratorium and to the losses it had experienced, it proved more willing to undertake some adjustment. Although the banks responded with some concessions of their own, the outcome proved unstable. By the end of the period, Brazil and the banks found themselves deadlocked at the two-actor Nash equilibrium (LA..., LC...).

Situational changes

Although Brazil made some efforts in early 1989 to alter its economic capabilities by unilaterally pursuing economic adjustment, it failed to improve its financial health. Brazil also attempted to secure allies by garnering support from the U.S. For example, Nóbrega said in early January 1989 that the debt crisis had entered a phase where "the solution will necessarily come from the governments, not the banks."[165] In addition, Sarney warned that IMF inaction in September 1989 "certainly doesn't contribute to the democratic process, it hurts the democratic process."[166] Beyond encouraging the U.S. to pressure Brazil as well as the banks, however, this situational effort came to nought. For their part, the stable and financially strong banking coalition continued to protect itself from possible default by increasing its capital.

In December 1989, the populist Fernando Collor de Mello was swept into the presidency. With him, Brazil's debt and economic policies shifted to reflect an

[160] *Wall Street Journal*, July 20, 1989. [161] *LAWR*, July 20, 1989.
[162] *LAWR*, September 21, 1989; *Wall Street Journal*, September 27, 1989.
[163] *Wall Street Journal*, September 27, 1989. [164] *LAWR*, October 26, 1989.
[165] *LAWR*, January 10, 1989. [166] *Wall Street Journal*, September 27, 1989.

aggressive situational change strategy. Collor's victory created a new wave of anticipation and support that bolstered Brazil's coalition stability. The changes had an anticipated impact: the Brazilian government gained the independent authority needed to implement a new austerity plan, and the public demonstrated a willingness to suspend judgement for several months. Nonetheless, the public decided that this plan, like the others before it, had not generated the economic stability they demanded. Brazil was also hindered by a lack of support from banks and indifference by the international community, which wanted Brazil to follow a traditional IMF adjustment program.

Continuing its effort to secure creditor governments as allies, Brazil reinstituted payments to Paris Club creditors in February. This entailed an immediate $980 million payment on February 9, 1990, and regular payments throughout the year.[167] Internationally, private bankers were incensed that Brazil had chosen to stay on schedule with the Paris Club, yet not diverted a single cruzeiro to the private bankers. The reason was obvious to everyone concerned: Collor believed that the support of foreign governments would enable him to squeeze greater concessions out of private bankers. On March 16, 1990, one day after his inauguration, Collor proposed a massive readjustment program and decided to postpone any negotiations with the banks, as inflation ran at a monthly rate of over 70%. His approval rating immediately skyrocketed to over 90% and remained above 70% for the next few months.[168] Even after people began to feel the pain of the program, they remained confident that short-term sacrifice would lead to longer-term gain. They recognized the political role of opinion surveys and, even when in a literal sense it was not true, they answered "yes" to the question "Are you better off now than you were before Collor's adjustment program was initiated?"[169]

The adjustment program was wide-ranging. Citizens and corporations all faced steep new income taxes; many export-oriented firms lost government subsidies (a total of $2.2 billion was cut); utility rates were brought closer to market levels; and the government was drastically reorganized, including a cut of 10% (80,000) of government jobs and privatization of several government enterprises. The plan also included a new currency that floated on the international currency market, and a freeze on personal bank accounts in excess of $1,200.[170] The plan had its intended immediate effect. In April, the budget went from an 8% deficit to a 1% surplus, and inflation was cut from a monthly rate of 84 to 3%.[171] However, the cost of this effort was great: it slowed the economy to a standstill. April saw industrial production fall by 15%, the industrial sector was operating at 62.5% of capacity,[172] half of unionized workers were laid off,[173] and the auto industry was threatening a 20% wage cut for those still going to work.[174]

167 *Financial Times*, February 9, 1990.

168 *International Herald Tribune*, March 24–25, p. 1; *New York Times*, December 3, 1990, p. C1.

169 *Financial Times*, June 1, 1990.

170 *International Herald Tribune*, March 17–18, 1991, p. 11.

171 *Financial Times*, July 6, 1990.

172 *Financial Times*, June 1, 1990.

173 *New York Times*, April 10, 1990.

174 *Financial Times*, May 18, 1990.

Despite these efforts, Brazil's financial position improved only slightly. The government's cash flow situation brightened for a few months, but this was offset by two difficulties. First, exports were slashed, which caused a substantial fall in foreign exchange reserves. Second, the plan effectively discouraged the offer of fresh international money. In the interim, Brazil attempted to improve its financial situation independently, and refused to negotiate with the banks.

Brazil's individual situation did change, but not in the way the government had hoped it would. After several months of anxious expectation, Brazilian citizens began to lose faith in the economic reform program. By late May, support for Collor's plan had fallen from 81 to 54% approval,[175] and rapidly continued its downward course. Collor's coalitional stability weakened sharply, as rifts within the government became more difficult to smooth over. Inflation crept back up to 11% in June and July, far above the 2% target, and economic indicators in general were dismal. Although reserves had increased overall because Brazil had stopped paying interest on its foreign debt, the economy as a whole was seriously ill. By mid-1990, an unstable, issue, and overall weak Brazil that was over $8 billion in arrears needed both new loans and rescheduling.[176] It limped back to the negotiating table, requesting an 18-month standby credit from the IMF in July 1990.

Meanwhile, the banks began to stabilize their coalition somewhat following the successful Mexican Brady Plan negotiations. Although the agreement had come with difficulty, the bankers' positions began to converge.

Period 8, July 1990–July 1991: waiting for Brady

This period was marked by an abundance of negotiations, fueled in part by increasing pressure from the U.S. government and the IMF to find some sort of resolution to the debt problem. Brazil, sensitive to the fact that Mexico and Argentina had already concluded favorable agreements along the lines of the Brady initiative, was anxious to close a deal itself before the Brady Plan lost momentum.

Deals were conducted over the course of two rounds. The first round saw posturing by Brazil and the private banks, but also the conclusion of an IMF adjustment program. This agreement provided the impetus for second-round negotiations between Brazil, the banks, and official creditors, which resulted in a rescheduling of interest payments and an end to the second interest moratorium. These interest accords, which rescheduled $6 billion in private bank interest and $11 billion in Paris Club principal, represented some adjustment and some concessions by both parties, and set the stage for negotiation of a Brady Plan accord.

Identifying individual situations

Collor's policies became increasingly inconsistent and ineffective after the March 1990 economic reforms failed to do any good. The government's coalitional

[175] *LAWR*, May 31, 1990. [176] *LAWR*, June 28, 1990.

instability continued. Foreign exchange reserves improved slightly, but not enough to raise Brazil from a position of economic or overall weakness (IS 8). The banks became coalitionally medium, but remained issue strong, and overall medium during this period (IS 1/6).

Brazil. The most important characteristic of this period was Brazil's coalition instability, which continued into the ninth period as well. Instability manifested itself in two ways: popular support for the Collor government plummeted and Collor's own administrators registered their disagreements with his policies by resigning en masse. Public support was the lifeblood of Collor's populist government, but following the failed economic reforms, Brazilian citizens would not give his administration the time of day. By November 1990, Brazil was well on its way to completing another year with more than 300% inflation, and Collor's approval rating had fallen to 26%.[177] Collor's popularity remained low for the rest of his term. This popular dissatisfaction reflected and fostered increasing instability and inconsistency within the Collor government. Although an accord was reached with bankers regarding interest rescheduling in April 1991, the economic team, including the Economic Minister and the Central Bank Governor, resigned as a group declaring the accord a sell-out to the banks.

Collor had hoped to make beneficial economic changes. Generally speaking, he failed. As late as September 1990, however, the adjustment program had generated some positive overall and debt-specific effects. Inflation over the summer ran at 11% per month. Although this was far higher than he had hoped for, it was also far lower than the 84% inflation of February 1990, the month immediately before the shock plan was implemented. Also, foreign exchange reserves had risen to $7.5 billion in July. This was not comfortable, but it was above the perceived danger level.[178] In general, however, the Brazilian economy was on a sharp downward trajectory, leading to diminished expectations. The Persian Gulf crisis threatened to cost Brazil between $3–4 billion annually,[179] and inflation continued to rise to 15% in October, 17% in November,[180] and upward in early 1991. Moreover, by the end of 1990, GDP was 4.6% lower for the year.[181]

Lenders. The banks were able to prevent efforts to destabilize their coalition. In early September 1990, Brazil's efforts to split the banks in the advisory committee failed. Only 12 of 30 banks agreed to separate negotiations in Brasilia.[182] In addition to a strong loan-loss position, slow economic growth (or even recession) in the U.S., Japan, and Europe left the banks with a surplus of lending power. This meant they were not in immediate need of debt repayments. Finally, low inflation rates in the United States bolstered overall bank profits.

[177] *New York Times*, December 3, 1991, p. C1. [178] *Financial Times*, July 6, 1990.
[179] *Financial Times*, September 27, 1990. [180] *Financial Times*, November 10, 1990.
[181] *LAWR*, March 21, 1991; *New York Times*, March 14, 1991.
[182] *Financial Times*, September 12, 1990.

Creditor governments and international organizations. The Bush Administration increasingly involved itself in Latin American debt affairs, to the benefit of the debtor countries. Because the international financial community was no longer threatened, the U.S. could focus its attention on buttressing fragile democracies in Brazil, Argentina, and Chile by throwing itself behind debt relief. The IMF and the World Bank soon followed with their own "relief" plans, but they demanded levels of fiscal restraint and inflation that Brazil was unable to provide.

Debt game and predicted outcome

From the codings for period eight, we arrive at the debt game shown in Figure 14.8. In the two-actor game, we expect Brazil and its bankers to find themselves deadlocked. With IMF and U.S. intervention, however, we expect higher concessions from the banks and adjustment by Brazil. In short, we predict a MA..., MC... outcome in the game with intervention.

The negotiations and outcome

Collor's failed effort to foster situational change left Brazil in need of new loans, but with an increasingly unstable government that was unable to implement austerity programs. At the same time, the significantly stronger banks were unwilling to make concessions to Brazil. Hoping for third-party intervention to help its plight, Brazil used government-to-government negotiations to propel private negotiations throughout this period. We consider two rounds, the first from August to October 1990, and the second from that point to early April 1991.

Round one. Both sides used preliminary meetings in August 1990 to stake out their initial bargaining positions (there had been no discussions since Brazil implemented the second interest payment moratorium in June 1989). Each quickly discovered that the other was in no mood to acquiesce.

Brazil entered the negotiations aggressively, expecting to be rewarded for its self-imposed austerity program, despite the program's utter failure. Having selectively paid back the Paris Club in February 1990, Brazil also expected support from creditor governments.

The IMF experimented with two tactics designed to improve the negotiating climate. First, it wielded the stick used frequently throughout Latin America: withholding new IMF money until private bank payments were on a mutually acceptable track.[183] When Brazil refused to budge, cemented by Economy Minister Zélia Cardoso de Mello's statement in August that Brazil would not make any debt payments for the rest of the year,[184] the IMF tried a carrot. It recognized that the negotiations were stalled because the bankers had no confidence in either Brazil's ability or its willingness to repay according to an acceptable schedule. The IMF bolstered Brazil's credibility on September 10 by tentatively

[183] *New York Times*, August 14, 1990. [184] *LAWR*, August 30, 1990.

Cardinal Payoff Matrix,
Intervention Expected

		Lenders IS 1/6		
		HC...	MC...	LC...
	HA...	0, –7.5	–3.5, –4.83	–4, –2.17
Brazil IS 8	MA...	4, –7.25	<u>0, –5</u>	–2, –2.75
	LA...	8, –4.5	3.5, –3.5	**0, –2.5**

Note: Nash equilibrium bolded; expected outcome with intervention underlined.

Ordinal Payoff Matrix,
Intervention Expected

		Lenders IS 1/6		
		HC...	MC...	LC...
	HA...	5, 1	2, 4	1, 9
Brazil IS 8	MA...	8, 2	<u>5, 3</u>	3, 7
	LA...	9, 5	7, 6	**5, 8**

Note: Nash equilibrium bolded; expected outcome with intervention underlined.

Figure 14.8. *Play phase, period eight: July 1990–April 1991*

agreeing to grant a $1.4 billion standby loan starting in October. The IMF reasoned that if it issued the loan, the banks would know that an outside party would have influence in assuring continued fiscal restraint from Brazil.

The strategy failed. Brazil responded by trying to divide the coalition in two ways. First, it tried unsuccessfully to negotiate with individual banks. Second, it tried to create dissension between the banks and their governments by reiterating a willingness to be flexible regarding the Paris Club debt. The second strategy was somewhat more successful than the first. Following intense government pressure, the banks and Brazil resumed negotiations in October.

The first month of talks was acrimonious. Brazil continued attempting to divide the banking coalition and separate the issues of principal rescheduling and interest payment (the moratorium was still on). On September 30, a week before talks were to resume following the August fiasco, Brazil unilaterally raised the number of banks represented on the advisory committee from 16 to 22.[185] All of the new members came from Europe because Brazil expected to receive gentler treatment from them than from the U.S. members. A confident Brazil then demanded that principal restructuring negotiations begin immediately. Brazilian chief negotiator Jório Dauster said haughtily that if the banks insisted on payment of overdue interest before renegotiating the principal, "I will close the drawer and that's it. What are they going to do? The days of gunboats are gone. No one forces Brazil to pay, which doesn't mean Brazil doesn't want to pay."[186] In addition, bankers were angered by evidence that Brazil was using its reserves to buy back its debt at a highly discounted rate.

In October 1990, Brazil asked the bankers for three concessions: (1) new loans, (2) separate negotiations on interest, private bank principal, and Paris Club principal, and (3) the parceling of the old principal into three bundles of new bonds, none of which would be backed by Brazilian collateral.[187] The bankers showed little interest in this proposal, which led to deadlocked negotiations. Their response was to quickly increase their pressure on the U.S. government, and soon all new loans were blocked. Said one U.S. representative from an international organization, "There is a limit to everything. We cannot wait any more for the good will of Brazil."[188] Shortly before this announcement Brazil had paid a debt of $270 million it owed to three Japanese companies in an attempt to split the creditor government coalition, but this action yielded few changes. The IMF quickly withdrew its loan when it realized that Brazil would not come close to fiscal and inflation targets. In short, despite continued pressure from the IMF and creditor governments, the outcome remained at no adjustment and no concessions.

Round two. The second round, which ran from mid-November 1990 until April 9, 1991 when the interest rescheduling deal was signed, saw much more aggressive management by the United States government as well as by several international organizations. The basic conflict between the two major players was straightforward: the bankers demanded that Brazil clear up its interest arrears before they would agree to a broad debt accord; Brazil wanted to see an accord before it paid up its arrears.

The bankers opened negotiations on November 19 with a softer position: Brazil was to pay one-third (about $2.5 billion) of back interest before a comprehensive debt accord would be signed. Also, the remaining two-thirds could

[185] *Los Angeles Times*, October 2, 1990. [186] *Los Angeles Times*, October 2, 1990.
[187] *The Economist*, October 27, 1990. [188] *New York Times*, November 19, 1990.

be capitalized in the context of the broader agreement.[189] Thus, although interest and principal rescheduling would still be linked, they would be linked in the form of a short-term $5.5 billion concession from the bankers.

Brazil responded by showing some flexibility of its own. It pleaded its inability to pay more than $1.1 billion in 1991, but pointed out that its cash flow problems would be alleviated if loans from the World Bank and the Inter-American Development Bank were allowed to go through ($2.2 billion worth of loans were in the pipeline).[190] The concession was provided: on November 30, $700 million in World Bank and IDB loans were cleared.[191] Still, Brazil offered to pay only $900 million in interest arrears before December 31, 1990. When banks rejected this offer, Brazil responded by raising it to $1.2 billion. Under persistent pressure from creditor governments, it paid about $400 million to satisfy its January 1991 interest obligation, although it still did not reduce its arrears from the previous year.[192]

On January 4, 1991, the banks responded to Brazil's decision to end its interest payments moratorium with a more concessionary interest rescheduling offer. They asked that Brazil pay $3.4 billion immediately, but only $5.7 billion over three years, with the remainder of the $2 billion in arrears to be paid after a three-year grace period.[193] Brazil did not accept this proposal, but negotiations continued. In the meantime, the government announced an encore to the Collor Plan of 1990 – a plan which had done little to improve the government's popularity or the economy's health.

On April 9, 1991, the parties reached an accord on interest payments: Brazil agreed to pay $2 billion within one year of ratifying the accord with the remaining $6.5 billion in arrears to be swapped for new bonds. The accord was ratified by the Brazilian Senate on June 19 and the first payment, $900 million, cleared on June 29.[194] More than 95% of the bankers agreed to the interest accord by mid-August.

Summary. In this period, Brazil and the banks continued to clash, and the initial outcome of their negotiations was a deadlock. By the second round, active intervention by the U.S. government and international organizations propelled the negotiations toward an agreement on interest arrears, and an outcome of MA..., MC..., setting the stage for a Brady Plan accord.

Situational changes

During this period, Brazil made various efforts to play off the banks and creditor governments, but failed to achieve much success from this effort. Economically

[189] *Financial Times*, November 19, 1990.
[190] *Financial Times*, November 16, 1990 and November 20, 1990.
[191] *Financial Times*, November 30, 1990. [192] *New York Times*, April 9, 1991.
[193] *Financial Times*, January 24, 1991.
[194] *Financial Times*, June 26, 1991. The remaining $1.1 billion interest payment was received on November 20, 1992 (five months behind schedule) and, as agreed, $7.1 billion in new bonds were then capitalized. See *LAWR*, December 3, 1992.

Brazil continued to be beset by high inflation, and the second Collor Plan failed to improve Brazil's economic performance.

Over the months following the April agreement, the banks continued their disengagement from Latin American lending, and continued to strengthen their overall position. Brazil responded to a near crisis of decreasing foreign exchange reserves by shifting its policy to one of high interest rates. This policy attracted capital to Brazil, and dramatically increased its reserves. Politically, Brazil continued to be unstable, and the replacement of Collor by his Vice-President, Itamar Franco, did little to help.

Period 9, August 1991–April 1994: I did it my way

The interest accord, combined with U.S. government pressure, fueled third-round negotiations that ended in a rescheduling of principal consistent with the Brady Plan. The fourth round involved the implementation failure that kept the provisions of the Brady Plan from being executed. Brazil failed to meet the IMF's typically strict fiscal targets. Continued pressure from the U.S. and an IMF monitoring agreement in early 1994 did lead to an agreement, but with a twist. Brazil, in keeping with its previous distaste for IMF agreements, agreed to fund collateral for the Brady bonds out of its own reserves and purchased U.S. Treasury bills in the open market. An accord was finally concluded in April 1994.

Identifying individual situations

Brazil was issue strong in this period, but remained unstable domestically and overall weak (IS 2). The banks became overall strong and remained coalitionally medium and issue strong during this period (IS 5/6).

Brazil. Political instability continued to haunt Brazil. The international community approved of new Finance Minister Marcilio Marques Moreira's arrival in May 1991, but Moreira was hamstrung by the increasingly fragmented nature of the administration's economic policy formulation.[195] Moreira's job was made even more difficult after a strong political opposition emerged. Opposition candidates had won 10 out of 15 statewide gubernatorial elections in December 1990. By October 1991 these governors, as well as other politicians and businessmen, were creating an alternative economic plan to fight inflation. Collor had dropped the reigns of economic policymaking.[196]

Another source of instability resulted from government corruption. Collor had risen to power billing himself as a clean young face, different from the typically corrupt Brazilian politician. By the beginning of 1992, however, the shine had begun to wear off. Several of his ministers were accused of corruption and were replaced in the next few months.[197] On May 30, 1992, scandal-mongering caught

[195] *Financial Times*, May 30, 1991. [196] *Financial Times*, October 29, 1991.
[197] *The Economist*, April 4, 1992.

up to the president himself. Collor's own brother accused the president of shady dealings.[198] Most people dismissed this charge as yet another salvo in a continuing family feud, but the problem refused to go away. It decreased government stability because Collor was forced to yield a greater share of power to Congress to appease them while the corruption investigation was underway.[199] Eventually, the scandal led to Collor's impeachment.

The installation of Itamar Franco (Collor's Vice-President) as President toward the end of 1992 failed to stabilize Brazil's political situation significantly. Franco came to power with an unstable power base and proceeded to go through five economic ministers, decreasing popular confidence in his ability to govern and leading to calls for his resignation.

Economically, Brazil managed to increase its foreign reserves to $13 billion by May 1992 through a policy of high interest rates. These reserves continued to rise and reached nearly $35 billion in early 1994. Although Brazil continued to face high inflation rates, it did manage to achieve 5% growth in 1993 and record exports, but only after several years of stagnation. Overall, however, Brazil continued to face problems with a high fiscal deficit and experienced a dramatic increase in its short-term internal debt.[200] Moreover, it hoped to increase its access to foreign capital markets and cut its foreign debt.

Lenders. Banks continued to increase their overall strength as they raised considerable amounts of capital and resolved outstanding debt problems with almost all significant debtors except Brazil.[201] Although the banks had been able to maintain a significant degree of coalitional stability, individual variation in banks' positions and financial strategies, as well as disputes over menu choices in the Brady debt rescheduling accords, continued to leave them with medium coalitional stability.

Creditor governments and international organizations. The U.S. government continued to have an interest in resolving the outstanding debt problems of Brazil to stabilize its economic relationship with the largest country in Latin America. For its part, the IMF also wished to complete the last of the major rescheduling agreements, but was reluctant to endorse policies that did not conform to Brady Plan guidelines.

Debt game and predicted outcome

Based on Brazil's and the lenders' classifications, we predict the matrix shown in Figure 14.9. As in the eighth period, we expect a deadlock in the two-actor game. The growth of Brazil's debt resources in the form of growing reserves, however, only made the deadlock worse as Brazil became even more resistant to making concessions. With intervention, however, we expect sustained pressure by the U.S. and international financial organizations to lead to a more

[198] *The Economist*, May 30, 1992, p. 44. [199] *The Economist*, July 4, 1992.
[200] *LAWR*, April 1, 1993. [201] *The Economist*, September 21, 1991.

Cardinal Payoff Matrix,
Intervention Expected

		Lenders IS 5/6		
		HC...	MC...	LC...
	HA...	−12, −7.5	−11.5, −4.33	−8, −1.17
Brazil IS 2	MA...	−8, −8	−8, −5	−6, −2
	LA...	−4, −7.5	−4.5, −5	**−4, −2.5**

Note: Nash equilibrium bolded; expected outcome with intervention underlined.

Ordinal Payoff Matrix,
Intervention Expected

		Lenders IS 5/6		
		HC...	MC...	LC...
	HA...	1, 2.5	2, 6	4, 9
Brazil IS 2	MA...	4, 1	4, 4.5	6, 8
	LA...	8.5, 2.5	7, 4.5	**8.5, 7**

Note: Nash equilibrium bolded; expected outcome with intervention underlined.

Figure 14.9. *Play phase, period nine: August 1991–April 1994*

cooperative outcome. But in view of the strong deadlock, cooperation would not be an easy matter.

The negotiations and outcome

As early as June 14, 1991, Brazil indicated that it wished to negotiate along the lines of the Brady initiative. This was the first time since Collor came to office in 1990 that Brazil considered linking economic adjustment directly to loan negotiations. Still, Brazil took an aggressive stance, arguing that it should receive better terms than either Mexico or Venezuela. It reasoned that unlike these countries, Brazil did not have a readily exportable commodity owned by the state, such as oil, that could be used to generate surpluses.[202] U.S. President George Bush sweetened the deal on July 19, when he suggested that a successful debt deal would lead directly to increased trade with the United States.[203]

Round one. Negotiations began in earnest on August 23, 1991, when Brazil laid out a menu of four options for bankers: They could (1) issue discounted bonds with a 37.5% principal reduction but market rates of interest, (2) collateralize debt with 30-year bonds paying a fixed 4.8%, (3) issue new loans equivalent to 30% of existing exposure, and/or (4) lower interest rate bonds over 15 or 35 years. The details of Brazil's economic adjustment would be subject to negotiations with the IMF. On the strength of this proposal, Brazilian debt gained nearly 40% on the secondary market, from 27 to 38 cents on the dollar.

In October, the banks countered Brazil's proposal by calling for only a 30% discount on principal, an interest rate of 6.2%, a six-year reduction of interest rates before a return to the market rate, and the establishment of a fund to guarantee payments. The next several months were spent negotiating the details of these arrangements. In particular, the bankers were waiting for Brazil and the IMF to come to an agreement on a $2.1 billion stabilization loan/adjustment package. The IMF, for its part, showed signs of accommodation. Michel Camdessus, head of the IMF, argued for an IMF program, worrying that Brazil was "too big to fail."[204] He pressed on with the negotiations, ignoring Brazil's accumulated arrears with creditor governments.

The new year brought further progress in the negotiations. First, on January 29, 1992, the IMF announced that an accord had been reached. It would distribute $2.1 billion in seven tranches, each dependent on compliance with agreed policy targets. For their part, the bankers were pleased to see stringent targets: Brazil was required to achieve a fiscal surplus equivalent to 2.4% of GDP, as well as bring the monthly inflation rate down to 2% by the end of 1992.[205] Thus, Brazil committed itself to making significant adjustments, anticipating that this commitment would pave the way for bankers' concessions outlined in the Brady Plan. Further enhancing the prospects for a general agreement with the bankers was the February 28 Brazil/Paris Club accord. Payment of half of the $21 billion debt Brazil owed was rescheduled over an additional 14 years.[206] On the strength of these two deals, the commercial bankers resumed negotiations with Brazil on March 17.

Because of domestic instability, Brazil found it hard to maintain its economic adjustment program and fell out of compliance with its IMF mandate by mid-May. It did, however, make continued efforts to come back into compliance. By

[202] *LAWR*, June 27, 1991. [203] *Washington Post*, June 19, 1991.
[204] Quoted in the *Financial Times*, December 2, 1991. [205] *LAWR*, February 13, 1992, p. 7.
[206] *Wall Street Journal*, February 28, 1992.

July 9, 1992, Brazil had tentatively agreed to a Brady Plan accord with the steering committee to address $44 billion in debt. Under the plan, bankers could choose from among six options: two would recapitalize 80% of the old debt under new bonds, one would allow for new money, and the rest would provide Brazil with temporary interest relief. The accord would cut Brazil's debt by as much as 35% over 30 years, as well as protect it from interest rate fluctuations by fixing rates.[207] The deal was also good for the banks. They would not need to de-capitalize bad debt, so they could draw on as much as $1 billion in loan-loss reserves for additional profit-making ventures. In addition, they would receive $600 million in annual interest income, up from $300 million in even the best of pre-Brady Plan years. Finally, the agreement bolstered the value of the old debt in the secondary market. Since the banks owned much of this debt, they benefited when its value rose.[208] At the same time, the deal hinged on a Brazilian "protocol of intentions," stipulating that the agreement would only go into effect if Brazil came back into compliance with the IMF program.

This accord concluded the first round of the negotiations. On paper, the agreement seemed like medium concessions by the banks and medium to high adjustment commitment by Brazil as its payments to banks would increase as it cleared up its arrears. It was widely hailed as heralding the end of the Latin American debt crisis because every major debtor in the region had concluded a Brady Plan agreement. As we shall see, however, signing the agreement was one thing; implementing it was quite another.

Round two. Although creditor government and the IMF could push Brazil and the banks to negotiate a debt accord, they could not guarantee Brazilian compliance with an adjustment program. Brazil's ruling coalition was weak and simply could not muster the political support or economic wherewithal to impose the fiscal discipline required by the IMF. By the end of July 1992, the IMF had suspended disbursement of its loan because Brazil had failed to meet almost all of its economic targets.

Meanwhile, tainted by accusations of corruption and facing impeachment proceedings, Collor was temporarily replaced on October 2, 1992 by Itamar Franco, his vice-president. Economically, Brazil faced inflation at an average of 22% per month, a fiscal deficit of 7% of GDP, sharply falling tax receipts, and per capita GDP 10% lower than in 1990.[209] Its reserves continued to increase, however, as a result of its high interest policy, and totaled nearly $24 billion by the end of 1992. Domestic economic problems were serious because they triggered suspension of the IMF loan disbursal. This suspension was critical because the IMF loans were to be used as collateral for the Brady bonds. Without collateral, no bonds would be issued and the entire Brady Plan would fall through the floor.

[207] *Wall Street Journal*, July 10, 1992. [208] *Washington Post*, July 10, 1992.
[209] *Financial Times*, December 3, 1992.

Following Collor's replacement by Franco in December 1992, the government went through four finance ministers in the space of seven months in the first part of 1993.[210] Economic policy was in flux, with overt disagreements between Franco and his economic advisers. Brazil continued to meet with IMF officials in January in an effort to reach a new accord with the Fund.

In mid-March, over 800 banks, accounting for nearly all private lenders, agreed in principle to the debt accord negotiated between the steering committee and Brazil in July 1992, although an agreement between Brazil and the IMF had still to be signed. But a snag immediately developed. In response to the various options for debt conversion that had been proposed, bankers leaned heavily toward fixed rate bonds. Brazil was unhappy that 60% had chosen such bonds, but only 18% had agreed to the discounted but floating rate interest bonds. The debt deal once again appeared to be in jeopardy. The deadline for implementation of the agreement was repeatedly postponed as the banks awaited an accord between Brazil and the IMF, and Brazil requested that the banks restructure their choice of debt reduction options.

By June 1993, the banks had agreed to a distribution of 40% in par bonds and 35% in discounted bonds, and the IDB indicated willingness to come up with $500 million in financing guarantees following an IMF accord.[211] Once again, however, Brazil asked for a delay in the signing deadline, this time until November 1993, while it attempted to stabilize its economy sufficiently to secure the IMF's blessing. Finance Minister Cardoso developed a new economic adjustment program that appeared to be more promising than previous plans. Still, the plan failed to yield immediate results, and Brazil came under increasing pressure from the U.S. government and the IMF to undertake more significant adjustment. But adjustment continued to be stymied by a new corruption scandal and congressional opposition.

On November 29, 1993, as planned, the commercial banks signed a Brady Plan accord that restructured $52 billion in debt, including funds held by foreign branches of Brazilian banks. Still, the final accord was contingent on an IMF accord and funding to purchase Treasury bills to provide collateral for part of the interest payments that Brazil would owe under the accord. Brazil continued its negotiations with the IMF, but failed to secure a standby agreement. In March 1994, the best the IMF would do was to give Brazil an informal blessing and promise future cooperation. Brazil responded by seeking a waiver of a clause in the November 1993 agreement that linked the deal to an IMF standby agreement and banks agreed to this demand. Finance Minister Cardoso also let it be known that Brazil had already purchased the needed Treasury zero-coupon bonds in secret open market operations that had been taking place since October 1993. By April 15, 1994, the banks and Brazil initialed the final agreement on schedule. The final outcome can be coded as MA..., MC..., in view of the absence of a binding IMF accord and somewhat lesser concessions made by

[210] *Financial Times*, May 12, 1993. [211] *LAWR*, June 3, 1993.

banks as compared to concurrent cases such as Polish debt rescheduling (40% principal reduction and 20% write-down of interest arrears).

Summary. This period saw a final accord between Brazil and its bankers under the auspices of the Brady Plan. Unlike Argentina and Mexico, negotiating an agreement proved particularly difficult, as continued political instability hampered Brazil's ability to develop a sustained economic adjustment program that would meet the IMF's strictures. In the end, the best Brazil could get from the IMF was simply a blessing of its efforts. Finance Minister Cardoso simply took matters into his own hands and used Brazil's large reserves to purchase Treasury bonds to back the agreement and satisfy the lenders.

As in the case of Argentina, the outcome appears consistent with my prediction, but the payoffs do not seem to reflect the willingness of both Brazil and the banks to make adjustment and concessions. Again, the Brady Plan strongly influenced payoffs. Although the final agreement did not include immediate financial backing by creditor governments and international organizations, the same menu of options was available to banks. Moreover, Brazil was able to secure both principal and interest reduction on its debt, as well as new money. Prospects for funding from third parties have also improved.

In terms of the model, the banks' collective action problem has been significantly overcome by the plan, because banks could choose among a variety of options and not fear free-riding. As one analyst of the Brady Plan notes, "the new approach addressed the contradiction between individual and collective interests that had increasingly troubled its predecessor."[212] At the same time, banks also would be motivated to sign onto the accord because the alternative was to be left out of a deal and not receive at least partial interest guarantees on the new bonds that replaced old debt. For its part, Brazil could be expected to be more willing to undertake adjustment, in view of the backing of the financial community for a Brady Plan accord, and the prospects of new capital inflows from official sources and private investors. In sum, agreement was facilitated by the Brady Plan, despite Brazil not having followed the same procedure as other debtors under this regime.

Conclusion

Throughout the dozen years of debt rescheduling examined here, Brazil proved to be a highly contentious opponent for the banks. It continuously attempted to thwart both the banks and the IMF by resisting the imposition of a traditional economic adjustment program. Even when Brazil did sign a Brady accord, it did so on its own terms. It used its reserves to back the accord, rather than by securing an IMF agreement which would trigger a special issue of bonds by the U.S. government.

212 Clark (1993).

What accounts for the difficult negotiations between Brazil and its creditors? Foremost among the factors underlying Brazil's intransigence has been its continued political instability. Except for brief periods of stability in the fourth and sixth periods, during which Brazil actually negotiated and then partially carried out its agreements, Brazil's polity remained in turmoil. Moreover, although Brazil's economy faced hyper-inflation almost continuously, it did manage to maintain a strong export position and was able to accumulate significant financial reserves at various points. Yet contrary to what most analysts might predict, my model suggested that such a development would only harden Brazil's negotiating position, and indeed such capabilities only made Brazil more resistant to traditional adjustment approaches.

The most significant situational change that Brazil attempted backfired – at least in the short run. Faced with worsening financial and political situations, Brazil declared a moratorium on interest payments in early 1987. It then made considerable efforts to play off the banks, to seek creditor government support, and to secure a fundamental change in the debt rescheduling game. Yet the banks responded to this action with counter-efforts to decrease their own vulnerability, taking large loan-loss reserves that would insulate them from such actions in the future. The net result was a harder stance by the banks as they became less concerned about debtors' threats to stop payments.

The immediate effect of the banks' increased reserves was a more stubborn U.S. position toward the debtors as its concerns about the vulnerability of the international financial system dissipated. In the end, the Brazilian action, along with serious political instability in Mexico and problems in Argentina and elsewhere, led to a rethinking of American policy. In 1989, U.S. announcement of the Brady Plan proved to be a significant shift in the terms of debt rescheduling. But whereas Mexico and Argentina, as well as Venezuela and several smaller debtors, came to relatively quick agreements under its auspices, Brazil once again pursued its own course. Continued instability marred by corruption, scandals, and fragmented political parties made it nearly impossible for the government to implement an economic program that would prove satisfactory to the IMF. Thus, as in previous periods, Brazil used its capabilities to pursue its own course – in this case, purchasing Treasury bonds to back the plan with its own reserves.

PART VI
Implications

15 Findings and avenues for future research

Over the last two centuries, bountiful years of lending have frequently been followed by retrenchment and default. Debt rescheduling has repeatedly involved bargaining between interdependent debtors and lenders, with the stakes being the division of the costs of restoring normal financial intercourse. These protagonists have sought to optimize their bargaining in light of their existing international power and domestic political positions. But debtors and lenders have also sought to improve their prospects through efforts to manipulate both their own and their opponents' bargaining position. Moreover, negotiations over repayment and lending have often attracted the interest and intervention of creditor governments and international organizations. Thus, what might be seen as a basically economic problem has been fraught with political repercussions.

Economists who have written about debt rescheduling generally focus on debtors' incentives to repay loans in view of prospects for additional financing and lenders' willingness to extend new loans in light of the probability that debtors will service their loans. But their analytical models have focused primarily on the economic calculations made by debtors and lenders, ignoring important political and strategic issues that sovereign debt rescheduling raises. In addition, these models have rarely been tested systematically across a range of cases. For their part, political scientists have studied the domestic consequences of adjustment programs, but have generally failed to link domestic adjustment decisions to an investigation of the international bargaining process.

This book has attempted to remedy these lacunae by constructing a model of debt rescheduling that draws on the insights of both political and economic analysts. I began with a focus on the systemic characteristics of broad time periods, which I refer to as epochs. Although this approach yielded some insights, an epochal analysis could not account adequately for patterns of international debt rescheduling. Thus, my major effort in this book has been to develop and test a "situational theory of payoffs" that links the factors of actors' overall capabilities, financial positions, and domestic stability – constraints which I refer to as their "individual situations" – to specify actors' payoffs in debt rescheduling. By then focusing on the likely equilibrium in these games, I predict the adjustment decisions of debtors and the choice of lending concessions by bankers and bondholders. In testing the model with cases over the last 170 years, I find that adjustment and concession decisions – as well as intervention by third parties – can be explained with a high degree of success. In addition, rather than examining these games only within fixed parameters, I present and evaluate a "theory of situational change" that focuses on the types of strategies that actors use in their efforts to manipulate their bargaining position to enhance their prospects for victory in future negotiations.

This chapter reviews my specific findings about debt rescheduling, as well as some general insights from my case analyses about lending, default, and efforts to resolve debt crises. After examining some policy implications of this work, it then considers how the model might be refined and generalized to other areas of international relations.

The findings

International debt crises have several components. The most central of these are: (1) the initial lending and borrowing, (2) the onset of financial crises and possible default, (3) bargaining between debtors and lenders to resolve debt problems, (4) the role of creditor governments and international institutions in negotiations, and (5) the development of plans to resolve debt problems. The primary objective of this book has been to examine the third and fourth of these components by assessing the performance of my situational theory of bargaining in explaining debt rescheduling outcomes and the role of creditor governments in this process. Before turning to the findings that emerge from my static and dynamic models of debt rescheduling, I begin with the results of my epochal inquiry of debt rescheduling.

The epochal analysis

For reasons of parsimony, I began with an aggregate epochal analysis in this book. I tried to gauge if such a focus would illuminate the process of debt rescheduling. My nested systems approach did yield some insights on competition among lenders and on the role of creditor governments in the rescheduling process. In using this approach, I defined epochs and looked at their implications by focusing on the distribution of capabilities, the types of actors, and the role of international organizations in three systems: the overall security-political system, the international economic system, and the financial subsystem. What findings emerge from this investigation?

The distribution of capabilities in the financial system has influenced the conclusion of debt agreements. For example, the appearance of new lenders sometimes encouraged debt settlements. In anticipation of loans from Germany, a newly emerging lender, the Mexicans concluded an agreement with their bondholders in 1886 to settle a default dating back to the 1820s. The distribution of capabilities in the overall system has also affected the behavior of creditor governments. After the onset of the Second World War, the U.S. pressed for a quick resolution of Latin American debt problems to cement its southern flank. For example, in 1941, the U.S. went ahead with an Export-Import Bank loan to Peru, at a time when Peru's negotiations with its bondholders were deadlocked. While not wholly sympathetic to debtors by any means – despite the global conflict – the U.S. refused to respond to bondholders' demands for sanctions against debtors and signaled that it was supportive of considerable write-downs of the outstanding debt.

The types of debtors and lenders found in different epochs has influenced debt rescheduling outcomes as well. As we saw in the first epoch, most newly emerging countries in the nineteenth century failed to service their debts in a timely manner and reneged on their agreements with bondholders. It is also noteworthy that when faced with creditors at their door, debtors have consistently failed to unite as a group. By contrast, in response to defaults, bondholders or bankers have generally grouped together.

In all epochs, united groups of lenders have often sought creditor governments as allies in their efforts to deal with debtors. My review of intervention decisions suggested that creditor governments appear to have responded to such pleas more willingly in the 1980s and 1990s than in earlier epochs. Others who have made a similar observation attribute this change to the shift in the nature of lending from the flotation of bonds to direct loans held by banks.[1] I find that concern about the stability of the financial system did indeed motivate creditor governments to intervene in negotiations more frequently in the current epoch. But they also responded to their concerns about issues such as trade losses, immigration worries, and domestic pressure to support emerging democracies. Moreover, the role of creditor governments in recent debt rescheduling episodes should not obscure the fact that they have often actively intervened for many of the same reasons in earlier epochs, and on rare occasions, used military force to do so. Lenders are not the only ones who have secured a sympathetic ear from creditor governments. I have found that in many cases, debtors succeeded in having creditor governments champion their cause. In the early 1980s, for example, the U.S., U.K., and others pressured the banks to continue lending. More recently, they encouraged debt write-downs through the Brady Plan.[2]

Although they were involved in some European debt rescheduling efforts, international organizations, such as the League of Nations, played a minor role in Latin America. In the 1930s, for example, the League of Nations acted much as the IMF has in the current epoch – imposing conditionality on governments in exchange for loans. My examination of Mexican negotiations in the third epoch focused on the International Committee of Bankers of Mexico, which sent experts to Mexico in 1927 to analyze its economy, just as IMF missions to debtors have done so recently. Our current epoch has seen an institutionally richer environment, populated by organizations such as the International Monetary Fund, the World Bank, and, in a lending role, the Bank for International Settlements. These organizations have frequently influenced the nature of rescheduling agreements. But in contrast to many dependency theorists' view of the hand-in-glove coordination of the IMF and the major capitalist countries, I

[1] See Fishlow (1985a), Lipson (1989), and Eichengreen (1991) on this issue.

[2] Thus, I do not share Eichengreen's (1991) assessment that the 1980s can be distinguished from the 1930s by the lack of pressure on lenders in the current epoch. See his discussion on p. 164.

found numerous instances where the IMF and the U.S. were at odds in the 1980s and early 1990s. But the U.S. or other creditor governments have rarely discussed their differences with the IMF openly. For example, the statement by U.S. officials that the IMF might not have a significant role to play in Argentine rescheduling efforts in 1985 (see Chapter 13) is more the exception than the rule.

In short, an epochal approach proved useful, but gave us only limited insight into patterns of debt rescheduling. I also included an economic analysis of lending cycles as part of this endeavor. Although I found that we could better understand patterns of lending and default, a focus on cycles still did not yield much additional insight into the process of rescheduling itself. Other avenues to improve the epochal analysis by incorporating domestic or cognitive factors also did not help very much. On the whole, then, this aggregate level approach does not adequately explain the high degree of variation in outcomes of rescheduling in both the nineteenth and twentieth centuries. This may be true because rescheduling outcomes have not been strongly influenced by any type of international debt regime, with the exception of the Brady Plan of the last few years.[3] The lack of success of an epochal approach has motivated my analysis of the debt renegotiation process using my situational theory of bargaining, the topic to which we now turn.

The static analysis

My effort to predict debtors' adjustment choices and lenders' concession decisions using my situational theory of payoffs proved highly successful, with these choices being predicted over 85% of the time. The appendix tables to this chapter summarize the cases, the codings for each actor, their preference orderings, the resulting game type, the predicted outcomes with and without intervention, and the actual outcomes of the negotiations. Four tables, beginning with Table 15.1, present a synopsis of these results.

Table 15.1 summarizes the predictive success of the model. In numerical terms, the model proved successful in 52 out of 61 cases. It performed somewhat worse in the second and third epochs. Following an extended discussion of some other findings, we will consider the cases both in these two epochs and the others identified in the table where the model fell short.

Table 15.2 focuses on the role of creditor governments and international organizations in the negotiations. Out of 61 periods, I predicted some intervention in 35 cases, but expected third parties to have a significant effect in pushing the outcome to one different from the Nash equilibrium in the two-player game in 20 of the cases. Intervention took place in all 35 cases, but in eight of those

[3] Although Biersteker (1993), pp. 2–6 discusses the "global debt regime" of the 1980s and 1990s, he also notes that "there has been wide variation in the outcome of different negotiations." I have argued (1987), pp. 49–50 that until about 1986, there was a "distinctive pattern" of debt rescheduling, but it partly stemmed from a meta-regime on debt rescheduling rather than a regime. The Brady Plan, however, has provided more of a regime. Biersteker and I seem to agree on the need for analysis of specific cases in view of the high variance in debt rescheduling outcomes.

Table 15.1. *Success rate of predictions for debt games*

Case	Number of periods	Correctly predicted outcomes	Percentage	Problem case
Epoch 1				
Mexico	3	3	100	none
Peru	5	5	100	none
Epoch 2				
Mexico	5	4	80	1911–1914
Peru	7	5	71	1876–1880
				1887–1889
Epoch 3				
Mexico	8	5	75	1916–1920
				1934–1936
				1937–1940
Peru	8	7	88	1939–1943
Epoch 4				
Mexico	5	5	100	none
Peru	4	4	100	none
Argentina	7	6	85	1984–1985
Brazil	9	8	89	1982–1983
Total	61	52	85	9 cases

cases (the column labelled "unexpected outcome"), the outcome differs from the one predicted. In the remaining 26 cases where the model predicted that intervention would not take place, unanticipated intervention occurred in one case. In total, third parties intervened 36 times in the 61 cases. This high frequency of intervention by creditor governments and international organizations in debt rescheduling cases supports my choice of not simply focusing on bilateral interaction between debtors and lenders to examine debt rescheduling.

It is worth asking why creditor governments and international organizations intervene to "bolster" the existing two-actor Nash equilibrium (14 cases). If these actors can anticipate the outcome of negotiations between debtors and lenders, as Chapter 3 postulates, why do they play a role in these cases? To answer this question, we can examine negotiations in the cases where third-party intervention simply maintained the Nash equilibrium. In almost every one of these bargaining episodes, intervention came about because of either conflicts among creditor governments or differences between the IMF and the U.S. Intervention in such cases would make sense from the perspective of a powerful creditor government that was satisfied with the anticipated outcome of interaction between a debtor and lender. In such cases, by supporting its preferred outcome, it could deter others from intervening in a manner that could be detrimental to its interests.

Table 15.2. *Predicting intervention*

Case	No. of periods	Intervention (predicted/actual): Maintain Nash equilibrium	Intervention (predicted/actual): Move from Nash equilibrium	No intervention (predicted/actual)	Unexpected outcome
Epoch 1					
Mexico	3	1/1	1/1	1/1	0
Peru	5	2/2	0/0	3/3	0
Epoch 2					
Mexico	5	0/0	1/0	4/4	1
Peru	7	3/3	2/0	2/2	2
Epoch 3					
Mexico	8	3/2	2/1	3/2	3
Peru	8	2/2	1/0	5/5	1
Epoch 4					
Mexico	5	1/1	3/3	1/1	0
Peru	4	2/2	0/0	2/2	0
Argentina	7	0/0	4/3	3/3	1
Brazil	9	1/1	6/5	2/2	1
Total	61	15/14	20/13	26/25	9

Summary:

Total predicted interventions (intervention of some kind expected)	35/61 cases
Actual interventions (interventions that actually occurred)	36/61 cases
Correctly predicted interventions (intervention took place and led to the outcome I predicted)	27/61 cases

With respect to differences among epochs, the most significant finding is the large number of interventions by creditor governments or international organizations in the fourth epoch. Out of 25 periods in the fourth epoch, intervention of some type took place in 17 periods, compared to only 19 interventions for the 36 cases in the other three epochs. In the fourth epoch, the IMF also played an important role, and the Brady Plan has also affected debt rescheduling outcomes. These results are consistent with the view that creditor governments have been more prone to intervene in more recent debt negotiations because of their concern for risks to the financial system since banks hold debt on their own books.

Table 15.3 illustrates the types of games that I have derived in this study. These games are based on a combination of actors' preference orderings, which in turn are derived from an empirical analysis of actors' individual situations. Of

Table 15.3. *Summary of game types*

	Number of cases
Symmetrical	
Chicken	3
Prisoner's Dilemma	1
Harmony	2
Deadlock[1]	6
Prisoner's Dilemma-Deadlock	1
Total	13
Percentage of all cases	21
Asymmetrical	
Bully[2]	13
Called Bluff[3]	6
Asymmetrical Deadlock	14
Protector Analogue[4]	2
Pareto Suboptimal Asymmetry[5]	1
Bully-Called Bluff	5
Complex[6]	7
Total	48
Percentage of all cases	79

Note: The games of Called Bluff, Bully, and Deadlock include games with slightly similar payoffs that I refer to as "analogues." See Aggarwal and Allan (1993) for a discussion of such games. Also, I use the names for common 2×2 games that most closely approximate the logic in the 3×3 games in my analysis.

[1] Four out of six cases slightly asymmetrical.

[2] Bully is a combination of Deadlock and Chicken payoffs.

[3] Called Bluff is a combination of Chicken and Prisoner's Dilemma payoffs.

[4] Protector Analogue is a combination of Deadlock/PD and Apology.

[5] Pareto suboptimal asymmetry is a combination of Hero analogue and Harmony payoffs (similar to Game 47, Rapoport and Guyer, 1966).

[6] Complex refers to games with more than two equilibria in pure strategies.

the resulting games,[4] 79% are asymmetrical, while only 21% are symmetrical. Among the asymmetrical games, Asymmetrical Deadlock (14 cases) and Bully (13 cases) occur most frequently. The most common symmetrical game is Deadlock. Pure games of Chicken and Prisoner's Dilemma only accounted for a total of four cases. Of the 61 cases, 51 games are dominance solvable – in the sense that each actor has only one strategy after elimination by successive dominance.

In using game theory to analyze international bargaining, scholars in international relations have often used specific game types, such as the Prisoner's

[4] Although 3×3 games do not have formal names as do 2×2 games, I have used here the names of the 2×2 types to which they are comparable.

Dilemma or Chicken, as metaphors or analogies to investigate strategic interaction.[5] In addition, useful insights have also emerged from studies on the strategic implications of repeated play in such games.[6] While some scholars have also examined other game models,[7] for the most part these inquiries have been heuristic attempts to garner insights from this type of modeling, rather than an attempt to specify these games in advance and use them for predictive purposes. Both the variety of games that have emerged in the present analysis, as well as the fact that games are mostly asymmetrical in these debt rescheduling cases, casts doubt on the use of single symmetrical games such as Prisoner's Dilemma or Chicken as archetypal representations of bargaining in international relations.

Examples of different games. To underscore the way in which these alternative game models capture the diversity of the cases examined in this book,[8] I briefly review one example of each major distinct game type. Turning first to symmetrical cases, we can examine a classic game of Chicken, which is the game derived in the play phase of the third period of negotiations from September 1985 to March 1987 between Mexico and its bankers. In this bargaining episode, as in a typical game of Chicken, both the Mexicans and the bankers took a hard line in the negotiations in an effort to secure their favored outcome. Finance Secretary Silva Herzog warned that "cooperation between bankers and lenders will no longer be enough," and President de la Madrid followed with a warning about the danger that the international economic system might collapse if Mexico defaulted.[9] One banker who was participating in the negotiations commented that these statements were intended to "scare the bankers into living up to their side of the compromise" by increasing lending to Mexico.[10] But the bankers responded in kind, refusing to defer principal repayments and ruling out additional loans. While this game of Chicken could well have led to a collapse in the negotiations, I anticipated that in view of U.S. and IMF objectives, intervention would lead to a more cooperative outcome of medium concession and adjustment. In fact, this outcome did come about following considerable posturing and threats by both sides. It is noteworthy that the bankers responded to both the Mexican game as well as the dramatic Brazilian moratorium of February 1987, which occurred just at the end of this bargaining period, by taking large loan-loss reserves soon after the end of these negotiations. This action altered the basic game, and allowed them to escape from a potentially disastrous situation.

The game of Prisoner's Dilemma (PD), illustrated by the negotiations between Peru and the Foreign Bondholders Protective Council from 1948 to 1950, reflects the difficulties in attaining a beneficial outcome with joint gains for both

[5] See Snidal (1985a). [6] See Axelrod (1984).

[7] For good examples, are Snyder and Diesing (1977) and the articles in Oye (1985b).

[8] Given the relatively similar logic of play in Bully-Called Bluff and Prisoner's Dilemma-Deadlock in relation to the games of which they are composed, I do not give empirical examples of these in the discussion that follows.

[9] *Financial Times*, August 30, 1985, p. 1 and *Wall Street Journal*, September 26, 1985.

[10] *New York Times*, September 7, 1985, p. 21.

parties in an atmosphere of distrust. Following an aborted agreement between the Council and Peru, the Peruvian government bypassed the Council and went directly to the bondholders with its offer. This split the negotiations into two sets of games: one, an asymmetrical game between Peru and the bondholders, and the other, a PD game with the Council. Peru's action in making a direct offer to the bondholders – which the Council saw as a breach of normal protocol but which Peru saw as reasonable in view of its offer to make payments on its debt – led to a set of negotiations with the Council in which neither side was willing to trust the other. As a result, the outcome of this PD game was no concessions or adjustment, as both parties viewed the game purely as a one-shot affair.

Following Mexico's settlement of its debt with bondholders in 1886, the atmosphere for lending improved. Meanwhile, under Porfirio Díaz, Mexico sought new funds for railway construction and other projects requiring foreign capital. In this situation, a game of Harmony emerged for the period 1888–1893, with both sides finding it in their best interest to be concessionary toward one another. In this game, the best outcome for Mexico and the banks was continued high adjustment and lending. In fact, during these years, Mexico borrowed easily and at low rates while continuing to pursue economic adjustment. When Mexico faced bad harvests in the early 1890s, although it appeared that Mexico might default, José Yves Limantour, Díaz's Minister of Finance, responded rapidly to the economic crisis and achieved a budget surplus by 1894 – the first in Mexico's history. The lenders responded by offering additional loans, and foreign investment flows continued into Mexico.

Between 1841 and 1842, Peru and the bondholders were in a game of Deadlock. When the Peruvian government came into a sudden windfall with the massive exploitation of guano, rather than undertaking economic adjustment, the government simply used its control over guano to extract loans from guano contractors. The bondholders were divided, with loans being held by large numbers of individuals. Consequently, they could not extract any significant concessions from Peru, and the resulting game led to an outcome of no concessions or adjustment by either party.

Among the asymmetrical games, the game of Bully is well illustrated by negotiations between Mexico and the International Committee of Bankers of Mexico (ICBM) from 1941 to 1942. In this game, Mexico was clearly the "bully," and found itself in a strong and secure position against a fearful group of lenders. Having settled its problems with the U.S. government, the Mexicans aggressively pursued concessions from the ICBM. John Laylin, the American negotiator, recognized the bankers' weakness, with his views being reported by the State Department to the effect that "it was his [Laylin's] personal opinion that the Bankers' Committee should accept what it could and not hold out, as does the Foreign Bondholders Protective Council, for some unrealistic figure."[11] The bankers' request for better terms on writing down the debt were simply

[11] United States Department of State Archives (hereinafter SD) 812.51/2501.

rebuffed by the Mexicans. In the end, approximately $500 million of accumulated debt was written down to $50 million, finally resolving an on and off set of rescheduling negotiations to deal with loans dating back to the late nineteenth century.

Peru's negotiations with its bondholders in 1889 fit my expectations of a Called Bluff game. In this instance, Peru was highly concerned about reaching an agreement with its bondholders, as it attempted to secure foreign capital to recover from wartime destruction. Under a relatively stable government led by General Cáceres, Peru found itself in a preference ordering that corresponds to the game of Chicken. The bondholders, while relatively weak financially, were intent on securing an agreement. But their ability to block bond flotations on the London market gave them the upper hand, putting them in a PD preference ordering. In the end, the actual agreement proved highly favorable to the bondholders, but the negotiations leading up to the agreement were less lopsided than in a game of Bully.

From July 1985 to August 1986, Peru and the bankers found themselves in an Asymmetrical Deadlock. In this case, while Peru had a Deadlock Analogue preference ordering, the lenders were in a Prisoner's Dilemma. The predicted equilibrium in such a case is a deadlocked outcome. Given the poorer anticipated payoffs for the bankers, we might expect them to be more interested in negotiations. Indeed, during this period, Peru demonstrated a clear unwillingness to be conciliatory toward the international financial community. After rolling over interest payments without consulting the banks, President García bluntly told the IMF that "we will pay when Peru decides to."[12] He then proceeded to expel the IMF mission. The bankers were in a relatively strong position and were by no means desperate for a settlement. Still, while they continued to press for a meeting on debt negotiations, Peru simply refused to open talks with the bankers.

In a game from 1950 to 1953, culminating in the end of the third epoch of debt negotiations for Peru, it found itself in a game of "Protector Analogue." Here, Peru found itself in an Apology analogue preference ordering and the bondholders were in a Prisoner's Dilemma. In this game, which ended in high adjustment by Peru and few concessions from the lenders, Peru seemed oddly anxious to adjust. But in this case, following the two split games, and the PD game with the Council discussed above, the Council had secured an alliance with the World Bank and support from creditor governments. Thus, Peru found that its efforts to secure additional funds from official lenders were being blocked. The need for a settlement if Peru wished to obtain new funds became evident when the Bank tried to show some flexibility by offering Peru a very small loan. The British government immediately responded by "taking violent exception to the loan," warning that "the city [London financial interests] will have nothing further to do with the [World] Bank if the Bank pursues such a course."[13]

[12] *Latin American Weekly Report*, February 21, 1986, pp. 8–9. [13] SD 823.10/9–1351.

Seven games had more than two equilibria in pure strategies, and I have referred to these games as "complex." Among these cases, Mexican negotiations with bondholders from 1867 to 1876 illustrate the dynamics of this type of game. In this first period following the occupation of Mexico by the French, and the subsequent overthrow of Maximilian, Mexico had Deadlock preference orderings. President Benito Juárez assumed a tough stance, repudiating Maximilian's loans and the 1864 debt conversion. With the end of the U.S. Civil War, European powers were wary of further intervention, and Juárez had little to fear from these countries. Meanwhile, the lenders found themselves in a combination of PD and Chicken preference orderings. This put them in a more vulnerable position, and the three predicted equilibria were all unfavorable to the lenders. In this instance, Mexico had a dominant strategy of not adjusting and could secure relatively high payoffs by doing so, while the lenders were indifferent among very low payoffs associated with making high, medium, or low concessions in view of their stable coalitional position, overall strength, and financial need. While the lenders could help Mexico by making high concessions without lowering their own payoffs, they had little incentive to do so unless they believed that their concessions would lead Mexico to be more forthcoming. But a relatively unstable Mexico showed little interest in making any adjustments, and instead, began to purchase bonds on the open market at reduced prices rather than paying interest on its debt. In these circumstances, the lenders had little reason to help Mexico since it did not appear as if concessions on their part would be reciprocated. As a result, the game ended in a deadlock.

Three important implications emerge from these findings. First, the richness in game types derived from basic political and economic factors using my situational theory of payoffs provides a response to critics of game theory who see it as excessively limited in its application to real-world empirical problems. A great deal of the apparent complexity of international bargaining can be captured using game theoretic tools – especially if these are properly combined with an adequate approach to generating the games themselves. Second, as one can readily see from the Appendix, the games in which actors find themselves often change quite dramatically within epochs, as actors find themselves in new bargaining situations. Thus, when one observes different bargaining outcomes over time, it is imperative to differentiate between changes in strategy that result from different calculations in an iterated context, versus actual changes in underlying game payoffs that reflect shifting political and economic conditions. Third, the large number of games with single solutions suggests that using game theory in a predictive manner is indeed a feasible option. Once payoffs are specified in light of actors' power resources and domestic constraints, we can generally anticipate the bargaining outcome of the interaction between the two actors. Moreover, in this connection, when playing these games, the case studies suggest that debtors and lenders generally had considerable information about both their opponents' power position and domestic stability. Although there were instances of bluffing and posturing, for the most part, in game theory terminology, actors had a good sense of the "type" of opponent they were facing (for example, a more dovish or hawkish actor).[14]

Counterintuitive insights from the analysis. One's confidence in a theory is strengthened by not only a high rate of predictive success, but also by its ability to anticipate what might be seen as unexpected results. Scholars who use models of the general type employed in this book do not expect that all of the predictions of their model will run dramatically counter to what we would expect from common intuition. Nonetheless, my model generated several predictions that seem to be counterintuitive. I turn to a few examples of such instances below.

In the first epoch during the second and third periods of negotiation between Peru and its creditors (1841–1844), the Peruvian government came into a sudden windfall with the massive exploitation of guano. With these substantial new resources, one might expect Peru to become more amenable to servicing its debt. In fact, the model anticipated the opposite to occur in view of Peru's domestic instability and overall strength, despite an improving financial situation. In fact, rather than undertaking economic adjustment, Peru simply used its control over guano to extract loans from guano contractors, while ignoring the bondholders. And in the next period of negotiations from 1845 to 1847, a more politically stable Peru still refused to come to an agreement. Only when its overall capabilities declined as its dependence on guano contractors increased dramatically, and Peru became more politically stable and financially secure, did we see Peru negotiate a settlement of its long-standing debt with the bondholders. These two episodes illustrate the complex interplay of domestic political factors with financial and overall power in actors' calculations, which I have attempted to capture in deriving their payoffs in debt bargaining games.

The examination of Peruvian negotiations in this epoch also sheds light on a debate among historians as to the role of the British government in promoting a debt settlement. Whereas Jonathan Levin suggests that such intervention was decisive in leading to a debt settlement in 1849, the game I derived based on Peru's and the bondholders' political and economic situation supports William Mathew's contention that British intervention was helpful, but hardly decisive, in securing a rescheduling agreement. As the analysis for this period illustrates, the actual outcome of high adjustment and low concessions was one of the equilibria in the game between Peru and the lenders.

The analysis of a more recent episode involving Peruvian negotiations with its bankers from 1984 to 1985 illuminates the underlying structure of the bargaining game. Whereas Peru tried to misrepresent its payoffs by pretending that it was willing to adjust, the derived game for this period suggested that this was simply a ruse. Based on follow-up interviews with key participants, this interpretation would appear to reflect Peru's true motivations at the time. In addition,

[14] I will return to this issue below when discussing the question of what assumptions about information to use in my game theoretic modeling.

my view that actors rapidly develop good information about each other's situation is supported by this case. While in the first round of negotiations the banks appeared to be taken in by this strategy and became more conciliatory, they soon shifted to a more confrontational stance when they realized the true nature of the game in which they found themselves.

In Argentine negotiations from August 1989 to August 1991 when Carlos Menem, an avowed Peronist, came to power, many observers anticipated a deterioration in the negotiating climate and an inevitable deadlock. As *The Economist* bluntly summarized the view of many observers, the "know-nothing" Menem who had inherited General Peron's populist tradition would destroy Argentina's economy.[15] Based on Argentina's economic situation and political stability, however, the model suggested that Argentina would adopt a more conciliatory position. Indeed, Menem quickly proceeded to pursue significant and harsh adjustment, despite a run on the austral. By 1992, Argentina had come to an agreement with the banks under the auspices of the Brady Plan – a counterintuitive outcome from the perspective of analysts like *The Economist* who soon changed their tune and sang Menem's praises as he pursued significant economic adjustment.[16]

Learning from failed predictions. We turn next to an examination of the cases where the model failed. It is useful to consider two types of cases: those in which the game outcome reverts to the two-actor equilibrium, rather than the third-party intervention outcome (four cases); and those in which the model fails completely, with the outcome deviating from both the two-actor and third-party predicted outcome (five cases). Both sets of cases share three common elements that cause deviations from the predicted outcomes. First, the involvement of many creditor governments, or intervention by a single creditor government with many different objectives, sometimes made it difficult to anticipate their actions. In addition, predictions were more difficult when the U.S. and IMF were not in accord. A second factor, unanticipated domestic political changes or external shocks, also threw off predictions. Finally, a third factor is the unanticipated role played by individuals. In the second set of cases, a fourth factor – the presence of games with Chicken payoffs, when combined with creditor governments who lack a strong motivation to intervene or have multiple interests – also contributed to the model's failed predictions. Table 15.4 summarizes the role of these factors in these problematic cases.

I begin with the first set of cases where I did not accurately predict intervention. In Peru's negotiations with bondholders between 1876 and 1880 (period two in the second epoch), I predicted little adjustment by Peru and few concessions by lenders in the two-actor game. Because of the creditor governments' interest in Peruvian guano and concern over the war between Peru and Chile, I anticipated

[15] April 8, 1989.

[16] One could of course claim that his regime was "capitalist," but then from a coding perspective, it is not clear that one could use such an approach to make predictions.

Table 15.4. *Factors involved in problematic cases*

		Factors			
Type of failure	Case	Creditor governments with multiple competing concerns	Domestic political shocks or external shocks	Unanticipated role by individuals	Chicken-type game structure
Failure in predicting intervention	Peru (1876–1880)	yes	yes	yes	N.A.
	Peru (1887–1889)	yes	yes		N.A.
	Mexico (1916–1920)		yes		N.A.
	Brazil (1982–1983)		yes		N.A.
Predictions fail completely	Mexico (1911–1914)	yes		yes	
	Mexico (1935–1936)			yes	
	Mexico (1937–1940)		yes		yes
	Peru (1939–1943)	yes			yes
	Argentina (1984–1985)	yes	yes		

Note: N.A. = not applicable.

that intervention would lead to an outcome of medium adjustment and few concessions. Although Peru did agree to undertake servicing of its debt as anticipated, President Prado inexplicably and suddenly left the presidency and went to Europe. When Piérola came to power, he sought his own accord with French financiers, creating a conflict between the French and British governments. Shortly thereafter, Chile defeated Peru in the War of the Pacific and seized Peru's southern territories, leaving Peru in dire financial straits and unable to service its debt. As the British bondholders shifted their attention to Chile, the Peruvian game ended in deadlock, rather than the intervention outcome of medium adjustment and low concessions. In this bargaining episode, then, all three of the factors identified above played a role in leading to a misprediction of the correct outcome with intervention. Specifically, competing British and French government concerns, unanticipated actions by Peru's President, and the onset of war combined to confound my prediction.

The second problematic case in this category also involved Peru and the bondholders in negotiations in the second epoch from June 1887 to March 1889. In this sixth period, I expected an outcome with some intervention that would move the parties away from a position of few concessions and adjustment to a medium level of adjustment by Peru. Although Peruvian authorities formally signed the Grace contract in May 1887, the agreement quickly came under attack by the Chileans (who had assumed responsibility for half of Peru's debt in connection with the settlement that recognized its annexation of Peruvian territory). Still, the British seemed interested in settlement of the debt problem following the conclusion of the Pacific War, and, thus, would likely pressure Peru to accommodate the lenders. Although the British applied pressure, it took the form of blocking a Chilean loan flotation – an action that did decrease Chilean opposition to the accord. But in the meantime, opposition by the Peruvian Congress to the Grace contract led to growing domestic instability. As a result, the negotiations ended in stalemate, and final passage of the Grace contract would have to wait until the next period when Peruvian President Cáceras stabilized his coalition by replacing recalcitrant members of Congress. Thus, in this case, I mispredicted the locus of intervention and underestimated the degree to which domestic opposition would block the accord.

In negotiations between Mexico and the banks from 1916 to 1920 in the third epoch (period one), a major domestic political shift contributed to the model's failure to predict intervention. In this instance, Mexico and the banks were negotiating over possible loans and an adjustment of the debt payments suspended in 1914 by Huerta. My model predicted that the U.S. would push Mexico away from a deadlock to a medium level of adjustment. As anticipated, with the end of the First World War, by the end of 1918 and early 1919, the U.S. began to sharply pressure Mexico on a host of other issues, including oil and mineral rights. Soon, Carranza's government began to bend, announcing that it would resume debt service payments. But in April 1920, General Obregón revolted against the government and forced Carranza out of power. Carranza's unanticipated overthrow threw the game into a deadlock, rather than the medium level of Mexican adjustment predicted.

In the last case in this set, involving the first period of Brazilian negotiations in the fourth epoch (August 1982 to May 1983), domestic political shocks again proved to be a key factor. The model anticipated that intervention by the IMF would lead to some adjustment by Brazil and some concessions by the bankers, rather than the deadlock in which the parties found themselves. In this case, however, IMF pressure created an unsustainable agreement. Although both the U.S. and IMF pushed Brazil and the banks to sign an accord that would have provided new lending concessions and adjustment on Brazil's part, they overestimated both actors' ability to stick to their promises. When Brazil failed to continue with its adjustment program soon after signing the agreement, the IMF suspended its disbursements and the banks quickly followed suit, leaving the two protagonists deadlocked. In this example, intense domestic opposition and economic problems proved unexpectedly strong in neutralizing efforts by third parties to force adjustment on Brazil.

We turn next to the second set of five cases where the model failed entirely. In the fifth period of the second epoch, Mexico was involved in negotiations with bankers from 1911 to 1914. I anticipated that significant intervention by the U.S. would push the game outcome to high adjustment and concessions by both parties, rather than high concessions only by eager bankers. The American government had a strong interest in protecting its nationals' investments and preventing any involvement by other creditor governments. In the first round of negotiations, from 1911 to 1913, bankers showed a willingness to make new loans to Mexico. But President Woodrow Wilson's decision not to recognize General Huerta's government in February 1913 blocked any significant loans. Although Mexico received a small loan and pledged state revenues, the U.S. did not pressure Mexico into pursuing major economic adjustments. In the second round, the U.S. linked a large American loan to Huerta's resignation, but not unexpectedly, Huerta refused to agree to this arrangement. Following Huerta's dissolution of the Mexican Congress and the arrest of over a hundred top government officials, Wilson decided to topple Huerta's government by blocking all financial flows to Mexico. As the strategy began to weaken his position, the lenders feared a deadlocked outcome that would leave them with their worst payoff, and called for strong intervention by the U.S. to force high adjustment on Mexico. By April 1914, Huerta showed signs of making significant concessions to the lenders. Soon thereafter, however, the U.S. and Mexico found themselves on the verge of war over an incident involving an American warship in Tampico. Following mediation efforts by Argentina, Brazil, and Chile, war was avoided and Huerta resigned. The Mexican government, however, remained in default, and lenders desisted from making any loans to Mexico, leading to a deadlocked outcome. Thus, in this case, debt negotiations became linked to a more complex set of American concerns, dominated by Woodrow Wilson's interest in overthrowing Huerta.

In the second case involving Mexico from 1935 to 1936 (the sixth period of the third epoch), the actions of a single individual appears to have again played a crucial role in the model's failure. As anticipated by the model in view of the bankers' weak position, in 1935 the Mexican government and the International Committee of Bankers on Mexico (ICBM) completed a draft accord that was highly favorable to Mexico. The bankers waited for President Cárdenas's signature, but in March 1936, Mexico backed out of the agreement. In this unusual case, there is strong evidence – although not conclusive proof – that the U.S. ambassador in Mexico, Josephus Daniels, undermined the draft agreement. Archival documents suggest that Daniels told the chief Mexican negotiator, Finance Minister Eduardo Suárez, that the U.S. was not anxious to have the Mexicans conclude an agreement with the ICBM at that point because most of the debt was held by foreigners. In this case, unanticipated action by the U.S. ambassador explains the anomalous outcome.

Chicken-type games with multiple equilibria were an additional complicating factor in the next period of negotiations from 1937 to 1940 between Mexico and the ICBM. The game had three equilibria.[17] In view of relatively low levels of U.S. concern about the negotiations, and American government interest in the issue of oil rights, it is difficult to make predictions about which of the three possible outcomes would be more likely. Despite another agreement that appeared to be highly favorable to the Mexicans, Finance Minister Suárez refused to submit the accord for congressional ratification. In this case, Mexico's oil nationalizations appear to have sharply affected the negotiations, because Suárez was unwilling to accept any debt servicing as his government challenged the oil companies. Thus the actual outcome was a deadlock.

In the next problematic case, Peru and the lenders found themselves in a classic game of Chicken from 1939 to 1943. The model predicted that the U.S. might attempt to meet its conflicting strategic, political, and economic objectives by pressing for a compromise that would lead both actors to make moderate concessions. I could not be certain, however, of how the complex U.S. calculations would translate into pressure on the two parties. During the negotiations, the U.S. alternately pushed the Peruvians to adjust, while criticizing the lenders for not being more forthcoming. But the U.S. refused to get deeply involved, and did not take very aggressive measures in this effort. As both Peru and the banks jockeyed for position, and as they tried to enlist the U.S. government to advance their cause, neither proved willing to accommodate the other's demands. Because of mixed U.S. interests, and jockeying between the two parties, the outcome ended up with a deadlock – not an unusual occurrence in a game of Chicken.

The fifth and final case in this set involved Argentine debt negotiations from August 1984 to March 1985. I expected eager banks to make high concessions to an unstable Argentina, but anticipated that U.S. and IMF pressure would lead to medium adjustment in response. Following an agreement with the IMF, Argentina reached an accord with the banks that came close to fulfilling this latter prediction. Yet in this case, Argentina's highly unstable government began to back away rapidly from adjustment. By March 1985, when the IMF suspended Argentina's standby loan, the banks followed suit and the game ended in deadlock. Here, by playing the role of an enforcer of adjustment, and ignoring domestic political constraints faced by Argentina's leaders, the IMF may have damaged the likelihood of concessions by the banks.

The two most important factors in both sets of failed predictions were the unanticipated role that creditor governments sometimes played and sudden changes in domestic politics or economic shocks. An improved model of creditor government intervention, a topic addressed below, might help to eliminate some of the errors in predictions. Sudden political changes or unanticipated actions by individuals, however, are more difficult to incorporate into an improved analytical

[17] At LA..., HC...; HA..., LC...; and MA..., LC....

model. Moreover, given the relatively small number of cases where the model failed, the loss of parsimony that would come from adding more variables would appear to outweigh the benefits.

The dynamic analysis

The most common approach to examining actors in a dynamic context has been to focus on games they play repeatedly. The evidence of the many game changes that can be seen in this set of cases supports my view, developed in Chapter 4, that actors often do not simply play the same game repeatedly within fixed parameters. Instead, actors with lower payoffs should attempt to reset the parameters of the game in which they find themselves.

Empirically, the evidence mostly supports this supposition. In almost all the cases, actors with relatively poor payoffs made greater efforts to improve their individual situation or undermine that of their opponent than actors who received high payoffs. Still, there are two problems with assessing the model's success in predicting such dynamic strategic efforts. First, unlike debt rescheduling, which usually results in some type of formal agreement, situational change efforts are sometimes difficult to observe – unless they lead to new individual bargaining structures. Thus, although the model appears to be successful on this count, some types of change efforts could go undetected. Second, actors often attempt to improve their economy or to appeal to allies in connection with issues of concern unrelated to debt rescheduling. Without a highly detailed analysis of each case, it is difficult to ascertain if the motivation behind such efforts is directly related to their payoffs in a debt bargaining game.

The case of Mexican negotiations from March 1983 to August 1985 shows the difficulty of predicting when actors will change their bargaining position. Both actors received the highest payoffs in the play phase of this period, but subsequently their circumstances changed dramatically. Two exogenous shocks account for Mexico's new position: an earthquake that hit Mexico City in September 1985 and a sharp plunge in oil prices in January 1986. For their part, despite their high payoffs, some European banks attempted to improve their situation by taking loan-loss provisions. The result was a partial weakening of the bankers' coalition. In this case, there are two interconnected explanations for the banks' unanticipated efforts. First, many banks were involved in a number of different rescheduling efforts – with the Europeans most actively involved in Eastern Europe. Thus, they may have been responding to outcomes in a number of other debt rescheduling games. Second, the different regulatory environment of the European banks made it easier for them to bolster their financial position. Thus, predictions about game change that are tied only to the specific bargaining case can be confounded by the broader context to which actors respond.

In addition to focusing on the motivation for game changes, Chapter 4 also theorized about the types of power resources that actors would use and the elements of their or their opponents' individual situation that they would attempt to change. Moreover, I suggested that actors would engage in issue linkage and delinkage efforts and the "types of goods" involved in debt negotiations would constrain their efforts. I have found that change efforts included the full panoply of power resources of norms and rules, capabilities, and alliances. Exogenous shocks also produced changes in actors' individual situations. I will next examine some of the resources that actors draw upon in attempting to change games, including whether they proved successful or not in promoting situational change, and also focus on both the elements that actors tried to change as well as the constraints they faced in this effort.

In the nineteenth century, lenders often appealed to the "norms" that "civilized" states follow. They also sometimes attempted to take legal action through the courts to bolster their bargaining position, as in the twentieth century. Debtors such as Peru in the 1930s, and Argentina in the 1980s, pointed to "norms" of not honoring "illegitimately contracted" debt. Also, they have tried to use such norms to justify their calls for debt reduction, arguing that speculators were the beneficiaries of rescheduling arrangements – rather than poor individual bondholders who had tied up their life savings in a foreign bond. Although frequently used over the centuries by both lenders and debtors, by and large, these appeals have not borne much fruit. In some cases, however, as when Peruvian President García challenged the banks in the mid-1980s, such efforts have served to bolster domestic coalitions in the short run. In the 1880s, Chile used the terms of its debt agreement to force bondholders to group together instead of operating independently. In contrast, Peru in the 1940s attempted to weaken the Foreign Bondholders Protective Council by making a direct offer to bondholders, with only limited success. For their part, creditor governments have often used the tool of political recognition to bolster particular favored governments.

Actors have also commonly used their capabilities to alter their underlying bargaining resources. For example, debtors can strengthen (or sometimes undermine) their domestic coalitions by pursuing economic policies that favor particular groups. Creditor governments, however, have been far more effective than either lenders or debtors in promoting coalitional changes. Similarly, the IMF has used its leverage over financial resources to bolster particular societal groups, but its actions have often destabilized rather than stabilized debtors' governments. More commonly, both lenders and debtors have strengthened both their issue capabilities and overall capabilities by increasing financial reserves, making them less vulnerable to outright default or financial embargoes. In the 1840s, for example, Peru used its capability to control guano to extract financial concessions from contractors, which enabled it to resist pressures from bondholders for a rescheduling accord. Another quite common and effective strategy has been for debtors to secretly buy back bonds on the open market to weaken bondholders' groups.[18]

Finally, both debtors and lenders have often appealed to allies, attempting to

[18] On the financial implications of debt buybacks, see Bulow and Rogoff (1988a), Krugman (1988), Williamson (1988), Froot (1989), and Diwan and Rodrick (1992).

both influence the patterns of intervention and to foster situational changes. From the early part of the nineteenth century to the present, lenders have regularly formed alliances with each other in bondholders' committees and bankers' groups. They have often received unofficial, and sometimes official, encouragement to form such organizations (for example, the American government's promotion of the ICBM in 1919 or the actions in the 1980s by the U.S., U.K., and other creditor governments to foster unity among banks). Debtors have been considerably less successful in uniting, with little to show for their many discussions of forming a cartel in the 1980s.[19] Lenders and debtors have also attempted to develop transnational alliances with sympathetic groups of their counterparts in an effort to affect coalitional composition and stability.

In the fourth epoch, debtors commonly attempted to bolster their issue strength and overall capabilities by appealing to creditor governments' concerns about immigration and democracy. While somewhat effective in promoting creditor government pressure on lenders, these efforts have not succeeded in directly changing debtors' individual situations. Lenders have more often been successful at securing strong allies to alter their overall bargaining abilities, as in the case of the unusual direct involvement of creditor governments in the installation of Maximilian in Mexico in the nineteenth century.

Attempts to secure allies can also backfire. For example, in the 1840s, after continuous appeals from bondholders, the British government began taking a more active interest in their affairs, and negotiated the "English Convention Debt" which dealt with property claims. Shortly thereafter, the bondholders discovered that this intervention had its drawbacks. Because debt servicing was a collective good, the bondholders found themselves in competition with the British government for payment, while at the same time, they lacked a commitment that their own bonds would be covered by British diplomatic protection.

Finally, with respect to linkages, debtors such as Peru and Mexico in the 1930s and 1940s, and Mexico and Brazil in the 1980s have attempted to affect issue-capabilities by linking debt negotiations to trade. But while these connections sometimes helped debtors secure more favorable treatment from creditor governments, they generally did not fundamentally change the boundaries of the debt rescheduling issue-area. An unusual case in which lenders attempted to *delink* issues occurred in the early 1920s, when the International Committee of Bankers of Mexico attempted to discourage the U.S. government from linking debt rescheduling to issues of concern to the United States such as expropriation and property damage.

Despite such voluntary situational change efforts, the key source of change is often an external shock. Shocks include frequent changes in domestic coalitions. Sometimes, of course, changes are tied to a debtor's efforts to carry out an excessively severe adjustment program without having received comparable concessions from lenders. In general, however, changes in coalitional stability

[19] See Aggarwal (1987) for an analysis of why debtors' cartel formation efforts have failed.

usually relate to a host of other domestic political issues that may have little to do with debt rescheduling. Other types of shocks have been the discovery and exploitation of guano in Peru in the 1840s or of oil in the early 1900s in Mexico, changes in the international oil market, or the onset of wars.

In short, my attempt to examine how actors alter their bargaining constraints has yielded insights into many aspects of this process. Actors appear to react to lower payoffs by actively using power resources to modify the games in which they find themselves. From a predictive standpoint, however, I have found it difficult to anticipate the results of these efforts, and thus my situational theory of change does not fully capture the complexity of this phenomenon. In discussing avenues for further research below, I will consider how this part of my situational theory might be improved.

Other findings on lending, default, and crisis resolution[20]

My primary objective up to this point has been to evaluate the success of efforts to explain debt rescheduling and intervention by creditor governments and international organizations. In addition to these specific findings, other generalizations emerge from the assessment of the 61 cases and four epochs covered in this book.

I begin with the process of lending. My epochal analysis shows that for the most part, banks have directly loaned money to debtors or floated loans on their behalf when flush with deposits. But as we have seen, bondholders and bankers generally failed to analyze the risks they were taking when making foreign loans. False optimism was common, both with respect to each country's prospects for servicing their debt and how quickly debt defaults would be resolved. Of course, it is often in the interest of bankers to misrepresent the risks involved in lending, in their efforts to float bonds among a gullible public. Still, in some cases I found that bondholders managed to fare quite well, even after lengthy periods of rescheduling (e.g., Mexico 1825–1886). In other cases, the original bondholders received little return on their bonds (e.g., Mexico 1942).[21]

With respect to the borrowing practices of debtors, I found that most Latin American governments almost perpetually ran budget deficits and sought funds from international financiers as an alternative to generating additional tax revenues.

[20] This section draws on Aggarwal (1989), Section 6.1, for a discussion of parallels between earlier periods of indebtedness and rescheduling based on Mexican rescheduling efforts over the last two centuries. The empirical examples draw from the case study chapters. I also relate my findings here to two excellent surveys on parallels between earlier and current episodes of international lending and rescheduling written by Albert Fishlow (1985a) and Barry Eichengreen (1991).

[21] Barry Eichengreen found this kind of false optimism and lack of analysis on the part of lenders (1991), p. 154. Still, based on a review of quantitative studies on bondholders' returns over the last 150 years, Eichengreen concludes that an investor with a balanced portfolio might have done reasonably well on his or her investments. Thus, investors may have been wiser than would appear to be the case. But the high variance in returns suggests that lenders may not have been fully compensated by the eventual realized returns on foreign bonds. This applies to private bondholders who can be assumed to be risk averse, requiring a risk premium. Financial institutions with diversified shareholders are generally assumed to be risk neutral, caring only about expected returns.

As noted in Chapter 9, Mexico in the 1920s faced problems in servicing its debts because of declining oil revenues and difficulties in tax collection – a characterization that describes Mexican problems in the early 1980s as well. In the recent period, Latin American reliance in the 1960s and 1970s on inefficient state-owned enterprises has aggravated their need for capital.[22] As the case studies show, even sudden windfalls, such as the discovery of oil in Mexico or guano in Peru, have done little to bring government budgets into balance. Instead, as we have seen, they only served to whet politicians' appetites for foreign loans and encouraged even greater borrowing.[23]

The cyclical theories of lending examined in the first chapter suggest that default is likely when lenders cut back on their loans.[24] While the availability of capital is no doubt an important factor in stimulating default, countries have sometimes managed to avoid the "inevitable" through domestic adjustment programs. For example, Argentina, Australia, Canada, and others continued to service their debt when lenders retrenched in the early part of this century.[25]

Finally, with respect to debt reduction, most ideas proposed in the current epoch, whether specific to a particular set of negotiations or more global schemes, share a number of similarities to earlier plans.[26] Throughout the three prior epochs that I have examined, solutions involving interest capitalization, repurchase of bonds on the open market, debt-equity swaps, and debt payment guarantees from other countries were common. Interest capitalization has been the most common approach to dealing with overdue debts, with the new issue of bonds a common strategy as in Mexico in the 1830s and 1880s and in Peru in 1849. As seen in several cases, both (in the 1860s) Mexico and (in the 1840s and 1930s) Peru engaged in the secret repurchase of bonds at low prices. Although this was a common strategy used by debtors, they occasionally undertook such activities to prevent bondholders from becoming aware of their actions. One would naturally expect lenders to be concerned about the use of funds to eliminate debt at low prices, rather than to service outstanding debts.[27] With respect to debt-equity swaps, I noted that following the war between Mexico and Texas in the 1830s, for example, the Mexicans offered, but failed to secure, London bondholders' acquiescence to exchange land in Texas, Sonora, and the Californias for outstanding debts. Peru engaged in a more successful swap effort, offering bondholders guano concessions in exchange for debt in the 1870s with the Raphael

[22] See Frieden (1981) on "indebted industrialization."

[23] My observation is in line with many studies of "Dutch disease" among borrowers, which describes the growing uncompetitiveness of Dutch exports in reaction to its currency's appreciation as a result of natural gas exports. For a discussion of this phenomenon, and case studies of this problem, see Gillis et al. (1983), pp. 529–537.

[24] See Marichal (1989) and Suter (1992).

[25] Eichengreen (1991), p. 155. See also Fishlow (1985).

[26] See Aggarwal (1989) on specific efforts to reduce the debt burden. The Winter 1990 Symposium of the *Journal of Economic Perspectives* examines global debt reduction plans. See also Eichengreen (1991), pp. 165–167 for a summary of these plans.

[27] On the implications of bond buybacks, see Bulow and Rogoff (1988a) and Cohen and Verdier (1990).

Contract, and more complex debt for equity exchanges involving railroads, mines, steamers, and guano with the Grace Contract in 1889.

As Mexico's difficulties have illustrated, loan payment guarantees from creditor governments have been fraught with political intrigue. In an 1857 deal, which eventually fell through because of domestic political disagreements in the U.S., Mexico agreed to reduce customs barriers with the U.S. in exchange for a loan of $15 million. Soon thereafter, during an ongoing civil war in 1859, Mexico's Foreign Relations Secretary and the U.S. Ambassador to Mexico concluded an agreement for a loan that would have given the U.S. unlimited transit rights across Northern Mexico, free trade access, and the right to intervene in exchange for $4 million. The U.S. Senate rejected the treaty because there was domestic dispute in the U.S. over whether slaves would be permitted in "former" Mexican territory once the land fell into U.S. hands. The British also failed in their efforts to secure a reduction in trade duties from Mexico in exchange for debt concessions, shortly before the 1861 invasion of Mexico by British, French, and Spanish troops.

Although creditor governments discussed several global debt reduction schemes in the 1930s, none succeeded.[28] By contrast, while the 1985 Baker Plan did not significantly alter the course of debt negotiations, I argue that the 1989 Brady Plan appears to be a significant break from earlier efforts to develop global debt reduction schemes. This undertaking is politically backed by major creditor governments, provides a mechanism for debt reduction that the banks have by and large accepted, and involves the financial backing of governments as well as international organizations. As I have suggested in examining the implications of this accord for my model, this greater institutionalization significantly affects debtors' and lenders' calculations in their negotiation of debt agreements.

As I noted earlier, a combined epochal/economic cycles approach did not prove very helpful in explaining debt rescheduling. By contrast, when supplemented by insights from my empirical survey of a large number of cases of debt rescheduling, it does appear to be quite useful for advancing our understanding of indebtedness, default, and debt reduction efforts.

Policy implications

What are the implications of this study for how decisionmakers deal with the problems they face? While academics have the luxury of hindsight, policymakers must cope with their challenges with any tools they have at their disposal. On this score, my findings provide both good news and bad news for policymakers. Let me begin with the bad news.

My findings suggest, for the most part, that given the large number of games with determinate outcomes, tactical bargaining efforts do little to bring about an outcome which differs from the prediction based on the actors' individual

[28] Eichengreen (1991), p. 165.

situations. Because overall capabilities, financial resources, and domestic stability are often relatively immutable in the short run, actors may as well accept that they can do no better than the Nash outcome in any given negotiation. Because both lenders and debtors are generally aware of the game parameters, attempting to fool one's counterpart by misrepresenting one's payoffs is unlikely to succeed. With respect to intervention by third parties, some tactical efforts, such as appeals to norms, may occasionally bring about more favorable intervention in the game. But, as we have seen, both creditor governments and international organizations are primarily guided by their own agendas.

Now the good news. To advise that an actor should play as well as it can, given the circumstances in which it finds itself, is not to say that one should not study or seek help if one keeps losing at chess. Over time, situational change efforts *can* lead to radically different outcomes. We have seen successful appeals to norms and rules, and other efforts to promote situational changes. More importantly, regime construction has fundamentally altered actors' calculations and willingness to compromise, as with the Brady Plan. Actors also have been able to use their own capabilities to improve their strength, or to redefine bargaining games. Linkage strategies have sometimes worked, and substantive linkages can bring about more favorable intervention or even more fundamental game changes. Allies sometimes have been instrumental in altering games, although as we have seen, intervention by outside actors is often a mixed blessing. And while random shocks, by definition, are something that one cannot anticipate, some debtors and lenders have coped with such changes better than others.

My epochal and case study analysis also holds some lessons for policymakers. Lenders could benefit from more careful analysis of the risks involved in sovereign lending. Historically, it has been more difficult to ensure servicing of sovereign debt than private debts, because no international equivalent of receivership and Chapter 11 bankruptcy proceedings exist in lending to sovereign states. Borrowers have often misused funds, and have been overeager to meet shortfalls in their budgets through international financing rather than through increasing taxes. Debtors, for their part, should be wary of excessive private borrowing – particularly if they do not have reserves to weather shocks. While good economic policies should in principle encourage lenders to continue to provide funds, even in times of economic crises, such policies have not protected countries from the "redlining" we have commonly seen in Latin America. For example, even when Brazil pursued significant adjustment policies to ensure that it would remain attractive to lenders in 1982, the Mexican crisis led to a near cessation of voluntary lending – and forced Brazil into rescheduling negotiations of its own.

Lenders and debtors must also recognize that once defaults take place, rescheduling efforts will take time, and write-downs of some portion of the debt are nearly inevitable. Policymakers (and scholars) should also be aware of the many different approaches that have been used to cope with defaults historically, and learn from the successes and failures of such approaches. In particular, interest capitalization, and in many cases, interest forgiveness, has been an essential element in the resolution of debt crises.

Finally, international organizations and creditor governments can play useful roles in the process of debt rescheduling. In many cases, however, the excessive concern with fiscally prudent policies and the desire of international financial institutions to see rapid economic adjustment has destabilized governments and harmed prospects for steady repayment. In designing adjustment programs, the IMF must be responsive to the differing economic conditions of countries and attentive to the political constraints that governments face.

Avenues for future research

In this book, I have tried to develop a model to explain and predict international debt rescheduling outcomes in a variety of different cases. In view of both the substantial degree of predictive success achieved by the model, and its failure in 9 of the 61 cases, this section discusses how to refine my approach and considers how it might be used to explain other types of international bargaining.

Refining the static model

What avenues might be pursued to refine my static approach to construct bargaining games and predict outcomes in this context?[29] One improvement to the situational theory of payoffs might be to construct models with fewer, more, or different variables to derive actors' preference orderings. A number of economic models focus only on economic variables and model debt rescheduling by drawing an analogy to domestic negotiations over credit. But based on my case materials, I come to the same conclusion as Jonathan Eaton, Mark Gersovitz, and Joseph Stiglitz: "The central role of the enforcement problem and the absence of collateral make the international loan market fundamentally different from domestic credit markets."[30] Thus, I find that it is very important for models to differentiate among debtors' and lenders' domestic or coalitional characteristics, and not to ignore overall power factors.

What about the incorporation of additional variables into the definition of game payoffs? My experience in incorporating more than three variables has been that the consequent rapid growth in types of actors makes it difficult to derive payoffs systematically. On this question, however, I am rather agnostic, as there may be some relevant factors that might permit analysts to derive payoffs more accurately. Given the relatively successful performance of the

[29] With respect to types of models, one could also reject the strategic interaction approach I have taken here and develop econometric models to predict rescheduling outcomes. I find the game theoretic avenue more compelling, because as Martin Hellwig (1986) notes in commenting on Eaton, Gersowitz, and Stiglitz's paper (1986), "I agree with the authors that the problems of international borrowing and lending must be analyzed in terms of strategic behaviour rather than mechanical concepts of 'insolvency' or 'illiquidity.'"

[30] Eaton, Gersowitz, and Stiglitz (1986), pp. 511–512.

model, however, introducing greater complexity to increase its predictive ability would be a poor trade-off.

Another possibility would be to use different variables than the ones I have chosen to derive actors' preferences. For example, one of my key variables was the stability of actors' domestic coalitions. But why not consider the ideological complexion of the debtor's government? One might at first glance assume that stability is not as important as a government's progressive or conservative policy orientation.[31] But the belief that specific government types necessarily have an ideological propensity to adjust is suspect. As noted above in my discussion of Argentine negotiations in 1989, many, including *The Economist*, believed that newly elected Peronist Carlos Menem would pursue a populist course. But it appears that bankers had a better understanding of the prospects for reform in Argentina. Following Menem's victory in May 1989, one banker commented, "creditors might be better off in a situation where the party that comes to power comes decisively, and has the responsibility to govern."[32]

Recent literature on two-level games has introduced a different approach to examining payoffs.[33] Following Robert Putnam, analysts have focused on domestic and internationally relevant variables, in the sense that policymakers are seen to be attentive to both an "international" and "domestic" game. If developed carefully, this approach could provide an interesting alternative to my focus on factors reflecting domestic and international concerns into a single game. But in practice, this research has not been rigorously developed, and the choice of variables that one should focus on at the domestic or international level has not been clearly specified. Nor does this approach provide a method to reconcile the two different games in which actors are postulated to be involved. Furthermore, this method has not been systematically tested through careful specification of payoffs for different bargaining games.[34] In fact, many empirical studies of two-level games fail to explain exactly how decisionmakers make their calculations beyond informing us that policymakers face competing domestic and international concerns.[35] If studies in this genre were more rigorously developed

[31] Christian Suter (1992) argues that four ideal-type political regimes, classified by Pfister and Suter in 1991, will influence borrowing and adjustment patterns in conjunction with economic cycles. He classifies regimes as capitalist, populist, disarticulated, or based on state class. In examining Peruvian debt rescheduling since the 1820s, Suter argues that debt settlements were negotiated by regimes that were either capitalist or disarticulated. Although this provides an alternative conception of what domestic factors drive adjustment, I might note that in the Peruvian cases of adjustment that Suter and I have examined, the common factor is that the regimes were also politically stable.

[32] *Washington Post*, May 16, 1989. [33] See the overview for citations.

[34] See the studies in Evans, Jacobson, and Putnam (1993). In his introduction to this volume of "two-level" game studies, Marovcsik warns the reader that this approach is not formally developed, and that the empirical studies are "plausibility probes."

[35] Lehman and McCoy (1992) provide an example of the problems that may beset one's analysis in the absence of careful formalization. In their examination of Brazil's bargaining with the banks in 1985, they note that "Brazil perceived the costs of no-agreement to be sufficiently low to warrant this strengthened bargaining stance." They also argue that "The banks at that time also seemed to prefer no-agreement to agreement without IMF linkage." Thus their informal coding effort suggests that a deadlock in the negotiations will ensue. Yet in the following sentences, they tell us that

and tested, we would more readily be able to compare the merits of different formulations.

In addition to specifying payoffs, the second key aspect in my use of games concerns the types of assumptions I made in using game theoretic analysis. Chapter 2 briefly mentioned the possibility of incorporating varying assumptions about the information available to actors. I speculated that there was a trade-off between more empirically tractable models such as the one proposed here and more complex ones that assume that actors lack complete information about each other's payoffs. In contrast to the complete information models used in this book, incomplete information models deal with players who learn about how their opponent is likely to behave (as a function of their "type," which reflects different individual situations, following my terminology) during the bargaining process.

This modeling approach makes strong assumptions about actors' decision-making abilities and the types of calculations they make. If used in the framework of my situational analysis, each actor would be seen as facing an opponent in any one of eight pure different possible situations (and many more combinations of different hybrid situations), but would be uncertain about which type of opponent he is actually facing. Following this modeling technique, each player should be able to specify his own beliefs about the type of potential opponent he may be facing *prior* to play of the game.[36] In addition, each actor must have some information – full or partial – about the other's beliefs. Finally, each player should revise his beliefs about the type of opponent he faces after each of the latter's moves.[37] This revision of beliefs takes place through actors updating their initial beliefs as a result of their opponents' moves in accordance with Bayes's rule.[38] In sum, actors should be able to assign beliefs and change them – both in a static and dynamic context.

The assumption of incomplete information has theoretical advantages. Obviously such an approach allows us to more fully approximate actors' behavior in negotiations in which actors are uncertain about the type of opponent they face. It may also provide considerable heuristic power in developing more sophisticated models. The drawbacks of this approach, however, lie in its unparsimonious

"Nevertheless, faced with Brazil's tough stance on the IMF and recognizing the internal politics, the banks took a series of temporary measures . . ." (p. 613). These measures included a number of significant concessions followed by a rescheduling agreement in July 1986 without commitment by Brazil to submit to an IMF plan. Despite an erroneous prediction of deadlock, the authors identify this case in their conclusion as a success (pp. 637–638). I analyze this case quite differently in Chapter 13.

[36] In some cases, the situation is even more complex, because an actor may not have full information about his own type. In this case, one should model the bargaining situation with two sets of beliefs for each actor: one with respect to one's own type and another with respect to the opponent's type. Incomplete information models can also be extended to players' uncertainty about the strategic options available to them during the game.

[37] Of course, some moves do not convey information about the nature of one's opponent, or the information transmitted might not be sufficient to alter one's beliefs.

[38] For a discussion of Bayes's rule, see Ordeshook (1992), pp. 214–217.

formulation and its lesser predictive power in the face of the severe empirical demands it imposes. In analyzing a bargaining setting with a multiplicity of types of actors (as in, for example, debt rescheduling negotiations), the coding problem becomes extremely difficult, making operationalization a nearly impossible task. Moreover, with a large number of different types of actors, the analysis quickly becomes highly complex. Most incomplete information games of this type generally have a host of equilibria, and it is often difficult to select among them.[39] Consequently, many analysts use these games to focus on variation in families of outcomes, which depend on the variation of specific factors, rather than to predict a single outcome.

As it turns out, an incomplete information approach may also be *less* consistent with what we know about actual actors' behavior in relation to the process of decisionmaking. Indeed, as noted above, I found that actors involved in debt games during the play phase seemed to have an accurate sense of their opponents' payoffs. In a few instances, they did seek additional information about their opponents or update their views about the type of actor they faced during the game, but generally, judging from the negotiation pattern and outcomes, actors seem to have correctly assessed the debt game in which they found themselves. Thus, it appears that my assumption of complete information not only provides a more tractable model, but also more accurately reflects reality. In sum, although I would not deny the utility of developing incomplete information models,[40] it is questionable whether we should rush headlong into the empirical testing of such complex models.[41]

One area where further research could strengthen my modeling effort concerns the role of third party intervention. Although Chapter 3 specified the factors that will influence creditor governments' or international organizations' calculation, I often found it difficult to assess how actors weight these elements in choosing to intervene in rescheduling negotiations. As noted in my summary of findings, in five cases I predicted an intervention outcome that could not be sustained, and that reverted to the two-actor game. My decision-theoretic approach to intervention, in which third parties make their decisions to intervene after predicting the likely outcome of the two-actor game, could be formalized further with more systematic weighting of the factors that influence these choices.[42]

An alternate path would be to develop three or more person games from the start, including creditor governments and international organizations in negotiations with bankers and debtors. As I suggested in my discussion of debtors' and lenders' payoffs in games under the Brady Plan, my situational theory of payoffs

[39] One of the biggest concerns of game theorists is to find refinement criteria for equilibrium concepts in order to select among the multiple equilibria. At present most admit that this is a daunting task.

[40] For a rigorous and innovative effort to both develop and test incomplete information models empirically, see Dupont (1994).

[41] For an incomplete information model with apolitical assumptions about what motivated debtors and lenders, see Kletzer (1989).

[42] I have attempted to develop such a model but have not yet found it to be very satisfactory.

does not fully capture the changed calculations of these actors when a stable regime has been developed. Multi-actor games would allow us to contend with the different calculations that actors make in such cases. Unfortunately, such game models are not very tractable and are hard to use for predictive purposes because the outcome of which coalition will form appears indeterminate or is extremely hard to predict.[43]

Developing an improved theory of situational change

My effort to explain how actors might attempt to change the games in which they find themselves might be strengthened if I could predict patterns of how actors use norms and rules, capabilities, and allies, and identify which aspects of an actor's individual situation is likely to change. In other work that I have done singly and jointly, I have tried to develop such a model.[44] Unfortunately, these efforts have not yet yielded successful predictions. Still, because some of the insights apply to the cases examined here, I briefly review some of the points from my earlier work.

There are three important elements in analyzing situational changes. First, one might try to ascertain if some sequence is likely among the three power resources mentioned above. Second, one could gauge if actors attempt to change the three factors that define their or their opponent's individual situation in some particular order. Third, one could attempt to see if an actor's individual situation predicts his or her power resource use pattern.[45] Here, I focus on only the first question.

If one assumes that actors can correctly anticipate the results of the bargaining in specific games, but is unsure as to how successful they will be in changing either their own or their opponent's situation, one can construct a possible sequencing model of game change. We might, for example, expect actors to appeal first to international arrangements, then to capabilities, and lastly to alliances. The logic of this particular sequence is based on ideas developed by Alexander George. He has argued that the foreign policymaking process often does not allow for "purely rational" calculation. Unfortunately for policymakers, they often are beset by: (1) "uncertainty" about what is likely to be the result of a particular course of action (owing to lack of information and understanding of causal relationships), and (2) "value-complexity" about the tradeoffs they face in selecting a particular course of action, that is, "the presence of multiple, competing values and interests that are embedded in a single issue."[46] Consequently, a smooth, rational decisionmaking process that incorporates accurate information, knowledge of relationships, and rankings of one's goals is unlikely when actors are attempting to promote situational changes. Faced with these

[43] Bulow and Rogoff (1988b) develop a bargaining-theoretic model in which creditor governments are assumed to be part of three-way negotiations in which they seek to preserve some of the gains from trade.

[44] Aggarwal (1986) and Aggarwal and Allan (1990).

[45] I raised the possibility of this last issue in Aggarwal (1986), Chapter 4. Aggarwal and Allan (1990) develop a rigorous approach to examine this question.

[46] George (1980), p. 26.

impediments, decisionmakers often develop or use several coping mechanisms in foreign policy decisionmaking.

Based on these ideas, we can construct a sequential argument about the use of power resources, beginning with norms and rules, then escalating to the use of one's capabilities, and lastly to allies. If we only focus on costs, the use of capabilities or the addition of new issues will generally create a higher level of value-complexity because the problem of making trade-offs among goals becomes more difficult. The entrance of new actors will create greater uncertainty in the minds of policymakers since they may have their own goals. By contrast, appeals to meta-regimes and regimes do not necessarily introduce either new issues into the negotiations or new actors. If a bank asks a debtor to maintain its debt service in line with an agreed contract, negotiations remain restricted to financial issues and to the bank and debtor alone. The use of capabilities will generally introduce new issues. Lenders' efforts to undermine a debtor's government, for example, increases value-complexity as new issues are raised, forcing actors to make trade-offs. Lastly, employing alliances inevitably introduces new issues and, by definition, new actors into the picture. Securing allies, as we saw, often requires the use of capabilities and appeals to international arrangements. In this case, both the uncertainty level and the problem of value-complexity will be compounded.

This prediction of a likely sequence is complicated by the need to consider benefits – and not only costs. On the benefit side, it seems reasonable to assume that appeals to international arrangements will generally improve one's bargaining position less than the use of capabilities. Realists would, of course, subscribe to this notion. But even sophisticated Institutionalists see material capabilities as being more effective than appeals to norms and rules.[47] In general, at least for debt rescheduling involving banks or bondholders and indebted countries, it is also likely that allies such as creditor governments can bring considerable capabilities of their own to bear in negotiations, thus making this form of power use potentially more efficacious than using one's own capabilities. Thus, if we focused only on costs, we would then expect decisionmakers to turn to the most powerful approach to promote situational changes – namely allies and capabilities.

Given the diametrically opposite calculations for costs versus benefits, when actors make a direct cost-benefit analysis we could expect *any* sequence, because decisionmakers may not be able to accurately anticipate the costs and benefits of these measures. While they may suspect that capabilities are more powerful than appeals to international arrangements, they may be unsure of exactly how much more effective they really are, and must weigh the greater costs in using such power resources as compared to appeals to norms and rules. Moreover, if creditor governments already have a high propensity to intervene in one's favor, then one could well expect actors to appeal to allies quite readily.[48]

Although it is tempting to postulate some type of ordering in the use of power

[47] See Keohane (1984), Chapter 1. [48] This issue is treated formally in Aggarwal (1986).

resources (as well as in the aspects of one's own or opponent's situation that will be changed first), I have not found a method to accurately gauge the cost and benefit calculations that actors might use. Moreover, from my review of the empirical evidence presented in the cases in this book, there does not appear to be any obvious sequencing of situational change efforts. Both debtors and lenders commonly used more than one power resource at a time. For example, in the late 1980s, in their negotiations with Mexico as well as other debtors, banks attempted to improve their financial position, sought alliances with creditor governments and the IMF, and appealed to rules and procedures in their rescheduling arrangements. Still, my ideas about the higher costs of using capabilities and allies that result from increasing value-complexity and uncertainty might have some merit. When creditor governments became more intimately involved with debt rescheduling in the nineteenth century, and when the lenders actively sought U.S. pressure on debtors in the 1940s, they found creditor governments pursued their own objectives, often conflicting with the lenders' own goals.

In sum, I have identified several areas where refinements and changes to the approach developed in this book may prove fruitful. While I have shown some of the pros and cons of different approaches to examining strategic interaction, and have discussed my rationale for choosing the specific formulation in this book, those with somewhat different objectives may weigh the trade-offs differently. I hope to have demonstrated, however, that carefully specifying game payoffs and testing theoretical predictions against empirical cases is a fruitful avenue to pursue.

Generalizing the theoretical approach

The situational approach presented here can be usefully applied to other issue-areas in international relations. The specific variables and the way their interaction is modeled may vary, but the logic of constructing bargaining games and finding equilibria remains the same. In my collaborative research with Pierre Allan, for example, we have developed an ordinal, rather than a cardinal, model to construct game payoffs.[49] Our analysis focuses on the same three variables of coalitional stability, issue capabilities, and overall capabilities, and we operationalize these variables for different areas of international relations. We have shown that this model can successfully account for bargaining outcomes in cases involving international security, including the end of the Cold War, the Berlin Crises, and the Cuban missile crisis, as well as those dealing with economic issues such as U.S.–Hong Kong trade negotiations and Polish debt rescheduling.

In using a situational theory of bargaining to analyze international debt rescheduling or other areas of international relations, one could, of course, make different modelling assumptions and employ other analytical techniques. But the need to derive game payoffs systematically and to move beyond the illustrative use of game theory remains the central message of this book. Although few

[49] See Aggarwal and Allan (1991, 1992, 1993, 1994a, and 1994b).

would dispute that, in principle, rational choice approaches can provide a valuable instrument to analyze strategic interaction in international politics, in practice many remain skeptical of the empirical contributions of these efforts.[50] By melding theories from international politics and economics with rational choice tools, I have tried to illuminate the complex process of international debt rescheduling. I do not claim to have found the ideal path that addresses a host of competing theoretical and methodological concerns. But I do hope this work will encourage others to work toward more systematic development and testing of empirically grounded game models that integrate domestic and international factors to tackle the problems that confront the global political economy.

[50] In a recent book, Green and Shapiro (1994) criticize rational choice approaches for faulty empirical applications.

Mexico, epoch 1

	Individual situations		Preference ordering			Theoretical predictions[1]		
Bargaining period	Mexico	Lenders	Mexico	Lenders	Game type	Without intervention	With intervention	Empirical outcome
Period 1: 1827–1847	4	7	Deadlock	Harmony	Bully Analogue	LA, HC		LA, HC
Period 2: 1848–1863	4	3/7	Deadlock	Chicken	Bully	LA, HC	MA, HC	MA, HC
Period 3: 1863–1867	7	5	Harmony	Mix Deadlock, Deadlock Analogue	Bully Analogue	HA, LC	HA, LC	HA, LC

[1] Here and in subsequent tables, if no intervention is expected, then the "with intervention" column is left blank.

Peru, epoch 1

Bargaining period	Individual situations		Preference ordering		Game type	Theoretical predictions		Empirical outcome
	Peru	Lenders	Peru	Lenders		Without intervention	With intervention	
Period 1: 1823–1841	8	2/4	Mix Prisoner's Dilemma, Deadlock	Deadlock	Asymmetrical Deadlock	LA, LC		LA, LC
Period 2: 1841–1842	6	2/4	Mix Deadlock, Deadlock Analogue	Deadlock	Deadlock	LA, LC		LA, LC
Period 3: 1842–1844	4	2/4	Deadlock	Deadlock	Deadlock	LA, LC		LA, LC
Period 4: 1845–1847	3/4	1/8	Prisoner's Dilemma	Mix Hero, Deadlock	Complex	LA, H/M/LC	LA, MC	LA, MC
Period 5: 1848–1851	1/5	1/8	Hero Analogue	Mix Hero, Deadlock Analogue	Complex	LA, HC LA, MC HA, LC	HA, LC	HA, LC

Mexico, epoch 2

	Individual situations		Preference ordering			Theoretical predictions		
Bargaining period	Mexico	Lenders	Mexico	Lenders	Game type	Without intervention	With intervention	Empirical outcome
Period 1: 1867–1876	4	3	Deadlock	Mix Prisoner's Dilemma, Chicken	Complex	LA, H/M/LC		LA, LC
Period 2: 1877–1887	7	3	Harmony	Mix Prisoner's Dilemma, Chicken	Called Bluff Analogue	HA, LC		HA, LC
Period 3: 1888–1893	7	7	Harmony	Harmony	Harmony	HA, HC		HA, HC
Period 4: 1894–1910	1/5	7	Hero Analogue	Harmony	Pareto Suboptimal Asymmetrical	LA, HC		LA, HC
Period 5: 1911–1914	8	7	Mix Prisoner's Dilemma, Deadlock	Harmony	Bully-Called Bluff Analogue	LA, HC	HA, HC	LA, LC

Peru, epoch 2

Bargaining period	Individual situations		Preference ordering		Game type	Theoretical predictions		Empirical outcome
	Peru	Lenders	Peru	Lenders		Without intervention	With intervention	
Period 1: 1875–1876	4/8	3/7	Deadlock	Chicken	Bully	LA, HC		LA, HC
Period 2: 1875–1880	4/8	4/8	Deadlock	Deadlock	Deadlock	LA, LC	MA, LC	LA, LC
Period 3: 1880–1881 (Chile)	7	4/8	Harmony	Deadlock	Bully Analogue	HA, LC	HA, LC	HA, LC
Period 4: 1882–1886 (Chile)	5	3/8	Mix Deadlock, Deadlock Analogue	Prisoner's Dilemma	Asymmetrical Deadlock	LA, LC		LA, LC
Period 5: 1886–1887	7	3	Harmony	Mix Prisoner's Dilemma, Chicken	Called Bluff Analogue	HA, LC	HA, LC	HA, LC
Period 6: 1887–1889	8	3/4	Deadlock	Prisoner's Dilemma	Asymmetrical Deadlock	LA, LC	MA, LC	LA, LC
Period 7: 1889–1889	7/8	3/4	Chicken	Prisoner's Dilemma	Called Bluff	HA, LC	HA, LC	HA, LC

Mexico, epoch 3

	Individual situations		Preference ordering			Theoretical predictions		
Bargaining period	Mexico	Lenders	Mexico	Lenders	Game type	Without intervention	With intervention	Empirical outcome
Period 1: 1916–1920	4/8	5	Deadlock	Mix Deadlock, Deadlock Analogue	Deadlock	LA, LC	MA, LC	LA, LC
Period 2: 1921–1922	7/8	5	Chicken	Mix Deadlock, Deadlock Analogue	Bully	HA, LC	HA, LC	HA, LC
Period 3: 1923–1924	4/8	5	Deadlock	Mix Deadlock, Deadlock Analogue	Deadlock	LA, LC		LA, LC
Period 4: 1925–1926	2/5	5/7	Deadlock Analogue	Chicken	Bully	LA, HC	LA, MC	LA, MC
Period 5: 1927–1933	4/8	1/8	Deadlock	Mix Hero, Deadlock Analogue	Complex	LA, H/M/LC		LA, LC
Period 6: 1934–1936	2/5	7/8	Deadlock Analogue	Chicken	Bully	LA, HC		LA, LC
Period 7: 1937–1940	3	7/8	Mix Prisoner's Dilemma, Chicken	Chicken	Complex	LA, HC HA, LC MA, LC	LA, HC HA, LC MA, LC	LA, LC
Period 8: 1941–1942	5	7/8	Deadlock Analogue	Chicken	Bully	LA, HC	LA, HC	LA, HC

Peru, epoch 3

Bargaining period	Individual situations		Preference ordering		Game type	Theoretical predictions		Empirical outcome
	Peru	Lenders	Peru	Lenders		Without intervention	With intervention	
Period 1: 1930–1936	8, 2/8[1]	4/8	Mix Prisoner's Dilemma, Deadlock	Deadlock	Asymmetrical Deadlock	LA, LC		LA, LC
Period 2: 1936–1939	1/6	3/8	Deadlock	Prisoner's Dilemma	Asymmetrical Deadlock	LA, LC		LA, LC
Period 3: 1939–1943	3/7	3/7	Chicken	Chicken	Chicken	LA, HC HA, LC	MA, MC	LA, LC
Period 4: 1944–1945	3/5	3/7	Prisoner's Dilemma	Chicken	Called Bluff	LA, HC		LA, HC
Period 5: 1946–1947	4/8	3	Deadlock	Mix Chicken, Prisoner's Dilemma	Complex	LA, H/M/LC	LA, LC	LA, LC
Period 6a: 1948–1950	4/7	7	Prisoner's Dilemma	Harmony	Called Bluff Analogue	LA, HC		LA, HC
Period 6b: With Council	4/7	3/5	Prisoner's Dilemma	Prisoner's Dilemma	Prisoner's Dilemma	LA, LC	LA, LC	LA, LC
Period 7: 1951–1953	1	3/5	Apology Analogue	Prisoner's Dilemma	Protector Analogue	HA, LC		HA, LC

[1] The slight change is used for accuracy and technically should be a separate period.

Bargaining period	Individual situations		Preference ordering		Game type	Theoretical predictions		Empirical outcome
	Mexico	Lenders	Mexico	Lenders		Without intervention	With intervention	
Period 1: 1982–1983	7	8	Harmony	Mix Prisoner's Dilemma, Deadlock	Bully-Called Bluff Analogue	HA, LC	HA, MC	HA, MC
Period 2: 1983–1985	7	7	Harmony	Harmony	Harmony	HA, HC	HA, HC	HA, HC
Period 3: 1985–1987	7/8	7/8	Chicken	Chicken	Chicken	LA, HC HA, LC	MA, MC	MA, MC
Period 4: 1987–1988	2/8	2/6	Mix Deadlock, Deadlock Analogue	Deadlock Analogue	Deadlock	LA, LC		LA, LC
Period 5: 1988–1990	8	2/6	Mix Prisoner's Dilemma, Deadlock	Deadlock Analogue	Asymmetrical Deadlock	LA, LC	HA, HC	HA, HC

Peru, epoch 4

	Individual situations		Preference ordering			Theoretical predictions		
Bargaining period	Peru	Lenders	Peru	Lenders	Game type	Without intervention	With intervention	Empirical outcome
Period 1: 1983–1984	7	3	Harmony	Mix Chicken, Prisoner's Dilemma	Called Bluff Analogue	HA, LC	HA, LC	HA, LC
Period 2: 1984–1985	2/8	3	Mix Deadlock, Deadlock Analogue	Mix Chicken, Prisoner's Dilemma	Complex	LA, H/M/LC	LA, LC	LA, LC
Period 3: 1985–1986	5	3/5	Mix Deadlock, Deadlock Analogue	Prisoner's Dilemma	Asymmetrical Deadlock	LA, LC		LA, LC
Period 4: 1986–1990	8	5	Mix Prisoner's Dilemma, Deadlock	Mix Deadlock, Deadlock Analogue	Asymmetrical Deadlock	LA, LC		LA, LC

Argentina epoch 4

Bargaining period	Individual situations		Preference ordering		Game type	Theoretical predictions		Empirical outcome
	Argentina	Lenders	Argentina	Lenders		Without intervention	With intervention	
Period 1: 1982–1984	4/8	8	Deadlock	Mix Prisoner's Dilemma, Deadlock	Asymmetrical Deadlock	LA, LC	LA, MC	LA, MC
Period 2: 1984–1985	8	7/8	Mix Prisoner's Dilemma, Deadlock	Chicken	Called Bluff-Bully	LA, HC	MA, HC	LA, LC
Period 3: 1985	7/8	7/8	Chicken	Chicken	Chicken	LA, HC HA, LC	HA, HC MA, MC	MA, MC
Period 4: 1986–1987	8	7/8	Mix Prisoner's Dilemma, Deadlock	Chicken	Called Bluff-Bully	LA, HC		LA, HC[1]
Period 5: 1987–1989	8	2/6	Mix Prisoner's Dilemma, Deadlock	Deadlock Analogue	Asymmetrical Deadlock	LA, LC		LA, LC
Period 6: 1989–1991	7/8	1/6	Chicken	Deadlock Analogue	Bully	HA, LC		HA, LC
Period 7: 1991–1992	1/7	5/6	Apology	Mix Deadlock Analogue Deadlock	Protector Analogue	HA, LC	HA, MC	HA, MC

[1] Slightly different than predicted outcome. See text.

Brazil, epoch 4

Bargaining period	Individual situations		Preference ordering		Game type	Theoretical predictions		Empirical outcome
	Brazil	Lenders	Brazil	Lenders		Without intervention	With intervention	
Period 1: 1982–1983	8	8	Mix Prisoner's Dilemma, Deadlock	Mix Prisoner's Dilemma, Deadlock	Symmetrical Mixed Prisoner's Dilemma-Deadlock	LA, LC	MA, MC	LA, LC
Period 2: 1983–1984	8	7	Mix Prisoner's Dilemma, Deadlock	Harmony	Bully-Called Bluff Analogue	LA, HC	MA, HC	MA, HC
Period 3: 1984–1985	2	7	Variant of Deadlock, Deadlock Analogue	Harmony	Bully Analogue	LA, HC	LA, HC	LA, HC
Period 4: 1985–1987	2/8, 8[1]	7/8	Mix Deadlock, Deadlock Analogue	Chicken	Bully	LA, HC	MA, HC	MA, HC
Period 5: 1987	8	6/8	Mix Deadlock, Prisoner's Dilemma	Deadlock	Asymmetrical Deadlock	LA, LC		LA, LC
Period 6: 1987–1988	7/8	2/6	Chicken	Deadlock Analogue	Bully	HA, LC	HA, MC	HA, MC
Period 7: 1989–1990	8	2/6	Mix Deadlock, Prisoner's Dilemma	Deadlock Analogue Deadlock	Asymmetrical Deadlock	LA, LC		LA, LC

Period 8: 1990–1991	8	1/6	Mix Prisoner's Dilemma, Deadlock	Deadlock Analogue	Asymmetrical Deadlock	LA, LC	MA, MC	MA, MC
Period 9: 1991–1994	2	5/6	Mix Variant of Deadlock, Deadlock Analogue	Mix Deadlock, Deadlock Analogue	Asymmetrical Deadlock	LA, LC	MA, MC	MA, MC

[1] The slight change is used for accuracy and should technically be a separate period.

Appendix

This appendix will discuss how the bilateral model involving only a debtor and lenders, which might at first glance seem like a fairly simple one-shot game, compares to more elaborate models.[1] The discussion will show that the goodwill term, rather than representing a primitive element of a player's utility function, is a composite of several important features common in standard dynamic models of debt negotiation. These "off-the-shelf" models were not used in this book for two reasons. First, most existing models use only economic variables, failing to capture the political concerns that make international debt negotiations distinct from domestic debt relations. Second, most models do not allow for systematic coding of their variables. The model in this book has been driven by an interest in utilizing models that can be operationalized empirically by different scholars with a considerable degree of consistency.

The unenforceability of international debt contracts presents the modeler with the problem of explaining why agents ever agree to give anything away during rescheduling negotiations. Economists have been ingenious in designing models which can account for some of the phenomena observed in this issue area. For example, Bulow and Rogoff[2] use a bilateral bargaining game, which emphasizes the ability of players to impose costs on each other – not only through direct penalties but also by making counter-offers or imposing delays. Debtors and creditors vary in their ability to impose and to resist penalties. In my model, I generate a similar diversity of relations by explicitly coding both overall and debt-specific capabilities.

The classic article by Eaton, Gersovitz, and Stiglitz[3] includes the observation that penalty credibility (in a game-theoretic sense) requires an infinite two-way relation between debtor and lenders. This is true because, with strict rationality and a finite number of periods, cooperation can "unravel" starting in the last period (where there is no "shadow of the future") and working back. Rather than build such a model, which would require us to forecast how actor preferences will evolve over an infinite number of periods, I allow actors to calculate a value for interaction based on the play of the current round. In essence, the "goodwill" variable incorporates the "continuation payoffs" from future relations between actors into what would otherwise be a one-shot model. This will be demonstrated below in a sample model showing how actors incorporate possible situational change in their thinking.

The ability to impose penalties is generally considered central to understanding the willingness of banks to lend to sovereign debtors.[4] Where are the penalties in my model? They are implicit in the weights that I have assigned based on debt-specific and, especially, overall capabilities. A debtor (or a lender coalition) with high overall capabilities expects to be able to resist or counteract the penalty that will accompany low adjustment (by a debtor) or low concessions (by lenders). Their valuations of outcomes in which they "play low" are always higher over other outcomes ("strictly dominant" in the language of game theory) precisely because they can withstand the penalties that are assumed to follow non-cooperative behavior.

The model also treats another common feature of dynamic economic models – actors'

[1] I am deeply indebted to Greg Linden for helping me prepare this Appendix. I would also like to thank Cédric Dupont and Om P. Aggarwal for their comments.
[2] Bulow and Rogoff (1989b). [3] Eaton, Gersovitz, and Stiglitz (1986), p. 490.
[4] Eaton, Gersovitz, and Stiglitz (1986), Calvo et al. (1989).

time preferences. Time preferences capture an actor's subjective level of impatience. A very impatient actor would care only about what happens in the present (placing little value on the future) whereas a patient one gives more weight to future costs and benefits. For example, coalitionally unstable actors generally[5] place a lower weight (c or z) on the "goodwill" variable because they have a lower expectation of incumbency (debtor decision-makers) or of continuing as a bloc (lenders). Hence, they are less concerned about what transpires in future periods. Once again I have been able to replace an unobservable economic variable (discount rates) with an observable one (coalitional stability).[6]

The main difference between my model and most other treatments is the "goodwill" variable. Goodwill is not used here in the sense of a primitive concern for the welfare of others, but rather in a closely related sense of a derived concern for how one's actions will affect the future behavior of others.[7] However, instead of constructing an extensive-form model with multiple actors that tries to capture every factor of concern in debt rescheduling, I have found it more productive for my purposes to use a summary variable that I believe captures the richness of the bargaining while maintaining methodological tractability. Thus, goodwill serves as a repository for the potential penalties within a round and concern for possible situational change in future periods.

In this appendix, I do not show a one-to-one correspondence between the goodwill term in my model and some more complex game.[8] However, I will use the examples of penalties and concern about situational change to show how one of the more controversial features of the game – the willingness of some players to give more than they get ($A > L$ or $L > A$) – can be reproduced in a model with no goodwill term.

Penalties

To better see the connection between this model, in which the penalties are implicit, and the standard economic approach, we can consider a modified version of the debt game.[9] First, I will excise the implicit features of the model by simply truncating the goodwill term from each utility function, so debtors and lenders care only about getting more and giving less.[10] In game theoretic terms, this means that the lowest action will "strictly dominate" higher actions. For simplicity, I will use only a 2×2 matrix with only "high" and "low" choices, which preserves the essential features of the model. A typical matrix will look like Figure A.1, with the Nash equilibrium marked by an asterisk. In this instance the game is between an IS 2 debtor and IS 2 lender with the truncated utility functions.

In more general terms, the payoffs would be as shown in Figure A.2.

Next, we will assume that each player will try to punish the other any time its opponent plays "low."[11] Let Pd be the punishment imposed by the debtor on the creditor and Pc

[5] That this is not always the case (i.e., c and z are not strictly lower for unstable actors) is due to the fact that a single coefficient (the weight on "goodwill") is doing double duty. It captures both the concern for future penalties, and the desire of actors to "bribe" their counterpart to avoid instigating situational change and replaying the game (see Chapter 4). Users of the model with a theoretic orientation could explicitly separate these two characteristics.

[6] Note that coalitional stability has its primary effect on an actor's willingness to undertake economic adjustment.

[7] Such strategic considerations are at the heart of game theory, but in this case, the concerns extend to third parties or even members of one's own coalition.

[8] For an effort along these lines, see Aggarwal and Dupont (1992).

[9] The following model is meant to be suggestive of the relationship between the model used in this book and a more conventional theoretical approach. It is not intended as a comprehensive model of debt rescheduling.

[10] This makes the remaining model functionally similar to economic models in which banks seek to maximize profits and debtors seek to maximize consumption.

[11] For now, we will assume the credibility of this strategy by letting penalties be costless to impose. It will be shown that even with small costs, penalties are credible to the extent that they increase one's payoff by forcing an opponent to switch from "low" to "high."

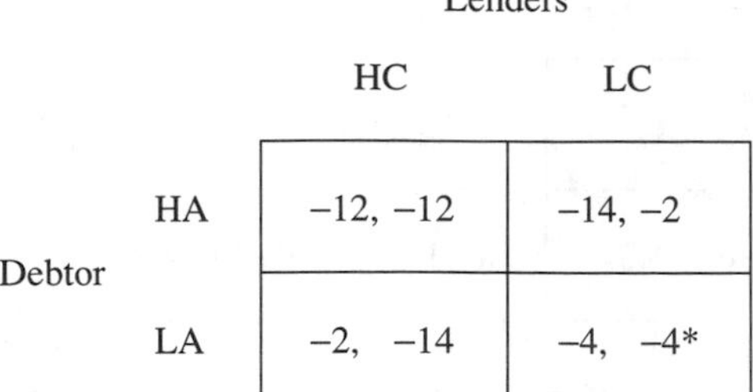

		Lenders HC	Lenders LC
Debtor	HA	−12, −12	−14, −2
	LA	−2, −14	−4, −4*

Figure A.1

	HC	LC
HA	aHC − bHA, yHA − xHC	aLC − bHA, yHA − xLC
LA	aHC − bLA, yLA − xHC	aLC − bLA, yLA − xLC*

Figure A.2

	HC	LC
HA	aHC − bHA, yHA − xHC	aLC − bHA, yHA − xLC − zPd
LA	aHC − bLA − cPc, yLA − xHC	aLC − bLA − cPc, yLA − xLC − zPd

Figure A.3

be the punishment imposed by the creditor. In order to be consistent, we need to provide a weight for the penalty, and the coefficients "c" and "z" used for the goodwill measure are suitable for demonstration purposes. The one-shot game with penalties is now as shown in Figure A.3.

Substituting 1 and 3 for "low" and "high," we get Figure A.4. There is now no longer an unconditional Nash equilibrium. If Pc < 2b/c and Pd < 2x/z, then (LA, LC) is still the Nash equilibrium. But if Pc > 2b/c and Pd > 2x/z, then (HA, HC) is the Nash. If Pd < 2x/z and Pc > 2b/c, then (HA, LC) is the Nash. And finally, if Pd > 2x/z and Pc < 2b/c, then (LA, HC) is the Nash.[12] This shows one of the ways in which play can be driven from (LA, LC) to one of the other outcomes, as occurs in the non-truncated model.

So far, we have treated penalties as though they can be imposed instantaneously. It is probably more realistic to model sanctions that take time to put in place. Doing so

[12] In practice, quantifying these penalties is extremely difficult.

	HC	LC
HA	$3a - 3b, 3y - 3x$	$a - 3b, 3y - x - zPd$
LA	$3a - b - cPc, y - 3x$	$a - b - cPc, y - x - zPd$

Figure A.4

requires us to construct an extensive form version of the truncated game with penalties. I make the following assumptions. First, I will assume that the creditor is able to inflict (costlessly, although this is not necessary)[13] a penalty on the debtor greater than 2b/c. And second, I will assume that the debtor is not able to inflict any penalty greater than 2x/z. Finally, we will assume that a penalty is slow to be imposed, but can subsequently be readily stopped if the other player behaves as desired.

I construct the game as follows. Play will occur in two parts (which are internal to the "rounds" discussed in the empirical chapters). Both players have the truncated version of the utility function. In the first part, the players play a simultaneous "high-low" game. In the second part, after penalties have or have not been put in place, the players renegotiate. If the opponent plays low and one of the players has decided to impose a penalty, he then does so.

The extensive form version of this game is presented in Figure A.5, in which simultaneous-move parts are shown by a normal-form matrix. Using the notion of subgame perfection (closely related to the Nash equilibrium concept used in this book), we can solve the tree. Based on our assumptions about penalty size, the Nash equilibrium for each of the possible second part games is indicated by an asterisk. Because the debtor is not able to penalize lenders enough to change their behavior, the debtor's decision to penalize will not change its own payoff. The opposite is true of lenders, who receive strictly larger payoffs by deciding to impose sanctions by forcing the debtor to change its choice. This means that in the second part of the game, the creditor will definitely punish and the debtor will not.[14] The equilibrium payoffs in the game on that branch are $a - 3b$ and $3y - x$.

In order to continue solving the model back through its first part, we must introduce an explicit discount factor δ ($0 < \delta < 1$) which will enable us to measure the present value of the second part payoffs as viewed from the first part.[15]

We can now move up the tree to part one and ask which actions will be optimal for both players. Now, instead of considering part one actions in isolation, the part one choice must take into account the discounted payoffs from the second part. Thus, $\delta(a - 3b)$ must be added to each of the debtor's first part payoffs and $\delta(3y - x)$ must be added to the creditor's first part payoffs in order to see the payoffs from the full round. Because these amounts are not contingent on first part actions, this is simply adding a constant to

[13] Letting the cost of sanctions be k, rearranging the condition $(3y - x - k) > (y - x)$ yields the necessary condition that sanctions will be credible provided they cost no more than 2y to impose. In the alternate case where penalties bring net benefits to the penalizer (e.g., confiscation of assets), they could be imposed even when they do not change the behavior of the other player.

[14] The debtor would be indifferent if penalties are costless to impose, so we will assume a small cost of imposing penalties to make the decision firm. This assumption will not affect the calculations for the creditor.

[15] In practice, each actor could have a different discount factor, but for ease of exposition, we will assume that actors share a common one.

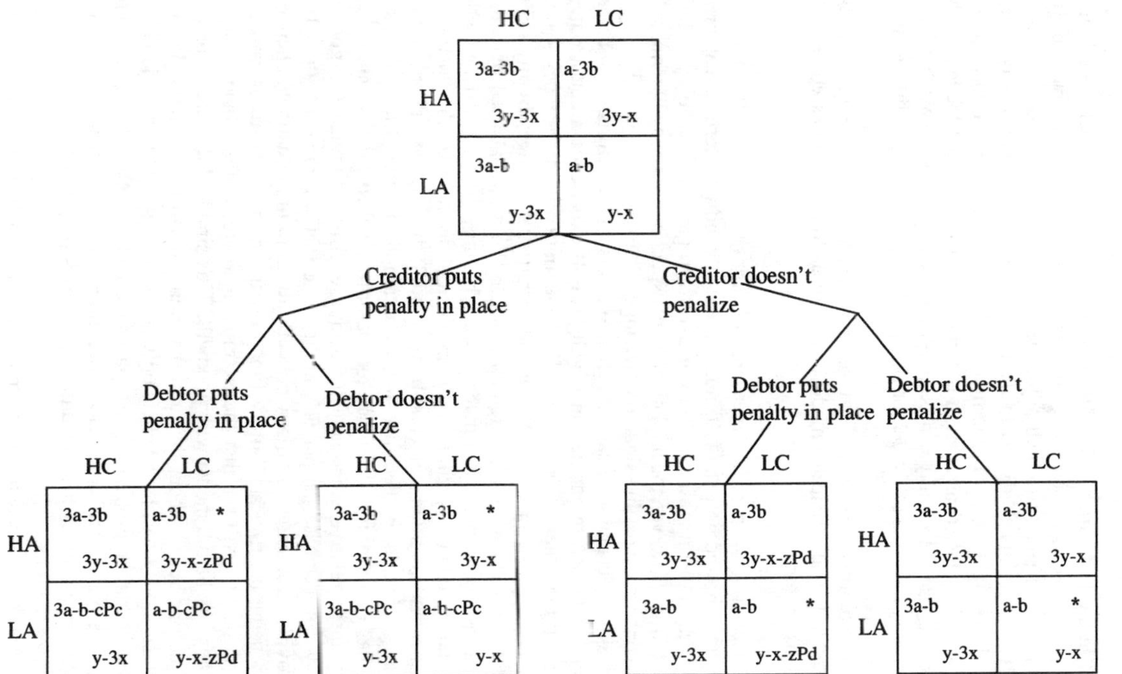

Figure A.5. *Two-part "truncated" model with penalties*

each payoff in the first part, which does not alter the game. In other words, the first part will still exhibit "low-low" behavior. Only when the penalty is in place (in the second part) will the debtor submit to high adjustment.

To clarify, the penalty that leads to the outcome of the second part is never actually imposed in this simple model. In the first part, players have no reason to play anything other than "low." By the second part, it is common knowledge that the lenders have done all they need so that the penalty can be imposed "at the flip of a switch," which makes the penalty unnecessary since the debtor changes from low to high adjustment rather than suffer the penalty.[16]

The simple extensive form game analyzed above shows one sense in which the impact of "goodwill" in the non-truncated model corresponds to the compressed result of a more explicit extensive form game.

Concern about possible situational changes

The last section showed how the full model uses a "goodwill" term to capture a fear of penalties that might be imposed in an extensive form game where utility functions have the truncated form. However, the implicit penalty aspect of the goodwill term is dominated by another concern – possible situational changes.

As described in Chapter 4, situational change refers to the efforts of an actor to move from one joint situation to another, in which he will experience a better outcome (and doesn't care if the other fares worse). We have built into the model – through the goodwill term (A/L – 1 or L/A – 1) – the idea that such changes by my opponent are more likely to succeed when the bargaining has led to an unbalanced outcome (A < L or A > L) favorable to me. When outcomes are balanced (e.g., LA, LC), both players, neither of whom are unitary, will find it more difficult to mobilize their power resources, including allies and coalition members. In my model, the relative outcome influences the optimal strategy, but not in the sense that, for example, Joseph Grieco argues. For him, actors may have a primitive preference for maximizing their relative gains.[17] In the full debt model, large relative gains actually decrease utility (through the goodwill term) because they will decrease the player's ability to effect favorable situational change.

I will provide an illustration of how concern about future situational change could be modeled by using the truncated utility functions in an extensive form game. As in the case of penalties, we will see that the example leads to results which are qualitatively similar to those in the full model with goodwill. This simple illustration already involves variables (such as beliefs about the future) which are virtually impossible to observe.

In this illustration, actors have beliefs only about four possible future joint situations.[18] The key idea is that the probability distributions about the future that follow unbalanced outcomes in the present are more heavily weighted (probabilistically) on joint situations with equilibrium outcomes that are unfavorable to a player with large relative gains in the current negotiations.

Figure A.6 shows a sequence of normal-form games between players whose utility functions are truncated versions of those in the full model (i.e., aL – bA and yA – xL).

[16] Obviously sanctions *are* imposed in the course of debt negotiations. This could occur for many reasons, among which are uncertainty by the debtor about the size of the penalty (a more complex modeling problem) or an action that brings net benefits to one of the players during negotiations. It is worth noting that the duration of "part one" clearly depends on the speed with which a player can put a penalty in place. With more complex penalties, we would expect to see some non-cooperation prior to an agreement. With instantaneous penalties, the game consists only of the second part.

[17] See Grieco (1988). For a criticism of this assumption, see Powell (1991), Snidal (1991a, 1991b).

[18] A truly general treatment of concern about situational change would be extremely difficult to illustrate because for each outcome of a single period, actors would need a probability distribution over the 64 possible joint situations that might emerge from situational change efforts.

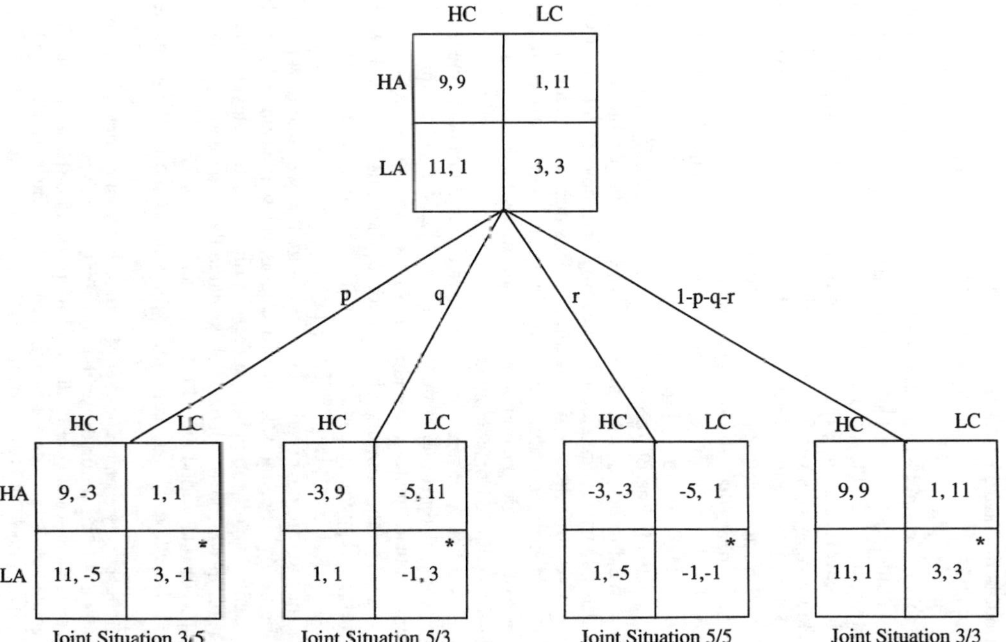

Figure A.6. *"Truncated" model with possible situational change*

In the first period, both players are in Individual Situation 3 (overall strong, issue weak, and stable), leading to the one-period payoffs shown in the upper 2 × 2 matrix.[19] In the second period, the two players will have made efforts to increase issue strength (i.e., trying to move to IS 5, overall strong, issue strong, and stable). Based on their success or failure, they will find themselves playing in new joint situation 3/5, 5/3, or 5/5, or they might remain in situation 3/3. Players will choose an optimal strategy by maximizing the sum of first period payoffs and the expected value of the second period payoffs. A careful inspection of Figure A.6 will reveal a problem: the payoffs to players in IS 3 range from 1 to 11 while those in IS 5 range from −5 to 1. Since the only difference in the two situations is that IS 5 has more debt-specific resources, it would clearly be a mistake to conclude from the numbers that IS 5 is everywhere worse off than IS 3. This incommensurability has not posed a problem before because we have not tried to add payoffs across situations as we are about to do.

The problem is actually one of "zero-point and unit interval,"[20] that is, the payoffs in the two situations need to be put into the same scale for comparability. As described in Chapter 3, the utility functions are cardinal, meaning that they are quantitative measures for which the relative differences have meaning.[21] This does not mean that payoffs can automatically be added across situations. The Fahrenheit and Celsius scales are also cardinal measures of a single phenomenon, but one needs to be converted to the other before they can be compared or combined.

Fortunately, all cardinal measures preserve their cardinality under linear transformations. Therefore, we can adjust one of the sets of payoffs. We will do this by finding the linear transformation that equates the endpoints of the two sets of payoffs (i.e., equates $\{-5, 1\}$ with $\{1, 11\}$).[22] The formula which accomplishes this is $1.67x + 9.33$, where x is the original value.[23] Applying this to each payoff in the truncated IS 5 utility function converts $\{-5, -3, -1, 1\}$ into $\{1, 4.33, 7.67, 11\}$.

Having done this, we are now ready to revise Figure A.6 with the new payoffs, which are shown in Figure A.7. For the sake of illustration, we will assume this to be a finite game. By the definition of sub-game perfect equilibrium, the players must play the unique equilibrium in whichever second-period game they find themselves.[24] Each Nash equilibrium in the second period is indicated by an asterisk.

During period one, players share common beliefs about the particular game that will

[19] As was done in the penalty example, the set of actions has been restricted to "high" and "low" for each player to simplify the illustration without loss of generality.

[20] The phrase is from the discussion of cardinality on pp. 14–15 of Hirshleifer and Riley (1992).

[21] The contrast would be with an ordinal function such as the function which assigns 1, 2, 3 . . . to a set of payoffs without respect to relative magnitudes. In such a case, the fact that 3–2 has the same value as 2–1 is of no interest since payoff #3 could be much larger than #2 or it could be nearly the same size. These ordinal utilities, unlike those used in this book, tell us nothing about the intensity of the preferences involved.

[22] I do not claim that this is an exact procedure. However, the payoffs apply to broad ranges ("high" and "low") to begin with. It is reasonable to proceed by equating the best and worst outcomes across the two situations and letting the intermediate values fall where they may. The argument that IS 5 is somehow richer or stronger than IS 3 and should therefore have higher utility overall is unconvincing because we are trying to measure how the players feel about outcomes, not the outcomes themselves. This is therefore similar to the debate whether a millionaire derives the same intensity of pleasure from an extra dollar of consumption as does a pauper.

[23] It is reasonable to ask why we are not performing this operation on the complete (i.e., including goodwill) versions of the same situational payoffs. If we did so, the transformation would be $1.9x + 9.7$, which is not sufficiently different to be of concern in this appendix.

[24] This is done for analytical convenience. An ideal model of situational change is potentially infinite. We could capture some of this by using the goodwill term to derive the second period payoffs, but this would be assuming what we are trying to prove, which is that actors might not play the one-shot Nash equilibrium in the first period when they are concerned about the future.

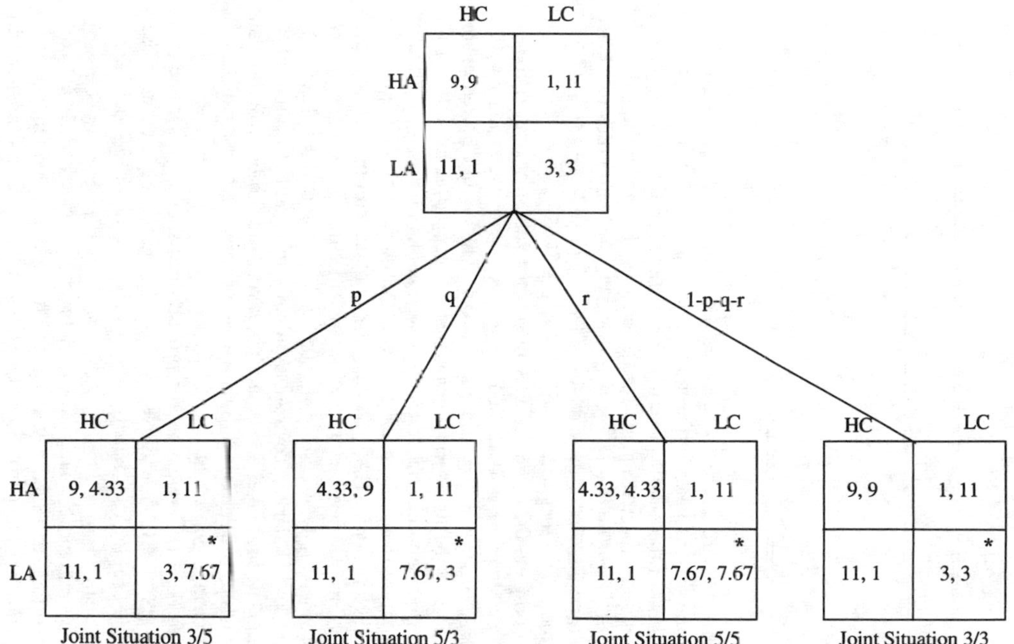

Figure A.7. *Adjusted "truncated" model with possible situational change*

Table A.1. *Probability distributions*

Period one outcome	p	q	r	1 − p − q − r
(LA, LC)	0.1	0.1	0.2	0.6
(HA, HC)	0.05	0.05	0.1	0.8
(HA, LC)	0.05	0.8	0.1	0.05
(LA, HC)	0.8	0.05	0.1	0.05

be played in period two. These probabilities are p, q, r, and 1 − p − q − r,[25] which are contingent on the actions taken in the first period. The total expected payoff for the two periods is the sum of the payoff in period one (denoted in the following formulas as P1) plus the discounted expected payoff for period two. For the debtor the total payoff is $P1 + \delta[p(3)q(7.67) + r(7.67) + (1 - p - q - r)(3)]$. This simplifies to $P1 + \delta(3 + 4.67q + 4.67r)$. The total payoff for the creditor is $P1 + \delta[p(7.67) + q(3) + r(7.67) + (1 - p - q - r)(3)]$, which simplifies to $P1 + \delta(3 + 4.67p + 4.67r)$.

In order to complete the example, we will specify values of p, q, r, and δ. First of all, if the period one outcome is (LA, LC), let us set p = q = 0.1 and r = 0.2, and if the outcome is (HA, HC), p = q = 0.05 and r = 0.1. This would be reasonable because a balanced outcome in the first period means that neither player has a better possibility for situational improvement than the other, and that it is more likely for both to improve their issue strength rather than only one. However, the most likely outcome is no change.

When period one play is (HA, LC), then the unbalanced outcome will give the debtor a better chance of (and greater motivation for) mobilizing resources to improve issue strength. Correspondingly, we set p = 0.05, q = 0.8, and r = 0.1. A player who has benefitted from an unbalanced contract is unlikely to be able to (or want to) move to a better situation. The high likelihood that the player with the unfavorable outcome in the first period will succeed in changing the situation leaves a low residual probability that no situational change will occur.

Following an (LA, HC) outcome, the probabilities should be symmetric to those just assigned: p = 0.8, q = 0.05, and r = 0.1. For clarity, we will restate these values in a probability table (Table A.1). Finally, we specify a common discount factor δ = 0.9 to complete this example.

We now have all the elements we need to complete a 2 × 2 matrix (Figure A.8) representing the total expected payoffs in the full game contingent on first period play. The strategy chosen by a player now has two parts: one for each period of play. As explained above, the second period action is always "low."

As indicated by the asterisks, there are two possible Nash equilibria in the full game, making this normal-form version of the dynamic game we are studying equivalent to the textbook case known as "Chicken." First period play has moved from its one-shot outcome (LA, LC) because each player's expected outcome in the second period is a function of the outcome in the first. The players cannot do better by "stalling" and striving for situational change immediately since this is like playing (LA, LC) in period one, and the probabilities for change are not as favorable as when one of the unbalanced outcomes occurs in the first period.

The 2 × 2 version of the full goodwill model of the joint situation 3/3 game has the payoffs and equilibria shown in Figure A.9. Although the two matrices differ by the presence of the LA, LC equilibrium in the goodwill model, the similarity is of greater interest – the goodwill model and the above illustration share "Chicken" equilibria.

[25] Probability distributions must always sum to unity. Therefore, with four possibilities, knowing any three probabilities determines the fourth.

	HC→ LC	LC→ LC
HA→ LA	12.33, 12.33	* 7.48, 14.33
LA→ LA	* 14.33, 7.48	6.96, 6.96

Figure A.8

	HC	LC
HA	9.0, 9.0	3.0, 10.3 *
LA	10.3, 3.0 *	3.0, 3.0 *

Figure A.9

Therefore, as we did for penalties, we have now shown the similarity between the full model with goodwill and an extensive form game built with truncated utility functions.

If our goal was to build a more complex model, we would next combine the separate penalty and situational change models in a single example. We should see, for instance, that concern about situational change lowers the threshold level of penalties that is necessary to change one's behavior. But in the end, we would only have a model that functions like the goodwill model in Chapter 3, but one which would be much less useful.

No claim is being made that goodwill corresponds precisely to the models of penalties and situational change that we have constructed here for explanatory purposes. The model used in this book was built from readily observable variables in a way that captures enough of the effect of broader concerns (like those described in this appendix) that meaningful predictions could be made. Researchers with goals other than the extended empirical analysis that is at the heart of this volume may choose to reverse the trade-off and build a theoretical model from first principles. If so, I hope this appendix will provide a basis for this effort.

Bibliography

Acharya, S., and I. Diwan, 1993. "Debt Buybacks Signal Sovereign Countries' Creditworthiness – Theory and Tests." *International Economic Review*, vol. 34, no. 4 (November), pp. 795–817.

Adler, Emanuel, 1987. *The Power of Ideology: The Quest for Technological Autonomy in Argentina and Brazil* (Berkeley: University of California Press).

Aggarwal, Vinod K., 1983. "The Unraveling of the Multi-Fiber Arrangement, 1981: An Examination of International Regime Change." *International Organization*, vol. 37, no. 4 (Autumn), pp. 617–645.

Aggarwal, Vinod K., 1985. *Liberal Protectionism: The International Politics of Organized Textile Trade* (Berkeley: University of California Press).

Aggarwal, Vinod K., 1986. *Defusing the Debt Bomb: Conflict, Cooperation and Costs in International Debt Rescheduling*. Unpublished manuscript.

Aggarwal, Vinod K., 1987. *International Debt Threat: Bargaining among Creditors and Debtors in the 1980's* (Berkeley: IIS Policy Paper, no. 29).

Aggarwal, Vinod K., 1989. "Interpreting the History of Mexico's External Debt Crises." In Eichengreen and Lindert, 1989, pp. 140–188.

Aggarwal, Vinod K., 1990. "Foreign Debt: The Mexican Experience." *Relazioni Internazionali* (September), pp. 26–33.

Aggarwal, Vinod K., 1991. "Debt Forgiveness: Dangerous Trend or Absolute Necessity?" *World Link*, vol. 4, no. 5 (September/October), pp. 37–39.

Aggarwal, Vinod K., and Pierre Allan, 1983. "Evolution in Bargaining Theories: Toward an Integrated Approach to Explain Strategies of the Weak." Paper presented at the American Political Science Association meetings, Chicago, September.

Aggarwal, Vinod K., and Pierre Allan, 1990. "Modeling Game Change: The Berlin Deadline, Berlin Wall, and Cuban Missile Crisies." Paper presented at the American Political Science Association meetings, San Francisco, August.

Aggarwal, Vinod K., and Pierre Allan, 1991. "Obiettivi, Preferènzie, e Giòchi: Verso una Teorìa della Contratazióne Internazionale." In Guerrieri and Padoan, 1991, pp. 39–70.

Aggarwal, Vinod K., and Pierre Allan, 1992. "Cold War Endgames." In Allan and Goldmann, 1992, pp. 24–54.

Aggarwal, Vinod K., and Pierre Allan, 1993. "Cycling over Berlin: The Deadline and Wall Crises." In Caldwell and McKeown, 1993, pp. 209–226.

Aggarwal, Vinod K., and Pierre Allan, 1994a. "The Origin of Games: A Theory of the Formation of Ordinal Preferences and Games." In Intriligator and Luterbacher, 1994, pp. 299–325.

Aggarwal, Vinod K., and Pierre Allan, 1994b. "Preferences, Constraints, and Games: Analyzing Polish Debt Negotiations with International Banks." In Allan and Schmidt, 1994, pp. 9–49.

Aggarwal, Vinod K., and Maxwell Cameron, 1994. "Modelling Peruvian Debt Rescheduling in the 1980s." *Studies in Comparative International Development*, vol. 29, no. 2 (Summer), pp. 48–81.

Aggarwal, Vinod K., and Cédric Dupont, 1992. "Modeling International Debt Rescheduling: Choosing Game Theoretic Representations and Deriving Payoffs." Paper presented at the American Political Science Association meetings, Chicago, September.

Aizenman, J., 1991. "Trade Dependency, Bargaining and External Debt." *Journal of International Economics*, vol. 31, nos. 1–2 (August), pp. 101–120.

Akerlof, George, 1970. "The Market for 'Lemons': Quality Uncertainty and the Market Mechanism." *Quarterly Journal of Economics*, vol. 84, no. 3 (August), pp. 488–500.

Aldcroft, Derek Howard, 1977. *From Versailles to Wall Street, 1919–1929* (London: Allen Lane).

Alford, A., and J. Lussier, 1993. "An Examination of the Price Discount on the External Debt of Developing Countries." *World Economy*, vol. 16, no. 6 (November), pp. 713–724.

Aliber, Robert Z., 1973. *The International Money Game* (New York: Basic Books).

Allan, Pierre, 1983. *Crisis Bargaining and the Arms Race: A Theoretical Model* (Cambridge, Mass.: Ballinger Publishing Co.).

Allan, Pierre, 1984. "Comment Négocier en Situation de Faiblesse? Une Typologie des Stratégies à Disposition." *Annuaire Suisse de Science Politique*, vol. 24, pp. 223–237.

Allan, Pierre, and Kjell Goldmann, eds., 1992. *The End of The Cold War: Evaluating Theories of International Relations* (Dordrecht: M. Nijhoff).

Allan, Pierre, and Christian Schmidt, eds., 1994. *Game Theory and International Relations: Preferences, Information, and Empirical Evidence* (Brookfield, Vt.: E. Elgar).

Altimir, Oscar, and Robert Devlin, eds., 1994. *Moratoria de la Deuda en América Latina* (Buenos Aires: Fondo de Cultura Económica de Argentina).

American Academy of Political and Social Science, 1914. *International Relations of the United States*, vol. 54, no. 143.

American Express International Banking Corp., 1982. *Sovereign Debt Rescheduling: The Implications for Private Banks* (London: The Amex Bank Review. Special papers, no. 4).

Ames, Rolando, 1980. "Gran Burguesia y Movimiento Popular: Las dos Fuerzas en Pugna." *Que Hacer*, vol. 50 (June), pp. 13–24.

The Andean Report (various).

Angell, Alan, 1984. "The Difficulties of Policy Making and Implementation in Peru." *Bulletin of Latin American Research*, vol. 3, no. 1 (January), pp. 25–43.

Angell, Alan, and Rosemary Thorp, 1980. "Inflation, Stabilization and Attempted Redemocratization in Peru, 1975–1979." *Bulletin of Latin American Research*, vol. 3, no. 1 (January), pp. 36–71.

Angell, James, 1933. *The Financial Policy of the United States* (New York: Russel & Russel).

Armendariz de Aghion, Beatrice, 1993. "Analytical Issues on LDC Debt: A Survey." *The World Economy*, vol. 16, no. 4 (July), pp. 467–482.

Aronson, Jonathan David, 1977. *Money and Power: Banks and the World Monetary System* (Beverly Hills: Sage Publications).

Aronson, Jonathan David, ed., 1979. *Debt and the Less Developed Countries* (Boulder: Westview Press).

Arora, Vivek B., 1993. *Sovereign Debt: A Survey of Some Theoretical and Policy Issues* (Washington, D.C.: International Monetary Fund, IMF working paper, WP/93/56).

Arrow, Kenneth 1968. "The Economics of Moral Hazard: Further Comment." *American Economic Review*, vol. 58, no. 3, pp. 537–539.

Asheshov, Nicholas, 1977. "Peru's Flirtation with Disaster." *Institutional Investor* (October), pp. 181–190.

Ashesov, Nicholas, 1988. "The 1987 Peruvian Bank Crisis." *The Andean Report* (October), pp. 233–247.

Axelrod, Robert, 1970. *Conflict of Interest: A Theory of Divergent Goals with Applications to Politics* (Chicago: Markham Publishing Co.).

Axelrod, Robert, 1981. "The Emergence of Cooperation among Egoists." *American Political Science Review*, vol. 75, no. 12 (June), pp. 306–318.

Axelrod, Robert, 1984. *The Evolution of Cooperation* (New York: Basic Books).

Axelrod, Robert, and Robert O. Keohane, 1985. "Achieving Cooperation under Anarchy: Strategies and Institutions." *World Politics*, vol. 38, no. 1 (October), pp. 226–254.

Bacha, E., 1992. "External Debt, Net Transfers, and Growth in Developing Countries." *World Development*, vol. 20, no. 8 (August), pp. 1183–1192.

Bagehot, Walter, 1873. *Lombard Street: A Description of the Money Market* (New York: Scribner; Armstrong & Co.).

Bailey, Norman, and Richard Cohen, 1987. *The Mexican Time Bomb* (New York: Priority Press Publications).

Baldwin, David A., 1979. "Power Analysis and World Politics: New Trends vs. Old Tendencies." *World Politics*, vol. 31, pp. 161–194.

Baldwin, David A., 1980. "Interdependence and Power: A Conceptual Analysis." *International Organization*, vol. 34, no. 4, pp. 471–506.

Baldwin, David A., 1985. *Economic Statecraft* (Princeton: Princeton University Press).

Baldwin, David A., ed., 1993. *Neorealism and Neoliberalism: The Contemporary Debate* (New York: Columbia University Press).

Baldwin, Robert, 1986. "Lobbying for Public Goods: The Case of Import Protection." Paper Presented at Conference on The Political Economy of Trade Policy, Massachusetts, January 10–11.

Ballon, Eduardo, ed., 1986. *Movimientos Sociales y Crisis: El Caso Peruano*. (Lima: Centro de Estudios y Promoción del Desarrollo).

Bambirra, Vania, 1974. *El Capitalismo Dependiente Latinoamericano* (Mexico: Siglo Veintiuno Editores).

Banco Central de Reserva, 1985. *La Renegociación de la Deuda Externa 1983–1984: El Caso Peruano* (Lima).

Banco de Credito del Perú, 1985a. "Foreign Investment 1985 – I." *Peruvian Quarterly Report*, New York.

Banco de Credito del Perú, 1985b. "The García Administration 1985 – II." *Peruvian Quarterly Report*, New York.

Banco de Credito del Perú, 1986. "The Banking System." *Peruvian Quarterly Report*, New York.

Bancroft, Hubert Howe, 1885. *History of Mexico*, vol. 5, 1824–1861 (San Francisco: A.L. Bancroft and Co.).

The Banker (various).

Bank for International Settlements. *Annual Reports* (Basel), various.

Basagni, Fabio, ed., 1983. *International Debt, Financial Stability, and Growth* (Paris: Atlantic Institute for International Affairs, no. 51).

Basu, Kaushik, 1991. *The International Debt Problem, Credit Rationing, and Loan Pushing: Theory and Experience* (Princeton: International Finance Section, Dept. of Economics, Princeton University, Princeton Studies in International Finance, no. 70).

Batista, Jorge Chami, 1992. *Debt and Adjustment Policies in Brazil* (Boulder: Westview Press).

Bazant, Jan, 1968. *Historia de la Deuda Exterior de México, 1823–1946* (Mexico: Colegio de México Centro de Estudios Historicos).

Becker, David, 1982. "Bonanza Development and the New Bourgeoisie: Peru under Military Rule." *Comparative Political Studies*, vol. 15, pp. 243–288.

Becker, David, 1983. *The New Bourgeoisie and the Limits of Dependency: Mining, Class and Power in "Revolutionary" Peru* (Princeton: Princeton University Press).

Berger, James O., 1980. *Statistical Decision Theory, Foundations, Concepts and Methods* (New York: Springer-Verlag).

Bergsten, C. Fred, 1975. *Dilemmas of the Dollar: The Economics and Politics of United States International Monetary Policy* (New York: New York University Press).

Bergsten, C. Fred, William R. Cline, and John Williamson, 1985. *Bank Lending to Developing Countries: The Policy Alternatives* (Washington, D.C.: Institute for International Economics, Policy Analyses in International Economics, no. 10, April).

Bester, Helmut, 1994. "The Role of Collateral in a Model of Debt Renegotiation." *Journal of Money, Credit and Banking*, vol. 26, no. 1 (February), pp. 72–86.

Biersteker, Thomas J., 1990. "Reducing the Role of the State in the Economy – A Conceptual Exploration of the IMF and World Bank Prescriptions." *International Studies Quarterly*, vol. 34, no. 4 (December), pp. 477–492.

Biersteker, Thomas J., ed., 1993. *Dealing with Debt: International Financial Negotiations and Adjustment Bargaining* (Boulder: Westview Press).

Bird, Graham R., 1989. *Loan-loss Provisions and Third-World Debt* (Princeton: International Finance Section, Dept. of Economics, Princeton University, Essays in International Finance, no. 176).

Blake, David H., and Robert S. Walters, 1992. *The Politics of Global Economic Relations*, 4th ed. (Englewood Cliffs: Prentice Hall).

Blakemore, Harold, 1974. *British Nitrates and Chilean Politics, 1886–1896: Balmaceda and North* (London: Athlone Press for the Institute of Latin American Studies, no. 4).

Block, Fred, 1977. *The Origins of International Economic Disorder: A Study of United States International Monetary Policy from World War II to the Present* (Berkeley: University of California Press).

Blunden, George, 1977. "International Cooperation in Banking Supervision." *Bank of England Quarterly Bulletin*, vol. 17, no. 3, pp. 325–329.

Bogdanowicz, Bindert C.A., 1985. "The Debt Crisis: The Case of the Small and Medium Size Debtors." *Journal of International Law and Politics*, vol. 17, no. 3 (Spring), pp. 527–532.

Bolivar, Símon, 1979. *Doctrina del Liberador*, ed. Manuel Pérez Vila (Caracas).

Boloña Behr, Carlos, 1993. *Cambio de Rumbo: El Programa Economico para los '90*, 2d ed. (Peru: Instituto de Economia de Libre Mercado).

Bonilla, Heraclio, 1974. *Guano y Burguesia en el Perú* (Lima: Instituto de Estudios Peruanos).

Bonilla, Heraclio, 1980. *Un Siglo a la Deriva: Ensayos sobre el Perú, Bolivia y la Guerra* (Lima: Instituto de Estudios Peruanos, Serie Estudios Historicos, no. 7).

Bonilla, Heraclio, ed., 1986a. *Las Crisis Económicas en la Historia del Perú* (Lima: Centro Latinoamericano de Historia Economica y Social).

Bonilla, Heraclio, 1986b. "La Crisis de 1872." In Bonilla, 1986, pp. 167–183.

Bonilla, Heraclio, ed., 1992. *Los Conquistados: 1492 y la Poblacion Indigena de las Américas* (Bogotá: Tercer Mundo Editores).

Booth, David, and Bernardo Sorj, eds., 1983. *Military Reformism and Social Classes: The Peruvian Experience, 1968–1980* (London: Macmillan).

Borchard, Edwin, 1951. *State Insolvency and Foreign Bondholders*, vol. 1 (New Haven: Yale University Press).

Bornschier, Volker, and Peter Lengyel, eds., 1990. *World Society Studies*, vol. 1 (Frankfurt and New York: Campus).

Boston Globe (various).

Bouchet, Michael Henri, 1987. *The Political Economy of International Debt: What, Who, How Much, and Why?* (New York: Quorum Books).

Bradlow, Daniel D., and Willis W. Jourdin, Jr., eds., 1984. *International Borrowing: Negotiation and Renegotiation* (Washington, D.C.: International Law Institute).

Brainard, Lawrence J., 1985. "Current Illusions about the International Debt Crisis." *World-Economy*, vol. 8, no. 1 (March 1985), pp. 1–9.

Brams, Steven J., 1975. *Game Theory and Politics* (New York: Free Press).

Brams, Steven J., 1985a. *Rational Politics: Decisions, Games, and Strategy* (Washington, D.C.: CQ Press).

Brams, Steven J., 1985b. *Superpower Games: Applying Game Theory to Superpower Conflict* (New Haven: Yale University Press).

Brams, Steven J., 1990. *Negotiation Games: Applying Game Theory to Bargaining and Arbitration* (New York: Routledge).

Brams, Steven J., 1993. "Theory of Moves." *American Scientist*, vol. 81, no. 6 (November/December 1993), pp. 562–570.

Brandes, Joseph, 1962. *Herbert Hoover and Economic Diplomacy: Department of Commerce Policy, 1921–1928* (Pittsburgh: University of Pittsburgh Press).

Brau, Eduard H., and R.C. Williams, with P.M. Keller and M. Nowak, 1983. *Recent Multilateral Debt Restructuring with Official and Bank Creditors* (Washington, D.C.: International Monetary Fund. Occasional Paper, no. 25).

Brimer, Andrew, and Frederick Dahl, 1975. "Growth of American International Banking: Implications for Public Policy." *Journal of Finance*, vol. 30, no. 2, pp. 341–363.

British and Foreign State Papers, London (various).

Buchanan, James, and Gordon Tullock, 1962. *The Calculus of Consent: Logical Foundations of Constitutional Democracy* (Ann Arbor: University of Michigan Press).

Bueno de Mesquita, Bruce, 1981. *The War Trap* (New Haven: Yale University Press).

Bueno de Mesquita, Bruce, and David Lalman, 1986. "Reason and War." *American Political Science Review*, vol. 80, no. 4 (December), pp. 917–931.

Bueno de Mesquita, Bruce, and David Lalman, 1989. "The Road to War Is Strewn with Peaceful Intentions." In Ordeshook, 1989, pp. 253–266.

Bueno de Mesquita, Bruce, and David Lalman, 1992. *War and Reason: Domestic and International Imperatives* (New Haven: Yale University Press).

Bueno de Mesquita, Bruce, David Newman, and Alvin Rabushka, 1985. *Forecasting Political Events: The Future of Hong Kong* (New Haven: Yale University Press).

Bulow, Jeremy, and Kenneth Rogoff, 1988a. "The Buyback Boondoggle." *Brookings Papers on Economic Activity*, vol. 2, pp. 675–704.

Bulow, Jeremy, and Kenneth Rogoff, 1988b. "Multilateral Negotiations for Rescheduling Developing Country Debt: A Bargaining-Theoretical Approach." *International Monetary Fund Staff Papers*, vol. 35 (December), pp. 644–657.

Bulow, Jeremy, and Kenneth Rogoff, 1989a. "Sovereign Debt: Is to Forgive to Forget?" *American Economic Review*, vol. 79 (March), pp. 43–50.

Bulow, Jeremy, and Kenneth Rogoff, 1989b. "A Constant Recontracting Model of Sovereign Debt." *Journal of Political Economy*, vol. 97, no. 1, pp. 155–178.

Bulow, Jeremy, and Kenneth Rogoff, 1991. "Sovereign Debt Repurchases – No Cure for Overhang." *Quarterly Journal of Economics*, vol. 106, no. 4 (November), pp. 1219–1235.

Burr, Robert N., 1965. *By Reason or Force: Chile and the Balancing of Power in South America, 1830–1905* (Berkeley: University of California Press).

Business Week (various).

Cabieses Cubas, Hugo, 1976. *Comunidad Laboral y Capitalismo: Alcances y Limites* (Lima: DESCO).

Cairncross, A.K., 1953. *Home and Foreign Investment, 1870–1913: Studies in Capital Accumulation* (London: Cambridge University Press).

Caldwell, Dan, and Timothy McKeown, eds., 1993. *Diplomacy, Force, and Leadership: Essays in Honor of Alexander L. George* (Boulder: Westview Press).

Callcott, Wilfred, 1926. *Church and State in Mexico, 1822–1857* (Durham: Duke University Press).

Calvo, Guillermo A., and Graciela L. Kaminsky, 1991. "Debt Relief and Debt Rescheduling: The Optimal-contract Approach." *Journal of Development Economics*, vol. 36, pp. 5–36.

Calvo, Guillermo A., Ronald Findlay, Pentii Kouri, and Jorge Braga de Macedo, eds., 1989. *Debt, Stabilization and Development: Essays in Memory of Carlos Diaz-Alejandro* (Oxford: Basil Blackwell).

Campbell, Bonnie, ed., 1989. *Political Dimensions of the International Debt Crisis* (New York: St. Martin's Press).

Caporaso, James A., ed., 1978. *Dependence and Dependency in the Global System*, Special Issue, *International Organization*, vol. 32, no. 1 (Madison: University of Wisconsin Press).

Caporaso, James, A., 1992. "International Relations Theory and Multilateralism: The Search for Foundations." *International Organization*, vol. 46, no. 3 (Summer), pp. 599–632.

Caporaso, James A., and David P. Levine, 1992. *Theories of Political Economy* (New York: Cambridge University Press).

Cardoso, Eliana A., and Albert Fishlow, 1992. "Latin-American Economic Development – 1950–1980." *Journal of Latin American Studies*, vol. 24, pp. 197–218.

Carey, James, 1964. *Peru and the United States, 1900–1962* (Notre Dame: University of Notre Dame Press).

Carr, E.H., 1946/1962. *The Twenty Years' Crisis, 1919–1939: An Introduction to the Study of International Relations* (New York: St. Martin's Press).

Carvounis, Chris C., 1986. *The Foreign Debt/National Development Conflict: External Adjustment and Internal Disorder in the Developing Nations* (New York: Quorum Books).

Casasus, Joaquin Demetrio, 1885. *Historia de la Deuda Contraida en Londres con un Apendice sobre el Estado Actual de la Hacienda Pública por el Lic. Joaquin D. Casasus* (Mexico: Impr. del Gorbierno Federal).

Caskey, J., 1989. "The IMF and Concerted Lending in Latin American Debt Restructurings: A Formal Analysis." *Journal of International Money and Finance*, vol. 8, pp. 105–120.

Cencini, Alvaro, and Bernard Schmitt, 1991. *External Debt Servicing: A Vicious Circle* (London and New York: Pinter Publishers).

Centeno, M., and Sylvia Maxfield, 1992. "The Marriage of Finance and Order – Changes in the Mexican Political Elite." *Journal of Latin American Studies*, vol. 24 (February), pp. 57–85.

Chamberlain, Edward, 1933. *The Theory of Monopolistic Competition: A Re-orientation of the Theory of Value* (Cambridge, Mass.: Harvard University Press).

Chang, Chun, 1990. "The Dynamic Structure of Optimal Debt Contracts." *Journal of Economic Theory*, vol. 52, no. 1 (October), pp. 68–86.

Charbaji, Abdulrazzak, Hamid F. Ali, and Mohammed Marash, 1993. "Predicting the Government's Decision to Seek a Rescheduling of External Debt." *Applied Economics*, vol. 25, no. 6 (June), pp. 751–757.

Chirinos Soto, Enrique, 1986. *Alan García: Análisis de su Gobierno* (Lima: Centro de Documentación Andina).

Christian Science Monitor (various).

Clark, John, 1993. "Debt Reduction and Market Reentry under the Brady Plan." *Federal Reserve Bank of New York Quarterly Review*, vol. 18, no. 4 (Winter), pp. 38–62.

Clark, John, Ajai Chopra, Mohamed A. El-Erian, Alessandro Leipold, Paul Mylonas, and Louis W. Pauly, 1991. *Private Market Financing for Developing Countries* (Washington, D.C.: International Monetary Fund).

Clarke, Stephen, 1967. *Central Bank Cooperation 1924–1931* (New York: Federal Reserve Bank of New York).

Clarke, William, 1877. *Peru: And Its Creditors* (London: Ranken and Co.).

Cline, Howard, 1953. *The United States and Mexico* (Cambridge, Mass.: Harvard University Press).

Cline, William R., 1983. *International Debt and the Stability of the World Economy* (Washington, D.C.: Institute for International Economics).

Cline, William R., 1984. *International Debt: Systemic Risk and Policy Response* (Cambridge, Mass.: MIT Press).

Cline, William R., 1988. "International Debt: Progress and Strategy." *Finance and Development*, vol. 25, no. 2 (June 1988), pp. 9–11.

Cohen, Benjamin J., 1977. *Organizing the World's Money: The Political Economy of International Monetary Relations* (New York: Basic Books).

Cohen, Benjamin J., 1982. "Balance-of-Payments Financing: Evolution of a Regime," *International Organization*, vol. 36, no. 2, pp. 457–478.

Cohen, Benjamin J., 1985. "International Debt and Linkage Strategies: Some Foreign-Policy Implications for the United States." *International Organization*, vol. 39, no. 4 (Autumn), pp. 699–727.

Cohen, Benjamin J., 1986. *In Whose Interest?: International Banking and American Foreign Policy* (New Haven: Yale University Press).

Cohen, Benjamin J., 1989. *Developing-Country Debt: A Middle Way* (Princeton: International Finance Section, Dept. of Economics, Princeton University, Essays in International Finance, no. 173).

Cohen, Benjamin J., 1990. "The Political Economy of International Relations." *International Organization*, vol. 44, no. 2 (Spring), pp. 261–281.

Cohen, Benjamin J., with Fabio Basagni, 1981. *Banks and the Balance of Payments: Private Lending in the International Adjustment Process* (Montclair N.J.: Allanheld, Osmun).

Cohen, Daniel, 1991. *Private Lending to Sovereign States: A Theoretical Autopsy* (Cambridge, Mass.: MIT Press).

Cohen, Daniel, 1993. "Low Investment and Large LDC Debt in the 1980s." *American Economic Review*, vol. 83, no. 3 (June), pp. 437–449.

Cohen, Daniel, and Thierry Verdier, 1990. "Secret Buybacks of LDC Debt," CEPR Discussion Paper, no. 462 (September).

Collier, Ruth B., 1982. "Popular Sector Incorporation and Political Supremacy: Regime Evolution in Brazil and Mexico." In Hewlett and Weinert, 1982, pp. 57–109.

Collier, Ruth B., 1992. *The Contradictory Alliance: State-Labor Relations and Regime Change in Mexico* (Berkeley: International and Area Studies, no. 83, University of California).

Collier, Ruth B., and David Collier, 1979. "Inducements Versus Constraints: Disaggregating 'Corporatism'." *The American Political Science Review*, vol. 73, no. 4 (December), pp. 967–986.

Collier, Ruth B., and David Collier, 1991. *Shaping the Political Arena: Critical Junctures, The Labor Movement, and Regime Dynamics in Latin America* (Princeton: Princeton University Press).

Comercio Exterior (various).

Committee of Mexican Bondholders, London (various).

Committee of Spanish-American Bondholders, London (various).

Congressional Research Service, 1984. *Issue Brief* (IB84105) (Octorber 16).

Contreras, Manuel E., 1990. "Debt, Taxes, and War: The Political Economy of Bolivia, c. 1920–1935." *Journal of Latin American Studies*, vol. 22, part 2 (May), pp. 265–287.

Conybeare, John A.C., 1985. "Trade Wars: A Comparative Study of Anglo-Hanse, Franco-Italian, and Hawley-Smoot Conflicts." *World Politics*, vol. 38, no. 1 (October), pp. 147–172.

Conybeare, John A.C., 1987. *Trade Wars: The Theory and Practice of International Commercial Rivalry* (New York: Columbia University Press).

Conybeare, John A.C., 1990. "On the Repudiation of Sovereign Debt – Sources of Stability and Risk." *Columbia Journal of World Business*, vol. 25, nos. 1–2 (Spring-Summer), pp. 46–52.

Coombs, Charles, 1976. *The Arena of International Finance* (New York: John Wiley and Sons).

Cooper, Richard, 1968. *The Economics of Interdependence: Economic Policy in the Atlantic Community* (New York: McGraw-Hill).

Cooper, Richard, 1972. "Economic Interdependence and Foreign Economic Policy in the '70s." *World Politics*, vol. 24, pp. 159–182.

Cooper, Richard, 1992. *Economic Stabilization and Debt in Developing Countries* (Cambridge, Mass.: MIT Press).

Cooper, Richard, and Jeffrey Sachs, 1985. "Borrowing Abroad: The Debtor's Perspective." In Smith and Cuddington, eds., 1985, pp. 21–60.

Corbridge, Stuart, 1993. *Debt and Development* (Oxford and Cambridge, Mass.: Blackwell).

Corden, W., 1991. "The Theory of Debt Relief – Sorting Out Some Issues." *Journal of Development Studies*, vol. 27, no. 3 (April), pp. 131–145.

Corporation of Foreign Bondholders, *Annual Reports*, London (various).

Cotler, Julio, 1978. *Clases, Estado y Nación en el Perú* (Lima: Instituto de Estudios Peruanos).

Cotler, Julio, 1981. "La Relacion Peligroso: Monetarismo y Democracia." *La Revista*, vol. 5 (June).

Cotler, Julio, 1986. "The Political Radicalization of Working-Class Youth in Peru." *Cepal Review*, vol. 29 (August), pp. 107–118.

Craig, Gordon A., and Alexander L. George, 1983. *Force and Statecraft: Diplomatic Problems of Our Time* (New York: Oxford University Press).

Cronon, E. David, 1960. *Josephus Daniels in Mexico* (Madison: University of Wisconsin Press).

Cuanto (various).

Culpeper, R., 1993. "A Note on the Multilateral Creditors and the Debt Crisis." *World Development*, vol. 21, no. 7 (July), pp. 1239–1244.

Czerkawski, Chris, 1991. *Theoretical and Policy-oriented Aspects of the External Debt Economics* (Berlin and New York: Springer-Verlag).

Dahl, Robert, 1961. *Who Governs? Democracy and Power in an American City* (New Haven: Yale University Press).

Darity, William, Jr., and Bobbie L. Horn, 1988. *The Loan Pushers: The Role of Commercial Banks in the International Debt Crisis* (Cambridge, Mass.: Ballinger Publishing Co.).

Davidson, Paul, and Jan Kregel, eds., 1989. *Macroeconomic Problems and Policies of Income Distribution: Functional, Personal, International* (Brookfield, Vt.: Gower).

Davis, Diane, 1990. "Social Movements and Mexico's Crisis." *Journal of International Affairs*, vol. 30, no. 2 (Winter), pp. 343–367.

Davis, Morton D., 1983. *Game Theory, A Nontechnical Introduction* (New York: Basic Books).

Dawson, Frank G., 1990. *The First Latin American Debt Crisis: The City of London and the 1822–25 Loan Bubble* (New Haven: Yale University Press).

Deaghion, B., 1990. "International Debt – An Explanation of the Commercial Banks' Lending Behavior after 1982." *Journal of International Economics*, vol. 28, nos. 1–2 (February), pp. 173–186.

Debs, Richard A., David L. Roberts, and Eli M. Remolona, 1987. *Finance for Developing Countries: Alternative Sources of Finance: Debt Swaps* (New York: Group of Thirty).

Delamaide, Darrell, 1984. *Debt Shock: The Full Story of the World Credit Crisis* (New York: Doubleday).

Dennis, William Jefferson, 1931/1967. *Tacna and Arica: An Account of the Chile-Peru Boundary Dispute and of the Arbitrations by the United States* (New Haven: Yale University Press).

Detragiache, Enrica, 1992. "Optimal Loan Contracts and Floating-Rate Debt in International Lending to LDCs." *European Economic Review*, vol. 36, no. 6 (August), pp. 1241–1261.

Deutsch, Karl, 1963. *The Nerves of Government: Models of Political Communication and Control* (New York: Free Press of Glencoe).

Devlin, Robert, 1983. *Transnational Banks and the External Finance of Latin America: The Experience of Peru* (Santiago: United Nations).

Devlin, Robert, 1987. "Los Procesos de Reprogramación de la Deuda Externa Latinoamericana 1982–1987: Tendencias y Perspectivas." Paper prepared for conference on *La Economía Mundial y el Desarrollo Latinoamericano, Problemas y Perspectivas*, Caracas, Venezuela, 4–8 May.

Devlin, Robert, 1989. *Debt and Crisis in Latin America: The Supply Side of the Story* (Princeton: Princeton University Press).

Devlin, Robert, and Enrique de la Piedra, 1985. "Peru and Its Private Bankers: Scenes from an Unhappy Marriage." In Wionczek, 1985, pp. 383–426.

Diaz-Alejandro, Carlos F., 1984. "Latin American Debt: I Don't Think We Are in Kansas Anymore." *Brookings Papers on Economic Activity*, no. 2, pp. 335–403.

Dillon, K. Burke, and Gumersindo Oliveros, 1987. *Recent Experience with Multilateral Official Debt Rescheduling* (Washington, D.C.: International Monetary Fund).

Diwan, I., 1990. "Linking Trade and External Debt Strategies." *Journal of International Economics*, vol. 29, nos. 3–4 (Fall), pp. 293–310.

Diwan, I., and K. Kletzer, 1992. "Voluntary Choices in Concerted Deals – The Menu Approach to Debt Reduction in Developing Countries." *World Bank Economic Review*, vol. 6, no. 1 (January), pp. 91–108.

Diwan, Ishac, and Dani Rodrik, 1992. "External Debt, Adjustment, and Burden Sharing: A Unified Framework." *Princeton Studies in International Finance*, no. 73 (November).

Diz, Aldofo C., 1983. "Economic Performance under Three Stand-by Arrangements: Peru, 1977–80." In Williamson, 1983, pp. 263–274.

Donaldson, John, 1928. *International Economic Relations: A Treatise on World Economy and World Politics* (New York: Longmans, Green, and Co.).

Dornbusch, Rudiger, 1989. *The Road to Economic Recovery: Report of the Twentieth Century Fund Task Force on International Debt: Background Paper* (New York: Priority Press Publications).

Dornbusch, Rudiger, 1993. *Stabilization, Debt, and Reform: Policy Analysis for Developing Countries* (Englewood Cliffs, N.J.: Prentice Hall).

Dornbusch, Rudiger, and Mario Draghi, 1990. *Public Debt Management: Theory and History* (Cambridge and New York: Cambridge University Press).

Dornbusch, Rudiger, and S. Edwards, 1990. "La macroeconomía del populismo en la América Latina." *El Trimestre Economico*, vol. 58, no. 1 (January–March), p. 158.

Dornbusch, Rudiger, John H. Makin, and David Zlowe, eds., 1989. *Alternative Solutions to Developing-country Debt Problems* (Washington, D.C.: American Enterprise Institute for Public Policy Research, AEI Studies, no. 494).

Downs, George W., and David M. Rocke, 1990. *Tacit Bargaining, Arms Races, and Arms Control* (Ann Arbor: University of Michigan Press).

Dupont, Cédric, 1994. *The Interplay of Domestic and International Factors in Negotiations: A Formal Approach* (Ph.D. dissertation, University of Geneva).

Durand, Francisco, 1977. *Estudio de las Relaciones Sociales en el Marco de la Empresa en el Sector Industrial, 1970–1976* (Unpublished manuscript, Pontificia Universidad Catolica del Perú, Lima).

Durand, Francisco, 1984. *Los Industriales, el Liberalismo y la Democracia* (Lima: Fundación Friedrich Ebert/DESCO).

Easton, David, ed., 1966. *Varieties of Political Theory* (New York: Prentice-Hall).

Eaton, J., 1990. "Debt Relief and the International Enforcement of Loan Contracts." *Journal of Economic Perspectives*, vol. 4, no. 1 (Winter), pp. 43–56.

Eaton, Jonathan, 1993. "Sovereign Debt – A Primer." *World Bank Economic Review*, vol. 7, no. 2 (May), pp. 137–172.

Eaton, Jonathan, and Mark Gersovitz, 1981. "Debt with Potential Repudiation: Theoretical and Empirical Analysis." *Review of Economic Studies* (Edinburgh), vol. 48 (April) pp. 289–309.

Eaton, Jonathan, Mark Gersovitz, and Joseph E. Stiglitz, 1986. "The Pure Theory of Country Risk." *European Economic Review*, vol. 30 (June) pp. 481–513.

Economic Commission for Latin America and the Caribbean, 1985. *External Debt in Latin America: Adjustment Policies and Renegotiation* (Boulder: Lynne Rienner Publishers).

Economic Commission for Latin America and the Caribbean, 1986a. *Economic Panorama of Latin America, 1986: Argentina, Brazil, Colombia, Chile, Mexico, Peru, Uruguay, Venezuela* (Santiago: United Nations).

Economic Commission for Latin America and the Caribbean (ECLAC), 1986b. *Debt, Adjustment, and Renegotiation in Latin America: Orthodox and Alternative Approaches* (Boulder: Lynne Rienner Publishers).

Economic Commission for Latin America and the Caribbean, 1990. *Latin America and the Caribbean: Options to Reduce the Debt Burden* (Santiago: United Nations).

Economic Commission for Latin America and the Caribbean, 1991. *Economic Survey of Latin America and the Caribbean*, vols. 1–2 (Santiago: United Nations).

Economic Commission for Latin America and the Caribbean, 1993. *Preliminary Overview of the Economy of Latin America and the Caribbean* (Santiago: United Nations).

The Economist (various).

Economist Intelligence Unit, various. *Country Report: Brazil* (London and New York: Economist Intelligence Unit).

Economist Intelligence Unit, various. *Country Report: Mexico* (London and New York: Economist Intelligence Unit).

Economist Intelligence Unit, various. *Country Report: Peru, Bolivia* (London and New York: Economist Intelligence Unit).

Economist Intelligence Unit, various. *Quarterly Economic Review of Mexico* (London and New York: Economist Intelligence Unit).

Edwards, George, 1938. *The Evolution of Finance Capitalism* (New York and London: Longmans, Green and Co.).

Edwards, Sebastian, 1993. *Latin America and the Caribbean a Decade after the Debt Crisis* (Washington, D.C.: World Bank).

Edwards, Sebastian, and Felipe Larraín, eds., 1989. *Debt, Adjustment, and Recovery: Latin America's Prospects for Growth and Development* (Cambridge, Mass.: Basil Blackwell).

Eichengreen, Barry, 1991. "Historical Research on International Lending and Debt." *Journal of Economic Perspectives*, vol. 5, no. 2 (Spring), pp. 149–169.

Eichengreen, Barry, 1993. Review of *Debt Cycles in the World-Economy: Foreign Loans, Financial Crises, and Debt Settlements, 1820–1990*, by Christian Suter. *The International History Review*, vol. 15, no. 2 (May), pp. 358–360.

Eichengreen, Barry, and Peter Lindert, eds. 1988. *The International Aspects of Current International Debt Problems: Is the Problem Insolvency or Illiquidity?* (Washington, D.C.: American Enterprise Institute for Public Policy Research).

Eichengreen, Barry, and Peter Lindert, eds., 1989. *The International Debt Crisis in Historical Perspective* (Cambridge, Mass.: MIT Press).

Eichengreen, Barry, and Richard Portes, 1986. "Debt and Default in the 1930s: Causes and Consequences." *European Economic Review*, vol. 30, pp. 599–640.

Eichengreen, Barry, and Richard Portes, 1989. "Settling Defaults in the Era of Bond Finance." *World Bank Economic Review*, vol. 3, no. 2 (May), pp. 211–239.

Einzig, Paul, 1932. *The Bank for International Settlements* (London: Macmillan).

Eskridge, William N., Jr., ed., 1985. *A Dance along the Precipice: The Political and Economic Dimensions of the International Debt Problem* (Lexington, Mass.: Lexington Books).

Esteves, L., 1882. *Apuntes para la Historia Económica del Perú* (Lima: Imprenta Calle de Huallaga, no. 139).

Euromoney (various).

Evans, Peter B., Harold K. Jacobson, and Robert D. Putnam, eds., 1993. *Double-edged Diplomacy: International Bargaining and Domestic Politics* (Berkeley: University of California Press).

Fagen, R., ed., 1979. *Capitalism and the State in U.S.-Latin American Relations* (Stanford: Stanford University Press).

Fearon, James, 1990. "Deterrence and the Spiral Model: The Role of Costly Signals in Crisis Bargaining." Paper presented at the 1990 Annual Meeting of the APSA, August 30–September 2.

Feinberg, Richard E., and Ricardo Ffrench-Davis, eds., 1988. *Development and External Debt in Latin America: Bases for a New Consensus* (Notre Dame: University of Notre Dame Press).

Feinberg, Richard E., and Valeriana Kallab, eds., 1984. *Adjustment Crisis in the Third World* (New Brunswick, N.J.: Transaction Books, U.S.–Third World Policy Perspectives, no. 1).

Feis, Herbert, 1930. *Europe: The World's Banker, 1870–1914: An Account of European Foreign Investment and the Connection of World Finance with Diplomacy before the War* (New York: A.M. Kelley).

Felix, David, 1984. "The Baring Crisis of the 1890s and the International Bond Defaults of the 1930s: Delphic Prophecies on the Outcome of the Current Latin American Debt Crises." Unpublished manuscript.

Felix, David, 1990. "Latin-America's Debt Crisis." *World Policy Journal*, vol. 7, no. 4 (Fall), pp. 732–771.

Felix, David, ed., 1990. *Debt and Transfiguration?: Prospects for Latin America's Economic Revival* (Armonk, N.Y.: M.E. Sharpe).

Fellner, William, 1949/1965. *Competition among the Few: Oligopoly and Similar Market Structures* (New York: Augustus M. Kelley, Reprints of Economic Classics).

Fernandez, Raquel, and David Kaaret, 1992. "Bank Heterogeneity, Reputation and Debt Renegotiation." *International Economic Review*, vol. 33, no. 1 (February), pp. 61–78.

Fernandez, R. and R. Rosenthal, 1990. "Strategic Models of Sovereign-Debt Renegotiations." *Review of Economic Studies*, vol. 57, no. 3 (July), pp. 331–349.

Ferner, Anthony, 1983. "The Industrialists and the Peruvian Development Model." In Booth and Sorj, 1983, pp. 40–71.

Ferrero Costa, Eduardo, ed., 1985. *El Perú Frente al Capital Extranjero: Deuda e Inversion* (Lima: Centro Peruano de Estudios Internacionales, Serie Simposios y Seminarios Internacionales, no. 2).

Financial Times (various).

Finifter, Ada W., ed., 1983. *Political Science: The State of the Discipline* (Washington, D.C.: American Political Science Association).

Finlayson, Jock, and Mark Zacher, 1983. "The GATT and the Regulation of Trade Barriers: Regime Dynamics and Functions." In Krasner, 1983b, pp. 273–314.

Fischer, Stanley, 1987. "Sharing the Burden of the International Debt Crisis." *American Economic Review*, vol. 77, no. 2 (May), pp. 165–170.

Fishlow, Albert, 1973. "Some Reflections on Post-1946 Brazilian Economic Policy." In Stepan, 1973, pp. 119–141.

Fishlow, Albert, 1985a. "Coping with the Creeping Crisis of Debt." In Wionczek, 1985, pp. 97–144.

Fishlow, Albert, 1985b. "Lessons from the Past: Capital Markets during the 19th Century and the Interwar Period." *International Organization*, vol. 39, no. 3, pp. 383–440.

Fishlow, Albert, 1989. "Conditionality and Willingness to Pay: Some Parallels from the 1890s." In Eichengreen and Lindert, 1989, pp. 86–105.

Fishlow, Albert, 1990. "The Latin American State." *Journal of Economic Perspectives*, vol. 4, no. 3 (Summer), pp. 61–74.

Fishlow, Albert, 1992. "International Capital Flows to Latin America – What Is the Promise?" *World Bank Economic Review*, pp. 337–339.

Fitzgerald, E.V.K., 1976. *The State and Economic Development: Peru since 1968* (Cambridge and New York: Cambridge University Press).

Fitzgerald, E.V.K., 1988. "The Fiscal Crisis of the Latin American State." In Toye, 1988, pp. 125–156.

Fitzgerald, E.V.K., 1983. "State Capitalism in Peru: A Model of Economic Development and Its Limitations." In McClintock and Lowenthal, 1983, pp. 65–93.

Fletcher, Richard D., 1984. *Implications of the Current Crisis for Latin America* (Washington, D.C.: Inter-American Development Bank, Reprint Series, no. 146).

Floud, Roderick, and Donald McCloskey, eds., 1981. *The Economic History of Britain since 1700, vol. 2, 1860 to the 1970s* (Cambridge and New York: Cambridge University Press).

Foreign Bondholders Protective Council, *Annual Reports*, New York (various).

Foreign Policy Notes, Institute of International Studies, University of California, Berkeley (various).

Foreign Relations of the United States (various).

Frankel, Allen, 1975. "The Lender of Last Resort Facility in the Context of Multinational Banking." *Columbia Journal of World Business*, vol. 10, no. 4, pp. 120–127.

Frankel, Jacob A., Michael P. Dooley, and Peter Wickham, eds., 1989. *Analytical Issues in Debt* (Washington, D.C.: International Monetary Fund).

Frieden, Jeffry A., 1981. "Third World Indebted Industrialization: International Finance and State Capitalism in Mexico, Brazil, Algeria, and South Korea." *International Organization*, vol. 35, no. 3 (Summer), pp. 407–431.

Frieden, Jeffry A., 1987. *Banking on the World: The Politics of American International Finance* (New York: Harper & Row).

Frieden, Jeffry A., 1991. *Debt, Development, and Democracy: Modern Political Economy and Latin America, 1965–1985* (Princeton: Princeton University Press).

Friedman, James W., 1986. *Game Theory with Applications to Economics* (New York: Oxford University Press).

Friedman, Milton, 1969. "The Euro-Dollar Market: Some First Principles," *The Morgan Guaranty Survey*, pp. 1–11.

Friedman, Milton, and Anna Schwartz, 1963. *A Monetary History of the U.S., 1867–1960* (Princeton: Princeton University Press).

Froot, Kenneth, 1989. "Buybacks, Exit Bonds, and the Optimality of Debt and Liquidity Relief." *International Economic Review*, vol. 30, no. 1 (February), pp. 49–70.

Fudenberg, Drew, and Jean Tirole, 1991. *Game Theory* (Cambridge, Mass.: MIT Press).

García Perez, Alan, 1986. "An Interview." *Third World Quarterly*, vol. 8, no. 4 (October), pp. 125–134.

Gardner, Richard N., 1969. *Sterling-Dollar Diplomacy: The Origins and the Prospects of our International Economic Order* (New York: McGraw-Hill).
Geddes, Barbara, 1990. "Building State Autonomy in Brazil, 1930–1964." *Comparative Politics*, vol. 22, no. 2 (January), pp. 217–235.
Geddes, Barbara, 1991. "A Game Theoretic Model of Reform in Latin-American Democracies." *American Political Science Review*, vol. 85, no. 2 (June), pp. 371–392.
Geddes, Barbara, and J. Zaller, 1989. "Sources of Popular Support for Authoritarian Regimes." *American Journal of Political Science*, vol. 33, no. 2 (May), pp. 319–347.
Gellman, Irwin F., 1979. *Good Neighbor Diplomacy: United States in Latin America, 1933–1945* (Baltimore: Johns Hopkins University Press).
Gentleman, Judith, ed., 1987. *Mexican Politics in Transition* (Boulder: Westview Press).
George, Alexander L., 1979. "Case Studies and Theory Development: The Method of Structured, Focussed Comparison." In Lauren, 1979, pp. 43–69.
George, Alexander L., 1980. *Presidential Decisionmaking in Foreign Policy: The Effective Use of Information and Advice* (Boulder: Westview Press).
George, Alexander L., ed., 1983. *Managing U.S.-Soviet Rivalry: Problems of Crisis Prevention* (Boulder: Westview Press).
Gerschenkron, Alexander, 1962. *Economic Backwardness in Historical Perspective, A Book of Essays* (Cambridge, Mass.: Belknap Press of Harvard University Press).
Gersowitz, Mark, 1986. Review of *International Debt: Systemic Risk and Policy Response*, by William Cline, *Journal of Economic Literature*, vol. 24, no. 1, pp. 108–110.
Gibbons, Robert, 1992. *Game Theory for Applied Economists* (Princeton: Princeton University Press).
Gibson, Quentin, 1960. *The Logic of Social Enquiry* (London: Routledge and Kegan Paul).
Gilbert, A., 1990. "The Provision of Public Services and the Debt Crisis in Latin-America – The Case of Bogotá." *Economic Geography*, vol. 66, no. 4 (October), pp. 349–361.
Gilbert, Milton, 1980. *Quest for World Monetary Order: The Gold-Dollar System and Its Aftermath* (New York: John Wiley and Sons).
Gillis, Malcolm, Dwight H. Perkins, Michael Roemer, and Donald R. Snodgrass, 1983. *Economics of Development* (New York and London: W.W. Norton and Co.).
Gilpin, Robert, 1981. *War and Change in World Politics* (Cambridge and New York: Cambridge University Press).
Gilpin, Robert, 1987. *The Political Economy of International Relations* (Princeton: Princeton University Press).
Glasberg, D., and K. Ward, 1993. "Foreign Debt and Economic Growth in the World System." *Social Science Quarterly*, vol. 74, no. 4 (December), pp. 703–720.
Goldstein, Joshua S., and John R. Freeman, 1990. *Three-way Street: Strategic Reciprocity in World Politics* (Chicago: University of Chicago Press).
Goldstein, Judith, 1986. "The Political Economy of Trade: Institutions of Protection." *American Political Science Review*, vol. 80, no. 1, pp. 161–184.
Goldstein, Judith, 1993. *Ideas, Interests, and American Trade Policy* (Ithaca: Cornell University Press).
Goldstein, Judith, and Robert O. Keohane, eds., 1993. *Ideas and Foreign Policy: Beliefs, Institutions, and Political Change* (Ithaca: Cornell University Press).
Gooptu, Sudarshan, 1993. *Debt Reduction and Development: The Case of Mexico* (Westport, Conn.: Praeger).
Gourevitch, Peter, 1986. *Politics in Hard Times: Comparative Responses to International Economic Crises* (Ithaca: Cornell University Press).
Grant, Arthur James, and Harold Temperley, 1952. *Europe in the Nineteenth and Twentieth Centuries (1789–1950)* (London and New York: Longmans, Green).

Green, Donald P., and Ian Shapiro, 1994. *Pathologies of Rational Choice Theory: A Critique of Applications in Political Science* (New Haven: Yale University Press).

Grieco, Joseph M., 1988. "Anarchy and Cooperation." *International Organization*, vol. 42, no. 3 (Summer), pp. 485–507.

Grieco, Joseph M., 1990. *Cooperation among Nations: Europe, America and Non-tariff Barriers to Trade* (Ithaca: Cornell University Press).

Griffith–Jones, Stephany, ed., 1988. *Deuda Externa, Renegociación y Ajuste en América Latina* (Mexico: Fondo de Cultura Económica, El Trimestre Económico, no. 61).

Griffith–Jones, Stephany, 1991. "Creditor Countries' Banking and Fiscal Regulations – Can Changes Encourage Debt Relief?" *Journal of Development Studies*, vol. 27, no. 3 (April), pp. 167–191.

Gruber, Herbert, 1971. "Risk, Uncertainty and Moral Hazard." *Journal of Risk and Insurance*, vol. 38, no. 1, pp. 99–106.

Guerrieri, Paolo, and Pier Carlo Padoan, eds., 1991. *Politiche Economiche Nazionale e Regimi Internazionali* (Milan: Franco Angeli Publishers).

Guttman, William, 1989. *Between Bailout and Breakdown: A Modular Approach to Latin America's Debt Crisis* (Washington, D.C.: Center for Strategic and International Studies, Significant Issues Series, vol. 11, no. 2).

Haas, Ernst, 1964. *Beyond the Nation-State: Functionalism and International Organization* (Stanford: Stanford University Press).

Haas, Ernst, 1980. "Why Collaborate? Issue Linkage and International Regimes." *World Politics*, vol. 32, pp. 357–405.

Haas, Ernst, 1982. "Words Can Hurt You: Or Who Said What to Whom about Regimes." *International Organization*, vol. 36, no. 2, pp. 207–244.

Haas, Ernst, 1990. *When Knowledge Is Power: Three Models of Change in International Organizations* (Berkeley: University of California Press).

Haggard, Stephan, 1985. "The Politics of Adjustment: Lessons from the IMF's Extended Fund Facility." *International Organization*, vol. 39, no. 3 (Summer), pp. 505–534.

Haggard, Stephen, and Robert R. Kaufman, eds., 1992. *The Politics of Economic Adjustment: International Constraints, Distributive Conflicts, and the State* (Princeton: Princeton University Press).

Haggard, Stephen, Chung H. Lee, and Syliva Maxfield, eds., 1993. *The Politics of Finance in Developing Countries* (Ithaca: Cornell University Press).

Hall, Alan R., ed., 1968. *The Export of Capital from Britain, 1870–1914* (London: Methuen).

Hall, John A., ed., 1986. *States in History* (New York: Basil Blackwell).

Hamilton, Nora, 1982. *The Limits of State Autonomy: Post-Revolutionary Mexico* (Princeton: Princeton University Press).

Hansen, Roger, 1971. *The Politics of Mexican Development* (Baltimore: Johns Hopkins University Press).

Hardin, Russell, 1982. *Collective Action* (Baltimore: Johns Hopkins University Press for Resources for the Future).

Hardy, Chandra S., 1982. *Rescheduling Developing-Country Debts, 1956–1981: Lessons and Recommendations* (Washington, D.C.: Overseas Development Council, no. 15).

Harsanyi, John C. 1977. *Rational Behavior and Bargaining Equilibrium in Games and Social Situations* (Cambridge: Cambridge University Press).

Harsanyi, John C., and Richard Selten, 1988. *A General Theory of Equilibrium Selection in Games* (Cambridge, Mass.: MIT Press).

Hart, Jeffrey, 1976. "Three Approaches to the Measurement of Power in International Relations." *International Organization*, vol. 30, pp. 289–305.

Hawtrey, Ralph G., 1962. *The Art of Central Banking* (London: Frank Cass).

Head, J.G., 1972. "Public Goods and Public Policy." *Public Finance*, vol. 12, no. 3, pp. 197–221.

Helleiner, Gerald K., ed., 1982. *For Good or Evil: Economic Theory and North-South Negotiations* (Buffalo: University of Toronto Press).

Helleiner, Gerald K., 1990. *The New Global Economy and the Developing Countries: Essays in International Economics and Development* (Brookfield, Vt.: E. Elgar).

Hellwig, Martin, 1986. "Comments on 'The Pure Theory of Country Risk,' by J. Eaton, M. Gersovitz and J. Stiglitz." *European Economic Review*, vol. 30, pp. 521–527.

Helpman, Elhanan, 1989a. "Voluntary Debt Reduction: Incentives and Welfare." In Frenkel, Dooley, and Wickham, 1989, pp. 279–310.

Helpman, Elhanan, 1989b. "The Simple Analytics of Debt Equity Swaps." *American Economic Review*, vol. 79, no. 3 (June), pp. 440–451.

Herrera, Cesar, 1985. *Inflacion, Politica Devaluatoria y Apertura Externa en el Perú: 1978–1984* (Lima: Instituto de Estudios Peruanos).

Hewlett, Sylvia Ann, and Richard S. Weinert, eds., 1982. *Brazil and Mexico: Patterns in Late Development* (Philadelphia: Institute for the Study of Human Issues).

Hirsch, Fred, 1969. *Money International* (Garden City: Doubleday).

Hirsch, Fred, 1977. "The Bagehot Problem." *The Manchester School*, vol. 45, no. 3, pp. 241–257.

Hirschman, Albert, 1945. *National Power and the Structure of Foreign Trade* (Berkeley and Los Angels: University of California Press).

Hirshleifer, Jack, and John G. Riley, 1992. *Analytics of Uncertainty and Information* (Cambridge: Cambridge University Press, Cambridge Surveys of Economic Literature).

Hobsbawm, Eric J., 1962. *The Age of Revolution, 1789–1848* (Cleveland: World Publishing Co.).

Hobsbawm, Eric J., 1969. *Industry and Empire* (Harmondsworth: Penguin Books, The Pelican Economic History of Britain, vol. 3).

Hobson, Charles K., 1914/1963. *The Export of Capital* (London: Constable Co., Studies in Economic and Political Science, no. 38).

Holsti, Ole, Randolph Silverson, and Alexander George, eds., 1980. *Change in the International System* (Boulder: Westview Press).

Hopkins, Raymond, 1992. "Reform in the International Food Aid Regime: The Role of Consensual Knowledge." *International Organization*, vol. 46, no. 1 (Winter), pp. 225–244.

Huntington, Samuel, 1968. *Political Order in Changing Societies* (New Haven: Yale University Press).

Husain, Ishrat, and Ishac Diwan, eds., 1989. *Dealing with the Debt Crisis* (Washington, D.C.: World Bank).

Institute for International Studies Notes (various issues) (Berkeley: Institute for International Studies).

Institutional Investor (various).

Inter-American Development Bank, 1984a. *External Debt and Economic Development in Latin America: Background and Prospects* (Washington, D.C.: IADB).

Inter-American Development Bank, 1984b. *Round Table on the External Debt of Latin America*. 25th Annual Meeting of the Board of Governors. (Washington, D.C.: IADB).

International Herald Tribune (various).

International Monetary Fund (various). *International Monetary Fund Survey* (Washington, D.C.: International Monetary Fund).

International Monetary Fund, 1990. *Balance of Payments Statistics* (Washington, D.C.: International Monetary Fund).

Intriligator, Michael, and Urs Luterbacher, eds., 1994. *Cooperative Models in International Relations Research* (Boston, Mass.: Kluwer Academic Publishers).

Islam, Shafiqul, 1988. *Breaking the International Debt Deadlock* (New York: Council on Foreign Relations).

Jenks, Leland, 1927/1973. *The Migration of British Capital to 1875* (New York: Barnes and Noble).

Jervis, Robert, 1976. *Perception and Misperception in International Politics* (Princeton: Princeton University Press).

Johnson, Harry, 1968. "Problems of Efficiency in Monetary Management." *Journal of Political Economy*, vol. 76, no. 5, pp. 971–990.

Jorge, Antonio, and Jorge Salazar-Carrillo, eds., 1992. *The Latin American Debt* (New York: St. Martin's Press).

Journal of Commerce (various).

Kahler, Miles, ed., 1986. *The Politics of International Debt* (Ithaca: Cornell University Press).

Kaletsky, Anatole, 1985. *The Costs of Default* (New York: Priority Press Publications).

Kaneko, Mamoru, and Jacek Prokop, 1993. "A Game Theoretical Approach to the International Debt Overhang." *Journal of Economics–Zeitschrift für Nationalokonomie*, vol. 58, no. 1, pp. 1–24.

Katzenstein, Peter J., 1976. "International Relations and Domestic Structures: Foreign Economic Policies of Advanced Industrial States." *International Organization*, vol. 30, no. 1 (Winter), pp. 1–46.

Katzenstein, Peter J., ed., 1977. "Between Power and Plenty: Foreign Economic Policy of Advanced Industrial States." *International Organization*, special issue, vol. 31, no. 4, pp. 587–606.

Katzenstein, Peter J., 1985. *Small States in World Markets: Industrial Policy in Europe* (Ithaca: Cornell University Press).

Kaufman, Robert, 1985. "Democratic and Authoritarian Responses to the Debt Issue." *International Organization*, vol. 39, pp. 473–503.

Kaufman, Robert, 1986. "Democratic and Authoritarian Responses to the Debt Issue: Argentina, Brazil, Mexico." In Kahler, 1986, pp. 187–217.

Kaufman, Robert, 1988. *The Politics of Debt in Argentina, Brazil, and Mexico: Economic Stabilization in the 1980s* (Berkeley: Institute of International Studies, University of California).

Keller, Peter M., and Nissanke E. Weerasinghe, 1988. *Multilateral Official Debt Rescheduling: Recent Experience* (Washington, D.C.: International Monetary Fund).

Kelly de Escobar, Janet, 1977. *Bankers and Borders: The Case of American Banks in Britain* (Cambridge, Mass.: Ballinger Publishing Co.).

Kenen, Peter, 1989. *Debt Buybacks and Forgiveness in a Model with Voluntary Repudiation*. Working Paper 89–91 (Princeton: International Finance Section, Princeton University).

Keohane, Robert O., 1980. "The Theory of Hegemonic Stability and Changes in International Economic Regimes, 1967–1977." In Holsti, Silverson, and George, 1980, pp. 131–162.

Keohane, Robert O., 1982. "The Demand for International Regimes." *International Organization*, vol. 36, no. 2, pp. 325–355.

Keohane, Robert O., 1983. "Theory of World Politics: Structural Realism and Beyond." In Finifter, 1983, pp. 503–540.

Keohane, Robert O., 1984. *After Hegemony: Cooperation and Discord in the World Political Economy* (Princeton: Princeton University Press).

Keohane, Robert O., ed., 1986. *Neorealism and Its Critics* (New York: Columbia University Press).

Keohane, Robert O., 1989. *International Institutions and State Power: Essays in International Relations Theory* (Boulder: Westview Press).

Keohane, Robert O., and Stanley Hoffmann, eds., 1991. *The New European Community: Decisionmaking and Institutional Change* (Boulder: Westview Press).

Keohane, Robert O., and Joseph S. Nye, Jr., eds., 1972. *Transnational Relations and World Politics* (Cambridge, Mass.: Harvard University Press).

Keohane, Robert O., and Joseph S. Nye, Jr., 1974. "Transgovernmental Relations and International Organizations," *World Politics*, vol. 27, no. 1, pp. 39–62.

Keohane, Robert O., and Joseph S. Nye, Jr., 1977. *Power and Interdependence: World Politics in Transition* (Boston: Little, Brown).

Keohane, Robert O., and Joseph S. Nye, Jr., 1989. *Power and Interdependence*, 2nd ed. (Glenview, Ill.: Scott, Foresman).

Keynes, John M., 1920. *The Economic Consequences of the Peace* (London: Macmillan).

Kindleberger, Charles, 1973a. *The World in Depression, 1929–39* (Berkeley: University of California Press, History of the World Economy in the Twentieth Century, vol. 4).

Kindleberger, Charles, 1973b. *International Economics* (Homewood, Ill.: Richard D. Irwin).

Kindleberger, Charles, 1978. *Manias, Panics, and Crashes: A History of Financial Crises* (New York: Basic Books).

Kindleberger, Charles, and Jean-Pierre Laffargue, eds., 1982. *Financial Crises: Theory, History, and Policy* (Cambridge: Cambridge University Press).

Kisic, Drago, 1987. *De la Corresponsibilidad a la Moritoria: El Caso de la Deuda Externa Peruana 1970–1986* (Lima: Fundación Friedrich Ebert/Centro del Estudios Internacionales).

Kletzer, Kenneth, 1989. "Sovereign Debt, Renegotiation under Asymmetric Information." In Frankel, Dooley, and Wickham, 1989, pp. 208–241.

Knorr, Klaus, 1975. *The Power of Nations: The Political Economy of International Relations* (New York: Basic Books).

Kraft, Joseph, 1984. *The Mexican Rescue* (New York: Group of Thirty).

Krasner, Stephen D., 1976. "State Power and the Structure of International Trade." *World Politics*, vol. 28, no. 3 (April), pp. 317–343.

Krasner, Stephen D., 1978. *Defending the National Interest: Raw Materials Investments and U.S. Foreign Policy* (Princeton: Princeton University Press).

Krasner, Stephen D., 1981. "Transforming International Regimes." *International Studies Quarterly*, vol. 25, pp. 119–148.

Krasner, Stephen D., 1982. "Structural Causes and Regime Consequences: Regimes as Intervening Variables." *International Organization*, vol. 36, no. 2, pp. 185–205.

Krasner, Stephen D., 1983a. "The Tokyo Round: Particularistic Interests and Prospects for Stability in the Global Trading System." *International Studies Quarterly*, vol. 23, no. 4, pp. 491–531.

Krasner, Stephen D., ed., 1983b. *International Regimes* (Ithaca: Cornell University Press).

Krasner, Stephen D., 1985. *Structural Conflict: The Third World against Global Liberalism* (Berkeley: University of California Press).

Krasner, Stephen D., 1991. "Global Communications and National Power: Life on the Pareto Frontier." *World Politics*, vol. 43, no. 3 (April), pp. 336–366.

Kratochwil, Friedrich V., 1989. *Rules, Norms, and Decisions: On the Conditions of Practical and Legal Reasoning in International Relations and Domestic Affairs* (Cambridge: Cambridge University Press).

Krause, Lawrence B., and Kim Kihwan, eds., 1991. *Liberalization in the Process of Economic Development* (Berkeley: University of California Press).

Krugman, Paul, 1985. "International Debt Strategies in an Uncertain World." In Smith and Cuddington, eds. 1985, pp. 79–126.

Krugman, Paul, 1988. "Financing versus Forgiving a Debt Overhang: Some Analytical Notes." *Journal of Development Economics*, vol. 29 (November), pp. 253–268.

Krugman, Paul, 1989. "Market Based Debt-Reduction Schemes." In Frankel, Dooley, and Wickham, 1989, pp. 258–278.

Krugman, Paul, 1990. "Debt Relief Is Cheap." *Foreign Policy*, no. 80 (Fall), pp. 141–152.

Kuczynski Godard, Pedro-Pablo, 1977. *Peruvian Democracy under Economic Stress: An Account of the Belaunde Administration, 1963–1968* (Princeton: Princeton University Press).

Kuczynski Godard, Pedro-Pablo, 1982–1983. "Latin American Debt." *Foreign Affairs*, vol. 61, no. 2 (Winter), pp. 344–364.

Kuczynski Godard, Pedro-Pablo, 1988. *Latin American Debt* (Baltimore: Johns Hopkins University Press).

Kuhn, Harold, 1953, "Extensive Games and the Problem of Information." In Kuhn and Tucker, 1953, pp. 193–216.

Kuhn, Harold, and A. Tucker, eds., 1953. *Contributions to the Theory of Games*, vol. 2 (Princeton: Princeton University Press, Annals of Mathematics Studies, no. 28).

Kurth, James, 1979. "The Political Consequences of the Product Cycle: Industrial History and Political Outcome," *International Organization*, vol. 3B, no. 1 (Winter), pp. 1–34.

Laitin, David, 1993. "The Game Theory of Language Regimes." *International Political Science Review*, vol. 14, no. 3 (July), pp. 227–239.

Lakatos, Imre, 1970. "Falsification and the Methodology of Scientific Research Programmes." In Lakatos and Musgrave, eds., 1970, pp. 91–196.

Lakatos, Imre, and Alan Musgrave, eds., 1970. *Criticism and the Growth of Knowledge* (Cambridge: Cambridge University Press).

Lake, David A., 1988. *Power, Protection, and Free Trade: International Sources of U.S. Commercial Strategy, 1887–1939* (Ithaca: Cornell University Press).

Lama, Abraham, 1993. "Peru: Government Sets out to Placate Its Private Creditors." *Inter Press Service* (August 17).

Langoni, Carlos G., 1985. *A Crise Do Desenvolvimento, Uma Estrategia para O Futuro* (Rio de Janeiro: Jose Olympio Editora).

Larraín, Felipe, and Jeffrey D. Sachs, 1991. "International Financial Relations." In Paredes and Sachs, 1991, pp. 344–373.

Latin American Weekly Report (various).

Latsis, Spiro, ed., 1976. *Method and Appraisal in Economics* (Cambridge: Cambridge University Press).

Laudan, Larry, 1977. *Progress and Its Problems: A Theory of Scientific Growth* (Berkeley: University of California Press).

Lauren, Paul Gordon, ed., 1979. *Diplomacy: New Approaches in History, Theory, and Policy* (New York: Free Press).

League of Nations, Secretariat, Financial Section and Economic Intelligence Service, 1942. *The Network of World Trade: A Companion Volume to "Europe's Trade"* (Geneva: League of Nations).

Lee, Boon-Chye, 1993. *The Economics of International Debt Renegotiation: The Role of Bargaining and Information* (Boulder: Westview Press).

Lee, S., 1991a. "Using Terms of Rescheduling as Proxy for Partial Reneging on LDCs Debt in a Test of Willingness-to-Pay Model." *Journal of International Money and Finance*, vol. 10, no. 3 (September), pp. 457–477.

Lee, S., 1991b. "Ability and Willingness to Service Debt as Explanation for Commercial and Official Rescheduling Cases." *Journal of Banking & Finance*, vol. 15, no. 1 (February), pp. 5–27.

Lefler, Melvyn, 1972. "The Origins of the Republican War Debt Policy, 1921–33: A Case Study in the Applicability of the Open Door Interpretation." *Journal of American History*, vol. 59 no. 3, pp. 585–601.

Lehman, Howard P., 1993a. *Indebted Development: Strategic Bargaining and Economic Adjustment in the Third World* (New York: St. Martin's Press).

Lehman, Howard P., 1993b. "Strategic Bargaining in Brazil's Debt Negotiations." *Political Science Quarterly*, vol. 108, no. 1 (Spring), pp. 133–155.

Lehman, Howard P., and J. McCoy, 1992. "The Dynamics of the 2-Level Bargaining Game – The 1988 Brazilian Debt Negotiations." *World Politics*, vol. 44, no. 4 (July), pp. 600–644.

Leipold, Alessandro, et al., 1991. *Private Market Financing for Developing Countries* (Washington, D.C.: International Monetary Fund).

Levi, Leone, 1880. *The History of British Commerce and of the Economic Progress of the British Nation, 1763–1878* (London: John Murray).

Levin, Jonathan V., 1960. *The Export Economies: Their Pattern of Development in Historical Perspective* (Cambridge, Mass.: Harvard University Press).

Levy-Leboyer, Maurice, 1982. "Banking and Foreign Trade – The Anglo American Cycle in the 1830's." In Kindleberger and Laffargue, 1982.

Lewis, Arthur, 1978. *The Evolution of the International Economic Order* (Princeton: Princeton University Press).

Lewis, Cleona, 1938. *America's Stake in International Investments* (Washington, D.C.: Brookings Institution).

Li, Carmen A., 1992. "Debt Arrears in Latin America: Do Political Variables Matter?" *Journal of Development Studies*, vol. 28, no. 4 (July), pp. 668–688.

Lindblom, Charles, 1977. *Politics and Markets: The World's Political-Economic System* (New York: Basic Books).

Lindert, Peter, 1989. "Response to the Debt Crisis: What Is Different about the 1980s?" In Eichengreen and Lindert, 1989, pp. 227–275.

Lipman, Bart, 1983. "Cooperation among Egoists in Prisoner's Dilemma and Chicken Games." Paper presented at the American Political Science Association meetings Chicago, August.

Lipschutz, R., 1991. "Bargaining Among Nations – Culture, History, and Perceptions in Regime Formation." *Evaluation Review*, vol. 15, no. 1 (February), pp. 46–74.

Lipschutz, R., 1993. "Bargaining among Nations" (correction). *Evaluation Review*, vol. 17, no. 6 (December), p. 663.

Lipson, Charles, 1981. "The International Organization of Third World Debt." *International Organization*, vol. 35, no. 4 (Autumn), pp. 603–631.

Lipson, Charles, 1985. *Standing Guard: Protecting Foreign Capital in the Nineteenth and Twentieth Centuries* (Berkeley: University of California Press).

Lipson, Charles, 1989. "International Debt and National Security: Comparing Victorian Britain and Postwar America." In Eichengreen and Lindert, 1989, pp. 189–226.

Lipson, Charles, 1991. "Why Are Some International Agreements Informal?" *International Organization*, vol. 45, no. 4 (Fall), pp. 495–538.

Lloyd, Ellis H., G.W. McKenzie, and S.H. Thomas, 1989. "Using Country Balance Sheet Data to Predict Debt Rescheduling." *Economics Letters*, vol. 31, no. 2, pp. 173–177.

Lloyd, Ellis H., G.W. McKenzie, and S.H. Thomas, 1990. "Predicting the Quantity of LDC Debt Rescheduling." *Economics Letters*, vol. 32, no. 1 (January), pp. 67–73.

Los Angeles Times (various).

Loveman, Brian, 1979. *Chile: The Legacy of Hispanic Capitalism* (New York: Oxford University Press).

Luce, R. Duncan, and Howard Raiffa, 1957. *Games and Decisions* (New York: Wiley).

Luebbert, Gregory M., 1986. *Comparative Democracy: Policy Making and Governing Coalitions in Europe and Israel* (New York: Columbia University Press).

Lustig, Nora, 1992. *Mexico: The Remaking of an Economy* (Washington, D.C.: Brookings Institution).

Macdonald, Scott B., Jane Hughes, and Uwe Bott, eds., 1991. *Latin American Debt in the 1990s: Lessons from the Past and Forecasts for the Future* (New York: Praeger).

Madden, John T. Marcus Nadler, and Harry C. Sauvin, 1937. *America's Experience as a Creditor Nation* (New York: Prentice-Hall).

Madura, J., A. Tucker, and E. Zarruk, 1992. "Reaction of Bank Share Prices to the Third-World Debt Reduction Plan." *Journal of Banking & Finance*, vol. 16, no. 5 (September), pp. 853–868.

Mailath, George J., Larry Samuelson, and Jerome M. Swinkels, 1993. "Extensive Form Reasoning in Normal Form Games." *Econometrica*, vol. 61, no. 2 (March), pp. 273–302.

Malloy, James, ed., 1977. *Authoritarianism and Corporatism in Latin America* (Pittsburgh: University of Pittsburgh Press).

Malpica Silva Santisteban, Carlos, Oscar Ugarteche, and Augosto Zuniga, 1985. *Deuda Externa: Problemas y Soluciones* (Lima: Servicios Populares).

Mann, Michael, 1986. "The Autonomous Power of the State: Its Origins, Mechanisms and Results." In Hall, 1986, pp. 109–136.

Manning, William R., 1916/1968. *Early Diplomatic Relations between the United States and Mexico* (New York: Greenwood Press).

March, James, 1966. "The Power of Power." In Easton, 1966, pp. 39–70.

March, James, and Herbert Simon, 1958. *Organizations* (New York: John Wiley and Sons).

Mares, David, 1987. *Penetrating the International Market: Theoretical Considerations and a Mexican Case Study* (New York: Columbia University Press).

Marichal, Carlos, 1989. *A Century of Debt Crises in Latin America: From Independence to the Great Depression, 1820–1930* (Princeton: Princeton University Press).

Markham, Clements R., 1892. *A History of Peru* (Chicago: Charles H. Sergel and Co.).

Martin, Lisa, 1992. "Interests, Power, and Multilateralism." *International Organization*, vol. 46, no. 4 (Fall), pp. 765–792.

Mascarenhas, Briance, and Ole Christian Sand, 1989. "Combination of Forecasts in the International Context: Predicting Debt Reschedulings." *Journal of International Business Studies*, vol. 20, no. 3 (Fall), pp. 539–552.

Mason, Edward, 1939. "Price and Production Policies of Large-Scale Enterprises." *American Economic Review*, Supplement, pp. 61–74.

Mathew, William, 1968. "The Imperialism of Free Trade: Peru, 1820–1870." *Economic History Review*, 2d series, vol. 21 (December), pp. 562–579.

Mathew, William, 1970. "The First Anglo-Peruvian Debt and Its Settlement, 1822–1849." *Journal of Latin American Studies* (May), pp. 81–99.

Mathew, William, 1977. "Antony Gibbs & Sons, the Guano Trade and the Peruvian Government, 1842–1861." In Platt, 1977, pp. 337–370.

Mathew, William, 1981. *The House of Gibbs and the Peruvian Guano Monopoly* (London: Royal Historical Society).

Maxfield, Sylvia, 1990. *Governing Capital: International Finance and Mexican Politics* (Ithaca: Cornell University Press).

Maxfield, Sylvia, 1991. "Bankers' Alliances and Economic Policy Patterns: Evidence from Mexico and Brazil." *Comparative Political Studies*, vol. 23, no. 4 (January), pp. 419–458.

Maxfield, Sylvia, 1992. "The International Political Economy of Bank Nationalization – Mexico in Comparative Perspective." *Latin American Research Review*, vol. 27, no. 1, pp. 75–103.

Mayer, Thomas, 1975. "Should Large Banks Be Allowed to Fail?" *Journal of Financial and Quantitative Analysis*, vol. 10, no. 4, pp. 603–610.

McCaleb, Walter, 1921. *The Public Finances of Mexico* (New York and London: Harper and Brothers).

McClintock, Cynthia, and Abraham F. Lowenthal, eds., 1983. *The Peruvian Experiment Reconsidered* (Princeton: Princeton University Press).

McKenzie, George, 1976. *The Economics of the Euro-Currency System* (London: Macmillan).
McKeown, Timothy, 1986. "The Limitations of 'Structural' Theories of Commercial Policy." *International Organization*, vol. 40, no. 1 (Winter), pp. 43–64.
McKinnon, Ronald, 1979. *Money in International Exchange: The Convertible Currency System* (New York: Oxford University Press).
McQueen, Charles, 1926. *Peruvian Public Finance* (Washington, D.C.: Government Printing Office, Department of Commerce, Trade Promotion Series, no. 45).
Mendelsohn, Stefan, 1983. *Commercial Banks and the Restructuring of Cross-border Debt* (New York: Group of Thirty).
Mendelsohn, Stefan, 1984. *The Debt of Nations* (New York: Priority Press Publishers).
Meyer, Michael, and William Sherman, 1987. *The Course of Mexican History* (New York: Oxford University Press).
Middlebrook, Kevin, 1989. "The Sounds of Silence: Organised Labour's Response to Economic Crisis in Mexico." *Journal of Latin American Studies*, vol. 21, part 2 (May), pp. 195–220.
Miller, Rory, 1976. "The Making of the Grace Contract: British Bondholders and the Peruvian Government, 1885–1890." *Journal of Latin American Studies*, vol. 8, no. 1, pp. 73–100.
Miller, Rory, 1983. "The Grace Contract, The Peruvian Corporation, and Peruvian History." *Ibero-Amerikanishes Archiv*, vol. 9, nos. 3/4, pp. 319–347.
Millington, Herbert, 1948. *American Diplomacy and the War of the Pacific* (New York: Columbia University Press).
Milner, Helen V., 1988. *Resisting Protectionism: Global Industries and Politics of International Trade* (Princeton: Princeton University Press).
Milner, Helen V., 1992. Review of *Cooperation among Nations* by J. Grieco. *World Politics*, vol. 44, no. 3 (April), pp. 466–496.
Ministry of Labor, 1983. *Empleo e Ingresos en el Contexto de la Crisis: Perú, 1983* (Lima: Ministry of Labor).
Mishan, E.J., 1969. "The Relationship between Joint Products, Collective Goods, and External Effects." *Journal of Political Economy*, vol. 77, no. 3, pp. 329–348.
Mishan, E.J., 1971. "The Postwar Literature on Externalities: An Interpretative Essay." *Journal of Economic Literature*, vol. 9, no. 1, pp. 1–28.
Moghadam, Mashalah Rahnama, and Hedayeh Samavati, 1991. "Predicting Debt Rescheduling by Less-Developed Countries: A Probit Model Approach." *Quarterly Review of Economics and Business*, vol. 31, no. 1 (Spring), pp. 3–14.
Mohr, Ernst, 1991. *Economic Theory and Sovereign International Debt* (London and New York: Academic Press).
Monteón, Michael, 1982. *Chile in the Nitrate Era: The Evolution of Economic Dependence, 1880–1930* (Madison: University of Wisconsin Press).
Morgenstern, Oskar, 1959. *International Financial Transactions and Business Cycles* (Princeton: Princeton University Press).
Morrow, James D., 1986. "A Spatial Model of International Conflict." *American Political Science Review*, vol. 80, no. 4 (December), pp. 1131–1150.
Morrow, James, 1989. "Capabilities, Uncertainty, and Resolve – A Limited Information Model of Crisis Bargaining." *American Journal of Political Science*, vol. 33, no. 4 (November), pp. 941–972.
Morrow, James, 1992. "Signaling Difficulties with Linkage in Crisis Bargaining." *International Studies Quarterly*, vol. 36, no. 2 (June), pp. 153–172.
Murphy, Craig N., and Roger Tooze, eds., 1991. *The New International Political Economy* (Boulder: Lynne Rienner Publishers).
Myerson, Roger, 1991. *Game Theory: Analysis of Conflict* (Cambridge, Mass.: Harvard University Press).

Nagy, Sandor, 1989. "The International Debt Trap: External and Internal Redistribution of Incomes." In Davidson and Kregel, 1989, pp. 174–178.

Nalebuff, Barry, 1991. "Rational Deterrence in an Imperfect World." *World Politics*, vol. 43, no. 3 (April), pp. 313–335.

Nash, John F., 1950. "The Bargaining Problem." *Econometrica*, vol. 18, pp. 155–162.

Nash, John F., 1951. "Non-Cooperative Games." *Annals of Mathematics*, vol. 54, pp. 286–295.

Nelson, Joan M., 1989. *Fragile Coalitions: The Politics of Economic Adjustment* (New Brunswick: Transaction Books, U.S.-Third World Policy Perspectives, no. 12).

Nelson, Joan M., ed., 1990. *Economic Crisis and Policy Choice: The Politics of Adjustment in the Third World* (Princeton: Princeton University Press).

New York Times (various).

Newsweek (various).

Oberholtzer, Ellis P., 1968. *Jay Cooke, Financier of the Civil War* (New York: A.M. Kelley).

O'Brien, Thomas F., 1982. *The Nitrate Industry and Chile's Crucial Transition: 1870–1891* (New York: New York University Press).

O'Connell, Stephen A., and Stephen P. Zeldes, 1988. "Rational Ponzi Games." *International Economic Review*, vol. 29, no. 3 (August), pp. 431–450.

Odell, John S., 1982. *U.S. International Monetary Policy: Markets, Power, and Ideas as Sources of Change* (Princeton: Princeton University Press).

Odell, John S., and Thomas D. Willett, eds., 1990. *International Trade Policies: Gains from Exchange between Economics and Political Science* (Ann Arbor: University of Michigan Press).

O'Donnell, Guillermo A., 1973. *Modernization and Bureaucratic-Authoritarianism: Studies in South American Politics* (Berkeley: Institute of International Studies, University of California, Politics of Modernization Series, no. 9).

O'Donnell, Guillermo A., 1985. "Deuda Externa: Por Qué Nuestros Gobiernos No Hacen lo Obvio?" *CEPAL Review*, vol. 27 (December), pp. 27–33.

Oliveri, Ernest J., 1992. *Latin American Debt and the Politics of International Finance* (Westport, Conn.: Praeger).

Olson, Mancur, Jr., 1965. *The Logic of Collective Action: Public Goods and the Theory of Groups* (Cambridge, Mass.: Harvard Univesity Press).

Olson, Mancur, 1971. "Increasing Incentives for International Cooperation." *International Organization*, vol. 25, pp. 86–974.

Ordeshook, Peter, ed., 1989. *Models of Strategic Choice in Politics* (Ann Arbor: University of Michigan Press).

Ordeshook, Peter, 1992. *A Political Theory Primer* (New York: Routledge).

Oye, Kenneth, Donald Rothchild, and Robert J. Lieber, eds., 1979. *Eagle Entangled: U.S. Foreign Policy in a Complex World* (New York: Longman).

Oye, Kenneth, 1983. *Belief Systems, Bargaining and Breakdown: International Political Economy 1929–1934* (Ph.D. dissertation, Harvard University).

Oye, Kenneth, 1985a. "Explaining Cooperation under Anarchy: Hypothetical Strategies." In Oye, 1985b, pp. 1–24.

Oye, Kenneth, ed., 1985b. "Cooperation under Anarchy." Special Issue, *World Politics*, vol. 38, no. 1 (April).

Palacios Moreyra, Carlos, 1983. *La Deuda Anglo Peruana: 1822–1890* (Lima: Libreria Studium).

Palmer, David Scott, 1980. *Peru: The Authoritarian Tradition* (New York: Praeger Publishers).

Papi, Giuseppe, 1951. *The First Twenty Years of the Bank for International Settlements* (Rome: Bancaria).

Paredes, Carlos E., and Jeffrey D. Sachs, eds., 1991. *Peru's Path to Recovery: A Plan for Economic Stabilization and Growth* (Washington, D.C.: Brookings Institution).
Pareto, Vilfredo, 1971. *Manual of Political Economy*, Translated by Ann J. Schwier (New York: A.M. Kelley).
Parkes, Henry, 1938/1969. *A History of Mexico* (Boston: Houghton Mifflin Co.).
Parodi, Jorge, 1986. "La desmoilización del sindicalismo industrial peruano en el segundo belaundismo." In Ballon, 1986, pp. 45–68.
Pauly, Mark, 1968. "The Economics of Moral Hazard: Comment." *American Economic Review*, vol. 58, no. 3, pp. 528–529.
Payer, Cheryl, 1991. *Lent and Lost: Foreign Credit and Third World Development* (London and Atlantic Highlands, N.J.: Zed Books).
Payno, Manuelo, 1862. *Mexico y Sus Cuestiones Financieras con la Inglaterra, la España, y la Francia* (Mexico: I. Cumplido).
Pennano, Guido, ed., 1980. *Cronica de un Colapso Económico, Perú, 1974–1979* (Lima: Universidad del Pacifico Centro de Investigacion, Serie Cuadernos Documento de Trabajo, no. 6).
Perkins, Dexter, 1927. *The Monroe Doctrine 1823–1826* (Cambridge, Mass.: Harvard University Press, Harvard Historical Studies, vol. 29).
Pettis, M., 1991. "Using Mexican Debt Prices as a Proxy for the Economy." *Columbia Journal of World Business*, vol. 26, no. 2 (Summer), pp. 116–123.
Phelps, Clyde, 1927. *The Foreign Expansion of American Banks: American Branch Banking Abroad* (New York: Ronald Press Co.).
Pike, Frederick B., 1967. *The Modern History of Peru* (London: Weidenfeld and Nicolson).
Pinzas García, Teobaldo, 1981. *La Economia Peruano, 1950–1980: Un Essayo Bibliografico* (Lima: Instituto de Estudios Peruanos).
Platt, Desmond C.M., 1968. *Finance, Trade and Politics in British Foreign Policy, 1815–1914* (Oxford: Clarendon Press).
Platt, Desmond C.M., ed., 1977. *Business Imperialism, 1840–1930: An Inquiry Based on British Experience in Latin America* (Oxford: Clarendon Press).
Portocarrero, Felipe, 1982. "The Peruvian Public Investment Programme, 1968–1978." *Journal of Latin American Studies*, vol. 14, no. 2 (November), pp. 433–454.
Powell, Robert, 1990. *Nuclear Deterrence Theory: The Search for Credibility* (Cambridge: Cambridge University Press).
Powell, Robert, 1991. "Absolute and Relative Gains in International Relations Theory." *American Political Science Review*, vol. 85, no. 4 (December), pp. 1303–1320.
Powell, Robert, 1994. "Anarchy in International Relations Theory: The Neorealist-Neoliberal Debate." *International Organization*, vol. 48, no. 2 (Spring), pp. 313–344.
Priestley, Herbert I., 1923/1969. *The Mexican Nation, A History* (New York: Cooper Square Publishers, Library of Latin American History and Culture).
Putnam, Robert D., 1988. "Diplomacy and Domestic Politics: The Logic of Two-Level Games." *International Organization*, vol. 42 (Summer), pp. 427–460.
Quijano, Anibal, 1971. *Nationalism and Capitalism in Peru: A Study in Neo-Imperialism*, trans. Helen R. Lane (New York: Monthly Review Press).
Rahnama Moghadam, Mashahla, Hedayeh Samavati, and Lawrence Haber, 1991. "The Determinants of Debt Rescheduling: The Case of Latin America." *Southern Economic Journal*, vol. 58, no. 2 (October), pp. 510–517.
Ramamurti, R., 1992. "The Impact of Privatization on the Latin American Debt Problem." *Journal of Interamerican Studies and World Affairs*, vol. 34, no. 2 (Summer), pp. 93–125.
Rapoport, Anatol, and Melvin Guyer, 1966. "A Taxonomy of 2 × 2 Games." *General Systems*, vol. 11, pp. 203–204.

Rapoport, Anatol, Melvin Guyer, and David Gordon, 1976. *The 2 × 2 Game* (Ann Arbor: University of Michigan Press).

Raw, Silvia, ed., 1987. "The Debt Crisis in Latin America." *International Journal of Political Economy*, vol. 17, no. 1, pp. 5–14.

Res, Zannis, and Sima Motamen, eds., 1987. *International Debt and Central Banking in the 1980s* (New York: St. Martin's Press).

Ridley, Jasper, 1970. *Lord Palmerston* (London: Constable).

Rieffel, Alexis, 1985. *The Role of the Paris Club in Managing Debt Problems* (Princeton: International Finance Section, Dept. of Economics, Princeton University, Essays in International Finance, no. 161).

Rippy, J. Fred, 1929/1964. *Rivalry of the U.S. and Great Britain over Latin America (1808–1830)* (New York: Octagon Books, The Albert Shaw Lectures on Diplomatic History).

Rittberger, Volker, ed., 1990. *International Regimes in East-West Policies* (London and New York: Pinter Publishers).

Rittberger, Volker, ed., 1993. *Regime Theory and International Relations* (New York: Oxford University Press).

Roett, Riordan, ed., 1976. *Brazil in the Seventies* (Washington, D.C.: American Enterprise Institute for Public Policy Research).

Roett, Riordan, 1985–1986. "Peru: The Message from García." *Foreign Affairs*, vol. 64, no. 2 (Winter), pp. 274–286.

Rogoff, K., 1992. "Dealing with Developing Country Debt in the 1990s." *World Economy*, vol. 15, no. 4 (July), pp. 475–486.

Rogovitsky, A., 1990. "Bank Lending to LDCs – From the Euphoria of Credit Syndication to the Debt Problems Implications." *Development and Change*, vol. 21, no. 4 (October), pp. 621–636.

Romero, Matías, 1871. *Memoria de Hacienda y Crédito Público* (Mexico).

Rosecrance, Richard, 1986. *The Rise of the Trading State: Commerce and Conquest in the Modern World* (New York: Basic Books).

Rosenthal, R., 1991. "On the Incentives Associated with Sovereign Debt." *Journal of International Economics*, vol. 30, nos. 1–2 (February), pp. 167–176.

Rotemberg, J., 1991. "Sovereign Debt Buybacks Can Lower Bargaining Costs." *Journal of International Money and Finance*, vol. 10, no. 3 (September), pp. 330–348.

Rothschild, Kurt W., ed., 1971. *Power in Economics: Selected Readings* (Harmondsworth: Penguin).

Rothstein, Robert L., 1979. *Global Bargaining: UNCTAD and the Quest for a New International Economic Order* (Princeton: Princeton University Press).

Rothstein, Robert L., 1984. "Consensual Knowledge and International Collaboration: Some Lessons from the Commodity Negotiations." *International Organization*, vol. 38, no. 4 (Autumn), pp. 733–762.

Rowlands, D., 1993. "Constitutional Rules, Reputation, and Sovereign Debt." *Journal of International Economics*, vol. 35, nos. 3–4 (November), pp. 335–350.

Ruggie, John G., 1972. "Collective Goods and the Future of International Cooperation." *American Political Science Review*, vol. 66, pp. 874–893.

Russett, Bruce, and John Sullivan, 1971. "Collective Goods and International Organization." *International Organization*, vol. 25, no. 4 (Autumn), pp. 845–865.

Sachs, Jeffrey D., 1984. *Theoretical Issues in International Borrowing* (Princeton: International Finance Section, Dept. of Economics, Princeton University Press, Princeton Studies in International Finance, no. 54).

Sachs, Jeffrey D., 1985. "External Debt and Economic Performance in Latin America and East Asia." *Brookings Papers on Economic Activity*, vol. 2, pp. 523–564.

Sachs, Jeffrey D., 1986. "Managing the LDC Debt Crisis." *Brookings Papers on Economic Activity*, vol. 2, pp. 397–431.

Sachs, Jeffrey D., 1989a. *New Approaches to the Latin American Debt Crisis* (Princeton: International Finance Section, Dept. of Economics, Princeton University, Essays in International Finance, no. 174).

Sachs, Jeffrey D., ed., 1989b. *Developing Country Debt and Economic Performance* (Chicago: University of Chicago Press).

Sachs, Jeffrey, 1989c. "Making the Brady Plan Work." *Foreign Affairs*, vol. 68, no. 3 (Summer), pp. 87–104.

Sachs, Jeffrey, 1989d. "Efficient Debt Reduction." In Husain and Diwan, 1989, pp. 239–257.

Sachs, Jeffrey, 1989e. "The Debt Overhang of Developing Countries." In Calvo et al., 1989, pp. 80–102.

Samuelson, Paul A., 1954. "The Pure Theory of Public Expenditure." *Review of Economics and Statistics*, vol. 36, no. 4, pp. 387–390.

San Francisco Examiner (various).

Sater, William F., 1979. "Chile and the World Depression of the 1870s." *Journal of Latin American Studies*, vol. 11, no. 1, pp. 67–99.

Sayers, Richard, 1976. *The Bank of England, 1891–1944* (Cambridge: Cambridge University Press).

Scheetz, Thomas, 1986. *Peru and the International Monetary Fund* (Pittsburgh: University of Pittsburgh Press).

Schelling, Thomas, 1960/1963. *The Strategy of Conflict* (New York: Oxford University Press).

Scherer, Frederic M., 1970/1980. *Industrial Market Structure and Economic Performance* (Chicago: Rand McNally College Publishing Co.).

Schloss, Henry, 1958. *The Bank for International Settlements: An Experiment in Central Bank Cooperation* (Amsterdam: North-Holland Publishing Co.).

Schydlowsky, Daniel M., 1986. "The Macroeconomic Effect of Nontraditional Exports in Peru." *Economic Development and Cultural Change*, vol. 34, no. 3 (April), pp. 491–509.

Sebenius, James K., 1984. *Negotiating the Law of the Sea* (Cambridge, Mass.: Harvard University Press).

Selten, Reinhard, 1965. "Spieltheoretische Behandlung eines Oligopolmodelles mit Nachfragetragheit." *Zeitschrift für Gesamte Staatswissenschaft*, vol. 121, pp. 301–324.

Selten, Reinhard, 1975. "Re-Examination of the Perfectness Concept of Equilibrium Points in Extensive Games." *International Journal of Game Theory*, vol. 4, pp. 25–55.

Selten, R., 1978. "The Chain Store Paradox." *Theory and Decision*, vol. 9, no. 2, pp. 127–159.

Serven, Luis, and Andres Solimano, 1993. "Debt Crisis, Adjustment Policies and Capital Formation in Developing Countries: Where Do We Stand?" *World Development*, vol. 21, no. 1 (January), pp. 127–140.

Sheahan, John, 1980. "Peru: Economic Policies and Structural Change, 1968–1978." *Journal of Economic Studies*, vol. 7, no. 1, pp. 3–27.

Shubik, Martin, 1959. *Strategy and Market Structure: Competition, Oligopoly and the Theory of Games* (New York: John Wiley and Sons).

Shubik, Martin, 1982. *Game Theory in the Social Sciences: Concepts and Solutions*, vols. 1 and 2 (Cambridge, Mass.: MIT Press).

Simon, Herbert, 1962. "The Architecture of Complexity." *Proceedings of the American Philosophical Society*, pp. 467–482.

Simon, Herbert A., 1982. *Models of Bounded Rationality* (Cambridge, Mass.: MIT Press).

Simon, Matthew, 1968. "The Pattern of New British Portfolio Foreign Investment, 1865–1914." In Hall, 1968, pp. 15–44.

Skidmore, Thomas E., 1977. "The Politics of Economic Stabilization in Postwar Latin America." In Malloy, 1977, pp. 149–190.

Skidmore, Thomas E., and Peter H. Smith, 1984. *Modern Latin America* (New York: Oxford University Press).

Smith, Gordon W., and John T. Cuddington, eds., 1985. *International Debt and the Developing Countries* (Washington, D.C.: World Bank).

Smith, Robert F., 1972. *The United States and Revolutionary Nationalism in Mexico, 1916–1932* (Chicago: University of Chicago Press).

Snidal, Duncan, 1979. "Public Goods, Property Rights, and Political Organization." *International Studies Quarterly*, vol. 23, no. 4, pp. 532–566.

Snidal, Duncan, 1985a. "The Game *Theory* of International Politics." *World Politics*, vol. 38, no. 1 (October), pp. pp. 25–57.

Snidal, Duncan, 1985b. "The Limits of Hegemonic Stability Theory." *International Organization*, vol. 39 (Autumn), 25–57.

Snidal, Duncan, 1991a. "Relative Gains and the Pattern of International Cooperation." *American Political Science Review*, vol. 85, no. 3 (September), pp. 701–726.

Snidal, Duncan, 1991b. "International Cooperation among Relative Gains Maximizers." *International Studies Quarterly*, vol. 35, no. 4 (December), pp. 387–403.

Snider, Lewis, 1990. "The Political Performance of the Third-World Governments and the Debt Crisis." *American Political Science Review*, vol. 84, no. 4 (December), pp. 1263–1280.

Snyder, Glenn, and Paul Diesing, 1977. *Conflict among Nations: Bargaining, Decision Making, and System Structure* (Princeton: Princeton University Press).

Solberg, Ronald L., 1988. *Sovereign Rescheduling: Risk and Portfolio Management* (London and Boston: Unwin Hyman).

Solomon, Robert, 1989. *An Overview of the International Debt Crisis* (Washington, D.C.: Brookings Institution, Brookings Discussion Papers in International Economics, no. 74).

South (various).

Sorj, Bernardo, 1983. "Public Enterprises and the Question of the State Bourgeoisie, 1968–76." In Booth and Sorj, 1983, pp. 72–93.

Spero, Joan, 1977. *The Politics of International Economic Relations* (New York: St. Martin's Press).

Srack, Dieter, and Siegfried Schonherr, eds., 1990. *Debt Survey of Developing Countries* (Boulder: Westview Press, Westview Special Studies in International Economics and Business).

Stallings, Barbara, 1979. "Peru and the U.S. Banks: Privatization of Financial Relations." In Fagen, 1979, pp. 217–253.

Stallings, Barbara, 1983. "International Capitalism and the Peruvian Military Government." In McClintock and Lowenthal, 1983, pp. 144–180.

Stallings, Barbara, 1987. *Banker to the Third World: U.S. Portfolio Investment in Latin America 1900–1986* (Berkeley: University of California Press).

Stallings, Barbara, 1990. "The Reluctant Giant – Japan and the Latin American Debt Crisis." *Journal of Latin American Studies*, vol. 22 (February), pp. 1–30.

Stallings, Barbara, and Robert Kaufman, eds., 1989. *Debt and Democracy in Latin America* (Boulder: Westview Press).

Stein, Arthur A., 1980. "The Politics of Linkage." *World Politics*, vol. 33 (October), pp. 62–81.

Stein, Arthur A., 1983. "Coordination and Collaboration: Regimes in an Anarchic World." In Krasner, 1983b, pp. 115–140.

Stein, Arthur A., 1990. *Why Nations Cooperate: Circumstance and Choice in International Relations* (Ithaca: Cornell University Press).

Stepan, Alfred, ed., 1973. *Authoritarian Brazil: Origins, Policies, and Future* (New Haven: Yale University Press).

Stepan, Alfred, 1978. *The State and Society: Peru in Comparative Perspective* (Princeton: Princeton University Press).

Stephens, Evelyne Huber, 1983. "The Peruvian Military Government, Labor Mobilization and the Political Strength of the Left." *Latin American Research Review*, vol. 18, no. 2, pp. 57–93.

Stewart, Watt, 1946/1968. *Henry Meiggs: Yankee Pizarro* (New York: AMS Press).

Story, Dale, 1987. "The PAN, the Private Sector, and the Future of the Mexican Opposition." In Gentleman, 1987, pp. 261–280.

Strange, Susan, 1970. "International Economics and International Relations: A Case of Mutual Neglect." *International Affairs*, vol. 46, pp. 304–315.

Strange, Susan, 1976a. *International Economic Relations of the Western World, 1959–1971* (New York: Oxford University Press for the Royal Institute of International Affairs).

Strange, Susan, 1976b. *International Monetary Relations* (London and New York: Oxford University Press for the Royal Institute of International Affairs).

Strange, Susan, 1986. *Casino Capitalism* (Oxford and New York: B. Blackwell).

Strange, Susan, 1988. *States and Markets* (London: Pinter Publishers).

Strange, Susan, 1991. "Big Business and the State." *Millennium-Journal of International Studies*, vol. 20, no. 2 (Summer), pp. 245–250.

Strange, Susan, 1992. "States, Firms, and Diplomacy." *International Affairs*, vol. 68, no. 1 (January), pp. 1–15.

Suratgar, David, ed., 1984. *Default and Rescheduling: Corporate and Sovereign Borrowers* (London: Euromoney Publications, and Washington, D.C.: International Law Institute).

Suter, Christian, 1992. *Debt Cycles in the World-Economy: Foreign Loans, Financial Crises, and Debt Settlements, 1820–1990* (Boulder: Westview Press).

Taffler, R.J., and B. Abassi, 1987. "Country Risk: A Model for Predicting Debt Servicing Problems in Developing Countries." In Res and Motamen, 1987, pp. 187–273.

Taylor, Michael, 1976. *Anarchy and Cooperation* (New York: John Wiley and Sons).

Telhami, Shibley, 1990. *Power and Leadership in International Bargaining: The Path to the Camp David Accords* (New York: Columbia University Press).

Temperley, Harold, 1925. *The Foreign Policy of Canning, 1822–1827: England, the Neo-Holy Alliance and the New World* (London: G. Bell and Sons).

Thomas, J., 1992. "Sovereign Debt – Ignorance Can Be Bliss." *Journal of Development Economics*, vol. 39, no. 2 (October), pp. 389–396.

Thorp, Rosemary, 1983. "The Evolution of Peru's Economy." In McClintock and Lowenthal, 1983, pp. 39–64.

Thorp, Rosemary, 1985. "Endeudamiento o Inversion Directa: Consideraciones a Partir del Caso Peruano." In Ferrero, 1985, pp. 25–38.

Thorp, Rosemary, and Geoffrey Bertram, 1978. *Peru 1890–1977: Growth and Policy in an Open Economy* (London: Macmillan).

Thurow, Lester, 1980. *The Zero-Sum Society: Distribution and the Possibilities for Economic Change* (New York: Basic Books).

The Times, London (various).

Tollison, Robert D., and Thomas D. Willett, 1979. "An Economic Theory of Mutually Advantageous Issue Linkages in International Negotiations." *International Organization*, vol. 33, no. 4, pp. 425–449.

Toye, J.F.J., ed., 1988. *Taxation and Economic Development* (London and Totowa, N.J.: Frank Cass).

Tsebelis, George, 1990. *Nested Games: Rational Choice in Comparative Politics* (Berkeley: University of California Press).

Turlington, Edgar, 1930. *Mexico and Her Foreign Creditors* (New York: Columbia University Press, Mexico in International Finance and Diplomacy, vol. 1).

Ugarteche, Oscar, 1980. *Teoria y Practica de la Deuda Externa en el Perú* (Lima: Instituto de Estudios Peruanos).

Ugarteche, Oscar, 1986. *El Estado Deudor: Economía Política de la Deuda: Perú y Bolivia* (Lima: Instituto de Estudios Peruanos).

Ugarteche, Oscar, 1988. "El Perú: La Deuda y el Ajuste Heterodoxo con Alan García." In Griffith-Jones, 1988, pp. 188–218.

Ullmann-Margalit, Edna, 1977. *The Emergence of Norms* (Oxford: Clarendon Press).

Unal, H., A. Demirguckunt, and K. Leung, 1993. "The Brady Plan, 1989 Mexican Debt-Reduction Agreement, and Bank Stock Returns in United States and Japan." *Journal of Money, Credit and Banking*, vol. 25, no. 3 (August), pp. 410–429.

United Kingdom, 1875. "Loans to Foreign States." *Parliamentary Papers*, Reports from Committees, vol. 11 (London).

United Nations, 1955. *Foreign Capital in Latin America* (New York: Department of Economic and Social Affairs).

United States Congress, 1984. Subcommittee on International Finance and Monetary Policy of the Committee on Banking, Housing, and Urban Affairs, U.S. Senate. *The Argentinian Debt*. 98th Congress, 782 (Washington, D.C.: U.S. Government Printing Office).

United States Congress, 1985. Joint Economic Committee, Subcommittee on Economic Goals and Intergovernmental Policy, 98th Congress. *Dealing with the Debt Problem of Latin America* (Washington, D.C.: U.S. Government Printing Office).

United States Department of State, archives (various).

United States House of Representatives, 1988. Committee on Banking, Finance, and Urban Affairs, Subcommittee on International Finance, Trade, and Monetary Policy, 100th Congress. *Report on an International Debt Management Authority* (Washington, D.C.: U.S. Government Printing Office).

United States *Treasury Notes* (various years).

Uriarte, J. Manuel, 1986. *Transnational Banks and the Dynamics of the Peruvian Foreign Debt and Inflation* (New York: Praeger).

Uriona, Ramiro Cavero, 1992. Review of *Developing Country Debt and Economic Performance, Country Studies: Argentina, Bolivia, Brazil, Mexico*, vol. 2, by J. Sachs. *Journal of Latin American Studies*, vol. 24, no. 1 (February), pp. 214–215.

van Wijnbergen, S., 1991. "Debt Relief and Economic Growth in Mexico." *World Bank Economic Review*, vol. 5, no. 3 (September), pp. 437–455.

Varian, Hal R., 1990. *Intermediate Microeconomics: A Modern Approach* (New York: W.W. Norton).

Vázquez, Josephina, and Lorenzo Meyer, 1985. *The United States and Mexico* (Chicago: University of Chicago Press).

Velasco Alvarado, Juan, 1972. *Velasco: La Voz de la Revolución; Discursos del Presidente de la Republica General de Division Juan Velasco Alvarado, 1968–1970* (Lima: Oficina Nacional de Difusión del SINAMOS).

Verba, Sidney, 1967. "Some Dilemmas of Comparative Research." *World Politics*, vol. 20, pp. 111–128.

Versluysen, Eugene, 1981. *The Political Economy of International Finance* (Westmead: Gower Publishing Co.).

von Neumann, John, and Oskar Morgenstern, 1944. *Theory of Games and Economic Behavior* (Princeton: Princeton University Press).

Wagner, R. Harrison, 1983. "The Theory of Games and the Problem of International Cooperation." *The American Political Science Review*, vol. 77, no. 2 (June), pp. 330–346.

Wagner, R. Harrison, 1991. "Nuclear Deterrence, Counterforce Strategies, and the Incentive to Strike First." *American Political Science Review*, vol. 85, no. 3 (September), pp. 727–749.

Wall Street Journal (various).

Waltz, Kenneth, 1959. *Man, the State, and War: A Theoretical Analysis* (New York: Columbia University Press).

Waltz, Kenneth, 1964. "The Stability of a Bipolar World." *Daedalus*, vol. 93, pp. 881–909.

Waltz, Kenneth, 1979. *Theory of International Politics* (Reading, Mass.: Addison-Wesley Publishing Co.).

Waltz, Kenneth, 1986. "Reflections on Theory of International Politics: Response to My Critics." In Keohane, 1986, pp. 322–345.

Washington Post (various).

Watkins, Alfred J., 1986. *Till Debt Do Us Part: Who Wins, Who Loses, and Who Pays for the International Debt Crisis* (Washington, D.C.: Roosevelt Center for American Policy Studies).

Webb, Richard C., 1988. "Domestic Crisis and Foreign Debt in Peru." In Toye, 1988, pp. 241–253.

Weber, Cynthia, 1990. "Representing Debt: Peruvian Presidents Belaúnde's and García's Reading/Writing of Peruvian Debt." *International Studies Quarterly*, vol. 34, no. 3 (September), pp. 353–365.

Weeks, John F., 1985. *Limits to Capitalist Development: The Industrialization of Peru, 1950–1980* (Boulder: Westview Press).

Weeks, John F., 1989. *Debt Disaster?: Banks, Governments, and Multilaterals Confront the Crisis* (New York: New York University Press).

Weisz, G.N. Schwarzkopf, and M. Panitch, 1991. "Selected Issues in Sovereign Debt Litigation." *University of Pennsylvania Journal of International Business Law*, vol. 12, no. 1, pp. 1–49.

Wellons, Philip A., 1985. "International Debt: The Behavior of Banks in a Politicized Environment." *International Organization*, vol. 39, no. 3 (Summer), pp. 441–471.

Werlich, David P., 1978. *Peru: A Short History* (Carbondale: Southern Illinois University Press).

Wesson, Robert, ed., 1988. *Coping with the Latin American Debt* (New York: Praeger).

Whitehead, Laurence, 1989. "Latin American Debt: An International Bargaining Perspective." *Review of International Studies*, vol. 15, pp. 231–249.

Wiesner, Eduardo, 1985. "Latin American Debt: Lessons and Pending Issues." *American Economic Review*, vol. 75, no. 2 (May), pp. 191–195.

Wilensky, Harold L., 1981. *Leftism, Catholicism, and Democratic Corporatism: The Role of Political Parties in Welfare State Development* (Berkeley: Institute of Industrial Relations).

Williams, John Fischer, 1923. *International Law and International Obligations Arising from Contract* (Lugdini Batavorum: E. J. Brill).

Williamson, John, ed., 1983. *IMF Conditionality* (Washington, D.C.: Institute for International Economics).

Williamson, John, 1988. *Voluntary Approaches to Debt Relief* (Washington, D.C.: Institute for International Economics, Policy Analyses in International Economics, no. 25).

Williamson, John, ed., 1990. *Latin American Adjustment: How Much Has Happened?* (Washington, D.C.: Institute for International Economics, April).

Williamson, Oliver, 1975. *Markets and Hierarchies, Analysis and Antitrust Implications: A Study in the Economics of Internal Organization* (New York: Free Press).

Winkler, Max, 1933. *Foreign Bonds, An Autopsy: A Study of Defaults and Repudiations of Government Obligations* (Philadelphia: Roland Swain Co.).

Wionczek, Miguel S., ed., 1985. *Politics and Economics of External Debt Crisis: The Latin American Experience* (Boulder: Westview Press).

Wise, Carol, 1989. "Democratization, Crisis, and the APRA's Modernization Project in Peru." In Stallings and Kaufman, eds., 1989, pp. 163–180.

Wolfers, Arnold, 1962. *Discord and Collaboration: Essays on International Politics* (Baltimore: Johns Hopkins University Press).

Wolfinger, Raymond E., 1960. "Reputation and Reality in the Study of 'Community Power.'" *American Sociological Review*, vol. 25, no. 5 (October), pp. 633–644.

Wood, Bryce, 1961. *The Making of the Good Neighbor Policy* (New York and London: Columbia University Press).

World Bank (various). *World Debt Tables* (New York and Oxford: Oxford University Press).

The World Today (various).

Wyllie, Robert Crichton, 1840. *A Letter to G.R. Robinson, Esq., Chairman of the Committee of Spanish American Bondholders, on the Present State and Prospects of the Spanish American Loans* (London: A.H. Baily & Co.).

Wyllie, Robert Crichton, 1845. *Mexico. Noticia sobre su Hacienda Publica bajo el Gobierno Espanol y despúes de la Independencia . . . Calculos sobre la deuda Pública Interior y Esterior. Presupuestos Aprocsimados de sus Ingresos y Egresos* (Mexico: I. Cumplido).

Wynne, William H., 1951. *State Insolvency and Foreign Bondholders*, vol. 2 (New Haven: Yale University Press).

Yarbrough, Beth V., and Robert M. Yarbrough, 1991. *The World Economy: Trade and Finance*, 2nd ed. (Chicago: Dryden Press).

Yepes del Castillo, Ernesto, 1972. *Perú 1820–1920: Un Siglo de Desarrollo Capitalista* (Lima: Instituto de Estudios Peruanos).

Young, Oran, ed., 1975. *Bargaining: Formal Theories of Negotiation* (Urbana: University of Illinois Press).

Young, Oran, 1980. "International Regimes: Problems of Concept Formation." *World Politics*, vol. 32, no. 3, pp. 331–356.

Zacher, Mark W., 1987. "Trade Gaps, Analytical Gaps: Regime Analysis and International Commodity Trade Regulation." *International Organization*, vol. 41, no. 2 (Spring), pp. 173–202.

Zagare, Frank C., 1984. *Game Theory: Concepts and Applications* (Beverly Hills: Sage Publications).

Zagare, Frank C., 1990. "Rationality and Deterrence." *World Politics*, vol. 42, no. 2 (January), pp. 238–260.

Zartman, I. William, and Maureen R. Berman, 1982. *The Practical Negotiator* (New Haven: Yale University Press).

Zeitlin, Maurice, 1984. *The Civil Wars in Chile, or, The Bourgeois Revolutions That Never Were* (Princeton: Princeton University Press).

Zeuthen, Frederik, 1930. *Problems of Monopoly and Economic Warfare* (London: Routledge & Sons).

Index